Law, Labor, and Ideology in the Early American Republic is a fundamental reinterpretation of law and politics in America between 1790 and 1850. The most detailed study yet available of the basic legal relationships involving working people at work in an industrializing economy, the book also reveals the crucial political and social significance of those relationships and the law's role in their creation. Not just for those interested in the history of law or the history of labor, this is a book for anyone interested in the broad stream of American political and social history.

Law, Labor, and Ideology
in the Early American Republic

Law, Labor, and Ideology
in the
Early American Republic

CHRISTOPHER L. TOMLINS

CAMBRIDGE
UNIVERSITY PRESS

Published by the Press Syndicate of the University of Cambridge
The Pitt Building, Trumpington Street, Cambridge CB2 1RP
40 West 20th Street, New York, NY 10011-4211, USA
10 Stamford Road, Oakleigh, Victoria 3166, Australia

First published 1993

Printed in the United States of America

Library of Congress Cataloging-in-Publication Data
Tomlins, Christopher L., 1951–
Law, labor, and ideology in the early American republic /
Christopher L. Tomlins.
p. cm.
ISBN 0–521–43278–2 (hc). – ISBN 0–521–43857–8 (pb)
1. Labor laws and legislation – United States – History – 19th
century. 2. Industrial relations – United States – History – 19th
century. I. Title.
KF3369. T65 1993
344.73'01 – dc20
[347.3041]   92–17452

A catalog record for this book is available from the British Library.

ISBN 0–521–43278–2 hardback
ISBN 0–521–43857–8 paperback

For Sheila Tomlins, for Jean Douglas,
and, especially, for Ann and Jasmin and Meredith

Contents

It is common that those who labor should
feel some enmity toward those who do not.
Pennsylvania Packet, 4 March 1780

Preface and acknowledgments

This is a book about the interaction between law, labor, and society in the early republic, that period of American history beginning in the immediate aftermath of the Revolution and extending through the mid-nineteenth century. It is a book for people interested in legal and labor history, but it is also intended as a demonstration of how research undertaken under the auspices of those disciplines can inform the broad stream of American political and social history. It is a book, then, which seeks an audience with American historians at large.

My most substantive concern in undertaking the research that has produced this book has been to provide a detailed analysis of developments during the early republic in the three areas of law that had the clearest and most direct impact on the lives of working people *at work*. These were the law of criminal conspiracy, under which both journeymen and factory operatives were tried and convicted for combining against their employers; the law of master and servant, under which the relations of parties to employment contracts were construed to be relations of domination and subordination; and the several common law rules which immunized employers from liability to their employees for accidental injuries occurring in the course of employment. This analysis is undertaken at some length in Parts 2, 3, and 4 of the book. In each area I describe the broad circumstances in which cases arose and the doctrinal discourses to which courts and lawyers had resort in deciding them. I seek to show how these discourses depicted the actors involved, why they were chosen, what alternatives existed, and what social and political significance inhered in the outcomes. Fundamentally, my goal throughout is to demonstrate how law was integral to the process of establishing factitious categories for work relations in an industrializing society. In this way I seek to clarify the contribution which legal discourse made to the construction of the new nineteenth-century world of production and employment.

In Part 1, however, this detailed analysis is preceded by an exploration of the wide context in which I believe such analysis must necessarily be set – that of the development of the American polity in the colonial and early national periods. Put straightforwardly, I believe it impossible to understand outcomes in the interaction between law and labor during the early republic unless one also comes to grips with the preeminent position which legal discourse was assuming at the time in American society as a whole, and with the particular reasons for that preeminence. That belief is based on two related propositions that have informed my own previous work and also, to some extent, the work of others in this field: first, that as a matter of fact demonstrable by reference to specific historical occasions, the distinctive role occupied by law in the American polity has, from that polity's inception, had quite crucial implications for the institutions and ideologies through which laboring people in America have identified and pursued their interests;[1] but also, second, that this intimate interaction between law and labor has taken place because, quite apart from the exigencies of specific occasions, labor has throughout been positioned in legal discourse as the preeminent liability of the polity which the American legal order epitomizes.[2]

In short, one might best characterize this book by saying that its purpose is to describe the course of law's interaction with labor during the first half of the nineteenth century but also and simultaneously to offer as a major factor

---

[1] On this, see generally Christopher L. Tomlins, *The State and the Unions: Labor Relations, Law, and the Organized Labor Movement in America, 1880–1960* (New York and Cambridge, 1985); Victoria C. Hattam, "Unions and Politics: The Courts and American Labor, 1806–1896" (Ph.D. diss., MIT, 1987), now published in a revised version as *Labor Visions and State Power: The Origins of Business Unionism in the United States* (Princeton, 1992); William E. Forbath, "Law and the Shaping of the American Labor Movement," *Harvard Law Review*, 102, 6 (Apr. 1989), 1109–256, also published in a revised version as *Law and the Shaping of the American Labor Movement* (Cambridge, Mass., 1991). Hattam develops some qualifications of this position in "Economic Visions and Political Strategies: American Labor and the State, 1865–1896," *Studies in American Political Development*, 4 (1990), 82–129, at 128–9. For a response, see William E. Forbath, "Law and the Shaping of Labor Politics in the United States and England," in Christopher L. Tomlins and Andrew J. King, eds., *Labor Law in America: Historical and Critical Essays* (Baltimore, 1992), 225–7.

[2] As Adam Smith put it in the opening sentence of *The Wealth of Nations*, "The annual labour of every nation is the fund which originally supplies it with all the necessaries and conveniences of life" (*An Inquiry into the Nature and Causes of the Wealth of Nations* [New York, 1937], 3). My translation of this observation into the language of liability is adapted from Stanley Vittoz, *New Deal Labor Policy and the American Industrial Economy* (Chapel Hill, 1987), 9, where labor is referred to as "the preeminent material liability" and also "the foremost ethical liability" of *capital*. My adaptation of Vittoz's conceptualization is intended, not to alter its implication of antagonistic relations, but to widen its focus from the economy to the polity as a whole. In this way I seek to establish an avenue for historical analysis of the specific discourse of labor law and also for investigation of the relationship of that discourse to the more general world of eighteenth- and nineteenth-century American legal discourse and, more widely yet, to law's relationship with politics in the American context.

Other scholars investigating these matters have also been drawn in this general direction. In *Belated Feudalism: Labor, the Law, and Liberal Development in the United States* (New York and Cambridge, 1991), e.g., Karen Orren has embraced "the primacy of labor" as her point of departure, "based on the premise that labor is a bridge between the realm of state elites and institutions and the ongoing activities of social life" (21, and see generally 21–4). See also her essay "Metaphysics and Reality in Labor Adjudication," in Tomlins and King, eds., *Labor Law in America*, 160–79, esp. 167. For a rather different example of how to pursue what is essentially the same agenda, see Anthony Woodiwiss, *Rights v. Conspiracy: A Sociological Essay on the History of Labor Law in the United States* (New York, 1990). For a more traditional intellectual history which nevertheless demonstrates how central the examination of labor was to the early republic's mainstream discourses, see Jonathan A. Glickstein, *Concepts of Free Labor in Antebellum America* (New Haven, 1991).

in explaining the course of that interaction the pivotal role which law assumed in the production and reproduction of a particular kind of postrevolutionary society.[3]

Legal historians have, over the last thirty-odd years, successfully focused scholarly attention on the importance of placing law among the social and ideological structures that shaped the United States between the Revolution and the Civil War.[4] To assert law's centrality to the period's history in light of this historiography, therefore, seems uncontentious. To date, however, legal history's most lasting achievement has been the development of "instrumentalist" hypotheses which have dwelt on law's reflection of more fundamental social processes, in particular those founded in the economy.[5] In reaction, recent years have seen attempts to head in a somewhat different direction, one that has emphasized law's constructive or constitutive aspect.[6] This study has benefited from the example of both approaches but cleaves fully to neither. Instead, it follows a third, possibly idiosyncratic, way. Through an investigation of the relationship between legal categories, political and economic discourses, and concrete struggles, it attempts to establish how the postrevolutionary legal order was constitutive of social relations; but it also seeks to emphasize how, in arising at a particular historical moment to become the most important conveyance for the constitution of those relations, law in America may be seen as in itself an expression of historically contingent purposes.[7]

[3] In this way I seek to draw attention to (1) the considerable power that official capacity to "name" social actors, roles, and processes lends the namer; and (2) the consequences of vesting much of this discursive authority in the least-accountable, least-democratic institutions in the American polity. In concentrating upon official discourse, however, one must not forget that those "named" could explore and agitate for alternatives. As part of the process of its own creation, the post-revolutionary legal order could – and did – disempower or render invisible (or at least inarticulate) names or meanings chosen by actors for themselves, but it could not altogether eliminate them. Instead they formed part of an essential "other," a submerged, perpetually threatening netherworld created in the very decisions to define *this* institutional and imaginative alternative as orderly rather than *that* one, a world with which official discourse had necessarily to become paired in a perpetual struggle of self–other, order–disorder definition. Dirk Hartog, "Pigs and Positivism," *Wisconsin Law Review*, July 1985, no. 4:899–935, and Gary Wills, "Talking Ourselves Out of a Fight," *William and Mary Quarterly*, 3d ser., 44, 3 (July 1987), 623–7, are both quite suggestive on this score.

[4] See, generally, J. Willard Hurst, *Law and the Conditions of Freedom in the Nineteenth Century United States* (Madison, 1956); Perry Miller, *The Life of the Mind in America: From the Revolution to the Civil War* (New York, 1965), 99–265; Lawrence M. Friedman, *A History of American Law* (New York, 1973); Morton J. Horwitz, *The Transformation of American Law, 1780–1860* (Cambridge, 1975). For more recent examples see R. Kent Newmyer, *Supreme Court Justice Joseph Story; Statesman of the Old Republic* (Chapel Hill, 1985); G. Edward White, *The Marshall Court and Cultural Change, 1815–35* (New York, 1988).

[5] For a comprehensive summary and restatement of this approach see Kermit Hall, *The Magic Mirror: Law in American History* (New York, 1989).

[6] See, e.g., Michael Grossberg, *Governing the Hearth: Law and the Family in Nineteenth Century America* (Chapel Hill, 1985). This approach is most usefully laid out in Robert W. Gordon, "Critical Legal Histories," *Stanford Law Review*, 36, 1–2 (Jan. 1984), 57–124. See also the short discussion in Forbath, *Law and the Shaping of the American Labor Movement*, ix–xiii.

[7] Anthony Woodiwiss has recently made a basically similar point this way: "In the same way that a particular legal system as an ideological and political element represents a condition of the existence of

In furtherance of this project I have sought, first and fundamentally, to investigate the implications, political and ideological, of the turn to *legal* ordering and *legal* discourse, as opposed to other modes and discourses of social ordering, during the period under discussion. I present law in the early republic as neither epiphenomenal nor relatively autonomous but rather as the modality of a particular vision of rule.[8] Second, I have sought to show how the depiction of labor and employment in particular substantive areas of legal doctrine impacting upon work relations – criminal conspiracy, contract, tort – comported with those political and ideological considerations; to show in detail, that is, how the law characteristic of these areas of doctrine did in fact function as a modality of rule.[9]

In the highly visible area of criminal conspiracy the connections between these two levels of analysis are relatively clear, for here the social actors were to an important extent explicitly engaged in public contestation over how democracy and justice were to be embodied in a republican polity and over their relevance to economic as well as to political life. Hence it is to this substantive area that I move first after my opening discussion. As I seek to demonstrate in Parts 3 and 4, however, the same connections exist in the more mundane legal routines of the employment relationship. Here, as in the conspiracy cases, courts and treatise writers who were engaged in the resolution of disputes and the description of legal relationships were of necessity allocating power, authority, and responsibilities. Their choices of lines of reasoning and action thus involved them in implicit or explicit

an economy, then so too economic as well as other political and ideological elements represent the conditions of existence of the legal system. It is for this reason that one has to look beyond the law if one wishes to understand fully such signifying chains as are contained in constitutions, statutes and juristic arguments, and such disciplinary effects as are exemplified by decisions to proceed or not, degrees of enforcement and even judgements themselves" (*Social Theory after Postmodernism: Rethinking Production, Law, and Class* [London, 1990], 120). For a more structural approach, see Orren, *Belated Feudalism*, 1–28.

[8] My concern here is to avoid theoretical formulae which impute transhistorical characteristics to law. In the case of "relative autonomy," e.g., my argument is not with its implication of causal distance between legal events and the social environment in which they occur but rather with what I see as its more general implication that "law" per se is a phenomenon with constant attributes whose nature places it in a constant structural relationship with the contexts in which it is located. Approached historically, law's relative autonomy seems to me not to be a constant at all but a characteristic of particular times and places. That being the case, I prefer to concentrate on what can be stated about the particularities of law's historical role in the times and places in which I am interested.

[9] Here, then, I part company, at least to a degree, with those who stress law's discursive indeterminacy, its "open-endedness and mutability." I do, of course, acknowledge that law has "ambiguities" and "recessive radical strains" that can be mobilized by oppositionists to support their programs of revision and reform. On this see, in particular, William E. Forbath, "The Ambiguities of Free Labor: Labor and the Law in the Gilded Age," *Wisconsin Law Review*, July 1985, no. 4:767–817; also the conclusion to his *Law and the Shaping of the American Labor Movement*, at 171–2. See also David Thelen, *Paths of Resistance: Tradition and Dignity in Industrializing Missouri* (New York, 1986), 77–85, 217–19, 225–7, 274. Only rarely, however, do we observe those ambiguities and radical strains achieving any kind of "official" discursive status. Their role instead is almost invariably one of informing opposition. Recognizing, then, that what is law at any moment has been selected from a rich diversity of available legal cultures and consciousnesses, it is surely important to go on to explain how what becomes official discourse differs from what does not. I canvass this issue in "A Mirror Crack'd? The Rule of Law in American History," *William and Mary Law Review*, 32, 2 (Winter 1991), 353–97, at 364–5.

endorsements of one kind of political economy rather than another, one set of social relations or vision of social order over another.[10]

As we shall see, in each of the areas of law examined here legal discourse exhibited an overall consistency of choice, tending during the period under study to move toward a representation of working life in voluntaristic terms, as a network of self-interested relationships created more or less spontaneously by the participants themselves, whose capacity so to act was guaranteed by their constitution as homogeneous participants in a universalistic legal order – formally equal citizens benefiting equally from protection of their private rights.[11] In this tendency we see the emergence and realization of liberal legal discourse's fundamental distinction between public and private spheres of social action, perhaps the most important characteristic of the categorical schema characterizing the legal order to emerge during the early republic.

This apparently empowering definition of individual freedom, however, was beset by powerful anomalies and contradictions. Most obvious were the growing disparities of material capacity rendered immune from meliorative intervention by the legal order's careful cabining of the state's redressive potentialities.[12] Their development both accounts for and to an important extent justifies the traditional Marxist critique of "bourgeois law" as "a formal framework for the realization of private power and domination."[13] Yet such a critique does not quite get to the heart of the matter. What were ostensibly "bourgeois" freedoms – independence, competency – were as highly valued by working people as anyone. Rather, the point is that their enjoyment of such freedoms was all too often countermanded not just by burgeoning material inequalities but by doctrinal constructions of social roles interpolating *legal* conditions of existence directly belying independence and competency. Even as it declared its embrace of autonomy and spontaneity in the private sphere, that is, law showed itself not just as a *framework* for the realization of private power and domination but in fact as an element integral to their construction.[14]

The postrevolutionary legal order's fondness for one kind of freedom relativizes law's familiar metanarrative – its claim to discursive universality. That fondness, however, identifies the legal order not so much as a consequence of the development

[10] For a stimulating case study, see Robert J. Steinfeld, "The *Philadelphia Cordwainers' Case* of 1806: The Struggle over Alternative Legal Constructions of a Free Market in Labor," in Tomlins and King, eds., *Labor Law in America.*, 20–43.

[11] Gordon Wood has recently sought to persuade us of the overweening centrality of this vision to the politics and culture of the early republic in his passionately argued *The Radicalism of the American Revolution* (New York., 1992).

[12] The process of "cabining" is explored at length below. For a useful introduction, see Joyce Appleby, "The American Heritage: The Heirs and the Disinherited," *Journal of American History*, 74, 3 (July 1987), 798–813.

[13] For a recent exposition, see Gerald Turkel, "The Public/Private Distinction: Approaches to the Critique of Legal Ideology," *Law and Society Review*, 22, 4 (1988), 801–23.

[14] This process was not one in any sense restricted to working life. Thus, for an exploration of the early republic's legal discourse undertaken from the standpoint of gender relations, see Linda K. Kerber, "The Paradox of Women's Citizenship in the Early Republic: The Case of *Martin v. Massachusetts*, 1805," *American Historical Review*, 97, 2 (Apr. 1992), 349–78.

of a particular political economy, as instrumentalists would have it, but rather as in itself an integral element in that political economy's constitution. Establishing the how and the why of this is the task of the pages that follow.

I have accumulated many debts in the course of writing this book. Colleagues at La Trobe University – Tony Blackshield, Kit Carson, Martin Chanock, Adrian Howe, and Pat O'Malley – read and commented on parts of the project in its initial stages as a series of research papers; Denise Lumsden, Kelly McMurtry, Christine Shortal, and Martha Lord all lent a hand by typing one or another of those papers. Since then I have done my own typing, but the intellectual and emotional debts have continued to grow. Any number of people have made helpful suggestions, pointed out errors, offered encouragement, or in some fashion lent assistance at one time or another: Joyce Appleby, Chandos Brown, Elisabeth Cawthon, Saul Cornell, Nancy Cott, Christine Daniels, Stanley Engerman, Dan Ernst, Leon Fink, Robert Fogel, Willy Forbath, Lawrence Friedman, David Galenson, Bob Gordon, Bob Gross, Dirk Hartog, Vicky Hattam, Douglas Hay, Wythe Holt, Morty Horwitz, Richard Johns, Stan Katz, Fred Konefsky, David Konig, Gary Kornblith, Mark Kornbluh, Lisa Lubow, Staughton Lynd, Michael Merrill, David Montgomery, Bill Novak, Karen Orren, John Orth, David Rabban, Stephen Reams, Gary Schwartz, Ray Solomon, Amy Stanley, Robert Steinfeld, Stephan Thernstrom, David Trubek, Bob Wiebe, Bob Zieger, and David Zonderman. I am also indebted to those others, not mentioned here by name, who have taken part in the various conference sessions and seminars at which I have presented portions of the work.

Staffs of a number of libraries and institutions have been of enormous assistance to me. Pride of place must go to everyone at the Social Law Library in Boston. I cannot think of a more accommodating, or diverting, place to work in. Close behind come the staffs of the Rare Books and Manuscripts Division of the Boston Public Library; the Manuscripts and Archives Division of the Baker Library, Harvard Business School; the Kress Library, Harvard Business School; the Treasure Room, Harvard Law School; the Houghton Library; the Judicial Archives Reclamation Project, Suffolk County Court House, Boston; the office of the Clerk of Court, Supreme Judicial Court, Suffolk County; and the office of the Clerk of Court, Boston Municipal Court. Particular mention should be made of the help given me by John E. Powers (Clerk of Court, SJC), Francis X. Shields (Clerk of Court, BMC), and Kay Menand (Director, JARP) in expediting access to materials within their jurisdiction. Lynn Kincaid of Northwestern University Law Library was of enormous assistance during the first half of 1989 in tracking down and securing the extended loan of numerous books, articles, and microfilms. I have also been greatly aided by the staffs of the Law, Rare Books, and Schwem libraries of the College of William and Mary; of Melbourne University Law Library; and in particular of the Borchardt Library, La Trobe University. Finally, I should acknowledge the assistance of the Massachusetts Historical Society, the Massachusetts State Archives, the Massachusetts State Library, the Newberry Library, the Regenstein Library of the University of Chicago, and the Library of Congress Newspaper Division, all of which proved crucial at strategic moments.

That the debts which have accrued over the last eight years have been intellectual rather than financial is the happy consequence of the generosity of a number of institutions. At an early stage the American Bar Foundation and the Charles Warren Center, Harvard University, both provided fellowship support which enabled me to spend an extended period of time working in Massachusetts archives and libraries. That work established an essential foundation upon which much of my subsequent research was built. I am extremely grateful to Jack Heinz, then Director of the ABF, and Bernard Bailyn, then Director of the Warren Center, for expediting my visit to the Warren Center in 1984–5, and I should like to acknowledge a particular debt to Bernard Bailyn, whose expressions of interest and encouragement when the project was in its very early stages were most welcome. Others then at the Warren Center or close by – Chris Miller, Barbara DeWolfe, Catherine Clinton, Judy Coffin, James Henretta – were always good company. I received further assistance from the ABF in 1989, this time in the shape of a visiting resident fellowship, and my thanks go to Jay Casper, Bill Felstiner, and Ray Solomon for all their help in bringing that fellowship to fruition. Together with my time at the ABF, a subsequent joint fellowship during 1989–90 at the Commonwealth Center for the Study of American Culture and the Institute for Bill of Rights Law, College of William and Mary, was invaluable in providing an extended period for final research and for undertaking the bulk of the writing of the manuscript's first draft. I am very grateful to Law School Dean Tim Sullivan and to Center Director Thad Tate for making that visit to William and Mary possible. Between 1985 and 1989 my work was sustained by grants from the Australian Research Grants Committee and from the School of Social Sciences, La Trobe University. Because for most of this period I was occupied almost continuously throughout the year in chairing the Legal Studies Department, these grants were particularly important in enabling me to take off on brief, intensive research trips in the United States when opportunities presented themselves at (inevitably) fairly short notice. These grants and a grant from the Littleton–Griswold fund of the American Historical Association also enabled me to employ Ruth Adler as a research assistant during 1988–89, and I am grateful for her help in certain key aspects of the project. I am also very grateful to Ann Tomlins for her assistance in uncovering what turned out to be some absolutely critical details, and to Professor Emeritus John Falconieri of the American University in Rome for helping with a translation. At Cambridge University Press, Frank Smith's sustained interest and enthusiasm over several years were a great encouragement. I also want to thank Pamela Bruton for her superb copyediting. Finally, I want to thank some dear and valued friends: Bill Harris and Terry Rockefeller for their patient hospitality on the many trips I have made to Boston and Cambridge; and Fredrika Teute and Clyde Haulman for making my family and myself feel so much at home in Williamsburg.

Since I finished the final draft of my last book, in 1984, Ann and I have between us lost three parents but gained two daughters. I dedicated that last book to our two fathers, both then very ill. This one, with the exception of my mother, who died suddenly in the very early morning of New Year's Day, 1989, is for the living.

The errors of fact or interpretation that have crept into this book despite the best efforts of all the above are, as ritual rightly requires, my responsibility.

Elements of the research presented here first appeared in more abbreviated form in the following articles: "Law, Police and the Pursuit of Happiness in the New American Republic," *Studies in American Political Development*, 4 (1990), 3–34; "Criminal Conspiracy and Early Labor Combinations: Massachusetts, 1824–1840," *Labor History*, 28, 3 (Summer 1987), 370–85; "The Ties that Bind: Master and Servant in Massachusetts, 1800–1850," *Labor History*, 30, 2 (Spring 1989), 193–227; and "A Mysterious Power: Industrial Accidents and the Legal Construction of Employment Relations in Massachusetts, 1800–1850," *Law and History Review*, 6, 2 (Fall 1988), 375–438. This material is incorporated here, in revised form, by permission of the respective journals. A highly condensed version of Chapters 7 and 8 also appears in *Labor Law in America: Historical and Critical Essays* (Baltimore, 1992), edited by Andrew King and me.

Prologue: two moments of the republic

THE FIRST MOMENT

1798 was the year of XYZ, of the Alien and Sedition acts, of the "Federalist Reign of Terror," of the Kentucky and Virginia Resolves – a year of dramatic events that congealed into one of the most severe of the many moments of crisis that haunted the early history of the American republic. 1798 was also the year William Manning of Billerica, Massachusetts, laboring in obscurity, completed a remarkable work of politics, which he called *The Key of Libberty*. Dubbed somewhat condescendingly the work of a "village Hampden" by the youthful Samuel Eliot Morison ("we do not claim to have discovered a forgotten Locke or a homespun Montesquieu," wrote Morison a shade regretfully, contemplating Manning's untutored scrawl), *The Key of Libberty* instances its author's growing concern that what little was left of the revolutionary achievement two decades past was about to disappear beneath a rising tide of Federalist reaction. *What* Manning wrote, however, is misunderstood if thought of simply as the gloomy response of a staunch Jeffersonian to the contemporary travails of his party: *The Key of Libberty* was no humdrum partisan tract but a detailed critical constitutional commentary designed both to address "the causes why a free government has always failed" and to suggest "a remidy against it." Nor was it an expression of the "profound distrust of governors and government" which, Morison claimed, was the typical attitude of "the average American farmer" of Manning's day and which he attributed to Manning himself. In fact, *The Key of Libberty* took for granted the inevitability of government in human affairs. Its purpose was constructive: to show how the Revolution had created conditions whereby "free" government might be realized, why despite this the result thus far had been something other than free government, and what Manning's constituency – he addressed himself specifically to "all the Republicans, Farmers, Mecanicks, and Labourers In Amarica" – might do to remedy a state of affairs so clearly inimical to their happiness. "Seeing the unweryed pains & the unjustifyable masures taken by large numbers of all ordirs of men who git a living without labour in Elections & many other things to ingure the interests of the Labourer & deprive us of the priviledges of a free government," Manning wrote, "I came to a resolution (although

1

I have neither larning nor lasure for the purpose) to improve on my Constitutional Right & give you my sentiments on what the causes are & a remidy."[1]

All government, Manning argued, was founded upon the fundamental need to restrain the human propensity to selfishness, a propensity which "may be deserned in all persons, let their conditions in life be what they will," and which tended to be encouraged rather than sated by the acquisition of power and wealth.[2] This, however, was but the point of departure: Governments came in many different forms and varieties with very different attendant consequences. Most forms of government were unfree, "Dispotick, Monorcal, & Aristocraticle." But some were free, "such as Democratical, Republican Elective." All the latter, Manning said, "I take to be senominus tarmes, [f]or that all those nations who ever adopted them aimed at nearly the same thing, viz. to be governed by known Laws in which the hole nation had a Voice in making."[3]

[1] William Manning, *The Key of Libberty: Shewing the Causes Why a Free Government has always Failed, and a Remidy Against It*, with notes and foreword by Samuel Eliot Morison (Billerica, Mass.: Manning Association, 1922) (written in 1798), vi, viii, xii, 3–5. (The Morison text represents one draft of *The Key of Libberty*; Manning wrote the first version of his commentary in February 1797 and subsequently revised it more that once.) Morison found Manning "rather narrow and partisan" on current politics. "His mind was evidently of a type not yet wholly extinct in rural New England; misinformed and prejudiced on particular issues, but shrewd and penetrating on general principles." Morison, however, was able to surmount his own prejudices sufficiently to take pleasure in the discovery "of so much political acumen and originality in so obscure a source" (xiii–xiv). For a more recent and more thorough discussion of Manning's life and political thought, see Michael Merrill and Sean Wilentz, "William Manning and the Invention of American Politics," in idem, eds., *The Key of Liberty: The Life and Democratic Writings of William Manning, a Laborer, 1747–1814* (Cambridge, Mass., 1993). See also Sean Wilentz's references to him in "Against Exceptionalism: Class Consciousness and the American Labor Movement, 1790–1920," *International Labor and Working Class History*, 26 (Fall 1984), 1–24, at 6–8.

[2] "A persons being raised to stations of high Honour & trust doth not clear him from this selfishness. But on the conterary it is a solemn truth that the higher a Man is raised in stations of honour power and trust the greater are his temtations to do rong & gratify those selfeish prinsaples" (Manning, *Key of Libberty*, 8–9).

A considerable body of work, much of it by Joyce Appleby, argues that the late eighteenth century saw a growing challenge to "the traditional wisdom that men and women were incapable of self-restraint and that elaborate institutions were required to control human vice." Appleby in particular has written eloquently of the radical potential of this new regard for human autonomy and self-government, which she has seen as the essence of Jeffersonian republicanism and also – more controversially in my estimation – as the key to understanding the transformative vision embodied by liberal political economy. See Joyce O. Appleby, "The Radical *Double-Entendre* in the right to Self-Government," in Margaret Jacob and James Jacob, eds., *The Origins of Anglo-American Radicalism* (London, 1984), 275–83, at 275; and, generally, Joyce O. Appleby, *Capitalism and a New Social Order: The Republican Vision of the 1790s* (New York, 1984). See also Hendrik Hartog, "Imposing Constitutional Traditions," replying to Morton Horwitz, "Republicanism and Liberalism in American Constitutional Thought," both in *William and Mary Law Review*, 29, 1 (Fall 1987), 57–74 and 75–82 respectively. In this light, Manning's radical and Jeffersonian argument for government seems anomalous.

Like Thomas Paine in *Common Sense*, however, Manning combines in his text elements both of traditional skepticism at aspects of human motivation and of the newer democratic faith in human capacities that Appleby describes. The result is suspicion not so much of government per se but rather of forms of government that are not democratic in character. Like Paine, and like Jefferson, Manning's principal concern was the promotion of forms of government that were popular and enabling rather than distant and oppressive. It was this, indeed, that led him to write of "the advantage" and not merely of "the absolute nesecaty" of civil government (8–9).

[3] Ibid., 10.

From here it was but a short jump to an identification of "free government" with legislative supremacy and majoritarian representative democracy. "A free Government is a government of laws made by the free consent of a majority of the hole people, But as it is Impossable for a hole Nation to meet together & deliberate, So all their laws Must be made judged & executed by men chosen & appointed for that purpose. And the duty of all those men are to act & do in makeing judging & executing those laws just as all the people would." The appropriate form for such a government was a bicameral legislature, each house elected on an identical franchise, with a separate executive and a separate judiciary. Each element should have distinct functions and powers. The scope of the judicial power, for example, properly extended to the hearing and determination of all complaints and breaches of the law but not to an examination of "the law wheather it is good or not" itself. The scope of the executive, likewise, extended to execution of the laws but "without any reference to their being right or ronge in his opinnon." Manning made it quite clear where supreme power lay. It was solely "the bisness and duty of the Lejeslative Body to determine what is Justis or what is Right & Rong," obedient to constitutions established by the people, and it was the duty of every individual in the nation "to regulate his conduct according to their detisions." Provided that "the Many were always fully & fairly represented in the Lejeslative Body they neaver would be opresed or find fault so as to trouble [such a] Government, but would always be zelous to seport it."[4]

The guiding star of such a government would be "the safry & hapyness" of the whole population. Manning defined "safty & hapyness" in an ostensibly uncontroversial Lockean mode as "the protection of Life, Liberty & property" but immediately showed that his understanding of the formula gave it a decidedly radical cast. "The poor mans shilling aught to be as much the care of government as the rich man's pound. Every person in the Nation aught to be compeled to do justis & have it dun to him promptly & without delay. All taxes for the seport of government aught to be layed equilly according to the property each person purseses & the advantages he receives from it."[5] Throughout his text – in his labor theory of

---

[4] Ibid., 11–12, 13, 18. Manning identified the Massachusetts Constitution – "the compleatest modle of a free government of any existing" – as the source of many of his ideas. The identification is significant, in that recent scholarship has concluded that the Massachusetts Constitution was animated by a model of strong government responsive to popular majorities and dedicated to the vindication of communal rights of well-being, rather than by one of restrained government checked by antecedent individual rights. (Manning reflects this approach in his description of the Massachusetts Declaration of Rights as establishing "all men to be free and equel as to their rights *in & under* the government" [11, emphasis supplied].) On the character of the Massachusetts Constitution, see, generally, Ronald M. Peters, Jr., *The Massachusetts Constitution of 1780: A Social Compact* (Amherst, Mass., 1978). See also Robert C. Palmer, "Liberties as Constitutional Provisions, 1776–1791," in William E. Nelson and Robert C. Palmer, *Liberty and Community: Constitution and Rights in the Early American Republic* (New York, 1987), 55–148, esp. 69–75. (Palmer offers the important qualification that "communal rights were for the benefit of individuals as well, so that individual and community were not in opposition. One was not sacrificed, in theory, to the other" [72]. As we shall see in Chapters 2–3, Massachusetts was not alone in this communal orientation.)

[5] Ibid., 13.

3

value,[6] his contempt for those who lived without laboring,[7] his sensitivity to the fragility of "justis" and the potential for oppression in exchange relationships[8] – Manning made it clear that his definition of safety and happiness as protection of life, liberty, and property conveyed a concern that all be protected not in their enjoyment of an assumed right to unrestricted accumulation but rather in their enjoyment of independence and a "competency" in their lives.[9] "For the prinsapel hapiness of a Man in this world is to eat & drink & injoy the good of his Labour, & to feal that his Life Libberty & property is secure, & not in the abundance he poseses nor in being the instrument of other mens miseryes."[10]

Left to itself, Manning argued, all this would add up to a government "In which all the laws are made judged & executed according to the will & interest of a majority of the hole peopel and not by the craft cunning & arts of the few." Unfortunately, it was precisely that craft and cunning – "the unreasonable demands and desires of the few," their "ungoverned dispositions & Combinations" – which had thus far always proven fatal to such free governments.[11]

In general, Manning attributed the ruin of republics, to "a Conceived Difference of Interests Between those that Labour for a Living & those that git a Living without Bodily Labour."[12] In America, much had been heard from the latter since the Revolution of "the Licentiousness of the Many" and of their representatives, of the necessity that, to preserve free government, the few be guaranteed "wait or influence in the Government according to their property & high stations in life." The remedies they proposed – so-called "ballenced" government, measures to design parliamentary structures to represent property rather than people, the executive veto – were all, however, "directly contrary to the prinsaples of a free government & no doubt written to destroy it." The real issue was far simpler:

They cant bear to be on a leavel with their fellow cretures, or submit to the determinations of a Lejeslature whare (as they call it) the Swinish Multitude are fairly represented. . . .

___

[6] "Labour is the sole parrant of all property – the land yealdeth nothing without it, & their is no food, clothing, shelter, vessel, or any nesecary of life but what costs Labour & is generally esteemed valuable according to the Labour it costs" (ibid., 14).

[7] "No person can posses property without labouring, unless he git it by force or craft, fraud or fortun, out of the earnings of others" (ibid., 14).

[8] "The Labourer being contious that it is Labour that seports the hole, & that the more there is that live without Labour & the higher they live or the grater their salleryes & fees are, so much the harder he must work, or the shorter he must live . . . If the prices of labour & produce should fall one halfe it would be just the same to the few as if their rents fees & salleryes ware doubled, all which they would git out of the many. Besides the fall of Labour and produce & scarsety of money always brings the many Into destress & compels them into a state of dependance on the few for favours & assistance in a thousand ways" (ibid., 15–17).

[9] For discussion of this mentality see Gary B. Nash, "Artisans and Politics in Eighteenth-Century Philadelphia," in Jacob and Jacob, eds., *Origins of Anglo-American Radicalism*, 162–7; Daniel Vickers, "Competency and Competition: Economic Culture in Early America," *William and Mary Quarterly*, 3d ser., 47, 1 (Jan. 1990), 3–29. On the rootedness of Manning's political economy in a localized culture of reciprocal exchange rather than in the political economy of transnational commerce and capital movements, see Merrill and Wilentz, "William Manning and the Invention of American Politics."

[10] Manning, *Key of Libberty*, 66, and see 13–17.

[11] Ibid., 14, 7, 18.   [12] Ibid., 5.

those that live without Labour are ever opposed to the prinsaples & operation of a free Government, & though the hole of them do not amount to one eighth part of the people, yet by their combinations, arts and skeems have always made out to destroy it soner or later.[13]

Among "the few" Manning listed merchants and physicians, lawyers and ministers, "letirary men and the over grown rich." He gave particular attention to the judicial and executive officers of the government itself, however, for in his opinion it was primarily through the self-aggrandizement of these branches at the expense of the legislature that "the few" promoted their interests.[14] Most commonly this was accomplished through a spurious assertion of executive/judicial authority to interpret the will and acts of the people "by construing & explaining away the true sence and meening of the constitutions and laws."[15] In this move he detected the hand of lawyers – "the most formidable and influential ordir of any in the Government . . . a kind of Mule ordir ingendered by [the executive and judicial officers of government], & many times overawing both." In Manning's theory lawyers and the government's judicial and executive officers lived in a symbiotic relationship in which lawyers took advantage of "the intricacy of our Laws" and in the process furnished the judicial and executive branches "with the chief of their bisness & imploy." They were all, as a result, "bound together by the strongest bonds of union"; in other words, by their mutual self-interest in keeping the laws "numerous, intricate & as inexplicit as possable."[16]

The disproportionate influence of the few was attributable to two major and related weaknesses of the many: ignorance and lack of organization. These weaknesses left the many easy prey to oppression on the part of those notables (mostly lawyers) to whom in their naiveté they turned to act as their representatives. The result was that constitutions and laws embodied the interests of the few not only in their interpretation but in their actual form and content.[17] Manning's remedy was twofold: first, publicly funded schooling for all to bring opportunities to acquire "Larning" within reach of the commonality; and, second, the widest-possible promotion and dissemination of political knowledge and information through a mass press

---

[13] Ibid., 6–7, 18.   [14] Ibid., 20.

[15] Ibid., 30. Manning's objection to constitutional interpretation was very plain indeed. "The people excepted of it as it is," he wrote of the federal Constitution, "and no other way" (ibid., 42). Manning thought it the responsibility of the legislative branch to resolve any conflicts which might arise between "the Constitution, tretyes and [federal] laws." He was particularly opposed to any reference to the deliberations of the Philadelphia Convention. "As to the mening of the Convention that formed it, it has nothing to do in the question, & it was an insult on the people to keep their debates secret at that time, & a grater one to site us to them now for an explanation, as Worshington did to the house of Representatives" (41). On the issue of constitutional interpretation at the time of the federal Constitution's drafting and ratification see H. Jefferson Powell, "The Original Understanding of Original Intent," *Harvard Law Review*, 98, 5 (Mar. 1985), 885–948.

[16] Manning, *Key of Libberty*, 33–4, 21.

[17] Ibid., 21, 34. Manning appears originally to have given cautious support to the idea of a federal Constitution but to have become very disillusioned with its operation by the time he wrote *Key of Libberty*. See below, Chapter 3, n. 106.

published by a national "Sociaty of Labourers." "We see all the ordirs of the few completely organised," Manning observed, referring to the several associations of bench and bar, of doctors, of divines, and to the Society of the Cincinnati. "I would not be understood to be against the associations of any ordirs of men, for to hinder it would hinder their improvements in their professions, & hinder them from being servisable to the Many. Their need ondly one Society more being established, or proper means of information amongue the Many to hinder their being daingerous in politicks."[18] Far from seeing association as a threat, Manning regarded it as a salutary lesson. Organization begetting autonomous knowledge would be the Many's salvation.[19]

How shall we assess the significance of Manning's text? We might treat such observations simply as one more illustration of the eighteenth century's tendency to employ conspiratorial modes of explanation.[20] Or we might cite

[18] Manning, *Key of Libberty*, 20–1, 35–7, 61–7. In their essentials Manning's recommendations for the organization of public schooling reproduced Jefferson's scheme for a general education as set forth in his "Bill for the More General Diffusion of Knowledge." See below, the section entitled Democratic Politics, State, and Police, in Chapter 3. See also Thomas Cooper, *Lectures on the Elements of Political Economy* (Columbia, S.C., 1826), 264–71 ("Of Police Laws Relating to Instruction and Education"). Given the nature of the argument to be advanced in Part 1 of this book, it is worth briefly comparing Manning's proposal for a continent-wide "Munthly Magazein" and weekly newspaper, to be published and distributed by his society of laborers, and the proposal by the British theorist of police, Patrick Colquhoun, that the government publish a national "police gazette." Manning indicated that the first numbers of his magazine would print the federal and state constitutions, complete with all amendments and a description of the principles on which they were founded; a federal register, showing the names of each member of Congress since 1789, the votes cast for and against them in elections, their own record of voting on major issues, and a digest of the most important speeches made on both sides; and a state register with similar information (see William Manning, *The Key of Libberty* draft MSS [Houghton Library, Harvard University], preface). In Colquhoun's case, the object was to ensure wide dissemination of salutary and "improving" information among the common people of England, particularly knowledge of municipal and administrative regulations, health codes, and the provisions of the criminal law. Details of Colquhoun's proposal can be found in his *Treatise on Indigence* (London, 1806), 97–108. I discuss Colquhoun further in Chapter 3, in the section entitled Markets, Liberty, and Security. Of interest here are the contrasting visions of law and society that inhabit two superficially similar proposals for the dissemination of useful knowledge. Manning's proposal was intended to assist "the many" in organizing themselves to protect the democratic promise of "free government" and to participate in its production of law. Colquhoun's, in contrast, was a prescription for the maximization of social efficiency, informing the many of the details of their regulation, from above.

[19] For a general study of the conditions governing the existence and diffusion of knowledge in colonial and republican America, see Richard D. Brown, *Knowledge Is Power: The Diffusion of Information in Early America, 1700–1865* (New York, 1989). In "Polite Foundation: Citizenship and Common Sense in James Wilson's Republican Theory," *Supreme Court Review*, 1984, 359–88, at 372–3, Stephen Conrad draws our attention to Benjamin Rush's conviction that a revolution in "knowledge" was necessary to safeguard the revolutionary heritage of 1776. "We have only finished the first act of the great drama. We have changed our forms of government, but it remains yet to effect a revolution in our principles, opinions and manners so as to accommodate them to the forms of government we have adopted." Like Manning, Rush clearly appreciated the strategic political importance of "knowledge." But Rush's understanding of knowledge was elitist; Manning's, plebeian. Like Jefferson, Manning argued that the mass of ordinary citizens needed to have command of the guts of law and politics if they were to stave off threats to popular rule. Rush sought safety in refinement, the propagation of a new *politesse* for the new nation.

[20] On which, generally, see Gordon S. Wood, "Conspiracy and the Paranoid Style: Causality and Deceit in the Eighteenth Century," *William and Mary Quarterly*, 3d ser., 39, 3 (July 1982), 401–41.

Manning's clear intellectual debts to "country" rhetoric, his allusions to moral sense philosophy, his religiosity, his clear Painite sympathies, his exemplification of yeoman or artisan republicanism, or his nascent liberalism (his search for equality of opportunity in the acquisition of knowledge, his varied defenses of liberation from the shackles of privilege) in assimilating him to one or other of the prevailing interpretive paradigms which historians have employed so creatively and perceptively in analysis of the history of politics in the early republic.[21] Yet Manning's idiom is unassimilable in toto to any single interpretation of late eighteenth-century political discourse, evidence reinforcing what appears to be the emerging perception of the era as one of contentious disputation conducted in a variety of polyvalent sublanguages.[22] Let us then focus first on what he wrote and then attempt to find a way of understanding it. This was an urgent, at times caustic, disquisition upon the necessity of government, one that condemned the careful checks and balances of late eighteenth-century constitutionalism, together with the elegant juridical–legal discourse in which they were constructed and defended, as little more than the machinations of a crafty elite, and instead identified majoritarian democracy as the only genuine expression of the ideal of free republican government, the only basis upon which citizens could be required *and expected* to submit to government.

William Manning's Billerica farm had not prepared him to be party to a world of "polite" conversation on politics.[23] Manning, though, was no eccentric rural iconoclast; as we shall see, his keen appreciation of the strain between popular rule and law rule reproduced in some respects the concerns of far more prominent figures. Yet Manning's perspective on that strain was rather different from theirs: We cannot, that is, simply sum up his contribution as a "rude" variation on one

[21] On the persistence of court and country ideology in the politics of the early republic see Lance Banning, *The Jeffersonian Persuasion: Evolution of a Party Ideology* (Ithaca, N.Y., 1978); Drew R. McCoy, *The Elusive Republic: Political Economy in Jeffersonian America* (Chapel Hill, 1980). The issue is debated by Lance Banning and Joyce Appleby in their companion essays "Jeffersonian Ideology Revisited: Liberal and Classical Ideas in the New American Republic" (Banning) and "Republicanism in Old and New Contexts" (Appleby), both in *William and Mary Quarterly*, 3d ser., 43, 1 (Jan. 1986), 3–19 and 20–34. On artisan republicanism see principally Sean Wilentz, *Chants Democratic: New York City and the Rise of the Working Class, 1788–1850* (New York, 1984); and idem, "Against Exceptionalism." On yeoman republicanism see James T. Henretta, "Families and Farms: *Mentalité* in Pre-Industrial America," *William and Mary Quarterly*, 3d ser., 35, 1 (Jan. 1978), 3–32. On liberalism see Appleby, *Capitalism and a New Social Order*; John Patrick Diggins, *The Lost Soul of American Politics: Virtus, Self-Interest, and the Foundations of Liberalism* (New York, 1984).

[22] On political language see J. G. A. Pocock, "The Concept of a Language and the *Metier d'Historien*: Some Considerations on Practice," in Anthony Pagden, ed., *The Languages of Political Theory in Early-Modern Europe* (Cambridge, 1987), 19–38. For evidence of the level of contention see John R. Howe, Jr., "Republican Thought and the Political Violence of the 1790s," *American Quarterly*, 19, 2, pt. 1 (Summer 1967), 147–65. For examples of the turn to polyvalency in analysis of late eighteenth-century political language see James T. Kloppenberg, "The Virtues of Liberalism: Christianity, Republicanism, and Ethics in Early American Political Discourse," *Journal of American History*, 74, 1 (June 1987), 9–33; Isaac Kramnick, "The 'Great National Discussion': The Discourse of Politics in 1787," *William and Mary Quarterly*, 3d ser., 45, 1 (Jan. 1988), 3–32.

[23] On the theme of "politeness" in eighteenth-century political discourse, see Conrad, "Polite Foundation," 361–5.

7

species of elite discourse.[24] If we are fully to understand Manning's commitment to resolution of the strain between popular rule and law rule in favor of the former, we must admit his text as the representative articulation of a further distinct language in the late eighteenth-century's polyphonic political discourse. Unlike the liberal tradition it was a language which could convey a vision of government, once guaranteed not to be tyrannous, as the key to individual and collective welfare rather than a potential threat to it. Unlike the classical republican tradition it sited the guarantee of freedom in mass participation in democratic politics rather than in the enlightened activities of a political nation whose membership was limited to a virtuous and independent minority. Above all, unlike both those traditions it envisaged the motor of future social development as an inevitable contest of interests between the powerful and monied but unproductive few and the weakly organized and poor but productive many. Twenty years after the Revolution, William Manning, Billerica farmer, had begun to talk law, government, and politics from a distinguishably plebeian standpoint, and in a republican language that was also a language of class.[25]

[24] In a superficial way, Manning had a counterpart in "polite" discourse in James Wilson. According to Stephen Conrad, Wilson, one of the firmest advocates of direct popular democracy at the Philadelphia Convention, expounded a popular constitutionalism predicated on a faith in the moral and intellectual capacities of the people at large and on the active facilitation of their further development. In all this his optimistic constitutionalism contrasted sharply with the profoundly skeptical, disenchanted conclusions built into the federal Constitution under Madison's tutelage. See generally ibid., 359–88; idem, "Metaphor and Imagination in James Wilson's Theory of Federal Union," *Law & Social Inquiry*, 13, 1 (Winter 1988), 1–70. For a lengthy recent analysis of Wilson's constitutionalism, see Jennifer Nedelsky, *Private Property and the Limits of American Constitutionalism: The Madisonian Framework and Its Legacy* (Chicago, 1990), 96–140. Manning, however, did not share Wilson's regard for the law's republican potential, and in his concern for the capacity of elites to manipulate the ignorant and suborn government he emphasized issues that Wilson ignored or downplayed. Manning's resolve that an informed majoritarian democracy was the only sure guarantee against manipulation set his constitutionalism apart. For comments on the tension between popular rule and law rule, see Frank Michelman, "Law's Republic," *Yale Law Journal*, 97, 8 (July 1988), 1493–537, at 1499–522. For skeptical assessments of Wilson's commitment to popular government and a politicized citizenry, see Steven Rosswurm, *Arms, Country, and Class: The Philadelphia Militia and the "Lower Sort" during the American Revolution* (New Brunswick, N.J., 1987), 254–5; Saul Cornell, "Reflections on 'The Late Remarkable Revolution in Government': Aedanus Burke and Samuel Bryan's Unpublished History of the Ratification of the Federal Constitution," *Pennsylvania Magazine of History and Biography*, 112, 1 (Jan. 1988), 103–30, at 116–17.

[25] For discussion of the Anglo–American constitutional tradition of government as threat to be restrained, see John P. Reid, *The Concept of Liberty in the Age of the American Revolution* (Chicago, 1988). On the incorporation of that tradition into American constitutional discourse, see Stanley N. Katz, "The American Constitution: A Revolutionary Interpretation," in Richard Beeman et al., eds., *Beyond Confederation: Origins of the Constitution and American National Identity* (Chapel Hill, 1987), 23–37. Katz concludes that "the revolutionary origins of American constitutionalism now look like a fundamentalist, antirevolutionary tradition, the bold assertions of the Declaration of Independence to the contrary. The Constitution stands as a bulwark against revolution on the one hand and legislative sovereignty on the other" (37). See also Mark Tushnet, *Red, White, and Blue: A Critical Analysis of Constitutional Law* (Cambridge, Mass., 1988), 4–16. On the varieties of liberty in eighteenth-century political ideology, see Appleby, *Capitalism and a New Social Order*, 16–23. For an interpretation of Manning's place in late eighteenth-century political debate not dissimilar to mine, see Merrill and Wilentz, "William Manning and the Invention of American Politics." (Merrill and Wilentz put Manning on the "left wing" of the Jeffersonian "democratic nationalist" coalition, the exponent of a radical, small-producer agrarianism.)

THE SECOND MOMENT

By the middle of the nineteenth century, William Manning's republican identification of labor with *production*, the engagement of members of a community in the individual or collective creation of useful artifacts to the general benefit of their society, had been significantly overshadowed among those who labored by a distinctly different identification of labor with *exploitation*, the accumulation of capital and the securing of profit by employers at the expense of those who worked for them.[26] Accompanying this change, and a key element in it, was the growth of an awareness that the supposedly freely bargained relationship into which workers entered with their employers was in all essentials one of structured inequality. A contemporary vignette – imaginary, meant as a metaphor – will illustrate. "Here goes a poor operative," wrote Jacob Frieze in 1844, "to find a situation in which he can obtain more wages. Let us slip on our magic rings, and, in our shadowy state, follow him in his rounds, and learn how he succeeds:

> "Mr. A——," says the applicant, addressing a pampered agent, "do you want to hire a good hand in your establishment?"
> "Yes," is the reply.
> Now mark. The agent does not condescend to inquire the poor man's terms. He does not ask, as though he were about to bargain for a barrel of flour, "what price do you ask?" This makes up no part of the bargain-making for labor. No – the question is by the poor operative himself, and until that is put the lips of the agent are sealed – "What wages *do you pay?*" The reply is seventy-five cents a day – and the hours of labor from sunrise in the Morning to seven at night with a deduction of thirty minutes for breakfast and forty for supper. The operative finds the wages and the hours the same as at the place at which he now labors. Aware that these are as fixed, and for the time as unalterable, as the laws of the Medes and Persians, you observe the operative says no more. It is now nearly night. We have followed him from place to place through the day. In every counting room we have heard him put the same well conned question, "what *wages do you pay?*" and heard returned the same everlasting reply. . . . This is the system which prevails everywhere, and in almost every branch of labor. This is the manner in which *bargains* are made.[27]

Frieze's apocryphal tale was intended to illustrate the lack of any equality of exchange in the wage bargain. It was a tale of power – the employer's possession of it, the operative's lack of it – consequent upon the different resources the parties were able to bring to bear in their bargaining. This was *private* power, emanating from what has been termed "monetary exchange asymmetry"; that is, from the discrepancy in material consequences that failure to enter into exchange visits upon

---

[26] See, e.g., Wilentz, *Chants Democratic*; Alan Dawley, *Class and Community: The Industrial Revolution in Lynn* (Cambridge, Mass., 1976); Jonathan A. Glickstein, *Concepts of Free Labor in Antebellum America* (New Haven, 1991), 4.

[27] Jacob Frieze, *The Elements of Social Disorder; A Plea for the Working Classes in the United States. By A Mechanic* (Providence, R.I., 1844), 64 (emphasis in original).

the different parties.[28] It was a power of which its subjects had become all too well aware and one they had begun increasingly during the 1830s to protest. In 1840, assembling in a "Grand Rally" only a few miles from Manning's Billerica farmhouse, the Workingmen of Charlestown declared in "An Address To Their Brethren Throughout the Commonwealth and the Union" the "direct opposition" between their interests and those of the purchasers of their labor.

We are men with the rights of men, with rights equal to those of the wealthiest and the proudest; but we are poor men; men obliged to labor for our daily bread; dependent on those who choose to employ us, and compelled by the invincible law of hunger to accept the wages they offer. They hold us then at their mercy, and make us work solely for their profit. . . . The capitalist has no other interest in us, than to get as much labor out of us as possible. We are hired men, and hired men, like hired horses, have no souls. . . . If we sicken and die, the loss is ours, not the employers. *There are enough more ready to take our places.*[29]

In important respects the language of the address of the Workingmen of Charlestown was far more overtly a language of class than Manning's had been forty years before. It was, for example, a language of irreconcilable division between working people and "capitalist" employers and manufacturers, of opposition to employers' increasing tendency to pool their capital in corporations in order to establish "sovereign control over the prices of labor." It was a language that flatly asserted the impossibility of accommodation between employer and employee, capital and labor: "their interests as capitalists, and ours as laborers, are directly opposite, and mutually destructive. . . . in the nature of things, hostile, and irreconcileable."[30] Yet the continuities were also clear. Like Manning, for example, the Workingmen of Charlestown saw themselves as part of a natural majority: "the real Workingmen . . . the great majority of the population . . . the real producers"; a majority, that is, composed of those whose labor had "done it all." Those to whom they counterposed their interests – "the capitalist, the accumulator, contractor, and employer," who grew "fat on our labors and sufferings" – were a small minority, "the few," the "aristocracy." And again like Manning, the Workingmen concluded that in association lay their best opportunity to counter the power of the few.

Brethren, in order to be able to assume this position, we must organize ourselves, and act in concert. The privileged classes have always prevailed against us, though we are the many and

---

[28] William M. Reddy, *Money and Liberty in Modern Europe: A Critique of Historical Understanding* (New York, 1987), 64–73, and see, generally, 62–106. As Reddy has shown, this asymmetry has a formidable disciplinary effect not only at the point of entry but also once employment has commenced, in that the consequences of failing to maintain the relationship, like the consequences of failing to enter into it in the first place, are far more serious for the employee than the employer. "The notion of monetary exchange asymmetry points to the imbalance of any relationship between large employer and penniless worker and to the disciplinary potential set up by formalizing such a relationship as a free contract to deliver labor for money. This imbalance arises out of the brute fact that equal amounts of money cannot possibly mean the same thing to different individuals" (94).

[29] *Third Grand Rally of the Workingmen of Charlestown, Mass., Held October 23d, 1840*, Kress Library, Harvard Business School, Cambridge, 8, 12 (emphasis in original).

[30] Ibid., 9–13.

they the few, because they have combined their numbers and acted together. We must not disdain to follow their example, so far as to combine in our own defence. We would, therefore, recommend to our brethren throughout the Commonwealth and the Union, to organize themselves into associations, which, by mutual correspondence, may bring about a concert of action between all the workingmen of the country.[31]

To the Workingmen of Charlestown, one clear consequence of association – a consequence which Manning forty years before had not dwelt on and indeed had had no reason to think about – was that it offered them an opportunity to countermand the power of their employers at the point of production and employment itself. In a world in which new forms of power were daily sprouting in locations beyond the established ambit of civic observation and authority, in which "the multiplication of large corporations" was "rapidly changing the whole character of our laboring population, by bringing them under the control of corporate bodies," this was a matter of no little importance. Hence, when passing resolutions intended to implement the principles contained in their address, the Workingmen gave prominent place to the endorsement of attempts on the part of journeymen, mechanics, and laborers to combine to fix the price of their labor and to refuse to work with those not belonging to their associations. It was "our right and our duty to combine to protect our rights and interests, and keep ourselves from being ground down into slavery."[32]

Along with that heightened consciousness of the asymmetries of power confronting them at work went a considerable skepticism about the capacity of existing political institutions to furnish redress. Where Manning's was a commentary upon the

[31] Ibid., 5–7, 17, 18.

[32] Ibid., 10, 3–4. On white workers' use of the language of slavery, see David Roediger, *The Wages of Whiteness: Race and the Making of the American Working Class* (London, 1991). See also Part 3 – Introduction: The Nomenclature of Power. Roediger comments: "Labor republicanism inherited the idea that designing men perpetually sought to undermine liberty and to 'enslave' the people. Chattel slavery stood as the ultimate expression of the denial of liberty. But republicanism also suggested that long acceptance of slavery betokened weakness, degradation and an unfitness for freedom. The Black population symbolized that degradation. Racism, slavery and republicanism thus combined to require comparisons of hirelings and slaves, but the combination also required white workers to distance themselves from Blacks even as the comparisons were being made" (66).
Labor republicanism's language of slavery does not feature prominently in the Charlestown address. References to slaves and slavery were few and not explicitly racialized. In commenting on their exploitation by capitalists and manufacturers, the Workingmen's dominant reference was to the degraded condition of the laboring classes of Europe. Their claim was for recognition of the rights of all, as "men" and as "human beings," to enjoy an unqualified equality (7–8).
Nevertheless, the address does include a few references akin to those Roediger describes. For example, "There is a spirit within us, that assures us we were not born to be slaves; that we were not made merely to toil and sweat, to endure hunger and cold, and nakedness and death, that the few might grow fat on our labours and sufferings, and then turn round and kick us. We feel that we were made for something better, and that we have a right to aspire to something higher" (6–7). And again (somewhat different from the sense of the first usage, suggesting that here "slave" refers specifically to American chattel slavery), "There is less identity of interest between the capitalists and us, than there is between the master and the slave. The slave is the master's property, and it is for the master's interest to take care of his property . . . for the sickness or death of his slave would be a loss of property. . . . But the capitalist has no other interest in us, than to get as much labor out of us as possible" (12).

11

realization of democracy, of achieving government in the hands of the people, the Workingmen's was a commentary, a half-century later, upon its failure. "Shall we look to politicians? What have politicians done for us, during the last fifty years? They have talked much about the rights, interests and dignity of labor; they have had smiling faces, soft voices, and fair speeches for us; but what have *they* DONE for us?" Yet the Workingmen's skepticism did not lead them to abandon politics. Rather, what they wanted from it was "DEEDS, not *words*; *deeds*, not promises."[33] And like Manning, they saw association as the means by which they might counterpose from an independent position of collective strength "the interests of labor" to the conventional wisdoms which serviced the interests of the few.[34] Nor was theirs to be a politics of nostalgia for days of artisan virtue lost, but a hardheaded politics of countervailing power. "What avails the acknowledgement of our *rights* when we want the MIGHTS to maintain them. It is with us a question as to our MIGHTS, rather than as to our RIGHTS." Rather than artisan participation in a continuing civic discourse of politics, the Workingmen's solution was a self-conscious "labor" discourse. Through association "we shall constitute ourselves a power in the State, and a power which no party will dare offend."[35]

The forum for the realization of the interests of labor which the power of association would allow was thus to be the private realm of production and employment but also the realm of law, government, and constitution. The two, indeed, were seen as interwoven, public authority impinging vitally on social relations. It was perhaps for this reason as much as any other that the *Boston Quarterly Review* subsequently dubbed the Workingmen "social Democrats."[36] In the Workingmen's discourse government was represented (in a fashion not dissimilar to Manning's) as "the agent of society," and its responsibility was to "secure to each individual member of society the full enjoyment of his rights," to ensure "the due performance of each

[33] *Third Grand Rally*, 13 (emphasis in original).

[34] "We must take our own stand, independent of both existing parties; adopt our own principles; propose our own measures; and support this or that party only so far as we have the surest pledges the nature of the case will admit, that by so doing we shall be doing something for the interests of labor" (ibid., 17).

[35] Ibid., 8, 18 (emphasis in original).

[36] *Boston Quarterly Review*, 4 (Jan. 1841), 116. According to the *Quarterly*: "Democracy as a form of government, *political* democracy, as we call it, could not be the term of popular aspiration. Regarded in itself, without reference to anything ulterior, it is no better than the aristocratic form of government, or even the monarchical. Universal suffrage and eligibility, the expression of perfect equality before the State, and which with us are very nearly realized, unless viewed as means to an end, are not worth contending for. What avails it, that all men are equal before the State, if they must stop there? If under a Democracy, aside from mere politics, men may be as unequal in their social condition, as under other forms of government, wherein consist the boasted advantages of your Democracy? Is all possible good summed up in suffrage and eligibility? Is the millennium realized, when every man may vote and be voted for? Yet this is all that political Democracy, reduced to its simplest elements, proposes. Political Democracy, then, can never satisfy the popular mind. This Democracy is only one step, – a necessary step, – in its progress. Having realized equality before the State, the popular mind passes naturally to equality before Society. It seeks and accepts *political* Democracy only as a means to *social* Democracy, and it cannot fail to attempt to realize equality in men's social condition, when it has once realized equality in their political condition" (113–14, emphasis in original).

one's social duties," and in particular to allow no one to live "in a *condition* below that which is proper to man," unable to attain "the full development of his nature as a moral, intellectual and physical being."[37] The Workingmen gave concrete embodiment to this perceived interrelationship of public and private, of law with the social relations of production and employment, by passing resolutions denouncing the state's "partial and oppressive" courts for their antagonism to the combinations formed by journeymen to confront their employers and by declaring the necessity of legislative reform of the courts and the judiciary to render them answerable to the electorate.

CLASS, POWER, LAW

Neither *The Key of Libberty* nor the Workingmen of Charlestown's "Address" has featured very prominently in the history of the early republic. Manning's tract was not admitted to the known universe of late eighteenth-century political discourse and remained mute for over a century until discovered by a descendant.[38] As for the Workingmen of Charlestown, their address was printed and circulated and their activities noted, at least by Orestes Brownson and the *Boston Quarterly Review*. But there matters rested. The 1840s swallowed the Workingmen of Charlestown (like so many other labor associations) whole: There is no indication that any further rallies took place.

Yet obscurity does not prevent these texts from providing an avenue of admission to the conceptual and social lives of their authors. Follow that avenue and one may discover something of the institutional and imaginative contexts in which working people lived, in which they came to understand themselves and to be understood, and with which they struggled, in the eighty-odd years between the Revolution and the Civil War, the years of the early republic when America underwent its industrial birth.

First, these texts help to demonstrate the growing salience during this period of

[37] *Third Grand Rally*, 8 (emphasis in original). In light of the argument developed in Chapter 3 (see the section Democratic Politics, State, and Police) regarding Jeffersonian conceptions of federalism and the merits of "energy" in local, relative to national, levels of government, it is worth noting here that the Workingmen did not look to "the General Government" but to "State Governments" for the action necessary to realize these ends. The general government's "aid to us can be at best only negative." What they sought at state level, in contrast, were "actual measures" implementing "the duty of government to aim to introduce the greatest practicable equality among all the members of the community" (15–16).

[38] Manning sent his essay to Thomas Adams, the editor of Boston's only Jeffersonian newspaper, *The Independent Chronicle*. Adams, at the time under arraignment for seditious libel for publishing material in support of the Virginia Resolves, replied that ill health and the pressures of his work prevented him from giving Manning's essay any attention and sent it back. Adams died later that year before his trial, but his brother, Abijah, was subsequently jailed on the seditious libel charge. Manning offered *The Key of Libberty* to Abijah Adams again the following year and professed his willingness to have it "drafted over & corected by some Larned Republican," but Morison was unable to discover any reply. See Manning, *Key of Libberty*, xi–xi.

class as a standpoint from which working people observed and understood their world. Manning's consciousness, close to the beginning of our period, is best described as plebeian; certainly his was not a working-class standpoint, nor would it make much sense to infer such a consciousness in such an individual at such a time. In contrast, the standpoint embraced by the Workingmen, who were far more sharply informed by their experience of the asymmetries of wage labor, comes much closer to evincing a working-class consciousness. This consciousness was not fully apparent until the midcentury decades or after; nevertheless we shall find evidence here suggestive of its emergence during the first half of the nineteenth century and of the influence of class standpoints on developments taking place during that period.[39]

Second, Manning and the Workingmen help to demonstrate why questions of power – its location and its expression in ideas, institutions, and relations – will be central to my analysis of the contexts in which labor appears. Perhaps the clearest theme shared by these texts after all is their anxiety concerning the power of the few and the powerlessness, whether as individuals or as a collective, of the many. Their authors' primary motivation, widely shared as we shall see, was their desire to see that powerlessness redressed. At the same time, comparison of the two texts also helps underline important shifts in how power was conceptualized. Manning's understanding of power, for example, was thoroughly republican. Power was primarily a creature of the polity; its possession a consequence of a bestowal of sovereign right through public decision; its exercise accountable to and within the public sphere. The weakness of the many was attributable to their inability, due to disorganization, to bring their majority status in the polity to bear on the pursuit of their interests. The power of the few lay in their monopolization of the high ground of government. Redress lay in organization to seize the high ground and impose "government" upon the "dispositions and combinations of the few." Forty years later, although the authority of that republican frame of reference was still clearly in evidence, the outlines of a different discourse about power had also been established. Concerned about their powerlessness in the polity, the Workingmen were also concerned about what was portended by the relativities of power in the employment relationship. "We must labor more hours, or with greater intensity, and increase the amount of our production; and this increased amount of production, returns upon us again in the shape of a still farther reduction of our wages. . . . We

---

[39] On class and working-class consciousness in the first half of the nineteenth century, see Wilentz, *Chants Democratic*, 14–17; idem, "Against Exceptionalism," 9–13; Bryan D. Palmer, "Social Formation and Class Formation In North America, 1800–1900," in David Levine, ed., *Proletarianization and Family History* (Orlando, 1984), 229–309, at 234–68; Richard J. Twomey, *Jacobins and Jeffersonians: Anglo-American Radicalism in the United States, 1790–1820* (New York, 1989). See also Amy Bridges, "Becoming American: The Working Classes in the United States before the Civil War," in Ira Katznelson and Aristide R. Zolberg, eds., *Working-Class Formation: Nineteenth-Century Patterns in Western Europe and the United States* (Princeton, 1986), 157–96. If the Workingmen of Charlestown are any guide, the development of the "new sense of class" which Bridges sees as a post-1850 phenomenon must be allowed to have been under way at least a decade earlier. For a different assessment, see Victoria Hattam, *Labor Visions and State Power: The Origins of Business Unionism in the United States* (Princeton, 1992).

stand on the declivity; we have already begun to descend!" The power of the employer, the capitalist, the manufacturer, and their corporations – their capacity to exert "sovereign control" over the hired employee *at work* – was increasingly uppermost in their minds.[40]

Finally, these texts help point up the decisive importance of law in the construction of the contexts in which labor appears. Here again we encounter both continuity and transformation. Both Manning and the Workingmen expressed considerable antipathy to the law and its agents – the bar and the judiciary. Theirs was both a sociological suspicion of the members of the species – the "mule Ordir" – and an ideological suspicion of their product. But there were also differences. To Manning, as we have seen, the law was suspect because lawyers and judges kept it "numerous, intricate & . . . inexplicit" while simultaneously claiming exclusive authority to interpret what it meant. All this suborned democratic government in the interests of the few.[41] To the Workingmen, in contrast, law visited disadvantage upon them, not in the polity principally, but at work. "Partial and oppressive," it was the means whereby "journeymen, mechanics and laborers" could be and were prevented from organizing to establish their own independent standpoint in their relationships with their employers.[42] Yet neither Manning nor the Workingmen set their faces against law in its "proper" form of democratically constituted laws – majoritarian legislative government. Both saw such government as an essential party in the achievement of "happiness." Both, hence, were at some pains to distinguish between these two manifestations of public authority in their views of the world.[43]

CONCLUSION

These three dimensions – class, power, and law – form the context in which labor changed, during the years of the early republic, from being primarily an activity into a central and essential category of social action.[44] In what follows we will explore these dimensions and the context they helped to construct.

---

[40] *Third Grand Rally*, 11.

[41] Manning, *Key of Libberty*, 33–4, 21. "The Free Republican in N°9 saith that in many of the antiant Republicks the Juditial power became the mear instruments of tirony, & proposes lawyors as a nesecary ordir in a free government, to curbe the arbitrary will of the Judge. But that appears to me like seting the Cat to watch the Creem pot" (ibid., 30).

[42] *Third Grand Rally*, 3.

[43] Discoursing upon the "Knowledge nesecary for every freeman to have" Manning stressed the importance of "A Knowledge that when laws are once constitutially made, they must be obayed, let them be neaver so rong in his mind, and that their is no remidy for greevences but by petitioning the authority that made them & useing his Right in Elections" (*Key of Libberty*, 61). Though nowhere as succinctly stated, it is clear from their address that the Workingmen of Charlestown did not regard government as a problem as such but rather as a mobilizable resource, one that, through association, they might turn to their own advantage.

[44] This transformation provides the centerpiece to much recent writing. See Gordon S. Wood, *The Radicalism of the American Revolution* (New York, 1992); Glickstein, *Concepts of Free Labor in Antebellum America*.

15

Of the three, however, primacy will be accorded to law. Underlying this entire exercise is the hypothesis that one of the most significant characteristics of the period under examination is the establishment, during its initial phase, of law as the official discourse (so to speak) of the early republic. As such, law (legal ideas, legal institutions, legal personnel) furnished the principal medium through which discourses of class and power gained expression. Further, because law was not simply a medium, a means to implement ideas or ambitions or desires originating elsewhere, but rather was a distinct mode of operation, a structure, a discourse in itself, it did not simply and passively convey those other discourses but informed and helped constitute them.

There is, however, more to it than that. As these introductory texts have helped both explicitly and implicitly to demonstrate, law is, but simultaneously is much more than, *the* law.[45] That is, law is an official discourse but is also a plurality of unofficial discourses existing in apposition and in political contest, an array of alternative possibilities for social knowledge, alternative ways of constituting "the facts of life." Importantly, only some of these gain admission to rule as *the* law. The rest do not. In concentrating here upon the decisive significance of "the rule of law" as the official discourse of the early republic, then, I do not seek to represent law as an ontological singularity. Rather, I seek to describe the particular characteristics of what emerged as the republic's modality of rule.[46] Because that task is fundamental to everything that follows, it is the appropriate place to begin.

[45] On this distinction, see Gary Wickham, "Cautious Postmodernism and Legal Truths," *Law in Context*, 7, 2 (1989), 39–53.

[46] Christopher L. Tomlins and Andrew J. King, "Introduction: Labor, Law, and History," in Christopher L. Tomlins and Andrew J. King, eds., *Labor Law in America: Historical and Critical Essays* (Baltimore, 1992), 15–16.

PART 1

Law and the facts of American life

If knowledge be power, it must be so emphatically, when it is law knowledge in constant action, in the midst of a community being under the government of laws. The history of the *American* republics is already replete with illustrations of this truth.

James Kent, *A Lecture Introductory to a Course of Law Lectures in Columbia College, Delivered February 2, 1824*

Law: the modality of rule

Men generally set up the most solid embankments against open tyranny, but do not see the imperceptible insect that gnaws at them and opens to the flooding stream a way that is more secure because more hidden.

Cesare Beccaria, *Dei Delitti e delle Pene* (trans. Henry Paolucci)

In conceptualizing social institutions and the action they envelop, recent trends in contemporary social theory have tended to reinforce the historian's more intuitive proclivity to take nothing for granted. The relationship between human activity and its context, we are warned, is problematic and indeterminate. Society and its cognates – economic processes, cultural traditions, values, and mores – are ultimately contingent upon the epistemological speculations in which all human beings must engage in order to establish sufficient common ground to enable each other's actions to be observed, described, categorized, debated, and, ultimately, understood. Contemporary social theory does not deny that the relationship between human action and social context is amenable to explanation, but it does seek to restore the contingency attendant upon an appreciation of human agency to that task of explanation. Society must be understood as the expression neither of an all-pervading underlying natural order nor of irresistible material forces. Rather, society "is made and imagined . . . a human artifact."[1]

---

[1] Roberto Mangabeira Unger, *Social Theory: Its Situation and Task* (New York and Cambridge, 1987), 1. See also John Dunn, "Social Theory, Social Understanding, and Political Action," in his *Rethinking Modern Political Theory: Essays, 1979–83* (Cambridge, 1985), 119–38. According to Antonio Gramsci, "most men [*sic*] are philosophers in as much as they operate on the practical level and in their practice (in the controlling pattern of their conduct) have a conception of the world, a philosophy that is implicit" (as quoted in James Henretta, "Social History as Lived and Written," *American Historical Review*, 84, 5 [Dec. 1979], 1309). See T. J. Jackson Lears, "The Concept of Cultural Hegemony: Problems and Possibilities," *American Historical Review*, 90, 3 (June 1985), 570.

The antideterminism of contemporary social theory surely comes as a relief to intellectual historians such as Thomas L. Haskell, who feared some years ago for the impact of "radical contextualism" on assessments of the potential for voluntarism in human action. See his "Deterministic Implications of Intellectual History," in John Higham and Paul K. Conkin, eds., *New Directions in American Intellectual History* (Baltimore, 1977), 132–48. To his credit, however, Haskell also observed at that time that to present human action as absolutely voluntaristic and the actor as wholly accountable would be as misleading as the determinism which he fears. Indeed, "if intellectual historians tend toward a comparatively

Thus apprehended, human activity recaptures dynamic qualities of unruliness and unpredictability from the necessitarian constraints of yesteryear, while at the same time due recognition is given to the way in which humans, most of the time, are motivated to avoid or at least finesse that unruliness through theorizing the meaning of human activity. Our theorizing encourages the appearance and informs the development of conceptual structures-in-common, or paradigmatic discourses, which furnish the institutional and imaginative contexts that give meaning to human action and thereby establish what I will refer to here, with intentional irony, as "the facts of life."[2]

It is important that we recognize these facts of life as conditional statements, albeit conditionals of considerable authority, for "occasionally . . . we push the given contexts of thought, desire, and practical or passionate relations aside."[3] Instances in which transformative change is actually accomplished may well be exceptional. "A conceptual or social context may remain relatively immunized against activities that bring it into question and that open it up to revision and conflict."[4] Contrary to classic theories of revolution,[5] however, transformative action does not need to be qualitatively distinct from the normal or routine activities which reinforce contexts. "Pushed far enough, the small-scale adjustments and revisions that accompany all our routines may turn into chances for subversion."[6] Those who disregard this potential in everyday life risk turning conditional contexts into absolutes and "established modes of thought and human association" into "natural forms of reason or relationship."[7]

deterministic view of human affairs, that may be no defect but an advantage if it lends balance to a profession otherwise inclined toward voluntarism. One might on that account even welcome a broader alliance under the rubric of 'social and intellectual history' of all those historians whose curiosity centers not on events but on the circumstances underlying and shaping events, regardless of whether the circumstances are social or intellectual in character" (145).

[2] Unger, *Social Theory*, 18–25. See also, generally, Anthony Giddens, *New Rules of Sociological Method: A Positive Critique of Interpretative Sociologies* (London, 1976); and idem, *Central Problems in Social Theory: Action, Structure, and Contradiction in Social Analysis* (London, 1979); John B. Thompson, *Studies in the Theory of Ideology* (Berkeley, 1984), 148–72. There are similarities here with Durkheim's theory of "social facts." For Durkheim, however, the relationship of social fact to human action was that of an independently existing exogenous constraint (Emile Durkheim, *The Rules of Sociological Method* [New York, 1964], 1–13). See also Joyce Appleby, "Value and Society," in Jack P. Greene and J. R. Pole, eds., *Colonial British America: Essays in the New History of the Early Modern Era* (Baltimore, 1984), 290–316.

[3] Unger, *Social Theory*, 18.   [4] Ibid., 21.

[5] E.g., V. I. Lenin, *What Is to Be Done? Burning Questions of Our Movement* (Peking, 1973), 122–188.

[6] Unger, *Social Theory*, 21, 152–3. And see Robert W. Gordon, "New Directions in Legal Theory," in David Kairys, ed., *The Politics of Law: A Progressive Critique* (New York, 1982), 286–92.

[7] Unger, *Social Theory*, 18–25. For critiques of Unger's theory of formative contexts see John Dunn, "Unger's *Politics* and the Appraisal of Political Possibility," and David Van Zandt, "Commonsense Reasoning, Social Change, and the Law," both in *Northwestern University Law Review*, 81, 4 (Summer 1987), 732–50 and 894–940. Dunn argues that, like Barrington Moore, Unger sees "the human imagination as the site where human history is finally determined," a view he sustains "while attending to the heavy weight of power and the raw urgency of material need" (739). Van Zandt's appraisal is more negative. Arguing that Unger portrays formative contexts as restraints "external to and alien from individual interaction" (905), Van Zandt proposes instead that formative contexts "are individuals' own products whose pragmatic utility is constantly reaffirmed through daily use" (921). Differential outcomes in this pragmatic search for utility maximization, says Van Zandt, explain the incidence of inertia and change in social formations.

LAW'S REVOLUTION

Between the Revolution and the beginning of the nineteenth century, law became *the* paradigmatic discourse explaining life in America, the principal source of life's "facts."[8] Only gradually during the first half of the eighteenth century but with increasing rapidity thereafter, law moved from an essentially peripheral position as little more than one among a number of authoritative discourses through which the social relations of a locality were reproduced – religion, family, community, clientage[9] – to most of which it was effectively subsidiary in influence and standing[10] and from which it derived most of its normative content, to a position of supreme imaginative authority from which, by the end of the century, its sphere of institutional and normative influence appeared unbounded.[11] The features by which this move may be recognized were shifts in law's internal intellectual organization, from a series of discrete and loosely connected discourses to one holistic, "scientific," Anglocentric

---

[8] See, e.g., A. G. Roeber, *Faithful Magistrates and Republican Lawyers: Creators of Virginia Legal Culture, 1680–1810* (Chapel Hill, 1981). See also Richard D. Brown, *Knowledge Is Power: The Diffusion of Information in Early America, 1700–1865* (New York, 1989), 82–109, 116–22.

[9] Ibid., esp. 73–111. See also Rhys Isaac, *The Transformation of Virginia, 1740–1790* (Chapel Hill, 1982); William E. Nelson, *Dispute and Conflict Resolution in Plymouth County, Massachusetts, 1725–1825* (Chapel Hill, 1981); idem, "The Eighteenth Century Constitution as a Basis for Protecting Personal Liberty," in William E. Nelson and Robert C. Palmer, *Liberty and Community: Constitution and Rights in the Early American Republic* (New York, 1987), 15–53; Stephen C. Innes, *Labor in a New Land: Economy and Society in Seventeenth Century Springfield* (Princeton, 1983); Christine L. Heyrman, *Commerce and Culture: The Maritime Communities of Colonial Massachusetts, 1690–1750* (New York, 1984). In 1821 Joseph Story told his colleagues that before the Revolution, "the resources of the country were small, the population was scattered, the business of the courts was limited, the compensation for professional services was moderate, and the judges were not generally selected from those, who were learned in the law." As a result, "our progress in the law was slow" ("An Address delivered before the Members of the Suffolk Bar, at their anniversary, on the fourth of September, 1821, at Boston," in *American Jurist*, 1, 1 [Jan. 1829], 12).

[10] Some years ago, e.g., Alan Heimert noted that "in pre-revolutionary America, lawyers seemed, as they certainly were, of mere secondary importance as spokesmen for the elements of American society whom the Liberal [Old Light] clergy otherwise so well represented" (*Religion and the American Mind: From the Great Awakening to the Revolution* [Cambridge, 1966], 182–3).

[11] Controversy over the precise timing of the beginnings of this change (which of course has implications for causal argument) has heightened recently as a result of Bruce Mann's excellent book, *Neighbors and Strangers: Law and Community in Early Connecticut* (Chapel Hill, 1987). In contrast to the earlier arguments of William Nelson in *Americanization of the Common Law: The Impact of Legal Change on Massachusetts Society, 1760–1830* (Cambridge, Mass., 1976), and Morton Horwitz in *The Transformation of American Law, 1780–1860* (Cambridge, Mass., 1977), both of whom find little alteration in an essentially static and communitarian legal system prior to the 1780s, Mann finds that by the middle of the eighteenth century, a system "that allowed litigants to address their grievances in ways that were essentially communal" was already being replaced, at least in Connecticut, by one "that elevated predictability and uniformity of legal relations over responsiveness to individual communities" (*Neighbors and Strangers*, 9–10). On the relationship between law and communitarian strategies of social discipline see Alfred F. Young, "English Plebeian Culture and Eighteenth Century American Radicalism," in Margaret Jacob and James Jacob, eds., *The Origins of Anglo-American Radicalism* (London, 1984), 185–212, at 191. For one example of the imaginative authority attained by legal discourse by the late eighteenth century, see Rhys Isaac, "'The Rage of Malice of the Old Serpent Devil': The Dissenters and the Making and Remaking of the Virginia Statute for Religious Freedom," in Merrill D. Peterson and Robert C. Vaughan, eds., *The Virginia Statute for Religious Freedom: Its Evolution and Consequences in American History* (New York and Cambridge, 1988), 139–69.

discourse;[12] in its social focus and resonance, from the parochial particularities of landed property and debt litigation to the sweeping, courtroom-transcending metaphysics of contract;[13] in its geographical and institutional focus, from local to translocal;[14] in the standing of its exponents, from a certain shabby notoriety to the social authority of an intellectual elite;[15] and, among those exponents, from unselfconscious disorganization to professional self-awareness.[16] The clearest manifestation of this enhanced authority was the restatement of the new republic's institutional and imaginative life in terms of a superordinate ideology of "the rule of law."

Whig history notwithstanding, law's achievement and retention of this preeminence were not straightforward.[17] First, law's rise to prominence was socially controversial. It remained so. Evidence of the persistence of antilegalism in American culture cautions us against assuming too readily a general popular acceptance of the rule of law as "an unqualified human good."[18]

[12] R. Kent Newmyer, *Supreme Court Justice Joseph Story: Statesman of the Old Republic* (Chapel Hill, 1985), xiv; Duncan Kennedy, "The Structure of Blackstone's Commentaries," *Buffalo Law Review*, 28, 2 (Spring 1979), 205–382. According to Kennedy, Blackstone's "is the only systematic attempt that has been made to present a theory of the whole common law system" aside from Kent's *Commentaries*. Kennedy continues that Blackstone's treatise (published between 1765 and 1769 and with numerous American editions thereafter) was "the single most important source on English legal thinking in the 18th century, and . . . has had as much (or more) influence on American legal thought as it has had on British" (209).

[13] Compare Mann, *Neighbors and Strangers*, 11–46, with Horwitz, *Transformation of American Law*, particularly 160–210. See also Patrick S. Atiyah, *The Rise and Fall of Freedom of Contract* (Oxford, 1979), esp. 102–12.

[14] See Mann, *Neighbors and Strangers*, 47–66; Stephen Botein, *Early American Law and Society: Essays and Documents* (New, York, 1980), 42–67; David G. Allen, *In English Ways: The Movement of Societies and the Transferal of English Local Law and Custom to Massachusetts Bay in the Seventeenth Century* (Chapel Hill, 1981); Nelson, *Americanization of the Common Law*, 3–10; G. Edward White, *The Marshall Court and Cultural Change, 1815–35* (New York, 1988), vol. 3–4 of *History of the Supreme Court of the United States*, 11–156.

[15] See, generally, Robert A. Ferguson, *Law and Letters in American Culture* (Cambridge, Mass., 1984).

[16] Gerard W. Gawalt, *The Promise of Power: The Emergence of the Legal Profession in Massachusetts, 1760–1840* (Westport, Conn., 1979); Roeber, *Faithful Magistrates and Republican Lawyers*. See also Stephen Botein, "The Legal Profession in Colonial North America," in Wilfrid Prest, ed., *Lawyers in Early Modern Europe and America* (New York, 1981), 129–46; John Murrin, "The Legal Transformation: The Bench and Bar of Eighteenth Century Massachusetts," in Stanley N. Katz, ed., *Colonial America: Essays in Politics and Social Development* (Boston, 1971), esp. 417–31; Charles R. McKirdy, "Massachusetts Lawyers on the Eve of the American Revolution: The State of the Profession," in Daniel R. Coquillette, ed., *Law in Colonial Massachusetts, 1630–1800* (Boston, 1984), 313–58; Magali Sarfatti Larson, *The Rise of Professionalism: A Sociological Analysis* (Berkeley, 1977), 111. Bruce Mann finds that by the middle of the eighteenth century, a "fledgling legal profession" in Connecticut was beginning to approach law "as an autonomous system rather than as a contingent social process" (*Neighbors and Strangers*, 9).

[17] The teleological smoothness of law's ascension is one of the main themes of nineteenth- and early twentieth-century evolutionary–functionalist legal historiography. See Peter Stein, *Legal Evolution: The Story of an Idea* (Cambridge, 1980); Robert W. Gordon, "Historicism in Legal Scholarship," *Yale Law Journal*, 90, (1981), 1017–56. On the later twentieth-century reception of this tradition in legal history, and on reactions to it, see Robert W. Gordon, "Critical Legal Histories," *Stanford Law Review*, 36, 1–2 (Jan. 1984), 57–125.

[18] For the affirmation of the rule of law as "an unqualified human good" see E. P. Thompson, *Whigs and Hunters: The Origin of the Black Act* (New York, 1975), 266, and generally 258–69. In the course of an otherwise unexceptionable critique of instrumentalism, Thompson wrote of *the* law as "a genuine forum" within which "certain kinds of class conflict" could take place and which, because it elaborated rules and procedures and an ideology ("the rule of law") that regulated and reconciled those conflicts, therefore could, and should, be seen as a categorical benefit. This judgment both trivializes antilegalism and, more

Second, insofar as the revolutionary commitment to "life, liberty, and the pursuit of happiness" disclosed serious ambitions for a new and distinctively American and positive constitutionalism, the rule of law was hardly the obvious vehicle for its realization. The eighteenth century's Anglocentric common law tradition implied a constitutionalism which "could not contemplate the use of government to work for equality in the form of social or economic justice, because it could not trust government."[19] Law's rise was therefore conditional upon either a transformation of that common law tradition into something radically different or the adjustment of such revolutionary goals as contradicted it. Adjustment duly took place.[20] As the writings of William Manning and the Charlestown "social Democrats" signal, however, adjustment was not uncontested. An alternative oppositional constitutionalism was articulated both during the revolutionary era and again, with much vigor, in the late 1820s and 1930s.[21]

important, treats law as a metanarrative. For critiques of Thompson see Morton J. Horwitz, "The Rule of Law: An Unqualified Human Good?" *Yale Law Journal*, 86, 3 (Jan. 1977), 561–66; Karl Klare, "Law-Making as Praxis," *Telos*, 40 (1979), 133–4; Adrian Merritt, "The Nature and Function of Law," *British Journal of Law and Society*, 7, 2 (1980), 194–214. On antilegalism, see Christopher Hill, *The World Turned Upside Down: Radical Ideas during the English Revolution* (New York, 1972), 216–22. On the English antinomian tradition ("a wide movement that questioned all kinds of authority: of the law, of the King, of Scripture, of property, of patriarchy") and its Atlantic diaspora, see Peter Linebaugh, "All the Atlantic Mountains Shook," in Geoff Eley and William Hunt, eds., *Reviving the English Revolution: Reflections and Elaborations on the Work of Christopher Hill* (London, 1988), 193–219. On American antilegalism see Heimert, *Religion and the American Mind*, 179–82; Perry Miller, *The Life of the Mind in America: From the Revolution to the Civil War* (New York, 1965), 99–265; Gerard W. Gawalt, "Sources of Anti-Lawyer Sentiment in Massachusetts, 1740–1840," *American Journal of Legal History*, 14 (Oct. 1970), 283–307; Maxwell Bloomfield, *American Lawyers in a Changing Society, 1776–1876* (Cambridge, Mass., 1976), 32–90; Robert W. Gordon, "Review: The American Codification Movement," *Vanderbilt Law Review*, 36, 2 (Mar. 1983), 431–58.

[19] John Phillip Reid, *The Concept of Liberty in the Age of the American Revolution* (Chicago, 1988), 114.

[20] For a celebration of the postrevolutionary assimilation of the American system of judicature "to that of England" see Isaac Parker, "A Sketch of the Character of the Late Chief Justice Parsons, Delivered at the Opening of the Supreme Judicial Court at Boston, on the Twenty-Third Day of November, 1813," in Theophilus Parsons [Jr.], *Memoir of Theophilus Parsons* (Boston, 1859), 403–22, at 411.

[21] On these points see, generally, J. R. Pole, *The Pursuit of Equality in American History* (Berkeley, 1978), 11; Shannon C. Stimson, *The American Revolution in the Law: Anglo-American Jurisprudence before John Marshall* (Princeton, 1990); Christopher L. Tomlins, "Law, Police, and the Pursuit of Happiness in the New American Republic," *Studies in American Political Development*, 4 (1990), 1–34; Joyce Appleby, "The American Heritage: The Heirs and the Disinherited," *Journal of American History*, 74, 3 (Dec. 1987), 798–806; Gary B. Nash, "Also There at the Creation: Going beyond Gordon S. Wood," *William and Mary Quarterly*, 3d ser., 44, 3 (July 1987), 602–11; Steven Rosswurm, "'As a Lyen Out of His Den': Philadelphia's Popular Movement, 1776–80," in Jacob and Jacob, eds., *Origins of Anglo-American Radicalism*, 300–23; Ruth Bogin, "Petitioning and the New Moral Economy of Post-Revolutionary America," *William and Mary Quarterly*, 3d ser., 45, 3 (July 1988), 391–425. For the adjustment of American constitutionalism toward a common law paradigm see Jennifer Nedelsky, "Reconceiving Autonomy: Sources, Thoughts, and Possibilities," *Yale Journal of Law and Feminism*, 1, 1 (Spring 1989), 15–19, and idem, "Law, Boundaries, and the Bounded Self," *Representations*, 30 (Spring 1990), 163–7, each of which foreshadows arguments developed more fully in her *Private Property and the Limits of American Constitutionalism: The Madisonian Framework and Its Legacy* (Chicago, 1990). For hints of continued openings toward a subordinated "positive" American constitutionalism see Harry Scheiber, "Public Rights and the Rule of Law in American Legal History," *California Law Review*, 72, 2 (Mar. 1984), 217–51; William J. Novak, "Intellectual Origins of the State Police Power: The Common Law Vision of a Well-Regulated Society," *Legal History Program Working Papers* (Madison), ser. 3, no. 2 (June 1989). The issues adverted to in this paragraph and the next are pursued at length in Chapters 2 and 3.

23

That this alternative existed underlines the importance of recognizing that for much of the latter half of the eighteenth century the complex of common law ideas and institutions associated with the rule of law lived in competition with other potentially paradigmatic political discourses – of republicanism, of evangelical Christianity, of commerce or political economy, and, above all, of "police" – all of which can themselves be considered candidates for ideocultural hegemony. To understand the circumstances of the rise of the rule of law, and its significance, one must therefore consider the relationship between law and these other discourses, and their fate.

The burden of that inquiry will be picked up during the remainder of Part 1. Here we should simply note, as a preliminary, that the basic point of departure was an increasing consciousness, at the dawning of the eighteenth century, of the world's accessibility. This prompted a proliferation of theorizing – at first predominantly religious and scientific, later increasingly political and economic – about the relationship of human action to context and the means by which that relationship might be managed. "At the opening of the modern era," writes Gordon Wood, Protestant reformers had "invoked divine providence and the omnipotence of God in order to stamp out the traditional popular reliance on luck and magic and to renew a sense of design and moral purpose in the world." Subsequently natural philosophers like Newton effected the diminution of this absolute (and therefore necessarily arbitrary) divine authority by positing invariant natural laws of mechanism. Fear of chaos and contingency gradually ebbed. "The world lost some of its mystery." In particular the world of human affairs became manipulable, the new science promising human beings "the capacity to predict and control not only nature but [their] own society."[22]

Scientific thinking having "created a new world of laws, measurements, predictions, and constancies or regularities of behavior" that enabled human comprehension and governance of social no less than physical phenomena, finding these laws "became the consuming passion of the Enlightenment." At the same time, because in human affairs scientific thinking's mechanistic approach to causation was corrosive of the very notion of human capacity for self-determination which it had helped to popularize, the moral status of action became an all-consuming preoccupation. "If human affairs were really the consequence of one thing repeatedly and predictably following upon another, the social world would become as determined as the physical world seemed to be." In these circumstances investigation of the extent and limits of human agency – voluntarism and free will – moved to the forefront of philosophical inquiry. The result was a denial of the possibility of unintended consequences. All action, it was argued, was the product of intention. "Only by identifying causes with motives was any sort of human science and predictability possible, and only then could morality be preserved in the new, mechanistic causal world." Never before or since in Western history, says Wood, had human

---

[22] Gordon S. Wood, "Conspiracy and the Paranoid Style: Causality and Deceit in the Eighteenth Century," *William and Mary Quarterly*, 3d ser., 39, 3 (July 1982), 412–13.

beings "been held so directly and morally responsible for the events of [their] world."[23]

In the Atlantic world, classical republicanism, evangelical Christianity, police, and political economy all emerged during the course of the eighteenth century (roughly in that order) as viable modes of discourse addressing this problematic relationship between human action and context.[24] Simplifying for the moment, and ignoring for the sake of clarity their interrelationships,[25] one may distinguish these modes of discourse principally by their conceptions of how, now handed the opportunity, human action should be moderated and how the capacity to moderate should be sustained. Thus, classical republicanism proposed the moderation of action by a secular civic-minded virtue, sustained by propertied independence;[26] evangelical Christianity proposed moderation by the individual's redemptive commitment to a transcendent Christian morality – "enthusiasm" – sustained by strict new codes of self-conduct;[27] political economy proposed moderation by the pursuit of individual self-interest, sustained by the equilibrating effects of the market;[28] and police proposed moderation by the pursuit of safety and happiness – individual and communal welfare – sustained (in America) by the promise of "free" governments embodying the sovereignty of the people.[29]

Although the degree of influence enjoyed by each of these modes of discourse in the colonies can be explained, at least in part, by their capacity to articulate established routines of colonial culture, each also stood for a route to be followed in realization of or reaction to an unfolding process of context *transformation*.[30] Each, that is, also offered a distinctive perception of the deficiencies of established institutions and routines, and of their inability to provide clear explanations of and maps

---

[23] Ibid., 413–17.

[24] Kramnick, "The 'Great National Discussion'," 3–32; Ruth H. Bloch, "The Constitution and Culture," and John Howe, "Gordon S. Wood and the Analysis of Political Culture in the American Revolutionary Era," both in *William and Mary Quarterly*, 3d ser., 44, 3 (July 1987), 550–5 and 569–75; James T. Kloppenberg, "The Virtues of Liberalism: Christianity, Republicanism, and Ethics in Early American Political Discourse," *Journal of American History*, 74, 1 (June 1987), 9–33; Tomlins, "Law, Police, and the Pursuit of Happiness," 3–16.

[25] On the relationship between political economy and police, e.g., see the sensitive discussion of Michael Ignatieff and Istvan Hont, "Needs and Justice in the *Wealth of Nations*: An Introductory Essay," in Michael Ignatieff and Istvan Hont, eds., *Wealth and Virtue: The Shaping of Political Economy in the Scottish Enlightenment* (Cambridge, 1983), 1–44. See also, Chapter 2, this volume.

[26] J. G. A. Pocock, *The Machiavellian Moment: Florentine Political Thought and the Atlantic Republican Tradition* (Princeton, 1975), 184.

[27] Heimert, *Religion and the American Mind*, 27–58. See also David Lovejoy, "'Desperate Enthusiasm': Early Signs of American Radicalism," Patricia U. Bonomi, "'A Just Opposition': The Great Awakening as a Radical Model," and Rhys Isaac, "Radicalized Religion and Changing Lifestyles: Virginia in the Period of the American Revolution," all in Jacob and Jacob, eds., *Origins of Anglo-American Radicalism*, 230–42, 243–56, and 257–67. On the evangelical contribution to revolutionary and postrevolutionary politics see Ruth H. Bloch, *Visionary Republic: Millennial Themes in American Thought, 1756–1800* (New York and Cambridge, 1985).

[28] Joyce Appleby, *Capitalism and a New Social Order: The Republican Vision of the 1790s* (New York, 1984), 25–50.

[29] Tomlins, "Law, Police, and the Pursuit of Happiness," 16–20; and Chapter 2, this volume.

[30] See, generally, Kloppenberg, "Virtues of Liberalism," 11–24.

for human action. As the process of transformation intensified in the late eighteenth century, lent extraordinary focus first by the political and social pressures of imperial crisis, then by revolution and war, and finally by the process of creating new frames of government, so competition among these different routes intensified, culminating in a period of acute ideological strife whose reverberations extended well into the nineteenth century. The eventual outcome was the efflorescence of a new institutional and imaginative context, normally denominated "liberal," which eclipsed (where it did not absorb and rearrange) most aspects of the previous half-century's competing alternatives and which simultaneously spawned a new series of reinforcing routines constitutive of a market society with, however, distinctly asymmetrical social relations: social and economic individualism, the protection of property, a filtered democracy, and a hobbled state.[31]

LAW'S REPUBLIC

Law was central to the efflorescence of this new institutional and imaginative context during the early republic. By the early nineteenth century the rule of law had assumed a vital role as the integral constituting element of the society that had come into being over the previous seventy-odd years, a role that it had not previously played in American society and politics.[32] Subsequent chapters will demonstrate this by filling in the outlines of processes simply alluded to here, all the time using the experience of labor and the social relations of employment as the point of reference.

Right at the beginning, however, it is worth pointing out that the hypothesis here on display, that during the revolutionary and postrevolutionary epochs law gained a particular centrality in American life that it had not enjoyed before, is hardly novel. Over the years, historians of American law have voted with their feet in dedicating almost all their considerable energy to the period starting with the

---

[31] See, e.g., Joyce Appleby, "The Radical *Double-Entendre* in the Right to Self-Government," in Jacob and Jacob, eds., *Origins of Anglo-American Radicalism*, 275–83; idem, *Capitalism and a New Social Order*, passim; idem, "The Heirs and the Disinherited," 803–6. See also Steven J. Watts, *The Republic Reborn: War and the Making of Liberal America* (Baltimore, 1987); Cathy Matson and Peter Onuf, "Toward a Republican Empire: Interest and Ideology in Revolutionary America, *American Quarterly*, 37, 4 (Fall 1985), 496–531; Morton J. Horwitz, "Republicanism and Liberalism in American Constitutional Thought," *William and Mary Law Review*, 29, 1 (Fall 1987), 57–74; Nedelsky, "Reconceiving Autonomy," 15–19.

[32] See e.g., Allan C. Hutchinson and Patrick Monahan, "Democracy and the Rule of Law," in Hutchinson and Monahan, eds., *The Rule of Law: Ideal or Ideology* (Toronto, 1987), 97–123, at 104–5. Gordon Wood's recent description of the carving out of "an exclusive sphere of activity for the judiciary" during the 1780s and 1790s as "the most dramatic institutional transformation in the early Republic" – the high point of a "remarkable process by which the judiciary in America suddenly emerged out of its colonial insignificance to become by 1800 the principal means by which popular legislatures were controlled and limited" – is also noteworthy (*The Radicalism of the American Revolution* [New York, 1992], 323). Given these conclusions, it is puzzling that Wood's account of the politics and culture of the early republic in fact has almost nothing to say about law.

26

Revolution.[33] Clearly implicit in their accounts of the prominent role of law in molding the new nation's civic consciousness has been a judgment of its lesser previous importance.[34] Take, as a recent example, the opening paragraph of the first chapter of Robert Ferguson's elegant *Law and Letters in American Culture*:

The centrality of law in the birth of the republic is a matter of national lore. "In America the law is king," Thomas Paine the prophet of revolution proclaimed in 1776, and so it has remained ever since in the political rhetoric and governmental councils of the nation. Revolutionary orators and pamphleteers like John Dickinson, James Otis, John and Samuel Adams, Patrick Henry, Thomas Jefferson, James Wilson and Arthur Lee were members of the profession. Their writings were heavily scored with the citations and doctrines of legal study and contributed decisively to what historians have called the conceptualization of American life. Twenty-five of the fifty-six signers of the Declaration of Independence, thirty-one of the fifty-five members of the Constitutional Convention, and thirteen of the first sixteen presidents were lawyers. All of our formative documents – the Declaration of Independence, the Constitution, the Federalist Papers and the seminal decisions of the Supreme Court under John Marshall – were drafted by attorneys steeped in Sir William Blackstone's *Commentaries on the Laws of England* (1765–1769). So much was this the case that the *Commentaries* rank second only to the Bible as a literary and intellectual influence on the history of American institutions.[35]

What, though, was to be the substantive significance of law's centrality in the politics of the early republic? That is, what difference was it to make that this would be a law-centered polity? One could argue, after all, that what Ferguson is describing here is simply a somewhat amplified version of the role of providing a language for rule that law always seems to perform whatever interpretation of human action dominates society; or in other words that the key characteristic of legal discourse is

[33] This focus has been strongly criticized by colonial historians. See, e.g., Mann, *Neighbors and Strangers*; Botein, *Early American Law and Society*, 1–5; Katz, "The Problem of a Colonial Legal History," 457–89, esp. 470–4. Its persistence is nevertheless attested to in the continuity in emphasis accorded the postcolonial era in both of the major syntheses of American legal history to be published in the last twenty years: Lawrence M. Friedman, *A History of American Law* (New York, 1973; 2d ed., 1985); and Kermit L. Hall, *The Magic Mirror: Law in American History* (New York, 1989).

[34] As we have already noted, two of the most important interpretive texts of the 1970s – Nelson's *Americanization of the Common Law* and Horwitz's *Transformation of American Law* – both treat colonial and early national law as discontinuous, using the Revolution as a benchmark. In Horwitz's case the Revolution does not have causal significance, change being instead the consequence of a burgeoning judicial–commercial alliance under way from the 1780s. Nelson, in contrast, sees the revolutionary upheaval as the causal key to all of the changes in the role of law that both he and Horwitz see occurring over the following fifty years (*Americanization*, 5). See also Katz, "The Problem of a Colonial Legal History," 472–4.

[35] Ferguson, *Law and Letters in American Culture*, 11. As should be clear from the preceding section, although the position I take here adopts in broad outline the traditional chronological parameters which have focused our attention on the Revolution and early republic, I find very persuasive Bruce Mann's argument that (at least in New England) by the 1750s law was in the ascendancy as the technology of first resort in matters of dispute resolution. I do not believe, however, that ascendancy in itself can explain the discursive dominance that law was later to achieve as the postrevolutionary epoch's paradigmatic modality of rule. Evidence of law gaining its own agenda is a necessary but not a sufficient condition of its later supremacy. (The distinction I have in mind here is not dissimilar to Robert Ferguson's distinction between law as a means to social order and legal thought as a supplier of ideological coherence [*Law and Letters*, 10]. It is noteworthy that Mann himself alludes to, but does not attempt to grapple with, this issue [*Neighbors and Strangers*, 168].) This dominance, I argue in Chapter 2, was not ensured until the postrevolutionary period and was an outcome of postrevolutionary political debates.

its instrumental utility in assisting the task of penetrating and reorganizing the detail of social practice to bring action into conformity with current ruling ideas. Law does serve such a facilitative function, as we shall see later in this book.[36] But to see in law nothing more than a medium in which other-derived ideologies of rule or social values may be expressed would be to confine unduly one's comprehension of law[37] and, in the American case, thereby to miss one of the most important points of distinction between the postrevolutionary era and that which preceded it. Thus, to see law's prominence in the new order created after much conflict in the wake of the Revolution as nothing more than a consequence of technical facility in designing the appropriate institutional and imaginative structures for a new ruling "liberal" ideology does not give sufficient weight to the additional biases built into the design both explicitly and piecemeal by the increasingly self-conscious discourse and practices characteristic of *common law* personnel and institutions in themselves, biases which helped steer the early republic's unfolding new order in a particular direction: toward an ever more pronounced conceptual distinction between public and private realms of activity; toward confinement of legislative and administrative power and a vision of the legislative and administrative agencies of the state as threats to individual rights; toward a highly particularized meaning for such key general terms in revolutionary and immediately postrevolutionary political discourse as *democracy, sovereignty,* or *citizenship*; and above all toward an ascendant role in the American polity for the discourse and institutions of the common law itself.[38] Imaginatively and institutionally this was indeed to become, in Frank Michelman's memorable but distinctly double-edged phrase, "Law's Republic."[39]

In the past, some of the most influential explanations for this transformative rise of legal discourse to its position as *the* agency of rule of the postrevolutionary era have tended toward instrumentalism, most commonly taking commerce, social and economic development, or, most specifically, "the needs of capitalism," as their primary point of departure and viewing legal developments either as essentially epiphenomenal or functional consequences of activities occurring in society's engine room or – more sophisticatedly – as autonomously designed reforms initiated to facilitate those activities.[40] Thus law becomes of transcendent importance in

---

[36] Indeed, my interpretation of law's social significance in colonial American life, at least until the mid–eighteenth century, is very much that of law as largely a reflective, facilitative, nonautonomous discourse.

[37] See Richard A. Epstein, "Beyond the Rule of Law: Civic Virtue and Constitutional Structure," *George Washington Law Review*, 56, 1 (Nov. 1987), 149–71.

[38] These points are developed in Chapters 2 and 3. On the last point see, in addition, Horwitz, *Transformation of American Law*, xiii, 1–2; Nedelsky, "Reconceiving Autonomy," 17–18.

[39] Michelman, "Law's Republic." See also Reid, *The Concept of Liberty in the Age of the American Revolution*.

[40] As I hope this paragraph conveys, it is important to stress that instrumentalism and functionalism come wearing a variety of political colors. See J. Willard Hurst, *Law and the Conditions of Freedom in the Nineteenth Century United States* (Madison, 1956), esp. 3–32; idem, *Law and Economic Growth: The Legal History of the Lumber Industry in Wisconsin, 1836–1915* (Madison, 1964); Leonard Levy, *The Law of the Commonwealth and Chief Justice Shaw* (Cambridge, Mass., 1957), esp. 166–82; Friedman, *A History of*

modern society because the growth of commerce/economic change and expansion/ capitalist development "requires legal improvements that increase the certainty and predictability of exchange relationships."[41] In fact, that base proposition is not at all certain;[42] and as Robert Gordon has argued, even were it indisputable one would still have considerable difficulty in demonstrating that law had actually responded in any specifiable developmentally significant way.[43] Looser versions of the same argument are more defensible: for example, that whether there was a detectable functional outcome or not, legal elites were ambitious to create an accommodative environment for commercial/capitalist enterprise;[44] or (different again) that an essential systemic identity between law and capitalism can be inferred logically from the equivalent status accorded in each discourse to the primary unit of attention (in law, individuals; in capitalism, commodities) as objects of exchange relationships, guaranteeing law a central role in the reproduction of the overall conditions that make capitalism possible.[45] The cost of these qualified departures from reductionism, however, is heightened difficulty in making causal statements about the relationship between context and action. In the first version, for example, dysfunctional outcomes simply cease to prove anything; in the second version they can actually be recycled as system reinforcing in that by rendering mysterious in fact the law–capitalism relationship that logic tells us exists, they legitimate "law" by lending it the appearance of autonomy and thus enable it to continue to serve its inferred systemic purpose.[46] Nor does the latter leave any role for historical analysis – the imputed homology of legal and commodity forms simply *is* – except as a medium for illustration of the contention.

LEGAL DOMINATION

The chief problem with reductionist or protoreductionist explanatory strategies is not that they seek to uncover a relationship between law and economy where none exists but rather that the relationship which is uncovered tends to be unilinear and founded in the economy. More fruitful are analyses which concentrate upon law as first and foremost a modality of rule, whose particular practices at any one time will

American Law, 2d ed., 12, 114; Horwitz, *Transformation of American Law*; Michael E. Tigar and Madeleine R. Levy, *Law and the Rise of Capitalism* (New York, 1979); Hall, *Magic Mirror*; Charles Sellers, *The Market Revolution: Jacksonian America, 1815–1846* (New York, 1991), 47–59.

[41] This summary evaluation is Robert Gordon's. See his "Critical Legal Histories," 64, 78.

[42] See, e.g., Robert B. Ferguson, "Legal Ideology and Commercial Interests: The Social Origins of the Commercial Law Codes," *British Journal of Law and Society*, 4 (1977), 18–38.

[43] Gordon, "Critical Legal Histories," 78–81, and see generally 63–87.

[44] See, e.g., Horwitz, *Transformation of American Law*, 1–30; Ferguson, "Legal Ideology and Commercial Interests," 22–32.

[45] Isaac Balbus, "Commodity Form and Legal Form: An Essay on the 'Relative Autonomy' of the Law," *Law and Society Review*, 11 (Winter 1977), 571–88.

[46] Ibid., 585.

have determinable consequences for human action, not least those actions which constitute the practice of rule itself.[47]

Such an approach is suggested in the legal sociology of Max Weber. In Weber's view, structures of authority in complex industrial societies increasingly come to approximate *legal domination*. Legal domination is distinguishable from other forms of domination both by the mentality which it implies in rulers and ruled and by the structures through which it operates. Weber's other types of domination, well known, are *charismatic* and *traditional* authority, respectively embodied in the rule of the personal charismatic leader and the rule of the patriarch or patrimonial prince. The ideational characteristic of legal domination, in contrast, is rationality and its structural characteristic is bureaucracy, each embodying forms of stability independent of emotional, personal, and/or traditional ties of authority. In the case of a state, these characteristics translate into "a political association with a rational, written constitution, rationally ordained law, and an administration bound to rational rules or laws, administered by trained officials."[48]

Making use of the idea of legal domination is not unproblematic. For example, although Weber's forms of domination are ideal types rather than descriptions of actual historical circumstances, it is clear that legal domination and its reflection of (and in) increasing rationality is, as Roger Cotterrell has it, "the consequence of particular historical developments" derived specifically from the unique experience of the West.[49] Used uncritically, therefore, Weber's sociology of law would simply direct us to the theory of modernization, in particular to that peculiarly desiccated etiology in which rationalization appears "the sole consistent and ubiquitous motor of change, removed from all human choice and struggle."[50]

Just as problematic is the specific character of the legal domination that Weber derived from these Western historical experiences, for it actually reflects only one form of Western experience. Weber's stress on the formally rational and bureaucratic character of legal domination articulates quite satisfactorily with German legal science, with pandecticism, with the idea of the *Rechtsstaat*, with such developments as the Napoleonic Code, and, to a degree, with those aspects of the British constitution transformed by Benthamite reform. As Weber himself recognized, however, it does not articulate very satisfactorily with the

---

[47] Michael Grossberg's critique of Lawrence Friedman's important and influential *History of American Law* has a particular resonance in this regard. See Grossberg, "Legal History and Social Science: Friedman's *History of American Law*, the Second Time Around," *Law and Social Inquiry*, 13, 2 (Spring 1988), 359–84, at 368–74, esp. 373.

[48] Roger Cotterrell, "Legality and Political Legitimacy in the Sociology of Max Weber," in David Sugarman, ed., *Legality, Ideology, and the State* (London and New York, 1981), 69–93, at 75–6. There is, of course, no particular reason why we should consider either charismatic or traditional authority incompatible with the use of legal institutions to exercise rule per se. That is, legal institutions can and do facilitate the projection of distinctly nonlegal forms of domination.

[49] Ibid., 76.

[50] Ibid., 81. As Cotterrell suggests, used thus, legal domination cannot be mobilized as a concept "which allows us to reach an analysis of law's ideological functions which could explain their relevance for political action and social change."

"irrational" unreconstructed aspects of the British state – notably, a substantively eclectic common law and judge-centered decision making – or, one may add, with the early American republic's diffuse and decentralized "state of courts and parties."[51] That is to say, it does not articulate very satisfactorily with institutions and practices of governance associated with the Anglo-American common law "rule of law."

By no means, however, do these problems imply dispensing with the concept of legal domination. Rich dividends may be obtained by treating the historical fact of institutional variations departing from Weber's concept of rationality not as a fatal blow to his sociology of law but rather as a recommendation that closer attention be paid to the particular historical circumstances of a polity in defining the forms in which legal domination will appear. Having pursued such an analysis in the British case, David Sugarman has found ample reason to conclude that although in formal Weberian terms the legal system was genuinely nonrational, considered on its own terms it was "functionally and rationally successful."[52] This leads Sugarman to the observation "that irrationality may have a rationale ... that it may also constitute a structure for securing wealth, power and status – a system whereby certain groups maintain and legitimate themselves," an insight that Weber, ensnared by nineteenth-century historiographical and sociological traditions which structured scholarship around the "antinomies separating pre-modern from modern, pre-industrial from industrial ... artificially separat[ing] out the rational from the irrational features of society, marginalising the latter," was not in a position to glimpse.[53]

---

[51] David Sugarman, "In the Spirit of Weber: Law, Modernity, and 'The Peculiarities of the English,'" *Legal History Program Working Papers* (Madison), ser. 2, no. 6 (1987), 6–16. For the characterization of the early republic as a state of courts and parties, see Stephen Skowronek, *Building a New American State: The Expansion of National Administrative Capacities* (New York, 1982), 19–35.

[52] Sugarman "In the Spirit of Weber," 43. As Sugarman points out (at 44–6), the legal system consisted in (1) a form of social organization (the bar) that, though archaic, helped barristers and judges achieve a high degree of autonomy and that facilitated internal consistency in the expression of expertise (technical legal development) and in the bar's own ideology; and (2) a common law tradition willfully confusing code and custom that rendered law irrational and incoherent, and thereby mysterious, and thus not only actually assisted the bar's appropriation of legal knowledge but also proved remarkably flexible in providing cover for an endless variety of political, social, and economic changes. Indeed, concludes Sugarman, it was the legal system's flexibility, a flexibility ultimately derived from its articulation with rather than its replacement of nonlegal sources of power (social, cultural, economic), which was the priceless rationale of English irrationality. It was this "that put you in the position of an entrepreneur if you desired it, that gave you the legal regime you wanted, that allowed you to avoid the state legal order when you wanted to, but to use its coercive might when you needed it."

[53] Ibid., 43, 41. Weber certainly grappled with the problem and Sugarman credits his discussion of England as "of special interest precisely because it is a unique instance of Weber conceding in rich and suggestive vein, the importance and roles of irrationality in modern western society. Indeed, it can be interpreted as arguing against his own thesis – not only the causal importance of rational law; but also as disproving or deconstructing his association of modernity with rationality in any simple sense" (52). See also Maureen Cain, "The Limits of Idealism: Max Weber and the Sociology of the Law," *Research in Law and Sociology*, 3 (1980), 53–83, esp. 70–6. But Weber could not accommodate irrationality theoretically in his account of modernity. Though his general theory is not one of teleological modernization (the ideal types of domination do not form a sequential or developmental hierarchy) and rationalizing routines are always vulnerable to the intervention of charismatic authority, these interventions are still

Discard the antinomies, then, and legal domination ceases to be recognizable by reference to the embodiment of governance in a particular configuration of institutions. Instead legal domination may be seen more as the creation of a new context for action through the empowerment of a particular form of "creative imaginary activity" – legal discourse – as the modality of rule in a society. Furthermore, to be effective (functionally and rationally successful) as a modality of rule, legal domination will take idiomatic forms – institutional and imaginative – peculiar to that society's history and intimately related to its other structures of wealth, power, and status.

This is, as a matter of fact, precisely what we observe occurring in the American case. In the early republic, enshrining the rule of law through constitutional innovation appeared to mean locating legal domination in institutions and ideas which represented the track of formal rationality and bureaucracy, creating "a country founded upon explicit constitutions and bills of rights, and governed by statute";[54] in other words, the track which Weber held to be the characteristic of legal domination. As it turned out, however, enshrining the rule of law also meant the simultaneous empowerment of the very opposite: the institutions and track of the common law. As important, it meant enshrining that common law tradition's determinedly antihistoricist view of its own history[55] and (a crucial concession in the new republic) bowing before its obstinate determination to locate its own legitimacy and autonomy in that history rather than in the institutions developed in the postrevolutionary polity. This amounted to recognizing a claim to the legitimacy of legal domination established in a location quite separate and distinct from that "rational, written constitution, rationally ordained law, and an administration bound to rational rules or laws, administered by trained officials"; a location, further, which was safely under the control of the claimants themselves.[56]

treated as interruptions in a process rather than elements of it. Moreover, Weber characterizes the emergence of the charismatic leader not only as irrational but also as unpredictable (i.e., not theorizable). For an account of the "constructive incoherence" of Weber's sociology of law see David Trubek, "Reconstructing Max Weber's Sociology of Law," *Stanford Law Review*, 37, 3 (Feb. 1985), 919–35. But see also Stephen M. Feldman, "An Interpretation of Max Weber's Theory of Law: Metaphysics, Economics, and the Iron Cage of Constitutional Law," *Law & Social Inquiry*, 16, 2 (Spring, 1991), 205–48.

[54] Miller, *The Life of the Mind in America*, 127.

[55] On the emergence and refinement of this historical genre in the seventeenth century, see J. G. A. Pocock, *The Ancient Constitution and the Feudal Law: A Study of English Historical Thought in the Seventeenth Century: A Reissue with a Retrospect* (New York, 1987), 30–69, 240–3, 261–78, 290–6, 302–4, 338–40. Pocock finds "what is unmistakably a recrudescence of the prescriptive and immemorial character of the law and the constitution" occurring in the latter part of the eighteenth century (379–80). For acerbic commentary on the more recent manifestations of this genre in American writing, see Morton J. Horwitz, "The Conservative Tradition in the Writing of American Legal History," *American Journal of Legal History*, 17, 3 (July 1973), 275–94. See also Gordon, "Historicism in Legal Scholarship," 1038–40.

[56] Contemporary critics were, of course, well aware of this. See, e.g., the letters of Honestus [Benjamin Austin], published in the *Independent Chronicle* (Boston), March–June 1786, and reprinted thirty years after as *Observations on the Pernicious Practice of the Law . . . By Honestus* (Boston, 1819). Honestus commented: "One reason of the pernicious practice of the law, and what gives great influence to the 'order' [of lawyers] is, that we have introduced the whole body of English laws into our Courts; why should these states be governed by British laws? Can we suppose them applicable to the circumstances of this

From the beginning, then, the idea of the rule of law concealed a major duality in the institutional and imaginative structure of legal domination in the early republic. The rule of law seemed to be the voice of the institutions comprising the several polities (state and federal) created in the aftermath of the Revolution. Simultaneously it was the distinctly different voice of the Anglocentric common law: undemocratic, often hectoring, often speaking on its own behalf and often in order to override the other. As the medium in which both voices were expressed, moreover, legal discourse became an easy portal through which the common law's particular professional, organizational, and ideological preoccupations – its presuppositions about the role of courts, the judiciary, and the legal profession; its views of other social institutions; its notions about causation, social relations, and social processes; its commitments in legal reasoning to teleology, taxonomy, categorization, and conceptual hierarchy; its pretensions to scientism mixed with its genuflections before custom and tradition – could all leak into the wider and contested discourse of legal domination, where they could become established as an "expertise" mediating the early republic's political, social, and economic debates, interpreting the functions of institutions, translating rule of law generalities into usable behavioral particularities, and creating the appearance of legal–cultural–political–economic homologies.[57] One might indeed argue that thus enshrining the common law, in a context of written constitutions and relatively representative legislatures, was akin

country? Can the monarchical and aristocratical institutions of England be consistent with the republican principles of our constitution? Why should a young Republic be ruled by laws framed for the particular purpose of a monarchical government, or can laws which are applicable to Kings, Lords, and Commons of England, be any way consonant to the Republican establishment of this Commonwealth? We may as well adopt the laws of the Medes and Persians. A great error, therefore, lies in our want of a proper system of laws, adapted to our particular state and circumstances: the numerous precedents brought from 'Old English Authorities,' serve to embarrass all our judiciary causes, and answer no other purpose, than to increase the influence of lawyers; as from such authorities they can cull and select precedents to answer every purpose: the omnipotence of their laws can reconcile all contradictions; how absurd, therefore, to introduce into our young republic, the whole body of English laws!"

"Is it not melancholy to see such numerous volumes, brought into our Courts, arranged in formidable order, as the grand artillery to batter down every plain, rational principle of law? As we have framed our own constitution, and mean to support our independence as a nation, why should the people of this Commonwealth, be subjected to these English codes? Would it not be more for the honour and happiness of this State, to establish a system of laws of our own, dictated by the genuine principles of Republicanism, and made easy to be understood by every individual in the community? By this means we should destroy the wonderful misery of law craft, and the whole science would be adapted to the most simple understanding" (15–16).

For later examples of such criticism see *The English Practice: A Statement Showing Some of the Evils and Absurdities of the Practice of the English Common Law . . . By a Lover of Improvement* (New York, 1822); William Sampson, *An Anniversary Discourse before the Historical Society of New York . . . Showing the Origin, Progress, Antiquities, Curiosities, and Nature of the Common Law* (New York, 1824); Stephen Simpson, *The Working Man's Manual: A New Theory of Political Economy on the Principle of Production the Source of Wealth* (Philadelphia, 1831), 18–19, 136–8; [David Henshaw], *The Common Law of England* (Boston 1839).

[57] On the interface between constitutional and common law discourse see, e.g., H. Jefferson Powell, "The Original Understanding of Original Intent," *Harvard Law Review*, 98, 5 (Mar. 1985), 885–948; Novak, "Intellectual Origins of the State Police Power," 70–3. For contemporary commentary extolling that interface see, e.g., James Kent, *An Introductory Lecture to a Course of Law Lectures, Delivered November 17, 1794* (New York, 1794).

to sanctioning a state within a state. Certainly, to allow the common law its own foundation of existence independent of that upon which legal domination (in the Weberian sense) was established in the postrevolutionary polities was to guarantee the common law a decisive degree of influence over the form and substance of the rule of law, and thus over the "facts of life," in the new nation.

CONCLUSION

In furnishing the crucial element in the context framing life in the new nation, the common law rule of law furnished the early republic with a set of institutional procedures and a set of images. Immanent in these was a society – a structure of wealth, power, and status, of relationships, of conflicts and modes of resolution, of values (what was good and what was not, what was orderly and what was disorderly) and ambitions (both personal and societal) – represented by and in the rule of law as collectively constituting material reality, or "fact."

In both their collective and their individual aspect, the circumstances of work and employment relationships in the early republic, and the ideas and ambitions of their participants, conveyed an image of a society in which the facts of life differed, strikingly in some cases, in fundamental respects from those suggested in the descriptions immanent in the framework furnished by the rule of law. As such, work and employment furnished a prime site for instability or dissonance between dominant context and lived experience, one where, as a result, weaknesses and contradictions in the institutional and imaginative fabric of the rule of law – constituted in the uneasy, dualized form just described – might be likely to show up with particular clarity.[58]

Beginning in Part 2, I pursue a detailed assessment of the postrevolutionary legal order's apprehension of collective and individual labor and of its assiduous (and successful) attempts to reconceive both in forms which comported with, rather than challenged, the institutional and imaginative context to whose supremacy the legal order was committed. Law, we will see, played a major role in concretizing, while simultaneously obscuring, asymmetries of power and exchange arising in the social relations of employer and employee and the organization of employment.

First, though, I want to look more closely at some topics that so far have only been outlined: the contexts in which action was beginning to be understood by the second half of the eighteenth century, the circumstances of the claim to a preponderance of interpretive authority entered on behalf of the rule of law as I have described it, and the reasons for the success of that claim in the face of alternative contexts for action.

---

[58] Predictably, race and slavery provided another prime site where a similar dissonance between context and action bred contradictions. See, e.g., Mark Tushnet, *The American Law of Slavery, 1810–1860: Considerations of Humanity and Interest* (Princeton, 1981). As predictably, gender relations provided a third. See, e.g., Linda K. Kerber, "The Paradox of Women's Citizenship in the Early Republic: The Case of *Martin vs. Massachusetts*, 1805," *American Historical Review*, 97, 2 (Apr. 1992), 349–78.

2

Police: the pursuit of happiness

But where say some is the King of America? I'll tell you Friend, he reigns above, and doth not make havoc of mankind like the Royal brute of Britain. Yet that we may not appear to be defective even in earthly honours, let a day be solemnly set apart for proclaiming the charter; let it be brought forth placed on the divine law, the word of God; let a crown be placed thereon, by which the world may know, that so far as we approve of monarchy, that in America THE LAW IS KING. For as in absolute governments the King is law, so in free countries the law *ought* to be King; and there ought to be no other. But lest any ill use should afterwards arise, let the crown at the conclusion of the ceremony be demolished, and scattered among the people whose right it is.

Thomas Paine, *Common Sense*

Consider *police*. The word is hardly a stranger. Policing is an essential component of the institutional architecture of contemporary society, and American historians have devoted much energy to its origins and development.[1] Paradoxically, however, that energy has created a series of obstacles to a successful recovery of *police* in its original incarnation as a key term of political discourse. What historians have traced is the genealogy – and principally an institutional not a conceptual genealogy at that – of what *police* has become in the years since the middle decades of the nineteenth century. Admittedly historians have usually felt compelled to undertake a preliminary investigation of a premodern ("pre-uniformed") era, in which *police* is recognized to have been endowed with less precise a meaning than today's. But this kind of obligatory encounter with unfamiliar conceptual roots is not an unusual chore for historians of institutions, and generally it has been negotiated without much fuss by charting the development of the modern police institution out of a congeries of (increasingly outmoded and inefficient) English offices – (constables, sheriffs, watches, and so forth); by noting in passing without much comment the broader definitions of *police* supplied by such as Samuel Johnson ("the regulation and government of a city or country") and Noah Webster ("the government of a city or

---

[1] For a useful review of the development of police historiography see Robert Liebman and Michael Polen, "Perspectives on Policing in Nineteenth Century America," *Social Science History*, 2, 3 (Spring 1978), 346–60.

town" and "the administration of the laws and regulations of a city"); and by then proceeding with some relief to the stage of real debate for which all this has been scene setting and curtain raising: what uniformed police forces do, and why.[2] Within this scholarship there has been considerable variation and considerable debate, particularly over the reasons influencing the appearance of police forces – crime, riot, control of social deviance, control of the working class, the professionalization of urban government, the rise of the administrative state – and over their social role.[3] But throughout, *police* has been treated as an institutional phenomenon, to be addressed in terms of its evolution and function.

Here I wish to revisit a less-familiar vocabulary of *police*, vital to the politics of the eighteenth century but since then largely lost. William Manning would no doubt have recognized the word, although its current meaning would have been alien to him. He did not in any case use it in *The Key of Libberty*. Thomas Jefferson[4] did use it, however, and in a setting which underlines the importance of its recovery to the further refinement of our understanding of late eighteenth-century political discourse. Shortly after he became Virginia's second governor in 1779, Jefferson was elected to the Board of Visitors of the College of William and Mary and promptly set out to transform the college's organization and curriculum along lines which he had earlier promoted, unsuccessfully, while engaged in his mammoth revision of the laws of Virginia. Because the goal of Jefferson's proposed reforms was the creation of an educational system which would be a training ground for republican citizenship, it has long been considered significant that among the innovations he chose to press on the College of William and Mary was the establishment of the first professorial chair in law in North America – indeed, the only such position anywhere apart from the Vinerian chair at Oxford. What has been less remarked is that the chair which Jefferson pioneered was not a chair of *law*, as such, at all. It was a chair of "Law and Police."[5]

---

[2] See, e.g., Roger Lane, *Policing the City: Boston, 1822–1885* (Cambridge, Mass., 1967); James E. Richardson, *Urban Police in the United States* (Port Washington, N.Y., 1974); Wilbur R. Miller, *Cops and Bobbies: Police Authority in New York and London, 1830–1870* (Chicago, 1977); Eric H. Monkkonen, *Police in Urban America, 1860–1920* (New York and Cambridge, 1981). See also Leon Radzinowicz, *A History of English Criminal Law and Its Administration from 1750* (New York, 1957), vol. 3, *Cross-Currents in the Movement for the Reform of the Police*, 1–8. For the Johnson quotation see *A Dictionary of the English Language* (London, 1755), II, pt. 1, unpaginated; for Webster see *An American Dictionary of the English Language* (New York, 1882), II, unpaginated.

[3] See, e.g., Allen Steinberg, *The Transformation of Criminal Justice: Philadelphia, 1800–1880* (Chapel Hill, 1989), 119–232. See also Liebman and Polen, "Perspectives on Policing," 346–60; Lawrence Friedman, "The Long Arm of the Law," *Reviews in American History*, 6, 1 (Mar. 1978), 225–8; Samuel Walker, "Counting Cops and Crime," *Reviews in American History*, 10, 2 (June 1982), 212–17; Michael Brogden, "The Emergence of the Police – The Colonial Dimension," *British Journal of Criminology*, 27, 1 (Winter 1987), 5–7.

[4] Jefferson was dubbed Manning's "hero" by Samuel Eliot Morrison. See his foreword to William Manning, *The Key of Libberty* (Billerica, Mass., 1922), xi.

[5] Alonzo T. Dill, *George Wythe: Teacher of Liberty* (Williamsburg, 1979), 41–2. (Here I am indebted to David Konig, who first drew the full title of Wythe's foundation chair to my attention.) Herbert Baxter Adams is one of the few historians to have seen any significance in the title Jefferson chose for the William and Mary chair. Adams used it to point to Jefferson's curricular innovations at the college

Police: the pursuit of happiness

As we have seen in Chapter 1, historians of American law have dedicated considerable energy to detailing the prominent role of law in the formation of the early republic. They have, however, told us little of police. If we are to understand the full significance of law's domination of the republic, and of labor's emergence as its preeminent liability, it is past time to repair this deficiency. To this end I seek here to take advantage of the growing body of historical literature, to date mostly European in origin and focus, that is critical of the institutional bias of the history of police and that seeks instead to ferret out the term's conceptual and ideological meaning. My particular point of departure is the silence in the Anglo-American historiographical canon, to which Keith Tribe has adverted, on police as a strategy in the regulation of populations whose objective is not the achievement of security as such but rather what Manning described in 1798 as "safty and hapyness," or, as the *Boston Quarterly Review* would put it forty-odd years later, "equality before Society."[6]

This silence has a particular resonance when we encounter it in the history of the early republic. For some time now, American historians have been engaged in a painstaking reconstruction of the variety of ideological parameters within which, in the last quarter of the eighteenth century, the architects of the new republic debated the construction of a new social order.[7] It is indisputable that the question of the power of the state to order civil society – its origins, its extent, the forms in which it was to be expressed, the uses to which it could legitimately be put – was absolutely central to those debates. Yet despite this, despite the key role of enlightenment discourse on public happiness in those debates, despite the prominence accorded *police* in that discourse, despite the considerable sensitivity in American constitutional law subsequently on the subject of the state's police power, the historiography of the founding of the American state has failed to pay any attention at all to the conceptual genealogy of *police*. This is somewhat akin to writing a

as a contribution to the teaching of the "science of administration," a connection to which his Germanic bent made him sensitive. But Adams was also sensitive to the nearly complete burial of an earlier vocabulary of police beneath that of his own day. That "excellent term" [police] would, he said "probably suggest nothing but constabulary associations to most college faculties in these modern days" ("The College of William and Mary: A Contribution to the History of Higher Education," *Circulars of Information of the Bureau of Education* no. 1 [Washington, 1887], 39).

[6] Keith Tribe, "Introduction to Knemeyer," *Economy and Society*, 9, 2 (May 1980), 168–71. See also Prologue, n. 36.

[7] For useful recent surveys of this literature see James T. Kloppenberg, "The Virtues of Liberalism: Christianity, Republicanism, and Ethics in Early American Political Discourse," *Journal of American History*, 74, 1 (June 1987), 9–33; Lance Banning, "Jeffersonian Ideology Revisited: Liberal and Classical Ideas in the New American Republic," and Joyce Appleby, "Republicanism in Old and New Contexts," both in *William and Mary Quarterly*, 3d ser., 43, 1 (Jan. 1986), 3–19 and 20–34. For earlier surveys that were of some influence in shaping the development of the field see Robert E. Shalhope, "Toward a Republican Synthesis: The Emergence of an Understanding of Republicanism in American Historiography," *William and Mary Quarterly*, 3d ser., 29, 1 (Jan. 1972), 49–80; idem, "Republicanism and Early American Historiography," *William and Mary Quarterly*, 3d ser., 39, 3 (July 1982), 334–56. For a pithy summary of the results of this two-decade reinterpretive encounter with the political culture of the early republic, see Daniel T. Rodgers, "Republicanism: The Career of a Concept," *Journal of American History*, 79, 1 (June 1992), 11–38.

history of the American economy without discussing capitalism: Where there should be an intersection, there is instead a hole.

Historiographical silences are rarely the creatures of happenstance. Here the absence of *police* is in part at least explained by the presence of *law*, for in the political discourse of the late eighteenth century, law and police occur as distinguishable conceptual bases suggesting distinct paradigms of postrevolutionary socioeconomic order.[8] The police paradigm offered a conception of democratic political management of society and economy: in other words purposeful action by a democratic state for the promotion of human happiness and the maximization of individual and collective creative energies.[9] What Americans like William Manning saw as the promise inherent in the dynamic interplay of a broad-based democracy and the newly legitimated authority of the state, however, others interpreted as presaging a majoritarian assault on vested interests. The outcome was the ascendancy of a different paradigm, in which the social order was constituted principally by protecting property rights from the expanded political nation through constitutional confinement of the scope of democratic politics accompanied by invocation of the independent authority of the common law. In this law paradigm economic activity was labeled a "private" realm and segregated from purposeful public direction: By the early nineteenth century, property rights had effectively been removed from the realm of politics

[8] By *law*, as I have indicated in Chapter 1, I mean the array of common law ideas and institutions that furnished the key interpretive elements of the process of state formation in the new republic in the half-century after the Revolution: the ideology of limited (especially limited legislative) government, the protection of property, and judicial ascendancy. See, generally, G. Edward White, *The Marshall Court and Cultural Change, 1815–1835* (New York, 1988), vol. 3–4 of *History of the Supreme Court of the United States*, 76–156, 195–200. By *police* I mean an array of ideas and institutions predicated on the necessity of government in enhancing the general welfare. The particular meaning of *police* in the context of the democratic promise of the American Revolution is explored at length in the course of this chapter.

The existence of two such paradigms is acknowledged, at least implicitly, by Robert Ferguson. "Conservative members of the early American bar all believed in what they called 'an empire of laws, not of men.' Their republic enshrined the law of nature, a rule of right and reason, within organs of government that protected the rights of men against the encroachment of minorities *and* majorities. . . . From the beginning, however, another theory of republicanism influenced post-Revolutionary politics. This second theory looked to the inalienable power of the people as the source of all government" (*Law and Letters in American Culture* [Cambridge, Mass., 1984], 278). See also Richard E. Ellis, *The Jeffersonian Crisis: Courts and Politics in the Young Republic* (New York, 1971), 250–84; Harry Scheiber, "Public Rights and the Rule of Law in American Legal History," *California Law Review*, 72, 2 (Mar. 1984), 217–51; Frank Michelman, "Law's Republic," *Yale Law Journal*, 97, 8 (July 1988), 1493–537, at 1499–501.

[9] Resort to such a paradigm was a real possibility, I shall argue, particularly in a new American republic where, Joyce Appleby has told us, Jeffersonian republicans desired to realize the full potential of democracy by using "constitutional and statutory measures to make the poor independent." She continues, "What today would appear as social engineering presented itself to Jefferson as a liberation of those natural forces long held in check by the Old World artifices of monarchy, nobility and established religion" ("What Is Still American in the Political Philosophy of Thomas Jefferson?" *William and Mary Quarterly*, 3d ser., 39, 2 [Apr. 1982], 295). See also Joyce O. Appleby, "The Radical *Double-Entendre* in the Right to Self-Government," in Margaret Jacob and James Jacob, eds., *The Origins of Anglo-American Radicalism* (London, 1984), 281, where she describes Jefferson as "never loath to use legislation to achieve the institutional framework for a free society."

altogether.[10] Simultaneously, the administrative capacity of the state – "the police power" – was reinvented within this law paradigm and made an object of judicial contemplation, its legitimate use an issue for juridical, not political, determination.

The ascendancy of the law paradigm did not mean an end to police, and though the discourses of law and police are separable, one should hesitate to insist on too rigid a separation lest their subsequent close relationship seem anomalous. As we shall see, the issue is ultimately one of ideational hegemony. Which discourse would establish the intellectual and political context within which the other must exist? Thus posed, we can see that *police* was double-bound. First, it was constrained by a constitutional discourse increasingly influenced during the 1780s by elite concerns to fashion fundamental laws capable of harnessing the potential of state power let loose by the Revolution's surging democratic politics to knowable and nonthreatening objects before it escaped altogether out of control. Second, the law paradigm offered the further agency of the common law as an independent harness both on democratic politics and on constitutionalism itself. In this atmosphere *police* became extraordinarily difficult to maintain as an independent and autonomous political language, and in the realm of official discourse *police* became drawn into a complementary relationship with *law*, in which it became, as in England, increasingly a matter of security rather than happiness, an institutional instrument for the facilitation of individual transactions among absolute proprietors and for suppressing alternative modes of conducting human affairs.

A RENEWAL OF ACQUAINTANCE

Over the last fifteen years or so, European historians and social scientists have begun to uncover a concept of police current in eighteenth-century political and jurisprudential discourse quite unlike that suggested by the word's later history. W. G. Carson's comments in a recent study of the history of Scottish policing are typical. "Time and again," he notes, "the notion [of police] refers to a [broad] conception of policing for the public good, the public interest or public happiness . . . [to a] concern to promote happiness or the public good as opposed to concern to avert the ills to come or the maintenance of order."[11] As evidence Carson alludes specifically to John Erskine's reference, in his *Institute of the Law of Scotland*, to laws of police "calculated for the providing all the members of the community with a sufficient

---

[10] Jennifer Nedelsky, "Confining Democratic Politics: Anti-Federalists, Federalists, and the Constitution," *Harvard Law Review*, 96, 2 (Nov. 1982), 340–60; and in particular idem, *Private Property and the Limits of American Constitutionalism: The Madisonian Framework and Its Legacy* (Chicago, 1990). See also idem, "The Ideology of Property and the Structure of Power in the U.S. Constitution" (unpublished paper, Davis Center Seminar, Princeton University, 27 Feb. 1981).

[11] W. G. Carson, "Policing the Periphery: The Development of Scottish Policing, 1795–1900, Part I," *Australian and New Zealand Journal of Criminology*, 17, 4 (Dec. 1984), 207–32, at 210. See also, generally, idem, "Policing the Periphery: The Development of Scottish Policing, 1795–1900, Part II," *Australian and New Zealand Journal of Criminology*, 18, 1 (Mar. 1985), 3–16.

quantity of the necessaries of life at reasonable rates, and for the preventing of dearth." He also notes Adam Smith's lengthy critical commentary, in the *Lectures on Jurisprudence*, on police as "the proper means of introducing plenty or abundance into the country," a means of satisfying "the natural wants and demands of mankind."[12]

Michael Ignatieff and Istvan Hont have also stressed the centrality of the concept of police to eighteenth-century discourse on distributive justice. "Given the recurrence of dearth, even famine, and the omnipresence of underemployment in the European economies of their day," they argue, "it was natural for even those who styled themselves political economists to suppose that the subsistence of the labouring poor could only be safeguarded by a 'police' of the market in grain." In the face of Smith's innovative insistence on reliance on the market mechanism, the Scottish political economist James Steuart, for one, denied that "the natural course of things" should be allowed to determine outcomes where these would be unjust or otherwise morally illegitimate. "It was the local government's job to make economic circumstances conform to justice."[13]

These British examples underscore the conceptual identity of police, not with security as such, but with "the public good" as an end and with the administrative means of achieving that end. In so doing, they reveal important connections between concepts of police in eighteenth-century political discourse and the communal dynamics of "moral economy" as identified by E. P. Thompson and others. As Robert Malcolmson has put it, "almost all popular protests and collective actions were informed by certain clearly defined moral concerns and social expectations . . . as to the proper arrangement of economic affairs, the correct observance of priorities during times of hardship or the responsible exercise of magisterial authority." Together, such concerns and expectations added up to a generalized "popular desire for a welfare-oriented management of economic affairs."[14]

The ubiquity of this discourse of police, and the potential of its linkage to discourses of community and moral economy, can more readily be seen in histories of continental Europe, where scholars have given the genealogy of police extensive attention. Take, for example, Kaplan's comments on police in ancien régime France:

Under the old regime police meant managing and maintaining the life of the community, as Plato was understood to have defined it. It embraced, in the words of one writer, "everything

[12] John Erskine, *An Institute of the Law of Scotland* (Edinburgh, 1773), 714; Adam Smith, *Lectures on Jurisprudence*, ed. R. L. Meek, D. D. Raphael, and P. G. Stein (Oxford, 1978), 333, 334.

[13] Michael Ignatieff and Istvan Hont, "Needs and Justice in the *Wealth of Nations*: An Introductory Essay," in idem, eds., *Wealth and Virtue: The Shaping of Political Economy in the Scottish Enlightenment* (Cambridge, 1983), 13–15, 18–19.

[14] Robert W. Malcolmson, *Life and Labour in England, 1700–1780* (New York, 1981), 114–15, 123. See generally E. P. Thompson, "The Moral Economy of the English Crowd in the Eighteenth Century," *Past and Present*, 50 (Feb. 1971), 76–136; John Brewer and John Styles, eds., *An Ungovernable People: The English and Their Law in the Seventeenth and Eighteenth Centuries* (New Brunswick, N.J., 1980). Detailed exploration of these connections is here confined to the American case; see below, section entitled Police in America and section entitled Divergent Goals and the American Revolution, both in this chapter.

which treats of the public good." Indeed, it *was* the public good, for it was an end as well as means, an ideal type as well as a method for achieving it, a political as much as an administrative notion. As noun, verb, and adjective, it was used to describe the way in which social and civil life should be organized. It was also a measure of the progress of civilization, for nations without a police were viewed as barbarous. States with a vicious or imperfect police perished quickly while those with a "good police" endured. Without proscribing growth or change, police implied a social process which tended inevitably toward equilibrium and continuity. The vocation of police, according to one jurist, was to assure that "harmony and concord" prevailed among citizens.[15]

Scholars addressing the origins of cameralism and in particular *Polizeiwissenschaft*, or the "science of police," in the German states of the eighteenth century have come to comparable conclusions. Prior to the eighteenth century, *Polizei* (police) described less the institutions whose object was the establishment or preservation of communal order and prosperity than the condition of good order and prosperity in the community itself. "*Polizei* existed when freemen or subjects conducted themselves in an orderly, modest, courteous, and respectable fashion wherever human life was organised communally." State and society were not conceptually separate. *Polizei* was "either the community, republic, forms of government . . . or also the laws, institutions and regulations given to and prescribed a town or province."[16] Even after cameralist theorists began, during the eighteenth century, to articulate a more rigorous conception of police as means, the idea retained a powerful communitarian or organic orientation. For German police theorists, Mack Walker has written, "society was integral in character, described by the contributing relations of one group with another and with the whole."[17] In their hands police became an explicit ideology of the general good – of safety and happiness – and a strategy for implementing it, but they also represented it as a condition of the community's very being, an essential prerequisite of its continued existence.

Police appears to have gained its specifically "public" institutional expression as a matter of means as well as ends, together with an array of specifically "public" responsibilities, as a result of the decay of a more traditional social order based on estates. "The more the distinctions between estates became blurred and the estates were no longer able to fulfil their function of regulation, the more the responsibility for legislation devolved to the [state]."[18] State regulation (*Polizeigesetze*) then became in large part an attempt to reproduce the order (*Polizei*) of the estates, which the estates themselves were no longer capable of achieving (for example, sumptuary legislation attempting to preserve estate-derived definitions of social rank and regulation of transactions and trade practices that had been intra- or inter-estate matters). *Polizeiwissenschaft* became the attempt to give rigorous theoretical expression to the

[15] Steven L. Kaplan, *Bread, Politics and Political Economy in the Reign of Louis XV* (The Hague, 1976), 12.

[16] Franz-Ludwig Knemeyer, "Polizei," *Economy and Society*, 9, 2 (May 1980), 174, 176.

[17] Mack Walker, "Rights and Functions: The Social Categories of Eighteenth-Century German Jurists and Cameralists," *Journal of Modern History*, 50, 2 (June 1978), 241.

[18] Knemeyer, "Polizei," 178.

administrative practices of rulers seeking the maximization of the human and social resources under their control, at first in order to strengthen the state and benefit the ruler and, later, under the influence of the Enlightenment, in order to increase the welfare and prosperity of the population as an end in itself.[19]

This theme has been taken further by Pasquale Pasquino, who proposes that the "field of reality" addressed by the police regulations of territorial states extended "wherever the feudal world's traditional customs, established competences and clear relations of authority, subordination, protection and alliance cease[d] to hold sway."[20] Such is hinted by Nicolas Delamare's widely read *Traité de police*, published in Paris in 1722, which foreshadowed the Enlightenment's imminent discovery of police as a science of administration. "The purpose of all government is to maximize resources and unfold the potential of energies of a nation," writes Marc Raeff in seeking to convey the gist of Delamare's work, "and to this end the government should have concern for the general welfare, both spiritual and material, of the population. Police is the means by which this goal is best pursued. But the implication clearly seems to be that where the pattern of traditional institutions has broken down or is nonexistent, the function of police is to create or re-create it."[21]

In the hands of such as Delamare police became elaborated as a body of learning descriptive of a social order whose prosperity came to be perceived as requiring explicit institutional intervention for its preservation and advancement.[22] By midcentury this process of subjecting the institutional patterns constitutive of social order to scientific inspection and, increasingly, to administrative reconstruction could be found underway in every corner of human affairs. Take, for example, this passage from Cesare Beccaria's *Elementi di economia pubblica*:

---

[19] Marc Raeff, "The Well-Ordered Police State and the Development of Modernity in Seventeenth- and Eighteenth-Century Europe," *American Historical Review*, 80, 5 (Dec. 1975), 1221–43. See also his *The Well-Ordered Police State: Social and Institutional Change through Law in the Germanies and Russia, 1600–1800* (New Haven, 1983); Mack Walker, *Johann Jakob Moser and the Holy Roman Empire of the German Nation* (Chapel Hill, 1981), 199–208.

[20] Pasquale Pasquino, "Theatrum Politicum. The Genealogy of Capital – Police and the State of Prosperity," *Ideology and Consciousness*, 4 (1978), 47.

[21] Raeff, "Well-Ordered Police State," 1235. As I have shown here, however, and as Thomas Brennan has also recently pointed out in an analysis of police in prerevolutionary France, Raeff is in error in regarding police as such as a "modern" innovation: "Both the seigneur and the municipality in the middle ages exercised a 'police' over the economy and the public way [*voirie*], having thereby the power to regulate the economic and civic life of the community" ("Police and Public Power in Ancien Régime France" [paper read at the American Society for Legal History Annual Meeting, Atlanta, Feb. 1990]).

[22] Delamare summarized the subject matter of police under twelve headings as follows: religion, morals, health, the supply of food, streets, public tranquillity, the arts and sciences, commerce, manufacturing and mechanical arts, servants, domestics and laborers, the poor. Kaplan says of Delamare that he "tried to place the full range of options, strategies, precedents, and laws, along with explicit instructions on how to use them in different circumstances, at the disposition of all public authorities." The *Traité de police* was "a staggering monument to the range, complexity, and pretension of the police enterprise," an intellectual foundation for conceptualization of police as "the *science* of governing men" (*Bread, Politics and Political Economy*, 13; emphasis in original). Similarly, Walker defines cameralism as "the science of administrative economy" (*Johann Jakob Moser*, 88).

But, neither the products of the earth, nor those of the work of the hand, nor mutual commerce, nor public contributions can ever be obtained from men with perfection and constancy if they do not know the moral and physical laws of the things upon which they act, if the increase of bodies is not proportionately accompanied by the change of social habits; if, among the multiplicity of individuals, works and products one does not at each step see shining the light of order, which renders all operations easy and sure. Thus, the sciences, education, good order, security and public tranquility, *objects all comprehended under the name of police*, will constitute the fifth and last object of public economy.[23]

Having constituted humanity as an object of knowledge, the Enlightenment decreed its patterns of social relations susceptible to political intervention and re-formation. In this enlightened pursuit of happiness, police, now conceived of as the science of government, had become the strategic key to success.[24]

POLICE, CONSTITUTION, REPUBLIC

The eighteenth century's science of government was, we have seen, rooted instrumentally in the decay of estates-based social order and philosophically in the concept of the general good or public happiness. The latter, indeed, was of particular significance, for it anchored the science of government in the mainstream of a venerable and authoritative tradition in European political discourse which can be traced to the revival of Aristotelian thought in the late thirteenth century. In this tradition there appears a clear discursive identification of such terms as *polis, police, politics*, and *polity* with the idea of government by the many for the common good, with republicanism, and eventually with constitutionalism.[25]

---

[23] Cesare Beccaria, "Parte prima: Principi e viste generali," from the *Elementi di economia pubblica*. See Cesare Beccaria, *Opere* (Firenze, 1971), 1:385. The translation here is by Pasquale Pasquino and appears in his "Theatrum Politicum," 45 (emphasis supplied).

Like Adam Smith's *Lectures on Jurisprudence*, the *Elementi* were in fact transcribed notes, based on Beccaria's inaugural course of lectures on public economy delivered in 1767/68 at the Palatine School of Higher Learning in Milan but never repeated. Unreworked and unpublished in Beccaria's lifetime, the lectures appeared in book form as the *Elementi* for the first time in 1804, minus the "fifth and last object," which Beccaria, his best intentions notwithstanding, apparently had not had time to cover in his course. Fragments of other writings on police do, however, appear in the *Opere*. See, e.g., the "Piano delle lezioni di pubblica economia," in *Opere*, vol. 1, esp. 355–6, where Beccaria defined *police* as "all the regulations that contribute to public order and all the economic affairs of the State," and extending to "health services, safety, and the provision of goods" (unpublished translation by Professor John Falconieri, president emeritus of the American University in Rome).

Beccaria's first thoughts on the matter of police can be found in his most famous work, *Dei delitti e delle pene*, first published in 1764. See Cesare Beccaria, *On Crimes and Punishments*, trans. Henry Paolucci (New York, 1963), 79. On Beccaria's theory of public economy, particularly on his antagonism to laissez-faire ideology, see Marcello Maestro, *Cesare Beccaria and the Origins of Penal Reform* (Philadelphia, 1973), 81–117. Maestro also establishes the acquaintance of leading revolutionary intellectuals in the American colonies with Beccaria's work (viii).

[24] Pasquino, "Theatrum Politicum," 45. On France, see Brian W. Head, "The Origins of 'La Science Sociale' in France, 1770–1800," *Australian Journal of French Studies*, 19, 2 (May–Aug. 1982), 115–32. See also, however, Kaplan, *Bread, Politics and Political Economy*, 13.

[25] This connection was noted by Adam Smith: "Police, the word, has been borrowed by the English immediately from the French, tho it is originally derived from the Greek [*politeia*] signifying policy, politicks, or the regulation of a government in generall" (*Lectures on Jurisprudence*, 486).

43

Take, for example, Nicolai Rubinstein's observations on William of Moerbeke's thirteenth-century translation of Aristotle's *Politics*, the source of much of Europe's political vocabulary over the next four centuries. "In the *Politics*," says Rubinstein, "the adjective *politikos* shares with the other derivatives from *polis* a variety of meanings. The word could relate to the *polis* – the city or state – to its constitution, and to one of the three 'true' constitutions, that is the constitution in which the many rule with a view to the common interest. . . . Another derivative of *polis* is *politeia*, which can signify the constitution in general, or the constitution under which the many rule with a view to the common good." In the latter sense, says Rubinstein, Aristotle's definition of *politeia* becomes: "When the masses govern the state for the common interest, the government is called by the generic name common to all constitutions – a politeia."[26]

William of Moerbeke's translation assisted an appropriation of *politicus* and its derivatives for republican and constitutional discourse. "By the beginning of the fourteenth century, the word *politicus*, and its Latin and Italian equivalents *civilis* and *civile*, had been squarely pre-empted for the republican regime. As a constitutional term, its principal features were the institutional restraints to which the government was subjected, and the popular source of its authority."[27] This discourse also had a major influence in France and England, where it was employed to criticize absolutist trends in theorizing on monarchy. In France, for example, early in the sixteenth century Claude de Seyssel used the term *la Police* to describe measures which, he argued, composed one of the three bridles (*freins*) by which the sphere of royal power in France was restrained.[28] According to Rubinstein the writings of Sir John Fortescue, some forty years previously, may be seen as holding similar implications for English monarchical theory. Fortescue adopted the republican distinction between *regimen regale* (monarchy) and *regimen politicum* (republic) but argued that the latter might as well describe that form of monarchy – *dominium regale et politicum* – based on the people's constituting itself as a "body politic" and electing a king to rule "by suche lawes as thai all wolde assent unto." As Rubinstein puts it in discussing Fortescue, "the king who rules *politice* may not, like the one ruling *principatu regali*, change laws without the assent of the people, nor burden it against its will with taxes."[29]

[26] Nicolai Rubinstein, "The History of the Word Politicus in Early-Modern Europe," in Anthony Pagden, ed., *The Languages of Political Theory in Early-Modern Europe* (Cambridge, 1987), 41–56 (quotations from 42–3).

[27] Ibid., 45.

[28] Ibid., 52. Seyssel's three bridles were religion, justice, and police. Like the earlier German usages described by Knemeyer, Seyssel's usage of *police* dates from the period prior to the decay of the estates and refers simultaneously to "laws, institutions, and regulations," creating good order, and the condition of good order itself. Thus to Seyssel police was "the harmony of this monarchy of France achieved by the maintenance of the subjects of all estates in true accord to the satisfaction of each of them." To preserve harmony, "it is only necessary to maintain each estate in its liberties, privileges, and praiseworthy customs and so to superintend all of them that one cannot lord it over the others excessively nor all three join against the head and monarch" (Claude de Seyssel, *The Monarchy of France*, trans. J. H. Hexter and Michael Sherman [New Haven, 1981], 94).

[29] Ibid., 50–1.

Fortescue used *dominium regale et politicum* to convey a sense of protoconstitutionalist restraint on monarchy but without any direct translation of the classical vocabulary of Aristotelian political science into a discourse of constitutionalism. This was also the case in France, where, we have seen, Seyssel chose *la Police* to convey the same sense of restraint on monarchy. In both countries, that is, the meaning of *politeia* – fundamental settlement of public authority – was conveyed into contemporary political discourse by means other than a language of constitutions.[30] Instead the operative language in sixteenth-century French political discourse became the language of *police*, while in England the transition was to the idiom of commonwealth, made possible via the closely related language of *policy*. Thus the earliest (1598) English-language translation of Aristotle's *Politics* translates *politeia* as *policy* and defines it as "the order and description, as of other offices in a city, so of that which hath the greatest and most soveraine authority: for the rule and administration of a Commonweale, hath evermore power and authority joined with it: which administration is called policie in Greek, and in English a Commonweale."[31] From here to Samuel Johnson's and Noah Webster's eighteenth-century definitions of *police* is but a very short step.[32]

Police, then, is a term of considerable importance in the political vocabulary of early modern Europe. Prior to the eighteenth century it denoted both the condition of public order and tranquillity – safety and happiness – and the means to which resort was made to attain and preserve that condition, the "management of the public weal." During the eighteenth century the latter meaning became particularly prominent as *police* was rendered increasingly explicit as a science of government. Throughout, however, the unity of police as condition with police as means to attain that condition was ensured by the term's central location in a tradition of European political discourse which featured it as a description – like *commonwealth, polity, body politic, government*, and, by the eighteenth century, *constitution* – of the fundamental settlement and distribution of public authority.

Even in its Continental strongholds, however, by the eighteenth century *police* lived in tension with an equally powerful but distinct conceptual framework implying a different set of assumptions about social relations: that of *law*. "Rule of law and rule of police are two different ways to which history points, two methods of development between which peoples must choose and have chosen," wrote the German liberal, Eduard Lasker, from the vantage point of the

---

[30] Gerald Stourzh, "*Constitution*: Changing Meanings of the Term from the Early Seventeenth to the Late Eighteenth Century," in Terence Ball and J. G. A. Pocock, eds., *Conceptual Change and the Constitution* (Lawrence, Kans., 1988), 35–54, at 35.

[31] Quoted in ibid., 35.

[32] Stourzh demonstrates just how short in the course of quoting from the commentary to the previous passage: "Policy is the order and disposition of the city in regard of Magistrats & specially in regard of him that hath soveraine authority over all, in whose government the whole commonweale consisteth." He tells us that this English version was translated from an earlier French translation of the Latin version. The first direct translation into English, in 1776, rendered *politeia* as "form of government . . . the ordering and regulating of the city, and all offices in it, particularly those wherein the supreme power is lodged" (quoted in ibid., 36).

1860s.[33] The difference was marked. Where cameralism, for example, imagined a commonwealth, law stood instead for "an aggregate of individual and corporate rights, valid autonomously, each for its own, severally adjudicable by right and known procedures, but not subject to unilateral modification or violation in the name of participation in the common good."[34] Such a conceptual framework implied a shift "from intervention to laissez-faire, from police to political economy."[35] For Lasker the rule of law meant that "the true man is the independent citizen. . . . He has no other claim on the state than protection from injurious force; for this he has to sacrifice nothing to the state but his desire to attack the rights of others."[36]

In continental Europe and in England the ascendancy of the law paradigm and its discourse of rights remained in tension with police. In England the ascendancy of the law paradigm was more complete than elsewhere in Europe, built as it was on a common law constitutionalism which taught suspicion of government[37] and on a political economy, culminating in Smith, skeptical of attempts to legislate the common weal and mindful that there were benefits to be had from accommodating private selfishness.[38] Nevertheless, *police* retained some purchase on nineteenth-century British political discourse in the form of Benthamite utilitarianism, particularly Bentham's constitutional doctrine.[39] As Chapter 1

---

[33] Quoted in William Reddy, *Money and Liberty in Modern Europe: A Critique of Historical Understanding* (New York and Cambridge, 1987), 16.

[34] Walker, "Rights and Functions," 241.

[35] Kaplan, *Bread, Politics and Political Economy*, xxvi.

[36] Quoted in Reddy, *Money and Liberty in Modern Europe*, 16. According to Knemeyer, hostility to *Polizei* had become the dominant tendency among German liberals by the early nineteenth century. In part this can be explained by the tendency of autocratic continental regimes to copy Napoleonic France's resort to secret-police institutions devoted to internal security. But although liberals took exception to secret-police institutions, they largely accepted *Polizei*-as-security and reserved their opprobrium for *Polizei*-as-welfare. Thus according to the *Staatsrecht der constitutionellen Monarchie* (1839): "No governmental power is more dangerous to freedom than that of *Polizei* – not simply the so-called superior or secret police, but the so-called welfare 'Polizei' above all. The prime function of the state *should be solely* to secure the domination of Law. According to basic constitutional principles *there is only one possible* place for *Polizei*, and that is the responsibility for security and order in the state; What is known as welfare 'Polizei' . . . is nothing but open interference with the freedom of the citizen" (Knemeyer, "Polizei," 188; emphasis in original).

[37] See, e.g., Sir Edward Coke in *Bonham's Case*, 77 E.R. 638 (1610) (vacating the power claimed by the College of Physicians according to Act of Parliament to regulate the practice of physic in the City of London), at 652: "The Common Law will controll Acts of Parliament, and sometimes adjudge them to be utterly void: for when an Act of Parliament is against common right and reason, or repugnant or impossible to be performed, the common law will controul it, and adjudge such Act to be void." See also Allan C. Hutchinson and Patrick Monahan, "Democracy and the Rule of Law," in idem, eds., *The Rule of Law: Ideal or Ideology* (Toronto, 1987), 97–123, at 102–4.

[38] See, e.g., John Phillip Reid, *The Concept of Liberty in the Age of the American Revolution* (Chicago, 1988); M. M. Goldsmith, "Liberty, Luxury, and the Pursuit of Happiness," in Pagden, ed., *The Languages of Political Theory*, 225–51.

[39] See Thomas P. Peardon, "Bentham's Ideal Republic," in Bhikhu Parekh, *Jeremy Bentham: Ten Critical Essays* (London, 1974), 120–44. On the links between Bentham and Continental theorists of public happiness, notably Beccaria, see Robert Shackleton, "The Greatest Happiness of the Greatest Number: The History of Bentham's Phrase," *Studies on Voltaire and the Eighteenth Century*, 90 (1972), 1461–82. In *Bentham's Theory of the Modern State* (Cambridge, Mass., 1978), at 9–26 and 78–80, Nancy Rosenblum stresses Bentham's well-known antagonism to the common law and his commitment to the absolute

suggested in outline, the law paradigm's major nineteenth-century triumphs were to be celebrated elsewhere in the world – notably in the new American republic.

Yet even here tension between the paradigms of law and police was marked. This tension is a noticeable feature of the political and constitutional exchanges of the last quarter of the eighteenth century. Rooted in the colonial period, its resolution bore major implications for the subsequent nineteenth-century pattern of social, political, and economic relations.

POLICE IN AMERICA

Thus far, an examination of the conceptual genealogy of *police* in early modern Europe has demonstrated the many instances in which *police* stands not solely for institutions dedicated to the securing of the streets but rather for an institutionally inchoate ideology of collective responsibility for the reproduction of the well-ordered community, an ideology expressible in a political language giving pride of place to an ideal of the public good or happiness.

Over the last twenty years, historians of colonial America have begun to describe an environment for which such an ideology and language has considerable resonance. Noticing that, compared with Europe, colonial American society could often appear lacking in the "permanent structural institutions" which endow societies with "stable order in social, economic and political relations," scholars have begun to look beyond institutions to uncover the sources of social stability in ideas and meanings. The maintenance of order in colonial America, it has been suggested, was dependent upon "close attention to prescribed forms of public conduct. Every social act . . . conveyed a political message."[40]

Among the prescriptions shaping the colonial social order, none has been given

---

supremacy of the legislature, a command theory of law, and an active welfarist state. She also stresses Bentham's antagonism to the politics of classical republicanism – the virtuous legislator, the ideal of an unchanging order, and so forth – in favor of a politics of popular sovereignty and representative democracy. On Bentham's critique of the common law and its reception see David Sugarman, "Legal Theory, the Common Law Mind, and the Making of the Textbook Tradition," in William Twining, ed., *Legal Theory and Common Law* (Oxford, 1986), 35–43. See also, generally, David Lieberman, *The Province of Legislation Determined: Legal Theory in Eighteenth Century Britain* (Cambridge, 1989).

[40] Joyce Appleby, James Jacob, and Margaret Jacob, "Introduction," in Jacob and Jacob, eds., *The Origins of Anglo-American Radicalism*. 7, 11; G. B. Warden, "Inequality and Instability in Eighteenth Century Boston: A Reappraisal," *Journal of Interdisciplinary History*, 6, 4 (Spring 1976), 614. See also John B. Blake, *Public Health in the Town of Boston, 1630–1822* (Cambridge, Mass., 1959), 1–116. Appleby, Jacob, and Jacob observe that "the multiple settlements in the English colonies led to an inadvertent pluralism which made it easy to imagine alternatives to any particular institutional arrangement. In America, too, neither the coercion of economic dependence nor the persuasion of majestically ritualised power was ready at hand to reinforce the dictates of society's arbiters. Nor were there in the colonies the cathedrals, royal palaces or country estates to remind the many of the superior position of the few. Invisible social norms were not made visible on every community landscape" (11).

47

greater attention in recent years than those that scholars have associated with the paradigm of community.[41] Originally developed by historians of colonial New England in search of a means of conveying what they saw as the "closed, corporate and cohesive" reality of that region's "isolated, small, stable, homogeneous agricultural" towns, and more recently extended to the Chesapeake, the community paradigm has sometimes appeared to critics to be a rather superficial oversimplification of a more discordant reality.[42] Insofar as the objective of the idea's original proponents seemed at times to be to establish as a matter of fact that colonial communities remained peaceable kingdoms throughout the colonial era, the critics have a point. Yet explorations of communitarian "peace and unitie" dwell on it as a matter of value as much as of fact, of ideal as much as of reality. And indeed, considered as such, recent studies have shown that throughout the colonial period communal "bonds of affection," expressed in "patterns of association and inherited beliefs and values," gave life in New England and elsewhere much of its moral content and shared meaning.[43]

Whereas in the more highly developed political cultures of western Europe, accountability to the community increasingly meant accountability to the state and, formally at least, governmental responsibility for order in all areas of life, in colonial America, where the state was so much less developed, this broad conception of accountability was expressed in a widespread discourse of communalism. Hence, like police in its original incarnation, "peace and unitie" describes a condition of good order which was an end in itself. "In a variety of times and places, styles and situations, the townsmen of provincial Massachusetts acknowledged the primacy of peace and unity in the conduct of the community. Over and over again they were granted to be goals of public life which were good intrinsically rather than instrumentally. They did not have to be justified as ends of action; rather, other ends were justified in terms of them." The achievement of that condition of good order, moreover, was self-consciously a collective responsibility. "In other communities and cultures law and order could be conserved by custom or, in the failure of such traditional regulation, by institutional coercion. In the towns of Massachusetts peace was a preoccupation for the strikingly simple reason that there were no other adequate agencies of enforcement. Without an inner acceptance of the canons of concord by the villagers there could scarcely have been

<hr/>

[41] Rhys Isaac, *The Transformation of Virginia, 1740–1790* (Chapel Hill, 1982), 115–38. See also idem, "Order and Growth, Authority and Meaning in Colonial New England," *American Historical Review*, 76, 3 (June 1971), 728–37. On the persistence of communitarian ideas in the revolutionary era see Edward Countryman, *The American Revolution* (New York, 1985); Gordon S. Wood, *The Creation of the American Republic, 1776–1787* (Chapel Hill, 1969), 53–70, 114–24. See, generally, Richard Beeman, "The New Social History and the Search for 'Community' in America," *American Quarterly*, 29, 4 (Fall 1977), 422–43.

[42] See, e.g., Stephen Innes, *Labor in a New Land: Economy and Society in Seventeenth Century Springfield* (Princeton, 1983), xv–xxi.

[43] See, e.g., Melvin Yazawa, *From Colonies to Commonwealth: Familial Ideology and the Beginnings of the American Republic* (Baltimore, 1985), 9–27; Christine Leigh Heyrman, *Commerce and Culture: The Maritime Communities of Colonial Massachusetts, 1690–1750* (New York, 1984), 20.

concord at all, since there was no external agency powerful enough to compel compliance."[44]

New England's founding ethos of overt communitarianism, it has been argued, was exceptional in British North America. Outside that region colonial societies were from the beginning marked by the individualism, opportunities for personal autonomy, and social fluidity thought to have been characteristic of seventeenth-century English society. Over time, however, these diverse social patterns converged: Commercial and demographic developments initiated departures from communitarianism in New England while elsewhere social and institutional maturation was reflected in a growing ethos of communalism.[45] Perhaps for this reason one may detect by the eighteenth century a distinctly communal ethos in the representations of good order current in colonial societies outside New England. As Rhys Isaac has shown in his ethnographic study of colonial Virginia, for example, whatever the forum – land use or architecture, the dramas of religion and law, or the roughhouse of popular entertainments – the conduct prescribed proclaimed the stable order of Virginian society; everyday life itself became an essential mode of displaying and reproducing a well-ordered community.[46]

The ambition to achieve a life of mutual connection and harmony existed in perpetual tension with doubt of the possibility of achievement. In a developing society, bonds of affection constituted a fragile form of authority. Their capacity to compel conformity was not the power of institutionalized coercion but rather of social and moral obligation.[47] As such, theirs was a self-conscious harmony, its ultimate measure the demeanor of all concerned toward each other,[48] vulnerable to

[44] Michael Zuckerman, *Peaceable Kingdoms: New England Towns in the Eighteenth Century* (New York, 1970), 51, 65, 85.

[45] Jack P. Greene, *Pursuits of Happiness: The Social Development of Early Modern British Colonies and the Formation of American Culture* (Chapel Hill, 1988), 7–54, 170–206.

[46] Isaac, *Transformation of Virginia*, 115–38.

[47] As Joyce Appleby put it in a 1976 article, "Because law enforcement had always been weak in the Anglo-American colonies, community coercion had supplied the social control normally exercised by superior authorities. Local autonomy had served group, not individual goals, but the effectiveness of such a system of control depended upon the capacity of the larger society to create new locales of community control to keep pace with growth" ("Liberalism and the American Revolution," *New England Quarterly*, 49, 1 [Mar. 1976], 3–26, at 24). Although Appleby here appears to use "locale" to mean a geographically located place, her point is no less appropriate if one substitutes a less-physical sense of locale. Daniel Vickers, e.g., has pointed to how colonial society managed and reproduced itself "largely at the level of ritual" directed to "the preservation of local and family consensus" ("Competency and Competition: Economic Culture in Early America," *William and Mary Quarterly*, 3d ser., 47, 1 [Jan. 1990], 3–29, at 26–7). More generally, Gordon Wood deftly conveys the thinness of institutionalized authority in colonial America in his *The Radicalism of the American Revolution* (New York, 1992), 78, 109–24.

[48] Yazawa, *From Colonies to Commonwealth*, 31–81. "Demeanor" is at once compatible with the more venerable concept of "deference" and at the same time more subtle. It is also worth noting that historians have begun to question the extent of deference, particularly in later colonial society. See, e.g., Steven Rosswurm, *Arms, Country, and Class: The Philadelphia Militia and the "Lower Sort" during the American Revolution* (New Brunswick, N.J., 1987), 27; Billy G. Smith, *The "Lower Sort": Philadelphia's Laboring People, 1750–1800* (Ithaca, N.Y., 1990), 24–5; Richard R. Beeman, "Deference, Republicanism, and the Emergence of Popular Politics in Eighteenth-Century America," *William and Mary Quarterly*, 3d ser., 49, 3 (July 1992), 401–30.

disruption, particularly by the fear – ever-present in the idiom of communal order – of declension or corruption, of the loss of the public virtue of mutuality, the victory of selfishness or tyranny.

By the mid–eighteenth century such fears were working their way to the surface of the colonial consciousness, fueled, particularly in New England, by a continuing ambivalence about how best to accommodate economic activity to the communal social order:

Since the beginnings of the colonies, Americans had engaged in commercial life, but they persistently had difficulty in accommodating themselves intellectually to its effects. They were aware of commerce and the imperatives it posed for men's work, and they recognized that self-interest was the motive force in a life of trade. But they continued to adhere to an ethics which could give explicit legitimization only to activity which benefitted the public.[49]

The specter of social disruption was accompanied by the equally unsettling specter of major upheavals in the imperial relationship with Britain consequential upon the reorganization of British commercial, naval, and colonial power following the Seven Years' War. Symbolic of these were the new revenue-raising policies initiated in the years after 1763 by George Grenville and, later, Charles Townshend which forced the issue of the location of the parliamentary power to tax.[50] As important, however, was the mode of implementing Britain's new imperial policies, portending a dramatic erosion of local autonomy in favor of new networks of metropolitan administrative power. The hordes of customs agents and other petty officials that began descending on North America in the 1760s were, after all, intrusions of the British state into the domestic life of the colonies. In particular, the implementation of customs procedure and, after 1765, the enforcement of the Stamp Act through Vice-Admiralty courts were intended quite specifically to keep these essential vehicles of imperial policy outside the purview of locally answerable institutions; these courts provided colonial administrators with a parallel official universe immune from local influences and responsive only to representatives of the metropolis.[51]

Reflecting a trend also manifested in British domestic affairs toward the creation of a more centralized British state with real administrative capacities,[52] these new policies and administrative measures had profound consequences so far as the colonial

---

[49] J. E. Crowley, *This Sheba, Self: The Conceptualization of Economic Life in Eighteenth Century America* (Baltimore, 1974), 96. Recently, Daniel Vickers has argued that early Americans were less concerned about the legitimacy of commerce than about achieving "competency" or "a degree of comfortable independence" while at the same time finding ways to manage the social tensions arising from what he sees as an inevitable contradiction between their competitive drive to achieve competency and their desire to live in communal and cooperative surroundings ("Competency and Competition," 3–29).

[50] See, e.g., Countryman, *American Revolution*, 41–73.

[51] Hendrik Hartog, "Losing the World of the Massachusetts Whig," in idem, ed., *Law in the American Revolution and the Revolution in the Law* (New York, 1981), 143–66. See, generally, John P. Reid, *In a Defiant Stance: The Conditions of Law in Massachusetts Bay, the Irish Comparison, and the Coming of the American Revolution* (University Park, Pa., 1977).

[52] See, e.g., John Styles, "The Emergence of the Police – Explaining Police Reform in Eighteenth and Nineteenth Century England," *British Journal of Criminology*, 27, 1 (Winter 1987), 21–2.

relationship was concerned. The particular result was an "alienation of affection" in the imperial dimension of the communal paradigm of rule no less irrevocable than that already under way in its local dimension. The final outcome, unsurprisingly, was the crumbling of the paradigm itself and the beginnings of a fundamental reconceptualization of social order in America.[53]

DIVERGENT GOALS AND THE AMERICAN REVOLUTION

The predominantly localized organization of prerevolutionary America and the weakness of institutions enmeshing its communities in webs of power orienting localities one to another and to a center proved a decisive context when it came to the exertion of authority. Thus in Massachusetts, for example, "authority was diffuse and decentralized; the legitimacy and potency of local legal institutions were not dependent on the support and acquiescence of a central authority."[54] Similarly in Virginia the elaborately ritualized culture of Christian gentility existed amid an all-pervasive localism that rejected as alien and immoral the idea of government arranged in a hierarchy of institutions "culminating in a central nation-state."[55]

Considered formally, the practise of "politics" was confined more or less exclusively to the provincial level. Provincial elites apart, this was not a culture characterized by a widespread political mentality. According to Gordon Wood, colonial politics was "a highly personal business, essentially involving bitter rivalry among small elite groups." Kenneth Lockridge, similarly, has stressed the absence of any kind of generalized discourse of politics in colonial culture prior to the Revolution. The only serious contender for recognition as a pancolonial political ideology, classical republicanism or "civic humanism," had a currency largely restricted to elites.[56]

By its very nature, however, colonial culture was highly participatory in a direct and local fashion. "Institutions of government could not function at all without the involvement and the participation of local publics. And insofar as local institutions could hope to perform their 'jobs' – the maintenance of peace and order, the suppression of crime and violence, the administration of public works and so forth – they needed to enlist the support and the interest of their constituencies."[57] This

---

[53] Yazawa, *From Colonies to Commonwealth*, 87–135; Hartog, "Losing the World of the Massachusetts Whig," 158–66.

[54] Hartog, "Losing the World of the Massachusetts Whig," 147.

[55] Kenneth A. Lockridge, *Settlement and Unsettlement in Early America: The Crisis of Political Legitimacy before the Revolution* (Cambridge, 1981), 103. See also, generally, 4, 7–104.

[56] Wood, *Creation of the American Republic*, 76; idem, *Radicalism of the American Revolution*, 87–8, 91–2; Lockridge, *Settlement and Unsettlement in Early America*, 46–9, 102–4; Edmund S. Morgan, *Inventing the People: The Rise of Popular Sovereignty in England and America* (New York, 1988), 148, 173. Ronald P. Formisano writes of prerevolutionary Massachusetts: "To speak of eighteenth-century Massachusetts political culture is to invoke a realm of thought and activity in which very few persons actually dwelt. Those few were a select group, drawn largely from the colony's gentry and leaders" (*The Transformation of Political Culture: Massachusetts Parties, 1790s–1840s* [New York, 1983], 25).

[57] Hartog, "Losing the World of the Massachusetts Whig," 153.

was no less true when it came to oversight of the realm of economic exchange than it was, for example, of the regulation of crime and punishment. In both, historians have shown, popular participation was always marked, and frequently decisive.[58]

During the revolutionary epoch continued elite domination of politics and the ethos of popular participation came into conflict, the latter becoming the foundation and the point of departure for assertions of a right of direct involvement in the new and more distinctively *popular* culture of governance then in the process of creation.[59] Popular sovereignty, which Edmund Morgan has described as "the prevailing fiction in a society where government was traditionally the province of a relatively small elite," took on a wholly new aspect as the quasi-politics of "moral economy" and crowd action – the characteristic of which, both in England and the colonies, had been that the conflicts which took place had limited objectives and were bounded by overall acceptance of the prevailing social order – was increasingly replaced by an explicit and less-restrained politics of popular rights, both collective and individual.[60]

This upsurge of popular assertiveness raises the general question of the extent to which internal political conflict at the time of the Revolution had deep social roots that influenced the course the Revolution took. Historians have indeed long claimed a direct relationship between the occurrence of the Revolution and growing domestic social crisis. In 1973, for example, Kenneth Lockridge suggested that the coming of the Revolution in New England could be explained by alterations in the social structure toward greater inequality and differentiation caused by an agricultural crisis resulting from population pressure on a fixed quantity of productive land and from the general commercialization of the economy. More recently Gary Nash has argued that in the colonial port cities (Boston, New York, and Philadelphia) a narrowing of opportunities and rising poverty in the prerevolutionary period created conditions in which the War of Independence became also "a profound

---

[58] See, e.g., Barbara Clark Smith, "Markets, Streets, and Stores: Contested Terrain in Pre-industrial Boston," in Elise Marienstras and Barbara Karsky, eds., *Autre temps, autre espace: Etudes sur l'Amerique pre-industrielle* (Nancy, 1986), 181–97; Countryman, *American Revolution*, 74–104; Dirk Hoerder, *Crowd Action in Revolutionary Massachusetts, 1765–1780* (New York, 1977), 40–84. Hendrik Hartog concludes that overall, "in the absence of effective instruments of centralized control, in the absence of a positivist monopoly of violence by the state, a 'Whig' model of decentralized, locally responsive institutions might have been the only available model for reasonably effective government" ("Losing the World of the Massachusetts Whig," 153).

[59] Jackson Turner Main, "Government by the People: The American Revolution and the Democratization of the Legislatures," *William and Mary Quarterly*, 3d ser., 23, 3 (July 1966), 391– 407; Ruth Bogin, "Petitioning and the New Moral Economy of Post-revolutionary America," *William and Mary Quarterly*, 3d ser., 45, 3 (July 1988), 392–425.

[60] Morgan, *Inventing the People*, 148. See also Barbara Clark Smith, "The Politics of Price Control in Revolutionary Massachusetts, 1774–1780" (Ph.D. diss., Yale University, 1983). Ruth Bogin remarks that "where the English 'moral economy of the crowd' built on the concepts that the upper class had an obligation to relieve the impoverished in times of dearth and that the poor retained a reciprocal right to enforce both a fair price and the local distribution of scarce necessities, America's free working people introduced new ideological themes to buttress their concrete demands" ("Petitioning and the New Moral Economy," 394).

social upheaval" that "erupted along the lines of the deep faults that had existed within colonial society for generations."[61]

The extent of social division during the colonial period and its impact on the Revolution are matters of continuing debate. Attempting to summarize the direction of recent findings, James Henretta has pointed to rough consensus on two basic points: that per capita production of wealth remained relatively stable during the colonial period and that the distribution of wealth, at least in the northern colonies, also remained relatively stable. Such changes as were in train prior to the Revolution "did not constitute a basic social and economic transformation." That would come later – a sharp rise in economic stratification during the first half of the nineteenth century, culminating, between 1860 and 1930, in a plateau of the most marked inequality in American history.[62] On the basis of this literature, Jack P. Greene has argued that to interpret the revolutionary epoch as one of endemic internal social crisis, of division between those driving toward self-interest, profit maximization, and economic competition on the one hand and proponents of a traditional culture on the other, is to advance a version of history that is simply at variance with actual social experience, one that has taken an extravagant Puritan rhetoric of declension at face value and visited it upon the whole population of the American colonies.[63] The principal motivation of late colonial Americans in general, Greene writes, was an expansive individualism, a quest for personal independence, not a drive to satisfy a narrow economic self-interest. That quest, he emphasizes, was not one that "whittle[d] away at the foundations of the family, community, church, and other institutions of the social order." Rather its ethos was one of *improvement*, defined broadly as a process of metropolitan emulation and acculturation. "An *improved* society was one defined by a series of positive and negative juxtapositions. Not wild, barbaric, irregular, rustic, or crude, it was settled, cultivated, civilized, orderly, developed,

---

[61] Kenneth A. Lockridge, "Social Change and the Meaning of the American Revolution," *Journal of Social History*, 6 (1973), 403–39; Gary B. Nash, *The Urban Crucible: Social Change, Political Consciousness, and the Origins of the American Revolution* (Cambridge, Mass., 1979), 339–84. Such arguments have a venerable heritage. As Carl Becker put it so well in 1909 (so well, indeed, that he has been quoted repeatedly ever since), two questions, "about equally prominent," dominated the politics of the revolutionary era. "The first was the question of home rule; the second was the question, if we may so put it, of who should rule at home" (*The History of Political Parties in the Province of New York, 1760–1776* [Madison, 1968], 22).

[62] James Henretta, "Wealth and Social Structure," in Jack P. Greene and J. R. Pole, eds., *Colonial British America: Essays in the New History of the Early Modern Era* (Baltimore, 1984), 262–89. On rising inequality during the early republic, see Jackson Turner Main, "Trends in Wealth Concentration before 1860," *Journal of Economic History* 31, 2 (June 1971), 445–7; Edward Pessen, *Riches, Class, and Power before the Civil War* (Lexington, Mass., 1973); Jeffrey G. Williamson and Peter H. Lindert, *American Inequality: A Macroeconomic History* (New York, 1980), esp. 36–46; Robert W. Fogel, *Without Consent or Contract: The Rise and Fall of American Slavery* (New York, 1989), 354–62. See also Richard L. Bushman, " 'This New Man': Dependence and Independence, 1776," in Richard L. Bushman et al., eds., *Uprooted Americans: Essays to Honor Oscar Handlin* (Boston, 1979), 70–93, at 92–3. On the differing trajectory of wealth concentration in the South, see Lee Soltow, "Economic Inequality in the United States in the Period from 1790 to 1860," *Journal of Economic History*, 31, 4 (Dec. 1971), 822–39.

[63] Greene, *Pursuits of Happiness*, 55–100, 170–206.

and polite."[64] Congruent with but surpassing the English economic literature's emphasis on "schemes, devices or projects" for building national productivity and furnishing economic infrastructure, the ideology of improvement meant above all a strengthening and elaboration – a refinement – of prevailing social institutions.

With re-creation and not innovation as their aim, colonial British Americans generally aspired to a fully developed market society with credit, commercial agriculture, slavery, and a rapid circulation of money and goods. They wanted a settled and hierarchical social structure with social distinctions ranging from the genteel down to the vulgar. In particular they wanted a social structure that would enable successful independent and affluent people, in conformity with the long-standing traditions of Western civilization, . . . to exploit dependent people. They desired authoritative, if not very obtrusive, political institutions that could facilitate their socioeconomic and cultural development and would be presided over by people whose very success in the private realm testified to their merit and capacity and gave them a legitimate claim to political leadership. They wanted vital traditional social institutions that would contribute to and stand as visible symbols of their improvement, including churches, schools, and towns.[65]

This developmental model accords with the absence of basic discontinuities in social structure during the prerevolutionary period as described by Henretta. Henretta, however, was also careful to note that "an incipient polarization of the social order" was ongoing in colonial cities by midcentury. "Whatever the distribution of urban wealth, class differences obviously were felt with greater intensity and received more institutional expression as the eighteenth century advanced."[66] These differences suggest that the ideological consensus posited by Greene was probably less encompassing, and certainly more susceptible to interpretation in accordance with a variety of shades of meaning and perspective, than he allows.

The point is important. If discontinuity in social structure and growing social division were principally features of the postrevolutionary, particularly post-1790, period, then the revolutionary epoch may be seen as a period of opportunity when white male Americans, still relatively undifferentiated in social and economic power, could engage in a genuine exploration of alternative routes for the improvement of their society. The promise of personal independence, in other words, did not imply a single track of "development" toward "modernity" for its realization. Different elements of this relatively homogeneous, relatively equal society had different ideas about where it should go. "Even before the Revolution, drawing on both experience and theory, [America's working people] began to transform the moral content of their economic outlook from acceptance of a hierarchical structure to invocation of political rights . . . including the right to participate *as equals* in the political

---

[64] Ibid., 197 (emphasis in original). There is an important similarity between the language of *improvement* and the language of *police*. The antinomy of barbarity and police, e.g., is clear in Samuel Johnson's dictionary definition of *police*. See his *Dictionary*, II, pt. 1, unpaginated. One should also note that in Scottish usage the improvement of land is one of the meanings of *police* (*Oxford English Dictionary* [Oxford, 1933], 7:1070).

[65] Greene, *Pursuits of Happiness*, 198.

[66] Henretta, "Wealth and Social Structure," 278.

forums where economic policy was hammered out." Some quite specifically "demanded a new role for government – intervention on behalf of the vulnerable to promote their equal access to opportunity and personal independence."[67] When, in short, at their moment of national independence Americans began a heated twenty-five year discussion of the social, political, and institutional course that their societies would thenceforth follow under *their* control, they had a range of alternatives open to them to consider.

POLICE IN AMERICAN REVOLUTIONARY DISCOURSE

The language of *police* appears explicitly for the first time in American discourse precisely at this moment. Usage suggests that it entered the North American lexicon during the debates of the 1770s and 1780s as a discursive translation of the older communal ethos of "safety and happiness" into the newer secular language of revolutionary politics.[68] As such it features at all levels of the epoch's domestic controversies over the basis, institutional expression, and proper sphere of government and administration, conceptually coextensive with the idea of "the state" (whether in local, regional, or national guise) itself.[69] In Boston, for example, debates

[67] Bogin, "Petitioning and the New Moral Economy," 394–5, 402–3, 422–5 (emphasis in original). See also Gary B. Nash, "Also There at the Creation: Going beyond Gordon S. Wood," *William and Mary Quarterly*, 3d ser., 44, 3 (July 1987), 602–11; Steven Rosswurm, "'As a Lyen out of His Den': Philadelphia's Popular Movement, 1776–80," in Jacob and Jacob, eds., *Origins of Anglo-American Radicalism*, 300–23. See also Rosswurm, *Arms, Country, and Class*, 49–108.

[68] Thus note, e.g., the assumption of "police powers" by the popular committees that, in so many localities, took and wielded public power during the Revolution. See Willi Paul Adams, *The First American Constitutions: Republican Ideology and the Making of the State Constitutions in the Revolutionary Era* (Chapel Hill, 1980), 35; Richard D. Brown, *Revolutionary Politics in Massachusetts: The Boston Committee of Correspondence and the Towns, 1772–1774* (Cambridge, Mass., 1970), 210–47; Oscar Handlin and Mary Flug Handlin, *Commonwealth, a Study of the Role of Government in the American Economy: Massachusetts, 1774–1861* (Cambridge, Mass., 1969), 1–31; Hoerder, *Crowd Action in Revolutionary Massachusetts*, 311–89; Smith, "Politics of Price Control," 80–141, 166–209, 265–528.

[69] Later constitutional commentary on the police power underscores this. Thus according to J. I. C. Hare's *American Constitutional Law* (Boston, 1889), 2:766, "the police power may be justly said to be more general and pervading than any other. It embraces all the operations of society and government." Such commentary also goes a considerable distance toward confirming police's conceptual provenance in the communal responsibility for the production of good order which characterized prerevolutionary society by emphasizing its priority over individual rights. "The recognition that there exist rights of life, liberty, property and happiness which are possessed by the individual and which are guaranteed against arbitrary and unreasonable invasion by other persons, public or private, does not imply that these rights are absolute in character.... This is so for the reason that, more fundamental than the right of the private individual, is the right of the public person, the State, and, more important than the convenience or even the existence of the citizen, are the welfare and life of the civic whole" (Westel W. Willoughby, *The Constitutional Law of the United States* [New York, 1929], 3:1588). Similarly, according to Lemuel Shaw in *Commonwealth v. Alger*, 61 Mass. 53 (1851), a case widely cited as the first extended discussion of the meaning of the police power in constitutional law: "Rights of property, like other social and conventional rights, are subject to such reasonable limitations in their enjoyment as shall prevent them from being injurious, and to such reasonable restraints and regulations established by law as the legislature, under the governing and controlling power vested in them by the Constitution, may think necessary and expedient." That power extended to "mak[ing], ordain[ing], and establish[ing] all manner

55

over what would be the most appropriate "police" for the town preoccupied its citizens from the 1780s onward. Throughout participants resorted to the concept to convey a distinctively public dimension of community. Thus in 1784 it was voted "that a Committee be appointed to take into consideration . . . whether an alteration in the present Government of the Town be eligible, and to report if necessary a plan for a different Police." In 1791 a petition "for altering the Police of the town" was received from a number of inhabitants complaining of "the difficulties that arise from the defect of a regular and energetic system of police." The term was clearly understood to convey a sense of public administrative capacity: In 1786 the town appointed "Inspectors of the Police" to perform a general regulatory function as the administrative arm of the town's selectmen in matters of market regulation, sanitation, street lighting, and disease control. But it was also used coextensively with "government" to denote the presence of legitimate public authority in social life.[70]

Police also featured prominently in the same connection in the national debates of the 1780s, notably in the commentaries of Federalist and Anti-Federalist writers during exchanges over the adoption of the federal Constitution. In the letters of the Federal Farmer, for example, "internal police" appears to comprehend governmental power to regulate in pursuit of "peace, order and justice in the community"; the actual process of implementation and administration of regulatory measures; and the constitutional structures through which the concerns of the community gained articulation and were translated into action.[71]

Specifying police to be the community's capacity to ensure good order, or to govern the course of "improvement" (as rewritten in the new secular political language of revolutionary America), however, begs the question of how the good to be thus sustained or the course to be followed was to be defined, and by whom. In the heated debates of the 1770s and 1780s, as American revolutionary discourse appeared to give ever-greater stress to the primacy of politics in the construction of the social order, this was precisely the issue.

Throughout the revolutionary era, as committees and conventions of the people created new forms of institutionalized secular and democratic authority to replace

of wholesome and reasonable laws, statutes, and ordinances, either with penalties or without, not repugnant to the Constitution, as they shall judge to be for the good and welfare of the Commonwealth, and of the subjects of the same" (85). See also Leonard W. Levy, *The Law of the Commonwealth and Chief Justice Shaw* (New York, 1967), 229–65.

[70] "Petitions for City Incorporation" (May 1784, Oct. 1785, Dec. 1791) and "Report of a Committee Relative to Police" (Jan. 1792), all in *Boston Town Records*, Rare Books and Manuscripts Division, Boston Public Library. See also *Report of the Record Commissioners of the City of Boston* (Boston, 1887–), vol. 25, "Selectmen's Minutes 1776–86," 292, 295, 303; and vol. 27, "Selectmen's Minutes, 1787–98," 104, 156, 197. Roger Lane has noted that the first "official" use of the term *police* in New York occurred in 1778 with the appointment by the British occupation forces of a "Superintendent General of the Police," with supreme authority over "all . . . matters, in which the economy, peace, and good order of the City of New York and its environs are concerned." He adds, unfortunately without giving the matter any further attention, that "unofficial use in the same period is often quite confusing" (*Policing the City*, 249, n. 2).

[71] "Letters from the Federal Farmer," 1 and 2 (8 and 9 Oct. 1787), in Herbert J. Storing, ed., *The Complete Anti-Federalist* (Chicago, 1981), 2:223–30, 233, 239.

communal social and moral obligation as the embodiment of legitimate rule, Americans engaging in the attempt to define the foundation and purposes of that rule increasingly located it in the people at large and made their happiness its object.[72] Police featured in this discourse as a means of giving voice to a concept of governance expressing the community's right of response to communal necessity recast in the language of *inherent* popular rights of control and direction of government.[73] Thus in the Delaware Declaration of Rights, adopted in September 1776, it was stated "that the people of this State have the sole exclusive and inherent Right of governing and regulating the internal Police of the same." Pennsylvania (September 1776) and Maryland (November) used the same formulation, and North Carolina (December) and Georgia (February 1777) guaranteed the people's control of "internal government and police." Virginia's Declaration of Rights and Massachusetts's 1780 Constitution both underwrote the popular right of government. Rhode Island (which adopted no new constitution but retained its prerevolutionary charter) and New Jersey both reserved their police powers. New Jersey, for example, drew no explicit constitutional link between the sovereignty of the people and police, but the state's delegates to the Continental Congress were instructed to ensure that the Congress enacted no measures which might infringe on the state's sovereignty, defined as "all the Powers of Government, so far as relates to its internal Police and Conduct of our own Affairs, civil and religious."[74]

The state governments framed on this basis were strictly majoritarian, with few limits on legislative authority. Republican government as extolled in state constitutions and declarations of rights meant adherence to forms – notably popular participation in government or, at least, participation through representative democracy – underlining the unity of people and government rather than the people's distrust of government. Thus in May 1776 when the Boston town meeting instructed its representatives in the General Court on how to respond to proposals then current for a new state constitution (one of the "most important Questions that ever were agitated by the Representative Body of this Colony touching its internal

---

[72] "Popular sovereignty, the location in the people themselves of the ultimate decision-making authority for the new nation . . . [w]as the decisive achievement of the American political imagination" (Kloppenberg, "Virtues of Liberalism," 24). Note also the sentiments of the Bostonian Benjamin Hichborn, who in 1777 defined civil liberty to be "not 'a government by laws,' made agreeable to charters, bills of rights, or compacts, but a power existing in the people at large, at any time, for any cause, or for no cause, but their own sovereign pleasure, to alter or annihilate both the mode and essence of any former government, and adopt a new one in its stead" (quoted in Forrest McDonald, *Novus Ordo Seclorum: The Intellectual Origins of the Constitution* [Lawrence, Kans., 1985], 158). See also Russell L. Hanson, " 'Commons' and 'Commonwealth' at the American Founding: Democratic Republicanism as the New American Hybrid," in Ball and Pocock, eds., *Conceptual Change and the Constitution*, 165–93; Donald H. Meyer, *The Democratic Enlightenment* (New York, 1976), 150–1 (on the "demystification" of government); Wood, *Creation of the American Republic*, 306–89. See also David F. Epstein, *The Political Theory of the Federalist* (Chicago, 1984).

[73] See, generally, Robert C. Palmer, "Liberties as Constitutional Provisions, 1776–1791," in William E. Nelson and Robert C. Palmer, *Liberty and Community: Constitution and Rights in the Early American Republic* (New York, 1987), 61–86.

[74] Adams, *First American Constitutions*, 135–36.

Police") it emphasized that guarantees of a just and equal representation of the people in the legislature provided the appropriate basis for the exercise of legislative power. "It is essentially necessary, in Order to preserve Harmony among ourselves, that the constituent Body be satisfied, that they are fully and fairly represented. The Right to legislate is originally in every member of the Community; which Right is always exercised of a State: But when the Inhabitants are become numerous, 'tis not only inconvenient, but impracticable for all to meet in One Assembly; and hence arose the Necessity and Practice of legislating by a few, freely chosen by the many. When this Choice is free, and the Representation equal, 'tis the People's Fault if they are not happy."[75] In Pennsylvania, "government by representation, structured to retain the interest of the legislators in the people and thus to retain the unity between people and government, was the essential liberty" that gave the Revolution its real "intellectual content."[76]

State legislative majoritarianism did not go completely unchecked, for state constitutional protections of liberties enumerated popular rights. The rights and liberties acknowledged in state constitutions and declarations of rights were both individual *and* communal, however, expressing the "values that had to be taken into consideration when the individual and the collectivity confronted *each other*." Rather than "rigid exceptions to power," in other words, enumerated rights were conceived of as "serious principles of governmental propriety," enabling rather than disenabling devices that reflected a conception of the positive relationship pertaining between government power and collective need. As Robert Palmer has put it, stressing in particular the significance of declarations of the people's (collective) right of police, "state constitutions found no great dichotomy between individual rights and communal needs" for "communal powers, when exercised in a properly structured republican government, maximized freedom."[77]

CONCLUSION

The discourse of *police* that emerged after 1776 in the new American states gave political voice to a conception of republican government – government as a means, informed by constitutional declarations of communal as well as individual rights, of maximizing opportunities for the sovereign people to participate in the framing of

[75] "Boston's Instructions to Its Representatives" (30 May 1776), in *Report of the Record Commissioners of the City of Boston* (Boston, 1887–), vol. 18, "Town Records, 1770–77," 236–9. Barbara Clark Smith concludes that the Massachusetts Constitution of 1780 "established a form of government . . . resting entirely on the premise of popular consent" ("Politics of Price Control," 170, and generally 142–209).
[76] Palmer, "Liberties as Constitutional Provisions," 62, 64. See also Wood, *Creation of the American Republic*, 162–73; Joshua Miller, "The Ghostly Body Politic," *Political Theory*, 16, 1 (Feb. 1988), 99–119.
[77] Palmer, "Liberties as Constitutional Provisions," 55, 82 (emphasis supplied), 84. See also Rosswurm, *Arms, Country, and Class*, 194–9. And see William Treanor, Note: "The Origins and Original Significance of the Just Compensation Clause of the Fifth Amendment," *Yale Law Journal*, 94, 3 (Jan. 1985), 694–8.

the collective good – grounded in the older communitarian idiom of "peace and unitie" or "safety and happiness" but shaped by a developing consciousness of popular right. That conception was always contested in the states by those who spoke in the more conventional political idiom of elite dominion.[78] This contest, however, was played out more completely at the national level, where Federalist preoccupations with majoritarian tyranny led them to identify the common good with government distanced from significant democratic participation.[79] At the national level, as a consequence, a different conception of government was advanced, one articulating a fresh perception of the postrevolutionary social order, of the relationship between people and government, of the proper sphere of government action, and of the appropriate roles of its constituent elements. In this conception we see the discourse of *law* begin to emerge as the paradigmatic discourse of the American state.

[78] See, e.g., Rosswurm, *Arms, Country, and Class*, 228–56.

[79] "Central features of the framers' thought," writes Cass R. Sunstein, "consisted of fears about the consequences of decentralization and widespread citizen participation" ("Beyond the Republican Revival," *Yale Law Journal*, 97, 8 [July, 1988], 1558).

3

An excess of democracy

I am not among those who fear the people. They, and not the rich, are our dependence for continued freedom.

Thomas Jefferson to Samuel Kercheval (12 July 1816)

The earliest phase of the new republic, we have seen, was one in which the essentially hierarchical and localized society of prerevolutionary America experienced processes of politicization and democratization. In Robert Wiebe's words, in the 1770s and early 1780s "a multitude of small political units, governmental and quasi-governmental, rushed to fill the vacuum of British authority." During the 1770s, he continues, "the resistance to Britain and then revolution had unleashed a great range of popular assertions, triggering protests among hitherto passive farmers and townspeople and elevating a number of their spokesmen to office. Occasionally their wartime committees resembled direct government by the people." This democratic ferment continued to characterize popular participation through much of the 1780s, giving politics a robust "raucous" tone foreign to the elite's polite pretensions.[1]

The content of popular politics was as important as its tone. To meet the expenses of the war, for example, state legislatures showed a distinct preference for currency finance and paper money emissions as opposed to raising loans repayable in hard currency. They occasionally rebelled against levying taxes for debt retirement, relying instead on depreciation.[2] All this was held to be injurious to the interests of creditors and in violation of their property rights. To add to the injury state legislatures passed force laws which mandated the acceptance of their depreciated paper currencies; they enacted stay laws and various other forms of debtor relief legislation; they confiscated Loyalist property and sought to avoid altogether debts to

---

[1] Robert H. Wiebe, *The Opening of American Society: From the Adoption of the Constitution to the Eve of Disunion* (New York, 1984), 3, 22.

[2] E. James Ferguson, "Political Economy, Public Liberty, and the Formation of the Constitution," *William and Mary Quarterly*, 3d ser., 40, 4 (July 1983), 389–412; Ruth Bogin, "Petitioning and the New Moral Economy of Postrevolutionary America," *William and Mary Quarterly*, 3d ser., 45, 3 (July 1988), 392–425, at 412–17.

British subjects; and they adopted measures to control litigation costs. Informing most of these proposals was "a belief in government's moral obligation to sustain citizens who were caught in the web of economic woes." The expression of that belief in state action called forth strong condemnation. "The internal police, as it would be called and understood by the States ought to be infringed," Gouverneur Morris told the Philadelphia Convention, "as in the case of paper money and other tricks by which Citizens of other States may be affected."[3]

The revolutionary elite found the demeanor and general behavior of the state legislatures deeply offensive to the virtuous ideals of classical politics. They were partial; they were parochial; they were small-minded; they pandered to popular opinion. Madison freely advertised his disgust and disillusionment. Henry Knox thought the state legislatures "vile." Knox also feared they were encouraging the people at large in sinister levelling "agrarian" designs – the equalizing of property, the abolition of private rights, the redistribution of wealth. At the time of the western Massachusetts agitations that would culminate in Shays's Rebellion (and that threatened also in Connecticut and New Hampshire), Knox told George Washington that some people in the state believed "the property of the United States, has been protected from confiscation of Britain by joint exertions of *all* and therefore ought to be the *common property* of all." Washington could only shudder his agreement.[4]

The dismay of the revolutionary elite may in part be attributed to the relative atrophy of their political influence in the years after 1780 when the Continental Congress's control of the war was to all intents and purposes ceded to the states. To this must be added the maturing of a conviction on the part of significant numbers of them – notably, Hamilton and Robert Morris – that the future of the revolutionary polity lay in the creation of a national state, a perspective which placed these

[3] Bogin, "Petitioning and the New Moral Economy," 408, 407–11. See also Michael Merrill and Sean Wilentz, "William Manning and the Invention of American Politics," in idem, eds., *The Key of Liberty: The Life and Democratic Writings of William Manning, a Laborer, 1747–1814* (Cambridge, Mass., 1993). Gouverneur Morris's statement may be found in Max Farrand, ed., *The Records of the Federal Convention of 1787* (New Haven, 1937), 2:26.

[4] Knox is quoted by Janet A. Riesman, "Money, Credit, and Federalist Political Economy," and by Gordon Wood, "Interests and Disinterestedness in the Making of the Constitution," both in Richard Beeman et al., eds., *Beyond Confederation: Origins of the Constitution and American National Identity* (Chapel Hill, 1987), 150–1 (emphasis in original) and 76; see generally 72–7. See also Gordon Wood, *The Creation of the American Republic, 1776–1787* (Chapel Hill, 1969), 403–25; William Treanor, Note: "The Origins and Original Significance of the Just Compensation Clause of the Fifth Amendment," *Yale Law Journal*, 94, 3 (Jan. 1985), 699–708. Edmund Morgan notes that Virginia also experienced serious debtor agitation at this time. As in New England "the western counties clamored for more paper money, and mobs closed the courts and burned courthouses and prisons." All this led Henry Lee to write to Madison in the same tones as Knox had expressed himself to Washington, predicting an imminent "abolition of debts public and private, a division of property and a new government founded on principles of fraud and iniquity." See Edmund Morgan, *Inventing the People: The Rise of Popular Sovereignty in England and America* (New York, 1988), 266. See, generally, Joyce Appleby, "The American Heritage: The Heirs and the Disinherited," *Journal of American History*, 74, 3 (Dec. 1987), 798–803; Jennifer Nedelsky, *Private Property and the Limits of American Constitutionalism: The Madisonian Framework and Its Legacy* (Chicago, 1990), 25–8, 161–2.

leading Federalists increasingly at odds with those revolutionaries dedicated to the principle of local sovereignty as the repository of the public happiness. Such different perspectives entailed major differences in conceptions of appropriate government structure and power, perspectives that were fought out in the aftermath of the Philadelphia Convention.[5]

The debate, however, was more complicated than whether or not to create a federal system centered on a national government, for there were differences of opinion within each side.

On the Federalist side there were essentially two positions: one Hamiltonian, the other Madisonian.[6] Both centered on the restraint of existing state sovereignties, hence their common federalism. But where Hamilton saw that restraint as a precondition for the creation of an energetic and vigorous state at the national level, Madison – not particularly entranced by the prospect of "energetic government" at *any* level – saw it more as an end in itself.[7] As we shall see, it was the latter, Madisonian, model of governance which would come to exercise predominant influence on the course of state formation in the early republic. Both in its political implications and in its relationship to the early republic's social and economic future, the emergence of that model constitutes a fact of major significance.

The Federalist assault on the states was blunt. Nationalist reformers "had long been convinced that state sovereignty was the fundamental problem of American politics and that federal supremacy was the only solution." Popular attachments precluded some steps – thus the convention resisted "ultranationalist" calls to do away with the states altogether. The Federalists insisted, however, that the states submit to the legitimate authority of the general government. Hence the convention agreed that the central government's powers should extend to legislation "in all cases for the general interests of the Union, and also to those in which the States are separately incompetent, or in which the harmony of the United States may be interrupted by the exercise of individual legislation."[8]

[5] See, generally, Riesman, "Federalist Political Economy," 128–61; Saul Cornell, "Aristocracy Assailed: The Ideology of Backcountry Anti-Federalism," *Journal of American History*, 76, 4 (Mar. 1990), 1148–72; Carol M. Rose, "The Ancient Constitution vs. the Federalist Empire: Anti-Federalism from the Attack on 'Monarchism' to Modern Localism," *Northwestern University Law Review*, 84, 1 (Fall 1989), 74–105.

[6] The two positions are discussed in Isaac Kramnick, "The 'Great National Discussion': The Discourse of Politics in 1787," *William and Mary Quarterly*, 3d ser., 45, 1 (Jan. 1988), 3–32. See also John R. Nelson Jr., *Liberty and Property: Political Economy and Policy Making in the New Nation, 1789–1812* (Baltimore, 1987).

[7] On Madison's distaste for energy in government see Lance Banning, "The Hamiltonian Madison: A Reconsideration," *Virginia Magazine of History and Biography*, 92, 1 (Jan. 1984), 8–9.

[8] Peter S. Onuf, "State Sovereignty and the Constitution," in Terence Ball and J. G. A. Pocock, eds., *Conceptual Change and the Constitution* (Lawrence, Kans., 1988). 79–80. In so resolving, the Philadelphia Convention rejected an alternative description of national government powers that would allow the national government "to make laws binding on the People of the United States in all cases which may concern the common interests of the Union: but not to interfere with the government of the individual States in any matters of internal police ... wherein the general welfare of the United States is not concerned" (Farrand, ed., *Records of the Federal Convention*, 2:21). The division of powers between national and state governments, described in Art. 1, Secs. 8–10, of the federal Constitution, granted the national

Hamilton and Madison were later to develop the Federalist critique of the states at some length in the *Federalist*. To Hamilton the issue appears primarily to have been one of creating a vehicle for the projection of *raison d'état*. In Hamilton's discourse, writes Isaac Kramnick, "the separate American states were intermediate 'political bodies' like 'principal vassals' and 'feudal baronies,' each 'a kind of sovereign within . . . particular demesnes.'" Through the Constitution Hamilton sought to mold these separate bodies in accordance with European patterns, so that the ascendancy of "coercive centralized national-states" would be repeated in America. The result would be the subjugation "on both sides of the Atlantic . . . [of] the 'fierce and ungovernable spirit'" and its reduction "'within those rules of subordination' that characterize 'a more rational and more energetic system of civil polity.'"[9]

Madison's critique of the states was no less trenchant:

> Was then the American revolution effected, was the American confederacy formed, was the precious blood of thousands spilt, and the hard earned substance of millions lavished, not that the people of America should enjoy peace, liberty and safety; but that the Governments of the individual States, that particular municipal establishments, might enjoy a certain extent of power, and be arrayed with certain dignities and attributes of sovereignty? We have heard of the impious doctrine in the old world that the people were made for kings, not kings for the people. Is the same doctrine to be revived in the new, in another shape, that the solid happiness of the people is to be sacrificed to the views of political institutions of a different form?[10]

Madison's critique, however, was grounded upon foundations different from Hamilton's. Whereas Hamilton "held the new American state valuable for its own sake

---

government extraordinarily wide taxing authority while at the same time "remov[ing] a broad range of legislative powers in the economic domain from the state legislatures where popular majorities most effectively wielded power" (Appleby, "American Heritage," 811, and see 805–6). See also Isaac Kramnick, "Editor's Introduction," in idem, ed., *The Federalist Papers* (Harmondsworth, England, 1987), 33–4. On the federal taxation power and its subsequent employment see Thomas P. Slaughter, *The Whiskey Rebellion: Frontier Epilogue to the American Revolution* (New York, 1986), 12–27 and passim. See also, generally, Mark V. Tushnet, "The Constitution as an Economic Document: Beard Revisited," *George Washington Law Review*, 56, 1 (Nov. 1987), 106–13.

[9] Kramnick, "The 'Great National Discussion,'" 26. See also Alexander Hamilton in *Federalist*, no. 17: "The separate Governments in a Confederacy may aptly be compared with the feudal baronies" (in *The Federalist*, ed. Henry B. Dawson [New York, 1863], 111). On Hamilton's political economy see Nelson, *Liberty and Property*, 22–8. See also Rose, "The Ancient Constitution vs. the Federalist Empire," 85.

[10] *Federalist*, no. 44, in *The Federalist*, ed. Dawson, 318–19. See also Russell L. Hanson, "'Commons' and 'Commonwealth' at the American Founding: Democratic Republicanism as the New American Hybrid," in Ball and Pocock, eds., *Conceptual Change and the Constitution*, summarizing Madison's complaints against the states under the Confederation: "the failure of the states to comply with constitutional requisitions; encroachments by the states on the federal authority; violations by the states of the laws of nations and treaties; trespasses by the states on the rights of each other; the lack of concert in matters where common interest requires it; the lack of any guarantee in states' constitutions and laws against internal violence; the lack of sanctions to the laws and of coercion in the government of the confederacy; want of ratification by the people of the Articles; the multiplicity of laws in the several states; the mutability of states' laws; and the injustice of states' laws" (179).

as assertive power" – as a means, that is, once control of the agenda had been wrested from the several states, of projecting power in pursuit of the good of the nation – for Madison the utility of the new American state was heavily bound up in the prospect that it could offer a new model of governance to check unrestrained popular majorities.[11] By responding to the debt crisis of the Confederation period with paper money acts, stay acts, and force acts, the states had encouraged the violation of property rights; when challenged in the courts they had represented themselves as unrestrained by any law.[12] They had been guilty, as Noah Webster put it, of "so many legal infractions of sacred right – so many public invasions of private property – so many wanton abuses of legislative powers!"[13] All this Madison saw as proof that the seeds of tyranny were to be found in unchecked majoritarian legislative governments and the resultant pandering to popular sentiment. "Wherever the real power in a Government lies, there is the danger of oppression," he wrote in 1788. "In our Governments the real power lies in the majority of the Community, and the invasion of private rights is *chiefly* to be apprehended not from acts of Government contrary to the sense of its constituents, but from acts in which the Government is the mere instrument of the major number of the Constituents."[14] The goal, then, was to restrain government at any level from behaving as the state governments had during the previous decade. The means were an enlargement of the geographic sphere within which political activity would have to be pursued, attenuating local connections, and the establishment of a governing model of checks and balances. Each move would hinder majoritarianism.[15]

The overall Federalist demand that the states submit to a general government was fiercely controversial. "The most important end of government," wrote the Anti-Federalist commentator Brutus, "is the proper direction of its internal police and oeconomy; this is the province of the state governments. . . . Is it not then preposterous, and in the highest degree absurd, when the state governments are vested with powers so essential to the peace and good order of society, to take from them

[11] Kramnick, "The 'Great National Discussion,'" 30; Nedelsky, *Private Property and the Limits of American Constitutionalism* 1–66, 141–276. As Joyce Appleby has pointed out, "America in the 1780s had constitutions . . . but not a culture of constitutionalism" ("American Heritage," 800). The true mark of Madison's genius was that he fashioned one. We should not, however, believe that what Madison fashioned was the only culture of constitutionalism possible.

[12] Riesman, "Federalist Political Economy," 150. See also Kramnick, "Editor's Introduction," 21–8; Wythe Holt, "'To Establish Justice': Politics, the Judiciary Act of 1789, and the Invention of the Federal Courts," *Duke Law Journal*, Dec. 1989, no. 6:1421–531, at 1427–58.

[13] Quoted in Kramnick, "The 'Great National Discussion,'" 7.

[14] James Madison to Thomas Jefferson (17 Oct. 1788), in Gaillard Hunt, ed., *James Madison: Writings* (New York, 1904), 5:272 (emphasis in original).

[15] Wiebe, *Opening of American Society*, 28–30; Nedelsky, *Private Property and the Limits of American Constitutionalism*, 142–9. Within this framework Federalists were to deny that in a republican government, popular participation could in fact extend to any species of political action beyond the unique acts of framing or dissolving the constitution which constituted "the people" as "sovereign" and as citizens without becoming an assault on that sovereignty. See Joshua Miller, "The Ghostly Body Politic," *Political Theory*, 16, 1 (Feb. 1988), 99–119.

the means of their own preservation."[16] If there were to be a general government, commented the Federal Farmer, its powers should be carefully limited "to all foreign concerns, causes arising on the seas, to commerce, imports, armies, navies, Indian affairs, peace and war, and to a few internal concerns of the community; to the coin, post-offices, weights and measures, a general plan for the militia, to naturalization, *and perhaps to bankruptcies.*" In all other respects "the internal police of the community" (which meant among other things "the administration of justice in all causes arising internally, the laying and collecting of internal taxes, and the forming of the militia according to a general plan prescribed") should be left exclusively to the states. The Philadelphia Convention, the Federal Farmer asserted, had ignored this careful division, proposing to lodge "all the essential powers in the community" with the general government.[17]

As on the Federalist side, however, this Anti-Federalist argument in fact had two aspects. First, Anti-Federalists criticized the proposed Constitution for threatening republican liberties. The creation of a national "consolidated" government remote from local populations was detrimental to the capacity of the people to oversee government and safeguard their freedom through established mechanisms of popular control. It thus threatened oppression. The proposed architecture for popular representation in the federal government (large constituencies for the House of Representatives, an electoral college for the presidency, an unelected Senate) was symptomatic of the problem,[18] for to Anti-Federalists the goal should be as far as possible to prevent mediating structures of representation from diluting popular oversight of government. "Representation was at best a necessary evil, and its risks were

---

[16] "Essays of Brutus," 7 (3 Jan. 1787), in John P. Kaminski et al., eds., *The Documentary History of the Ratification of the Constitution*, vol. 15 (*Commentaries on the Constitution* vol. 3) (Madison, 1985), 234–40, at 236. The same essay also appears in Herbert J. Storing ed., *The Complete Anti-Federalist* (Chicago, 1981), 2:400–5, where "police" is rendered as "policy." Brutus evinces a particular concern at the states' loss of the powers enumerated in Art. 1, Sec. 8, of the federal Constitution. See in particular essays 5 and 6, in Storing, ed., *Complete Anti-Federalist*, 2:388–93 and 393–400.

[17] "Letters From the Federal Farmer," 1 (8 Oct. 1787), in Storing, ed., *Complete Anti-Federalist*, 2:229 (emphasis in original). The Federal Farmer chose a moderate tone compared with some other Anti-Federalist writers, representing himself as standing for the opinion of "the honest and substantial people" trapped between two unscrupulous and unprincipled parties. "One party is composed of little insurgents, men in debt, who want no law, and who want a share of the property of others; these are called levellers, Shayites, &c. The other party is composed of a few, but more dangerous men, with their servile dependents; these avariciously grasp at power and property; you may discover in all the actions of these men, an evident dislike to free and equal government, and they will go systematically to work to change, essentially, the forms of government in this country; these are called aristocrats, Morrisites, &c. &c. Between these two parties is the weight of the community; the men of middling property, men not in debt on the one hand, and men, on the other, content with republican governments, and not aiming at immense fortunes, offices, and power. In 1786, the little insurgents, the levellers, came forth, invaded the rights of others, and attempted to establish governments according to their wills. Their movements evidently gave encouragement to the other party, which, in 1787, has taken the political field, and with its fashionable dependents, and the tongue and the pen, is endeavoring to establish in great haste, a politer kind of government" (ibid., 2:253).

[18] See "Letters from the Federal Farmer," 2 (9 Oct. 1787) and 7 (31 Dec. 1787), both in ibid., 2:230, 268; Robert H. Webking, "Melancton Smith and the *Letters from the Federal Farmer*," *William and Mary Quarterly*, 3d ser., 44, 3 (July 1987), 510–28, at 513; Wiebe, *Opening of American Society*, 26–8.

to be limited by ensuring that public officials would be tightly controlled by the citizenry." Remoteness of government from popular control was also signified in the very idea of government as a balance of multiple institutions in which the actions of popular branches were checked by others altogether insulated from popular oversight. Not surprisingly, therefore, the proposed separation of powers excited Anti-Federalist opposition in direct proportion to the remoteness of each locus of power from popular influence. Anti-Federalists were "least suspicious of the House of Representatives"; they treated the Senate as "an intermediate case"; and they regarded the institution of the presidency and the unelected federal judiciary with greatest alarm.[19]

Some Anti-Federalists stopped here, theirs "the traditional republican fear of corruption."[20] Anti-Federalist discourse also implied, however, that proponents of the new government were in fact chiefly motivated by solicitude for the rights and property of a privileged minority – so much so that they had designed the new Constitution specifically to curb the capacity of the people acting through their existing local governments to exercise communal powers *positively* in response to popular concerns in ways that might prove detrimental to the interests of that minority. As Saul Cornell has put it, "one could attack the new Constitution for concentrating too much power in the hands of government and thus establishing an aristocracy of government officials, or one could attack the Constitution for favoring the interests of a specific social class, loosely defined as the natural aristocracy," a group thought of by Anti-Federalist writers as encompassing such persons as prominent politicians and officers of the new government, the officer corps, superior judges, eminent professionals, wealthy merchants, and large property holders.[21] This "plebeian populist" strain of Anti-Federalism, a response principally to the Madisonian conception of governance, evinced less a concern about how to protect against the threat that "consolidated government" per se might pose to "liberty" than a concern that the citizenry at large should continue to be able through their local governments to determine for themselves the outcomes of issues vital to the substance of their existence as populations free from the machinations of the few – should continue, that is, to control their political structures, the decisions taken in those structures, and the implementation of those decisions; in other words, their police and their pursuit of happiness.[22]

---

[19] Cass Sunstein, "Beyond the Republican Revival," *Yale Law Journal*, 97, 8 (July 1988), 1556. See also Kramnick, "Editor's Introduction," 40–7.

[20] Cornell, "Aristocracy Assailed," 1168 (describing George Mason).

[21] Ibid., 1157–8. Cornell takes his description of a natural aristocracy favored by the Constitution from the Federal Farmer. See "Letters from the Federal Farmer," 7 (31 Dec. 1787), in Storing, ed., *Complete Anti-Federalist*, 2:267. It is worth noting that William Manning's description of "the few" in *Key of Libberty* conforms almost exactly to these Anti-Federalist descriptions of the natural aristocracy. See the Prologue, this volume.

[22] Cornell, "Aristocracy Assailed," 1167–8. Robert Wiebe writes, "In comparison with a national government . . . every part of a state government seemed strikingly popular: close to the people, intimate with their concerns, ready to voice their wishes." From this perspective a state government appeared "an undifferentiated unit of democracy, and its actions expressed, in a common phrase, 'the will of the community'" (*Opening of American Society*, 23).

The tension between the Federalist project and communal conceptions of governance becomes particularly evident when we consider the role in government of what the Federalists called the "judiciary department."[23] As "majoritarian, popular sovereignty governments," governments of "inherent authority" with the duty of "caring for all the needs of society," the state governments had asserted an authority based on the communal right of police.[24] Because state constitutional declarations of rights and liberties voiced not absolute rights of individuals against government but principles intended to inform and guide legislatures in liberty-enhancing exercises of government for the good of all, the supremacy of the state legislatures was not conceived of as subject to check, least of all by the judiciary. "States were governments dedicated to popular sovereignty and structured so as to retain an identity between the people and their representatives in assembly. As in Britain, the fight for liberty had taken the form of empowering elected representatives at the expense of the executive. The judiciary was perceived as an arm of the executive; a free judiciary, then, was one less subject to executive interference, not one which could override the people acting through their representatives. Thus when, during the Confederation period, state judges invalidated state law, they could be attacked for defeating the will of the people."[25]

Proponents of the federal Constitution argued for a very different relationship between judicial and legislative authority, one expressing a different view of constitutions. Courts, said Hamilton in *Federalist*, no. 78, were intermediate bodies positioned between the people and their legislatures and charged with determining whether legislative action comported with constitutional intent. "The interpretation of the laws is the proper and peculiar province of the Courts. A Constitution is, in fact, and must be regarded by the Judges as a fundamental law. It therefore belongs to them to ascertain its meaning, as well as the meaning of any particular Act proceeding from the Legislative body. If there should happen to be an irreconcilable variance between the two, that which has the superior obligation and validity ought, of course, to be preferred; or in other words, the Constitution ought to be preferred to the statute."[26]

Hamilton portrayed the courts as protectors of the popular will, as embodied in constitutions, from illicit exercises of authority by the representatives in the legislature. Those protectors, however, were totally insulated from popular oversight:

---

[23] For the most thorough recent discussion of the general political and jurisprudential issues surrounding the creation of federal judicial authority, see Shannon C. Stimson, *The American Revolution in the Law: Anglo-American Jurisprudence before John Marshall* (Princeton, 1990). See also Sylvia Snowiss, "From Fundamental Law to the Supreme Law of the Land: A Reinterpretation of the Origin of Judicial Review," *Studies in American Political Development*, 2 (1987), 1–67.

[24] Robert C. Palmer, "Liberties as Constitutional Provisions, 1776–1791," in William E. Nelson and Robert C. Palmer, *Liberty and Community: Constitution and Rights in the Early American Republic* (New York, 1987), 86.

[25] Ibid., 82–3. See also Julius Goebel, Jr., *Antecedents and Beginnings to 1801* (New York, 1971), vol. 1 of *History of the Supreme Court of the United States*, 98–100; J. M. Sosin, *The Aristocracy of the Long Robe: The Origins of Judicial Review in America* (Westport, Conn., 1989), 203–26.

[26] *Federalist*, no. 78, in *The Federalist*, ed. Dawson, 538–48, at 542.

unelected, appointed during good behavior, "independent." Nor was their protectorate a restricted one, confined to excesses perpetrated by the legislature in defiance of the popular will. Rather it was to extend to circumstances where "the major voice of the community" itself sought to spur their representatives to action in derogation of other interests.

This independence of the Judges is equally requisite to guard the Constitution and the rights of individuals, from the effects of those ill humors, which the arts of designing men, or the influence of particular conjunctures, sometimes disseminate among the People themselves, and which, though they speedily give place to better information, and more deliberate reflection, have a tendency, in the mean time, to occasion dangerous innovations in the Government, and serious oppressions of the minor part in the community.[27]

Nor, significantly, was the projected constitutional role of judicial oversight confined to issues of constitutional infraction. It was to extend wherever "the private rights of particular classes of citizens" were injured by "unjust and partial laws."[28] As Hamilton put it in *Federalist*, no. 69, one of the main reasons the public interest required governments to be instituted was in order to furnish "protection of property against those irregular and high-handed combinations which sometimes interrupt the ordinary course of justice."[29] Applying this general argument to the judiciary extended its constitutionally sanctioned protectorate beyond the guarantee of the popular will in constitutional cases to a guarantee of property from "unjust" or "partial" legislative interventions in general. Here "the firmness of the Judicial magistracy" would be "of vast importance in mitigating the severity, and confining the operation of such [unjust] laws." That magistracy would "moderate the immediate mischiefs of those [laws] which may have been passed," and it would also operate "as a check upon the Legislative body," compelling them to "qualify their attempts."[30]

The Federalists' proposals for the new government's judiciary department provoked considerable criticism among Anti-Federalists aroused by the possibility that the new federal judiciary would make inroads upon local concerns, in particular through its extensive diversity and alienage jurisdiction. Thus the Federal Farmer

---

[27] Ibid., 544. [28] Ibid., 545. See also Holt, " 'To Establish Justice,' " 1459–66.

[29] *Federalist*, no. 69, in *The Federalist*, ed. Dawson, 486–96, at 487.

[30] *Federalist*, no. 78, in ibid., 538–48, at 545. What Hamilton had in mind is perhaps best illustrated by his contention in debate in the New York Assembly (6 Feb. 1787) that the provision of the state constitution preventing deprivation of one's rights except by "the law of the land" meant, quite precisely, except according to juridical proceedings and decision. The words, said Hamilton, could never refer "to an act of the legislature." See Gordon S. Wood, *The Radicalism of the American Revolution* (New York, 1992), 324. Wood calls Hamilton's claim "astonishing and novel" and the general move to restraint of which it was a sign "a long way from the 1776 republican confidence in popular legislative law-making" and "a severe indictment of democracy" (324, 325). On the removal of property from politics see Jennifer Nedelsky, "Confining Democratic Politics: Anti-Federalists, Federalists, and the Constitution," *Harvard Law Review*, 96, 2 (Nov. 1982), 340–60, and her more recent and more complete account in *Private Property and the Limits of American Constitutionalism*. On the embodiment of an absolute right of property in the federal Constitution, see Richard Epstein, *Takings: Private Property and the Power of Eminent Domain* (Cambridge, Mass., 1985), 16–18, 22–3.

criticized the judiciary department's enjoyment of "powers respecting questions arising upon the internal laws of the respective states"; according to Centinel, "the objects of jurisdiction . . . are so numerous, and the shades of distinction between civil causes oftentimes so slight, that it is more than probable that the state judicatories would be wholly superceded."[31] Like Centinel, Brutus also expected that the proposed federal judiciary would "swallow up all the powers of the courts in the respective states."[32] Federalists responded to this criticism by stressing that the federal judiciary's jurisdiction had been kept as limited as feasible. As stated by Madison, however, their goal was still the establishment of means whereby "improper Verdicts in State tribunals obtained under the biassed directions of a dependent Judge, or the local prejudices of an undirected jury," could be overturned.[33]

Anti-Federalists, however, also criticized the extent of the powers accorded the judiciary as such. Much, for example, was made of the absence from the draft Constitution of provision for jury trials. This point was pressed as a substantive issue: If federal judges were to have jurisdiction as to fact as well as law, jury trials should be guaranteed in all causes, civil and criminal. But it was also treated as symptomatic of the Federalist model of governance, and therefore an occasion for more general commentary. "It is essential in every free country, that common people should have a part and share of influence, in the judicial as well as in the legislative department," wrote the Federal Farmer. The common people could not realistically expect to occupy the high offices of state – senators, judges, and so forth – for which an expensive education (and therefore extensive property) was required. "These, and most other offices of any considerable importance, will be occupied by . . . the few, the well born, &c. as Mr Adams calls them, [who] in judicial decisions as well as in legislation, are generally disposed . . . to favour those of their own description." Those elements of juridical and legislative practice guaranteeing the people's voice therefore took on a major significance.

The trial by jury in the judicial department, and the collection of the people by their representatives in the legislature, are those fortunate inventions which have procured for them in this country, their true proportion of influence, and the wisest and most fit means of protecting themselves in the community. Their situation, as jurors and representatives, enables them to acquire information and knowledge in the affairs and government of the society; and to come forward, in turn, as the centinels and guardians of each other. I am very sorry that even a few of our countrymen should consider jurors and representatives in a

---

[31] "Letters From the Federal Farmer," 3 (10 Oct. 1787), in Storing, ed., *Complete Anti-Federalist*, 2:234–45, at 243; "Essays of Centinel," 1 (5 Oct. 1787), in Kaminski et al., eds., *Documentary History of the Ratification*, 13:328–36, at 333.

[32] "Essays of Brutus," 1 (18 Oct. 1787), in Storing, ed., *Complete Anti-Federalist*, 2:363–72, at 367.

[33] See Holt, " 'To Establish Justice,' " 1464–6. In his discussion of the federal court jurisdiction which emerged from the Philadelphia Convention, Holt argues, " 'Questions involving the national peace and harmony' turned out to include controversies between citizens and foreigners (alienage jurisdiction), controversies between citizens of different states (diversity jurisdiction), and 'all' admiralty cases." According to Holt, "pressure to facilitate debt recovery in forums not subject to local debtor pressures" featured prominently in the determination of a federal jurisdiction of this ambit.

different point of view, as ignorant, troublesome bodies, which ought not to have any share in the concerns of government.[34]

Other Anti-Federalists voiced direr suspicions. Brutus, for example, warned that the federal judicial power would "operate to effect . . . an entire subversion of the legislative, executive and judicial powers of the individual states."[35] Montezuma, more explosively, represented the judiciary as a "masked battery" primed and ready to decimate popular rule with the proverbial whiff of grapeshot.[36]

By creating a "judiciary department" insulated from popular inspection and by giving it authority over the institutional structure and powers of the state itself, Federalists ensured that *legal* discourse would be rendered central to the future of the American polity. Some of the immediate heat over the considerable power to be given to the judiciary in the new state was temporarily abated in the aftermath of ratification by the passage of the Judiciary Act of 1789, which receded in a number of respects from the expansive federal jurisdiction adumbrated during the ratification debates.[37] This notwithstanding, however, the Constitution had still created a state in which the judiciary occupied the pivotal position, its aegis extending to the prescribing and establishing of the powers and relationships among the polity's constituent elements, nation and states, and also of the private rights whose protection had so animated discussion of the Constitution's purposes, notably the deference of government to property, which the founders desired to establish.[38] Moreover, as the controversy over jury trials indicated, the law to which the judiciary would have resort in the execution of this role was law of a particular kind: uniform and homogeneous, untouched by "the local knowledge of ordinary people."[39] The "fundamental" law of the Constitution, then, was to be mapped in the polite, juristic, common law–indebted discourse of

[34] "Letters From the Federal Farmer," 4 (12 Oct. 1787), in Storing, ed., *Complete Anti-Federalist*, 2:245–51, at 249–50.

[35] "Essays of Brutus," 11 (31 Jan. 1788), in ibid., 417–22, at 420. See also "Essays of Brutus," 12 (7–14 Feb. 1788), 13 (21 Feb. 1788), 14 (28 Feb.–6 Mar. 1788), and 15 (20 Mar. 1788), in ibid., 422–42. In these essays Brutus continued his attack on the federal judicial power, concentrating first on its potential to elevate central government over local, resulting in the subversion and eventual abolition of local governments, and second on its potential to elevate the judicial power above all other powers in government, local *and* central. On Brutus, see Sosin, *Aristocracy of the Long Robe*, 259–61.

[36] "Letter of Montezuma" (17 Oct. 1787), in Cecelia Kenyon, ed., *The Antifederalists* (Indianapolis, 1966), 61–7, at 64–5. And see Hanson, "Democratic Republicanism as the New American Hybrid," 182.

[37] Holt, "'To Establish Justice,'" 1478–1521.

[38] On early cases illustrating the position of the judiciary, with specific reference to Pennsylvania, see Stephen Presser, "A Tale of Two Judges: Richard Peters, Samuel Chase, and the Broken Promise of Federalist Jurisprudence," *Northwestern University Law Review*, 73, 1 (1978), 26–111, at 40–6.

[39] Rose, "The Ancient Constitution vs. the Federalist Empire," 91, and cf. 79. On the role of the jury in prerevolutionary politics and law, and its transformation in Federalist theory from an agency determinative of law to one subject to judicial direction, see Stimson, *American Revolution in the Law*, 34–147. See also Forrest McDonald, *Novus Ordo Seclorum: The Intellectual Origins of the Constitution* (Lawrence, Kans., 1985), 289–91. Unlike the perspective adopted here, where the transformation of the jury is seen as symptomatic of a generalized political contest over the location of power, McDonald argues from an evolutionary perspective that a local jury's authority to determine law was an anachronism, a barrier, as he puts it, "to the onward flow of history."

the profession.[40] Julius Goebel has stressed the paucity of institutional borrowings from the common law in the Constitution, arguing that "reluctance to let the past take too great a command of the future may account for the Convention's judicious restraint in selecting only specific items from the vast storehouse of the mother law."[41] The absence of a mentality, however, cannot be assumed from the absence

---

[40] See H. Jefferson Powell, "The Original Understanding of Original Intent," *Harvard Law Review*, 98, 5 (Mar. 1985), 885–948, esp. 894–913.

[41] Goebel, *Antecedents and Beginnings*, 230. During the ratification debates, Federalists and Anti-Federalists did not often divide on the issue of the common law as such. Indeed, many Anti Federalists centered their critiques of the draft Constitution on its failure to protect particular common law rights, such as local jury trials (see, e.g., ibid., 296). Where they did divide was on the set of relationships between (1) individual common law rights, (2) communal or collective rights as embodied in the sovereignty of state governments, and (3) the sphere of power to be accorded the federal judiciary. Here it is important to consider the Bill of Rights. Long represented as the "price" paid to the Anti-Federalists to obtain ratification, the Bill of Rights as it emerged from the first session of the new Congress in fact recognized only individual common law rights while ignoring communal or collective rights and widening further the ambit of federal judicial power. In all three respects it was to the detriment of the Anti-Federalist position.

The amendments to the federal Constitution promoted in several states (notably Pennsylvania, Massachusetts, South Carolina, New Hampshire, Virginia, and New York) constituted the same mix of individual and collective rights as appeared in state declarations. Protections of the collective rights of state citizenries appeared in the form of substantive changes in the Constitution's division of powers between the national and the state governments, intended to restore to the states many of the powers taken from them under Art. 1, Secs. 8–10. Anti-Federalists pressing the amendments were seeking at the same time to safeguard individual popular liberties from a national government dangerously remote from the people and to preserve the freedom of state governments (governments, unlike the national government, in close proximity to the people and founded, as we have seen, on principles expressive of the comity of people and government) to act on behalf of the collectivity.

The amendments as adopted by the new Congress reflected a different logic. There was no amendment of the substance of the Constitution to alter the balance of national and state powers. Instead, amendments appended to the original document (i.e., the Bill of Rights) enumerated exceptions to the powers of the national government protecting individual rights. They were conceived of by Madison as putting a further "legal check [on government's infringement of essential rights] . . . into the hands of the judiciary" (Wood, *Creation of the American Republic*, 543). See also Bernard Schwartz, *The Great Rights of Mankind: A History of the American Bill of Rights* (New York, 1977), 200. Madison also sought to extend that legal check so that the rights enumerated in the amendments to the federal Constitution should also be secured against the state governments. See Francis Newton Thorpe, *The Constitutional History of the United States* (Chicago, 1901), 2:245–6. Gordon Wood comments that "because the Antifederalists in their demand for amendments and a bill of rights had actually been more concerned with weakening the power of the federal government in its relation to the states in matters such as taxation than with protecting 'personal liberty alone,' they found even this, the strongest of their objections to the Constitution, eventually turned against them" (543). Robert Wiebe has put it thus: "Madison . . . carefully discarded every proposal 'abridging the sum of power transferred from the States to the general Government' and even tried to insert one – 'the most valuable amendment on the whole list' – empowering the national government to police state actions." As to provisions protecting individual rights: "Referring to such lists of basic liberties as the 'personal rights of individuals,' [Madison] divorced the collective people from state government and construed the Bill of Rights as a direct relationship between the national government and its atomized citizenry" (Wiebe, *Opening of American Society*, 32–3). See also Treanor, "Origins and Original Significance of the Just Compensation Clause," 710–16, particularly 713–14; Stanley N. Katz, "The Strange Birth and Unlikely History of Constitutional Equality," *Journal of American History*, 75, 3 (Dec. 1988), 747–62, at 748; Nedelsky, *Private Property and the Limits of American Constitutionalism*, 187–9, 281n. On the amending process and the substance of the amendments see generally Palmer, "Liberties as Constitutional Provisions," 87–148; Thorpe, *Constitutional History of the United States*, 199–263.

of an explicit institutional trail. The judiciary department would be a site of common law practices and procedures populated by common law minds,[42] so much so that within ten years Jeffersonian republicans reviving fears of the power of the judiciary were stressing the danger of the judges' invention of a second constitution to rival the first, one built out of the "dark and barbarous pages of the common law" itself.[43]

Here, then, brought to a particularly sharp contrast, we see the same tension that appears to run through the whole Anti-Federalist–Federalist debate, a tension between the maximization of opportunities for popular government (or self-rule) and

[42] Note, e.g., the opinion of the jurist Peter S. Du Ponceau, writing in 1824. Du Ponceau argued that "at the very moment when independence was declared, the common law was claimed by an unanimous voice as the birth right of American citizens." Subsequently the Revolution had led to the promulgation of written compacts and these, Du Ponceau conceded, had replaced the common law as the source of the powers of American political institutions. He then promptly reestablished the common law as "source," however, by insisting that these compacts were themselves expressions of America's common law heritage. "We need but open the Constitution of the United States and the laws which have been made in pursuance of it, and we shall find the common law almost in every line." Hence, "the common law of England" was established as the law of the United States "for all national purposes and for all cases in which the local law is not the exclusive rule." See Peter S. Du Ponceau, *Dissertation on the Nature and Extent of the Jurisdiction of the Courts of the United States* (Philadelphia, 1824), ix, 91–2.

[43] Albert Gallatin, quoted in Goebel, *Antecedents and Beginnings*, 654. On the influence of common on constitutional law see R. Kent Newmyer, *Supreme Court Justice Joseph Story: Statesman of the Old Republic* (Chapel Hill, 1985), 98, 101; Stephen A. Conrad, "James Wilson's 'Assimilation of the Common-Law Mind,'" *Northwestern University Law Review*, 84, 1 (Fall 1989), 186–219. Conrad shows Wilson's anxiety at the potentially "despotick" implications of Blackstonian common law but also his desire to confirm its authority, once sufficiently "republicanized," as an inherited legal system.

Jeffersonian republican criticism of the common law mentality of the judiciary increased greatly during the 1790s, particularly in light of Federalist assertions in defense of the Alien and Sedition acts (1798) that the acts were founded on the principle that English common law was in force under the government of the United States and that the federal judiciary therefore enjoyed a common law jurisdiction over crimes. Jeffersonians attacked the Federalist position as a further attempt at consolidation. On the debate over federal common law crimes, and in general on the role of the judiciary in the republic's first two decades, see Presser, "A Tale of Two Judges," 26–111. See also Kathryn Preyer, "Jurisdiction to Punish: Federal Authority and the Criminal Law," Robert C. Palmer, "The Federal Common Law of Crime," and Stephen Presser, "The Supra-Constitution: The Courts and the Federal Common Law of Crimes," all in "Symposium: Federal Common Law of Crime," *Law and History Review*, 4, 2 (Fall 1986), 223–336.

Asserting a "federal common law" power meant a considerable widening in the ambit of the federal judiciary's jurisdiction. As Morton Horwitz has shown, however, criticism of the assertion was in large part founded upon a more general concern about judicial discretion and its capacity to undermine legislative authority. See Morton Horwitz, *The Transformation of American Law, 1780–1860* (Cambridge, Mass., 1977), 9–18; Goebel, *Antecedents and Beginnings*, 608–61. Madison of course joined Jefferson in the campaign against the Alien and Sedition acts, denying the establishment of the common law by the Constitution. Goebel, however, condemns Madison's denial as sheer casuistry inspired by little other than the politics of the moment (*Antecedents and Beginnings*, 652–3). And in fact, where Jefferson's Kentucky Resolves invoked the special relationship of the people with their particular state government by asserting the right of any state legislature to judge whether the national government had transgressed its delegated powers and if necessary *void* the offending action within the limits of its own jurisdiction, Madison's Virginia Resolves, while condemning the acts, avoided the Jeffersonian invocation of local sovereignty and instead located a right of redress against the national government in the states acting collectively. As Preyer, among others, shows, and as we shall see in this and the next chapter, the issue of the common law remained a live one long after the Alien and Sedition acts. See her "Jurisdiction to Punish," 238–65.

restraint of the people by law.[44] Obviously these were two premises with very different implications for the discourse of rule in the new republic. The former, prevailing in conceptions of republican government prior to the Constitution debate, had been founded on a general presumption of an identity of people and legislature, a presumption locating responsibility for realizing "the public happiness" in the actions of majoritarian popular-sovereignty governments. The latter, emerging most clearly during the Constitution debates, reveals a new model of governance growing out of the experiences of the Confederation period and expressing a desire to limit popular participation.[45] Its flavor is nicely conveyed by the Federalist model of an unelected elite judiciary[46] situated between people and legislature, with power to invalidate or render inoperative legislative action according to its own canons of interpretation.[47]

[44] In this connection it is appropriate to note conclusions reached recently by Shannon Srimson in regard to the Bill of Rights. "From the Anti-Federalist perspective," she writes, "the substance of a bill of rights should serve as an epistemological replacement for the certainty of political and legal judgment based on local standards and community norms . . . which they rightly believed national government would supersede." Its role would be to "provide a perpetual set of 'certain,' if generally worded, standards by which continually to judge government and, if necessary, resist it." To the Anti-Federalists, "The certainty of such a bill of rights . . . lay in the fact that *they* were left to judge, as they had been at local levels, the content as well as the application of the limits of government." This understanding, however, "struck at the very stability Madison hoped to produce by restricting, not enlarging, the space for exercise of popular judgment about law." For Madison, the purpose of "a strictly enumerated bill of rights" was to create "a double-edged political limit," one that not only would teach legislatures the limits of their powers but would also and simultaneously teach the people that "the area over which they could judge the law" also had limits. See Stimson, *American Revolution in the Law*, 120–1 (emphasis in original).

[45] "The Constitution closed the door on simple majoritarian government in the United States. Popular majorities animated by what people wanted to do at a particular moment would be forever constrained. The Constitution created a fundamental law, and that law severely restricted the range of government power. The same founding document made it extraordinarily difficult to change the distribution of power. Despite the celebration of popular sovereignty in America, the sovereign people were restrained once the Constitution was ratified" (Appleby, "American Heritage," 804).

[46] As Hamilton put it in *Federalist*, no. 78, "there can be but few men in the society, who will have sufficient skill in the laws to qualify them in the stations of Judges." These few, furthermore, would all undoubtedly be engaged in "lucrative" practices whence they would have to be prised by appointments offered on good behavior, immune from the "encroachments and oppressions of the representative body" (in *The Federalist*, ed., Dawson, 547, 539). On James Wilson's vision of the judiciary and its role and on Madison's more cautious views, see Nedelsky, *Private Property and the Limits of American Constitutionalism*, 119–24, 64–5.

[47] Forrest McDonald notes "general agreement" at the Philadelphia Convention "that, despite the shakiness of the precedents for the doctrine, the [federal] courts would by the very nature of their function have the power to strike down legislative acts if they were in violation of the Constitution." Indeed, McDonald continues, Madison through the creation of a federal council of revision "wanted to give the judges even greater power, that of vetoing legislation on policy grounds as well as on constitutional grounds" (*Novus Ordo Seclorum*, 254). Madison himself wrote Jefferson that "the Judicial authority under our new system will keep the States within their proper limits, and supply the place of a negative on their laws." He indicated, however, that he would have preferred a federal veto through a council of revision on the ground that "it is more convenient to prevent the passage of a law, than to declare it void after it is passed" (James Madison to Thomas Jefferson [24 Oct. 1787], in Julian P. Boyd, ed., *The Papers of Thomas Jefferson* [Princeton, 1950–82], 12:270–86, at 275–6). On the precedents see Goebel, *Antecedents and Beginnings*, 96–142.

MARKETS, LIBERTY, AND SECURITY

Although Federalists continued throughout the debate on the Constitution to speak of their goals in the same eudaemonic idiom of public happiness and the common good employed by their rivals, their diverging perspective on the means of achieving "the public happiness" marked a major difference on how the concept was to be understood. Hamilton's state-centered discourse of national power, we have already seen, continued to place considerable emphasis on politics and the public sphere and "shared the reading of man as a political animal, as a community-building creature," with Anti-Federalist republicans. But Hamilton did not share their "participatory ideals of moral citizenship," thereby quite dramatically differentiating his discourse from theirs.[48] Madison's position, meanwhile, suggested a substantial erosion of the primacy which politics and government had enjoyed since the Revolution as spheres for constitutive public action. The primary sphere of action in the Madisonian conception of human society was private, not public. The proper role of government was not to determine the course of society but instead to oversee ("umpire," "regulate") the competition of the many interests inhabiting the private sphere.[49] Its end was "justice," by which Madison meant the security of private rights, particularly rights of property. Interferences with such rights, he told the Philadelphia Convention, were the "evils which had more than perhaps anything else" brought about their meeting.[50] His own model of government sought to give recognition to the imagined plurality of interests in society, all of which, he implied, shared a common interest in forestalling intrusions.

Madison's influence in these debates helped bring about a major shift in expressions of the common good. Between the Revolution and the end of the eighteenth century there occurred a subtle elision of its collective aspect, one that saw the concept couched increasingly in individual, rather than communal, terms. Willi-Paul Adams, for example, notes that formulations of the common good characteristic of the period increasingly expressed the common good as the guaranteed right to

---

[48] Kramnick, "The 'Great National Discussion,'" 24–5.

[49] Madison could be quite cynical about this. "Divide et impera, the reprobated axiom of tyranny, is under certain conditions, the only policy, by which a republic can be administered on just principles" (Madison to Jefferson [24 Oct. 1787], quoted in ibid., 6). As Daniel Walker Howe has put it: "Madison . . . believed in an elite of the wise and the virtuous, whose government would be best. He hoped that enlarging the size of the body politic by creating an effective national government over the states would help ensure that members of this elite would be elected as rulers. Enlarging the commonwealth would also, he hoped, so multiply selfish special interests and their political expression in 'factions' that they would cancel each other out, leaving the wise and virtuous to govern in the interest of the community as a whole. . . . The rhetorical strategy of *The Federalist Papers* is to appeal, on behalf of virtue, to the enlightened self-interest of this group of prudent men against the danger of the mob, the factious and passionate" ("European Sources of Political Ideas in Jeffersonian America," *Reviews in American History*, 10, 4 [Dec. 1982], 37).

[50] Farrand, ed., *Records of the Federal Convention*, 1:134. See also Kramnick, "Editor's Introduction," 6; Treanor, "Origins and Original Significance of the Just Compensation Clause," 708–13; Nedelsky, *Private Property and the Limits of American Constitutionalism*. As we have already seen (above, n. 30) Hamilton was as concerned for the security of private property as Madison, but this was not the issue that animated his overall vision of the Constitution as it was for Madison.

enjoyment of life, liberty, and property, "that is, claims made by the individual, not by the collective." As a result, the "common good and the sum of private interests were seen as synonymous, and the possibility of conflict between them was belittled."[51]

Joyce Appleby has also written extensively of this redefinition of the common good in terms of individual rights and has arrived at similar conclusions. Appleby points to the existence within the political discourse of the last quarter of the eighteenth century of three different concepts of liberty: first, the liberty of the classical republican tradition, which meant liberty to share in the political life of the community and implied no limitation on the power of government as long as it served the common good (and which, as we have seen, emerged from the Revolution in a distinctively popular as well as a more traditional elitist incarnation);[52] second, the liberty of the common law tradition, which meant liberty of secure possession, the protection of private, personal (vested) interests, and the delimitation of the scope of public authority; and third, the liberty of a new liberal tradition, developed in the works of Thomas Hobbes and John Locke, which "rationalized government by deriving its functions from general propositions about human nature and the formation of civil society" and on that basis deduced that liberty meant the protection of natural rights by government acting in the service of the convenience of society's members. "By giving up their private right to execute the law of nature they created government to do the policing, but civil society added nothing to their rights nor to the content of natural law; it existed only to implement what was already a part of God's creation. Its power . . . was limited to those measures necessary to protect the life, liberty, and property of the members of society." According to Appleby it was this last tradition of liberty – liberty as free enterprise – which informed the transformation of social and political institutions which took place in America in the decade following the Revolution, and which was entrenched by the Constitution.[53]

Appleby has located the origins of postrevolutionary America's natural law/free enterprise liberalism in the quickening reappraisal of economic life and the role of government which began in late seventeenth-century England and received its most comprehensive expression in Adam Smith's *Wealth of Nations*: that is, in the transcendent "system of natural liberty" which accompanied the eighteenth century's spreading "promise of prosperity."[54] Smith's fundamental purpose was to investigate the bases of happiness and justice in commercial society. In particular it was to explain the apparent paradox that even though commercial society was

---

[51] Willi-Paul Adams, *The First American Constitutions: Republican Ideology and the Making of the State Constitutions in the Revolutionary Era* (Chapel Hill, 1980), 218–29, 223.

[52] There was, of course, no *necessity* that classical republicanism be elitist in its implications. See e.g., Quentin Skinner, "Sir Thomas More's *Utopia* and the Language of Renaissance Humanism," in Anthony Pagden, ed., *The Languages of Political Theory in Early Modern Europe* (Cambridge, 1989), 123–57.

[53] Joyce Appleby, *Capitalism and a New Social Order: The Republican Vision of the 1790s* (New York, 1984), 16–23.

[54] Ibid., 25–50.

typically characterized by greater extremes of inequality in wealth and property than had previously prevailed, it was nevertheless evidently more successful in providing for the needs of all than any prior form of social organization. "There was no economic mystery in the material well-being of 'the rich and powerful.' In any society he 'who can at all times direct the labours of 1000's to his own purposes' could be expected to live well. The distinctive feature of 'commercial society' was that those who 'provide both for themselves and for the enormous luxury of their superiors' should themselves be able to retain from the produce of their labour both the necessities and many of the simpler conveniences of life." Smith's answer was bottomed on his innovative invocation of the concept of the division of labor. As his famous example of the pin factory was intended to demonstrate, productivity was the creature less of intensified commitment to unchanged patterns of activity than of a disciplined reorganization of action. Through the division of labor, commercial society was able to generate so superior an opulence that the standard of living of all was enhanced, thus more effectively guaranteeing the subsistence of the poor.[55]

The general origins of the impulse to labor division were to be found, Smith said, in the human propensity "to truck, barter, and exchange one thing for another." Crucially, however, realization of its full potential for universal improvement, particularly in the supply of food, depended upon the unhindered operation of market mechanisms to facilitate the redistribution of independent wage-earning labor both between town and country and within manufacturing, for this had to occur in such a way as would lead to increases in manufacturing productivity, permitting the production of goods at prices that would in turn act as an incentive for farmers to increase their incomes through the production of agricultural surpluses for sale.[56] Free markets in labor and in food were thus essential institutional complements to the division of labor in Smith's scheme and became the key features of the system of natural liberty which he propounded.

Working from this basis Smith proceeded to develop a wholesale critique of nonmarket techniques for attempting to achieve distributive justice that interfered with market operations and thus eroded market discipline. "To hinder . . . the farmer from sending his goods at all times to the best market, is evidently *to sacrifice the ordinary laws of justice to an idea of publick utility*, to a sort of reasons of state – an act of legislative authority which ought to be exercised only, which can be pardoned only in cases of the most urgent necessity." For Smith, in other words, political economy's central task became the constant counterposition of the superiority of the "system of natural liberty" to the system of "police" in the achievement of "public happiness."[57] Smith, it is important to note, did not ascribe commercial society's

[55] Michael Ignatieff and Istvan Hont, "Needs and Justice in the *Wealth of Nations*: An Introductory Essay," in idem, eds., *Wealth and Virtue: The Shaping of Political Economy in the Scottish Enlightenment* (Cambridge, 1983), 4–5.

[56] Ibid., 4–5; Adam Smith, *An Inquiry into the Nature and Causes of the Wealth of Nations* (New York, 1937), 13–21.

[57] Ignatieff and Hont, "Needs and Justice in the *Wealth of Nations*," 20 (emphasis supplied), 20–6, 11. See also Smith, *Lectures on Jurisprudence*, 486–541.

superior performance in feeding and clothing its poorest members to that society's conscious benevolence. It was "an outcome of unintended consequences." However unintended, the capacity itself remained a powerful argument for the moral as well as the economic superiority of the market mechanism over a traditionalist communitarian moral economy and reinforced the Smithian tendency to contrast the *natural necessity* of the system of natural liberty with the mere *historical contingency* of police.[58]

Far from a triumph of necessity over contingency, however, Smith's elevation of the system of natural liberty to the status of a new and transforming epistemology of "abstract universals"[59] was itself an outcome marked by the contingency of historical circumstance. First, as Nicholas Phillipson puts it, the Scottish Enlightenment's "critique of the classic language of civic morality," from which *The Wealth of Nations* sprang, was a critique being undertaken by men "living in a sophisticated but provincial community which had been stripped of its political institutions at the time of the Act of Union in 1707 and still hankered after an understanding of the principles of virtue which would make sense of their present provincial condition." The Scottish Enlightenment, that is, undertook a search for a new grounding for civic morality, not simply because its proponents had become convinced intellectually of the bankruptcy of politics, but rather because politics was simply not available after the institutional revolution of 1707. In Smith's hands commerce provided a new, different, but nonetheless satisfying foundation for the comprehension of human behavior, not insignificantly one that also denied the importance of what had been lost:

In commercial society men could confront each other as consumers and producers and could acquire a sense of fair play and propriety by "higgling and bargaining" in the market places of the towns and cities of a modern polity. In Smith's theory, the *polis* and the coffee-house had become a market place, the citizen had been redefined as *home economicus*, winning his sense of moral autonomy by participating in the regionally based economic life of the commercial world. Commerce, independence and happiness had become the watchwords of the citizen in the civic world of the Scottish Enlightenment.[60]

Second, for all Smith's avowal of the market system's natural necessity, the market strategy for achieving happiness was in fact one to which contingency – here in the sense of the salience of choice about appropriate uses of public power – remained

---

[58] On "inequalities occasioned by the policy of Europe," see Smith, *Wealth of Nations*, 118–43. On the new political economy as 'anti-model,' see E. P. Thompson, "The Moral Economy of the English Crowd in the Eighteenth Century," *Past and Present*, 50 (Feb. 1971), 89–91. But see also Laurence Dickey, "Historicizing the 'Adam Smith Problem': Conceptual, Historiographical, and Textual Issues," *Journal of Modern History*, 58, 3 (Sept. 1986), 579–609, esp. 585–7, 589–95, 608–9.

[59] Appleby, *Capitalism and a New Social Order*, 83. And see William Reddy, *Money and Liberty in Modern Europe: A Critique of Historical Understanding* (New York, 1987), 78–81.

[60] Nicholas Phillipson, "The Scottish Enlightenment," in Roy Porter and Mikulas Teich, eds., *The Enlightenment in National Context* (Cambridge, 1981), 22, 36. See also J. G. A. Pocock, *The Ancient Constitution and the Feudal Law: A Study of English Historical Thought in the Seventeenth Century: A Reissue with a Retrospect* (New York and Cambridge, 1987), 373–4.

absolutely central. The market order which Smith theorized, in contrast to police, as *nature's* route to happiness depended upon a conception of unqualified property right which was itself totally dependent upon the institution of government for maintenance and protection; that is, it depended on *police*, now redefined as security.[61] For Smith, the "essential function of government was to protect property 'from the indignation' of the poor. . . . 'It is only under the shelter of the civil magistrate that the owner of that valuable property, which is acquired by the labour of many years, or perhaps of many successive generations, can sleep a single night in security.' " Like Madison, then, Smith regarded justice as a matter of securing private rights. He "insisted that the only appropriate function of justice was 'commutative'; it dealt with the attribution of responsibility and the punishment of injury among individuals. Distributive justice, which dealt with the allocation of superfluity according to claims of need, or desert, or merit, was not properly in the domain of law, but of morality."[62] Yet in acknowledging, as he did, the historicity of the concept of property – even if only to discount it – Smith had to acknowledge that it was a social, rather than a natural, institution, the very existence of which was conditional upon protection.[63] That property should now, in the regime of markets, become an unqualified, rather than a relative, right, and that government should become a matter of security rather than distribution, could not be denied to be a product of the exercise of political power rather than a "natural" outcome of the "natural course of events."

The story, then, is not one of the displacement of *police* by "the system of natural liberty," because the regime of property rights upon which that ideology was founded was dependent upon policing. The issue is rather the extent of the transformation in the conception of *police* required before *police* and the market could complement rather than contradict each other.

Signs of such an adjustment begin to emerge in contemporary English opinion in the second half of the eighteenth century. The first hint appears in Blackstone's *Commentaries*. Here, Blackstone attributed to "the public police and oeconomy" the all-encompassing definition of "the due regulation and domestic order of the kingdom." Offenses against the public police, furthermore, fell under the generic title of offenses "as more especially affect the common-wealth, or public polity of the kingdom." The concrete examples of police regulation which Blackstone offered, however, concentrated on those aspects of human activity likely to be disruptive to the moral or social tenor of public life: clandestine or bigamous marriage, indigence or idleness, gambling, offenses against the game laws, sumptuary offenses. Only one

---

[61] Just how much this was the case in Smith's own backyard is powerfully illustrated by W. G. Carson. See his "Policing the Periphery: The Development of Scottish Policing, 1795–1900," in two parts, in *Australian and New Zealand Journal of Criminology*, 17, 4 (Dec. 1984), and 18, 1 (Mar. 1985), esp. pt. 2.

[62] Hont and Ignatieff, "Needs and Justice in the *Wealth of Nations*," 24–5. On the move of nineteenth-century European liberals to separate "security" from "welfare" in police discourse, see above, the section entitled Police, Constitution, Republic, in Chapter 2.

[63] See Morton Horwitz, "History and Theory," *Yale Law Journal*, 96, 8 (July 1987), 1831.

of Blackstone's categories of offenses against the public police – common or public nuisances – suggested that consideration of what made up "the common good" extended beyond issues of public order. For Blackstone, then, police comprised those facets of social life "whereby the individuals of the state, like members of a well-governed family, are bound to conform their general behavior to the rules of propriety, good neighbourhood, and good manners; and to be decent, industrious and inoffensive in their respective stations." Offenses against the police were only one of several categories of offenses against the state (the other categories being offenses against public justice, public peace, public trade, and public health).[64]

This tendency to focus on police regulation as a subspecies of state power concerned predominantly with issues of security (crime, public morality, and social order) rather than broader questions of civic welfare was reinforced in the works of the growing numbers of "police theorists" (Henry and John Fielding, Jonas Hanway, Patrick Colquhoun, to name but a few), whose ideas on public order and security stirred debate during the second half of the eighteenth century.[65] Although a highly diverse body of literature, these works had two concerns in common. First, they all attempted a reassessment of the incidence of crime in contemporary society; second, they all identified police with the provision of means for the resolution of the "crime problem," which their assessments of crime's incidence revealed. Thus for Colquhoun, perhaps the most interesting of these theorists and certainly one of the most prolific, "the foundation of all good police rests upon those regulations and establishments which tend to prevent crimes" for it was crime prevention that would "preserve the morals and consequently . . . promote the security and happiness of the people." The "prevention of crimes and misdemeanors" was the "true essence" of police.[66]

For Colquhoun, as for Smith, true liberty was a function of security, depending "on those fences which are established in every country, for the protection of the persons, and property of the people, against every attack whatsoever."[67] In its current state, London's "municipal police" (by which Colquhoun meant that sphere of metropolitan "oeconomy and government" concerned with the "comforts" and the

---

[64] Sir William Blackstone, *Commentaries on the Laws of England* (Chicago, 1979), 4:162–75, 127–62.
[65] See R. J. Terrill, "Police Theorists and the Enlightenment," *Anglo-American Law Review*, 13, 4 (Oct.–Dec. 1984), 39–55; Leon Radzinowicz, *A History of English Criminal Law and Its Administration from 1750* (New York, 1957), vol. 3, *Cross-Currents in the Movement for the Reform of the Police*, 1–8.
[66] Patrick Colquhoun, *Observations and Facts Relative to Public Houses: Interesting to Magistrates in Every Part of Great Britain . . . By a Magistrate* (London, 1796), 5; idem, *A Treatise on the Police of the Metropolis* (London, 1796), 18.
[67] Colquhoun, *A Treatise on the Police of the Metropolis*, 380. See also Jonas Hanway, *The Defects of Police the Cause of Immorality* (London, 1775), republished as *The Citizen's Monitor: Shewing the Necessity of a Salutary Police* (London, 1780). In the latter work (at iv–v, emphasis in original) Jonas Hanway sounded a similar note: "The fact is that in this land, so justly boasting of freedom, liberty is alloyed by terror, and the bright enjoyment of property by law, is darkened by rapine." Hanway goes on to advocate "*a plan of police . . . a more regular, strict, and consistent police*" by which thieves could be systematically hunted out, punished, and reformed.

"various accommodations and conveniences" of the population) totally failed to offer such protection. Property was overrun by crime. Colquhoun's innovation was to seek to recast municipal regulation, particularly insofar as it addressed the morals, education, charitable support, and industry of the lower orders of inhabitants, as a component of police-as-security, to be reformed in its methods and objectives insofar as it did not already meet this bill. "The adoption of these various remedies could not fail to have a very salutary effect in the prevention of crimes, in the security of life and property, and in the increase of that species of useful industry and sobriety, which constitutes the strength and happiness of a nation."[68] By 1806 his definition of police had broadened from its earlier concentration upon crime to "all those regulations in a country which apply to the comfort, convenience and safety of the inhabitants, whether it regards their security against the calamity of indigence, or the effects produced by moral and criminal offences." Ostensibly such a definition could have encompassed the eighteenth century's police, which, as we have seen, had been directly concerned with questions of distribution. Colquhoun's object, however, was the mobilization of police as a means to create a social environment conducive to the further development of a free market economy and particularly a "free circulation of labour." Arguing, like Smith, that security against indigence lay not in a distributive police but in greater all-round productivity, he now advocated a police that would "call forth the greatest possible proportion of industry, as the best and surest means of producing national happiness and prosperity."[69] In short, in Colquhoun's mind police's role was to be one complementing and facilitating the division of labor and the realization of the market's disciplinary potential. It was to underwrite the "free and independent man" by securing his property from the indignation of the poor, and it was to mobilize the poor for participation in the labor market in the service of their own good – the attaining of their independence – and for the benefit of society as a whole.[70]

---

[68] Colquhoun, *A Treatise on the Police of the Metropolis*, 404, 471. Reform would extend "great humanity . . . to labouring people, by removing those numerous temptations, which too often assail them, and induce many to become dishonest." It would resolve "the deficiency of the laws, in not advancing progressively in the means of prevention, in proportion to the introduction of luxury, and the additional temptations which the influx of wealth and the intercourse of commerce occasions in every country" (472).

[69] Patrick Colquhoun, *A Treatise on Indigence* (London, 1806), 82, 15–16, 9; and see generally 80–109.

[70] Colquhoun's concern to maximize the mobilization of labor appeared as full-blown political economy in his *Treatise on the Wealth, Power, and Resources of the British Empire* (London, 1814). On Colquhoun as political economist see Maxine Berg, *The Machinery Question and the Making of Political Economy, 1815–1848* (Cambridge, 1980), 79. On the relationship between (1) the re-creation of property offences as *public* wrongs, (2) the simultaneous assault on *public* provision of welfare, and (3) the impulse to market disciplining of labor, see Jeremy N. J. Palmer, "Evils Merely Prohibited: Conceptions of Property and Conceptions of Criminality in the Criminal Law Reform of the English Industrial Revolution," *British Journal of Law and Scoeity*, 3 (Summer 1976), 1–16. See also Michael Ignatieff, "State, Civil Society, and Total Institution: A Critique of Recent Social Histories of Punishment," in Stanley Cohen and Andrew Scull, *Social Control and the State* (New York, 1983), 75–105, at 86–9.

DEMOCRATIC POLITICS, STATE, AND POLICE

In Scotland and England the outcome Colquhoun and his fellows sought was contested both by a gentry jealous of its traditional paternalist role in the moral economy and by the nascent working class. By the early nineteenth century, however, the intellectual ascendancy of the market system's abstract universals, together with the weakness of democratic politics, augured a view of government as increasingly a matter of "managerial efficiency in the interests of preserving public order in an increasingly turbulent age."[71] By the 1820s, police-as-security had become the order of the day.[72]

In America the potential for the survival of a conception of police-as-happiness was substantially greater, for here the process whereby police and the market came to complement each other had to negotiate the enlivened democratic politics produced by the Revolution. Americans, in other words, had a unique opportunity, while abandoning the hierarchical and localized colonial world and its ligaments of mutual affection, deference, and moral uniformity for a world of natural rights, self-government, and equality, to insist that the duty and legitimacy of their new, depersonalized, institutionalized governments lay not only in ensuring the security of the community but also in enabling all "Equally to Enjoy all the Blessings and benfits resulting there from." As Willi-Paul Adams has observed, these were demands "not only that everyone enjoy equality before the law or have an equal voice in government but also that everyone have an equal share in the fruits of the common enterprise," an equality to be achieved if necessary through government acting as a distributive mechanism under the guidance of a population whose inalienable right to political participation was the Revolution's signal domestic achievement.[73] It was in that spirit, for example, that "Captain Welton" of Massachusetts argued that in a popular or democratic system "an equal distribution of property was necessary" and that Centinel informed his fellow Pennsylvanians that "a republican, or free

[71] Phillipson, "Scottish Enlightenment," 39–40. See also Palmer, "Evils Merely Prohibited"; Thompson, "Moral Economy of the English Crowd," 129–31; John Stevenson, "Social Control and the Prevention of Riots in England, 1788–1829," and A. P. Donajgrodzki, "'Social Police' and the Bureaucratic Elite: A Vision of Order in the Age of Reform," both in A. P. Donajgrodzki, ed., *Social Control in Nineteenth Century Britain* (London, 1977), 27–50 and 51–76.

[72] See, generally, David Philips, "'A New Engine of Power and Authority': The Institutionalization of Law-Enforcement in England, 1780–1830," in V. A. C. Gatrell et al., eds., *Crime and the Law: The Social History of Crime in Western Europe since 1500* (London, 1980), 155–89. See also Allan Silver, "The Demand for Order in Civil Society: A Review of Some Themes in the History of Urban Crime, Police, and Riot," in David J. Bordua, ed., *The Police: Six Sociological Essays* (New York, 1967), 1–24; Robert D. Storch, "The Plague of the Blue Locusts: Police Reform and Popular Resistance in Northern England, 1840–57," *International Review of Social History*, 20, 1 (1975), 61–90; idem, "The Policeman as Domestic Missionary: Urban Discipline and Popular Culture in Northern England, 1850–1880," *Journal of Social History*, 9, 4 (June 1976), 481–509; Michael Brogden, "An Act to Colonise the Internal Lands of the Island: Empire and the Origins of the Professional Police," *International Journal of the Sociology of Law*, 15, 2 (May 1987), 179–208.

[73] Adams, *First American Constitutions*, 188. See also Stanley N. Katz, "Republicanism and the Law of Inheritance in the American Revolutionary Era," *Michigan Law Review*, 76, 1 (Nov. 1977), 14–21.

government, can only exist where the body of the people are virtuous, and where property is pretty equally divided[;] in such a government the people are the sovereign and their sense or opinion is the criterion of every public measure."[74] It was in that spirit, too, that ten years earlier Virginians had petitioned their state legislature to provide for a mode of land alienation that would advantage ordinary citizens over monopolizers. Vacant lands should be sold at a publicly regulated price in small lots to actual settler-proprietors. Such legislation would sustain "the true Policy of a Republic" by enabling "the Poor and Needy to raise their Families to be reputable and useful Members of Society."[75] And it was in that spirit that in 1776 Pennsylvanians had proposed to use the state's Declaration of Rights to confer on the new state government the power to pass "agrarian" laws prohibiting excessive accumulation of property on the grounds that such accumulation was "dangerous to the Rights, and destructive of the Common Happiness, of Mankind."[76]

This novel twist on republican discourse, with its plain implication that the democratic control of the resource of government promised by the Revolution might enable mobilization of that resource in pursuit of egalitarian outcomes, was predominantly a popular phenomenon, a creation of the Mannings of the revolutionary era. Nevertheless, traces may be found in the ideas of at least some of the epoch's more prominent revolutionaries. Although Thomas Paine, for example, has been credited primarily as a radical theorist of the ascendancy of economy over polity, of markets, commerce, and free association over the classical politics of virtuous citizenship,[77] his conception of natural rights held them in crucial respects dependent for their actual realization on political revolutions and on the affirmative activities of the new democratic governments that he hoped to see created thereby. Paine, that is, may have assumed the moral equality of all as a self-evident given of the human condition, but he did not assume further that equality would necessarily be self-realizable. "Equality of rights alone might

---

[74] "Letters of Centinel," 1 (5 Oct. 1787), in Storing, ed., *Complete Anti-Federalist*, 2:139. "Captain Welton" is quoted in Sunstein, "Beyond the Republican Revival," 1553.

[75] Bogin, "Petitioning and the New Moral Economy," 405. Bogin comments that the petitioners "wove together the concept of republican justice and the obligations of a moral economy, no longer to be sought as a gift but as a right."

[76] On the Pennsylvania Declaration of Rights see Wood, *Creation of the American Republic*, 89. See also Steven Rosswurm, *Arms, Country, and Class: The Philadelphia Militia and the "Lower Sort" during the American Revolution* (New Brunswick, N.J., 1987), 194–5. And see Slaughter, *Whiskey Rebellion*, 207, quoting from an August 1794 petition to the federal government drafted by residents of Carlisle, Pennsylvania, which inter alia condemned prevailing federal land alienation policies as "destructive of an essential principle in every republican government [namely] the equal division of landed property." It is important to note that in December 1787 Carlisle had been the center of significant backcountry Anti-Federalist disturbances protesting Pennsylvania's ratification of the federal Constitution. Saul Cornell has described Carlisle's Anti-Federalists as "men of humble origins and modest wealth," highly representative of the strain of egalitarian plebeian populism in Anti-Federalist discourse ("Aristocracy Assailed," 1155). On backcountry agrarianism in the era of the American Revolution, see, generally, Alan Taylor, *Liberty Men and Great Proprietors: The Revolutionary Settlement on the Maine Frontier, 1760–1820* (Chapel Hill, 1990).

[77] See, e.g., Joyce Appleby, "Republicanism and Ideology," *American Quarterly*, 37, 4 (Fall 1985), 470; Michael Foot and Isaac Kramnick, "Editors' Introduction: The Life, Ideology and Legacy of Thomas Paine," in idem, eds., *The Thomas Paine Reader* (Harmondsworth, England, 1987), 22–9.

not be enough to protect the moral integrity of the individual in society. Government might have to take positive steps to secure an equality of condition as well."[78]

Such steps were most likely to be required to ensure the welfare of the mass of people, "the *general* happiness." In Paine's discourse this was no eleemosynary exercise; nor was it a Colquhoun-like disciplinary reformation of morals from above, a preparation for the mobilization of the poor in the economy. Rather, Paine's conception was of welfare as a matter of "rectificatory justice," a right to the return of property "that had been extracted in a way that violated the owner's natural right to equal treatment" through, for example, the coercive use of economic or political power; and not only current use but historic.[79] Indeed, Paine's radical contempt for the constitution of the British polity – its indifference to representative democracy, its hereditary rights principle, its elevation of the dead hand of the past over the living – was contempt for a polity built precisely upon a history of such coercion, one that had systematically "impede[d] the general happiness by operating 'to create and increase wretchedness' in parts of society" and that enabled a few "to live a 'civilized' life of 'felicity and affluence'" while the vast majority lived "an 'uncivilized' life of 'hardship and want' . . . in a 'state of poverty and wretchedness, far below the condition of an Indian.'"[80] But Paine's contempt for the role of government in the British constitution did not automatically translate into a jaundiced view of all governments, and in fact Paine's work gives considerable attention to the circumstances whereby democratic rights–protecting governments can be established. Overall, then, we find in Paine not simply a market economy and free association but a market economy established in the context of a rights-protecting state which defines rights substantively and protects them affirmatively as part of its overall responsibility for universalizing the "principles of civilization."[81]

---

[78] William Christian, "The Moral Economics of Tom Paine," *Journal of the History of Ideas*, 34, 3 (July–Sept. 1973), 377.

[79] John W. Seaman, "Thomas Paine: Ransom, Civil Peace, and the Natural Right to Welfare," *Political Theory*, 16, 1 (Feb. 1988), 120–42, 128. Paine recognized a natural right of property but not of possession, which he subordinated to the common good ("All property," he once wrote, "is safe under *the people's* protection" [quoted in Wood, *Creation of the American Republic*, 62, emphasis added]). All were possessed of an equal natural right not to be excluded from nature. "Because no person's claim to nature is superior to another's, no one will have a right to exclude another from nature. . . . Civilization may not violate this equal natural right to property in nature. That is, it may not (in Paine's words) place people in a condition worse than they would have been had they been born in the state of nature." Civilization, however, had done exactly that by permitting private proprietorship "because of the impossibility of separating the improvement made by cultivation (which is the individual property of the cultivator) from the earth itself (which is everybody's property)." Paine did not seek the abolition of private property in land as such, but he held that everyone's natural right not to be excluded from nature had nonetheless to be vindicated by having "the state guarantee the indemnification of those who have lost their natural inheritance" (Seaman, "Thomas Paine," 130–1).

[80] Seaman, "Thomas Paine," 124.

[81] Ibid. See also Thomas A. Horne, "Welfare Rights as Property Rights," in J. Donald Moon, ed., *Responsibility, Rights, and Welfare: The Theory of the Welfare State* (Boulder, Colo., 1988), 107–32, esp. 119–23. In effect Paine was offering a radical and democratic retort to the democratically etiolated ideology of improvement described by Jack P. Greene. See above, the section entitled Divergent Goals and the American Revolution, in Chapter 2.

The same is even truer of Jefferson. Joyce Appleby, for one, has compellingly delineated Jefferson's commitment to the use of government in the protection of natural rights of individual self-fulfillment and his corresponding denial that governments existed to protect vested interests. It was in deference to this, she argues, that Jefferson amended Locke's natural rights of "life, liberty and property" to make the Declaration of Independence instead affirm natural rights to "life, liberty and the pursuit of happiness."[82] Property in the Jeffersonian canon was not a natural right at all, "but one which is established by and subject to the civil power," and as such decidedly subordinate to the natural and inalienable right to pursue happiness.[83]

Appleby chooses to situate Jefferson's commitment to the protection of natural rights in the context of what she sees as the corrosion of the classical republican tradition of civic activity in favor of a vision of society reconstituted as a compound of individual human components whose relationships were irreducibly economic and whose freedom and happiness consist in their liberation from artificial restraints on self-realization, a "natural harmony of autonomous individuals freely exerting themselves to take care of their own interests while expanding the range of free exchange and free enquiry."[84] Jefferson's commitment to such an ideal of freedom is undoubted. Humans, according to Jefferson, had a substantive right to economic freedom, a right of access to the means of life.[85] But Jefferson's reaction to the corrosion

---

[82] Joyce Appleby, "What Is Still American in the Political Philosophy of Thomas Jefferson," *William and Mary Quarterly*, 3d ser., 39, 2 (Apr. 1982), 297.

[83] Jeffrey Barnouw, "The Pursuit of Happiness in Jefferson and Its Background in Bacon and Hobbes," *Interpretation: A Journal of Political Philosophy*, 11, 2 (May 1983), 225–48, at 229. See also Richard K. Matthews, *The Radical Politics of Thomas Jefferson: A Revisionist View* (Lawrence, Kans., 1984); Katz "Republicanism and the Law of Inheritance," 17–18. Cesare Beccaria, whose *Dei delitti e delle pene* Jefferson greatly admired, described therein the right of property as "a terrible and perhaps unnecessary right" (*On Crimes and Punishments* [*Dei delitti e delle pene*], trans. Henry Paolucci [New York, 1963], 74). Marcello Maestro writes that "Beccaria had doubts about the necessity, or legitimacy, of the right of property. In this his view was certainly far from Blackstone, who unhesitatingly described the right of property as 'one of the absolute rights, inherent in every Englishman'" (*Cesare Beccaria and the Origins of Penal Reform* [Philadelphia, 1973], 92).

[84] Appleby, *Capitalism and a New Social Order*, 94. Appleby has also emphasized the influence of the political economy of Destutt De Tracy in Jeffersonian thought, distancing Jefferson from the assumed primacy of Adam Smith. See, e.g., Appleby, "The Radical *Double-Entendre* in the Right to Self-Government," in Margaret Jacob and James Jacob, eds., *The Origins of Anglo-American Radicalism* (London, 1984), 281–2. (Others, however, have disagreed. See Horwitz, "History and Theory," 1831.) On Tracy, particularly his role in the development of *la science sociale* and *ideologie* both as theories of social action and as sciences of government, see Brian W. Head, "The Origins of 'La Science Sociale' in France, 1770–1800," *Australian Journal of French Studies*, 19, 2 (May–Aug. 1982), 115–32; idem, *Ideology and Social Science: Destutt De Tracy and French Liberalism* (Dordrecht, 1985).

[85] Two years before the Philadelphia Convention, in words recalling the sentiments of the Virginia petitioners of 1779 and also intimating a conception of human welfare in his thought strikingly similar to Paine's, Jefferson wrote: "Whenever there is in any country, uncultivated lands and unemployed poor, it is clear that the laws of property have been so far extended as to violate natural right. The earth is given as a common stock for man to labour & live on. If for the encouragement of industry we allow it to be appropriated, we must take care that other employment be provided to those excluded from the appropriation. If we do not, the fundamental right to labour the earth returns to the unemployed" (Thomas Jefferson to Rev. James Madison [28 Oct. 1785], in Boyd, ed., *Papers of Thomas Jefferson*, 8:682). See also Barnouw, "The Pursuit of Happiness in Jefferson," 229.

84

of classical republicanism was not to eschew altogether its devotion to the civic realm but rather to give his attention to the problem of creating a new "public space" that would complement the substantive human right to economic freedom, one where *all* citizens could "actively participate in governmental affairs, and thereby ensure their freedom and their pursuit of public happiness."[86] Indeed, key elements of Jefferson's great revision of the laws of Virginia – the interrelated bills abolishing entail and primogeniture, establishing religious freedom, and creating a general education system – together with his scheme for the creation of republican structures of self-government describe just how such a public space, once created, might be underpinned. Discussing the revision of the laws in his *Autobiography*, Jefferson had this to say:

I considered 4 of these bills, passed or reported, as forming a system by which every fibre would be eradicated of antient or future aristocracy; and a foundation laid for a government truly republican. The repeal of the laws of entail would prevent the accumulation and perpetuation of wealth in select families, and preserve the soil of the country from being daily more and more absorbed in Mortmain. The abolition of primogeniture, and equal partition of inheritances removed the feudal and unnatural distinctions which made one member of every family rich, and all the rest poor, substituting equal partition, the best of all Agrarian laws. The restoration of the rights of conscience relieved the people from taxation for the support of a religion not theirs; for the establishment was truly of the religion of the rich, the dissenting sects being entirely composed of the less wealthy people; and these, by the bill for a general education, would be qualified to understand their rights, to maintain them, and to exercise with intelligence their parts in self-government: and all this would be effected without the violation of a single natural right of any one individual citizen.[87]

[86] Matthews, *Radical Politics of Thomas Jefferson*, 81 (emphasis supplied). Matthews's analysis of Jefferson's radicalism contrasts in important respects with Appleby's, particularly in its attempt to establish the Jeffersonian individual as *homo civicus* rather than *homo oeconomicus*. To Matthews, Jefferson's perspective on human society was fourfold. "One, man is a developing, active, social creature who defines and improves himself through his interaction with nature and other human beings; two, a just society is based on cooperation and human sociability, rather than on competition and human antagonism; three, the economic exploitation and human deprivation created by the possessive market society must not be allowed to develop; and four, an egalitarian redistribution – and redefinition – of the social good(s) on an on-going basis is part of a good society" (122). See also David M. Post, "Jeffersonian Revisions of Locke: Education, Property-Rights, and Liberty," *Journal of the History of Ideas*, 47, 1 (Jan.–Mar. 1986), 147–57.

[87] Boyd, ed., *Papers of Thomas Jefferson*, 2:308. According to Herbert Baxter Adams, Jefferson's 1779 bill for a general system of education was "the historical basis of all that Jefferson subsequently accomplished for the educational cause in Virginia" and was "closely allied to his cherished scheme for local self-government" ("The College of William and Mary: A Contribution to the History of Higher Education," in *Circulars of Information of the Bureau of Education*, 1 [Washington, 1887], 37). "What Jefferson proposed to do in the 'Bill for the More General Diffusion of Knowledge'" says Rhys Isaac, "was to replace the old ecclesiastical community of the parish by a new one (with an old name revived), the 'Hundred,' and to replace the pulpits with publicly supported teachers' desks. Since instruction would no longer be combined with religious duty, it would have to be directed at the young and would be steeped in secular republican morality. . . . A new Virginia republican 'establishment' would replace the old Anglican Christian one. Community involvement in the moral formation of its members would be reaffirmed" (*The Transformation of Virginia, 1740–1790* [Chapel Hill, 1982], 294).

Neither the general-education scheme nor the civic reorganization which it entailed was adopted in 1779, but Jefferson maintained his zeal for both reforms, as an 1810 letter to John Tyler on the subject

This is the language less of unalloyed liberal individualism than of a new republican architectonics, a design for a social order at once secular and democratic, popular rather than classical, but still distinctively "public."

Jefferson's model of federalism — distinctive in several crucial respects when compared with those championed by Hamilton and Madison — illustrates further the continued vitality of the public sphere in his notions of governance, particularly in its local and participatory aspects. Unlike Hamilton's, Jefferson's federalism did not seek to make central government the locus of definition of the common good; rather, it sought to leave that to the actions of the people themselves. "It is not that government should be directly concerned with the happiness of the people (a characteristic assumption of 'benevolent' absolutism), but rather that it should be responsive to, and indeed rely on, their concern, their pursuit."[88] Jefferson, indeed, was suspicious of the government portrayed in the draft Constitution which Madison sent him after the closure of the Philadelphia Convention. "I own I am not a friend to a very energetic government. It is always oppressive."[89] Unlike Madison's federalism, however, Jefferson treated government not as a carefully distanced umpire balancing interests one against the other, segregated from popular passions, disciplining potentially tyrannous majorities and recalcitrant state legislatures, but as an active and present reality in life, a means of giving effect to popular pursuits. Jefferson's vaunted suspicion of "energy" in government, in fact, was directly proportional to the distance of government from the people.[90] He had no fear of energetic government if government were structured to ensure democratic participation in the definition of the objects to which its "energy" would be directed.[91] As he put it in 1816, in terms decidedly reminiscent of those used by the Federal Farmer thirty years before:

of the government of Virginia testifies: "I have indeed two great measures at heart, without which no republic can maintain itself in strength." These were, first, "general education, to enable every man to judge for himself what will secure or endanger his freedom," and, second, the division of the greater republic into ward-republics, replacing parishes, to create a secular self-governing democracy. As in 1779 the structure was to be mutually determinative: The "hundred," or ward-republic, was the repository of local self-government; the focus of each ward-republic was provided by one of the elementary schools that would collectively form the base of the general educational pyramid and furnish the civic training essential to the survival of the greater self-governing republic. Thus would "these little republics . . . be the main strength of the great one" (Thomas Jefferson to John Tyler [26 May 1810], in Andrew A. Lipscomb, editor-in-chief, *The Writings of Thomas Jefferson* [Washington, 1905], 11:391–4).

[88] Barnouw, "The Pursuit of Happiness in Jefferson," 232.

[89] Thomas Jefferson to James Madison (20 Dec. 1887), in Boyd, ed., *Papers of Thomas Jefferson*, 12:442. I am indebted to Joyce Appleby for bringing this statement to my attention.

[90] On that suspicion, see Joyce Appleby, "Historians, Community, and the Pursuit of Jefferson," *Studies in American Political Development*, 4 (1990), 35–44, at 40. In refining my ideas on this issue I have learned much from Garrett Ward Sheldon, *The Political Philosophy of Thomas Jefferson* (Baltimore, 1991). See in particular 53–94.

[91] Thus, in the course of a recapitulation of his scheme for decentralized republican local government, for example, Jefferson commented, "General orders are given out from a centre to the foreman of every hundred, as to the sergeants of any army, and the whole nation is thrown into energetic action, in the same direction in one instant and as one man, and becomes absolutely irresistible" (Jefferson to John Tyler [26 May 1810], in Lipscomb, ed., *Writings of Thomas Jefferson*, 11:143).

Let the national government be entrusted with the defence of the nation, and its foreign and federal relations; the State governments with the civil rights, laws, police and administration of what concerns the State generally; the counties with the local concerns of the counties, and each ward direct the interests within itself. It is by dividing and subdividing these republics from the great national one down through all its subordinations, until it ends in the administration of every man's farm by himself; by placing under everyone what his own eye may superintend, that all will be done for the best. . . . The elementary republics of the wards, the county republics, the State republics, and the republic of the Union, would form a gradation of authorities, standing each on the basis of law, holding every one its delegated share of powers, and constituting truly a system of fundamental balances and checks for the government.[92]

Jefferson's was thus a disassembled federalism of little democracies, each an arena for the active participatory politics that his "republican architectonics" – educational, political, and economic – was designed to undergird. Through this system of limited national government and energetic local republics would be realized "the mother principle, that 'governments are republican only in proportion as they embody the will of their people, and execute it.'"[93]

The key characteristic differentiating Jefferson's theories of governance from the other founders, however, is that unlike both Hamilton and Madison, Jefferson did not regard government's relationship with the citizenry as one of restraint but rather as one of realization.[94] "*Bonheur*, happiness, is man's *telos*. Rights – property and other – are mere instruments to aid men in their pursuit of happiness. And governments must either be structured or dissolved and restructured so that all men will have access to this pursuit."[95] This perspective suffused Jefferson's attitude to law, rights, and government and as much as anything prompted his "gentle antifederalist"[96] critique of the Constitution championed by Madison and Hamilton. "No society can make a perpetual constitution, or even a perpetual law," he wrote to Madison in September 1789. "The earth belongs always to the living generation. They may manage it then, and what proceeds from it, as they please, during their usufruct. They are masters too of their own persons, and consequently may govern them as they please. But persons and property make the sum of the objects of government. The constitution and the laws of their predecessors extinguished then

---

[92] Jefferson to Joseph C. Cabell (2 Feb. 1816), in Peterson, ed., *Thomas Jefferson: Writings*, 1380. "While many theorists and politicians wanted to keep 'the people' out of the political process," writes Richard K. Matthews, "Jefferson felt it to be crucial – for both the individual and the community – that all citizens become intimately involved in public life" (*Radical Politics of Thomas Jefferson*, 95). See also Lynton K. Caldwell, *The Administrative Theories of Hamilton and Jefferson: Their Contribution to Thought on Public Administration* (Chicago, 1944), 142.

[93] Jefferson to Samuel Kercheval (12 July 1816), in Peterson, ed., *Thomas Jefferson: Writings*, 1396.

[94] William Novak has recently argued that something of this nature may also be discerned in the thought of contemporary Federalists such as James Wilson and Nathaniel Chipman ("Intellectual Origins of the State Police Power: The Common Law Vision of a Well-Regulated Society," *Legal History Program Working Papers* [Madison], ser. 3, no. 2 [June 1989]).

[95] Matthews, *Radical Politics of Thomas Jefferson*, 122.

[96] Wiebe, *Opening of American Society*, 30.

in their natural course with those who gave them being. This could preserve that being till it ceased to be itself, and no longer. Every constitution then, and every law, naturally expires at the end of 19 years. If it be enforced longer, it is an act of force, and not of right."[97]

The Jeffersonian conception of the proper civic and governmental structure for a republican polity, and the prominent role given education in sustaining that structure, return us to the remodeled curriculum of the College of William and Mary – "the roof and crown of the entire educational system of Virginia" – and its chair of Law and Police.[98] The chair is symbolic of the relationship of *law* and *police* in Jeffersonian thought, signifying a state not built simply to realize liberal capitalism's security of property rights but rather to pursue a strategy of civic action intended – through education, a highly participatory polity, and curbs on the generational transmission of wealth – to effect a republic of natural rights and, by evoking in particular a natural right to the pursuit of happiness, to empower and invigorate the whole population.

Such a conception of the state, however, was not to prevail. The point for the most influential of the founders – Madison and Hamilton – was precisely to adopt a perpetual constitution, one dedicating government to the securing of absolute rights of property from popular excesses, real or imagined.[99] Pursuers of security rather than happiness,[100] they created a state whose discourse in crucial respects privileged law over politics.[101] Faced with the problem of reconciling private rights

---

[97] Jefferson to Madison (6 Sept. 1789), in Boyd, ed., *Papers of Thomas Jefferson*, 15:395–6. On the fundamental conceptual differences between Jefferson's theories of politics and governance and those of Madison and Hamilton see Stimson, *American Revolution in the Law*, 94–105. Critical of Jefferson, Stimson's account nevertheless shows quite clearly that Jefferson was prepared to give much greater weight to democratic politics in matters of republican constitutionalism than were his contemporaries. In regard to the constitutional role of the "judiciary department," in particular, Jefferson clearly believed that the Supreme Court should not be allowed "to occupy and develop the space for judgment about law." This should instead "be left to the determination of each individual and aggregately to the literal majority will of 'the people'" because for Jefferson, "judging for oneself the constitutionality of every law means determining for oneself its 'fitness' to serve our political needs, and as such is basic to democratic self-rule." In Jefferson's jurisprudence, then, "the space for reflective judgment about law is simply coextensive with the political sphere of clashing needs and demands" (Stimson, *American Revolution in the Law*, 102, 104–5).

[98] Adams, "College of William and Mary," 38.

[99] Wood, *Creation of the American Republic*, 410–11, 503–4; McDonald, *Novus Ordo Seclorum*, 3–4, 155–62.

[100] David Epstein concludes, "The object of 'safety' is the dominant element in *The Federalist*'s understanding of the public good" (*Political Theory of the Federalist*, 163).

[101] "This was the logic behind the innovation of constitution-making through conventions. The sovereign people convened to draw up the fundamental law, then adjourned to place themselves under that institutionalized authority" (Melvin Yazawa, *From Colonies to Commonwealth: Familial Ideology and the Beginnings of the American Republic* [Baltimore, 1985], 113). On the postrevolutionary triumph of a distinctively *legal* cultural of power see A. G. Roeber, *Faithful Magistrates and Republican Lawyers: Creators of Virginia Legal Culture, 1680–1810* (Chapel Hill, 1981), 231–61; and Perry Miller, *The Life of the Mind in America: From the Revolution to the Civil War* (New York, 1965), 99–265. Constitutional scholars have tended to treat this diminution of democracy as a necessary separation of law from politics in the service of the public good. See William E. Nelson, "Reason and Compromise in the Establishment of the Federal Constitution," *William and Mary Quarterly*, 3d ser., 44, 3 (July 1987), 483–4. (*continued on p. 89*)

and democracy the framers chose to confine tightly the scope of democratic politics by creating a highly mediated system of representation and a watchdog judiciary to stand guard over its legislative products. The result was removal of "the most important and contested issues from the sphere of politics" altogether.[102]

LAW RULES

Ratification of the new federal Constitution was celebrated on a massive scale in all major American cities. Between February and July 1788 thousands marched in major parades. 4,000 in Boston, 5,000 in New York and Philadelphia, 3,000 in Baltimore. Working people (prominent among those to whom William Manning would address his *Key* ten years later) were committed participants. "In every city," Alfred Young tells us, "artisans marched by trades, either with the tools of their craft or with floats depicting themselves at work at their trade." In a context "distinctly political," urban artisans expressed their communities' support for the creation of the national government that some "mechanic radicals" had been seeking since the Declaration of Independence.[103]

Even in the late 1780s artisan communities were beginning to experience the stirrings of that divergence of interests, that emergence of substantial inequalities of wealth and power among the self-employed, and between masters and journeymen where trades were thus organized, which was to become central in their collective experience during the formative years of the early republic. Thus in some cities, "the trade" marched not as a body but as separate divisions – masters, journeymen, apprentices – presaging the "great transformation" that was to come and "that would gradually erode self-sufficiency and remake yeomen, artisans, and their children into workers dependent upon wages."[104] The specter of internal disagreement notwithstanding, artisan communities seemed united in closing ranks behind the federal Constitution. In part they did so simply because it was their

Such was the success of the Federalist model of governance that by the end of the nineteenth century, scholars could be found writing of the concept of the police power as a nineteenth-century doctrinal *innovation* pioneered by the leading federal and state judiciary as "a branch of constitutional law peculiar to countries having legislatures with limited power . . . an outgrowth of the American conception of protecting the individual from the state" (W. G. Hastings, "The Development of Law as Illustrated by the Decisions Relating to the Police Power of the State," *Proceedings of the American Philosophical Society*, 39, 163 [July–Sept. 1900], 360).

[102] Nedelsky, "Confining Democratic Politics," 341. On suffrage restrictions and the limitation of representation in the interests of protecting property, see Matthews, *Radical Politics of Thomas Jefferson*, 98–108; Adams, *The First American Constitutions*, 196–217; and Robert J. Steinfeld, "Property and Suffrage in the Early American Republic," *Stanford Law Review*, 41, 2 (Jan. 1989), 335–76. On the radically enhanced role of the judiciary, see Wood, *Creation of the American Republic*, 453–63. See also Caldwell, *The Administrative Theories of Hamilton and Jefferson*, 155–8. For a sociocultural account of the turn away from a "public" conception of happiness, see Jan Lewis, *The Pursuit of Happiness: Family and Values in Jefferson's Virginia* (Cambridge, 1983).

[103] Alfred F. Young, "English Plebeian Culture and Eighteenth-Century American Radicalism," in Jacob and Jacob, eds., *Origins of Anglo-American Radicalism*, 185–212, at 186, 200–1. See also Bruce Laurie, *Artisans into Workers: Labor in Nineteenth Century America* (New York, 1989), 49.

[104] Young, "English Plebeian Culture," 201; Laurie, *Artisans into Workers*, 15.

patriotic pleasure to demonstrate their support for the new nation. More concretely they did so because adoption of the Constitution seemed to promise means of establishing protection from British manufactures; that is, because it promised a regulation of commerce for the common good by a central government equipped to wield power in a sphere – international trade – where no single state government could take effective action. Finally, artisans and mechanics marched in celebration of the democratic processes that had attended the Constitution's ratification and the democratic principle of popular sovereignty that it appeared to embrace.[105]

Abundant ironies lay in wait for the working people engaged in these celebrations. The most immediate revelation came only a few years later when the new central government dealt a major blow to artisan hopes for protection against British manufactures. In the keystone act of the new republic's commercial policy, the Jay Treaty of 1795, Washington's administration established close trading ties between America and Britain which "acknowledged wholesale the British rules for Atlantic commerce." In 1798, William Manning wrote that because of the treaty, "we shall be thronged with their manufactoryes, made by their slaves who by the oppression of their government are obliged to worke for a trifel & live upon less, so that they will undersell and destroy all our manifactoryes."[106] A more subtle irony, however, lies in the artisans' celebration of ratification and its discourse of popular sovereignty as an expression of the conjunction of power and their own participation, for here they were celebrating as a unity that which the framers had themselves just labored quite successfully to prise in two.

The Constitution separated power from participation in pursuit of an earlier and

---

[105] Young, "English Plebeian Culture," 201.

[106] William Manning, *The Key of Libberty: Shewing the Causes Why a Free Government has always Failed, and a Remidy Against It* (Billerica, Mass., 1922), 47–8 and generally 44–51. For Manning, the Jay Treaty ("the Monster") epitomized everything that was going wrong with the federal experiment. The *Key* expressed a sense of profound disillusionment on the matter:

"The Federal Constitution by a fair construction is a good one prinsapaly, but I have no dout but that the Convention who made it intended to destroy our free governments by it, or they neaver would have spent 4 months in making such an inexpliset thing. As one said at the time of its adoption, it is made like a Fiddle, with but few strings, but so that the ruling Majority could play any tune upon it they pleased. The trety-making power which has caused so much rout was as well garded as any part of it, but as it has bin exercised, destroys the hole foundation & end the peopel had in makeing of it. For the soul end the peopel had in vue was to establish a government for national purposes ondly, reserving local consarns to the State governments. . . .

"Much has bin said about treatys being the Supreem Law of the land, which if admited would finely inlarge the power of the Juditial & innable them by constructions to destroy all our laws. But I cant se a word of it in the Constitution. In part 6th their is a clause that plainly declares that the Federal Constitution, the federal laws, & all treetys shall be supreem to the state laws & constitutions, but nothing determining which of the three is supreem, excepting that it appears reasonable to take them as they stand, viz: – 1t the Constitution. 2dly, the Laws. 3dly, tretys.

"By such an explanation the Judge is bound by his oath not to give judgment against either of them in favour of a treaty. If he doth he pergures himselfe. I would not be understoot that I think tretyes are less binding than laws when they are constitutally made, for it is the duty of the federal Legeslature to see that the Constitution, tretyes and laws do not clash with each other, & as their objects of legeslation are few they are to blame if their is any clash. Consiquently the bisness of the Juditial & Executive powers must be clear & plane" (39–41).

more familiar pattern of elite rule in the American polity.[107] Beginning in the 1780s and with increasing fervor, Federalist elites decried the personal freedoms and passions "unloosed by the Revolutionary experience" and sought the reestablishment of "a more hierarchical political order with themselves at the top."[108] Writing of Federalist incantations of order during the Whiskey Rebellion, Thomas Slaughter has argued that they demonstrate how little in fact had changed "in the nature of conflict and the parameters of political discourse during three decades of Revolutionary upheaval." He continues:

There is little of substance to distinguish the rhetoric, perspectives, ideology, or methods of Tories and British bureaucrats in the earlier period from those of the friends of order thirty years later. There is an ideological identity between many of the suspicions, fears, diagnoses, and prescriptions for the cure of political ill-health in the writings of Thomas Hutchinson, James Otis, George Grenville, and Lord North in the years preceding the Revolution, and those of George Washington, Alexander Hamilton, Fisher Ames, and other Federalists after the war. The attitudes of the friends of order certainly had more in common with the enemies of America's Revolution than they did with the ideals of Stephen Hopkins, Thomas Paine, the Antifederalists, and the Republicans either before or after the War for Independence and the French Revolution.[109]

The postrevolutionary recrudescence of elite domination of politics was a somewhat more delicately negotiated process than this might imply, for it was taking place in a milieu whose chief characteristic was an enlivened popular determination to seek out opportunities in all corners of life for the expression and realization of the Revolution's promise of "sufficiency," freedom, and equality.[110] True enough, in

---

[107] Charles Bright has commented that the Constitution "represented a successful effort by colonial elites . . . to establish a mechanism for resolving conflicts among themselves, [and] to check dissident and democratic pressures in American society with a strong governing counterpoise" ("The State in the United States during the Nineteenth Century," in Charles Bright and Susan Harding, eds., *Statemaking and Social Movements: Essays in History and Theory* [Ann Arbor, 1984], 121–58, at 126). See also Wiebe, *Opening of American Society*, 35–41, 144.

[108] Slaughter, *Whiskey Rebellion*, 134, 138. See also Katz, "Strange Birth and Unlikely History of Constitutional Equality," 748–53. John Murrin has concluded, "Without contending for a nationalist conspiracy or *coup d'état* in 1787, let us nevertheless concede what Beard rather clumsily argued, that the United States Constitution was very much an elitist solution to the problems left by the Revolution and the popular turbulence of the 1780s," which "shifted the entire spectrum of national politics several degrees to the right" ("The Great Inversion, or Court versus Country: A Comparison of the Revolution Settlements in England [1688–1721] and America [1776–1816]," in J. G. A. Pocock, ed., *Three British Revolutions: 1641, 1688, 1776* [Princeton, 1980], 368–453, at 403–4).

[109] Slaughter, *Whiskey Rebellion*, 227.

[110] Wiebe, *Opening of American Society*, 143–6; Wood, "Interests and Disinterestedness," 81–109. See also Gordon S. Wood, "Ideology and the Origins of Liberal America," *William and Mary Quarterly*, 3d ser., 44, 3 (July 1987), 628–40, at 638–40. This process was of course directly related to the "stirrings of division" in artisan communities already commented upon. See also Christopher L. Tomlins, *The State and the Unions: Labor Relations, Law, and the Organized Labor Movement in America, 1880–1960* (New York and Cambridge, 1985), 34–5; Sean Wilentz, "Artisan Republican Festivals and the Rise of Class Conflict in New York City, 1788–1837," in Michael H. Frisch and Daniel J. Walkowitz, eds., *Working Class America: Essays on Labor, Community, and American Society* (Urbana, 1983), 37–77. See, generally, Sean Wilentz, *Chants Democratic: New York City and the Rise of the American Working Class, 1788–1850* (New York, 1984).

what amounted to a call for wholesale confrontation with the future, some Federalists simply decried this whole milieu as profane and licentious.[111] But as we have seen, those in the mainstream of Federalist constitutional discourse recognized the permanence of the alterations wrought by the Revolution and responded by seeking to establish a model of a republican polity in which popular vigor might be accommodated, in acceptable form, while retaining the essentials of a hierarchical mode of governance. So successful were they that their model – government distanced from participation and overseeing a society and economy of rights-bearing individuals intensively engaged in private action – became the American standard.[112]

Law, not politics, furnished the discourse of rule in this American model. Partly this was a matter of rhetoric, though rhetoric powerfully expressive of desires to limit popular participation in government. Politics smacked too much of popular passion, of "wild ranting fury." America was to be a polity of laws and not men, a polity of the rule of law.[113] But although rhetorical, this was speech informed by the institutional realities of governance, for indeed constitutionally it was law not politics that defined and delimited the social and economic territory upon which the revolutionary era's rights discourse would actually take effect. As provided for in the Constitution's "judiciary department," law became the decisive means and the medium of supervision over the actual institutional processes through which the popular will was expressed in the republican polity.[114] Further, as Federalist constitutionalism and the model of governance it embodied took hold at all levels of the American polity, this function was reproduced in the states, notwithstanding their markedly different heritage in most instances.[115]

---

[111] Wood, "Ideology and the Origins of Liberal America," 81–109.

[112] Jennifer Nedelsky, "Reconceiving Autonomy," *Yale Journal of Law and Feminism*, 1, 1 (Spring 1989), 15–20.

[113] Slaughter, *Whiskey Rebellion*, 134, 135, 139. In a letter to Benjamin Goodhue of Andover (August 1795), John Phillips of Boston condemned the town's democratic republicans for encouraging the mobs that had rioted during the previous year against the export of flour, for stirring up "public opposition to an important national measure" [the Jay Treaty], and in particular for creating a Jacobinical society "whose manifest object is to *make themselves* the *dictators* of the *Government* – the *Supreme Court* of the *Nation*," in Phillips MSS, Massachusetts Historical Society, Boston. See also, generally, Philip S. Foner, "The Democratic–Republican Societies: An Introduction," in idem, ed., *The Democratic–Republican Societies, 1790– 1800: A Documentary Sourcebook* (Westport, Conn., 1976), 3–51.

[114] On judicial review as the apogee and epitome of Madisonian constitutionalism, see Nedelsky, *Private Property and the Limits of American Constitutionalism*, 187–99.

[115] Morton Horwitz, e.g., cites a Pennsylvania statute of 1807 empowering the state Supreme Court to decide which English statutes were in force in the state; he comments that "the delegation of so explicit and self-conscious a legislative function to judges would have been inconceivable even two decades earlier" (*Transformation of American Law*, 23–4). But see also Stimson, *American Revolution in the Law*, 56–7. In *Eakin et al. v. Raub*, 12 Sergeant and Rawles 330 (1825), in which the Pennsylvania Supreme Court affirmed its right and duty to pronounce void acts of the state legislature that it judged to be contrary to the state constitution, Judge John Gibson (at 344–58) argued at length in dissent that although the right and duty of judicial review could be found in the federal Constitution, it had no parallel in the state constitution. "I am aware, that a right to declare all unconstitutional acts void, without distinction as to either constitution, is generally held as a professional dogma; but, I apprehend, rather as a matter of faith than of reason." In the absence of an explicit constitutional grant of powers giving the courts authority to supervise the legislature, so to act was to usurp legislative power. "It is

The preeminence of law in the early republic was not simply a consequence of the role assigned the judiciary in American constitutional discourse. As Morton Horwitz has shown, the Revolution having confronted an emerging Anglocentric colonial legal culture with the sudden problem of reconciling intellectual dependence on customary common law with a polity created explicitly on foundations of popular sovereignty, courts and jurists in all states sought to sustain the legitimacy of their common law jurisdiction by adjusting the conception of the common law as immemorial custom in order to found its authority on "the people" at large. Such an adjustment may be observed under way in James Wilson's justly famous 1790–1 lectures on law.

> How was a custom introduced? By voluntary adoption. How did it become general? By the instances of voluntary adoption being increased. How did it become lasting? By voluntary and satisfactory experience, which ratified and confirmed what voluntary adoption had introduced. In the introduction, in the extension, in the continuance of customary law, we find the operations of consent universally predominant.[116]

Following in Wilson's tracks, some jurists reclaimed authority for the common law by arguing that it represented that body of prevailing legal principle to which "the people" – in a mysterious process whose details they did not elaborate – had "consented";[117] others recast it more completely, also more abstractly, as the purest expression of the sovereign people's will, with the judiciary as the "trustees" or "agents" of the people in interpreting that will. From here jurists moved on to claim a legislative authority for the courts' common law jurisdiction, arguing that as embodiments of the sovereign will courts enjoyed an authority to expound that

---

the business of the judiciary to interpret the laws, not scan the authority of the lawgiver; and without the latter, it cannot take cognizance of a collision between a law and the constitution." Rather, "it rests with the people, in whom full and absolute sovereign power resides, to correct abuses in legislation, by instructing their representatives to repeal the obnoxious act" (345, 348, 355). For similar criticism in Massachusetts, see *A Stricture on the Judiciary of Massachusetts . . . By A Citizen* (Andover, 1843), esp. 15–21. On legislative opposition to court assertions of authority to review prior to the ratification of the federal Constitution, see Goebel, *Antecedents and Beginnings*, 137–41. On judicial review in the states, see William E. Nelson, "Changing Conceptions of Judicial Review: The Evolution of Constitutional Theory in the States, 1790–1860," *University of Pennsylvania Law Review*, 120, 6 (June 1972), 1166–85.

[116] Robert Green McCloskey, ed., *The Works of James Wilson* (Cambridge, Mass., 1967), 1:180, quoted in Horwitz, *Transformation of American Law*, 19. The significance of Wilson's lectures is further enhanced when we realize that they were a social and political event of considerable magnitude. According to Stephen Conrad, "Wilson's inaugural law lecture, delivered on December 15, 1790, was more than a ceremonial academic event; it was also something of a state occasion. A newspaper of the day records that those in attendance included '[t]he President of the United States, with his lady – also the Vice-President, and both houses of Congress, [t]he President and both houses of the Legislature of Pennsylvania, together with a great number of ladies and gentlemen . . . the whole comprising a most brilliant and respectable audience'" ("Polite Foundation: Citizenship and Common Sense in James Wilson's Republican Theory," *Supreme Court Review*, 8 [1984], 359–88, at 374).

[117] On the common law and consent, see Conrad, "James Wilson's 'Assimilation of the Common Law Mind,'" 186–219; Jennifer Nedelsky, "Democracy, Justice, and the Multiplicity of Voices: Alternatives to the Federalist Vision," *Northwestern University Law Review*, 84, 1 (Fall 1989), 232–49. As Nedelsky observes: "We can be confident that customs reflect the consent of the people only if we believe that all the people had equal access to the shaping of the customs. We know, of course, that the contrary is almost always true" (244).

sovereign will no less than legislatures. Common law was "equally responsible with legislation for governing society and promoting socially desirable conduct."[118] Indeed in important respects – flexibility in molding decision to circumstance, continuity of tenure and thus of policy perspective – judges held that their capacity to expound the sovereign will was greatly superior.

In the newly created republic, therefore, as the discourse of police emerged to give brief political expression to a democratized ideology of communal good order or collective happiness, it encountered the competing discourse of law claiming to provide the language of rule in the new polity and also invoking, hastily transmuted into a language of consent, its own independent heritage as a superordinate source or mode of rule *in itself*.[119] The subsequent nineteenth-century fate of police, indeed, is an apt illustration of the power of this ideology. As William Novak has recently shown, by the middle decades of the nineteenth century contemporary American jurisprudence was representing the conceptual genealogy of the state's police power as one with its origins in what Novak terms a distinctive *common law* vision of the "well-regulated society."[120] This, however, was a vision of police as a power of the state largely stripped of the language of democratic participation that had been so essential a component of the ideal of police-as-happiness current in the revolutionary era.[121]

---

[118] Horwitz, *Transformation of American Law*, 30 and, generally, 23–30.

[119] For an illustration of the dual conception of sovereignty to which this claim of common law independence gave rise, see, e.g., Francis Hilliard, *The Elements of Law: Being a Comprehensive Summary of American Civil Jurisprudence* (Boston, 1835), at 5: "the formation of the United States government gave rise to a system of laws peculiar in itself, and which neither confirms, contradicts, nor in any way changes the common law, but occupies or constitutes a new and independent department of jurisprudence." Indeed, jurists argued not simply for common law independence but common law preeminence. "The principles of the common law *form the basis of all our systems*, from the great confederacy of independent states, down to the smallest corporation" (Warren Dutton, *An Address Delivered to the Members of the Bar of Suffolk, at their Annual Meeting, in September 1819* [Boston, 1819], 18, emphasis supplied). See also Peter Du Ponceau, quoted in n. 42 above. In his *Principles of Government: A Treatise on Free Institutions* (Burlington, Vt., 1833), at 253–4, Nathaniel Chipman made the same point in much more detail, arguing that English common law was the only legitimate key to the meaning of the Constitution: "By the common law is here to be understood the common law of England, so called; its principles, its rules, and maxims. From that country it was brought by our fathers, – the country of their birth and education. Its language was to them their native language, – not merely the language of their lips, but of their thoughts upon law, government, and all institutions, civil and political. They claimed the common law as their birthright, and transmitted it to their posterity in this country. Such was the language, and such the habits of thinking, both of those who framed, and of those who ratified the constitution. To the common law we must resort to learn what is meant by a legislative, and executive, and a judicial power in government, by an impeachment, by a court of law, a jury, a Grand Jury, an indictment, and a trial by jury. The same observation will be found applicable to almost every clause of the constitution." See also Stimson, *American Revolution in the Law*, 144. At the risk of stating the obvious I should point out that what is under consideration here is not the oft-discussed contest between the different institutions among which the Constitution distributes the sovereign's authority but the claim for effective ideational preeminence mounted on behalf of a legal discourse founded altogether outside that constitutional structure.

[120] Novak, "Intellectual Origins of the State Police Power," 1–112, esp. 57–86.

[121] Key questions about the construction of the postcolonial social order – what was to be subjected to police and what not, and by what means and to what end – questions, that is, crucial to the process of creating, defining, and taking control of the "public" sphere (and thereby simultaneously defining the "private" sphere), were thus comprehensively distanced from democratic politics.

CONCLUSION

The conception of police that would come to predominate in the jurisprudence of the nineteenth century was the particular product of a society seeking, in an organically founded ideology of common law and government, protection from a second wave of democracy breaking in the 1830s and from the "aggressive natural rights radicalism" which it brought with it "from below."[122] As Peter Du Ponceau, an exemplar of common law theorizing on police, put it in 1834, "the political, like the natural body, is not immortal, and it will sink at last, if efficient means are not taken to prevent the recurrence of those disorders, which gradually weaken it." Like leading Federalists fifty years earlier, Du Ponceau despaired of the "deadly poison" of uninhibited politics, whose consequences made him "tremble for the stability of our institutions."[123]

Such a reading had, indeed, begun to emerge years earlier, while the reverberations of the revolutionary era's conflicts were still ringing in some minds. Take, for example, an oration delivered in May 1805 before the members of the Massachusetts Charitable Fire Society at their annual meeting in Boston by Peter Oxenbridge Thacher, up-and-coming attorney and future judge of the Boston Municipal Court.[124] Like his British contemporary, the magistrate Patrick Colquhoun, Thacher's objective was to enhance the prosperity of a metropolis – in his case, Boston. Like Colquhoun his primary concern was that the metropolis be granted efficacious means of dealing with those concomitants of commercial growth, notably poverty and threats to social order, which if left unnoticed would be "fatal to its duration."[125] And like Colquhoun he concluded that the answer lay in the nature and performance of municipal institutions: "the prosperity of every city . . . must depend on the excellence of its police." In Boston's case this meant concretely the abandonment of government by town meeting – "baseless, unballanced, inefficient, and liable to be

---

[122] Daniel T. Rodgers, *Contested Truths: Keywords in American Politics since Independence* (New York, 1987), 125, and see generally 112–43. For a taste of that 1830s radicalism see Stephen Simpson, *The Working Man's Manual: A New Theory of Political Economy, on the Principle Production the Source of Wealth* (Philadelphia, 1831):

"In this country we have no orders but the people – no sovereign but the people – no rule of action but the happiness and safety of the community; and under our constitution and laws, founded on those of nature, INDUSTRY, not law, is the rightful distributer of property. . . .

". . . [T]he laws and customs of society ought to conform to the dictates of natural equity, which ordains, that industry shall distribute the wealth it produces, for the common happiness and comfort of all the children of toil" (136, 138).

[123] Peter Du Ponceau, *A Brief View of the Constitution of the United States* (Philadelphia, 1834), xvi, xviii. On Du Ponceau see Novak, "Intellectual Origins of the State Police Power," 25.

[124] Peter Oxenbridge Thacher, *An Address to the Members of the Massachusetts Charitable Fire Society, at their Annual Meeting, In Boston, May 31, 1805* (Boston, 1805).

[125] Thacher spoke of Boston as a city "where great inequality of property exists, where the private wealth of some is equal to levelling mountains, and even to abridging the limits of the sea; where, associated with such abundance, you can find multitudes dependent on the smiles of the passing day, and almost without means of supplying the wants of life." In such a situation "we must expect to see great virtues and great vices; we shall find everything good likely to rise to perfection, and everything evil carried to excess" (ibid., 12).

moved about by every afflation of the popular breath" – for a mode of governance that would better reflect "the spirit of our republican constitutions" by providing "a simple, united and energetic government under the gravest and wisest of citizens."

What Thacher sought from such a government was greater "security to the lives and property" of the inhabitants. "Under a well-connected and energetic police, we may repose without fear of the incendiary or ruffian. We may trust to its care the honour and safety of those whom we love, and who look to us for protection." Boston would become "a well regulated city, where the citizens are happy in the enjoyment of their lives, their fortunes, and their means of happiness; where each knows and preserves his own place; and where the whole harmoniously unite to promote the general good." Such a government would reestablish the "regular gradation" and the "orderly distribution of duties" so obviously lacking during the town's recent history, achieving a "correct arrangement and subordination of the parts which constitute a magnificent whole." Some, Thacher confessed, would see in this "the spectre of despotism." But reform was essential, particularly when, as now, there was abroad "a prevalent spirit of bold and lawless innovation, which aims its sacrilegious attacks against the ark of our political safety."[126]

Thacher and his opinions will feature prominently in the next part of this book for he plays a significant role in the disputes which are its principal subject. As we shall see there, Thacher, like Du Ponceau, reposed enormous confidence in the common law. Reluctant to concede the value of any but the most restrained democracy, he embraced law as the vehicle for realization, indeed as itself the realization, of the republic's promise of civic virtue. In turn this meant that law and

---

[126] Ibid., 5–21. As in England, such an approach tended to result in the realignment of the concept of *police* with the promotion of a market economy and the mobilization of the poor. In Massachusetts, for example, Colquhoun's recommendations for an effective police of indigence were paralleled by changes shifting the emphasis of the poor laws away from the principle of local responsibility, which did not easily accommodate transience, toward measures much more facilitative of a "free circulation" of labor. See Douglas Lamar Jones, "The Strolling Poor: Transiency in Eighteenth Century Massachusetts," *Journal of Social History*, 8 (1975), 28–54; idem, "The Transformation of the Law of Poverty in Eighteenth Century Massachusetts," in *Law in Colonial Massachusetts, 1630–1800* (Boston, 1984), 153–90. The issue was further explored in the early 1820s by Josiah Quincy, who was to become Boston's mayor in 1823, in a series of reports and opinions addressing the state's poor laws. According to Quincy, the point of relief was to stimulate productive labor. Hence the state should make "industry, morality and economy" indispensable conditions to relief. "Indolence, intemperance, and sensuality, are the great causes of pauperism, in this country. Notwithstanding the imbecility induced by their habits and vices it is yet found by experience, that generally speaking, all this class can do something; and very many of them a great deal; and some of them fall little, and often not at all, short of the ability to perform, daily, the complete task of a day labourer." See *Report of a Committee of the General Court of the Commonwealth of Massachusetts on the Pauper Laws of this Commonwealth* [Josiah Quincy, Chairman] (Boston, 1821), 5; *Report of the Committee on the Subject of Pauperism and a House of Industry in the Town of Boston* [Josiah Quincy, Chairman] (Boston, 1821), 9–10. See also Josiah Quincy, *Remarks on some of the Provisions of the Laws of Massachusetts, Affecting Poverty, Vice, and Crime* (Cambridge, Mass., 1822). On the simultaneous process of *excluding* the poor from participation in the polity, see Steinfeld, "Property and Suffrage," 335–76. As Steinfeld puts it, "That all men were entitled to govern themselves, but that only property ownership allowed them actually to do so, was a potentially explosive combination of ideas" (376).

democracy were now to an important extent competing expressions of republican-ism. Police had become the ideal of the well-regulated society, and a well-regulated society, to Thacher as to many others of his generation, was one that carefully controlled its people, not one that maximized their opportunities to control their own destiny.

PART 2

Law, labor, and state

Trades' Unions . . . appear to us to represent some of the most striking tendencies, and to imbody some of the most dangerous heresies of the age. They exhibit, on a small scale, the disposition so widely prevalent in this country, to substitute the power of associations or parties for the authority of law, and to gain unrighteous advantages by means of disciplined and confederated numbers. . . . Dependant for all our order and future welfare on the due administration of law, we are yet constantly taking or submitting to measures which tend to prostrate the influence of courts and to overthrow the authority of magistrates. Allegiance to party is getting to be rewarded, we had almost said honored, before allegiance to country; while independence of individual opinion and feeling is crushed under the ruthless car of popular passion and prejudice. Is there nothing in such a state of things to excite alarm? Is it not time, more than time, that all who love their country should combine to stay the progress of dangerous errors, to allay the violence of faction, to promote kind feelings among the various classes of our people, and to build about our lovely heritage the sacred defences of piety and truth!

Alonzo Potter, *Political Economy: Its Objects, Uses, and Principles*

Introduction: dictates of wise policy

In November 1806, the *Monthly Anthology and Boston Review*, a newly established Bostonian literary miscellany, published a short review of a pamphlet recounting "The Trial of the Journeymen Boot and Shoemakers of Philadelphia." The pamphlet had appeared in May of that year in the wake of the journeymen's indictment and conviction on a charge of a combination and conspiracy to raise their wages. According to Thomas Lloyd, one of the pamphlet's publishers and the original transcriber of the court proceedings, the issues involved had made the trial "the most interesting law case which has occurred in this state since our revolution."[1] Certainly the result had excited much controversy and had led to pressure on the governor and General Assembly of Pennsylvania for legislation to curb the courts' assumption of authority to convict combining workmen of common law conspiracy.[2] "Hitherto we have travelled on the happy and level road of rational and equal justice," the editor of the staunchly Jeffersonian *Philadelphia Aurora*, William Duane, had written

---

[1] Thomas Lloyd, *The Trial of the Boot and Shoemakers of Philadelphia, on an Indictment for a Combination and Conspiracy to Raise Their Wages* (Philadelphia, 1806), title page. Lloyd, the "father of American shorthand reporting," was a radical Jeffersonian based in Philadelphia who had been active in Democratic-Republican politics in the 1790s. See Richard J. Twomey, *Jacobins and Jeffersonians: Anglo-American Radicalism in the United States, 1790–1820* (New York, 1989), 57–8.

[2] Lloyd's pamphlet was dedicated "To Thomas M'Kean, Governor, and the General Assembly of Pennsylvania . . . with the hope of attracting their particular attention, at the next meeting of the Legislature" (*Trial of the Boot and Shoemakers of Philadelphia*). Some time after the trial a committee was appointed by the Pennsylvania House of Representatives "to inquire whether and what amendments are necessary in the law, on the subject of conspiracy," and to recommend alterations. The committee found that "by the common law of England, adopted in Pennsylvania, an agreement and combination among workmen, not to work under certain wages, may be indicted and punished as a conspiracy." It recommended steps to disestablish the doctrine, notably a bill to define conspiracy and to provide in particular "that no act or thing attempted or done by two or more in concert, shall be punishable as a conspiracy when the same if done by one only would have been not unlawful." A bill to this effect was subsequently introduced and debated, but not acted upon. See *Journal of the Nineteenth House of Representatives of the Commonwealth of Pennsylvania*, for 16 and 21 Dec. 1808, and 13 and 20 Mar. 1809 (Lancaster, 1808), 65, 125, 655–6, 729; and *Journal of the Twentieth House of Representatives of the Commonwealth of Pennsylvania*, for 13 Dec. 1809, and 17 and 24 Jan. 1810 (Lancaster, 1809), 53–4, 272, 334. See also Elizabeth K. Henderson, "The Attack on the Judiciary in Pennsylvania, 1800–1810," *Pennsylvania Magazine of History and Biography*, 61, 2 (Apr. 1937), 113–36, at 134–5; and below, the section entitled The First Wave, 1806–1815, in Chapter 5.

following the journeymen's indictment. "The barbarous principles of feudal subjection no where appear but in the deplorable curse entailed upon us by what has been called the *'parent country'* – the slavery of the unfortunate Africans." But even as steps were at last being taken to expiate that curse, measures were being attempted "which, if they could be accomplished, would reduce the laboring whites to a condition still more despicable and abject." Working shoemakers had been thrown in jail simply "for meditating and proposing to demand an augmentation of the reward for their manual labor." Was there anything in the constitution of the Commonwealth of Pennsylvania or of the United States which gave one body of men a right to say to another, "contrary to the will of him who labors," what should be the price of labor? There was not. It was "another of the glorious *shoots* of the English *common law*" that made such things possible.[3]

The *Monthly Anthology*'s reviewer, however, saw things differently:

The cities of the United States flourish and rapidly increase in population, wealth, arts, and commerce. With these it is reasonable to expect an influx of their concomitant vices and inconveniences. Regular government and strict internal police are necessary to preserve order and administer justice, where the business and concerns of man are so multiplied and complicated. Gain is the occupation of all; and the powerful love of lucre, like the principle of gravitation, impels to action even stocks [*sic*] and stones. Cooperation and concert are so useful to a multitude, pursuing a common end, that we frequently find brethren of the same craft constituting communities, enacting by-laws, and sanctioning them by the severe penalties of ignominy and ruin to the disobedient. These associations frequently contravene the rights and are very vexatious to other classes of citizens.

Combinations of workmen, concluded the reviewer, were oppressive and highly injurious to society, "and wise policy dictates that they should be repressed." Combinations placed "all the members . . . on equality, and consequently ingenuity, skill, and diligence are deprived of their reward." They were an encouragement to "the ignorant and indolent, who compose the majority of every class," and who "naturally advocate measures which elevate them, and depress their superiors." The Philadelphia conviction was thus both timely and appropriate. "In the correctness of the decision all sound lawyers, and all who wish for internal peace and industry, will acquiesce."[4]

Although unattributed, the review was without a doubt the work of Peter Oxenbridge Thacher, a founder–member of the Society that published the *Monthly Anthology* and a frequent contributor to the journal.[5] Born in the year of the

---

[3] *Philadelphia Aurora*, 27 Nov. 1805 (emphasis in original).

[4] *Monthly Anthology and Boston Review*, 3 (1806), 609–10.

[5] I base this conclusion regarding authorship on the views Thacher was to express on the subject of journeymen's combinations later in his career, on his known close involvement with the Anthology Society and the *Monthly Anthology*, and in particular on a comparison of the abbreviated observations on urban government outlined in the review with those expressed at much greater length in Thacher's *Address to the Members of the Massachusetts Charitable Fire Society, at their Annual Meeting, In Boston, May 31, 1805* (Boston, 1805); for details of the *Address*, see Chapter 3. Thacher's views on journeymen's combinations are outlined in Christopher L. Tomlins, "Criminal Conspiracy and Early Labor Combinations:

Revolution into a prominent family of Bay State lawyers and divines, Thacher had graduated from Harvard in 1796 and had then taught for three years at Phillips Academy in New Hampshire while pondering whether or not to follow his father into the ministry. Eventually choosing law, Thacher entered the law office of Attorney General James Sullivan, whence he was admitted to the Suffolk County bar in 1802. In 1807 he became town advocate (public prosecutor) of Boston and fifteen years later was appointed to preside over the city's most important criminal bench, the Boston Municipal Court. For the next two decades Thacher labored unremittingly at this gloomy pinnacle to secure Boston against the multiplying "vices and inconveniences," the "torrent of misrule," attending its metropolitan growth.[6] Among the particular inconveniences against which Thacher marshalled the resources of the criminal law, none was more sternly reproved by him than those associations of journeymen whose existence he had censured in his youth. As we shall see, in the 1830s and early 1840s Thacher featured prominently in the continuing efforts in Massachusetts and elsewhere to utilize the common law of criminal conspiracy to "repress" journeymen's combinations.[7]

Thacher's identification of "regular government and strict internal police" as the instrumentalities whereby society might be protected from the depredations of the multitude's self-constituted regulatory communities helps underline the currency in early nineteenth-century Boston of the reconceptualization of government as security described in the previous chapter. As important, however, Thacher's whole career and consciousness exemplify the accompanying commitment to a discourse of specifically *legal* power – and of the courts' supervention in matters of *police*[8] – which, we have seen, was the Federalists' primary constitutional counter to the threatened ascendancy of democratic politics in the early republic. "We are a free people," Thacher told his fellow inhabitants of Boston on the thirty-first anniversary of independence. Popular freedom, however, consisted neither in the institutional forms of republican government devised in the aftermath of the Revolution nor in the

Massachusetts, 1824–1840," *Labor History*, 28, 3 (Summer 1987), 370–85. On Thacher's involvement with the *Monthly Anthology*, see S. K. Lothrop, *A Sermon Preached in the Church in Brattle Square, March 5, 1843, The Sunday After the Interment of Hon. Peter O. Thacher, Judge of the Municipal Court* (Boston, 1843), 15. On the relationship of law and literature in the early republic see Robert A. Ferguson, *Law and Letters in American Culture* (Cambridge, 1984); Perry Miller, *The Life of the Mind in America: From the Revolution to the Civil War* (New York, 1965), 99–155; Alfred S. Konefsky, "Law and Culture in Antebellum Boston," *Stanford Law Review*, 40, 4 (Apr. 1988), 1119–59.

[6] Lothrop, *Sermon*, 13–20; John M. Williams, *Proceedings in the Municipal Court of the City of Boston, Occasioned by the Sudden Death of Hon. Peter O. Thacher, Late Judge of that Court, with a Sketch of his Judicial Character* (Boston, 1843). Judge Thacher, it was said, was "often stigmatized as a very severe judge; but he was not more rigid than just. He was peculiarly qualified for the period and station, and wisely effected more in the restraint of crime among us than any other man on the bench" (James Spear Loring, *The Hundred Boston Orators* [Boston, 1854], 324).

[7] Tomlins, "Criminal Conspiracy and Early Labor Combinations," 375–85.

[8] See, e.g., Thacher's comments on the relative powers and responsibilities of executive and judicial authorities in local government in his *Charge to the Grand Jury of the County of Suffolk, for the Commonwealth of Massachusetts, at the Opening of the Municipal Court of the City of Boston, on the First Monday of December, A.D. 1831* (Boston, 1832), 13–17.

location of power in the sovereign people. Freedom was the creature of an omniscient and uniform law.

We need not search the records of history to discover, that freedom is not essentially dependent on the form of a government. Civil liberty consists in your being governed by laws, and not by men. The political liberty of a citizen consists in the tranquility of mind, which proceeds from the idea, that he has no reason to fear any one, provided he keeps a clear conscience. The first duty then, which, as good citizens, we must practise, is obedience to the laws of our country. For in proportion as these approach to perfection, and they are administered with purity, we may estimate the degree and worth of our freedom. Subordinate to this, but essentially connected with it, is the obligation to venerate the Lawgiver, and to protect the Judge. If there is then, in this community, any one, who is constantly insulting your civil institutions; if there is any one, who is engaged in the nefarious attempt to control, or to intimidate your courts of justice; if there is any one, who is not willing that the law should be supreme; he is a dangerous citizen; he is either a tyrant or a slave, equally ready to wield the sceptre of death, or to cringe at the feet of a despot.[9]

Stated early in his career, these remained Thacher's guiding principles. Thus when, locally, the politics of mass participation and popular sovereignty came to be pressed with growing persistence during the 1820s and, particularly, the 1830s, law in Thacher's discourse took on quite noticeably the character of a bulwark against the destructive tides of the passionate multitude, the only safeguard, indeed, against anarchy.[10] Law was "the ligament of society, binding the state together, preserving its peace, increasing its harmony, and adding to its happiness."[11] Law "preserves the order of all ranks and professions among men"; it "makes every man to know his own place, compelling him to move in it, and giving to him his due."[12] Without

---

[9] Peter Oxenbridge Thacher, *An Oration Delivered Before the Inhabitants of the Town of Boston, on the Thirty-First Anniversary of the Independence of the United States of America* (Boston, 1807), 8–10. Thacher's veneration for the law in this speech contrasts with his antagonism toward the caprice and fickleness of electoral politics and its "party spirit."

[10] See his *Charge to the Grand Jury of the County of Suffolk, for the Commonwealth of Massachusetts, at the Opening of the Municipal Court of the City of Boston, on Monday, December 7, A.D. 1835* (Boston, 1835), 32, 25–6. On Massachusetts politics see Ronald P. Formisano, *The Transformation of Political Culture: Massachusetts Parties, 1790s–1840s* (New York and Oxford, 1983); Robert A. McCaughey, "From Town to City: Boston in the 1820s," *Political Science Quarterly*, 88, 2 (June 1973), 191–213.

[11] Peter Oxenbridge Thacher, *An Address Pronounced on the First Tuesday of March, 1831 Before the Members of the Bar of the County of Suffolk, Massachusetts* (Boston, 1831), 17, and generally 16–19. Thacher's rhetoric on this occasion verged on the rhapsodic. "Individuals, families, the farmer, the merchant, the artist, the mechanic, the laborer and his employer, the members of the learned professions, the rich and the poor, the wise and the ignorant, great and small, all feel the power, and yield to the sway of the Law." Law (and lawyers) was everywhere: "what place is so barren, what village so small, in which is not found its lawyer. . . . Nothing human is foreign to their pursuits." Even God himself "acknowledges a rule of conduct." The latter is a doubly interesting observation, given Thacher's own decision earlier in life to employ his talents in the law rather than in the ministry.

[12] Peter Oxenbridge Thacher, *A Charge to the Grand Jury of the County of Suffolk, for the Commonwealth of Massachusetts, at the Opening of the Municipal Court of the City of Boston, on the First Monday of December, A.D. 1832* (Boston, 1832), 19; *Two Charges to the Grand Jury of the County of Suffolk, for the Commonwealth of Massachusetts, at the Opening of the Terms of the Municipal Court of the City of Boston, on Monday, December 5th, A.D. 1836, and on Monday, March 13th, A.D. 1837* (Boston, 1837), 28.

law, "every man's will would be the rule of his own conduct, which would produce a scene of universal confusion and violence."[13]

When you survey the society to which you belong, and consider the various wants of its members; — their numbers, their variety of occupation and character, — their conflicting interests and wants, — the multitudes who are idle and unwilling to labor, or who are poor and dependent, and cannot labor, — how many live by vice and plunder, and how many derive a revenue from the arts of deceit and corruption; — what is it, permit me to ask, preserves the common peace and safety? I know of no answer but THE LAW.[14]

Given the argument so far developed in this book, it is important to note that the law to which Thacher looked to sustain the early republic in its hour of democratic excess — "over every thing . . . pervad[ing] every thing . . . the life of every thing"[15] — was at least as much the common law, declared by judges and rooted in the "ancient books, written by learned judges and lawgivers of that nation, from which our ancestors emigrated," as it was the product of local legislatures. In Massachusetts "the common law . . . is as much our own, as any act of the legislature, and it is equally binding on courts of justice."[16] In comparison, indeed, the acts of the legislature could seem rather suspect, always prey to the spirit of party, the local whims and fickle inattentions of the electorate, the designs of the self-interested.

That legislation which would render property insecure, and make it the spoil of the multitude, would annihilate property, and involve society in a common ruin. Laws which make it for the interest of individuals to cultivate honesty, moderation, temperance, industry, and frugality, are most friendly to the best interests of society, and essential to maintain a free government. Unless you secure to the merchant his merchandize, to the farmer his produce, and to the professional man the rewards of his talents and study, as well as to the laborer his hire, there will soon be no labor to reward, no hire to be paid. And therefore it would be a great error in legislation, to deprive skill or labor, mental or physical, either of their reward or respectability.[17]

The common law — "the condensed wisdom of ages, founded on reason, and transmitted, as an invaluable inheritance, from remote antiquity" — was "always clearer and generally wiser than any statute."[18]

Thacher's repeated articulation of law, particularly the common law, as the only real glue holding the republic together was by no means unique. In fact it was rather typical of American legal discourse throughout much of the first half of the nineteenth century. At one and the same time both a defense and a justification of the ascendancy of the courts in the American state, the legal discourse of the early republic was also a continuation of the centralizing Federalist project to reject the

---

[13] *A Charge to the Grand Jury . . . on the First Monday of December, A.D. 1831,* 17.
[14] *Two Changes to the Grand Jury . . . on Monday, December 5th, A.D. 1836, and on Monday, March 13th, A.D. 1837,* 28.
[15] *A Charge to the Grand Jury . . . on the First Monday of December, A.D. 1832,* 9.
[16] Ibid., 18.
[17] *A Charge to the Grand Jury . . . on the First Monday of December, A.D. 1834,* 19.
[18] *A Charge to the Grand Jury . . . on the First Monday of December, A.D. 1831,* 12–13.

multiform polity bruited in the debates of the 1780s and 1790s,[19] and in the process to deny both legitimacy and opportunity to competing claims to the exercise of power based on alternative conceptions of republican politicoeconomic order.[20]

Nowhere is the exclusionary character of this discourse more clearly revealed than in the struggles of courts to apply the doctrine of criminal conspiracy to journeymen's combinations. Always offering a unique public forum for confrontations between the exponents of competing conceptions of republican political and economic power,[21] by the mid-1830s these struggles had become both pervasive and strenuous, attracting considerable popular attention and political significance. In each of the most important industrializing states – Pennsylvania., New York, and Massachusetts – labor conspiracy prosecutions became a major issue, a focus for those on every side of contemporary attempts to craft comprehensive restatements of the republic's political economy; exponents of "free" competition, advocates for working people, defenders of law and republican order.

---

[19] On this, see Carol M. Rose, "The Ancient Constitution vs. the Federalist Empire: Anti-Federalism from the Attack on 'Monarchism' to Modern Localism," *Northwestern University Law Review*, 84, 1 (Fall 1989), 74–105, esp. 75–85.

[20] See, generally, Miller, *Life of the Mind in America*, 109–16; Ferguson, *Law and Letters*, 273–80; Konefsky, "Law and Culture in Antebellum Boston," 1126–36; R. Kent Newmyer, *Supreme Court Justice Joseph Story: Statesman of the Old Republic* (Chapel Hill, 1985), 37–8, 63, 86–7, 114, 187; G. Edward White, *The Marshall Court and Cultural Change, 1815–1835* (New York and London, 1988), 76–156; Alexis de Tocqueville, *Democracy in America* (1835; New York, 1963), 1:272–80. "Revolutions, generally unfavourable to morals and often to liberty, are *now* no more necessary; nor their spirit and language proper," thankfully observed Nathaniel Freeman, first justice of the Court of Common Pleas for Barnstable, Massachusetts, in his *Charge to the Grand Jury, at the Court of General Sessions of the Peace, Holden at Barnstable, within and for the County of Barnstable, March Term, A.D. 1802* (Boston, 1802), 10 (emphasis in original).

[21] See, e.g., Robert J. Steinfeld, "The *Philadelphia Cordwainers' Case* of 1806: The Struggle over Alternative Legal Constructions of a Free Market in Labor," in Christopher L. Tomlins and Andrew J. King, eds., *Labor Law in America: Historical and Critical Essays* (Baltimore, 1992), 20–43.

4

Combination and conspiracy

A code of laws draws around [the mechanic] a magick circle, by making mechanical combinations punishable, lest they should check capitalist combinations; and he is reimbursed by penalties for the loss of hope.

John Taylor of Caroline, *Tyranny Unmasked*

Since the early 1900s, when John R. Commons first assembled most of them in one place, the early republic's labor conspiracy cases have attracted considerable attention from both labor and legal historians.[1] In the main – and notwithstanding that very

[1] The majority of the cases were published together for the first time as a set in John R. Commons et al., eds., *A Documentary History of American Industrial Society* (Cleveland, 1910), vols. 3–4. For relevant commentary see, e.g., William A. Purrington, "The Tubwomen v. The Brewers of London," *Columbia Law Review*, 3 (1903), 447–69; John R. Commons et al., *History of Labor in the United States* (New York, 1918), 1:138–52, 162–5, 404–12; Francis B. Sayre, "Criminal Conspiracy," *Harvard Law Review*, 35 (1922), 393–427; Edwin E. Witte, "Early American Labor Cases," *Yale Law Journal*, 35 (1925–6), 825–37; Walter Nelles, "The First American Labor Case," *Yale Law Journal*, 41, 2 (Dec. 1931), 165–200; idem, "Commonwealth v. Hunt," *Columbia Law Review*, 32, 7 (1932), 1128–69; John M. Landis, *Cases on Labor Law* (Chicago, 1934), 1–37; Richard B. Morris, "Criminal Conspiracy and Early Labor Combinations in New York," *Political Science Quarterly*, 52, 1 (1937), 51–85; Ludwig Teller, *Labor Disputes and Collective Bargaining* (New York, 1940), 1:31–66; Leonard W. Levy, *The Law of the Commonwealth and Chief Justice Shaw* (Cambridge, Mass., 1957), 183–206; Morris D. Forkosch, "The Doctrine of Criminal Conspiracy and Its Modern Application to Labor," *Texas Law Review*, 40, 3 (Feb. 1962), 303–35; Marjorie S. Turner, *The Early American Labor Conspiracy Cases: Their Place in Labor Law, A Reinterpretation* (San Diego, 1967); Stephen Mayer, "People v. Fisher: The Shoemakers' Strike of 1833," *New York Historical Society Quarterly*, 62, 1 (Jan. 1978), 7–21; Sylvester Petro, "Unions and the Southern Courts: Part III – The Conspiracy and Tort Foundations of the Labor Injunction," *North Carolina Law Review*, 60 (1982), 544–629; Ian M. G. Quimby, "The Cordwainers' Protest: A Crisis in Labor Relations," *Winterthur Portfolio*, 3 (1983), 83–101; Sean Wilentz, "Conspiracy, Power, and the Early Labor Movement: The People v. James Melvin et al., 1811," *Labor History*, 24 (1983), 572–9; Christopher L. Tomlins, *The State and the Unions: Labor Relations, Law, and the Organized Labor Movement in America, 1880–1960* (New York and Cambridge, 1985), 32–59; Wythe Holt, "Labor Conspiracy Cases in the United States, 1805–1842: Bias and Legitimation in Common Law Adjudication," *Osgoode Hall Law Journal*, 22, 4 (Winter 1984), 591–663; B. W. Poulson, "Criminal Conspiracy, Injunctions, and Damage Suits in Labor Law," *Journal of Legal History*, 7, 2 (Sept. 1986), 212–27; Christopher L. Tomlins, "Criminal Conspiracy and Early Labor Combinations: Massachusetts, 1824–1840," *Labor History*, 28, 3 (Summer 1987), 370–86; Raymond L. Hogler, "Law, Ideology, and Industrial Discipline: The Conspiracy Doctrine and the Rise of the Factory System," *Dickinson*

different theoretical, political, and moral stances have been embraced by different protagonists – the question of labor conspiracy has generally been approached on a relatively narrow front and with more than half an eye on the course of industrial relations after the Civil War, the cases treated as of lasting significance primarily for what they reveal about the evolution of the law's role and priorities in conflicts between labor and capital. Within these parameters commentators have debated the reasons for the courts' attribution of illegality to journeymen's combinations in the early nineteenth century, usually treating as the fundamental issue the question whether illegality is to be explained as the outcome of the application of normal processes of judicial reasoning to prevailing doctrine, or whether it is instead to be held up as a particularly egregious example of outright pro-employer bias and hostility to labor on the part of the judiciary. The argument usually culminates in a discussion of the extent to which the "leading" case of *Commonwealth v. Hunt* (1842) can be said to have bestowed recognition on unions as a constituent element of American industrial society, making it, in Leonard Levy's phrase, "the Magna Carta of American trade-unionism"; or alternatively whether continued resort to conspiracy doctrine in the years beyond *Commonwealth v. Hunt* evidences that the case made little difference and was thus an aberration – or indeed a subtle restatement of prevailing judicial biases – which left unions enjoying at best a highly contingent legitimacy.[2]

Unfortunately for this evolutionary perspective, whichever version of it one might prefer, the legal status of labor combinations and their activities in the period prior to *Hunt* eludes authoritative categorization along a labor–capital relations continuum. As known cases are reexamined, as additional instances of attempts to use or invoke prosecution for conspiracy are discovered and inspected, old generalizations have tended to break down.[3] This does not mean that the importance of the antebellum cases has been overstated. It does mean, however, that the thrust of historical analysis must be somewhat redirected, that the cases and the issues which they canvassed must be situated in wider arenas than the institutional

Law Review, 91, 3 (Spring 1987), 697–745; Herbert Hovenkamp, "Labor Conspiracies in American Law, 1880–1930," *Texas Law Review*, 66, 5 (Apr. 1988), 919–65, at 922–4; Alfred S. Konefsky, " 'As Best to Subserve Their Own Interests': Lemuel Shaw, Labor Conspiracy, and Fellow Servants – Rethinking an Old Problem," *Law and History Review*, 7, 1 (Spring 1989), 219–39; Robert J. Steinfeld, "The *Philadelphia Cordwainers' Case* of 1806: The Struggle over Alternative Legal Constructions of a Free Market in Labor," and Victoria C. Hattam, "Courts and the Question of Class: Judicial Regulation of Labor under the Common Law Doctrine of Criminal Conspiracy," both in Christopher L. Tomlins and Andrew J. King, eds., *Labor Law in America: Historical and Critical Essays* (Baltimore, 1992), 20–43 and 44–70.

[2] Levy, *Law of the Commonwealth*, 183; Holt, "Labor Conspiracy Cases," 592–7.

[3] Tomlins, "Criminal Conspiracy and Early Labor Combinations," 370–4. Hogler, "Law, Ideology, and Industrial Discipline," is a painstaking attempt at restatement of the "industrial relations" perspective. Recent legal scholarship has criticized labor historians for assuming that early American labor combinations were treated as conspiracies without undertaking a close examination of the doctrinal dynamics of the cases. Such an examination, it has been argued, shows that for all practical purposes the illegality of labor combinations was in fact consequential upon their use of coercive tactics vis-à-vis others rather than an expression of a per se conspiracy doctrine. See, e.g., Poulson, "Criminal Conspiracy, Injunctions, and Damage Suits," 213–15; Hovenkamp, "Labor Conspiracies in American Law," 922–4.

evolution of American industrial relations, if their significance is to be fully appreciated.[4]

Addressing the issue of labor conspiracy from outside the particularist nexus of labor–capital relation has the considerable merit of helping to explain the confusion and uncertainty apparent in the courts' administration of the doctrine by underlining that the configuration of American industrial society was not at all a given during this period. Rather than occurring within the context of a set of known and established conditions which collectively constituted "American industrial society" and defined its values, priorities, goals, institutional structures, and distributions of power, the conspiracy cases were events occurring during a process of formation, a process, moreover, with a variety of contesting themes. Indeed, they were themselves major contributors to that process, for as we shall see, the most fundamental issues in most of the cases were not issues in labor–capital relations as such, at all, but rather issues arising in the course of struggles to define and sustain rival visions of an appropriate postrevolutionary polity and economy for America.

At the same time it remains important to remember that these were still *labor* conspiracy cases. That is to say, in these cases – the primary forum during the formative period of American industrialism for formal encounters between a nascent labor movement and a nascent state – the attempt was made, usually successfully, to represent journeymen who combined in pursuit of their interests as criminals engaged in an activity as morally repugnant as cheating, fraud, or extortion. Such a representation underlines the way in which the early labor movement, as it emerged, found itself forced into a uniquely oppositional – almost an outlaw – role in the economic and especially in the legal arena, encouraging its development, by the 1830s, of a sustained critique of the course of early American industrialism.[5] Hence,

---

[4] Indeed, one such reappraisal has already been attempted, involving an examination of the major cases in terms not of their vindication of either a traditional liberal or a revisionist class-oriented version of industrial relations but instead in terms of their capacity to inform analysis of republican ideology in the postrevolutionary period and in particular of the emergence of a dominant role for legal institutions in the processes of state formation under way throughout that period. See, e.g., Tomlins, *The State and the Unions*, 34–44; idem, "Criminal Conspiracy and Early Labor Combinations," 377–82; Konefsky, "Labor Conspiracy and Fellow Servants," 221, 229–35; and esp. Victoria C. Hattam, "Unions and Politics: The Courts and American Labor, 1806–1896" (Ph. D. diss., MIT, 1987), now published in a revised version as *Labor Visions and State Power: The Origins of Business Unionism in the United States* (Princeton, 1992); idem, "Courts and the Question of Class."

[5] There is from the outset recognition of and protest at this "outlaw" fate in the journeymen's responses to conspiracy indictments. Note, e.g., the "Address of the Working Shoemakers of the City of Philadelphia to the Public" published in the *Philadelphia Aurora* (28 Nov. 1805) following notification that they were to be presented for indictment the following January by the grand jury: "In the constitution of this state, it is declared . . . 'that the citizens have a right in a peaceable manner to assemble together for the common good.' For fifteen years and upwards we have assembled together in a peaceable manner and for our common good, and to guard against the accidents to which industrious men are exposed to promote the happiness of the individuals of which our little community is composed, and to render service to those whom age or infirmity may have rendered incapable of labor. . . . The master shoemakers, as they are called after the slavish style of Europe . . . have their associations, their meetings, and they pass their resolutions; but as they are rich and we are poor – they seem to think that we are not protected by the constitution in meeting peaceably together and pursuing our own happiness. They suppose that they have a right to limit us at all times, and whatever may be the misfortune of society,

although the earliest conspiracy cases are seen here to be most significant for what they reveal about the processes of state formation, or of republican political economy, and although I argue that it is not until the 1830s that the salience of class conflict in the formation of early American labor law may readily be detected, we need to be aware throughout that what we are examining is successive phases of the same process: the encounter between a polity in formation and that which came increasingly explicitly to be defined as its preeminent liability.

HISTORY AND HERITAGE

Through the early 1840s, certain concerns cropped up constantly throughout the run of antebellum American labor conspiracy prosecutions: the interests of the community at large; the legitimacy of the common law in the wake of the revolutionary seizure of sovereignty; the location of power and the means by which it should be wielded; the liberty of the individual. In each case, courts dealt with the particulars arising in terms of their relationship to these more general concerns. But although constants, the relative importance of each of these concerns in relation to the others varied considerably. The essence of *Commonwealth v. Pullis* (1806) – a defense of the integrity of the community and of its juridical agencies against illegitimate self-constituted communities of workers – was vastly different from that of *Commonwealth v. Hunt*, in which the nub of the case was the behavior and goals of such self-constituted communities rather than their existence per se. Close analysis of the cases leads one to see differences more than commonalities.

the changes in the value of necessaries, the encrease or the decrease of trade, they think they have the right to determine for us the value of our labor; but that we have no right to determine for ourselves, what we will or what we will not take in exchange for our labor. . . . If the association of men to regulate the price of their own labor, is to be converted into a crime, and libeled with the same reproachful terms as a design against the freedom of the nation; the prospect is a very sad one for Pennsylvania. . . . [U]nder whatever pretences the thing is done, the name of freedom is but a shadow, if for doing, what the laws of our country authorise, we are to have taskmasters to measure out our pittance of subsistence – if we are to be torn from our fireside for endeavoring to obtain a fair and just support for our families, and if we are to be treated as felons and murderers only for asserting the right to take or refuse what we deem an adequate reward for our labor." Thirty years later a national convention of cordwainers held in New York voiced very similar sentiments. See the *Proceedings of the Convention of Cordwainers, Holden in the City of New-York, Commencing on the First Monday in March, 1836*, pamphlet, Massachusetts Historical Society, Boston: "Our government is one which was established for the protection of the rights of the whole people, and not to grant favors nor privileges to any particular class. In the administration of the government, however, the republican simplicity of its construction has been shamefully disregarded, and instead of protecting rich and poor alike, castes, classes and distinctions have been created – the rich made richer and more tyrannical; the poor poorer and more oppressed. The mechanics have been obliged to resort to combinations among themselves, to obtain that which the God of Nature intended as their right, but which avarice denies them – a comfortable subsistence. And after having been compelled to resort to such a measure, they are to be . . . incarcerated in a loathsome prison, while others, for infinitely worse combinations, escape unwhipped of justice" (16). The notoriety of using conspiracy prosecutions against labor combinations is also underscored by the high proportion of cases – approximately one-third – publicized in pamphlet form. Nothing like this frequency exists in any other class of litigation, with the possible exception of "crimes of passion."

110

The material context in which the labor conspiracy cases arose was the increasing functional stratification of the urban artisan trades occurring in all the eastern seaboard commercial–manufacturing ports in the half-century after the Revolution. Before then, the small artisan communities of the eastern ports had been predominantly communities of independent tradesmen. The traditional tripartite hierarchy of masters, journeymen, and apprentices had some relevance in these communities: Apprenticeship, for example, was a familiar institution. But until the second half of the century, journeymen – wage workers – were less well known in the trades. In the normal course of events the apprentice who had completed his training to his master's satisfaction, or not infrequently simply to his own, would set up as a sole trader almost immediately. Indeed, early in the century those who did become journeymen were treated as self-evidently deficient in their skills rather than simply in their capital.[6] These artisan communities were, of course, stratified by wealth – increasingly so as the century progressed – and the individual trades were ranked in a clear hierarchy of status. The important point, however, is that for most of the century the typical urban artisan was an independent petty producer.[7]

As the century progressed, dependence on wage labor clearly became relatively

[6] Cotton Mather, *A Good Master Well Served: A Brief Discourse on the Necessary Properties and Practices of a Good Servant in Every Kind of Servitude* (Boston, 1696), 13.

[7] Charles S. Olton, *Artisans for Independence, Philadelphia Mechanics and the American Revolution* (New York, 1975); Bruce Laurie, *Working People of Philadelphia, 1800–1850* (Philadelphia, 1980), 3–14; Samuel McKee, *Labor in Colonial New York, 1664–1776* (New York, 1935), 22–3, 27; Gary B. Nash, *The Urban Crucible: Social Change, Political Consciousness, and the Origins of the American Revolution* (Cambridge, 1979), xii; Sharon Salinger, *"To Serve Well and Faithfully": Labor and Indentured Servants in Pennsylvania, 1682–1800* (New York and Cambridge, 1987), 67–8; David Montgomery, "The Working Classes of the Pre-industrial American City, 1780–1830," *Labor History*, 9, 1 (Winter 1968), 3–5; Sean Wilentz, "Against Exceptionalism: Class Consciousness and the American Labor Movement, 1790–1920," *International Labor and Working Class History*, 26 (Fall 1984), 7–8; David Brody, "Time and Work during Early American Industrialism," *Labor History*, 30, 1 (Winter 1989), 13–15; Alfred F. Young, "George Robert Twelves Hewes (1742–1840): A Boston Shoemaker and the Memory of the American Revolution," in Herbert G. Gutman and Donald H. Bell, *The New England Working Class and the New Labor History* (Urbana, 1987), 11–21; Gary J. Kornblith, "From Artisans to Businessmen: Master Mechanics in New England, 1789–1850" (Ph.D. diss., Princeton University, 1983), 86–7; idem, "The Artisanal Response to Capitalist Transformation," *Journal of the Early Republic*, 10, 3 (Fall 1990), 315–21.

It is worth noting that even where journeymen existed in considerable numbers, as in the English cloth industry, their position in the social relations of production was one which afforded them considerable independence. Thus according to John Smail, describing the West Riding woolen industry, "the journeyman was, in one sense, in a wage relationship with his master. But this was an artisanal wage relationship; he worked with, not for, his master. . . . Significantly it was assumed that a journeyman could always aspire to the status of a master [and] . . . even those journeymen who never became masters gained a degree of independence once they had worked as a journeyman. They usually married, and if they spun and wove their master's wool, it was in their own cottage on their own jenny and loom" ("New Languages for Labor and Capital: The Transformation of Discourse in the Early Years of the Industrial Revolution," *Social History*, 12, 1 [Jan. 1987], 49–71, at 54). For earlier confirmation of the legal independence of journeyman weaver from master clothier, see Daniel Defoe, *The Great Law of Subordination Consider'd; or, The Insolence and Unsufferable Behavior of Servants in England duly Enquir'd into . . .* (London, 1724), 91–103. See also the images evoked in *An Address to the Cordwainers of the United States, and More Particularly the Eastern States. Done by Order of the Convention of Cordwainers Held in New York in March, 1836* (Philadelphia, 1836), 5. For a somewhat different view see Steinfeld, "The *Philadelphia Cordwainers'* Case," 24–6. I pursue this matter further in Chapter 7.

more important in the artisan trades. Billy G. Smith, for example, estimates that during the second half of the century, while anywhere between one-third and one-half of Philadelphia's cordwainers and tailors in any given decade were setting up as independent producers, a similar number were hiring themselves out to other craftsmen.[8] Once "master" status was achieved, however, downward mobility was rare.[9]

In other cities, the preponderance of independent over dependent tradesmen tended to be greater. In Boston, where the artisan population has been estimated at 1,300 in 1790, almost all were described locally as "Master Workmen."[10] This situation altered rapidly, however, over the following twenty-five years. Where there had been nearly eight master carpenters for every journeyman carpenter in Boston in 1790, the journeymen were in a majority by 1815.[11] By then journeymen also outnumbered masters across all trades in Philadelphia and, decisively, in New York. Although wage labor had become well known in the urban trades prior to the turn of the century, it had not then been the rule. By the 1820s it was.[12]

This sea change in the culture and organization of urban craft production was caused largely by transatlantic and rural–urban migration, which created a growing population of potential wage workers, and by increased commercial investment in local handicrafts and construction, which meant the creation of new enterprises on a significantly larger scale than had existed theretofore.[13] For most craft workers these developments meant lessened opportunities for mobility and growing insecurity. The more impecunious "masters," those most easily marginalized by the changing scale and growing division of labor of craft enterprise, faced an increasing risk of

[8] Billy G. Smith, *The 'Lower Sort': Philadelphia's Laboring People, 1750–1800* (Ithaca, N.Y., 1990), 120, 139–40. Smith's estimates are not based on contemporary self-descriptions of "masters" and "journeymen" in the trades, for as he notes, "records differentiating between masters and journeymen in any trade are usually nonexistent." Instead, Smith distinguishes master from journeyman within the population of trade members on the basis of tax assessment practices and other measures of wealth and status. See 140, n. 23.

[9] Ibid., 140. Kornblith argues that masters still outnumbered journeymen in Philadelphia trades at the end of the first decade of the nineteenth century ("Artisanal Response to Capitalist Transformation," 318).

[10] Kornblith, "From Artisans to Businessmen," 78. And see Allan Kulikoff, "The Progress of Inequality in Revolutionary Boston," *William and Mary Quarterly*, 3d ser., 28 (July 1971), 377.

[11] Lisa B. Lubow, "Artisans in Transition: Early Capitalist Development and the Carpenters of Boston, 1787–1837" (Ph.D. diss., UCLA, 1987), 190–224. As of the mid-1790s Kornblith estimates a ratio of masters to journeymen in leading Boston trades of 6:1 (carpentry), 5:1 (tailoring), and 3:1 (cooperage) ("Artisanal Response to Capitalist Transformation," 317–18).

[12] Kornblith, "Artisanal Response to Capitalist Transformation," 318; Sean Wilentz, *Chants Democratic: New York City and the Rise of the American Working Class, 1788–1850* (New York, 1984), 1–103; idem, "Artisan Origins of the American Working Class," *International Labor and Working Class History*, 19 (Spring 1981), 1–22; Salinger, *"To Serve Well and Faithfully,"* 137–71; Laurie, *Working People of Philadelphia*, 15–30. See also Amy Bridges, "Becoming American: The Working Classes in the United States before the Civil War," in Ira Katznelson and Aristide R. Zolberg, eds., *Working-Class Formation: Nineteenth-Century Patterns in Western Europe and the United States* (Princeton, 1986), 158–62.

[13] See, generally, Bruce Laurie, *Artisans into Workers: Labor in Nineteenth-Century America* (New York, 1989), 36–46; Sean Wilentz, "The Rise of the American Working Class, 1776–1877: A Survey," in J. Carroll Moody and Alice Kessler-Harris, eds., *Perspectives on American Labor History* (Dekalb, Ill., 1989), 86–7.

downward mobility toward wage labor as employees in the establishments of more secure masters or of the new entrepreneurs. Meanwhile, those completing apprenticeships found their opportunities for entering petty production ever more limited, while craft apprenticeship itself shed more and more of its fiduciary aspects, taking on in their place the appearance of cheap labor. All of this meant a rapidly growing journeyman work force made up of downwardly mobile independent craftsmen and younger men whose prospects of advancement to anything beyond wage labor (or in some trades piecemeal subcontracting) were poor and growing poorer, all of whom were thrown into competition with each other. In those circumstances friction over wages, prices, and hours – the parameters of this new commodified employment relationship – was inevitable. What was customary, what oppressive, what the appropriate measure, how standards should be set and enforced, all these became the object of intense and continuing scrutiny and debate among journeymen and masters, a debate increasingly characterized by resort to association on both sides and the attempted imposition of unilaterally determined standards on the trade as a whole throughout a given locality.[14]

The changes in social relations of production in the artisan trades that took place in the thirty years after 1790, and the "coercive, sometimes rude," and "unsentimental" trade unionism to which, on the journeymen's part, it gave rise, both replicated in important respects the experience of workers in the artisan trades in Britain over a rather longer period. In tactics and goals, in ideology, and indeed in some cases in membership, early American journeymen's associations reproduced English craft practice, helping to confirm the "striking dispositional and ideological similarities" between the American and English working classes at the outset of American industrialism and the existence of what has been called an "Anglo-American world of labor."[15]

The juridical responses they provoked likewise reproduced English practice. Beginning in 1806, American courts consciously seized upon English common law precedent to combat journeymen's associations. This resort to common law discourse

---

[14] Lubow, "Artisans in Transition," 190–224; Wilentz, *Chants Democratic*, 48–50; William J. Rorabaugh, *The Craft Apprentice: From Franklin to the Machine Age in America* (New York, 1988), 16–31. For illustration of the "mix" of the journeymen work force and the tensions which could erupt between older family men and young single men during disputes see Thomas Lloyd, *The Trial of the Boot and Shoe Makers of Philadelphia, on an Indictment for a Combination and Conspiracy to Raise Their Wages* (Philadelphia, 1806), 11–13 (testimony of Job Harrison) and 29–31 (testimony of William Logan). Note also the prosecution's and the court's references to the youth of the defendants and to the tensions between them and older journeymen in *Commonwealth v. Moore* (1827): see Marcus T. C. Gould, reporter, *Trial of Twenty-Four Journeymen Tailors, charged with Conspiracy, before The Mayor's Court of the City of Philadelphia, September Sessions, 1827* (Philadelphia, 1827), 55, 97, 162.

[15] Bridges, "Becoming American," 158; Wilentz, "Conspiracy, Power, and the Early Labor Movement," 578–9; Alfred F. Young, "English Plebeian Culture and Eighteenth-Century American Radicalism," in Margaret Jacob and James Jacob, eds., *The Origins of Anglo-American Radicalism* (London, 1984), 186, 200–4; Peter Linebaugh, "All the Atlantic Mountains Shook," in Geoff Eley and William Hunt, *Reviving the English Revolution: Reflections and Elaborations on the Work of Christopher Hill* (London, 1988), 193–219. See also Mary Roys Baker, "Anglo-Massachusetts Trade Union Roots, 1130–1790," *Labor History*, 14, 3 (Summer 1973), 352–96.

by American courts, however, was far more controversial in its implications than it ever was in England. In the context of the Revolution, the courts' mobilization of conspiracy doctrine amounted to an assertion of a unique and independent sovereign heritage for themselves outside the bounds of the institutions created in the wake of the breach with Britain.

CONSPIRACY AS A CRIME

The most important characteristic of English journeymen's associations, at least insofar as their encounters with the law were concerned, was that their practices were outgrowths of an ancient corporate tradition of craft government originating in the thirteenth-century guilds' control of work and trade. Essential elements in the "profoundly collective world" of medieval England's society of estates, the guilds were "communal and self-governing groups" that controlled production and trade in a given locality, say a town or borough, in the interests of the member–inhabitants.[16] Between the thirteenth and eighteenth centuries these communitarian origins were gradually obscured as the guilds underwent a continuous institutional evolution brought about by the effects on them of two long-term processes: first, the development of a conception of the state centered on the Crown and the accompanying efforts of the Crown and its agents to "reinvent" already-established group entities – boroughs, guilds, and so forth – as creations of royal prerogative through the issuance to them of franchises or charters affirming their rules and legitimating their existence; and, second, the growth of commerce, which brought about a continuous internal differentiation of wealth, interest, and organizational form.[17]

---

[16] Colin A. Cooke, *Corporation, Trust, and Company: An Essay in Legal History* (Manchester, 1950), 19–50; Susan Reynolds, "The Idea of the Corporation in Western Christendom before 1300," in J. A. Guy and H. G. Beale, eds., *Law and Social Change in British History* (London, 1984), 32. See also Susan Reynolds, *Kingdoms and Communities in Western Europe, 900–1300* (Oxford, 1984).

[17] See, generally, George Unwin, *Industrial Organization in the Sixteenth and Seventeenth Centuries* (Oxford, 1904); Robert A. Leeson, *Travelling Brothers: The Six Centuries' Road from Craft Fellowship to Trade Unionism* (London, 1979), 23–99; Stephen C. Yeazell, *From Medieval Group Litigation to the Modern Class Action* (New Haven, 1987), 38–159. In Yeazell's view a powerful centralized royal state was slow to appear in England, leading him to conclude that at least prior to the late sixteenth century the state was too weak seriously to contemplate a "grant" theory of group personality. Hence he interprets Crown behavior as an attempt to oversee the exercise of particular powers rather than to control the legal existence of groups. Yeazell's view of the early English state, however, contrasts quite markedly with that of John Brewer, who argues that an effective system of centralized royal administration, law, and governance was in place by the thirteenth century. "An emergent national identity became associated with a single, powerful ruler. Authority was concentrated and public; particularism harnessed or eclipsed" (*The Sinews of Power: War, Money, and the English State, 1688–1783* [New York, 1989], 3–5). To the extent that Brewer is right, Yeazell's conclusions on the Crown's failure to embrace a grant theory of the group may require restatement. The difference between them, however, may be no more than a creature of two different perspectives on state power, the one very much "top–down" (Brewer), the other "bottom – up" (Yeazell). On the development of national control by the Crown see also Cooke, *Corporation, Trust, and Company*, 21, 29–35.

The first process is of considerable importance, for it suggests that distinctions between legal and illegal trade combinations came to be erected not on the basis of what they did so much as whether what they did had been sanctioned or not. "No person should make congregations, alliances or covins of the people, privily or openly," declared the mayor of London in 1383 ("on behalf of the King"); and "those belonging to the trades, more than other men, should not, *without leave of the mayor*, make congregations, conventicles nor assemblies, alliances, confederacies or conspiracies, or obligations to bind men together."[18] Trade combinations exercising without leave powers claimed by the king to be within his grant were per se a challenge to royal prerogative.[19] Sanctioned combinations, likewise, were subject to the loss of their corporate privileges should they engage in illicit activities.[20] Both issues were addressed in the Bill of Conspiracies of Victuallers and Handicraftsmen of Edward VI (1548). The bill punished victuallers who should "conspire, covenant, promise or make any Oaths, that they shall not sell their Victuals but at certain prices," and also "Artificers, Workmen or Labourers" who should "conspire, covenant, or promise together, or make any Oaths, that they shall not make or do their Works but at a certain Price or Rate, or shall not enterprize or take upon them to finish that another hath begun, or shall do but a certain Work in a Day, or shall not work but at certain Hours and Times." It also made express provision, however, that if "any such Conspiracy, Covenant or Promise . . . be had and made by any Society, Brotherhood or Company of any Craft, Mystery or Occupation of the Victuallers above mentioned," in addition to the punishments appointed by the statute the offending corporation would immediately be dissolved.[21]

This link between conspiracy and challenge to royal authority appears in the common law of conspiracy as first explicitly articulated. Historians have tended to argue that the crime of conspiracy was a creature of the statutes of the late thirteenth century, notably Edward I's Ordinance of Conspirators of 1293 (clarified 1305).[22] Sufficient instances of concerted activity stimulating accusations of conspiracy can be found prior to the late thirteenth century, however, to justify a degree

---

[18] Quoted in Leeson, *Travelling Brothers*, 41 (emphasis supplied).

[19] Yeazell, *From Medieval Group Litigation to the Modern Class Action*, 67, 75–9.

[20] One of the earliest recorded instances of this involved a royal prosecution of a guild on a writ of conspiracy. See G. O. Sayles, "The Dissolution of a Gild at York in 1306," *English Historical Review*, 55, 217 (Jan. 1940), 83–98.

[21] Anno 2 & 3 Edw. VI, c. 15 (1548), An Act Touching Victuallers and Handicraftsmen, in John Raithby, ed., *The Statutes at Large of England and of Great Britain* (London, 1811), 2:281–2. It is worth noting that this statute actually attempted to render null and void corporate oversight of the employment of handicraftsmen altogether, but the Crown was unable to sustain this position and that section of the statute was repealed the following year. See Anno 3 & 4 Edw. VI, c. 20 (1549), An Act Touching the Repeal of a Certain Branch of an Act passed in the last Session of this Parliament, concerning Victuallers and Artificers, in Raithby, ed., *Statutes at Large*, 296.

[22] Anno 21 Edw. I, st. 2 (1293), De Conspiratoribus Ordinatio, and Anno 33 Edw. I, st. 2 (1305), Diffinitio De Conspiratoribus, both in Raithby, ed., *Statutes at Large*, 143, 164–5. And see R. S. Wright, *The Law of Criminal Conspiracies and Agreements* (Philadelphia, 1887), 5–6; Percy H. Winfield, *The History of Conspiracy and Abuse of Legal Procedure* (Cambridge, 1921), 29–37; David Harrison, *Conspiracy as a Crime and as a Tort in English Law* (London, 1924), 3–12.

of skepticism on this.[23] Attention should instead focus on how those statutes reinvented the offense. As defined in the Ordinance of Conspirators, conspiracy was given the particular coloration of unlawful combination "to hinder or pervert the administration of justice."[24] Justice here meant the king's justice: conspirators were those who combined unlawfully to abuse the procedures of the royal courts, and hence the authority of the Crown itself.[25] Thus, when we find unsanctioned trade combinations – or unsanctioned actions of sanctioned trade combinations – rather quickly becoming entangled in the law of conspiracy, we can interpret this as at least in part the outcome of attempts by the Crown to make itself the fountainhead of legitimate authority wherever, and by whomever, exercised and the arbiter of whether group authority has been exercised legitimately or not.[26]

The second process, of continuous institutional change in the modes of organization pursued by the craft communities, is closely related to the first and is of equal significance in explaining the relationship between state sanctioning of the exercise of concerted authority and the origins of journeymen's conspiracy prosecutions. During the fourteenth century, the fraternal craft guilds of England (the successors of the original merchant guilds) began to reestablish themselves as chartered craft companies under the aegis of municipal civil authority. In the process they formalized significant distinctions of status, function, and wealth that had already begun to emerge in the craft communities by creating "liveries" of merchant traders and larger craft masters distinct from the "yeomanries" of smaller masters, journeymen, and covenant servants, who made up the major part of the craft's work force. "By 1500 most of the new companies were divided into livery and yeomanry sections, with the new charters conferring 'perpetual succession' of the craft leadership, not on the masters as a body but on the richer section of

---

[23] Hampton L. Carson, *The Law of Criminal Conspiracies and Agreements As Found in the American Cases* (Philadelphia, 1887), 95–9; James W. Bryan, "The Development of the English Law of Conspiracy," in *Johns Hopkins University Studies in Historical and Political Science*, ser. 27, 4 (Apr. 1909), 9–11. As Victoria Hattam has stressed, American courts desirous of maintaining their access to the common law as an independent basis for authoritative decision making in the early republic had a vital interest in finding that the crime had prestatutory origins (*Labor Visions and State Power*, Chapter 2).

[24] Bryan, "Development of the English Law of Conspiracy," 11.

[25] As J. R. Pole notes, the common law originated "as the law that was common to the whole kingdom of England in the twelfth century when Henry II strove to extend royal authority throughout his realms at the assizes of Clarendon in 1166 and Northampton in 1176" (*The Pursuit of Equality in American History* [Berkeley, 1978], 16). See also Frederick W. Maitland, *The Constitutional History of England* (Cambridge, 1950), 18–23. In the case of the York conspiracy prosecution of 1306, the guild was held to have flouted royal authority by creating its own court to hear disputes among members and by proposing to act as a litigative entity (the members agreeing to maintain each other) in suits involving members against nonmembers. Its members were also found to have schemed to avoid their fair burden of taxation. See Sayles, "The Dissolution of a Gild at York," 85–7, 89. Abuse of royal authority remained a consistent theme. See, e.g., *R. v. Starling et al.*, 83 E.R. 331 (1665), 1164–5, 1167–8, 1179–80. Resort to the so-called Villainous Judgment to punish conspirators also carries with it this connotation in that the villainous judgment was representative of the Crown's power to deny legal personality to a subject. See Harrison, *Conspiracy as a Crime and as a Tort*, 9–10.

[26] For examples see Raymond W. Postgate, *The Builders' History* (London, 1923), 4; and above, nn. 21 and 25. Yeazell notes that Edward I was "the king most resolute in challenging the franchises of his subjects" (*From Medieval Group Litigation to the Modern Class Action*, 68).

them."[27] The distinction had profound strategic as well as status implications: The livery concentrated on the development of devices (notably the seven-year apprenticeship, three-year waiting periods after apprenticeship, and high upset fees) that would limit entry to mastership and inhibit entry to the livery, while the yeomanry attempted to safeguard its interests by strenuously pursuing the traditional tasks of craft government, militantly exercising charter rights to search out illegal products and illegally employed strangers and apprentices.[28]

In all the craft companies, the yeomanry's attempts to use the powers of the company charter to exclude intruders and to compel all the company's masters to respect the rules meant increasing conflict with the "non-manufacturing merchants and bigger craft masters who now controlled the top layer of city company organisation," whose interests lay increasingly in the evasion of limitations on production and employment. For them, by the late seventeenth century, "the usefulness of controls on the trade . . . was at an end."[29] The result was a period of rapid change in the crafts. In the Merchant Taylors' Company, for example, the yeomanry's determination to exercise the right of search led to a complete split between yeomanry and livery in 1696, the departure altogether of the livery merchants, and the fragmentation of the remainder of the craft into antagonistic combinations of master tailors and journeymen. The same process occurred in other crafts too, producing by the mid-eighteenth century a steady undercurrent of disputation across a broad front.[30]

Throughout the eighteenth century one of the most striking characteristics of the activities of the new separate journeymen's organizations was their continued assertion of the corporate rights of the traditional craft company as previously articulated by the company yeomanries: control of the availability of labor through regulation of the proportion of apprentices to journeymen; maintenance of houses of call and control of the movements of "interlopers," "strangers," or "foreigners"; and the right of search for and suppression of "illegal" goods and shops. Indeed, it was precisely the continued articulation of such pretensions which prompted attacks on journeymen's organizations as unlawful combinations. Take, for example, the Proclamation Against Combinations of Woollen Weavers issued in February 1718, which condemned as conspirators the "great numbers of Woolcombers and Weavers in several parts of the Kingdom [who have] lately formed themselves into lawless Clubs and Societies which ha[ve] illegally presumed to use a Common Seal, and to act as Bodies Corporate, by making and unlawfully conspiring to execute certain Bylaws

---

[27] Leeson, *Travelling Brothers*, 46. See also Unwin, *Industrial Organization*, 57–61. Forkosch ("Doctrine of Criminal Conspiracy," 311–12) suggests that yeomanry organizations within the chartered craft companies were treated as unlawful concerts of serving men. Leeson argues that the sections of the Act Touching Victuallers and Handicraftsmen (1548) aimed at handicraftsmen were in fact designed to combat associations of serving men within the companies (51).

[28] Leeson, *Travelling Brothers*, 41–58.

[29] Ibid., 75. See also J. R. Kellett, "The Breakdown of Gild and Corporation Control over the Handicraft and Retail Trade in London," *Economic History Review*, 10 (1958), 381–94.

[30] On the tailors see F. W. Galton, ed., *Select Documents Illustrating the History of Trade Unionism: The Tailoring Trade* (London, 1896), xiii–xxvii. In general see Leeson, *Travelling Brothers*, 59–78.

or Orders, whereby they pretend to determine who ha[s] a right to the Trade, what and how many Apprentices and Journeymen each man should keep at once, together with the prices of all their Manufactures, and the manner and materials of which they should be wrought." The proclamation called for putting the 1548 Bill of Conspiracies of Victuallers and Handicraftsmen in execution "against all such as should unlawfully confederate and combine for the purposes above mentioned in particular, or for any other illegal Purposes, contrary to the Tenour" of the said bill.[31] Seven years later, a woolcombers club in Alton, Hampshire, was prosecuted for exercising "unlawful" authority by presuming "to act as a Body corporate . . . electing two Supervisors and a Book keeper, using a common Seal, and making By Laws, or Orders, by which they pretend to determine who hath a right to the Woolcombers Trade, how many Apprentices each master should keep at one time, and who is qualified to take them." The following year Parliament sought to give teeth to the 1718 proclamation by passing An Act to Prevent Unlawful Combinations of Workmen Employed in the Woollen Manufactures, and for Better Payment of their Wages.[32]

As the 1718 proclamation tends to show, "conspiracy" was invoked as a charge against journeymen's organizations because of their bare assertion of concerted regulatory authority unsanctioned by the Crown. It was, indeed, this "outlaw" status that, even distinct from anything they actually did, enabled public authority to label journeymen's groups "unlawful" or "lawless" combinations. As such, as the organic world of medieval and early modern British crafts dissolved into warring factions during the eighteenth century, the country saw a rapid, if piecemeal, expansion in statutory condemnation of journeymen's organizations for their attempts to continue unilaterally the corporate traditions that had earlier structured intracraft social and economic relations.[33]

---

[31] G. D. H. Cole and A. W. Filson, eds., *British Working Class Movements: Select Documents, 1789–1875* (London, 1951), 86–7. Earlier, in 1707, the clothiers of Bristol had complained to the House of Commons that their journeymen had formed a confederacy to regulate apprenticeship and the employment of strangers and had elected "supervisors." See Robert W. Malcolmson, "Workers' Combinations in Eighteenth Century England," in Jacob and Jacob, eds., *Origins of Anglo-American Radicalism*, 149–61, at 160, n. 39.

[32] Anno 12 Geo. I, c. 34 (1726). See also Malcolmson, "Workers' Combinations in Eighteenth Century England," 157. Complaints about the woolcombers' corporate pretensions continued. In 1741, for example, it was asserted that the woolcombers had "for a Number of years past erected themselves into a Sort of Corporation (tho' without a Charter) . . . [and] gave Laws to their masters, as also to themselves." See [T. Cowper], *A Short Essay upon Trade in General* (London, 1741), 40. Similar complaints were made throughout the century about other groups of journeymen who confederated, combined, and conspired to promulgate by-laws for the regulation of their respective trades. According to a Manchester assize judge in 1759, such confederacies gave rise to "the greatest Confusion betwixt the lower Class of People and their Superiors, in all Trades and Occupations, in every Manufactory, and in every Employ. If Inferiors are to prescribe to their Superiors, if the Foot aspire to be the Head, if every Man is aiming to follow the Evil of his ways without Restraint or Controul, to what End are Laws enacted?" (quoted in Malcolmson, "Workers' Combinations in Eighteenth Century England," 157).

[33] On British statutory developments during the eighteenth century see John V. Orth, "English Combination Acts of the Eighteenth Century," *Law and History Review*, 5, 1 (Spring 1987), 175–211; idem, "The English Combination Laws Reconsidered," in Douglas Hay and Francis Snyder, eds., *Labour,*

The whole issue of conspiracy, however, was one played out in two universes of doctrine: the common law of the courts as well as statute. The ideology of sovereignty expressed in the attempt to reinvent all concerted action as the grant of prerogative and in the condemnation of that which was not authorized as an affront to prerogative had its parallel in the common law doctrine of per se conspiracy, which treated as criminal the act of combining in pursuit of any purpose deemed unlawful, irrespective of whether anything was done to realize the unlawful purpose.[34] What was an unlawful purpose was of course a matter for the courts. The parallel lay in the clear implication of the common law doctrine that concerted activity in itself was sufficiently controversial to require a capacity in the court to punish it as a distinct offense where unauthorized – that the gist of the crime was the conspiracy itself. It may also, however, be detected in the institutional circumstances in which the doctrine came into being, for per se conspiracy first saw the light of day in the Court of Star Chamber, an institution that was an outgrowth of the king's council and thus far more overtly an expression of royal power than the traditional common law courts of King's Bench and Common Pleas.[35]

Per se conspiracy originated with *The Poulterers' Case* in 1611. At issue was a confederacy falsely to accuse an innocent; that is, to deceive the king's courts. The issue as posed appeared to be squarely within the Plantagenet definition of conspiracy as concerted action "falsely and maliciously to indite or cause to be indited." Because no indictment had been procured, however, the defendants argued that their concert was not a conspiracy. Star Chamber disagreed, finding that although a writ of conspiracy could not issue unless the party seeking the writ had been indicted and lawfully acquitted, the court's capacity to proceed against the unlawful concerted action was unimpaired. "A false conspiracy betwixt divers persons shall be punished, although nothing be put in execution."[36] This was a conclusion of no little significance, as David Harrison explained some years ago:

Law, and Crime: An Historical Perspective (London, 1987), 123–49. See also C. R. Dobson, *Masters and Journeymen: A Prehistory of Industrial Relations, 1717–1800* (London, 1980), 121–50; John Rule, *The Experience of Labour in Eighteenth Century English Industry* (New York, 1981), 147–77, 188–90. It is important to note that the legal treatment of combinations in general became increasingly controversial following the South Sea Bubble. See Cooke, *Corporation, Trust, and Company*, 80–94. See also Yeazell, *From Medieval Group Litigation to the Modern Class Action*, 160–96.

[34] Sayre, "Criminal Conspiracy," 399.

[35] On Star Chamber's jurisdiction see Yeazell, *From Medieval Group Litigation to the Modern Class Action*, 125–31. Yeazell notes that beginning in the late fifteenth century, Star Chamber appeared to become the home for cases involving groups formerly heard routinely in the more traditional common law courts. More important, the nature of the hearings before Star Chamber was that of "inquiry into the causes of unrest," attesting to the increasingly controversial character before the law of assertions of group status.

[36] 77 E.R. 813, at 814. The court's reasoning is instructive. Because a conspiracy is forbidden by law, conspirators shall answer for it, even though the false design – the proof of the conspiracy – is never executed. The party offended against here is the state, not the innocent. The innocent cannot obtain a writ because he has not actually been damaged. But the state still obtains *its* remedy, in effect on the grounds that it is damaged simply by the existence of a confederacy which flouts its authority. "It is true that a writ of conspiracy lies not, unless the party is indicted, and *legitimo modo acquietatus*, for so are the words of the writ; but that a false conspiracy betwixt diverse persons shall be punished, although nothing be put in execution, is full and manifest in our books; and therefore in 27 Ass. p. 44 in the articles of

Once it was established that a conspiracy to indict falsely had been committed by the mere act of combination for that purpose, without any act in furtherance of the objects of the combination, it followed that nothing had been done which amounted to a complete crime under the statute, as it had always been interpreted. Therefore the agreement or act of combination must be in some sense criminal at common law. But if the agreement or combination to indict falsely was criminal at common law, there was no reason why other agreements containing some wrongful element should not also be criminal.[37]

In the wake of *The Poulterers' Case* the expansion of conspiracy proceeded on two fronts. First, what constituted conspiracy within its "traditional" narrow definition as abuse of legal procedure was subjected to progressively wider readings. Second, and far more significant, that definitional limitation was greatly relaxed, allowing "conspiracy" to be applied to any unlawful concerted action.[38] The importance of the latter is extreme indeed, for it coincided with a major expansion in the ambit of the criminal law, one proceeding throughout much of the seventeenth and eighteenth centuries and turning the courts in their own words into "custodes morum" of all the king's subjects. Originating in Star Chamber's championing of the Stuart monarchy's obsession with social order, and continued during the more sagacious balancing of parliamentary and monarchical claims to sovereignty by King's Bench, this steady widening of the social terrain subject to the sovereign's imprimatur exposed more and more realms of action to state oversight. Where action thus exposed was adjudged "contra bonos mores et decorum," it was held unlawful. And where that antagonism to the public good was adjudged to inhere in the unauthorized concurrence of several in promoting an otherwise innocuous outcome, the doctrine of criminal conspiracy was available to stamp it out simply by condemning the concert.[39]

Initially, the growth of this public sphere was relatively slow. Hence the expansion of conspiracy doctrine was correspondingly cautious. Where resort was had to it, however, the connection was explicit and overt. Thus in *R. v. Starling* (1665), where certain London brewers were convicted of a conspiracy for agreeing not to brew small beer for as long as it was subject to the excise, notwithstanding being found innocent of all acts alleged as in pursuit of that object, the case turned on the deleterious impact such an impoverishment of the excise would have had on the king's revenues. For the Crown it was argued that it was "an inevitable consequence

---

the charge of enquiry by the inquest in the King's Bench, there is a *nota*, that two were indicted of confederacy . . . and notwithstanding that nothing was supposed to be put in execution, the parties were forced to answer to it, because the thing is forbidden by the law."

[37] Harrison, *Conspiracy as a Crime and as a Tort*, 15.

[38] Ibid., 17–47.

[39] Sayre, "Criminal Conspiracy," 400–1. The sphere of activity "contra bonos mores et decorum" is basically that which Blackstone was later to define as 'such crimes and misdemeanors as more especially affect the common-wealth, or public polity of the kingdom," namely offences against public justice, public peace, public trade, the public health, and the public police or oeconomy. See William Blackstone, *Commentaries on the Laws of England* (Chicago, 1979), 4:127–75.

that the King must lose his rent where his fermors are depaupered; and although it may mitigate the matter, that the particulars are not found, yet it remains a great offence, and of publick concernment." The decision to uphold the conviction has been called "the origin of the view that a combination directed against the Government, or against the general public may be criminal."[40]

Yet even at this point a subtext with a far wider import may be detected: that "the very conspiracy to do a lawful act to the prejudice of a third person is enquirable and punishable," and thus, for example, that "the very conspiracy to raise the price of [a commodity] is punishable, or of any other merchandise."[41]

The key to this late seventeenth-century leap in conspiracy doctrine from vindication of public injuries to protection of all third persons is the parallel and related growth of the doctrine of restraint of trade. To some extent, the development of restraint of trade doctrine, like incorporation, may be seen as an expression of the state's attempts to reinvent society and economy as consequences of its legitimating authority rather than as historically autonomous of it. In this formulation, what exists is, on the one hand, the assemblage of individual economic bargainers and, on the other, the overseer state that observes the behavior of all bargainers and protects the "community" interest. Because the state supplies the bargainers with their legal identities as bargainers, together with all the transactional mechanisms that they employ to bargain, it can be said to have successfully "invented" them. Just as seventeenth- and eighteenth-century criminal law helped establish the state as sole custodian of its citizens' social behavior, so restraint of trade was a powerful means of establishing the state as sole custodian of their economic behavior. An echo of this is preserved in modern times: "the doctrine of restraint of trade is part of the wider rule of the relation of contracts to public policy. Legal public policy comprises the principles under which the freedom of contract or private dealings is restricted by law for the good of the community. And in general terms contracts are regarded

---

[40] 83 E.R. 1168; Harrison, *Conspiracy as a Crime and as a Tort*, 25. In *R. v. Daniell*, 87 E.R. 856 (1704), Lord Chief Justice Holt held that the decision in *Starling* had been an exception because the offense was "directly of a publick nature, and levelled at the Government; and the git of the offence was its influence on the public, and not the conspiracy, for that must be put in execution before it is a conspiracy." But in his judgment in *Starling* Justice Windham had stated that "I do conceive the defendants found guilty of confederacy, as in *The Poulterers Case*; also the ends for which these crimes are alledged to be done are discharged, as the defeating the King of his customs, and pulling down their houses, except only the depauperating of the customers, whom I think publick persons, and so they appear to us by their imployment set forth in the declaration, and in this respect we ought to aggravate the fine, as if the end were to beat a sheriff as a private person, yet he being a publick officer, it will aggravate the offence. I agree that general confederacy without designment to publick or private end, is punishable by action upon the case . . . or by indictment . . . and therefore I do conceive here is enough found to give judgment against them for a confederacy, by their assembling together, their consultation and conspiracy, which is as much a false alliance, as if they had bound themselves by oath" (1179).
[41] 83 E.R. 1164–5. The assertion was not directly addressed in *Starling*, although see Windham's judgment excerpted in n. 40. In *R. v. Daniell*, however, Chief Justice Holt specifically declined to rule out such an extension of the doctrine. See also Winfield, *History of Conspiracy*, 114–5.

as being in restraint of trade when their fulfilment would be injurious to the community."[42]

This, however, does not provide a full account of the seventeenth century's restraint of trade doctrine. The doctrine's earliest origins may be detected, rather, in confrontations arising in the process of reinventing the society of estates as a "ruled" society. Claims to the exercise of organic powers of self-rule over significant sectors of the economy by the descendants of guilds, claims that the state had theretofore dealt with by recognizing the self-asserted right to act organically as a corporate privilege, were increasingly controversial. This is what restraint of trade doctrine began to deal with: "In the seventeenth century the rule was wider than contract. It was also applied continuously to corporations, particularly in their relations with the general public outside their membership. . . . a corporation, whether trading or municipal, could not limit the freedom of trade of its members or non-members. By-laws purporting to do so were void."[43]

Restraint of trade doctrine was thus one of the means by which the state sought to advance its project of voiding autonomous areas of economic self-rule. Like conspiracy doctrine it expressed the sovereign state's antagonism to unauthorized concerted action. Indeed, from this perspective common law protection of unlawfully prejudiced third persons may be seen as simply the common law protection of the state's own public aspect writ large.[44] In light of this one may conclude that the much-maligned William Hawkins was after all simply reflecting the leading edge of contemporary thought in concluding, in his *Treatise of the Pleas of the Crown* (1716), that "all confederacies whatsoever, wrongfully to prejudice a third Person, are highly criminal at Common Law."[45]

R. v. JOURNEYMEN-TAYLORS OF CAMBRIDGE

These distinct but related paths – the decaying society of estates, the growth of sovereign power and a "public" sphere, the state's corresponding suspicion of unauthorized collective action in society and economy – together help explain *R.*

---

[42] Cooke, *Corporation, Trust, and Company*, 62.

[43] Ibid., 63–5. Kellett, "Breakdown of Gild and Corporation Control," 383–5. Winfield concludes on the basis of his examination of the Parliament Rolls, as distinct from court records, that from the fourteenth century "by far the commonest use of conspiracy and confederacy is in connection with combinations to restrain or to interfere with trade. . . . In fact, the prevailing idea was that trade combinations when they interfered with prices were an economic evil to be stamped out by the state" (*History of Conspiracy*, 111). On the changes in the pattern of "rule" alluded to here see Gianfranco Poggi, *The Development of the Modern State: A Sociological Introduction* (Stanford, 1978); Donald W. Hanson, *From Kingdom to Commonwealth: The Development of Civic Consciousness in English Political Thought* (Cambridge, Mass., 1970).

[44] Yeazell notes that by the early seventeenth century the state had "seized a monopoly in ratifying the recognition of groups," forcing "future groups that would seek litigative recognition first to seek state approval" and rendering suspect "any group that had not done so" (*From Medieval Group Litigation to the Modern Class Action*, 113).

[45] William Hawkins, *A Treatise of the Pleas of the Crown* (London, 1716), 1:90.

v. Journeymen-Taylors of Cambridge (1721), in which the common law of conspiracy was visited upon associated workers for the first time. Here the "yeomen journeymen taylors" had their attempts to sustain a claim to the exercise of self-regulatory trade customs, in this case wage regulation, dismissed as conspiracy. In London, where the handicraft trades had long been governed by explicit corporate privileges of self-regulation, the final collapse of guild and corporation consensus on the desirability of self-regulation in the tailoring trade late in the seventeenth century had left the company's yeomanry of serving tailors and masters at bitter odds over the continued exercise of craft privileges. The eventual outcome had been the act of 7 Geo. I, st. 1, c. 13 (1721), the first tailors' combination act, which substituted a structure of public regulation for the exploded guild and corporate by-laws.[46] This was the first of many eighteenth-century combination acts, which, piecemeal, effected similar substitutions of public regulation for decayed corporate regulation in the corporate handicraft trades or established de novo public regulation in industries beyond the corporate handicrafts where competing structures of self-regulation were threatening to arise on the crest of waves of artisan discontent. In the Cambridge case it is not clear whether the tailors were attempting to *retain* old established corporate practices or unilaterally *establish* new self-interested regulatory practices, but in either case they were outside the reach of the statute and there was no attempt to prosecute them on the basis of the statute. Rather the issue was whether they had the right to agree among themselves to refuse to work except at the wages they stipulated. The court's answer was that so to agree was a conspiracy, and "a conspiracy of any kind is illegal, although the matter about which they conspired might have been lawful for them, or any of them, to do, if they had not conspired to do it."[47] No less than the London brewers, they were an illegitimate collectivity, an affront to the public.[48]

[46] On this and subsequent eighteenth-century legislation see Orth, "English Combination Acts," 175–211.

[47] *R. v. Journeymen-Taylors of Cambridge*, 88 E.R. 9 (1721). It was not "for the refusing to work" that they were indicted, the court stressed, "but for conspiring." See also Orth, "English Combination Laws Reconsidered," 138.

[48] See also *R. v. Hammond and Webb*, 170 E.R. 508 (1799). In *R. v. Eccles*, 168 E.R. 240 (1783), an appeal against a conviction for conspiring to impoverish another by entering into a combination not to work under certain prices, Lord Mansfield stated that "the offence does not consist in doing the acts by which the mischief is effected, for they may be perfectly indifferent, but in conspiring with a view to effect the intended mischief by any means. The illegal combination is the gist of the offence" (241). In *R. v. Daniell*, 87 E.R. 856 (1704), Justice Powell offered an opinion which implied that any combination which manifested a tendency to interfere with the relation of master and servant was indictable as a conspiracy, "for it becomes a publick concern, that they should be kept in good order." In support he cited *The Poulterers' Case*, "where bare conspiracy without more was held indictable" (857). The majority, however, held that an indictment would not lie in this case (for enticing an apprentice to leave his master's service) "for it is of a private nature, and to the prejudice of a single person only." For a record of indictments for conspiracy arising from labor disputes in eighteenth-century England see Dobson, *Masters and Journeymen*, 127–9. Dobson lists thirty indictments occurring between 1720 and 1800, one-third scattered between 1720 and 1780, the remaining two-thirds concentrated in the last two decades of the century.

Conspiracy was thus one major doctrinal manifestation of the state-created and state-policed public sphere in the process of formation in England in the seventeenth and eighteenth centuries. In origin expressing no more than the Crown's desire to safeguard its courts – its initial foray into state building – from abuse, conspiracy quickly became a useful means of signifying the illegitimacy of unlicensed forms of collective power, employed in particular in condemnation of illicit concerts whether within or beyond the realm of guild government.[49] As the conception of a state governing a realm of public action through the assertion of a direct sovereign power over subjects replaced the medieval conception of a society of estates – of cooperating organic entities (partial or dual sovereignties) coordinated by a ruler – the role of conspiracy grew until it became one of the principal legal mechanisms arbitrating the legitimacy of collective action.[50]

CONCLUSION

The foregoing account of the origins of journeymen's combinations and of conspiracy doctrine in English law is of considerable assistance in helping us to understand the ancestry both of the "coercive, rude and unsentimental" unionism of early nineteenth-century America and of the hostile reception it provoked. Clearly there were important links between English and American practice on both sides of the issue. Although opponents described early American combinations as "alien" or "foreign" institutions in order to disparage and delegitimate them, for example, it remains clear on the evidence of the available conspiracy trial transcripts that English, Irish, and Scottish migrants were active participants in the early American labor movement. One may presume that they modeled their activities in part on their old-country experience, for the tactics of early American journeymen's associations clearly reveal corporative pretensions similar to those of English craft combinations. Attempts to exercise a corporate discipline over the craft through rights of search, involuntary membership, and control over interlopers and "strangers" are well evidenced in the trial transcripts. These, like tramping networks and houses of call,

---

[49] The allegation of conspiracy, of course, was used to express a social as well as a legal illegitimacy. Socially as well as legally, that is, combinations could be divided into the licit and the illicit, the virtuous and the immoral. Note, e.g., the 1798 toast of a "Society for Prosecuting Felons, Forgers etc." as recorded by David Philips: "This Society and may there always be good men to associate while there are bad men to conspire" ("Good Men to Associate and Bad Men to Conspire: Associations for the Prosecution of Felons in England, 1760–1860," in Douglas Hay and Francis Snyder, eds., *Policing and Prosecution in Britain, 1750–1850* [Oxford, 1989], 113–70, at 113). On the distinction between virtuous and illegitimate collectivities see Anthony Woodiwiss, *Rights v. Conspiracy: A Sociological Essay on the History of Labor Law in the United States* (New York, 1990), 22–3.

[50] Nor did matters rest with the regulation of collective action affecting the public interest. Thus early in the nineteenth century one begins to encounter expressions of concern among certain of the judiciary that conspiracy doctrine was being employed to oversee all forms of collective action whether a public interest could be shown or not. See, e.g., Lord Ellenborough's opinion in *R. v. Turner*, 104 E.R. 357 (1811). See also *R. v. Jones*, 110 E.R. 485 (1832). This matter is taken up in Chapter 5.

speak to a common Anglo-American heritage.[51] Similarly, the realms of doctrine invoked by American prosecutors and courts were, as we shall see, those already partially developed by their English counterparts.

At the same time, however, the debate over the legal status of journeymen's associations in the new republic was distinctive in two major and related respects. First, it was a debate decisively shaped (as no debate in England could have been) by the particular circumstances of the American Revolution and the battles of the postrevolutionary era over the future course of the republic, battles pitting against each other two contesting paradigms for postrevolutionary society, one premised upon the rapid extension of democratic politics, the other upon its restraint. Indeed, well before journeymen's combinations began to appear before the courts, these battles had already made the status of self-constituted groups a hotly contested issue. The oppositional Democratic-Republican clubs, which attracted increasing Federalist ire during the 1790s, for example, were assailed as "self-created societies" and usurpers of sovereignty. Whereas to their proponents the clubs were perfectly legitimate "combinations of men," recalling the revolutionary era's communal *police* fashioned through the patriot movement's multiple committees and conventions, to their antagonists they were dangerous unlicensed aggregations of power, outlaw collectivities that had no place in the scheme of things appropriate to an orderly republic and that "warred from the outside against the total structure of American society."[52] When journeymen's combinations began to fall foul of conspiracy indictments during the following decade, the cases traversed very similar territory, prosecutors and courts condemning the journeymen's associations as illegitimate encroachments of unlicensed power upon republican institutions, while the journeymen themselves held out their associations as fitting representations of revolutionary republicanism – a communal local police of their crafts dedicated to safeguarding the artisan, "the very axis of society," from a debased dependency – and condemned the attempt to eliminate them as an affront to the democratic principle of popular sovereignty.[53]

[51] See, e.g., Lloyd, *Trial of the Boot and Shoemakers of Philadelphia*, 9, 11, 14, 30–1, 67; William Sampson, reporter, *Trial of the Journeymen Cordwainers of the City of New York; For a Conspiracy to Raise Their Wages* (New York, 1810), 106, 167–8; *Thompsonville Carpet Manufacturing Company v. Taylor* (1836), in Commons et al., eds., *Documentary History*, vol. 4 (supp.), 29, 32, 34, 38–9; Tomlins, *The State and the Unions*, 38; Quimby, "Cordwainers Protest," 83–7; Young, "English Plebeian Culture," 185–212. For a contrary view see Fink, "Labor, Liberty, and the Law," 908–9.

[52] Robert H. Wiebe, *The Opening of American Society: From the Adoption of the Constitution to the Eve of Disunion* (New York, 1984), 73–4. See also Thomas P. Slaughter, *The Whiskey Rebellion: Frontier Epilogue to the American Revolution* (New York, 1986), 221. On the prerevolutionary patriot movement see Barbara Clark Smith, "The Politics of Price Control in Revolutionary Massachusetts, 1774–1780" (Ph.D. diss., Yale University, 1983); Gary B. Nash, "Artisans and Politics in Eighteenth Century Philadelphia," in Jacob and Jacob, eds., *Origins of Anglo-American Radicalism*, 162–82, esp. 175–6. Before the Revolution, of course, it was the British who denounced collective action. It is worth recalling Governor Thomas Hutchinson's remark in October 1769 that "a thousand acts of Parliament will never have the least force, if combinations to prevent the operation of them and to sacrifice all who will conform to them are tolerated" (quoted in Smith, "Politics of Price Control," 106).

[53] Howard B. Rock (*Artisans of the New Republic: The Tradesmen of New York City in the Age of*

By the 1830s, the contest between these two irreconcilable positions had become marked by levels of vehemence and rancor unknown in earlier years or – on this issue at least – in other places. In this light, much of the considerable significance historians have rightly accorded *Commonwealth v. Hunt* can be attributed to the capstone contribution the decision in that case made to the search begun during the 1830s in New York and Pennsylvania for a means of reconceptualizing both labor combination *and* the character of the prevailing political economy in a manner allowing their accommodation with each other. It is important to note, however, that the courts' capacity to join in such an accommodation was compromised by the second distinctive feature of the American debate: the overtly political role which the courts themselves played in it. Having assumed for themselves a position of considerable prominence in the postrevolutionary polity, courts were led for much of the first half of the nineteenth century to debate criminal conspiracy in a manner couched far more self-consciously in the language of legitimate power and its exercise than was ever the case in England.[54] Before they could convincingly

Jefferson [New York, 1979], 279) comments, "Economic issues were clearly at the center of the journeymen–master disputes. Yet to see these conflicts, as most historians have, only as struggles for economic leverage, or as financial disputes with political parallels, would be to miss an important dimension. To the journeymen, more than the wage was in jeopardy; their very standing in society was at risk."

[54] The nearest English parallel was the case of *R. v. Marks*, 102 E.R. 557 (1802) (affirming the applicability to journeymen's combinations of stat. 37 Geo. III, c. 123, which prohibited the administration of oaths tending to promote mutiny and sedition and to seduce soldiers, sailors, and others from their duty and allegiance to the king, and which also generally prohibited the administration of any oath "to obey the orders or commands of any committee or body of men not lawfully constituted"). Here, Lawrence J. stated as part of a unanimous court of King's Bench that such combinations, "which strike at the root of the trade of the kingdom . . . beget a danger to the State itself to an extent beyond the power of the Government to repress" (560). See also *R. v. Loveless and Five Others*, 174 E.R. 119 (1834).

The parallels are more pronounced in Scottish juridical discourse. (Scotland was another polity in which the courts had assumed a major role as the embodiment of the state, although in the Scottish case, of course, this was largely by default, as a consequence of the dissolution in the previous century of the Edinburgh Parliament and the relocation of most of the organs of Scottish state power at Westminster.) In *Taylor's Case* (1808), Lord Justice-Clerk Hope argued that a combination to raise wages by the sudden striking of work was "a measure of a compulsive character, and implies a deliberate and mischievous purpose to distress the employer and the public" and more generally amounted to "an assumption of sovereign authority inasmuch as there is here an attempt to set up an arbitrary and uncontrollable dominion in the State, which shall enforce a thing, at its own pleasure, which the Legislature have never thought it advisable to attempt." Any association, he continued, "which aims at power or permanency, or proposes to do its work by means of such instruments, requires his Majesty's authority, and without it is downright usurpation" and "an interference with the rights of Government." See *Hume's Commentaries on the Laws of Scotland*, 3d ed. (Edinburgh, 1844), 1:494–5.

Taylor's Case did not result in a conviction, a majority of the court doubting that a combination per se could be found indictable without any allegation of overt acts of violence, intimidation, or extortion. The strong statement of the minority led, however, to the issue being retested in the subsequent cases of *Mackimmie* (1813), *Ferrier* (1813), *Wilson and Ross* (1813), and *Wilson and Banks* (1818), all reported at 1 Hume's Commentaries 495–6, in all of which it was held that a combination to compel an increase of wages by striking was an indictable conspiracy without necessity of further alleging overt acts in aggravation. "This new point of dittay seems, therefore, now to be thoroughly established," commented Hume, "and it furnishes another illustration of the character of our common law, and of its power to chastise, of its own native vigour, all wrongs and disorders, as the state of society brings them forth, which are found to be materially dangerous to the public welfare" (496).

represent themselves as entertaining a goal other than the simple suppression of combinations, American courts had to find some judicious means of distancing themselves somewhat from that former discourse. This distancing became the second element of their revised approach to the problem of labor conspiracy.

5

The American conspiracy cases

In [England], the laws against combinations of journeymen to raise wages, have very lately been repealed. It was assuredly anything but even-handed justice, which made it an offence for journeymen to combine to raise their wages, while masters might combine with impunity for the purpose of lowering wages. Yet, in this country, in Philadelphia, in the Cordwainer's case, tried before Mr. Recorder Levy, and in a late case in New York, the principles of the English acts of Parliament were adopted, and journeymen were found guilty of entering into such a combination. Probably the spirit of those decisions would be construed in this country to extend to combinations for an opposite purpose, among masters. But all these legislations and decisions are needless: let the masters and the journeymen settle their own bargains, and they will settle them much sooner than a court of law; which ought not to be resorted to unless in cases of breach of contract. . . . If it be worth the while of those who have the labour to supply, or the money to give, to assent to the terms proposed, they will do so. If not, what greater tyranny can there be than to force them?

Thomas Cooper, Lectures on the Elements of Political Economy

During the first half of the nineteenth century, labor combinations in at least six American states – Pennsylvania, Maryland, New York, Louisiana, Massachusetts, and Virginia – were the subject of indictment and prosecution for criminal conspiracy, comprising twenty-three known cases.[1] The first case occurred in 1806: No

---

[1] The full list of directly relevant cases and verdicts is *Commonwealth v. Pullis* (Pa. 1806), defendants convicted; *State v. Powley* (Md. 1809), defendants convicted, judgment suspended; *Baltimore Cordwainers* (Md. 1809), case dismissed; *People v. Melvin* (N.Y. 1809), defendants convicted; *People v. Melvin* (N.Y. 1811), defendants acquitted; *Pittsburgh Cordwainers* (Pa. 1814), settled before trial; *Commonwealth v. Morrow* (Pa. 1815), defendants convicted; *Commonwealth ex rel. Chew v. Carlisle* (Pa. 1821), case remanded; *People v. Trequier* (N.Y. 1823), defendants convicted; *Buffalo Tailors* (N.Y. 1824), defendants convicted; *Balize Pilots* (La. 1826), defendants acquitted; *Commonwealth v. Moore* (Pa. 1827), defendants convicted; *Commonwealth ex rel. Kennedy v. Marshall and Treillou* and *Commonwealth ex rel. Campbell v. O'Daniel* (Pa. 1829), cases continued; *State v. Pomeroy* (Md. 1829), defendants acquitted; *Chambersburg Shoemakers* (Pa. 1829), defendants convicted; *People v. Fisher* (N.Y. 1834), case dismissed and appealed; *People v. Fisher* (N.Y. 1835), dismissal reversed on appeal; *People v. Faulkner* (N.Y. 1836), defendants convicted; *Commonwealth v. Grinder* (Pa. 1836), defendants acquitted; *Philadelphia Coalheavers* (Pa. 1836), defendants acquitted; *People v. Cooper* (N.Y. 1836), defendants acquitted; *Thompsonville Carpet Manufacturing Company v. Taylor* (Conn. 1836), defendants acquitted; *Commonwealth v. Hunt* (Mass. 1840), defendants convicted, verdict appealed; *Commonwealth v. Hunt* (Mass. 1842), conviction reversed on appeal; *Commonwealth v. McConnell* (Pa. 1842),

colonial era prosecutions have even been discovered.[2] In most instances the defendants were convicted, although both indictments and the reasoning in justification of convictions varied considerably over time and from state to state. Conviction almost invariably meant local political controversy, for whether explicitly or not the arguments advanced in each case presented opposing theories of social order and disorder corresponding to political cleavages in early republican society, and the verdicts themselves stood as authoritative statements about the location and exercise of power in the new republic.

In the mid-1830s controversy over conspiracy prosecutions became acute. In each of the country's three most industrialized metropolitan areas (New York, Philadelphia, and Boston) the issue served as a major rallying point for movements of working people, spilling over metropolitan frontiers, merging momentarily in an assault upon the course of the American political economy in general and upon the law and the judiciary in particular. The upshot was a restatement of the application of criminal conspiracy doctrine to labor combinations that proceeded more or less simultaneously in each of the major eastern states and that tended to reproduce piecemeal the outcome achieved the previous decade in England through parliamentary action.[3] First, by routinizing access to the doctrine (by presenting it, in Francis

---

defendants convicted; *Lehigh Boatmen* (Pa. 1843), settled before trial; *Tredegar Iron Workers* (Va. 1847), case dismissed. My tally, reported in the text, does not include double counts in the case of appealed cases, nor does it include *Commonwealth v. Carlisle* (which involved master shoemakers) or *Thompsonville Carpet Manufacturing Company v. Taylor* (which was a civil suit).

[2] Richard B. Morris, *Government and Labor in Early America* (Boston, 1981), 205–7.

[3] See Chief Justice Shaw's statement to this effect in *Commonwealth v. Hunt*, 45 Mass. 111 (1842), at 132. After eighty years of legislation addressing individual trades and industries, the British Parliament passed the general combination acts of 1799 (39 Geo. III, c. 81) and 1800 (39 and 40 Geo. III, c. 106), which outlawed collective action in labor disputes and voided collective agreements, positing in their place "the paradigmatic employment contract . . . between individuals: one employer contracting for the services of one workman." The acts also ended the Tudor–Stuart policy of wage regulation by justices of the peace, substituting a new policy of arbitration. See John V. Orth, "English Combination Acts of the Eighteenth Century," *Law and History Review*, 5, 1 (Spring 1987), 175–211, at 195–208. These acts were, however, repealed in 1824 (5 Geo. IV, c. 95) on the ground, according to Joseph Hume, M.P., that "every law ought to be repealed which shackled any man in the free disposition of his labour, provided that free disposition did not interfere with any vital interest, and thereby endanger the political interest of the state." The 1824 act also sought to exempt from prosecution workmen combining "to obtain an advance or to fix the rate of wages, or to lessen or alter the hours or duration of the time of working, or to decrease the quantity of work, or to induce another to depart from his service before the end of the time or term for which he is hired, or to quit or return his work before the same shall be finished . . . or to regulate the mode of carrying on any manufacture, trade, or business, or the management thereof."

The 1824 act was itself repealed in 1825 by a Parliament acting in the shadow of a substantial increase in the incidence of strikes. Legislation was substituted (6 Geo. IV, c. 29) that "permitted common action in pursuit of common claims for wages and hours" but otherwise reinstated the common law of criminal conspiracy. The 1825 act allowed two limited exemptions from prosecution for criminal conspiracy: for workmen "[1] who shall meet together for the sole purpose of consulting upon and determining the rate of wages or prices, which the persons present at such meeting or any of them, shall require or demand for his or their work, or the hours or time for which he or they shall work . . . or [2] who shall enter into any agreement, verbal or written, among themselves" for the purpose of fixing the rates of pay or hours agreed. Otherwise the new act placed particular stress on conspiracy prosecution where workers in combination had resort to violence, threats, or intimidation in the course of a dispute, or resort to

B. Sayre's word, as a "predicable" discourse), courts sidestepped criticism of the conspiracy doctrine's arbitrariness. Second, by employing new and different metaphors of social and economic order, judicial authorities successfully suggested an alteration in their comprehension of their public role. Neither step reduced the conspiracy doctrine's potential or the courts' authority over its employment: Indeed, in restating criminal conspiracy the courts made it a more usable means of disciplining collective action. At the same time, by allowing explicitly that collective action per se was permissible and focusing attention instead on the nature and consequences of that action, the courts' restatement assisted in defusing the 1830s confrontation between working people and the judiciary, emptying the conspiracy doctrine of much of its contemporary political symbolism as a doctrine antithetical to working people's freedom of association. As a result, when the incidence of prosecutions began to escalate again after the Civil War, conspiracy appeared at first as an issue arising in a private realm of "industrial relations" rather than in the public realm of constitutional law and democratic politics – the legality of particular acts in the course of labor disputes in doubt rather than the legality of collective action per se. So it remained until the 1880s and 1890s.[4]

The course of labor conspiracy doctrine in the law of the several states during the first forty years of the nineteenth century describes an evolution from the protection of the public to the protection of private interests, from viewing the "self-created societies" of urban journeymen primarily as a threat to the structure of the polity and the interests of the community at large to measuring instead their potential to injure their masters and fellow journeymen through coercive intrusions upon the employment relationship and disruption of private businesses. With this evolution came some indication of a consensus on the acceptability of a degree of social fragmentation – the decline of a communitarian ideal and recognition instead of society as a thing of diverse interests pursued at cross-purposes. Journeymen pursuing their interests in association, it appeared, could be acceptable to such a society as long as they were respectful of the competing interests of others.

This evolution in labor conspiracy doctrine occurred alongside and was closely

---

molestation, obstruction, or force against others – employers or workmen – in pursuit of their goals, for attempting to induce breach of contract or to induce other workmen to join or contribute funds to their club or association. This legislation remained in place until 1871. See, generally, John V. Orth, *Combination and Conspiracy: A Legal History of Trade Unionism, 1721–1906* (Oxford, 1991), 43–92. See, in addition, Patrick S. Atiyah, *The Rise and Fall of Freedom of Contract* (Oxford, 1979), 528–32, and in general 219–568; Maxine Berg, *The Machinery Question and the Making of Political Economy, 1815–1848* (Cambridge, 1980), 203–18.

[4] Francis B. Sayre, "Criminal Conspiracy," *Harvard Law Review*, 35 (1922), 393–427; B. W. Poulson, "Criminal Conspiracy, Injunctions, and Damage Suits in Labor Law," *Journal of Legal History*, 7, 2 (Sept. 1986), 214–27; Herbert Hovenkamp, "Labor Conspiracies in American Law, 1880–1930," *Texas Law Review*, 66, 6 (Apr. 1988), 922–5. On the postwar cases see Victoria C. Hattam, *Labor Visions and State Power: The Origins of Business Unionism in the United States* (Princeton, 1992), Chapter 2. See in general Christopher L. Tomlins, *The State and the Unions: Labor Relations, Law, and the Organized Labor Movement in America, 1880–1960* (New York and Cambridge, 1985), 44–68; Leon Fink, "Labor, Liberty, and the Law: Trade Unionism and the Problem of the American Constitutional Order," *Journal of American History*, 74, 3 (Dec. 1987), 904–25.

related to the growth of the metropolitan economies. More precisely it represented the influence of two phenomena inextricably bound up with the growth of the metropolitan economies: the growing salience of market reasoning and the competitive principle. The spread of these made it increasingly difficult to represent the interruption to the custom of any particular employer as of itself an assault upon the vital needs of the community, and interruption instead came to be seen as an assault upon the rights of the employer. But such interruption, as we shall see, remained sanctionable. Conspiracy doctrine had been successfully "privatized."

THE FIRST WAVE, 1806–1815

No separation between private and public spheres of action existed in the minds of any of the protagonists in the initial half-dozen cases occurring in the decade after 1806. The first American prosecution – of the journeymen cordwainers of Philadelphia on an indictment for a combination and conspiracy to raise their wages – was mounted, according to prosecutor Joseph Hopkinson, "not from any private pique, or personal resentment, but solely, with a view, to promote the common good of the community: and to prevent in future the pernicious combinations of misguided men, to effect purposes not only injurious to themselves, but mischievous to society." It was an action mounted "to maintain the cause of liberty and repress that of licentiousness." The journeymen cordwainers had formed an unincorporated society – a private confederacy ("this secret association, this private club") – through which they designed to regulate the trade of the city. This was highly injurious to the public good and against the public interest, put "in jeopardy the interest and wellbeing of the community," and was forbidden by law. "What may be lawful in an individual may be criminal in a number of individuals combined, with a view to carry it into effect. The law does not permit any body of men to conspire or to undertake to do any act injurious to the general welfare."[5] Disclaiming any intention to prevent individual defendants from regulating their own wages, Hopkinson placed the prosecution's emphasis on their combination to enforce a standard on all employers and journeymen throughout the trade. "This is the *git* of the prosecution, it is not for what any one man of them has done, that the state prosecutes: the offence is in the combination." He proceeded to discuss the implications of the state's position at some length, first in the relatively new secular language of a republic of known rights and laws, then in the older language of communitarian organicism:

We live under a government composed of a constitution and laws . . . and every man is obliged to obey the constitution, and the laws made under it. When I say he is bound to obey these, I mean to state the whole extent of his obedience. Do you feel yourselves bound to obey

---

[5] Thomas Lloyd, *The Trial of the Boot and Shoemakers of Philadelphia, on an Indictment for a Combination and Conspiracy to Raise Their Wages* (Philadelphia, 1806), 7–9, 67.

any other laws, enacted by any other legislature, than that of your own choice? Shall these, or any other both of men, associate for the purpose of making new laws, laws not made under the constitutional authority, and compel their fellow citizens to obey them, under the penalty of their existence? . . . [I]f private associations and clubs, can make constitutions and laws for us . . . if they can associate and make bye-laws paramount, or inconsistent with the state laws; what, I ask, becomes of the liberty of the people, about which so much is prated; about which the opening counsel made such a flourish?[6]

Supposing, however, the existence of such a combination were to be entertained, what would be its effect upon the community at large? "This is a large, encreasing, manufacturing city. Those best acquainted with our situation, believe that manufactures will, bye and by, become one of its chief means of support." The interest of the whole required protection from the self-interested rapacity of the few. "It is then proper to support this manufacture. Will you permit men to destroy it, who have no permanent stake in the city; men who can pack up their all in a knapsack, or carry them in their pockets to New York or Baltimore?"[7]

Despite the vigor with which he pressed the state's case, Hopkinson's statement of English common law precedents and his stress on the cordwainers' coercive tactics left in some doubt whether he was founding his argument on the claim that at common law any concert which promised to prejudice another or the public at large was to be considered criminal per se, or the somewhat less controversial claim that confederating with the intention of undertaking an unlawful act, or of using unlawful means in pursuit of a lawful objective, was a conspiracy. The presiding judge, Recorder Moses Levy, was less circumspect. Like the prosecution, he condemned the combination both as a selfish assault on the general interest and as an outlaw in the constitutional polity created by the founding fathers,[8] but Levy also found criminality in the mere fact of concert to raise wages:

[6] Ibid., 66–7. See also Hopkinson's statement at 72: "Shall a secret body exercise a power over our fellow-citizens which the legislature itself is not invested with? The fact is, they do exercise a sort of authority the legislature dare not assume."

[7] Ibid., 67–8. Note also the statement of Hopkinson's co-counsel, Jared Ingersoll, at 137: "If the journeymen cordwainers may do this, so may the employers; the journeymen carpenters, brick-layers, butchers, farmers and the whole community will be formed into hostile confederacies, the prelude and certain fore-runner of bloodshed and civil war."

[8] "Is this like the formation of a society for the promotion of the general welfare of the community, such as to advance the interests of religion, or to accomplish acts of charity and benevolence? Is it like the society for extinguishing fires? or those for the promotion of literature and the fine arts, or the meeting of the city wards to nominate candidates for the legislature or the executive? These are for the benefit of third persons the society in question to promote the selfish purposes of the members. . . . The journeymen shoemakers have not asked an encreased price of work for an individual of their body: but they say that no one shall work, unless he recieves the wages they have fixed, They could not go farther than saying, no one should work unless they all got the wages demanded by the majority; is this freedom? Is it not restraining, instead of promoting, the spirit of '76 when men expected to have no law but the constitution, and laws adopted by it or enacted by the legislature in conformity to it? Was it the spirit of '76, that either masters or journeymen, in regulating the prices of their commodities, should set up a rule contrary to the law of their country? General and individual liberty was the spirit of '76. It is our first blessing. It has been obtained and will be maintained" (ibid., 148).

[The common law] says there may be cases in which what one man may do with[out] offence, many may not do with impunity. It distinguishes between the object so aimed at in different transactions. If the purpose to be obtained, be an object of individual interest, it may be fairly attempted by an individual. . . . Many are prohibited from combining for the attainment of it. . . . What is the case now before us? A combination of workmen to raise their wages may be considered in a two fold point of view: one is to benefit themselves . . . the other is to injure those who do not join their society. The rule of law condemns both.[9]

Levy's attribution of such wide authority to the rule of law seemingly attests to a determination to see the defendants convicted. As the Jeffersonian *Aurora* commented after the trial. "A man who did not know the purposes for which the law contemplated the appointment of a recorder to preside in the mayor's court would unquestionably have concluded that Mr. Recorder Levy had been paid by the master shoe-makers for his discourse in the mayor's court Friday last – never did we hear a charge to a jury delivered in a more prejudiced and partial manner."[10] No less important, however, it was a decisive rebuff to the defense attorneys' attempt to destroy the very basis of the prosecution by calling into question the relevance to a postrevolutionary republican polity of an indictment – indeed of an entire proceeding – based on English common law foundations. This, indeed, was the issue which provoked the most unrestrained exchanges during the trial: The defendants' attorneys stressed the arbitrary and unknowable character of the common law, condemned the "disgusting catalogue" of its punishments, hinted broadly at its partiality, and pointedly emphasized the vital importance of the legislature as the embodiment of the democratic promise of the revolution,[11] while Levy just as extravagantly praised the common law as the embodiment of justice and fairness and showered contempt upon the legislature.

The acts of the legislature form but a small part of that code from which the citizen is to learn his duties, or the magistrate his power and rule of action. These temporary emanations of a body, the component members of which are subject to perpetual change, apply principally to the political exigencies of the day. It is in the volumes of the common law we are to seek for information in the far greater number, as well as the most important causes that come before our tribunals. That invaluable code has ascertained and defined, with a critical precision, and with a consistency that no fluctuating political body could or can attain, not only the civil rights of property, but the nature of all crimes from treason to trespass. . . . [I]t regulates with a sound discretion most of our concerns in civil and social life. Its rules are the result of the wisdom of ages.[12]

---

[9] Ibid., 146–7. [10] *Philadelphia Aurora*, 31 Mar. 1806.

[11] See in particular the statement of defendants' counsel Caesar Rodney in Lloyd, *Trial of the Boot and Shoemakers of Philadelphia*, 107–24.

[12] Ibid., 146. Note also the statement of Justice Buchanan in the leading Maryland case of *State v. Buchanan*, 5 H.&J. 317 (1821), at 357: "The common law . . . is a system of principles not capable of expansion, but always existing, and attaching to whatever particular matter or circumstances may arise and come within the one or the other of them; not that this or that combination, is by the common law in terms declared to be an indictable conspiracy, but that it falls within those principles of the common law, which have for their object the preservation of the social order, in the punishing such combinations as are calculated to threaten its well being."

In comparison, both prosecution and the court were relatively restrained in their condemnation of the defendants, disclaiming any desire for extravagant punishment and warning that combinations of masters in any trade would suffer like consequences. Upon conviction, the defendants were fined eight dollars apiece, with costs, and ordered to stand committed until their fines were paid.[13]

The defending attorneys' challenge to the capacity of the court to convict the journeymen of acts previously denominated criminal only in English courts,[14] and Levy's equally strong defense of the court's authority to do just that, need to be seen in the context of a decade-long campaign by Pennsylvania's radical republicans against the state's judiciary and legal profession for their "anti-republican" reliance on the common law.[15] According to the radicals, only "legislative law . . . enacted by our own legislators, chosen by the people for that purpose," could be deemed republican. The law of the courts – "lawyers law" – was "a mass of opinions and decisions, many of them contradictory to each other, which courts and lawyers have instituted themselves, and is chiefly made up of law reports of cases taken from English law books," a tribute to the bench and bar's "open enmity to the principles of free government."[16] In their turn, the radicals were accused of plotting the destruction of both the state and the national governments. Incumbent Governor Thomas McKean, sometime chief justice,[17] condemned the radicals as "a small but active *combination* of malcontents" who had "exposed the form and substance of our government, the code of our laws, the system of our jurisprudence, and the administration of justice . . . to the scorn of the world."[18]

Radical agitation reached its climax in the 1805 gubernatorial election, which coincided almost exactly with the cordwainers' indictment and saw McKean narrowly reelected with the help of Federalist votes. It continued unabated for some time thereafter. "The inroads of an artful body of men, encroaching by degrees on the public liberties, may as has been the course in England, totally undermine and destroy every vestige of liberty," commented William Duane's *Aurora* in August of 1806. "These desperate doctrines of common law are like the artillery of tyrants; the

[13] Lloyd, *Trial of the Boot and Shoemakers of Philadelphia*, 64, 141, 148.

[14] Ibid., 86–7.

[15] See generally Richard E. Ellis, *The Jeffersonian Crisis: Courts and Politics in the Young Republic* (New York, 1974), 157–83; Richard J. Twomey, *Jacobins and Jeffersonians: Anglo-American Radicalism in the United States, 1790–1820* (New York, 1989), 108–24. See also Allen Steinberg, *The Transformation of Criminal Justice: Philadelphia, 1800–1880* (Chapel Hill, 1989), 93–5. For details of the assertiveness of Pennsylvania's courts in matters of judicial power, particularly in regard to the right of judicial review and to the existence of a federal common law jurisdiction, see Stephen B. Presser, "A Tale of Two Judges: Richard Peters, Samuel Chase, and the Broken Promise of Federalist Jurisprudence," *Northwestern University Law Review*, 73, 1 (1978), 26–111. On the prerevolutionary roots of that assertiveness, see Shannon C. Stimson, *The American Revolution in the Law: Anglo-American Jurisprudence before John Marshall* (Princeton, 1990), 56–7.

[16] In Ellis, *Jeffersonian Crisis*, 176, 177.

[17] In which capacity he had been burnt in effigy by Carlisle's Anti-Federalist rioters in 1788. See Saul Cornell, "Aristocracy Assailed: The Ideology of Backcountry Anti-Federalism," *Journal of American History*, 76, 4 (Mar. 1990), 1152.

[18] In Ellis, *Jeffersonian Crisis*, 178, 179 (emphasis in original).

small guns are first brought to play upon those that are to be destroyed, the heavy artillery are planted behind masked batteries, ready to overwhelm as soon as the victim is brought to the proper point for destruction."[19] In the thick postelection atmosphere the cordwainers' case became an important rallying point for radical republicans.[20] For Recorder Levy it became an occasion to affirm the legitimacy and power of the courts and the judiciary in the postrevolutionary polity.

Beyond this, however, the trial was also a specific assertion of the authority of the courts over that of other claimants in matters of local social order; in matters, that is to say, of *police*.[21] In *Commonwealth v. Pullis*, Levy identified two challenges to that authority. the radical republican claim that the legislature, not the courts, was the appropriate forum for decision making on the disposition of the state's power of police, but also the distinct self-asserted collective right of the journeymen to act directly on behalf of the community of their trade.[22] He responded to each

[19] *Philadelphia Aurora*, 21 Aug. 1806.

[20] See the *Philadelphia Aurora* for 19 Aug. 1806 and for 31 Mar. 1806, both linking the cordwainers' conviction to the wider campaign against the common law. As I have already noted in the Introduction to Part 2 (n. 2) the conviction provided radicals with an occasion to attempt to establish a legislative definition of conspiracy in place of that to which the judiciary had had resort. Of all the elements of the commonwealth's criminal law, the Pennsylvania House was told, the common law of conspiracy "appears to be the most undefined, and leaven the widest latitude to the discretion of the court and jury." If left unamended it would bring "abuse and oppression," some authorities providing that *"no proof of any specific overt act"* was required in order to effect a conviction for conspiracy, and others holding that the mere combination to do a lawful act – and even to do it in a lawful manner – was a crime. Such a doctrine "appears evidently to have sprung from the fears and jealousies incident to a monarchical government; and as far as it is in force in this state ought . . . to be amended." In *Journal of the Nineteenth House of Representatives of the Commonwealth of Pennsylvania*, for 13 Mar. 1809 (Lancaster, 1808), 656 (emphasis in original).

[21] Note, e.g., Recorder Levy's statement that "the common law which relates to morals, is what is applicable here" (Lloyd, *Trial of the Boot and Shoemakers of Philadelphia*, 86). And see, generally, Levy's charge to the jury (140–1, 146). It is important to note in this connection that a key element in the radical campaign against the established legal system in Pennsylvania was the proposal to remove jurisdiction over a wide variety of disputes from the courts and lodge it instead with boards of arbitration "composed of merchants, farmers or mechanics" that would deal with disputes largely within each occupation. See Eric Foner, *Tom Paine and Revolutionary America* (New York, 1976), 260. See also the *Philadelphia Aurora*, 15 May 1805, 11 June 1806.

[22] The assertion of this right can best be found in the cordwainers' "Address of the Working Shoemakers of the City of Philadelphia, to the Public" published in the *Philadelphia Aurora*, 28 Nov. 1805. As the address indicates, the serving on employers of a demand for higher wages was not a preliminary to a round of bargaining but the journeymen's public declaration of the "just" price for their labor which they expected henceforth to receive.

"It is notorious that for many years back the working shoemakers have been associated and peaceably assembled together, and that they have regulated the wages which they ought to accept for their labor. It is notorious that the retailing or shopkeeping shoemakers have also had and now have a similar association in which they have regulated the prices for which they sell goods to the public.

"In both these cases we think the parties are justified and correct; because every man being the sole owner and master of his labor and of his property, has the right to affix the price of his own labor or his own property . . . it is not to us a matter to be submitted to, that because we are working men, that our labor is to be paid for not as we estimate it, but at the will of another person who may not know the value of labor. . . .

"As our claim was founded in right and justice, we have adhered to it, and shall abandon life before we depart from it, unless the circumstances of society itself should so change, as to render a reduction equally proper and just, as the encrease is now reasonable."

negatively, but separately in such a way as to use one to check the other. Thus to the claims of the journeymen, Levy counterposed the rule of law – embodied in constitutional polities of known laws enacted by legislatures – as the pinnacle of the revolutionary achievement:

> The journeymen shoemakers . . . say that no one shall work, unless he receives the wages they have fixed. They could not go farther than saying, no one should work unless they all got the wages demanded by the majority; is this freedom? Is it not restraining, instead of promoting, the spirit of '76 when men expected to have no law but the constitution, and laws adopted by it or enacted by the legislature in conformity to it? Was it the spirit of '76, that either masters or journeymen, in regulating the prices of their commodities should set up a rule contrary to the law of their country?[23]

When it came to the radical republican claim of a supervening authority located in the legislature, however, this "spirit of '76" was suddenly absent. Now, notwithstanding the manifest disjunction between the common law tradition and the constitutional polity of known laws which he so carefully invoked against the journeymen's claim, Levy insisted that common law and English precedents were at least as much an expression of the will of the people of Pennsylvania as any legislative act and that as such they provided a wholly sufficient authority for remedial action to be undertaken. "If the rule be clear, we are bound to conform to it even though we do not comprehend the principle upon which it is founded. We are not to reject it because we do not see the reason of it. It is enough that it is the will of the majority. It is law because it is their will."[24] Crucially, however, Levy lent legitimacy to the will of the majority only insofar as it was expressed in the law administered by the courts. "The law is the permanent rule. It is the will of the whole community." Will unmediated by the courts had no legitimacy, no matter how widely the sentiment expressed was felt:

> In forming this decision, we cannot, we must not forget that the law of the land is the supreme, and only rule. We live in a country where the will of no individual ought to be, or is admitted, to be the rule of action. Where the will of an individual, or of any number of individuals, however distinguishable by wealth, talents, or popular fame, ought not to affect, or controul, in the least degree, the administration of justice. There is but one place to determine whether violations or abuses of the law have been committed. It is in our courts

---

On the corporatist implications of journeyman discourse, see also Robert J. Steinfeld, "The *Philadelphia Cordwainers' Case* of 1806: The Struggle over Alternative Legal Constructions of a Free Market in Labor," in Christopher L. Tomlins and Andrew J. King, eds., *Labor Law in America: Historical and Critical Essays* (Baltimore, 1992), 20–43, esp. 36–40. For commentary on the strategies employed in antebellum labor disputes see David Grimsted, "Ante-bellum Labor: Violence, Strike, and Communal Arbitration," *Journal of Social History*, 19 (Fall 1985), 14–15, and generally 5–28.

[23] Lloyd, *Trial of the Boot and Shoemakers of Philadelphia*, 148.

[24] Ibid., 147, and generally 146–7. See also Morton J. Horwitz, *The Transformation of American Law* (Cambridge, Mass., 1977), 22, and generally 18–24. There was, of course, no empirical hook upon which Levy could hang his claim that the rule in question was "the will of the majority." It was simply an argument of assertion. As such, it was rather typical of the early republic's common law discourse of implied consent adverted to in Chapter 3 (see the section entitled Law Rules).

of justice: and there only after proof to the fact: and consideration of principles of law connected with it.[25]

By embracing a dual definition of the rule of law, as at one and the same time a phenomenon invented by the constitutional polity created in the wake of the Revolution and simultaneously as a phenomenon – the common law – distinct and independent of that polity, Levy was able to secure the policing claims of the courts from the counterclaims both of the journeymen and of their radical advocates. At the same time, Levy's dual response helps confirm that the counterclaims of journeymen and radicals *were* distinct, that the goals of the journeymen in defending their combination were different in important respects from those of the radical republicans who took up the issue after it had become a matter of political and legal controversy. For both, the law as enunciated by the court was oppressive. For the journeymen, however, it was oppressive because it undermined their attempts to impose their own explicit and group-constituted standards of fairness or "justice" on their relationships with their employers. Their goal in resisting indictment was protection of their capacity to use their collective power to inhibit individual dealing, thereby constraining the development of a market in their labor within boundaries set by their own conscious collective choice.[26] For the radicals, in contrast, the law was oppressive because by mobilizing common law precedents to prosecute combinations of journeymen while winking at the similar activities of others, it distorted the operation of the market. "Let them ask as freely as they breathe the air, wages for their services. No person is compelled to give them more than their work is worth, the market will sufficiently and correctly regulate these matters." This critique stressed the "unfair application of the law" rather than a defense of combination. Indeed, it implied that equality before the law would do away with conflict and remove the necessity for combination. "If you will take my advice," Caesar Rodney told the jury, "you will leave the regulation of these things to the open market. There every article, like water, acquires its natural level: adopt this rule and you will be more likely to get your boots much cheaper." In their opposition to common law harassment of the journeymen, then, the radicals' goal was an "evenhanded" facilitation of the market's operation, as exemplified in the legislature's *abstention* from statutory intervention.[27]

---

[25] Lloyd, *Trial of the Boot and Shoemakers of Philadelphia*, 141, 140.

[26] On this see also Steinfeld, "The *Philadelphia Cordwainers' Case*." As Steinfeld notes, at 39, and as we have already seen, the journeymen's defense of the legitimacy of *their* autonomous collective activity within their own sphere of interest led them readily to acknowledge the legitimacy of the autonomous collective activity of others within theirs. See above n. 22.

[27] Lloyd, *Trial of the Boot and Shoemakers of Philadelphia*, 78–81 (remarks of defendants' attorney Walter Franklin), 91–8, 104, 119–21 (remarks of defendants' attorney Caesar Rodney). This was also the line taken subsequently by those advocating reform in the legislature (in *Journal of the Nineteenth House of Representatives*, at 655–6): "Occasional and temporary evils may arise from such combination of workmen. So, it is evident, they may form a like combination among any other people interested in the same object. Among the raisers or venders of any commodity as well as among manufacturers; and regulation by indictment and punishment appears as necessary in one case as in the other.

"But the committee are of opinion that in neither case is such regulation wanted. It is supposed that

Richard Twomey has commented that the differences in position and perspective between journeymen trade unionists and ostensibly sympathetic radical advocates that may be found in the early conspiracy cases indicate "a growing conflict within the Jeffersonian republican coalition between masters and journeymen, between journeymen and their political leaders, and between capitalist and non-capitalist tendencies in republican thought." By the early nineteenth century, journeymen and radicals embraced diverging definitions of republican freedom and equality. For the journeymen, the promise of freedom and equality was bound up in the defense of localized corporate rights and practices. For the radicals, in contrast, freedom and equality were "indistinguishable from a market economy."[28] For as long as the public voice of the journeymen was being provided largely by their radical sympathizers, the distinction between these two perspectives would remain somewhat muted. Moreover, these was much in the radicals' Jacobinical antagonism to traditional hierarchies that resonated naturally with the artisans' discourse of independence and sufficiency. Nevertheless, where there are two voices one should listen for both. As we shall see, by the 1830s heightened political mobilization and, more important, systematic organization of trade unions had created a milieu where, momentarily, a distinctive plebeian republicanism gained a much greater degree of prominence.

The complex of issues featured in *Commonwealth v. Pullis* was revisited with some variation three years later in the New York case *People v. Melvin* (1809), in which a number of New York journeymen cordwainers were convicted of a conspiracy to raise their wages. Again the issue was posed as a matter of public welfare. Here, however, the court held that the conspiracy was proven on the basis of the unlawful means which had been agreed upon to effect the goal – refusing to work for any master who offered or with any journeyman who accepted wages lower than those

---

leaving trade completely free and unshackled by legal penalties, no combination or agreement for the purpose of extortion upon the public can prevail. Competition must soon reduce every thing to its just standard in the market."

See also the important work of Richard Twomey, "Jacobins and Jeffersonians: Anglo-American Radical Ideology, 1790–1810," in Margaret Jacob and James Jacob, eds., *The Origins of Anglo-American Radicalism* (London, 1984), 284–99, esp. 289–92; and idem, *Jacobins and Jeffersonians*, 193–213, esp. 202–5. See also Michael Durey, "Thomas Paine's Apostles: Radical Emigrés and the Triumph of Jeffersonian Republicanism," *William and Mary Quarterly*, 3d ser., 44, 4 (Oct. 1987), 661–87.

Caesar Rodney in fact pointed out to the jury (at 121) that in the cordwainers' case the market had already dealt with the disagreement between masters and journeymen over wages. Rodney's purpose was to emphasize the injustice of the prosecution, but the terms he used suggested that unlike the journeymen he saw nothing inappropriate in the treatment of wage determination as a matter of market outcomes, nor, indeed, that he saw anything inappropriate in the outcome which had transpired – namely, that the journeymen had been forced to concede defeat. This helps to illustrate the difference in perspective that was beginning to divide the radicals from the journeymen: "In this last contest between the journeymen and the masters, the weaker power against the stronger, (for whilst the masters *may* loose [sic] the profits on a good job, the journeymen may want bread) we have been unsuccessful, after a struggle to obtain the same wages with our fellow labourers in New-York and Baltimore: we have been compelled to yield and submit to the former reduced prices for our work. The masters have been completely triumphant, and victorious as they are, they persist in this cruel prosecution! They have already accomplished all they asked, what can they desire more? . . . They grasp at too much!"

[28] Twomey, "Jacobins and Jeffersonians," 291–2.

138

stipulated by the conspirators and requiring that all eligible join the society of journeymen without option of refusal – and forbore to decide whether a bare agreement to seek higher wages in the absence of any agreement on how to effect that object would constitute a conspiracy.[29] Again both court and prosecution avoided extravagant condemnation of the journeymen and warned masters that they were subject to the same rule. Again the penalty was relatively nominal. Again the issue that dominated argument was the relevance of the common law.[30] Again, within that issue, the question was whether courts or legislature had command of the state's power of police and whether courts should abstain from interference in market relationships.

For the defendants' attorney, the Irish exile and radical William Sampson, the arguments canvassed by the prosecution were arguments already settled by the Revolution, "which changed the entire form of government, from monarchy, the soul of common law, to a republic, which was a stranger to it."[31] In America "all are in one degree, that of citizens; and all equal in their rights," and the journeymen had the right to do that which neither Constitution nor statute forbade. "Where is the public law that prohibits any thing, or commands any thing, which these defendants are charged with having committed or omitted? The silence of our statutes, the silence of our records, shows that there is none." English law – "built upon the inequality of condition in the inhabitants" – was irrelevant except where expressly embraced by the sovereign people "unless the Court could make laws which none but the legislature can do, and this enlightened and patriotic tribunal will never do what is beyond its province. . . . [W]e had better be contented with the laws under which this country has so long enjoyed all its justly boasted prosperity, unless offences of this kind become enormous. Then let the legislature provide for them."[32]

For the prosecution the matter was rather different. "*Individual* rights are sufficiently secured by letting every man, according to his own will, follow his own pursuits." Public welfare, however, forbade "that *combinations* should be entered into for private benefit, by the persons concerned in any employment connected with the general welfare," for in such combinations they would "make common cause against

---

[29] William Sampson, reporter, *Trial of the Journeymen Cordwainers of the City New York; For a Conspiracy to Raise Their Wages* (New York, 1810), 165.

[30] In this case the defendants' attorneys' assault on the common law far exceeded in rhetorical extravagance anything said during *Commonwealth v. Pullis*. See, e.g., William Sampson in ibid., 45–6, to which prosecuting counsel Thomas Addis Emmet responded (94–95), and Sampson's reply (116), and compare the exchange between Caesar Rodney and Recorder Levy in *Trial of the Boot and Shoemakers of Philadelphia*, 122.

[31] Sampson, *Trial of the Journeymen Cordwainers of the City of New York*, 124. See also Sampson's later polemic, *An Anniversary Discourse before the Historical Society of New York . . . Showing the Origin, Progress, Antiquities, Curiosities, and Nature of the Common Law* (New York, 1824). For observations on the character of Sampson's radicalism, see Walter J. Walsh, "Redefining Radicalism: A Historical Perspective," *George Washington Law Review*, 59, 3 (Mar. 1991), 636–82. See also, generally, Twomey, *Jacobins and Jeffersonians*.

[32] Sampson, *Trial of the Journeymen Cordwainers of the City of New York*, 11, 139–40. See also 44–7. Note also the remarks of Sampson's co-counsel, Cadwallader Colden (81–5), and his statement (158) that "in this country" it was the legislature "which speaks the will and voice of the people."

the community at large" and infringe upon the "public police and prosperity," of which the courts were guardians.

These combinations are an infringement of that tacit compact which all classes reciprocally enter into, that when they have partitioned and distributed among them the different occupations conducive to general prosperity, they will pursue those occupations so as to contribute to the general happiness; and they are therefore at war with public policy.

When it was further considered that such combinations were "always accompanied with compulsory measures against those of the same class or trade, who would willingly pursue their occupation with industry and tranquillity," there could be no doubt that they also represented "most tyrannical violations of private right," tending to the "unjust impoverishment of multitudes, either of those against whom the confederacy is directed, or of those who are forced into it, *or devoted by it*, for exercising *their own individual rights*, and refusing to cooperate with the unlawful association." Both in their impact upon the general welfare and in their impact upon individual rights the journeymen were in derogation of "the laws and policy which must be maintained in every well regulated state."[33]

As a discourse specifically upon the legality or otherwise of journeymen's combinations, the judgment in *People v. Melvin* refrained from asserting the blanket illegality visited upon them in *Commonwealth v. Pullis*. Association was not condemned per se. Rather it was held that the legality of an association inhered in its objects and the methods it contemplated in achieving those objects. Whether objects or methods were unlawful, however, was dependent on whether they were adjudged prejudicial to the general welfare or to the community's interest in ensuring that particular individuals within the community were not prejudiced by the acts of others. Here, even though there had been no personal violence, outrage, or disorder, the society's constitution and by-laws were nonetheless held proof of a coercive, cruel, oppressive, and tyrannical nature in that they exhibited a tendency to interfere with the liberty of masters and other journeymen. The gist of the offense was the conspiracy, and the proof of the conspiracy was the manner in which the concert had been constituted. No overt act was necessary to precipitate its condemnation.[34]

By stressing a general-welfare justification for common law adjudication of the issue, *People v. Melvin* sharpened the conflict over the location and usage of the power of police. Courts, the prosecutors argued, had no need of recourse to "an express statute" in order to justify furnishing a remedy against the journeymen's combination, for "all the principles of the common law which are beneficial to the public, are in full force. . . . As such acts would be against the public good, and immoral in a high degree, they would therefore fall under the animadversions of the general law; and as offences against the whole community, be subject to public prosecution."[35] As in *Commonwealth v. Pullis*, the radical response was to concentrate on attempting to undermine the common law foundations of the court's claim of jurisdiction while

---

[33] Ibid., 98, 105–6 (emphasis in the original).
[34] Ibid., 160, 164, 165, 167–8.   [35] Ibid., 89, 88–9.

invoking the greater justice of market-determined outcomes. "Why call in the law to make artificial regulations? Why not let the thing naturally regulate itself? ... Muzzle but these prosecutions, and then, before we have gone long slipshod, the masters and the men will have come to an agreement, founded, like all bargains, on reciprocal need; the one giving as little as he can give, and the other taking as much as he can get."[36] In particular, defense attorneys made no attempt to take up and justify on its own terms the journeymen's counterclaim for the propriety of acting to impose their own distinctive forms of quasi-corporate regulation on the employment relationship in the interests of achieving outcomes conforming to their own collective standards of fairness.[37] Instead, they simply decried the unfairness of prosecutions which sought to cripple combinations of journeymen while leaving intact combinations of masters. In conjunction with their invocation of the market, this argument clearly implied not that journeymen's combinations were entirely legitimate in their own right but rather that one evil deserved another and that all would be better off without resort to combination by any party.[38] Indeed, as we have seen, in the course of stressing the responsibility of the legislature over the courts in matters of police, Sampson allowed that he could conceive of circumstances in which journeymen's combinations might become oppressive. "If the evil [of

---

[36] Ibid., 35, 36–7.

[37] Even more so than in *Commonwealth v. Pullis*, the report of hearings in *People v. Melvin* – cobbled together by William Sampson after the event, largely from his and Emmet's prepared remarks – concentrates heavily on legal argument, allowing one little direct access to the voices of the journeymen defendants themselves. It is nevertheless clear from the transcript that the Society of Journeymen Cordwainers of the City of New York sought to enforce rules governing the conduct of the trade upon the generality of masters, journeymen, and apprentices in the city, asserting jurisdiction over members and nonmembers alike. See ibid., 147–53. For confirmation, see "Constitution of the New York Cordwainers Society," in Howard B. Rock, ed., *The New York City Artisan, 1789–1825: A Documentary History* (Albany, 1989), 201–3, at 202: "*ARTICLE XI.* Any Journeyman Cordwainer, coming into this city, that does not come forward and join this society in the space of one month, (as soon as it is known,) he shall be notified by the Secretary, and for such notification he shall pay twelve and a half cents; and if he does not come forward and join the same on the second meeting of the society, after receiving the notice, shall pay a fine of three dollars. *ARTICLE XII.* Any member of this society having an apprentice or apprentices, shall, when he or they become free, report the same to the President, on the first monthly meeting following; and if the said apprentice or apprentices do not come forward and join the Society, in the space of one month from the time of the report, shall be notified by the Secretary, and if he does not come forward within two months after receiving the notification, shall pay a fine of three dollars." Note also the contemporaneous "Constitution and Bye-Laws of the United Society of Journeymen Cabinet and Chair-Makers of the city of Baltimore," which provided that any cabinetmaker coming to work as a journeyman in the city should within six weeks join the society or pay it a monthly fine for failing to comply (Charles F. Montgomery, *American Furniture: The Federal Period* [New York, 1966], 21–2). See also Christopher L. Tomlins, *The State and the Unions: Labor Relations, Law, and the Organized Labor Movement in America, 1880–1960* (New York, 1985), 38; Sean Wilentz, "Conspiracy, Power, and the Early Labor Movement: The People v. James Melvin et al., 1811," *Labor History*, 24 (1983), 57–9. In light of all this, it is not surprising that, as in *Commonwealth v. Pullis*, we find the prosecution in *People v. Melvin* accusing the journeymen of adopting measures "going to erect an *imperium in imperio*, and overbear the rights of the citizen, and the law of the land" (remarks of Thomas Addis Emmet, at 164; see also the remarks of Emmet's co-prosecutor, George Griffin, at 160–1).

[38] This, indeed, was the position taken by Thomas Addis Emmet, for the prosecution. The coincidence of views between counsel, both Irish exiles, both Jacobins, is remarked upon by Twomey (*Jacobins and Jeffersonians*, 204–5, and generally 199–213).

combination] requires a law we shall have a legislature to provide one in due time."[39]

The definition of conspiracy suggested in *People v. Melvin* was taken up and clarified in *Commonwealth v. Morrow* (Pittsburgh, 1815), where it was restated succinctly as "an agreement of two or more to the prejudice of the rights of others or of society." Invoking the same common law police power maintained in the preceding cases, prosecutors argued that concerted action was subject to indictment as a common law conspiracy if it "is against good morals, injures society, or is destructive to the trade of a place."[40] In other respects, too, the case largely followed what had by now emerged as a normal pattern – prosecution disclaimers of hostility to the journeymen and promises of a light penalty; defense protests against juridical "interference" in the marketplace determination of wages, condemnation of the importation of alien common law principles into local law, and invocations of legislative supremacy;[41] and the court's confident claim to authority based on the prior prosecutorial assertion of a common law–rooted power of police:

Confederacies of this kind have a most pernicious effect, as respects the community at large. They restrain trade: they tend to banish many artizans, and to oppress others. It is the interest of the public, and it is the right of every individual, that those who are skilled in any profession, art, or mystery, should be unrestrained in the exercise of it. It is peculiarly the interest of a trading and manufacturing town, (such as Pittsburg) that such freedom should exist.[42]

[39] Sampson, *Trial of the Journeymen Cordwainers of the City of New York*, 140. See also above, n. 27. Sampson also allowed that the defendants in *People v. Melvin* might well be civilly liable (ibid., 66).

[40] Charles Shaler, reporter, *Report of the Trial of the Journeymen Cordwainers, of the Borough of Pittsburgh* (Pittsburgh, 1817), reprinted in John R. Commons et al., eds., *A Documentary History of American Industrial Society* (Cleveland, 1910), 4:15–87, at 24, 71. Note also the opening statement of attorney General Jared Ingersoll that "every confederacy to injure individuals, or to do acts which are unlawful or prejudicial to the community, is a conspiracy. Journeymen who refuse to work in consequence of a combination, till their wages are raised, may be endicted for a conspiracy" (24).

[41] Ibid., 63–4, 70, 77. The court answered arguments for legislative supremacy with its own counterassertions of the "impracticability" of having resort to legislative action to declare the content of any particular branch of the common law. "Such is the variety of occurrences, which from time to time, take place in society: crimes and offences are so infinitely varied, and complicated, that no legislative provision could anticipate them, or sufficiently provide against them: but the common law affords ample provision. It abounds with principles, which, in their application, are calculated to attain and establish every right, and to redress every wrong, in a state of society. It is a system founded in reason: matured and corrected by constant investigation, and the decision of learned men, through a succession of ages. It is not as some have ignorantly represented it, vague, uncertain and incomprehensible. Its principles are well known to every lawyer; though the application of those principles, to particular cases, may embarrass the most learned" (79–80).

[42] Ibid., 81, and generally 82–6. The reporter, Shaler, approved the outcome: "The verdict . . . is most important to the manufacturing interests of the community; it puts an end to those associations which have been so prejudicial to the successful enterprize of the capitalists of the western country. But this case is not important to this country alone; it proves beyond the possibility of doubt, that notwithstanding the adjudications in New York and Philadelphia, there still exists in those cities, combinations, which extend their deleterious influence to every part of the union. The inhabitants of those cities, the manufacturers particularly, are bound by their interests, as well as the duties they owe community, to watch those combinations with a jealous eye, and to prosecute to conviction, and subject to the penalties of the law, conspiracies so subversive to the best interests of their country" (16–17).

Morrow, however, is notable for two departures from the pattern of the previous cases. First, even as they inveighed against the particulars of the indictment the defendants' attorneys nevertheless hinted (more broadly than had Sampson five years earlier) at their tacit acceptance of the legitimacy of applying the concept of conspiracy to journeymen's combinations under certain circumstances. They did so by offering an alternative definition of what the charge of conspiracy should entail in order for it to be maintainable. In this definition a conspiracy was a combination to effect an unlawful purpose or to effect a lawful purpose by unlawful means. Various tests were suggested by which unlawful means might be measured. Threats and violence would qualify, but not the simple act of writing and adopting a constitution or a collective refusal to work unless a nonmember were discharged. Their suggestion was not entirely ignored. As such it signaled traces of a consensus on the regulation of collective activity that was to emerge with fuller force in later years, a consensus built on foundations that, as we have already begun to see, would tend to exclude nonmarket justifications for regulatory action such as those generally embraced by the journeymen themselves.[43]

Morrow's second departure is not unconnected, in that by granting a degree of recognition in its jury charge to the defense attorneys' criticism of juridical interventions in market relations, the court suggested its own variation on that potential consensus:

It would be taking a very contracted, and by no means a just view of this case, to consider it as a controversy between the employers and the journeymen. And your time would be very unprofitably employed, in calculating the respective profits of the one or the other. With the regulation of wages, or the profit of the one or the other, you have nothing to do. It has been truly said that every man has a right to affix what price he pleases on his labor.

It was not for demanding high prices that the defendants had been indicted, said the court, but for employing unlawful means to extort those prices, "for using means prejudicial to the community." Inevitably the court's idea of unlawful means differed markedly from the defense's. Thus if some men conspired to compel others to work at certain prices or to compel an employer to hire certain persons and not others, they were indictable. If men conspired to prevent a man from freely exercising his trade or to compel him to join their association or even to support their association, they were indictable. Whether or not they used threats or violence was immaterial. The conspiracy was complete as soon as it was shown that it had a necessary tendency to impoverish or prejudice a third person or the community as a whole.[44] Nonetheless, there was now a degree of commonality in defining the issue over which the parties were at odds. From the beginning the issue of conspiracy had been perceived as one involving the regulation of behavior impinging upon the interests of "the community," with defendants, counsel, and courts quarreling over how those interests should be measured. By 1815 courts and counsel, although not

---

[43] Ibid., 59, 63–71, 74–7.   [44] Ibid., 81–5.

the journeymen themselves, had moved some distance toward a common definition of those interests in terms of the unrestricted operation of markets.

PUBLIC OR PRIVATE WRONGS?

To this point the formal legal status of associated journeymen had appeared precarious indeed. Courts had seemed determined to treat their combinations as conspiracies per se in all but the narrowest sense, in that they had required no evidence of compounding action to sustain the indictment once it had been shown that the object contemplated by the concert or the manner of its formation might be taken to imply some form of public prejudice or injury. On the other hand courts had not penalized the journeymen heavily and had been careful to warn master craftsmen against unlawful combinations on their part.[45] Seven prosecutions had been mounted, but two of these had apparently been dismissed.[46] Nor, finally, was there hard evidence that the effectiveness of journeymen's combinations had been materially impaired by their consignment to a shadow world of semi-illegality. "As in early 19th-century London and Paris, formal prohibition or limitation of trade union activities did not eradicate the journeymen's militancy: meeting quietly, in semi-secret and unreported by the press, the journeymen established and maintained a disciplined order of regulation within the shops, one which the masters . . . did not lightly transgress."[47]

Over the next few years, furthermore, the apparent precariousness of the journeymen's legal position would be somewhat qualified. First, the incidence of prosecution declined. After seven prosecutions in ten years across three states there was an eight-year lull, roughly coinciding with a downturn in journeymen's activities following the conclusion of the War of 1812. Prosecutions began again with the New York case *People v. Trequier* (1823) and became reasonably frequent during the next six years (seven in seven years across four states), before a further five-year hiatus. Second, during this later phase courts began to abstain from continued invocations of their guardianship of the common weal – the interest of the community at large in an unobstructed commerce, in social order, in "public police and prosperity" – in favor of a greater emphasis on the existence of actual prejudicial behavior and intent on the part of the alleged conspirators in their dealings with

[45] This quasi-educative stance was reproduced in other contemporary prosecutions of legally disapprobated social behavior. See e.g., Hendrik Hartog, "Pigs and Positivism," *Wisconsin Law Review*, July 1985, no. 4:899–935.

[46] *Baltimore Cordwainers* (Md. 1809) and *People v. Melvin* (N.Y. 1811). The occurrence of the Baltimore case has been established only indirectly. See Sampson, *Trial of the Journeymen Cordwainers of the City of New York*, 162. On the second *Melvin* case, recently come to light, see Wilentz, "Conspiracy, Power, and the Early Labor Movement," 572–9. The seventh case was a direct predecessor of *Commonwealth v. Morrow* involving the same society of cordwainers. Begun in 1814 it did not proceed to judgment, although clearly the journeymen would have been convicted had it done so. See Shaler, *Report of the Trial of the Journeymen Cordwainers*, 31.

[47] Wilentz, "Conspiracy, Power, and the Early Labor Movement," 578.

the parties said to have been injured. This in turn made it somewhat more likely that prosecutors would have to work harder for convictions.[48]

To some extent this change may have been caused by a shift in the conduct of journeymen's associations, for there is some evidence that during the 1820s journeymen began to present their combinations as voluntary associations rather than "self-created" quasi-corporate combinations, "conspiracies against society."[49] This placed greater pressure on the courts to find reasons why they should be considered to be engaging in forms of unlicensed association distinct enough from those practiced by others to constitute illegal activity. Alternatively, as we have just seen, the courts' growing concentration on journeymen's behavior in association as distinct from the very fact of their association may be thought of as acknowledgment of the growing respect accorded market, as opposed to political, determination of social relations. In either case the change had the beneficial effect of routinizing somewhat the courts' approach to what was clearly a matter of considerable political controversy, insofar as both the particular matter of labor combination and the more general issue of the courts' claim to an overweening police authority were concerned.

The appearance of a modified version of labor conspiracy doctrine was heralded in an 1821 opinion on a point of law delivered by Justice John Gibson of the Supreme Court of Pennsylvania in the case of *Commonwealth v. Carlisle*. Although delivered at a *nisi prius* sitting and therefore not officially reported at the time, Gibson's opinion became known and respected – at least in Pennsylvania – as the most authoritative local statement on the law of conspiracy as applied to labor combinations then available.[50] The occasion was a motion to discharge a group of master ladies shoemakers being held in custody on a charge of conspiracy to reduce the wages of their journeymen. The ground offered for the motion was that a combination to regulate wages was no offense by the common law of Pennsylvania.

---

[48] In the *Balize Pilots* case (La. 1826) seventeen deputy pilots were acquitted on a charge of entering into an unlawful combination (*Boston Courier*, 30 Mar. 1826). For details of this dispute see *Louisiana State Gazette*, 10, 20, 22–25 Feb. and 7 Mar. 1826. In *Commonwealth v. Moore* (Pa. 1827) the court dismissed counts in the indictment where actual threats and intimidation had not been shown. In *State v. Pomeroy* (Md. 1829) the defendants were acquitted, the prosecution being unable to show threats or intimidation. Also worth noting is the Boston case *Commonwealth v. Holmes* (1824), Police Court Docket no. 885, which, although not a conspiracy case, attests to a sense of uncertainty on the part of the court as to its capacity to entertain a complaint that the defendant had sought (apparently without accompanying threats or intimidation) to induce the complainant's employer to discharge him. See Tomlins, "Criminal Conspiracy and Early Labor Combinations," 371–2.

[49] See e.g., Marcus T. C. Gould, *Trial of Twenty-Four Journeymen Taylors Charged with Conspiracy: Before the Mayor's Court of the City of Philadelphia, September Sessions, 1827* (Philadelphia, 1827), 28 (testimony of Thomas Carr), 29 (testimony of James Sheridan), 30 (testimony of John Flaherty), 53 (testimony of Robert Scott), 122–4 (argument of defendants' counsel).

[50] In *Commonwealth v. Moore*, Recorder Joseph Reed stated that he felt "bound to take the law" from the decision in *Commonwealth v. Carlisle* as "respectable authority" in preference to the earlier cases in Pennsylvania and New York both because it was the most recent relevant decision and because "I consider it to contain the opinion of an eminent Judge, who has since attained the highest honours of his profession" (ibid., 156). Gibson's opinion was not reported officially until 1851 when it appeared in Brightly's *Nisi Prius Reports* (Philadelphia, 1851), 36–43. At the time the case was decided, however, it was reproduced in full and widely circulated in *Hall's Journal of Jurisprudence*, 1 (1821), 225–30.

"In no book of authority," Gibson stated, "has the precise point before me been decided." *R. v. Journeymen-Taylors of Cambridge* had been poorly reported, and subsequent British precedents had arisen in obedience to statutes that had never been given effect in America; *Commonwealth v. Pullis* had asserted no general principle; *People v. Melvin* had ultimately avoided the issue. "An investigation of the principles of the law which declares the offence, then, becomes absolutely necessary to a correct decision in this particular instance." The law was "unsettled"; it had suffered from "a gradual extension . . . each case having been decided on its own peculiar circumstances, without reference to any pre-established principle." Combinations to perform criminal acts or to achieve lawful goals but by unlawful means were clearly conspiracies; "but when the crime became so far enlarged as to include cases where the act was not only lawful in the abstract, but also to be accomplished exclusively by the use of lawful means, it is obvious that distinctions as complicated and various as the relations and transactions of civil society, became instantly involved, and to determine on the guilt and innocence of each of this class of the cases, an examination of the nature and principles of the offence became necessary." This examination had not yet been very accurately made. There was "an unusual want of precision" in the law.[51]

As with previous judgments in previous conspiracy cases, Gibson's discourse in *Carlisle* was in part overtly communitarian. Thus in offering examples of what could be considered indictable concerted activity he described primarily instances of disruption to the general welfare. At the same time Gibson noted that indictments had also been pressed successfully where individuals had been oppressed by concerted activity. This might well have been presented as another, less-direct form of assault on the general welfare – through, for example, restraint of trade doctrine – but Gibson noted that English courts had also allowed conspiracy indictments where there was no apparent detriment to the general welfare either directly or indirectly, but simply an advantage to the conspirators. Under Levy's per se doctrine all these classes of cases were reconcilable. Gibson, however, rejected Levy's approach lest the law "necessarily impart criminality to the most laudable associations." His particular problem, then, was to find a rule which could impose some degree of order on the several classes of cases under consideration, while at the same time allowing the community – and individuals within it – to benefit from "laudable" forms of combination, by which he meant primarily combinations of capital for purposes of "fair" competition. His solution was to point to the motive for combination – the nature of the object to be attained – as the key.

Where the act is lawful for an individual, it can be the subject of a conspiracy, when done in concert, only where there is a direct intention that injury shall result from it, or where the object is to benefit the conspirators to the prejudice of the public or the oppression of individuals, and where such prejudice or oppression is the natural and necessary consequence.[52]

---

[51] *Commonwealth v. Carlisle, Hall's Journal of Jurisprudence* 1 (1821), 226–7.
[52] Ibid., 227.

By placing the emphasis upon motive, lawful acts pursued in concert might continue to be subjected to criminal indictment and prosecution without any requirement for reference to actual or anticipated community injury.[53] At the same time, however, concert itself would not be prima facie justification for an indictment. Indeed, in acknowledging that "the mere act of combining to change the price of labour" was not conclusive of illegality – indeed could often be a response to oppressive behavior by another party – Gibson appeared to acknowledge that artisan combinations were not necessarily harmful per se at all, and that courts should not feel obliged to intervene against them if prejudice or oppression either to the community or to individuals could not be demonstrated.

Pennsylvania cases during the 1820s and after show Gibson's influence. "Resting, therefore, on this respectable authority, I am disposed to give the law of conspiracy a more liberal construction," said Recorder Joseph Reed in *Commonwealth v. Moore* (1827), "to leave every man in the community to exercise his faculties to regulate his conduct with as little restraint as possible, provided he permits others to do the same."[54] Other state courts also put greater emphasis on the question whether combination was accompanied by injury and whether injury was a necessary consequence of the object of the combination. Acquittals followed.[55]

None of this dislodged the courts from their position of decisive authority over the fate of combinations. Indeed, in its very reliance on judgments of motive, Gibson's approach if anything enhanced the courts' role. Yet an authority relying on discriminating among forms of collective behavior and ascribing legality on the basis of inferences as to their different meanings was an authority more easily cast into disrepute than one based on Levy's magnificently (if deceptively or erroneously) dogmatic pronouncement that all unlicensed concerted activity was presumptively illegal. As courts edged away from the automatic invocation of an organic general welfare in whose eyes all intermediate association was inherently suspicious and whose interest would form the test of whether collectivity would be sanctioned, and attempted instead to establish criteria of fairness or intent by which some concerts could be declared illegitimate and others not, the risk of appearing partial, and the desire to avoid that appearance, both increased.

The risk was further increased by the courts' continued attempts during the 1820s to redefine the ambit of conspiracy doctrine in nonlabor cases. As Gibson's opinion showed, given the impracticality of the per se rule once courts had decided to retreat from the iron logic of the organic community toward recognition of the existence of complex intracommunity interests, tests were needed of what should and should not be considered injurious concerts. In the leading Maryland case of *State v. Buchanan* (1821) – "one of the earliest as well as one of the most exhaustive examinations of the subject . . . one of the corner stones of our

<hr>

[53] Dicta in *R. v. De Berenger*, 105 E.R. 536 (1814), indicate that a similar alteration in emphasis was under way in English case law.

[54] Gould, *Trial of Twenty-Four Journeymen Tailors*, 156–7.

[55] See above, n. 48.

law"[56] – the leading opinion emphasized that criminal indictment would be available, notwithstanding the legality of the act itself, not only where the public was the victim of the concert but also where a private individual was injured without discernible public impact.[57] The decision made determination of motive decisive to the question of indictment, holding that "every conspiracy to do an unlawful act, or to do a lawful act for an illegal, fraudulent, malicious or corrupt purpose, or for a purpose which has a tendency to prejudice the public in general, is at Common Law an indictable offence."[58]

The direction of doctrinal development indicated by the decision in *Buchanan* was controversial and was disputed in subsequent decisions. "There are authors . . . who say that a combination to prejudice a *private person*, either in his property, trade or reputation, is indictable as a conspiracy," the New Jersey Supreme Court observed in *State v. Rickey* (1827). But this was to go beyond the outer limits, "the very *ne plus ultra*," of the doctrine. A conspiracy indictment, the New Jersey court insisted, could not be maintained in cases of "private injuries not otherwise of an indictable nature, and in which the public have no concern." The court suggested a categorical limitation of conspiracy to "combinations to commit *an act*, which, if committed, would be *an indictable offence*."[59]

In New York, in the crucial case of *Lambert v. The People* (1827), the Court of Errors revealed itself comprehensively split on the question of the doctrine's extent, some members denying its availability to vindicate merely private injuries, others favoring it.[60] John Canfield Spencer (senator), in the lead opinion, owned that he approached the matter "with great diffidence." It could not be denied that courts "have, in some instances, sustained such indictments." He was, however, unconvinced. He was also highly critical of the current state of the law:

---

[56] Hampton L. Carson, *The Law of Criminal Conspiracies and Agreements, As Found in the American Cases* (Philadelphia, 1887), 100.

[57] Ibid., 353–5.   [58] *State v. Buchanan*, 352.

[59] *State v. Rickey*, 9 N.J. L.R. 293 (1827), at 305 (emphases in original). Like the English decisions in which Lord Ellenborough similarly attempted to draw a line preventing the extension of conspiracy doctrine to vindicate private injuries – e.g., *R. v. Turner*, 104 E.R. 357 (1811) – this New Jersey decision was subsequently vilified as inconsistent "with the common law, and the general current of jurisprudence," (*Report of the Penal Code of Massachusetts* [Boston, 1844], tit. "Conspiracy," 2–3, 5). In 1850 *Rickey* was overturned by the New Jersey Supreme Court in *State v. Norton*, 23 N.J. L.R. 33. For English judicial commentary on Ellenborough's conspiracy jurisprudence see e.g., *R. v. Rowlands*, 117 E.R. 1439 (1851), at 1445.

[60] *Lambert v. The People* (a case of conspiracy to cheat and defraud certain incorporated companies and individuals of goods) came before the Court of Errors on appeal from a judgment of Chief Justice Savage in the New York Supreme Court, where it had been held that conspiracy indictments were available at common law to vindicate private injuries. The case was argued twice in the Court of Errors. After hearing all arguments of counsel and the opinions of three of its members (who divided 2–1 in favor of reversing the chief justice) the full bench of the Court of Errors divided equally for and against reversal. The matter was settled, in favor of reversal, by the casting vote of the president. See *Lambert v. The People*, 9 Cowen 577 (1827), 579–624. Savage's Supreme Court judgment is of considerable significance given his later involvement in the labor conspiracy case *People v. Fisher*, 14 Wend. 9 (1835), for details of which see below, this chapter.

If [as I believe to be the case] no general rule defining the offence of conspiracy exists in the law it presents a lamentable exception from the principles of our whole system. If the offence is to be declared after the fact, and cannot be ascertained before it, we may apply to ourselves the maxim, that miserable is the condition of a people where the law is so vague and uncertain as to rest only in the breast of the judge. I am unwilling to sanction any such principles. If it be consistent with the public feeling in England that judges should possess an indefinite power of extending a principle of criminal law to cases after the fact, so as to prevent what they may suppose a failure of justice, it is yet contrary to the first principles of our government, and subversive of the great object of our institutions.[61]

But others on the same bench had fewer qualms. "A conspiracy may be defined (so far as it is capable of a precise definition) as a confederacy to do an unlawful act, or a lawful act by unlawful means, whether to the prejudice of an individual or the public; and . . . it is not necessary, to render the conspiracy indictable, that its object should be the commission of a crime."[62]

The upshot of all this confusion in New York was action in the state legislature and the adoption there of a new statutory definition of the offense operative in all future conspiracy indictments, the effect of which was to criminalize conspiracies, inter alia, "to commit any act injurious to the public health or morals, or to trade or commerce, or for the perversion or obstruction of justice, or the due administration of the laws."[63] In so describing the offense the legislature clearly limited its ambit (other than in cases of fraud or abuse of legal procedure) to *public* wrongs, throwing out language which would have formalized extension to private injuries through the criminalization of conspiracies "to defraud or injure any person in his trade or business."[64] Thereby the legislature set itself against the direction taken in *Commonwealth v. Carlisle* and *State v. Buchanan* and urged by influential opinion in its own Court of Errors, all of which had implied a doctrine available for the vindication of private injuries, in favor of the adoption of statutory definitional limitations on the ambit of the offense (and hence on the "indefinite power" of the judiciary) similar to those suggested by the New Jersey court in *Rickey*. As we shall see, this was to create considerable uncertainty in the doctrine's application in New York.

There is no evidence to suggest that a desire to modify the conspiracy doctrine's impact on journeymen's combinations had any particular bearing on the New York legislature's action, and certainly those courts that had been critical of the doctrine's indiscriminate extension had carefully excepted its impact on journeymen's

---

[61] *Lambert v. The People*, at 597. On contemporary English developments, see R. S. Wright, *The Law of Criminal Conspiracies and Agreements* (Philadelphia, 1887), 33–4, 48–9.

[62] *Lambert v. The People*, 606.

[63] Act of 10 Dec. 1828, *New York Revised Statutes* (Albany, 1829), 2:691. The words quoted are from the fifth section of the statute. The first four sections criminalized conspiracies (1) to commit an offense; (2) to indict any person falsely and maliciously; (3) falsely to move or maintain a suit; and (4) to cheat and defraud any person by criminal means, or by means which, if executed, would amount to a cheat.

[64] Wythe Holt, "Labor Conspiracy Cases in the United States, 1805–1824: Bias and Legitimation in Common Law Adjudication," *Osgoode Hall Law Journal*, 22, 4 (Winter 1984), 633.

combinations from their critique. Concerts "such as journeymen combining not to work till they get an advance of wages, an offence in restraint of trade," were "public wrongs," said the New Jersey court.[65] As such they appeared to fall comfortably within the parameters of the definition chosen by the New York legislature.[66] Yet given the abandonment of the organic "community" and the legislative redrawing of the ambit of conspiracy to exclude concerted activities causing purely private injuries from criminal prosecution, what logic left journeymen's combinations on the inside, apparently alone in their "public," rather than merely private, impact? That uncertainty created at least the possibility that criminal conspiracy's availability for the vindication of injuries done by journeymen's combinations might be affected.

In fact this was precisely the issue addressed by the New York Supreme Court in 1835 in *People v. Fisher*.[67] The case came before the court on appeal from the Court of General Sessions of Ontario County, where the previous year the state had contended unsuccessfully that a combination to regulate the price of making boots and shoes in the village of Geneva, and to prevent by means of boycott any journeyman willing to accept a lower wage from being employed in the village, was injurious to trade within the meaning of the statute. The lower court had held the indictment insufficient, as unknown to the laws of the state, and the defense now renewed that argument. "The course of proceeding contemplated by the defendants was not 'injurious to trade or commerce,' within the meaning of the statute. . . . The act could never have been intended to apply to a controversy between master and journeymen mechanics, as to the price of making some particular article."[68] The Supreme Court, however, disagreed. Chief Justice John Savage concluded, first, that the statute had not abrogated the common law meaning of conspiracy except insofar as to render null an indictment for a conspiracy to effect a merely private injury (thus construing the legislative limitation on judicial discretion as narrowly as possible); and, second, that journeymen's combinations clearly produced public injuries. "That the raising of wages and a conspiracy, confederacy, or mutual agreement among journeymen for that purpose is a matter of public concern, and in which the public have a deep interest, there can be no doubt. That it was an indictable offence at common law is established by legal adjudications."[69]

---

[65] *State v. Rickey*, 307. So was "conspiring to hiss at a theatre, in order to put down an actor, obstruct the performance of a play, or compel the managers to lower the price of tickets."

[66] Note that in the abbreviated report of initial arguments before the Court of Errors in *Lambert v. The People*, counsel for the plaintiff contended that the only conspiracies indictable in New York, whether at common law or under the statute defining the crime of conspiracy then in effect, were inter alia "[c]onspiracy to do an act affecting the *public*; as a conspiracy among journeymen not to labor without a certain price" (*Lambert v. The People*, 585, emphasis in original). In the course of a subsequent Supreme Court case (*People v. Mather*, 4 Wend. 230 [1830], at 261), Marcy J., speaking for the court, opined that an agreement "to turn out for higher wages" on the part of "the journeymen of any particular mechanic art in a city" was indictable as a criminal act, with no more needed to convict defendants of the conspiracy than the act of turning out. "Concurrence, without any particular proof of an agreement to concur," would be conclusive.

[67] *People v. Fisher*, 14 Wend. 10 (1835).   [68] Ibid., 12–13.

[69] Ibid., 15.

Defining trade as "traffic or mutual dealings between members of the same community," Savage held that all that was necessary to support an indictment in conformity with the statute was a demonstration of the tendency of a combination to enhance the price of boots made in Geneva relative to those made elsewhere, thereby lessening their attractiveness. "It is important to the best interests of society that the price of labor be left to regulate itself, or rather be limited by the demand for it. Combinations or confederacies *to enhance or reduce* the prices of labor, or of any articles of trade or commerce, are injurious."[70] The point established, Savage proceeded to illustrate the threat to the public:

> In the present case, an industrious man was driven out of employment by the unlawful measures pursued by the defendants, and an injury done to the community, by diminishing the quantity of productive labor, and of internal trade. In so far as the individual sustains an injury, the remedy by indictment is taken away by our revised statutes, and the sufferer is left to his action on the case; but in so far as the public are concerned, in the embarrassment to trade by the discouragement of industry, the defendants are liable to punishment by indictment.[71]

In New York, *People v. Fisher* indicated, the applicability of criminal conspiracy to labor combinations was founded on the claim that such combinations injured the public through their threats to trade, not on private injuries done to innocents by coercion. The criminal courts could police the market but not individual transactions without public impact.[72]

People v. Fisher was the first recorded criminal conspiracy prosecution to arise in New York since the unreported *Buffalo Tailors'* case in 1824, and the first anywhere since 1829. More prosecutions quickly followed in 1836, two in New York and two in Philadelphia, with a further cluster in the early 1840s. These cases were very distinctive. First of all, the success rate of prosecutions dropped sharply. Of eight cases occurring between 1836 and 1843, only three resulted in convictions (including the initial trial of *Commonwealth v. Hunt*); four ended in acquittals (including the successful appeal in *Commonwealth v. Hunt*); and one was settled before

---

[70] Ibid., 17, 18 (emphasis in original). Savage continued as follows: "Without any officious and improper interference on the subject, the price of labor or the wages of mechanics will be regulated by the demand for the manufactured article, and the value of that which is paid for it; but the right does not exist either to enhance the price of the article or the wages of the mechanic, by any forced and artificial means. The man who owns an article of trade or commerce is not obliged to sell it for any particular price, nor is the mechanic, obliged by law to labor for any particular price. He may say that he will not make coarse boots for less than one dollar per pair, *but he has no right to say that no other mechanic shall make them for less*. . . . [I]f one individual does not possess such a right over the conduct of another, no number of individuals can possess such a right. All combinations therefore to effect such an object are injurious, not only to the individual particularly oppressed, but to the public at large" (18, emphasis in original).

[71] Ibid., 18–19.

[72] Herbert Hovenkamp's argument that the case "actually condemned the coercion directed at others, not the price-fixing agreement among the defendants" thus misstates the issue ("Labor Conspiracies in American Law, 1880–1930," *Texas Law Review*, 66, 5 [Apr. 1988], 919–65, at 935). It should also be clear, by now, that American courts did *not*, contra Hovenkamp, simply "toy" with a conspiracy theory of labor organizing during the first decades of the nineteenth century (922).

trial.[73] This compares with nine convictions and five acquittals among the previous recorded cases.[74]

Second, the political and economic environment in which conspiracy prosecutions took place in the 1830s was very different to that prevailing previously. In a trend first apparent in the mid-1820s, journeymen's organizations and strikes by the early 1830s were developing to a size and a level of organizational sophistication not previously seen in the metropolitan cities.[75] This tended both to raise considerably the stakes in any prosecution and to generalize issues and protests beyond specific localities. As we have already seen, labor conspiracy prosecutions always attracted considerable public attention and controversy within their particular city or town. The 1830s prosecutions, however, were given widespread publicity up and down the East Coast. They were attended by major protests and demonstrations and became an important focus for the period's endemic partisan political controversy. More important, their occurrence added momentum to an oppositional critique of the direction of the American political economy, and in particular of the role of juridical authority, which had begun to emerge at the time of the independent working men's political movements of the late 1820s and early 1830s and which was taken up in revised form by the Jacksonian union movement.

RADICALS, POLITICS, AND UNIONS

Before the late 1820s, a "labor movement" did not exist, as such, in any part of the United States. As we have seen, instances of journeymen combining in associated activity can be found in different parts of the country throughout the forty years separating the creation of the republic from the Age of Jackson. Further, although some of these combinations were doubtless short-lived, many showed considerable longevity.[76] Nevertheless, their activities were clearly restricted in geographic focus,

[73] For details see n. 1.

[74] This tally counts the first trial of *People v. Fisher* as an acquittal. It does not include *Commonwealth v. Marshall* (Pa. 1829), which was a hearing to continue recognizances and not a result. Nor does it include the first *Pittsburgh Cordwainers* case (1814), which was settled before trial. From the sentiments expressed in *Marshall*, however, it is fair to conclude that, like the first *Pittsburgh* case, had it gone to trial the result would most likely have been a conviction. Thus the balance of convictions and acquittals clearly alters markedly in the 1830s.

[75] See generally, John R. Commons et al., *History of Labor in the United States* (New York, 1918), 1:169–453; Philip S. Foner, *History of the Labor Movement in the United States* (New York, 1947), 1:97–120. On New York see Sean Wilentz, *Chants Democratic: New York City and the Rise of the American Working Class, 1788–1850* (New York, 1984), 219–54; on Philadelphia see Bruce Laurie, *Working People of Philadelphia, 1800–1850* (Philadelphia, 1980), 85–104; on Boston see Lisa B. Lubow, "Artisans in Transition: Early Capitalist Development and the Carpenters of Boston, 1787–1837" Ph.D. diss., UCLA, 1987), 493–600.

[76] The society of journeymen cordwainers indicted in *Commonwealth v. Pullis* had been in continuous existence for "fifteen years and upwards" at the time of indictment. See the "Address of the Working Shoemakers of the City of Philadelphia to the Public," published in the *Philadelphia Aurora* (28 Nov. 1805). See also Ian M. G. Quimby, "The Cordwainers Protest: A Crisis in Labor Relations," *Winterthur Portfolio*, 3 (1983), 83–101. Similar claims of longevity characterize the New York society indicted in

consisting largely of attempts by single, trade-specific combinations to establish or preserve their members' voice in determining the conditions of the trade within a specific locality. Almost invariably these combinations manifested a "civic," rather than an explicit class, orientation, asserting quasi-corporate or quasi-municipal rights of regulation founded on nonmarket concepts of republican justice (police) rather than exhibiting some kind of nascent collective bargaining mentality. In some cases they sought decisively to separate themselves from masters, but in others they did not. Nor does there appear to have been much communication among them, far less any explicit attempts at translocal organization.[77]

This situation, however, began to change in the second half of the 1820s. The immediate issue was agitation for the ten-hour day, occurring across a broad front of trades in all the eastern cities. The underlying cause was growing awareness among working people of the extent of the decomposition of the artisan mode of production that had occurred in the decade since the end of the War of 1812. Symptomatic of that decomposition was the growing concentration of wealth and the spreading influence of entrepreneurialism and liberal "free market" ideologies in the trades, and with it the growth of stratification in the employment relationship and increasing conflict between employing masters and journeymen. The response was a wave of organization. Beginning in 1827 in Philadelphia, "journeymen and factory hands . . . organized unions on a widening front that drew together in confederations as well as third parties with ambitious manifestos."[78]

This burgeoning movement did not long remain focused on workplace organization but instead quickly assumed an active role in local and state politics. In Philadelphia, the Mechanics' Union of Trade Associations, the first citywide federation of journeymen trade societies in the country, became the conduit for independent organized participation of working men in the 1828 city and state elections; it was soon overshadowed by that political activity. In 1829 and 1830 similar independent Working Men's parties developed in New York and Massachusetts, where, particularly in Massachusetts, they transcended a specifically urban base and attracted considerable support from rural artisans and farmers. All canvassed the same general concerns: a republican system of education – equal, general, and publicly funded – to break the aristocracy's monopoly of knowledge, rescue the working classes from the dependency of ignorance, and equip them for the full participation in the polity that was their right as republican citizens; a radical simplification of the legal system to establish a republic of known laws; lien laws to protect the working

---

People v. Melvin (Wilentz, "Conspiracy, Power, and the Early Labor Movement," 575, n. 7). The Pittsburgh cordwainers' society indicted in *Commonwealth v. Morrow* had been in existence for "about six years" at the time of that trial (Commons et al., eds., *Documentary History*, 4:25).

[77] In all these respects American combinations paralleled their English counterparts. See e.g., John Smail, "New Languages for Labour and Capital: The Transformation of Discourse in the Early Years of the Industrial Revolution," *Social History*, 12, 1 (Jan. 1987), 49–71.

[78] Bruce Laurie, *Artisans into Workers: Labor in Nineteenth Century America* (New York, 1989), 63, 50–1. See, generally, Tomlins, *The State and the Unions*, 35–7; Wilentz, *Chants Democratic*, 61–142; Grimsted, "Ante-bellum Labor," 14–15.

classes against victimization by speculators and capitalists; abolition of all chartered monopolies, particularly banks; abolition of compulsory militia duty; and abolition of imprisonment for debt and prison labor.[79]

Disputes over the direction of the reform thrust within this broad critical republican consensus, however, proved highly damaging to the Working Men's electoral campaigns. This was particularly the case in New York, where the Working Men's Party split over adoption of Thomas Skidmore's radical proposals to equalize property holding through expropriation of land monopolies, and again subsequently over Robert Dale Owen's "state guardianship" education plan. Late developing and never electorally strong in New England, ravaged by factionalism in New York, the Working Men's greatest successes came in Philadelphia. Even here, however, their influence was spent by 1831.[80]

Their articulation of broad reform programs and their attractiveness to an electorate transcending the urban trade origins of the movement suggest that the eclectically radical Working Men's parties should be considered as parts of a translocal insurgent political movement expressing a "catchall" anxiety about the course of the polity – the growing influence of special interests, the appearance of ever-greater concentrations of political and economic power, the deterioration of the public sphere – rather than a movement specific to urban journeymen. Just such a catch-all quality, indeed, is suggested by the permeability of the frontiers between the Working Men and factions in the mainstream parties and by the diversity of influences one may detect in the movement's various positions: the urban radicalism of middle-class intellectuals such as Cornelius Blatchly, Robert Dale Owen, and Frances Wright; the plebeian radicalism of Langton Byllesby, Thomas Skidmore, and William Heighton; the democratic political economy of Daniel Raymond and Stephen Simpson; the quasi-agrarianism of one-time Jacobin Thomas Cooper; even the late John Taylor of Caroline's civic republicanism. It is that catch-all quality, too, which helps explain the reappearance within the Working Men's republican discourse of tensions between antimonopolism and self-policing collectivism not unlike those hinted at during the early conspiracy trials separating the journeymen from their radical Jacobin advocates. Certainly, radical antimonopolism's more individualistic adherents did not feel particularly at ease with the rather different direction implied in, for example, some of the proposals for a publicly funded and publicly controlled education system.[81] New York's bitter faction fighting over Skidmore's assault on

[79] See, generally, Commons et al., eds., *Documentary History*, 5:75–199; Laurie, *Artisans into Workers*, 80.

[80] Laurie, *Artisans into Workers*, 63–73, 79–82; Wilentz, *Chants Democratic*, 172–216. On the somewhat different course of the Working Men in Massachusetts see Ronald P. Formisano, *The Transformation of Political Culture: Massachusetts Parties, 1790s–1840s* (New York, 1983), 222–44.

[81] See e.g., the Working Men's "Report of the Joint Committees of the City and County of Philadelphia, Appointed September, 1829, to Ascertain the State of Public Instruction in Pennsylvania" (Feb. 1830), recommending a system of publicly funded and equal education (in Commons et al., eds., *Documentary History* 5:94–107). The Working Men's proposals were later vilified as "agrarianism" in the *Philadelphia National Gazette*: "Government cannot provide for the necessities of the People ... it is they who maintain the government, not the latter the People. Education may be among their necessities; but

the legitimacy of private property, and subsequently over Owen's state guardianship system of education reform, both treated by some within the Working Men's movement as unacceptable intrusions of collective power into social life, is further evidence for this.[82]

The strength of radical antimonopolism in the Working Men's movement suggested by the outcome of intraparty squabbles in New York may also be detected in the lack, notwithstanding that this was a movement founded in the first instance on journeymen's associations, of any party programmatic commitment to a vision of the republican polity accommodative of trade unionism. Some scholars have concluded from this that, notwithstanding the substantial alteration in the scale of their activities in the 1830s, workingmen saw collective organization as but a temporary expedient, an expression not of a growing consciousness that exploitation and class division were becoming permanent characteristics of their situation but rather of their desire for a suitable means of agitation for the abolition of artificial privileges accumulated by self-interested monopolists and restoration of the early republic's holistic community of producers. Of the antebellum decades, Victoria Hattam has written that "workers' protest focused primarily on changing capital's behavior, on abolishing capital's special privileges rather than on trying to secure similar privileges of collective action for workers from the state."[83]

There is a lot to be said for this argument. Hattam can clearly demonstrate the persistence of "producer" ideology in the discourse of the 1830s, and her case is further strengthened by the failure of any of the Working Men's parties to adopt explicit endorsements of workers' collective action in their platforms.[84] But although defensible as a characterization of the position of the Working Men's movement on trade unions, Hattam's argument is less convincing as a blanket

it is one of that description which the state or national councils cannot supply" (12 July 1830); and "a direct tax for 'the equal means of obtaining useful learning' is . . . the action, if not the name, of the Agrarian system. Authority – that is, the State – is to force the more eligibly situated citizens to contribute a part (which might be very considerable) of their means, for the accommodation of the rest; and this is equivalent to the idea of an actual, compulsory partition of their substance" (19 Aug. 1830). See generally Commons et al., eds., *Documentary History*, 5:107–14.

[82] Commons et al., eds., *Documentary History*, 5:149–77. See, generally, Laurie, *Artisans into Workers*, 65–7; idem, *Working People of Philadelphia*, 75–83; Wilentz, *Chants Democratic*, 172–216.

[83] Victoria Hattam, "Unions and Politics: The Courts and American Labor, 1806–1896" (Ph.D. diss., MIT, 1987), 111. Hattam's argument is restated, in detail and at length, in *Labor Visions and State Power*, Chapter 3.

[84] The preamble of the Mechanics' Union of Trade Associations, out of which the Working Men's Party developed in Philadelphia, was somewhat more forthcoming (in Commons et al., eds., *Documentary History*, 5:89–90): "The real object, therefore, of this association, is to avert, if possible, the desolating evils which must inevitably arise from a depreciation of the intrinsic value of human labour; to raise the mechanical and productive classes to that condition of true independence and [equality] which their practical skill and ingenuity, their immense utility to the nation and their growing intelligence are beginning imperiously to demand: to promote, equally, the happiness, prosperity and welfare of the whole community – to aid in conferring a due and full proportion of that invaluable promoter of happiness, leisure, upon all its useful members; and to assist, in conjunction with such other institutions of this nature as shall hereafter be formed throughout the union, in establishing a just balance of power, both mental, moral, political and scientific, between all the various classes and individuals which constitute society at large."

characterization of the ideology of the Jacksonian labor movement, particularly when accompanied by the claim that antebellum workers *accepted* convictions for criminal conspiracy as "a legitimate form of government regulation" and "as a reciprocal restraint on their own collective action" – that is, as a quid pro quo logically implied by their own opposition to special privileges enjoyed by capital.[85] In fact, as we shall see, it was precisely during the years *after* the passing of the Working Men's parties that the labor movement began to show that, in a way never clearly articulated by those parties, it conceived of a properly republican polity and political economy as one in which trade societies and trades unions would play an essential, central, and permanent role. In other words, one finds for the first time in the 1830s a growing and explicit emphasis on the extension of organization and permanence of unions as the *only* basis upon which working people could expect to have any impact upon the polity.

The forums within which this new conception began to be hammered out were the urban federations of craft unions which began to appear in all the eastern seaboard centers during 1833 and 1834. The first, the General Trades' Union (GTU) of New York, was established by twelve craft societies in August 1833 in the wake of a major carpenters' strike. Within a year similar federations had appeared in upwards of a dozen cities. The biggest at the movement's peak, judged by number of affiliates, was the Trades' Union of the City and County of Philadelphia. Formed

---

[85] Hattam, "Unions and Politics," 111. See also idem, *Labor Visions and State Power*, Chapter 3. In the latter work, Hattam acknowledges that her claim "rests largely on an evaluation of what the producers did and did not demand" and that she "has not found any explicit statements to this effect in the antebellum era." I do not doubt the thoroughness of her evaluation, but I am not persuaded that the conclusion she has stated follows. It should be noted, however, that Hattam is not alone, for Steven J. Ross makes a similar argument in *Workers on the Edge: Work, Leisure, and Politics in Industrializing Cincinnati, 1788–1890* (New York, 1985), 62. As we shall see, such a "trade-off" was posited by adherents of both major parties during the mid-1830s, but there is little evidence of its acceptance in any of the pronouncements of the major city federations or nascent national unions of the period. Rather, as New York journeymen put it in the spring of 1836, theirs was "the only *justifiable* combination that exists" (quoted in Wilentz, *Chants Democratic*, 290).

One should note, as Louis Hartz did many years ago, that because workers "identified themselves with the only legitimate members of the community" they saw nothing inconsistent in condemning chartered corporations as legislated monopolies in the service of special interests while simultaneously pursuing their own prolabor measures: "they were able to argue that measures in their behalf were unsullied by class implications [because they] served the mass interest" (Louis Hartz, *Economic Policy and Democratic Thought: Pennsylvania, 1776–1860* [Cambridge, Mass., 1948], 195). As Ely Moore put it in his "Address Delivered before the General Trades' Union of the City of New York at the Chatham Street Chapel, Monday, December 2, 1833" (in Joseph L. Blau, ed., *Social Theories of Jacksonian Democracy: Representative Writings of the Period 1825–1850* [New York, 1954] 3:289–300, at 293): "Again; it is alleged, that it is setting a dangerous precedent for journeymen to combine for the purpose of coercing a compliance with their terms. It may, indeed, be dangerous to aristocracy – dangerous to monopoly – dangerous to oppression – but not to the general good, or the public tranquillity. Internal danger to a state is not to be apprehended from a general effort on the part of the people to improve and exalt their condition, but from an alliance of the crafty, designing and intriguing few. What! tell us, in this enlightened age, that the welfare of the people will be endangered by a voluntary act of the people themselves? That the people will wantonly seek their own destruction? That the safety of the state will be plotted against by three fourths of the members comprising the state! O how worthless, how poor and pitiful, are all such arguments and objections!"

by fifteen societies in November 1833, by August 1834 it had seventeen affiliates comprising a total of 6,000 organized journeymen. By 1836 the number of affiliates had grown to fifty-three, with a collective membership of 10,000. Meanwhile, in New York and Brooklyn the GTU quickly grew beyond its founding membership of twelve societies to twenty-one, with 4,000 members, by the end of 1833, and to twenty-nine, with 11,500 members, by August 1834. Over the next two years the number of affiliates expanded to fifty-two, one less than in Philadelphia, but it is likely that the membership by this time exceeded 20,000. Elsewhere, in Boston sixteen trades joined in March 1834 to call a founding convention of a citywide federation representing approximately 4,000 journeymen; a year later six new craft societies had been added. Baltimore also had a federation, smaller again but still thriving. Washington, Albany, Newark, Buffalo, and Cincinnati all also had well-established unions of trades. All told, at the movement's peak, "it is likely that between one-fifth and one-third of urban journeymen belonged to unions, the highest in antebellum history."[86] Appropriately symbolic of the unions' vitality and ambition, in mid-1834 a convention of delegates from all the major eastern union centers met in New York to create a National Trades' Union. In 1836 national conventions of cordwainers, carpenters, combmakers, weavers, and printers met to create national unions of their particular trades.[87]

In a fashion similar to the Working Men's parties, the union federations sought to mobilize an otherwise-fragmented plebeian opposition to the mainstream political economy. Indeed, there was a certain programmatic continuity between the "political" and "union" phases of activity: Like the parties, union federations debated republican schemes of education and voiced opposition to chartered monopolies, imprisonment for debt, and prison labor.[88] Unlike the parties, however, the union federations were by nature far more homogeneous and far more focused on the daily conflicts of the employment relationship. Too, the wrangling that had destroyed the Working Men's effectiveness had left the unions' leaders highly suspicious of further involvement in partisan politics.[89] The consequence, "since unions were only for

---

[86] Laurie, *Artisans into Workers*, 84; Commons et al., eds., *Documentary History*, 5:203–7, 325–6, and 6:73–5, 191; Wilentz, *Chants Democratic*, 220. It is worth noting that in June 1836 the *New York Evening Post* opined that at least two-thirds of the city's workingmen (then numbering about 50,000) had joined unions, which would place the New York unions' total membership close to 30,000.

[87] Commons et al., eds., *Documentary History*, 6:191–3 311–13.

[88] Amy Bridges, "Becoming American: The Working Classes in the United States before the Civil War," in Ira Katznelson and Aristide Zolberg, *Working Class Formation: Nineteenth Century Patterns in Western Europe and the United States* (Princeton, 1986), 157–96, at 163.

[89] See e.g., Commons et al., eds., *Documentary History*, 6:341. Something of the unions' complex relationship to politics – careful avoidance of party involvements combined with active interest in politics as *policy* – is revealed in the course of a debate on the meaning of politics that occurred at the 1834 National Trades' Union convention, pitting New York Journeymen House Carpenters delegate Robert Townshend and Boston Trades' Union delegate Charles Douglass against Philadelphia Trades' Union delegates William English, John Ferral, and Michael Labarthe, and Howard Schenk from Newark (in ibid., 211–16, 205–9, emphases in original). The question was the inclusion of the word "political" in a resolution to appoint a committee to draft resolutions expressing the views of the convention on "the social, civil, and political condition of the laboring classes of the country." All agreed that the National

workers and most political figures were critical of unions," was growing distance between the union movement and what had gone before, a separation manifested at first in tactics – "an upsurge of militancy on the job" – and then in strategy and, increasingly, theory as unions mounted a search for alternatives to market institutions and employment relations "that transcended anything political radicalism had to offer."[90]

The essential prerequisite both to the success of militancy in the short term and to success in developing policies capable of altering the polity's direction in the longer term was the extension of organization throughout each trade and the practice of solidarity among the trades, and between journeymen tradesmen and common laborers, through the instrumentality of the city federation.[91] Hence the increasing prominence given to *permanent* organization of all working people in the pronouncements of the various trade societies and city federations on the purpose and objectives of the union movement. Hence, too, their sensitivity to perceived encroachments on the right to organize. "What better means can be devised for promoting a more equal distribution of wealth," asked New York GTU president Ely Moore, speaking at a convocation of the associated trades in December 1833, "than for the producing classes to *claim*, and by virtue of union and concert, *secure* their claims to their respective portions" and thereby establish "the honor and

---

Trades' Union should avoid anything suggestive of involvement in partisan politics. Townshend and Douglass, however, argued that working people should maintain an active interest in "the science of government" and in agitation for measures to promote their "welfare and happiness." The convention had assembled, Douglass argued, "because the working classes were partially shorn of their rights, and because their interests had been neglected, to devise means to restore those rights and to have their interests attended to: this was their *policy*, this their *Politics*." Against this it was argued that a reference to politics would inevitably be construed to mean partisan involvement, and further that the experience of the Working Men's parties, particularly in Philadelphia, had shown that union organization could not coexist with partisan political involvement.

The latter position prevailed, and the word "intellectual" was substituted for "political" in the committee's brief. However the subsequently appointed committee (two delegates from New York, two from Philadelphia, one from Boston, chaired by Ferral – the only participant in the previous day's debate to be included) reported what was in fact a comprehensive policy program, endorsing inter alia an equal, universal, republican system of education; unrestricted access to public lands; factories legislation to limit children's hours of labor and provide for their education; and repeal of trade union conspiracy laws. The report was premised on a call for the complete organization of the working classes throughout the United States as the only sure foundation for "social happiness" and concluded with the resolution "that as productive labor is the only legitimate source of wealth, and as the productive laborers have been deprived of the advantages of their labor by bad legislation, it behooves this portion of the community to regain and maintain, by correct legislation, what they have lost by inattention to their own best interests."

[90] Laurie, *Artisans into Workers*, 84.

[91] For examples of the unions' stress on extensive organization and solidarity see "An Address to Mechanics and Working Men, by the Trades Union of the City and County of Philadelphia" (*Pennsylvanian*, 9 Jan. 1834), and "What Is the Trades Union?" (*Pennsylvanian*, 9 Feb. 1836), both in Commons et al., eds., *Documentary History*, 5:339–40, 389–92. See also "To the Journeymen Cordwainers of the City and County of Philadelphia" (*Pennsylvanian*, 4 Apr. 1835), "Report of the Delegated Members from the Several Associations of Journeymen Comb Makers" (*National Laborer*, 10 Sept. 1836), and "Report of Proceedings of the Convention of Journeymen House Carpenters" (*National Laborer*, 19 Nov. 1836), all in Commons et al., eds., *Documentary History*, 6:24–7, 333–4, 338–9.

safety of our respective vocations upon a more secure and permanent basis."[92] Six months later, the founding Declaration of Rights of the Trades' Union of Boston emphasized "that it is the right of workmen, and a duty they owe to each other, to associate together."[93] Similarly, the 1835 convention of the National Trades' Union resolved that only "the formation and permanency of Trade Societies and Trades' Unions" could provide "security against the entire degradation of the whole mass of the working men in the United States."[94] The first national convention of cordwainers, held in March 1836 in New York, likewise agreed that there was no possibility of regaining "our lost rights" other than "by combinations and associations among the mechanics and laboring poor" and therefore resolved "that the Journeymen Cordwainers represented in this Convention will never forego their right to form any society or association in conformity with the Constitution of the United States and fundamental principles of our Government, and will resist to the utmost of their power any attempt to wrest from them that right."[95]

Actions spoke as loud as all these words. In Philadelphia, for example, the 1835 general strike for a ten-hour day was touched off by a dispute initially involving unskilled coal heavers. Tradesmen joined in, "shouting 'we are all day laborers,'" and the strike subsequently spread to textile operatives and outworkers. This tentative journeyman–laborer alliance was reproduced the following year in New York.[96]

In most cases, the specific cause of tradesmen's protestations of their right to organize was, unsurprisingly, the willingness of local authorities to renew their resort to conspiracy indictments to countermand the growing power of the union movement. That willingness in turn prompted demands from the unions for legal reform. The common law doctrine of criminal conspiracy was "neither wise, just, nor politic" and was "directly opposed to the spirit and genius of our free institutions," argued Ely Moore in 1833. "[It] ought, therefore, to be abrogated." In the same vein the 1834 convention of the National Trades' Union resolved, more specifically, that "the laws existing in portions of our country, under which Trades' Unions among mechanics for the maintenance of their rights, and the correction of abuses, are declared illegal combinations, are a manifest violation of the Constitution of these United States, and an infringement on the lawful rights of every citizen," and urged their repeal. In July 1836 the Trades' Union of Philadelphia heard a similar demand that it petition the state legislature "for the passage of a definite law in

---

[92] Moore, "Address Delivered before the General Trades' Union," at 290–1 (emphasis in original).

[93] "Declaration of Rights of the Trades' Union of Boston and Vicinity" (June 1834), in Philip S. Foner, ed., *We, the Other People: Alternative Declarations of Independence by Labor Groups, Farmers, Woman's Rights Advocates, Socialists, and Blacks, 1829–1975* (Urbana, 1976), 52–4, at 54.

[94] Commons et al., eds., *Documentary History*, 6:241.

[95] *Proceedings of the Convention of Cordwainers, Holden in the City of New-York, Commencing on the First Monday in March, 1836*, pamphlet, Massachusetts Historical Society, Boston, 17. See also the "Report of the Committee on Trades' Unions," from the Third Annual Convention of the National Trades' Union, *National Laborer*, 26 Nov. 1836, in Commons et al., eds., *Documentary History*, 6:294–7.

[96] Laurie, *Working People of Philadelphia*, 91; Sean Wilentz, "The Rise of the American Working Class, 1776–1877: A Survey," in J. Carroll Moody and Alice Kessler-Harris, eds., *Perspectives on American Labor History: The Problems of Synthesis* (DeKalb, Ill., 1989), 96.

relation to combinations and conspiracies, so far as relates to the operations of Mechanics in regard to their wages or hours of labor."[97]

The situation came to a head in the summer of 1836 – the climax of three years of considerable tension and drama for the Jacksonian labor movement – as local prosecutors in New York and Pennsylvania pressed a series of conspiracy indictments against trade societies in both states. Clearly intended as a challenge to the unions, the 1836 conspiracy cases provoked a massive reaction in which the specific issue of conspiracy merged with the Jacksonian labor movement's general indictment of existing structures of political and juridical authority.

THE NEW YORK CASES

The four 1836 cases in New York and Pennsylvania were crowded into a three-month period beginning in late May. The first, and in many ways the most notorious, was *People v. Faulkner*, in which twenty New York tailors were tried for an illegal combination to raise their wages, for conspiring to intimidate other journeymen from laboring at lower rates, and for using force and violence to effect their purposes. Occurring at the height of New York's "year of the strikes," the case grew out of a major confrontation earlier the same year between the city's journeymen tailors and their employers, themselves combined in the Union Association of Master Tailors. In turn, this confrontation had itself been but one element in a general conflict between masters and journeymen, and between masters and the New York GTU, which had spread all across the city during the early months of 1836.[98]

The journeymen tailors had been indicted by a New York grand jury in late March in a prosecution pressed by the masters, in light of the outcome in *People v. Fisher*, as a "test" of the legality of trades unions. The particular occasion for the indictment was a strike called by the journeymen's society to protest the master tailors' repudiation of a standing agreement on prices and their accompanying declaration that they would no longer employ society members.[99] That kind of antagonism toward society members was not all that unusual: Almost from the moment in the early 1830s that labor activism had begun to be a significant factor across the generality of New York trades, reports had circulated of instances of harassment. The 1833 carpenters' strike out of which the GTU was born, for example, had prompted elements in the press to advise the master carpenters and the

---

[97] Moore, "Address Delivered before the General Trades' Union," 292. On the National Trades' Union convention of 1834, see Commons et al., *Documentary History*, 6:208. On the Philadelphia Trades' Union, see Commons et al., eds., *Documentary History*, 5:373, 375. The Philadelphia Trades' Union did not act on the petition request, no doubt because of the successful outcome in *Commonwealth v. Grinder*. Protest against oppressive laws did, however, form a significant element of the Trades' Union's August 1836 rally against the indictment of the Schuylkill laborers. For details of the *Grinder* and *Schuylkill Laborers* prosecutions, see below, this chapter, section entitled The Pennsylvania Cases.

[98] Wilentz, *Chants Democratic*, 286–90.

[99] Commons et al., eds., *Documentary History*, 5:287–8; Wilentz, *Chants Democratic*, 290.

citizenry at large that it was "their duty . . . to set their faces like flint against all such combinations." The following year the journeymen hat makers reported to the GTU that employers in that trade had declared they would discharge all men suspected of being society members. As a delegation to the New York GTU from the Newark Trades' Union put it in May 1835, describing similar experiences in that city, "the Employers are not so much against the advance of wages, as they are against the formation of a 'Trades' Union" among the Journeymen – which they are determined to oppose with their united influence."[100] The master tailors' action, however, appeared to be the first move in a more deliberate campaign; within a month employers in two other well-organized trades called meetings and adopted similar declarations.[101]

Popular opposition to the tailors' conspiracy prosecution was pronounced and sustained. The indictment alone provoked a parade of several thousand workers from all trades, and when the case came to trial in the last week of May in the Court of Oyer and Terminer it was attended by "a large concourse of persons."[102] Proceedings commenced with an impassioned speech by Associate District Attorney Joseph Blunt, a prominent local Whig, in condemnation of unions for the "injustice, illiberality and tyranny" which attended their organization, for their alien origins,

---

[100] *New York Journal of Commerce*, 1 June 1833, in Commons et al., eds., *Documentary History*, 5:211 (see also 5:222, 241). The *Journal of Commerce*, we should note, professed antipathy to all combinations, whether of masters or journeymen, whether "by simple individual pledges, or legislative enactments, or menaces and violence." See its issues of 1 June 1833 and 10 June 1835 (in Commons et al., eds., *Documentary History*, 5:209–11 and 308–9).

[101] These were the Curriers and Leather Dealers (meeting on 24 March 1836) and the Manufacturing and Retailing Cordwainers (meeting on 8 April 1836). Employer groups with similar goals were in the process of formation at this time in other trades, and this circumstance was acknowledged and welcomed at the cordwainers' meeting, which resolved "that we cordially invite the employers in the different branches of the mechanic arts to hold meetings expressive of their views in relation to the oppressive operations and proceedings of the Trades Union, and such other matter as they shall deem expedient for their future welfare" and called upon "the different societies of employers to appoint delegates to hold a general convention." See Commons et al., eds., *Documentary History*, 5:309–13.

[102] Describing the postindictment parade, Wilentz notes that "individual unions hurled abuse at banks, party politicians, and chartered corporations, as well as that combination of men 'who have evinced an unrepublican taste in dubbing themselves *master tailors*'" (*Chants Democratic*, 290). On the atmosphere of the tailors' trial see *New York Transcript*, 26 May 1863. The *Transcript* report made reference to "the excitement which had been caused in reference to this prosecution (in consequence of its supposed aim to annihilate the existence of Trades Unions)."
From early on in the year the unions had shown themselves well aware of the threat that the decision in *People v. Fisher* posed. A committee appointed to consider the decision's implications by the Cordwainers' National Convention in New York in 7–10 March 1836 reported back to the convention that the decision invoked "the tyranny and oppression of British law" and that it was "odious and despotic . . . aristocratic in the extreme – subversive of republican principles, and cannot receive the sanction or approval of any friend of free government or equal rights" (*Proceedings of the Convention of Cordwainers*, 17). (The committee's report on *People v. Fisher* and its implications occupied fully one quarter of the convention's printed proceedings.) On the same day that the cordwainers' committee reported (9 March) the New York GTU also appointed a committee of three to report on the decision. The committee presented an interim report on 23 March and reported in full the following week. It was in response to the interim report that the GTU called "a general meeting of mechanics and workingmen," which in turn resulted in the subsequent parade and demonstration of opposition to the tailors' indictment. See Commons et al., eds., *Documentary History*, 5:294–5, 296, 298.

and for the "ruinous and pernicious" and "oppressive" consequences with which their existence threatened individuals and communities. A verdict against the defendants, Blunt informed the jury, would "lay the foundation for the overthrow of those institutions which had already attained a wide, extended and giant strength, and which, if permitted still to progress, would ultimately spread devastation and misery around, and be as fatal and pestilential in their effects as the deadly *upas* tree of eastern growth."[103] In its turn, the defense challenged the validity of the indictment under New York law.

In his charge, delivered after a trial of three days, Judge Ogden Edwards told the jury that the Supreme Court's decision in *People v. Fisher* confirmed that the indictment was sustainable under the New York Revised Statutes. The defense had attempted to argue that this prosecution was naught but "a spiteful proceeding between the Masters and the Journeymen." But this was "but a narrow and partial view of the subject, and not what the legislature had in view when they established a law for the community at large."[104] Edwards then proceeded to deliver a denunciation of unions which quite matched the associate district attorney's opening in its extravagance. If such institutions were tolerated, he was reported to say, "the constitutional control over our affairs would pass away from the people at large, and become vested in the hands of conspirators. We should have a new system of government, and our rights be placed at the disposal of a voluntary and self-constituted association." The jury should consider "whether any body of men could raise their crests in this land of law, and control others by self-organized combination."[105]

The jury duly found the defendants guilty but recommended leniency.[106] The *New York Transcript* opined that, given the recommendation, it was probable that "the judgment of the Court . . . will not amount to more than a fine of six cents against each of the defendants."[107] Edwards, however, had other ideas. He was, he said at the sentencing on 11 June, "at a loss to know what degree of severity may be necessary to rid society" of combinations. Influenced by the jury's recommendation, he was disposed to impose only "a very mild punishment." He then fined the twenty defendants a total of $1,150.[108]

---

[103] *New York Transcript*, 26 May 1836. For the unknowing, like me, Blunt's arboreal metaphor refers to "a tall Asian and East Indian tree (*Antiaris toxicaria*) of the mulberry family with a latex that contains poisonous glucosides used as an arrow poison" (*Webster's Ninth New Collegiate Dictionary*, 1296).

[104] Although framed in terms of the court's jurisdiction in light of the statute, Edwards's comments in this portion of his charge may also be seen as an echo of the older republican discourse of civic welfare that animated earlier courts. For this argument see Victoria C. Hattam, "Courts and the Question of Class: Judicial Regulation of Labor under the Common Law Doctrine of Criminal Conspiracy," in Tomlins and King, eds., *Labor Law in America*, 44–70, at 55. See also below, Chapter 6, where I find a similar echo in the case of Peter Oxenbridge Thacher. Hattam argues that the same mentality applies to Chief Justice Savage, but this seems to me unlikely on the evidence of his Supreme Court opinion in *Lambert*.

[105] *People v. Faulkner* (1836), in Commons et al., eds., *Documentary History*, 4:315–33, at 321–5.

[106] *New York Mercantile Advertiser*, 31 May 1836. [107] *New York Transcript*, 31 May 1836.

[108] *People v. Faulkner*, in Commons et al., eds., *Documentary History*, 4:332; *New York Mercantile Advertiser*, 11 June 1836.

The tailors' conviction was greeted with widespread condemnation and major demonstrations of opposition from working people both in New York and elsewhere. Originally scheduled for 6 June, the sentencing hearing had to be abandoned because of widely publicized plans for a major protest against the verdict.[109] Sentencing eventually took place the following Saturday (11 June) before a crowd of several hundred mechanics and amid widespread fears of violence. The following Monday (13 June) a parade and demonstration of nearly thirty thousand people jammed into City Hall Park and burned Judge Edwards in effigy, along with the Supreme Court's Chief Justice Savage, the author of *People v. Fisher*, for good measure.[110] Other attacks followed: The *New York Union*, organ of the GTU, called upon the population to arrest "the enemies of the working classes" in their "schemes of oppression." The *Long Island Democrat* denounced "the ministers of our common laws" for their gross violation of the rights of fellow citizens. "It is time for the people to take the subject in hand, and place such unprincipled, miscreant judges in a position to smart under the just indignation of an offended public." Delivering a July Fourth address before the Mechanics and Working Men of Brooklyn, the New England radical Seth Luther ridiculed Edwards as "an imbecile old man" and "one of the sappers and miners of despotism . . . at work destroying the very foundations of liberty."[111]

---

[109] *Boston Courier*, 8 June 1836. At the conclusion of the trial on Monday 30 May, Edwards set Monday 6 June for sentencing. The weekend prior to the scheduled sentencing hearing, however, the following handbill (known as the "coffin" handbill) was widely distributed throughout the city:

> The RICH against the POOR! Judge Edwards the tool of the Aristocracy, against the People! Mechanics and Workingmen! a deadly blow has been struck at your LIBERTY! The prize for which your fathers fought has been robbed from you! The Freemen of the North are now on a level with the slaves of the South! – with no other privileges than laboring that drones may fatten on your life-blood! Twenty of your brethren have been found guilty for presuming to resist a reduction of their wages! and Judge Edwards has charged an Ameirican [sic] Jury, and agreeably to that charge, they have established the precedent, that workingmen have no *right to regulate the price of labor*! or, in other words, the Rich are the only judges of the wants of the Poor Man! – On Monday, June 6, 1836, at 10 o'clock, these Freemen are to receive their sentence, to gratify the hellish appetites of the Aristocracy! On Monday, the Liberty of the Workingmen will be interred! – Judge Edwards is to chant the Requiem! – Go! Go! Go! every Freeman, every Workingman, and hear the hollow and the melancholy sound of the earth on the Coffin of Equality! Let the Court-Room, the City-Hall – yea the whole Park, be filled with MOURNERS! But, remember, offer no violence to Judge Edwards! Bend meekly, and receive the chains wherewith you are to be bound! Keep the peace! Above all things keep the peace!
>
> '76.

During the week following the postponement of sentencing sympathizers collected funds to pay the anticipated fines. As a result, despite the severity of the sentence when finally delivered, the men's fines were paid immediately and they walked free from the courtroom rather than having to stand committed. It is perhaps worth noting the report in the *New York Evening Post* of 13 June, 1836 that "while the journeymen tailors were paying their fines, one of the officers [of the court] stepped up, said he had been employed three weeks at 10s per day, and wished to give the whole as a donation to assist the men."

[110] On fears of violence see *New York Evening Post*, 13 June 1836. On the City Hall Park meeting see Commons et al., eds., *Documentary History*, 5:318–22.

[111] *New York Union* and *Long Island Democrat*, both excerpted in the *Philadelphia Public Ledger*, 13 June 1836. Seth Luther, *An Address delivered before the Mechanics and Working-Men of the City of Brooklyn, on the Celebration of the Sixtieth Anniversary of American Independence* (Brooklyn, 1836), 8, 17.

The reverberations of the tailors' conviction spread far beyond New York. The Trades' Union of Philadelphia, for example, protested the trial's outcome as one more example of the "shameful maladministration" of law which seemed, with increasing frequency, to await working people in their encounters with the judiciary and announced "that a crisis has arrived in which the Workingmen must either tamely yield their dearest rights" or make a stand against the "thraldom" of biased legislation. "We have seen in this and other states, journeymen mechanics indicted, tried and imprisoned for combining to protect their interests, while capitalists, for infinitely worse combinations, have not only escaped the censure of the law, but have been held up as public benefactors. . . . It is with painful solicitude that we have watched the rapid advance of inequality in our beloved country, and while we remember that foreign tyranny found a limit in 1776, we yet hope that domestic oppression may find a stern and as successful a foe in the strong union of the Working Men."[112] At the Pittsburgh Trades' Union's Independence Day celebration, resolutions were adopted attacking the "corrupt judiciary" and calling for "the English common law, as respects the prohibition of laboring men's combinations," to be "effectually kicked out of these free states."[113] In Newark, mechanics greeted the tailors' sentencing by hanging an effigy of Edwards from the town's liberty pole. "When an attempt was made . . . by order of the municipal authorities, to cut down the counterfeit presentment of his Honor, the pole was found to be so completely

---

[112] Commons et al., eds., *Documentary History*, 5:362–3. The reference to imprisonment here is noteworthy, in that none of the labor conspiracy cases so far recovered by historians involves a sentence of imprisonment. Most likely the statement refers to known cases in which defendants were committed for trial either at exorbitant bail or without opportunity to offer bail in lieu of physical committal, resulting in their imprisonment awaiting trial; or to defendants sentenced to be fined and to stand committed until the fines were paid. On the former see, e.g., the *Philadelphia Coalheavers'* case (1836) and *Commonwealth v. McConnell* (1842), both described below. On the latter see, e.g., Lloyd, *Trial of the Boot and Shoemakers of Philadelphia*, 149. There is always the possibility, although this is less likely, that the statement refers to sentences of imprisonment passed on convicted defendants in cases yet undiscovered. Thus, one should note Orestes Brownson's statement, in 1840, that in New York, "laborers have been fined *and imprisoned* for . . . agreeing together, not to sell their labor unless at higher price than they had hitherto been paid" (Orestes Brownson, *Defence of the Article on the Laboring Classes, From the Boston Quarterly Review* [Boston, 1840]. 50, emphasis supplied).

One can, of course, find examples of sentences of imprisonment passed on defendants convicted of engaging in violent or riotous behavior in the course of a strike. See e.g., the report of the trial and conviction of eight New York riggers and stevedores on riotous conduct charges arising from a confrontation on the east side of Manhattan. The confrontation involved between two and three hundred strikers engaged in the "forcible remov[al] from vessels [of] people of their own occupation who were willing to work . . . for wages less than the rioters seemed to consider a proper remuneration" (see *Boston Courier*, 17–19 July 1828, carrying reports from New York papers). There is, however, no indication in the newspaper reports that riot charges were accompanied by conspiracy indictments.

[113] Quoted in Foner, *We, the Other People*, 9. Similar sentiments had been expressed on the subject of *People v. Fisher* at the Cordwainers' National Convention in New York the previous March: "To sustain the positions taken, the Judge quotes freely the ancient and modern law of the British empire, and the inference is too plain that he wishes the courts of this country to be ruled by the decisions of the British courts, notwithstanding it was the tyranny and oppression of British law that drove our pilgrim fathers to seek an asylum in this country, and afterwards prompted them to resist still further the tyranny of their native land, and to establish, in '76, a government and laws for their own protection" (*Proceedings of the Convention of Cordwainers*, 14–15).

slushed with grease that an ascent to it was found to be neither easy nor agreeable."[114] In Washington, workmen staged a "burial of liberty" featuring Edwards as the executioner.[115] Up and down the East Coast the decision was discussed and condemned in the democratic press.[116] By mid-July, according to the *Philadelphia Public Ledger*, Edwards was under considerable public pressure to resign from the bench.[117]

In its unrestrained condemnation of the threat posed by journeymen's "self-created societies" Edwards's opinion in *People v. Faulkner* was very much a creature of the conflicts that had been sweeping the trades in New York and in all of the East Coast's major metropolitan areas since 1833.[118] Certainly these had been of a nature and of a scale such that the subtleties and qualifications which some of the more carefully crafted opinions had been introducing into criminal conspiracy doctrine threatened to become lost as panicky courts set about achieving a cruder agenda. "Judging from what we have witnessed within the last year, we should be led to the conclusion that the trades of the country . . . is [*sic*] rapidly passing from the control of the supreme power of the state into the hands of private societies," Edwards had stated at the tailors' sentencing.

Every American knows, or ought to know, that he has no better friend than the laws, and that he needs no artificial combination for his protection. Our experience never manifested their necessity, and I may confidently say that they were not the offspring of necessity. They are of foreign origin, and I am led to believe are mainly upheld by foreigners. If such is the fact, I would say to them, that they mistake the character of the American people, if they indulge a hope that they can accomplish their ends in that way. No matter how crafty may be their devices, nor how extensive may be their combinations, or violent may be their conduct, yet such is the energy of the law, and such the fidelity of the people to the

---

[114] *Philadelphia Public Ledger*, 15 June 1836.   [115] Witte, "Early American Labor Cases," 827.

[116] Ibid., 827. Note, e.g., the following editorial in the *Essex Gazette* of 23 July 1836, written by John Greenleaf Whittier (extracted in John A. Pollard, "Whittier on Labor Unions," *New England Quarterly*, 12,1 [Mar. 1939], 99–102, emphasis in original): "We have been desirous for some time past to say a word or two in regard to the decision of Judge Edwards of New York, in the case of certain journeymen tailors, who have been indicted, tried and convicted before the criminal court of the city of New York for a conspiracy to procure higher wages. The crime is thus described by Judge Edwards. 'These men are charged with entering into *a conspiracy not to work for any master which did not give them certain rates which they demanded*, or for any master who employed men that worked for a less rate, or who were not members of their society.' In favor of this most absurd charge of 'conspiracy' the judge argues at length. So then it has come to this, that in a land of equal rights a laborer cannot fix the amount of his wages in connection with his fellow laborer, without being charged as a criminal before our courts of law. The merchants may agree upon their prices; the lawyers upon their fees; the physicians upon their charges; the manufacturers upon the wages given to their operatives; but the LABORER shall not consult his interest and fix the price of his own toil and skill. If this be LAW, it is unjust, oppressive and wicked. It ought not to disgrace the statute book of a republican state. . . . We are no advocate of disorderly conduct on the part of any portion of the community. But to brand laborers as criminals for *peaceably* requiring an increase of their wages, we hold to be an outrage on the rights of man, and a disgrace to a community professing to be free."

[117] *Philadelphia Public Ledger*, 19 July 1836.

[118] On New York see Wilentz, *Chants Democratic*, 219–96. On Philadelphia see Laurie, *Working People of Philadelphia*, 85–106. On Boston, see below, Chapter 6.

government, that they will soon find their efforts as unavailing as the beating of frothy surges against a rock. It is a sentiment deeply engrafted in the bosom of every American, that he ought and must submit to the laws, and that to its [*sic*] mandates all stubborn necks must yield. Self-created societies are unknown to the constitution and laws, and will not be permitted to rear their crest and extend their baneful influence over any portion of the community.[119]

The antagonism toward the existence of unions manifested in Edwards's opinion – his concern, in particular, to speak to what he represented as their fundamental challenge to a law-constituted republic – evidences the depth of the social and political anxieties to which the previous three years of trades union growth and activity in New York had given rise. His example, however, was not followed. Undoubtedly this was in part a consequence of the outcry against it. But it is also important to recognize, in order to understand its subsequent evolution, that the particular direction in which Savage's opinion in *People v. Fisher* had pointed the conspiracy doctrine in New York – the foundation upon which Edwards had built his denunciation – was in fact highly vulnerable. Indeed, within a month of *People v. Faulkner*'s decisive affirmation of *Fisher*, the precedent had been effectively distinguished in *People v. Cooper*, heard in the Court of Oyer and Terminer for Hudson.[120]

Cooper involved an indictment pressed against eight journeymen cordwainers on the strength of *People v. Fisher* for a conspiracy to raise their wages through a combination and to coerce noncompliant masters and journeymen, to the injury of trade and commerce. Although unable to produce evidence of actual coercion (even the district attorney admitted that the journeymen's society "was scarcely an evil of itself"), the prosecution sought to sustain the allegation of injury to trade by introducing evidence to show that the society was in league with the New York GTU (represented as an organization embracing a hundred other societies and extending throughout the United States) and was thus part of a grand conspiracy injurious to the public by its very nature.[121] The court, however, excluded the evidence as not material to the indictment, and the defense then pilloried *People v. Fisher*, suddenly rendered vulnerable by the exclusion, for criminalizing lawful activity, for "saying in plain language that it is a criminal act – a conspiracy for men to combine together to attain a lawful end by lawful means," and invited the jury to disregard it. Importantly, the defendants' attorneys did not deny the salience of conspiracy as such. "I suppose a true definition of a conspiracy to be this," said counsel John W. Edmonds, "that it must be a combination of two or more, to obtain an unlawful end

---

[119] *People v. Faulkner* (1836), in Commons et al., eds., *Documentary History*, 4:330–1.

[120] *People v. Cooper* (1836), in ibid., 227–312.

[121] Ibid., 285. The report of the case shows that in opening the case the district attorney observed "that the offence against the law consists alone in the conspiracy. The crime did not consist in asking for an increase of wages; that they had a right to do, but they had not a right to meet together and to fix those prices by combination – they had no right to say that boss shoemakers should not employ men not belonging to their society. The tendency of these societies was to restrain the free circulation of wealth through the country, and the powerful arm of the law had a right to put them down before the land was swelling with the injuries resulting from them" (279).

by lawful means, or a lawful end by unlawful means." This, Edmonds claimed, was the definition settled upon by the Court of Errors in *Lambert v. People*. In *Fisher* the Supreme Court had taken it upon itself to "declare a conspiracy to consist in itself – in the very fact of combination – notwithstanding the end and the means are both lawful." But the Supreme Court was subordinate to the Court of Errors, and Edmonds invited the jury to follow the superior authority of the latter and restore the proper meaning of conspiracy doctrine in New York law.[122] After hearing a rather tepid defense of *People v. Fisher* from the presiding judge,[123] the jury did precisely what Edmonds asked and acquitted the defendants. "This is an important decision," stated the *New York Herald*. "It throws in the wind all the law of Judge Savage and Judge Edwards and begins a new era in conspiracies."[124]

The *Herald* was right. As it seemed to recognize, however, the new era was an alteration in New York's criminal conspiracy jurisprudence, not an excision. It constituted, one might say, a reversal of the polarity of *People v. Fisher*, the test of criminality now clearly agreed to be the resort of a combination to injurious behavior rather than the "threat" to the public perceived by a court to inhere in the combination's goals, regardless of injury.[125] This new trajectory was outlined and

---

[122] Ibid., 292, 300–1. Edmonds here misrepresented the decision of the Court of Errors in *Lambert v. People*, which, as we have seen, produced no clear voice on the matter. In fact, the position which Edmonds here recommended was doctrinally very similar to that adopted by Savage in the original Supreme Court judgment in *Lambert*. It was the statutory limitation on the courts' conspiracy jurisdiction, and Savage's attempt to get round it in *Fisher*, which were falling by the wayside in New York, not Savage's initial (and, one therefore assumes, preferred) position.

[123] The substance of the judge's charge is reported (ibid., 301–11) as follows:

"He took a review of the Statute under which the indictment was found, and observed that the indictment could only be made out under the 6th subdivision which declares it unlawful to commit any act injurious to trade and commerce. The cases at New-York and at Ontario County had been read to them, when it was shown that more violence was used than in the present case, and when compulsion had been used to prevent others from working who were not members of the societies. Heretofore all combinations of this nature have been deemed unlawful, and he could not but think that the gentlemen who were witnesses of this trial saw that it was a most serious combination. . . .

"If they would confine their operations to themselves they would be less obnoxious, but they struck at the boss shoemakers to their loss as it had been shown in the evidence. But if their proceedings had not a tendency to injure trade, it was of no consequence what the amount of the loss was to the bosses, they ought not to be found guilty, but if it could be shown that the measures adopted by the defendants, and the course pursued by them were injurious to trade and commerce, then it would be the duty of the Jury to find them guilty. Reference had been made to the Supreme Court of New-York. He would explain the nature of that Court. It was composed of three Judges, whose duty it was to lay down and expound the laws. They had expounded this law, and in a case parallel with the one now before them, they had decided it was a violation of the Statute. He did not know but that he had a right to advise them [i.e., the jury] of the law, but it was their right and their duty to judge of the law, and if they thought that the reason assigned for the conviction of the defendants was not satisfactory, and were willing to assume the responsibility and to say that the Supreme Court were wrong, they had a right to do so."

[124] As copied in the *Philadelphia Public Ledger*, 2 July 1836.

[125] It also meant that the Revised Statutes' limitation of the availability of indictment to the vindication of public wrongs had been rendered moot. What was now in effect an agreed "test" of what constituted sufficient evidence for the conviction of combined journeymen on criminal conspiracy charges – that they be shown to have formed a combination of two or more, to obtain an unlawful end by lawful means, or a lawful end by unlawful means – was silent on the requirement of public injury, in effect

endorsed by the *Philadelphia Public Ledger* in a lengthy editorial comment on *People v. Faulkner*:

So far as we can learn from the report of the decision of Judge Edwards, his opinion is against law. We understand him to say that combinations for regulating any department of business, among those who carry it on, are unlawful. If this be true, scarcely any man of any occupation is exempt from liability to indictment for conspiracy; for not an occupation can be mentioned, in which combinations to regulate prices have not occasionally appeared. Lawyers settle their prices by combination or agreement among themselves; so do booksellers; so do auctioneers; so, occasionally, have dealers in dry goods, and indeed in every other species of merchandise; in every department of mercantile business. No one has ever thought of indicting the bar of New York, for adopting rules to regulate fees; or the booksellers, for establishing scales of prices and discounts. No such indictments would be sustained; for such proceedings are perfectly lawful. Then why should journeymen tailors be indictable for doing the same thing? Every citizen has the right of determining the prices of his own labor or merchandise, and the right of agreeing with his neighbor upon such prices.

But while we contend that all men have a perfect right, by agreement, to settle the prices of their labor or merchandise, we contend that they have no right to coerce others into such agreement. Such coercion is a violation of the very principle upon which they claim the right of making such agreements. The right is to agree or not to agree, according to their own views of expediency. But by claiming the right to coerce others into their arguments, they deny to those coerced the very right of agreement which they claim for themselves.

The substance of the controversy between the trades unions and their opponents was in fact contained within a very narrow compass, the *Public Ledger* continued. All trades had a perfect right to settle the prices of labor or merchandise by voluntary agreement among themselves. None had any right to go further and molest in any way those who would not subscribe to the agreement. "If the journeymen agree to demand certain prices, and to refuse to work for less, they do not exceed in the least, their constitutional and legal rights. But if they insist that other journeymen tailors shall subscribe to their prices, and undertake to annoy, harass, perplex or molest them for refusing, and more especially to prevent them from working for prices chosen by the latter, then the assailants are guilty, *not* of conspiracy, against their employers or the public peace, but of *trespass against the other journeymen tailors.*"[126]

The position suggested by Edmonds in *People v. Cooper*, taken up in the *New York Herald* and endorsed at length in the *Public Ledger*, was the position of the generality of the Democratic Party press. Interestingly enough, as we have seen, it was also the position of the Whig press, even of that "most vociferous journalistic foe of trade

---

markedly *broadening* the ambit of the doctrine to encompass precisely that vindication of private injuries which a reluctant Chief Justice Savage had decided, in *People v. Fisher*, was beyond reach.

[126] *Philadelphia Public Ledger*, 13 June 1836. On American courts' adoption of a "tort" theory of labor activities see Hovenkamp, "Labor Conspiracies in American Law," 924. On the reemergence late in the nineteenth century of disparities between New York jurisprudence and that of other eastern states on the question of the legality of collective action in the course of labor disputes, see Poulson, "Criminal Conspiracy," 220–3; Charles O. Gregory and Harold A. Katz, *Labor and the Law*, 3d ed. (New York, 1979), 76–82.

unionism,"[127] the *New York Journal of Commerce*. "All combinations to *compel* others to give a higher price or take a lower one, are not only inexpedient, but at war with the order of things which the Creator has established for the general good, and therefore wicked," declared the *Journal* back in 1833. "*The means resorted to*, to cement and sustain the combinations, whether they are simple individual pledges, or legislative enactments, or menaces and violence, are all wrong, and in spirit equally so."[128] Such a convergence on the extent and limits of trades union legality suggests the growing strength in this hotly controversial area of that "liberal capitalist" ideological consensus which John Ashworth has elsewhere found to be so compelling a feature of American political culture in the late Jacksonian period.[129]

Yet although the story of the conspiracy doctrine in New York and, as we shall shortly see, elsewhere is one of growing consensus that the criminality of workers' combinations was best measured by the means they adopted, one should note that this was a consensus to which the unions themselves were not party. Their position continued to be outright opposition to any legal imposition on their proclaimed right to organize permanent associations and to use their collective strength to defend their interests. The City Hall Park meeting of 13 June called for independent political action to redress "partial administration of the laws engendered by unequal legislation." It condemned the judiciary for its encroachment on legislative power, for "making laws instead of declaring them"; condemned too the system of laws that resulted, "so mystified that men of common understandings, cannot unravel them – construction is forced upon construction – mystification is heaped upon mystification, and precedent furnished upon precedent, to show that what the people thought was liberty, bore not a semblance to its name"; and condemned finally "the close alliance which we have witnessed between the leaders of the two great political parties of this State, to crush the laboring men." The meeting resolved that a convention should meet at Utica three months later to form "a separate and distinct party, around which the laboring classes and their friends, can rally with confidence," and established a Correspondence Committee to plan the convention and to draft an address on the "common grievances" of workingmen as its keynote.[130]

---

[127] Wilentz, *Chants Democratic*, 265.

[128] *New York Journal of Commerce*, 1 June 1833 (emphasis supplied).

[129] John Ashworth, *"Agrarians" and "Aristocrats": Party Political Ideology in the United States, 1837–1846* (London, 1983), 132–73.

[130] Commons et al., eds., *Documentary History*, 5: 318–22. The Correspondence Committee address concentrated on three issues: currency regulation, convict labor, and criminal conspiracy. On the currency question the address called for legislation to take control of the state's money supply away from the banks and return it to the people. Control of the money supply meant control of trade and commerce, wages and prices. Placing that control in the hands of the banks meant giving control of the economy to "*chartered combinations* . . . spread over our country like swarms of locusts, preying on the fruits of our industry." On conspiracy, the address condemned the "decisions of our Judges, founded on forced constructions of the statute, and on precedents of British courts of law, which are hung over our heads as grim skeletons to frighten us into the deep vortex of subjection and degradation." Capitalists and employers might combine with impunity, but "if the humble operative dare to oppose, in order to counteract these petty tyrants, they are prosecuted and punished as 'conspirators against the peace and

The favorable outcome for the Hudson cordwainers in *People v. Cooper* intervened between the City Hall Park meeting and the Utica convention and lessened somewhat the GTU's immediate anxiety at the potency of the conspiracy weapon. Nevertheless, when it met, on 15 September, the convention still adopted a platform giving prominent place to condemnation of the courts and the legal system. "There has been less improvement in the proceedings of courts of law in the United States since our separation from Great Britain than in either of the other branches of government – the same forms, the same unintelligible and unmeaning jargon and special pleadings which were imported with our ancestors still prevail, and although we have a republican theory the practices of our courts of law are as aristocratic, arbitrary and oppressive as they were in the dark ages of feudalism." The convention called for the election of all judges and the limitation of their terms of office, condemned "the use of decisions of the aristocratic courts of Europe, as evidence of law in this country where the principles of government are so essentially different," and pledged amendment of the Revised Statutes so that "the construction given by the courts of law in this State to the statute on 'Trade and Commerce,' so as to make it an indictable offence for mechanics to combine to raise their wages, or fix a price on their labor," would be rendered null and void. Such a construction was "manifestly unjust, oppressive, and a violation of the first law of nature – self-preservation."[131]

The Utica platform suggests that the apparent ideological convergence on the conspiracy issue in mainstream politics was accompanied by ideological divergence on the part of "the laboring classes." Seemingly Whigs and Democrats alike could now agree that, if not association per se, then certainly attempts by associated journeymen to enforce their collective decisions on others should be condemned as antirepublican and coercive. In contrast, the unions' position remained unyielding: protection of the right of organization, self-preservation, and collective self-rule in the face of harassment, whether from judges or employers. Admittedly the evidence for this divergence derived from the Utica platform cannot be considered wholly conclusive. The Utica convention itself was in large part a vehicle for the views of the antimonopoly, antibank "Loco-Foco" faction of the New York Democratic Party, and in many respects the business of the convention revisited the complex factional maneuvering within the same general field occupied by the main-line parties that a few years before had been so characteristic of the Working Men's movement. Yet even as union advocates joined with the Loco-Focos in these maneuvers to press a

---

safety of the state.'" For details of the Correspondence Committee address, see Hattam, *Labor Visions and State Power*, Chapter 3. Both in its language and in its concerns, the address is highly reminiscent of the report of "the Committee appointed to examine and report upon the opinion of Judge Savage" to the Cordwainers' National Convention in New York, March 1836. See *Proceedings of the Convention of Cordwainers*, 13–17, quoted in part above, n. 113.

[131] On the Utica convention see F. Byrdsall, *The History of the Loco-Foco or Equal Rights Party, its Movements, Conventions and Proceedings* (New York, 1842), 73–4. See also Fink, "Labor, Liberty and the Law," 910.

renewed politics of republican antimonopolism,[132] they did so with no more indication than before that they regarded antimonopolism as a valid critique of their own activities. Rather, as the assembled delegates of the several societies of journeymen comb-makers showed while meeting five days before the Utica convention to create a national union of their own, unionists by 1836 had developed a distinct consciousness of their own essential place within the republican political economy they hoped to create:

Though we boast of our republic, its laws administered by the servants of the people, its liberal Institutions &c.; how do we enjoy ourselves under its laws? how [sic] do we feel the benefits of its public Institutions? First, by being indicted as conspirators, for contending for what is right, and repelling what is tyrannical and unjust – for asking a fair remuneration for our services, and for supporting the weak against the strong. . . . Under consideration of these facts, we urge upon the working classes the necessity of forming themselves into Societies, *as it is the only means by which we can obtain our object.* . . . [O]ur cause is a just one, and can be obtained only by union among ourselves.[133]

THE PENNSYLVANIA CASES

In Pennsylvania, as we have seen, the situation entering the 1830s as regards conspiracy doctrine differed somewhat from that in New York. There, courts had already moved quite far toward an examination of means in determining the criminality of a combination.[134] The trend was reinforced in both the 1836 and the 1842 cases. In addition, these cases also confirmed the availability of conspiracy doctrine for the vindication of purely private injuries.

A concise commentary on the law of criminal conspiracy as then prevailing in Pennsylvania was delivered before Philadelphia's grand jury in March 1836 by the city's newly elected recorder, John Bouvier. Bouvier's commentary came in the wake

---

[132] Wilentz disputes that they did. See his account of the Utica convention in *Chants Democratic*, 293–4. For an alternative view see Hattam, "Unions and Politics," 107–10.

[133] In Commons et al., eds., *Documentary History*, 6:333–4 (emphasis supplied).

[134] See above on *Commonwealth v. Moore* (Pa. 1827). In a preliminary hearing to continue defendants' recognizances in the joint matter of *Commonwealth ex rel. Kennedy v. Marshall and Treillou* and *Commonwealth ex rel. Campbell v. O'Daniel* (the so-called *Philadelphia Spinners'* cases) in January 1829, the issue was Kennedy's and Campbell's allegations that the defendants had threatened them with violence should they continue to seek employment at the cotton-spinning factory with which the defendants were in dispute. "The ends of public justice will be most effectually served by imposing a salutary restraint, which may tend to check the illegal measures which seem to be in progress," stated the court in granting the application for continuation. The law "will not permit any man or body of men to redress their own injuries, whether imaginary or real, and will promptly repress all acts of violence, whatever may be the pretext of their adoption" (Commons et al., eds., *Documentary History*, 4:67–8). In the *Chambersburg Shoemakers'* case (Pa. 1829), the charge against the journeymen shoemakers' society was "conspiracy to raise their wages, and prejudice such as were not members of their association." According to the brief newspaper report, the jury "found the Society [of journeymen shoemakers] guilty of conspiring to raise their wages" on the basis of "rules that were unwritten but acknowledged and practised by the Society" (ibid., 273).

of a year of considerable upheaval in the city, marked by strikes and walkouts involving many thousands of workers and by rapid increases in the numbers and influence of trade societies and the city's central trades' union.[135] Coinciding with expressions of rising antagonism toward journeymen's societies on the part of employers,[136] the recorder's charge advertised the availability of his court for the entertainment of conspiracy prosecutions. Requests for indictment were promptly presented. Knowing that these were to be considered, Bouvier repeated his comments to the grand jury at the opening of its next scheduled session in June.

Criminal conspiracies, said Bouvier, came in two varieties: conspiracies against individuals, which were "such as have for their object to injure them in their persons, characters or property"; and crimes against the public, which Bouvier described, as had his predecessors, in terms of threats to local police: "such as endanger public health, violate public morals, insult public justice, destroy public peace, and affect public trade or business." Bouvier placed journeymen's combinations in the latter category, as earlier courts had done, but his charge failed to locate the precise basis for their criminality there – that is, as a distinct category of conspiracy – instead defining conspiracy as in general "an agreement between two or more persons to do an unlawful act, or any of those acts which become, by the combination, injurious to others." As other courts were finding, it was becoming increasingly difficult to maintain journeymen's conspiracies on the "unlawful" side of the line of demarcation between those acts for the performance of which men might lawfully combine and those for which they might not simply on the basis of a general assertion that journeymen's combinations "prejudiced" the public. As Bouvier's charge hinted strongly, the alternative was to find criminality in the tendency of journeymen's combinations to interfere with "freedom of action . . . the principles of free exertion, free use of capital, and free competition" through their oppressive *behavior*. "The law does not sanction the combination of two or more

---

[135] As we have seen, in the years following its creation in November 1833 the Trades' Union of Philadelphia grew from fifteen trade society affiliates to more than fifty, boasting in excess of 10,000 members. By 1836, according to Bruce Laurie, it had become "the most impressive city central union in Jacksonian America " (*Working People of Philadelphia*, 87). For details of striking trades during 1835 see Commons et al., eds., *Documentary History*, 5:326–7.

[136] On 14 March 1836 a meeting of more than 130 master carpenters condemned the Trades' Union as "arbitrary" and "subversive" and as a "secret conclave" that presumed "to regulate and controul the private concerns of private citizens." The meeting resolved "that we claim the right as Free Citizens, to make our contracts with the journeymen mechanics themselves without the intervention of the Trades' Union; and that we do not recognize the right of any association or combination of men, to interfere in the ordinary transaction of our business," and called on all the city's master mechanics to join with them in creating an "Anti-trades' Union Association" (*Pennsylvanian*, 17 Mar. 1836, in Commons et al., eds., *Documentary History*, 6:50–4). Similarly, on 23 March 1836 a meeting of more than 80 employing shoemakers likewise condemned the journeymen's coercive interferences in their affairs, "fostering oppression, tyranny and misrule" and "obstructing the free course of trade," complained that they had been prevented from being masters of their own business, and called for action "to oppose every injurious combination, connected with the Trades' Union" (*Pennsylvanian*, 28 Mar. 1836, in ibid., 32–5).

individuals, who unite for the purpose of obtaining [higher] wages, and of compelling others to join them." The decisive test now was whether combinations had a tendency to control others and deprive them of their rights, rather than whether they "prejudiced" the public or not.[137]

The immediate consequence (undoubtedly unintended) of this explicit shift in emphasis was the first ever acquittal in Pennsylvania of journeymen indicted on a charge of criminal conspiracy. As in *People v. Cooper* in New York, the case of *Commonwealth v. Grinder* found a Philadelphia jury unwilling, despite the most extravagant declamations of the attorney general, to find a combination of journeymen to be a criminal conspiracy without evidence of deleterious consequences for some identifiable individual.[138]

The outcome in *Grinder* was significant, but its significance remained unclear in the short term, for the apparently favorable result was promptly swallowed up in a larger controversy. Again as in New York, the atmosphere in Philadelphia in the summer of 1836 was extremely tense. Working people were incensed at what appeared to have been a calculated decision by the attorney general to use the *Grinder* indictment to attack the Philadelphia Trades' Union, just as the *Faulkner* prosecution had incensed New York's workingmen. Barely a month after the acquittal in *Grinder*, a crowd numbering in excess of 5,000, described as one of the largest ever assembled in the city's history, gathered in Independence Square to demonstrate opposition to a second conspiracy indictment. Redolent with symbolism for the previous year's exhibition of solidarity between journeymen and laborers, the new indictment singled out a group of Schuylkill coal heavers. The crowd protested the indictment and also the "enormous and unconstitutional bail" of $2,500 demanded of the indicted laborers by the mayor, which had necessarily resulted in the committal of all the defendants to jail to await trial. More generally they condemned the application to working people of "unjust, unequal" laws "in their operations calculated to destroy . . . that spirit of liberty co-existent with the republic."[139]

The coal-heavers case has been described as "a clumsy attempt at discrediting" – and, one may add, intimidating – the Trades' Union. In indicting the defendants on riot and conspiracy charges and setting bail at a level causing them to be imprisoned, Philadelphia Mayor John Swift had declared his intention to strike at the root of the Trades' Union and to "fell the tree that it might lay and rot." As in the *Grinder* prosecution, the attempt failed, the coal heavers being acquitted on all counts.[140] Nevertheless the threat was plain. It should surprise no one, therefore,

---

[137] *Philadelphia Public Ledger*, 27 June 1836.

[138] *Commonwealth v. Grinder* (1836), in the Mayor's Court of Philadelphia. The indictment was brought against the defendants on the evidence of their former employer, one Cowperthwaite, alleging that they had injured John Smith, a fellow employee, by refusing to work with him because he was not a member of the Trades' Union. Smith had remained in Cowperthwaite's employment, however, and the defendants had left (*Philadelphia Public Ledger*, 14–15 July 1836).

[139] "Grand Meeting of the Workingmen," *Philadelphia Public Ledger*, 25 Aug. 1836.

[140] Laurie, *Working People of Philadelphia*, 99.

that the language of the 25 August demonstrators was apocalyptic. "The people will not always cry for justice and get mockery for their portion – the day may be near at hand when justice will not answer. Let our foes look to it in time – convulsion is ripening to perfection. The people will not always watch the Avalanche. The day of retribution may come!" The grievances listed were many, but among them the following were notable.

We complain of the protection given unnecessary and soul destroying monopolies – of the protection given to capital at the expense of labor – the consequent withdrawal of favour from labor – the existence of rotten monarchical laws, expressly applied to destroy the last prop and support of the hard working man, their right to sustain themselves. . . .

We complain, because our legislative halls are filled with lawyers, whose interest it is, when forced to adopt wholesome laws, to mystify those laws in such a manner that they may receive high salary to explain them to the people for whom they were made. . . .

And, lastly, we complain that, in direct violation of the letter and spirit of our laws, we are subject at any moment to be dragged from our hearths and families, and thrown into a prison, the receptacle of the associate of the knave, and that too without any other cause than what malignant hate may devise; because, under the sanction of the law, men have been so base as to threaten free citizens for the expression of their opinions.[141]

As in New York, Philadelphia workingmen considered the redress of such griev-ances through a return to politics. Thus, as in the Utica platform, the August meeting's "bill of violated rights" – described as "our rallying point of action, our cloud by day and pillar of fire by night," the basis upon which government should be thenceforth established – saw the conspiracy controversy joined with other well-thumbed issues, of public education, antimonopoly, and legal reform. Organizers promised a major campaign by working people against the erosion of their rights as citizens of a republican polity, against their loss not only of opportunities but of the very capacity for meaningful civic participation. In this company the conspiracy prosecutions played the role primarily of exemplar of antidemocratic tendencies among employers and the judiciary, further evidence of the necessity for a general reform and democratization of social and political institutions.[142]

The capacity of political action to achieve such a program for the labor movement, however, was doubted. Instead, as Bruce Laurie has recently shown, segments of the Jacksonian labor movement showed a growing interest in cooperative production, an interest clearly apparent in the proceedings of the Third Annual Convention of the National Trades' Union held in October 1836 in Philadelphia. Cooperation,

---

[141] "Grand Meeting of the Workingmen," *Philadelphia Public Ledger*, 25 Aug. 1836. The meeting re-solved, inter alia, that "it is an insult to our feelings as well as our common sense, to say we have no right to labor for whom we please, when we please, for what wages, and to refuse and give our reasons for refusal, whenever we may please" and that "we would do injustice to the memory of the great dead, and commit treason to the living, were we to suffer this monstrous outrage on our personal freedom, to pass unnoticed."

[142] Hattam in particular stresses the broad and reformist-political rather than class-oriented and industrial character of the workingmen's movements of the mid-1830s (*Labor Visions and State Power*, Chapter 3).

says Laurie, offered "a major tactical departure" representing "a collective project to achieve social equality and worker control." Until then, radicals "had warred against the market economy with the feeble politics of antimonopoly. Now they were armed with a cause that offered a closer, if by no means perfect, fit between means and ends, a different means of structuring productive relations."[143] In fact, whether the route was to be politics or cooperation was a moot choice. Neither could survive a collapsing economy. In 1837 mobilization became disbandment in both New York and Pennsylvania as depression bit deeply into the labor movement.

In Pennsylvania, however, there was a sequel, bringing a renewed and somewhat-altered focus on the issue of labor conspiracy. In May 1842, six years after the Schuylkill affair, eighteen Rockdale millworkers were brought before the Court of Sessions of Delaware County in the case of *Commonwealth v. McConnell* on an indictment charging them with counts of conspiracy and riot arising from a strike earlier that year provoked by the millowners' decision to reduce wage rates. "The prices of labor must be regulated by the manufacturers," it was stated for the commonwealth. Here, however, a combination of operatives had been formed and had passed "severe and arbitrary rules." The whole neighborhood having been kept in a constant state of alarm, "a sense of justice has led the well disposed part to urge forward this suit."[144] As in preceding cases, the proceedings attracted attention far beyond the immediate locale. The *Philadelphia Public Ledger* devoted considerable attention to the case, retaining a correspondent in Chester to cover it and printing daily reports and lengthy extracts from the trial testimony. The paper reported that the trial itself was attended by "hundreds from all parts of the country."[145]

Notwithstanding its general statement of the issue, the prosecution presented its case in *Commonwealth v. McConnell* as one seeking conviction of conspiracy to assault nonstrikers, not as a conspiracy to strike against a reduction of wages as such. This approach was endorsed by the presiding judge, Thomas S. Bell, who quite explicitly denied that combinations to alter the price of labor – whether of laborers to raise it or of employers to reduce it – were criminal in Pennsylvania, or even that their existence was particularly regrettable. Not surprisingly, given the position it had espoused in reaction to the conviction of the New York tailors six years

---

[143] Laurie, *Artisans into Workers*, 89–90. For details of debates on cooperation at the convention and subsequently, see Commons et al., eds., *Documentary History*, 6:58–65, 291–7, 298–9.

[144] *Commonwealth v. McConnell* (1842), reported in the *Philadelphia Public Ledger* 30–1 May and 1–3 June (proceedings) and 30 July (the bench's charge to the jury) 1842. The trial began on Friday 27 May and lasted five days. The jury charge was actually delivered on the morning of 2 June but not printed by the *Public Ledger* until 30 July. (See n. 147 for an explanation of this oddity.) The verdict was returned on the afternoon of 2 June. The prosecution in *Commonwealth v. McConnell* was conducted by "the prominent Chester attorney and politician" Samuel Edwards. Edwards "had served in Congress and was a close friend of James Buchanan; he was reported to be one of the most influential background advisers in the Democratic national machine." Joseph S. Lewis of West Chester and William D. Kelly of Philadelphia were counsel for the defense. The trial was before a bench of three judges, presided over by Judge Thomas S. Bell. Bell, says Anthony Wallace, "bore a reputation for learning, for courtesy, and for severity" (*Rockdale, The Growth of an American Village in the Early Industrial Revolution* [New York, 1978], 364).

[145] *Philadelphia Public Ledger*, 1 June 1842.

before, this was also the position of the *Public Ledger*. "The principle of natural and equal right, is this," the paper editorialized. "[A]ll combinations or agreements among any persons, to fix the price of their property, whether it be land, merchandise, or labor of head or hand, are lawful, are in pursuance of the natural and equal rights which God gave to *all* men. But all combinations to coerce others into such agreements, by punishing or annoying them in *any* mode for their refusal, are *unlawful*."[146]

It is noticeable that, in delivering its version of this message, the court had resort to a discourse critical of past conspiracy doctrine that in a sense echoed the position espoused by Philadelphia's trade unionists six years before. In its use of that discourse, however, all the court's stresses were on how the capacity to repudiate earlier ill-considered decisions demonstrated the genius of *existing* institutions, thereby rebuffing rather than by implication endorsing the calls for trenchant reform of the polity made by the workingmen during the previous decade. "The equal, and therefore equitable distribution of the rights and duties of man in society, recognised by a structure of government based on the maxim that all men are, politically, equal, and sanctioned by laws having for their object the moral elevation of all, has gradually but steadily operated to repudiate a doctrine which in respect to the offence of conspiracy would place the employed on ground less eligible than the employer, by subjecting the former to criminal punishment for any combination to procure an advance of wages, while, it would seem, the latter were left free to regulate the price of labor as the exigencies of trade or the suggestions of personal interest dictated," stated Judge Bell in his jury charge.[147] The outcome was still conviction of the strike's leaders for participation in a criminal conspiracy. But the court now placed the criminality of the defendants' offense wholly on the unlawfulness of the means – threats and violence – that had been contemplated and used.

In Bell's charge we see ousted completely from consideration the notion, hotly debated by courts ten years earlier, that there was something sufficiently distinctive about the "public sphere" as to require distinct measures of protection. Conspiracy was now presented wholly as a matter consequent upon investigation of means and ends. Were the actors' objects illegal or their methods coercive? If so, they were guilty of a criminal conspiracy. Did they contemplate an act illegal or criminal per

---

[146] *Philadelphia Public Ledger*, 8 June 1842 (emphasis in original). The *Public Ledger* had previously commented (31 May): "This will be found a highly interesting case, and will go to test whether operatives have the right to combine among themselves to keep up the price of their own labor, and also prevent others, by force, from working at less prices than they fix. The right of workmen to fix the value of their own labor can not be disputed, but they have no right to force another, who [is] willing to work at a less rate, to subscribe to their terms. Each man is the best judge of what his labor is worth, and it is his liberty to get just as much as he can, and no more."

[147] *Philadelphia Public Ledger*, 30 July 1842. A transcript of Bell's charge was given to the *Public Ledger* in late July. It had originally been the defendants' intention to produce a pamphlet account of the trial. Circumstances, however, had made this impossible. "In consequence of the indisposition of the reporter, the preparation of the matter was unusually delayed, during which time most of the operatives on Chester creek having been thrown out of employment, they now find it impossible to raise funds to complete the publication."

se, such as murder or robbery? If so, nothing more was needed. Where, however, the act contemplated was not criminal per se, as in effecting an alteration in the rate of wages, attention centered on the means. Here the principal means had been collective action. Was such collective action "in itself, and without more" indictable as illegal means? Quite decisively the court said not.

With us, every citizen, either singly or in combination with others, has a right to decide whether he will or will not sell his time and labor at any particular rate of compensation. So, every employer may exercise the same right in determining the rate of wages he will give. However impolitic such agreements may be, as interfering with the free operation of the laws of trade and business, there is in Pennsylvania no legal objection against entering into them. The defendants were entirely at liberty to agree as a body, and having agreed, to say to their employers, we will not work for the wages you offer us, and to carry such determination into effect by retiring from their service; and for this, simply, they cannot be called on to answer criminally.

Nor, continued Judge Bell, did the defendants' act of assembling together for the purpose of consulting on the propriety of so agreeing render them liable to indictment. "Peaceably to meet and discuss the proper steps to be adopted for the protection and advancement of their common interests, can never be objected against American citizens as an offence, and we have already seen there is nothing in our law to restrain a free expression of resolutions produced by such discussion. If evil results from such agreements, it must necessarily, in a short time, work its own correction, and it is far better to endure a temporary inconvenience than to attempt to remedy it by the exercise of a power tending unnecessarily and, therefore, improperly to abridge freedom of action."

Alone, then, the defendants' concert could not constitute illegal means. Rather, the measure of illegality was the impact of their collective activity on others – their oppressive interference with their employers' right to engage in business activity. "Did they confederate to raise the wages beyond the rate the manufacturers were willing to pay by the application of means which the law deems dangerous to the community or oppressive to individuals, and, therefore, prohibits?"

Every association is said to be criminal whose object it is to raise or depress the price of labor beyond what it would bring if left without artificial excitement. [Here Bell cited Gibson's opinion in *Commonwealth ex rel. Chew v. Carlisle*.] Without attempting to describe by any generality, what would be deemed such artificial excitement as would amount to prohibited means, or the great variety of cases presented by different combinations of circumstances, it is sufficient for present purposes to instruct you that any means used to create inordinate and continued popular feeling, tending to breaches of the peace and productive of terror in a neighborhood, or to coerce employers by menaces or hostile demonstrations to give the wages demanded; or to compel workmen by threats or violence to leave their employment, with intent to foment the views of the conspirators, are such means as the law denominates illegal or criminal means, and an agreement to use them, though for an otherwise innocent purpose, makes the parties to the agreement conspirators, and subjects them to punishment as such.

177

It was for their oppression of others that the Delaware County defendants were convicted, and it was upon this basis, thenceforth, that criminal conspiracy charges would be sustained against striking journeymen in Pennsylvania.[148]

CONCLUSION

It is interesting to note that in the aftermath of *Commonwealth v. McConnell*, self-described "friends of the convicted" wrote to the *Public Ledger* to defend Judge Bell's "able and impartial" jury charge.[149] These friends sought the charge's widest possible dissemination, through the equally friendly *Public Ledger*, to counter the influence of others – "ignorant" elements – who had been attacking the defendants' conviction as merely the work of another hanging judge in the tradition of Edwards et al. No doubt it still aggrieved those directly involved, who had been, after all, involved in a strike against a unilaterally imposed wage *reduction*, that they could be prosecuted and some convicted of a conspiracy to *raise* their wages. Nonetheless, their "friends" preferred to emphasize, it was now established that unlawful means constituted the gist of the offense, not the combination as such. Why was this a demonstration of ability and impartiality? Because it was in tune with the jurisprudential consensus on means over per se illegality which had emerged decisively by the late 1830s. That consensus, as we have seen, had come to embrace prosecutors, defense attorneys, and latterly judges. It had been in the making since the far-off days of *Pullis* and *Melvin* and in the mid-1830s had gained enough of an edge from public outcry to prevail over alternative readings of conspiracy, particularly *People v. Fisher*'s statute-driven distinction between public and private wrongs.

Commonwealth v. McConnell thus confirmed that by the early 1840s conspiracy doctrine in Pennsylvania and New York was proceeding on parallel tracks. The intervention of "the friends of the convicted" to defend the fairness of the conviction (the convicted themselves remained silent) also confirmed how those tracks were leading the doctrine out of the arena of articulated public controversy, where it had been firmly ensconced for most of the previous forty years. Consensus on the

---

[148] *Philadelphia Public Ledger*, 30 July 1842. Initially the *Public Ledger* was highly suspicious both of the prosecution and of the verdict, interpreting the workers' conviction as one "for agreeing upon a price for their labor" and calling for prosecution of the manufacturers who had agreed on the joint wage reduction which had caused the strike for a like offense. "If this agreement among the laborers were criminal, so was that among the employers. If the law be unequal, it is unconstitutional, and courts have no right to act under it." In response to this report the deputy attorney general for Delaware County, P. Frazer Smith, wrote to advise the *Public Ledger* that the indictment had been "for conspiracy in combining to raise their wages and carrying into effect the object of their combination by unlawful means, such as threats, violence, &c., directed against either the employers or the hands who were willing to work at the reduced wages – the 'unlawful means' being the gist of the offence" (*Public Ledger*, 16, 18 June 1842). Although there is no indication to this effect in the *Ledger*'s reporting of *Commonwealth v. McConnell*, it is conceivable that Judge Bell may have had access to the Massachusetts Supreme Judicial Court's decision in *Commonwealth v. Hunt*, 45 Mass. 111, handed down at the Supreme Judicial Court's March 1842 term. For details of that case see Chapter 6.

[149] *Philadelphia Public Ledger*, 30 July 1842.

adoption of the "unlawful means" test and the extension of conspiracy to the vindication of private wrongs had routinized the doctrine's application, simultaneously depriving protests against it of public resonance.

Commonwealth v. McConnell is noteworthy for a second reason: As well as underlining the routinization of conspiracy, it was the first criminal conspiracy conviction to be recorded against striking factory workers. It also continued the trend toward more severe penalties that had become apparent in the 1830s. The three strike leaders – Hiram McConnell, Mark Wild, and Major Rowe – were fined $35, $30, and $30 respectively and, though acquitted on the accompanying riot charges, were ordered to pay the costs of that prosecution, a sum in excess of $1,000. Upon failure to pay their fines all were committed to prison, where they remained for two weeks until they had their punishment remitted by the governor.[150]

Both in its doctrinal and its punitive aspect, *Commonwealth v. McConnell* may be treated as an appropriate augury of conspiracy's future course.[151] *Commonwealth v. McConnell*, however, was a relatively obscure case, politically notorious in Pennsylvania but legally uninfluential. To understand the juridical course upon which labor conspiracy was embarked by the 1840s we must turn to the doctrine's pre–Civil War capstone, the Massachusetts case of *Commonwealth v. Hunt*. In considering that case we will find replayed many of the issues and themes already canvassed here but on a vastly more elevated stage. We will also meet more of labor's friends. And we will discover that at least some of them were not as complaisant as those who briefly embraced the millworkers of Rockdale.

---

[150] *Philadelphia Public Ledger*, 16 June 1842. A Subscription eventually raised the amount necessary to meet the costs of the riot prosecution. For further details of the strike, the trial, and its aftermath see Wallace, *Rockdale*, 355–74.

[151] I make this point in qualification of Victoria Hattam's argument that not until after the Civil War do we find defendants in labor conspiracy trials punished severely. On the one hand, she is quite correct that sentences of imprisonment were not handed down in any of the known antebellum cases and that fines tended on average to be low. On the other, it is also important to note that the tendency to impose light fines disappeared during the 1830s and that from the outset one encounters instances of defendants jailed on indictment (as in *Pullis*) or committed as a result of failure to meet intentionally excessive bail requirements (as in *Schuylkill Laborers*) or through failure to pay fines (as in *McConnell*). More generally, the evidence presented in this and the next chapter as to the "privatization" of conspiracy doctrine also qualifies somewhat Hattam's contention that not until after the Civil War did courts begin to accept the salience of "injury [to] particular individuals and their business enterprises." As in the matter of punishment, what is at issue here is not Hattam's characterization of the state of the doctrine postwar but the timing of the trends it exemplified. See Hattam, "Courts and the Question of Class," in Tomlins and King, eds., *Labor Law in America*, 44–70, at 56, 58. See also, *Labor Visions and State Power*, Chapter 2.

6

Commonwealth against Hunt

Our right then to wages steady and permanent is . . . a right to be prized, defended, and improved; and all laws intended to force capital, or talent, or labor, out of one pursuit into another, thereby producing ruinous fluctuations; and all combinations to raise violently one kind of wages, thereby producing a corresponding diminution in other kinds, are highhanded violations of this our undeniable right.

Robert Rantoul, Jr., "An Address to the Workingmen of
the United States of America" (1833)

The trend in labor conspiracy doctrine after the mid-1830s, we have seen, was away from singling out journeymen's combinations as in themselves exceptional threats to the public interest, and very much toward homogenizing them with other sorts of concerted activity whose alleged deleterious impact was to be tested through an inspection of the means employed in furtherance of the desired goal for evidence of injury or prejudice to the self-interest of others.[1] The most extensive restatement of conspiracy doctrine to this effect came from the pen of Chief Justice Lemuel Shaw in the Massachusetts case of *Commonwealth v. Hunt*, argued before the Supreme Judicial Court of that state in 1841 and decided the following year. This was only the third occasion in the United States on which labor conspiracy had been discussed by a superior court on a point of law (*Commonwealth v. Carlisle* and *People v. Fisher* were the previous instances) and the Massachusetts forum was by far the most authoritative. Both *Carlisle* and *Fisher* had been opinions of intermediate courts of appeal, whereas the Supreme Judicial Court was a final court of appeal. Furthermore, both it and its chief justice carried considerable weight outside the state.[2]

[1] In addition to the cases already discussed, see *Thompsonville Carpet Manufacturing Company v. William Taylor et al.* (Conn. 1836), in John R. Commons et al., eds., *A Documentary History of American Industrial Society* (Cleveland, 1910), vol. 4 (supp.), 15–115, at 113–14. Unlike other cases discussed this was a civil action for damages arising out of a strike. For another example of such an action, see the master stonecutters' January 1836 suit against the New York Journeymen Stonecutters' Society described in Sean Wilentz, *Chants Democratic: New York City and the Rise of the American Working Class, 1788–1850* (New York, 1984), 287. The potential liability of associated journeymen to such suits had long before been admitted by William Sampson in *People v. Melvin* (1810). See William Sampson, reporter, *Trial of the Journeymen Cordwainers of the City of New York; For a Conspiracy to Raise Their Wages* (New York, 1810), 66.
[2] For a general assessment of Shaw's influence see Leonard W. Levy, *The Law of the Commonwealth and Chief Justice Shaw* (Cambridge, Mass., 1957), 301–21.

Although *Commonwealth v. Hunt* was the first labor conspiracy case to arise in Massachusetts, it was not by any means the state's first conspiracy case. Nor was it the first occasion there upon which the application of the doctrine of criminal conspiracy to labor combinations had been given lengthy consideration. As in New York and Pennsylvania the issue had been debated heatedly and at times bitterly during the 1830s, and those debates had resulted in a degree of polarization between the state's courts and its incipient labor movement quite as pronounced as that which had come to exist in the other eastern centers. Indeed, if the rhetoric employed is at all a useful measure, the degree of polarization in Massachusetts was if anything more extreme than elsewhere.

CONSPIRACY AND COMBINATION IN MASSACHUSETTS

The Supreme Judicial Court of Massachusetts discussed the doctrine of common law conspiracy on several occasions early in the nineteenth century, all of them well prior to the leading 1820s cases of *Buchanan*, *Rickey*, and *Lambert*, which we have already examined.[3] It quickly committed itself to an extremely wide reading of the doctrine. All but one of these early Massachusetts cases involved conspiracies to defraud and turned on the question whether a confederacy was indictable per se absent the perpetration of an indictable act. As in the early labor conspiracy trials in other states, the Massachusetts court's discourse was communitarian, emphasizing the threat of mischief to the public.[4] Thus in *Commonwealth v. Boynton* (1803) it held that a confederacy to do an act prejudicial to another, even if that act were not itself indictable, was more than a merely private wrong and hence warranted more than a merely civil remedy. In *Commonwealth v. Judd* (1807) it went further, holding that a confederacy to do an unlawful act, or a lawful act for unlawful purposes, was indictable as a crime because it carried with it the threat of injury at large. "This rule of the common law is to prevent unlawful combinations. A solitary offender may be easily detected and punished; but combinations against the law are always

---

[3] *Commonwealth v. Boynton*, unreported case noted at 1 Thacher's Criminal Cases 640 (1803); *Commonwealth v. Pierpont*, unreported case noted at 1 Thacher's Criminal Cases 641 (1803); *Commonwealth v. Ward*, 1 Mass. 473 (1805); *Commonwealth v. Judd*, 2 Mass. 329 (1807); *Commonwealth v. Tibbetts*, 2 Mass. 535 (1807); *Commonwealth v. Kingsbury*, 5 Mass. 105 (1809); *Commonwealth v. Warren*, 6 Mass. 72 (1809). On *Buchanan*, *Rickey*, and *Lambert* see Chapter 5.

[4] See Hampton L. Carson, *The Law of Criminal Conspiracies and Agreements, As Found in the American Cases* (Philadelphia, 1887), 115. In Nathan Dane's *General Abridgment and Digest of American Law* (Boston, 1823–), at vol. 7, ch. 204, conspiracy was categorized as a "crime against the public polity" and "against public justice." The doctrine in these cases appears to have been consistent with unreported eighteenth-century cases. According to Gordon Wood, "with all social relationships in a free state presumably dependent on mutual trust, it is not surprising that the courts of eighteenth century Massachusetts treated instances of cheating and deception far more severely than overt acts of violence" ("Conspiracy and the Paranoid Style: Causality and Deceit in the Eighteenth Century," *William and Mary Quarterly*, 3d ser., 39, 3 [July 1982], 401–41).

dangerous to public peace and to private security." Citing *R. v. Journeymen Taylors* as authority, the court held the offense "greatly aggravated by the *undistinguishing mischief* that was designed. . . . There is justice due to the commonwealth for the protection of its citizens against fraud and deceit."[5]

The general suspicion of combinations evident in these early pronouncements was underlined on the particular matter of labor combinations, as we saw earlier from Peter Oxenbridge Thacher's observations on the Philadelphia cordwainers' trial. Thacher was by no means the only Bostonian to express antagonism at this time to the prospect of artisan combinations. Yet there was an important difference: The association that was the object of most suspicion in early nineteenth-century Boston was the Massachusetts Charitable Mechanics Association (MCMA), a body seeking to advance an ideology of the artisan trades as an essentially homogeneous community of interest rather than, as in the case of the journeymen's associations emerging elsewhere, symptomatic of the centrifugal tendencies increasingly endemic in the organization of craft work.[6] Though Thacher was concerned to express his suspicion of self-constituted communities within the commonwealth, he appeared to recognize a distinction between this group of worthy master craftsmen and the oppressive rabble of journeymen cordwainers abroad in Philadelphia and hinted his regret that the state legislature's persistent refusal to entertain the MCMA's requests for corporate status (it eventually received its charter in March 1806) has perpetuated an unwarranted image of illegitimacy that lumped it in indiscriminately with less-respectable groups and weakened it in its laudable ambition to reinforce the hierarchical organization of the fragmenting crafts. Without bodies like the MCMA, Thacher implied, one might see the development in Boston of those less-attractive solidarities among artisans that were emerging elsewhere, to the disservice of the community at large.[7]

For a while, at least, such anxieties proved groundless. Indeed, during the following decade the artisan corporatism represented by the MCMA became quite acceptable in the community at large. Not only did the association receive its long-sought-after charter, but other, trade-specific, bodies of master mechanics also became active. It is perhaps suggestive both of their goals and of the extent of their respectability that in 1815 a proposal to reestablish the town of Boston as a municipal corporation (only narrowly defeated) could include a provision empowering the municipality "to grant to any association of artists, artificers, or

---

[5] 2 Mass. 329, at 336–7 (emphasis supplied).

[6] See Lisa B. Lubow, "Artisans in Transition: Early Capitalist Development and the Carpenters of Boston, 1787–1837" (Ph.D. diss., UCLA, 1987), 378–9; Gary J. Kornblith, "From Artisans to Businessmen: Master Mechanics in New England, 1789–1850" (Ph.D. diss., Princeton University, 1983), 1:49–130. For isolated examples of early labor organization in Boston, see Victor S. Clark Papers, box 10, Baker Library, Harvard Business School.

[7] Thacher wrote in his 1806 *Monthly Anthology* review, "Unfortunately our legislature has not looked with an indulgent eye on all applications for incorporations, and has strengthened bonds, naturally too strong to be severed by the sword of justice" (*Monthly Anthology and Boston Review*, 3 [1806], 610).

mechanics, such power of regulating themselves in their several occupations, and of possessing such immunities and imposing such restrictions as the said Municipality shall consider for the benefit of the community and for the encouragement of industry."[8]

Within another decade, however, the skin of craft homogeneity had grown brittle to the point of cracking. The need apparently felt by the more-prominent master craftsmen to give their regulatory authority in the trade some structural existence, evident in their organizational activities from the late eighteenth century on, was as much a symptom of the atrophy of artisanal communitarianism as an example of its enduring value, an attempt to shore up through institutions what had hitherto been largely a moral community. As elsewhere, moreover, the same commercialization of their trades that was prompting defensive responses on the part of masters also prompted a distinct set of responses from their employees. Just how distinct became apparent in the 1820s and 1830s when, as in the other seaboard cities, the intensifying transformation of work in Boston's craft industries gave birth to major outbreaks of industrial conflict. In April 1825, six hundred journeymen house carpenters – virtually the entire body of journeymen carpenters resident in Boston – turned out against an attempt by employers to establish new wage and hour standards. Following more-limited strikes by local journeymen rope makers and plasterers, this was one of the largest strikes seen to that point anywhere on the eastern seaboard.[9] Seven years later, the establishment in February 1832 of the New England Association of Farmers, Mechanics and Other Workingmen in Boston presaged a further outbreak of wage and hour conflicts, which lasted throughout the spring and early summer.[10]

Unsurprisingly, the 1825 strike excited considerable antagonism toward the journeymen carpenters among employing master carpenters and merchant builders. There was, however, no resort to legal action. Indeed, there is no evidence that the 1825 strike was organized by a distinct journeymen's association as such, and as in other contemporary disputes the strikers' tactics convey the impression that they thought of themselves primarily as citizens of town and trade participating in an event of municipal significance rather than as some kind of fledgling industrial

[8] Henry H. Sprague, *City Government in Boston: Its Rise and Development* (Boston, 1890), 17. See, generally, Lubow, "Artisans in Transition," 375–431.

[9] David J. Saposs, "Colonial and Federal Beginnings," in John R. Commons et al., *History of Labor in the United States* (New York, 1918), 1:158. Saposs called this "one of the most notable strikes in American labor history." The most complete account of this strike – whose principal goal was to ensure a ten-hour working day – is to be found in Lubow, "Artisans in Transition," 494–549. According to Lubow there were at this time 651 journeymen carpenters in Boston, which means that more than 90 percent turned out. Lubow also argues that as the strike progressed many journeymen from other trades became involved. Confirmation of this may be seen in a report in the *Boston Courier* for 25 April which estimated that 1,200 men were by then on strike.

[10] For descriptions of this agitation see Ronald P. Formisano, *The Transformation of Political Culture: Massachusetts Parties, 1790s–1840s* (New York, 1983), 227–30; Lubow, "Artisans in Transition," 557–76.

proletariat engaging in collective bargaining with their employers.[11] Given that the strike involved almost the entire body of journeymen, there was little need for its "enforcement" against recalcitrants, and the house carpenters in any case gave some indication that they disclaimed a desire to impose on others the wage and hour standards they themselves sought.[12] When the employing masters and builders tried to break the strike by encouraging an influx of out-of-town journeymen, the striking journeymen sought a town meeting to deliberate on the justice of their stand. When the mayor and aldermen refused to cooperate in calling the meeting, the strike was abandoned.[13]

The rhetoric of the strike's opponents is, nevertheless, reminiscent of contemporaneous labor conspiracy trials. Boston's master carpenters advertised their "surprise and regret" at the action of the journeymen in entering into a combination. Such a measure was "fraught with numerous and pernicious evils, not only as respects their employers, but the public at large." Its consequences for the morals and well-being of society were to be dreaded. "We cannot believe this project to have originated with any of the faithful and industrious sons of New England, but are compelled to consider it an evil of foreign growth, and one which we hope and trust will not take root in the favoured soil of Massachusetts."[14] A meeting of the "gentlemen engaged in building" approached the strike more bluntly, their discourse more that of capitalists than communitarians.

These proceedings are a departure from the salutary and steady usages which have prevailed in this city, and all New England, from time immemorial. . . .

While it is admitted that every man is free to make such contract in respect to time and wages as he may think for his interest, it is also considered that all combinations by any Classes of Citizens, intended to regulate or effect the value of labor by abridging its duration, are in a high degree unjust and injurious to all other classes, inasmuch as they give an artificial turn to business, and tend to convert all its branches into monopolies.[15]

The 1825 strike ended after about three weeks, with the journeymen generally unsuccessful.[16]

---

[11] On the characteristics of the antebellum labor dispute, see David Grimsted, "Ante-bellum Labor: Violence, Strike, and Communal Arbitration," *Journal of Social History*, 19 (Fall 1985), 5–28. On the characteristics of this particular dispute, see Philip S. Foner, ed., "An Early Trade Union and Its Fate," *Labor History*, 14, 3 (Summer 1973), 423–4.

[12] The strikers' statement of 20 April 1825 resolved, in part, "that ten hours faithful labor shall hereafter constitute a day's work . . . not by any means taking from any Journeyman Carpenter the right of exercising his own judgement in working a longer time per day for a proportional equivalent in order to accommodate his employer" (in Lubow, "Artisans in Transition," 500).

[13] Ibid., 525–30.

[14] "Meeting of Master Carpenters," in *Boston Commercial Gazette*, 23 Apr. 1825.

[15] *Independent Chronicle and Boston Patriot*, 23 Apr. 1825.

[16] There is some difference of scholarly opinion over whether the strike was an attempt to establish the ten-hour day or to preserve it. See Commons et al., *History of Labor*, 158, and contrast Lubow, "Artisans in Transition," 501–2. See also, generally, David Brody, "Time and Work during Early American Industrialism," *Labor History*, 30, 1 (Winter 1989), 5–46. There is no disagreement that they were unsuccessful, however; the *Courier* reported (30 Apr. 1825) that the journeymen "have resumed their labour on the same conditions as formerly."

184

JUDGE THACHER'S CHARGE

When conflict revived in the 1830s things were clearly different. Self-organization was rife, expressed in strikes (almost every year between 1830 and 1836 saw significant numbers of journeymen involved in strikes, mostly focused on the ten-hour day), in independent workingmen's political activity, and in citywide trade organization.[17] By the middle of the decade, for instance, journeymen in numerous trades had announced the formation of associations – iron founders, masons, printers, rope makers, bakers, cabinet and pianoforte makers, boot and shoe makers, painters and glaziers, stonecutters, machinists, coopers, tailors, shipwrights, house carpenters, curriers, black & white smiths, papermakers, sail makers, plasterers. In March 1834, fourteen of these trade societies joined to form the Trades' Union of Boston.[18]

As elsewhere this heady brew attracted the attention of the judiciary. The first sign of this came in May 1832 when, in the course of a charge to the Essex County grand jury at the opening of the Supreme Judicial Court's term at Ipswich, Chief Justice Lemuel Shaw dwelt at some length on the danger which "the union of

[17] Lubow, "Artisans in Transition," 557–76. Formisano, *Transformation of Political Culture*, 222–67

[18] For details of the formation of individual trade societies, see announcements of meetings of individual trades called to form associations appearing throughout 1834 in the *Boston Morning Post*. For details of the formation of the Trades' Union of Boston see Commons et al., eds., *Documentary History*, 6:87–92. On 5 April 1834, the *Post* commented: "The mechanics are moving in good earnest. If the plan of forming a Trades' Union proves as successful as present appearances give us reason to anticipate, it will tend more to elevate the character and increase the personal and combined influence of the *Workingmen*, than anything which has heretofore been attempted for the purposes of effecting those objects. The different trades should give their earnest and prompt attention to this subject."
And again, on 14 June 1834: "We perceive among the dependants of the monied aristocracy, continued and systematic efforts to decry the Trades' Union, and to bring them into disrepute. We are not surprised at this, for the object of the Trades' Union is to guard and protect its members against the selfish proceedings of capitalists. The working classes, or in modern phrase, the operatives, see the 'Wealth Unions' united under legal, corporative associations, which unions, or companies, adopt rules and regulations, fixing the time the operative shall labor each day, and the rate of wages he shall receive, and the only effective antagonist measure the laborer can raise, is in the Trades' Union. Is it not as fair for the laboring mechanic to have a common understanding what they shall charge for their work, as for the manufacturer and merchant to agree what they will or will not give? This is often done on their part – nay more, it is always done in some of the large manufactories, which have a regular 'Union' and report from one factory to another, when they dismiss an operative, and the reasons why; and in this way effectually outlaw him. The ship builders, who have a 'Union,' agreed, for the purpose of aiding the panic, and to feather their own nests, this spring, to cut down the wages of their workmen – who having no 'Union' to oppose to the union of their employers, were obliged to yield. Have not the factories at Dover and Lowell cut down the wages of their operatives in like manner? And yet, notwithstanding the 'pressure,' they divide twelve percent, for six months, and probably keep a reserve fund besides. The moment the operatives declined taking the prescribed wages, they were reported by the 'union of corporate wealth,' to all those factories, and were, *de facto*, outlawed, until they would submit to work on such terms as would yield the capitalists some 25 percent, on their investments.
"If the capitalists will leave the work market open to free competition – if they did not combine to reduce the price of labor, there would be no occasion for Trades' Unions. But under the present organization of monied corporations and other capitalists, the safety of the working classes depends upon 'Unions' – united, concerted efforts, and it will not be surprising to find the female operatives organizing these Unions among their sex. It is but the dictate of self-interest and equal justice." See also the *New England Artisan*, 31 May 1834 and 7 June 1834, on "Trades Unions."

numbers, animated by a strong sense of common feeling and interest, and combined for the support of some common cause" posed to "the just and due execution of the laws." In the present condition of society, Shaw stated, "there is little danger that the law will be set at defiance, or its due administration prevented by the power and influence of individuals, however elevated in rank or wealth." Rather, the problem was "the general tendency of society in our times, to combine men into bodies and associations, having some object of deep interest common to themselves, but distinct from those of the rest of the community."[19]

Shaw had apparently been moved to offer the grand jury such advice as a result of the agitation for a ten-hour workday that had begun in March 1832 following the convention of the New England Association of Farmers, Mechanics and Other Workingmen. By the middle of May the campaign had become focused on the shipyards, where it would climax during the summer months in a major strike led by the Society of Journeymen Shipwrights and Caulkers of Boston and Charlestown.[20] Shaw, however, made no explicit reference to the activities of the workingmen, contenting himself with a more general warning that the grand jury should not allow itself to be distracted by the organized pursuit of particular interests and leaving aside completely the question whether the activities of such associations (or, indeed, their very existence) violated the law. It remained for Peter Oxenbridge Thacher of the Boston Municipal Court to confront the question directly. This he did by devoting three-quarters of his charge to the Suffolk County grand jury at the opening of the court's December 1832 session to the merits of applying the law of criminal conspiracy to labor combinations. The first attempt at an authoritative discourse upon the law of labor conspiracy offered in Massachusetts, Thacher's charge

---

[19] Lemuel Shaw, *Charge Delivered to the Grand Jury for the County of Essex at the Supreme Judicial Court Held at Ipswich, May Term, 1832* (Boston, 1832), 7–8.

[20] Formal notice of the formation of this society appears in the *Independent Chronicle and Boston Patriot*, 23 May 1832, as part of a statement issued by the journeymen "to the Merchants of the City of Boston" in response to resolutions condemning the society adopted at a meeting of Boston merchants and shipowners on 15 May and printed in the *Chronicle* on the 19 May. These resolutions read, in part, as follows:

"Inasmuch as it is the opinion of the undersigned that labour ought always to be left free to regulate itself, and that neither the employer nor the employed should have the power to control the other; and that all combinations to regulate the price and the hours of labour, nor [*sic*] to restrain individual freedom and enterprise, are at all times attended with pernicious consequences, and especially so to the individuals whose interests they are intended to promote. . . .

"RESOLVED, that we view with deep regret the course which some of our fellow citizens, journeymen ship carpenters, caulkers, and others, are pursuing, in the adoption and maintenance of a system of measures designed to coerce individuals of their craft, and to prescribe the time and manner of that labour for which they are liberally paid.

"RESOLVED, that in our opinion, the tendency of this combination of the ship carpenters, caulkers, and others, instead of benefitting them, has a direct tendency either to put their business into other hands, or seriously to injure it in this place. . . .

"RESOLVED, that we will so far discountenance all associations and combinations for the purposes before stated, that we will neither employ any journeyman who, at the time, belong to such combination, nor will we give work to any master mechanic who shall employ them while they continue thus pledged to each other."

was subsequently published in pamphlet form at the grand jury's request.[21] Significantly – in that it came at what we have seen was a moment of some considerable uncertainty as to the precise state of the law of labor conspiracy in Pennsylvania and New York – Thacher's charge was also publicized by a leading eastern practitioners' journal, *The American Jurist and Law Magazine.* "We copy the part of the charge relating to conspiracies," the journal informed its readers, "as it is applicable to transactions that have occurred in different parts of the United States during the past year."[22]

Thacher left the grand jury in no doubt that his decision to instruct it on the law of labor conspiracies had been precipitated by the events of the previous spring and summer, when "our community was . . . agitated by combinations, which, by interrupting the completion of contracts, produced, at the time, a sudden cessation of business, and implied a deliberate and mischievous purpose to distress both employers and the public." No conspiracy charges, however, were brought against journeymen at the December session.[23] Delivered well after the agitation had died down, Thacher's comments were likely motivated less by a desire to procure an indictment of journeymen involved in the 1832 strikes after the event than to affirm publicly that the law of conspiracy was available to be mobilized in future controversies.[24]

Thacher took his cue from Chief Justice Parsons in *Commonwealth v. Judd.* The gist of a conspiracy and the source of its criminality consisted in the agreement of several persons to do an act, which, if not unlawful in itself, became so by the combination. "In many cases, the agreement to do a certain thing is considered as the subject for an indictment for a conspiracy, though the same act, if done separately by each individual, without concert with others, would be innocent. This is very manifest

---

[21] Peter Oxenbridge Thacher, *A Charge to the Grand Jury of the County of Suffolk at the Opening of the Municipal Court of the City of Boston, on the First Monday of December, A.D. 1832* (Boston, 1832).

[22] *American Jurist and Law Magazine*, 9 (Jan.–Apr. 1833), 216–20.

[23] Although the shipowners and merchants' declaration of 19 May had denounced "combinations formed to control the freedom of individuals as to the hours of labour," there is no evidence that they sought or even contemplated seeking a conspiracy indictment, and an examination of the Boston Municipal Court docket reveals no conspiracy charges were brought against journeymen at the December session. See Boston Municipal Court Docket (1832–3), in *Records of the Massachusetts Superior Court, Suffolk County* (now in the Massachusetts State Archives, Boston).

[24] Indeed, Thacher's comments were notable for their stress on future developments, particularly the likelihood of unions appearing among factory operatives, and on the availability of the law of conspiracy to regulate any future deleterious conduct (in Thacher, *Charge to the Grand Jury . . . December 1832,* 8–9): "In proportion as our country, possessing inexhaustible sources of mechanical ingenuity, and wisely encouraging the inventive genius of its citizens, extends its manufacturing establishments, multitudes will be collected into confined situations, which will present facilities for acting in concert. Hence, the respective rights of laborers and employers acquire increased importance. The law, that universal guide, protector, and friend of human industry, is not silent on this subject: and although no complaint exists, and I am sure I would not make any, it yet seems to me not unseasonable, to state the principles which govern such cases. For every man is presumed to know the law, and required to observe it; because it would be an infinite evil, if men might escape from the consequences of their actions by the plea of ignorance. This maxim increases the obligation of a judge, to state with plainness, as he has opportunity, those legal principles, which must guide individuals in the performance of their duty, with the reasons on which they are founded, and for which they deserve our observance." See also *Boston Morning Post,* 14 June 1834, quoted in n. 18, on the issue of organization among operatives, and Seth Luther's comments, at n. 30, on Thacher's presentation of this charge.

in combinations amongst journeymen mechanics and laborers, to raise their wages, and regulate the hours of work."[25] Far more important than the statement, however, was Thacher's explanation of it. This was a highly sophisticated restatement of Parsons's doctrine of injury at large, couched in a discourse of political economy.

Attempts by journeymen to control the price of their labor were fruitless even though they might be attended by momentary success, Thacher argued, because the ultimate determinant of the price of labor was the value of other commodities in the market. Massachusetts, he implied, was a market society of atomized individuals whose social and economic lives were defined by the transactions into which they entered with each other. This market order, however, did not exist in nature but was rather a social phenomenon constituted by laws. These secured to everyone the right to put such value on their labor, ingenuity, and learning as they pleased, and thereby enabled all freely to contend together for profit in pursuit of their respective good. But as a social construct the market order was vulnerable to disruption and had to be protected. "The operations of society cannot proceed, unless the law, which, like the air, is over every thing, and pervades every thing, and is the life of every thing, protect, in full extent, the principle of equal and fair competition. If individuals may combine together, to gain an unfair advantage over others, it would violate this principle."[26]

Protection was not simply a matter of guarding against overt threats. "When such a project is attended, as has often been the case in older countries, with a tumultuous assemblage of the people, or violence to the persons or property of individuals, or the writing of incendiary letters, or threats of mischief to masters or employers, it never has been doubted, that it was sufficient matter for a criminal indictment." Thacher, however, stressed rather the absence of any necessity for an overt act, for

---

[25] Thacher, *Charge to the Grand Jury . . . December 1832*, 383. As authority Thacher cited *R. v. Mawbey And Others*, 101 E.R. 796 (1796). In the course of his charge Thacher cited *The Poulterers' Case* (1611), *R. v. Journeymen-Taylors of Cambridge* (1721), and *Hume's Commentaries on the Laws of Scotland*, all of which were discussed in detail in Chapter 4. In addition Thacher cited *R. v. Edwards et al.*, 88 E.R. 229 (1724) (a conspiracy among parish officials to cause a female pauper in their parish to be married to a male pauper in another parish, thus voiding their obligation to support her); and *Parker v. Lord Clive*, 98 E.R. 267 (1769), and *Vertue v. Lord Clive*, 98 E.R. 296 (1769) (the announcement of an intention to resign their commissions by military officers in the employment of the East India Company in protest at the company's order to its agents for the reduction of the officers' pay and perquisites was held to be a combination "to terrify and intimidate the Company" into maintaining their pay and perquisites at the preexisting level, and as such a criminal act). Thacher would also have been familiar with Nathan Dane's and Daniel Davis's citation of "conspiracy of journeymen to raise their wages" and "lessen the Time of Labor" or to "refuse to work in consequence of a combination, until their wages are raised" as indictable offenses, on the basis of English common law precedents. See Dane, *Abridgment*, 7:4–5; Daniel Davis, *Precedents of Indictments* (Boston, 1831), 101. (Davis was solicitor general of Massachusetts at the time. His sample conspiracy indictment was taken from Thomas Starkie's *Treatise on Criminal Pleading* [London, 1814], 2:694–6.) He would also, no doubt, have been aware of the dicta delivered in the course of the New York Supreme Court's opinion in *People v. Mather*, 4 Wend. 230, 261 (1830), for which see Chapter 5.

[26] Thacher, *Charge to the Grand Jury . . . December 1832*, 9. This was essentially the position that Chief Justice Savage took in the New York case *People v. Fisher* in 1835. See above, the section entitled Public or Private Wrongs? in Chapter 5.

unlawful or criminal means. The law punished a conspiracy, "although it be not carried into effect," because the conspiracy was criminal in its very nature – oppressive to individual rights to participate freely in the market; in itself a threat, through its interference with those rights, to the social system comprising market society; antagonistic to the very principles in pursuit of whose realization humans entered into "society" with each other at all; and above all a threat to the great ordering authority of government and law, which kept all from dissolving into chaos:

Our government was constituted for the good of all. . . . In declaring combinations of this character criminal, the law but utters the voice of reason and good sense. All such acts infringe upon the freedom of the market, which it is one main object of policy in every well-regulated state to secure. They violate the freedom of the citizen, which consists not in liberty of person only, but of conduct, and in the right to do as one pleases in all matters not commanded or forbidden by law. They essentially interfere too with the rights of the government. Whenever individuals array themselves against the law, they should be promptly met, before combination manifests itself in mobs, insurrections, and other civil commotions, which the strong arm of government only can repress.[27]

Here was an uncompromising vision indeed. Journeymen's combinations were injurious interferences with private right, *and* they were public wrongs. They were punishable on either basis.

Although traces of the hierarchical communitarian society exalted in some previous opinions yet remained,[28] Thacher's charge demonstrates how far, by the early 1830s, American common law had come toward incorporating the economic liberalism of classical political economy. It is crucial to note, however, that economic liberalism had blended with, it had not displaced, the elite republicanism characteristic of common law discourse in its earlier, Federalist, incarnation. As I have already argued at some length, market society had a vital interest in *safety*. A free market was the means through which the nineteenth century's transactional ideal might best be realized in social and economic life, and for this reason its maintenance should be an important object of policy. But it was law, not the market, which was constitutive of civil society. This of course gave Thacher an additional reason for condemning combinations: Not merely did their attempts to impose their own

[27] Thacher, *Charge to the Grand Jury . . . December 1832*, 12–13.

[28] Note, e.g., the following statement in which criticism of labor combinations for interference with contractual relations mingles indiscriminately with criticism of them for interference with status relations and with the organic unity of society: "Now who has the right to say that a workman may not agree, if he please, to work from sun-rise to sun-set for such sum as will satisfy him for his labor? Who may justly complain of the man, who shall refuse to employ another, who will not stipulate to work during certain hours of each day, or for any other period of time? While the parties are content, who may presume to interfere between the laborer and his employer? The claim to interfere is against the social compact, and violates the duty, which binds every man to maintain its principles. In society, the members are essentially dependent on each other. He who seeks to divide them, seeks to destroy them. If the blood will not flow to the heart, the body must perish. So, if members of the social system engage in mutual contest, the rich against the poor, the laborer against the employer, human industry will stop, to the ruin of individuals, if not of the system itself. But though the loss of any individual can hardly be perceptible in the system of society, it must never be forgotten, that one of the great ends of society is to protect and preserve individuals" (ibid., 12).

private regulations on others offend against the economic laws of the marketplace by interfering with the free interaction of private interests, they also posed a major threat to the law and its monopoly of legitimate coercion by assuming to exercise powers that none but the juridical structures built to sustain republican society could legitimately possess. One may, in short, acknowledge the considerable and growing correspondence between those structures and the competitive, capitalist society springing up in their midst, but still one must also appreciate that when judges like Thacher, and like his New York contemporary Ogden Edwards, condemned labor combinations, they did so not as the willing agents of employers but as ideologues committed to a particular conception of the role of law in republican society. Theirs, we have seen, was a republic constituted by the legitimate coercive power of an Anglocentric common law. They pursued labor conspiracies with particular intensity because in their minds that common law vision was at stake, and thus the commonwealth itself.

Thacher's vociferous condemnation of journeymen's combinations precipitated a major confrontation with the labor movement in Massachusetts. Earlier in the year, when journeymen and employers had clashed over the ten-hour question, the issue had been the employers' discriminatory refusal to countenance organization among their workmen. "Men of property find no fault with combinations to extinguish *fires*, and protect their *precious persons* from danger," Seth Luther had told the Working Men of Boston that July. "But if *poor men* ask JUSTICE, it is a most HORRIBLE COMBINATION. The Declaration of Independence was the work of a combination, and was as hateful to the TRAITORS and TORIES of those days as combinations among working men are now to the *avaricious* MONOPLIST and *purse proud* ARISTOCRAT."[29] After Thacher's pronouncement, however, the focus of the workingmen's critique switched from their employers' antagonism to combinations to the antagonism given voice by the courts. "I cannot see the consistency, or honor, or honesty, if any, in the course the Judge pursued," Luther argued early in 1834. "It seems that law, and lawyers, and judges, were all determined, by the help of gold, to crush the working class to the dust. They may tell us in their charges, and pleas, and messages, and speeches in Congress, how much labor is respected, and how much necessity there is for protecting laborers; it will never alter my opinion so long as I see so much real oppression by law, on working men and women."[30]

---

[29] Seth Luther, *An Address to the Working Men of New England, on the State of Education, and on the Condition of the Producing Classes in Europe and America . . . and on the Safety of our Republic*, 2d ed. (New York, 1833), 27 (emphasis in original).

[30] Seth Luther, *An Address on the Origin and Progress of Avarice, and its Deleterious Effects on Human Happiness . . . Delivered before the Union Association of Working Men, in the Town Hall, Charlestown, Mass., January 30, 1834* (Boston, 1834), 15–16. Luther returned to the matter later in his speech: "We have been officially accused of a malicious design to injure the public, by attempts to fix the hours of labor, during the hot and sultry summer months. . . . The Judge, who acted the part of an *informer*, jury and judge, in the charge I have brought to your notice, has publicly charged us with a mischievous design to disturb the public peace, and stigmatized the Mechanics of Boston with the name of a Combination. The Judge knew, at the same time that the Lawyers, and Doctors and Booksellers had a Combination, under various forms and names. He knew that the Merchants at that moment had a Combination, backed

Luther's theme was picked up and expanded upon later that year by Frederick Robinson, a radical Democrat and member of the Massachusetts state legislature from Marblehead, in the course of a passionate July Fourth address delivered before some two thousand artisans and mechanics assembled under the banners of the Trades' Union of Boston to reaffirm their commitment to the ten-hour day.[31] Like Thacher's charge, Robinson's address blended republican and market discourse. But the result was very different.

Robinson, it has been said, "was one of the few politicians who spoke directly to the reality of the workingmen's situation." The reality he described that day was one of unrelieved antagonism between "aristocracy" in its various political, social, and economic guises and the progress and happiness of the people. "The interests of the thousands are always contrary to the interests of the millions," he told the crowd. "The prosperity of the one always consists in the adversity of the other."

> The aristocracy of our country are well aware that their notions of government are unsound, and in order to prevent the true appellation of aristocracy from being attached to them, they continually contrive to change their party name. It was first Tory, then Federalist, then no party, then National Republican, now Whig, and the next name they assume will perhaps be republican or democrat. But by whatever name they reorganize themselves, the true democracy of the country, the producing classes, ought to be able to distinguish the enemy. Ye may know them by their fruit. Ye may know them by their deportment towards the people. Ye may know them by their disposition to club together, and constitute societies, and incorporations, for the enjoyment of exclusive privileges, and for countenancing and protecting each other in their monopolies.[32]

up by all the wealth and influence of that body of men, and signed by over one hundred, and published in the papers of the city. He knew that these Merchants issued what was called by the Mechanics, a Ukase, from its resemblance to the tyrannical acts of the Emperor of Russia, under that title. Why did not the *impartial* judge attack them. *He dare not do it.* This Ukase *permitted* the Mechanics of Boston to take time to escape the Cholera, – it met with the scorn, contempt, and deep curses of every man in the community who had a soul; and the Merchants of Boston engaged in that mean affair, enlightened as they are, met the utter detestation of all fair, candid minds, wherever this *unprecedented* document found its way, both in Europe and America. Why did not the Judge present to the grand jury the Lawyers who have a Combination under the head of Bar-Rules, by which they grind to powder the poor, and sell, *not justice*, but injustice to the indigent. Not a word about *that* Combination, *nothing* about it. The Mechanics, the men who daily, nightly, hourly, protect the property of the rich; the men who dragged the engines over Warren Bridge when the west end of it was in flames, to save property not their own: *these, these* are the men denounced by a grave Judge, who lowered himself from the high dignity of the bench to become an *informer*, when he himself in that charge said '*there was no complaint, and he was sure he did not wish to make any;*' but he did make it, to his everlasting dishonor, as an impartial man, as an unbiassed judge, and good citizen" (40–1, emphasis in original).

[31] Formisano, *Transformation of Political Culture*, 234–5. "The respective trades appeared in procession, embracing more than two thousand persons, with banners and emblems. A beautiful printing-press, and a superb frigate completely rigged and manned, drawn by twenty-four white horses, gave effect to the parade" (James Spear Loring, *The Hundred Boston Orators* [Boston, 1854], 525).

[32] Formisano, *Transformation of Political Culture*, 235; Frederick Robinson, *An Oration Delivered before the Trades' Union of Boston and Vicinity, on Fort Hill, Boston, on the Fifty-Eighth Anniversary of American Independence* (Boston, 1834), 4, 6. The parallels at this point between Robinson's oration and the plebeian republicanism articulated by such as William Manning and numbers of Anti-Federalists in the 1780s and 1790s are striking.

Among the measures Robinson deemed essential to the defense of the people against the oppression of this elite of wealth and power, none was more important than union among themselves ("in concert with the democracy of the country") and destruction of the power of the common law (the "unwritten law, deposited only in the head of the Judge") and of the judiciary. Union was essential because alone the individual worker was powerless to give any effect to rights essential to personal well-being. "In the savage state each individual produces for himself whatever he consumes, and of course no union with others is required to protect his labor. But in a state of society where no one labors for his own consumption alone, but each receives the labor of others in exchange for his own, the price of labor in each division of labor, to prevent fraud, ought to be fixed by agreement among the laborers themselves." Further, the right so to act in concert was "a social right," for "when men enter into a state of society, all those rights which it is impossible to enjoy without the aid of others, become social rights, and must be enjoyed if at all, by concert with others." Such rights, however, had been invaded and denied by aristocracy, through "the semblance of law." Hence Robinson's assault on the judiciary, "the headquarters of the aristocracy," where "every plan to humble and subdue the people originates."[33]

Robinson used Thacher's condemnation of journeymen's associations to illustrate the point. "One of the judges in this city, not long since, charged the grand jury to indict the working men who attempt by unions to fix the price or regulate the hours of labor. What then ought we to think of the man who, being a member of the secret trades union of the bar, calls upon the jury to indict the members of the open Trades Union of the people, who join not for the purpose of injuring others, but for the enjoyment of their most inestimable right, to be deprived of which must always keep them in want, ignorance and slavery? Does it not become us, fellow citizens, when we see the enemies of the equal rights of man everywhere combined to maintain their ascendancy, to unite and employ our power of numbers against the power of their wealth and learning, for the recovery and protection of our rights?" From here Robinson proceeded to an extended assault on lifetime judicial office holding; on common law adjudication, decrying it as a usurpation of popular sovereignty; on the organized bar and its domination of both legal and legislative process; and on the resultant unintelligibility – the "dark chaos" – of the law.[34]

---

[33] Robinson, *Oration*, 11–13.

[34] Ibid., 13–14, 15–17. For an earlier example of Robinson's antilegal invective, see Frederick Robinson, *A Letter to the Hon. Rufus Choate, Containing a Brief Exposure of Law Craft* (Boston, 1832). In the *Letter* (at 14–15), Robinson criticized the organized bar for restrictive practices. "You are . . . nothing more than the followers of a trade or calling like other men, to get a living, and your trade, like other employments, ought to be left open to universal competition. What right have you to form associations for the purpose of preventing others from competing with you, more than the followers of any other trade?" As we have seen, Robinson's *Oration* was couched in the same antiprivilege vein, assaulting "incorporate monopolies" for their promotion of "the ends of the few, the ignorance, degradation and

Thacher responded to his critics five months later at the opening of the December 1834 session of the Municipal Court. On this occasion his comments were rather briefer than before but no less censorious, somberly emphasizing the tangible threat which journeymen's combinations and their leaders presented to the capacity of legal institutions to maintain a fragile social order. "When one class of citizens is taught to consider another as enemies," he instructed the grand jury, "it will infallibly tend, in time, to disturb the peace of society. It has of late been fashionable, even in this Commonwealth, to excite the employed against their employers, and borrowers against lenders, and thus to lead the poor to wage a civil war against the rich. . . . [T]here is but one and the same law for employers and workmen, securing to the latter their wages, and to the former the produce of their skill and enterprise. Employers may not combine against their workmen to depress, by unfair means, their wages; nor may workmen combine against employers, unjustly, to raise them. This is even handed justice, and is as good for the laborer as for the employer."[35] Thacher prefaced this renewed assault on journeymen's combinations with a lengthy denunciation of the riot earlier that year at the Ursuline Convent, "a scene of popular madness" that he compared with the Reign of Terror during the French Revolution. The trial of the rioters had begun just two days before in Cambridge, and Thacher used it to illustrate the growing disarray of contemporary society. Riots and combinations were alike symptoms of "that levelling spirit, which would take from industry its incentive, from talent its reward, and which seems to grow out

---

slavery of the many" (18). It is therefore all the more significant that Robinson did *not* apply this logic to trades unionism. Nor did he portray trades unions as necessary but essentially negative counters to the superior power of elites. Rather, using the language of "social right" to describe unionism, he sought, like contemporary labor leaders in New York and Pennsylvania, to represent the collective action of working people as an "open" and positive force, a source of democratic power that contrasted with the secret concerts of aristocracy: "Well may the capitalists, monopolists, judges, lawyers, doctors, and priests complain of Trades Unions. They know that the secret of their own power and wealth consists in the strictest concert of action, – and they know that when the great mass of the people become equally wise with themselves, and unite their power of numbers for the possession and enjoyment of equal rights, they will be shorn of their consequence, be humbled of their pride, and brought to personal labor for their own subsistence. They know from experience that unions among themselves, have always enabled the few to rule and ride the people; and that, when the people shall discover the secret of their power, and learn to use it for their own good, the sceptre will fall from their hands, will become merged in the great 'vulgar' mass of the people" (14–15).

[35] Peter Oxenbridge Thacher, *A Charge to the Grand Jury of the County of Suffolk at the Opening of the Municipal Court of the City of Boston on the First Monday of December, 1834* (Boston, 1834), 16. Frederick Robinson, of course, did not see it this way: "The right of the producer to fix the price of his own labor is unquestionable; for its denial admits the right of slavery. But every effort which the producing classes have ever made for the enjoyment of this most obvious right has always met with the most determined opposition of the aristocracy. . . . Those that have not the unblushing confidence to deny this right altogether contend that it is an individual and not a social right. For although each individual may fix the price of his own labor, yet no two or more individuals have a right to agree among themselves to fix the price. But when men enter into a state of society, all those rights which it is impossible to enjoy without the aid of others become social rights and must be enjoyed, if at all, by concert with others. It is unreasonable to suppose that we are possessed of rights which we have not the power to enjoy" (*Oration*, 12).

of the abuse of liberty." Each made it more difficult to sustain "the regular current of society." Each promised to "array one portion of our free and happy society against the other," opening the way for those seeking "to rise upon the ruins of their country, and trample under feet its liberty and laws."[36]

A DISCOURSE OF REFORM

Criticism of the courts, of the legal profession, and of the administration of law had been important themes of the Working Men's movement in New England from the moment of its inception in August 1830.[37] As we have seen, this was also the case in New York and Pennsylvania. The controversy over criminal conspiracy gave these themes an added prominence in all three states.[38] In Massachusetts it also became the occasion for a renewal of the ad hoc rapprochement between workers and democratically inclined lawyers seeking reform of the common law's grosser inanities, which had made an appearance earlier in the century in Philadelphia and New York.[39] Emblematic of that rapprochement was the role of Robert Rantoul, Jr., in 1840 and 1842 in defending the Boston Society of Journeymen Bootmakers on a

[36] Thacher, *Charge to the Grand Jury . . . December, 1834*, 11–15, 20–3.

[37] On the origins of the Working Men's movement in Boston see Commons et al., eds., *Documentary History*, 5:185–99. The founding document of the movement in Boston criticized "the multiplication of statutes, and the mysterious phraseology in which they are ordinarily involved" and called for "the enactment of laws clearly defined and justly applied." See *The Committee appointed by the Working Men of Boston at their Meeting the 3d ultimo . . . REPORT*, Aug. 1830, Massachusetts Historical Society, Boston. See also Robinson, *A Letter to the Hon. Rufus Choate*.

In October 1834, the Northampton Convention of Farmers, Mechanics and Other Workingmen of Massachusetts drafted an "Address to the Workingmen of Massachusetts" which singled out the "law system" as one of its principal objects of criticism:

"Our law system . . . is based upon arbitrary principles that derive no origin from the free spirit of the government which our fathers sought to establish; but which have been introduced from abroad; and it is maintained among us, in defiance of the good sense and better judgment of the people. . . .

"The people are not in the habit of looking upon the laws as a subject which requires the attention of any beside lawyers by profession, when the fact is, that our laws should be so plain, and so universally promulgated, that every man in the nation might see and understand them. That man is not a republican, he cannot be justly called a freeman, who is controlled by laws he does not understand. – And is it not self-evident, that if we are under the control of a power that we cannot regulate, and which is managed by others who can, that it deprives us of our birthright of freedom with the same certainty, whether the usurpation is brought about by laws that we never made nor understood or by a standing army at the point of a bayonet. . . .

"It is not a little extraordinary that an intelligent people that have had the spirit to rend asunder the political ties which bound them to the old world, should have retained with so little modification the whole system of jurisprudence, which prevails under that arbitrary form of government which they have forever abjured . . . laws that a free people never made, never understood, never consented to, and should never be compelled to obey" (*New England Artisan*, 25 Oct. 1834).

[38] As, indeed, did the controversy over imprisonment for debt, which gave rise to one of Seth Luther's more memorable metaphors: "behold, the harpies of 'the law,' the ministers of 'JUSTICE,' entering the grave-yard like hyenas, in search of human flesh, to gorge the appetite on corruption" (*Address on the Origin and Progress of Avarice*, 29).

[39] See Chapter 5.

194

conspiracy indictment in *Commonwealth v. Hunt*. As had been the case on those earlier occasions in New York and Philadelphia, however, the collaboration of reformist lawyer and indicted journeymen seeking to avoid a criminal conspiracy conviction was as much an alliance of convenience as a meeting of minds.

Robert Rantoul, Jr., was the quintessential embodiment of the conjunction of law reform and negative liberty – the qualities which the Jacobins, Duane and Sampson, had brought to bear on the labor conspiracy issue thirty years before. An Essex County lawyer all his adult life, Rantoul was born in 1805 into a prominent Beverly family and attended Phillips Academy and Harvard before beginning his practice in Salem. Initially a National Republican in his politics, after moving to Gloucester in 1831 he became active in the town's Democratic Party and from 1835 to 1838 represented Gloucester in the state legislature.

Rantoul was a reformer in state politics and an identified opponent of the state's Whig elites, but unlike Marblehead's Frederick Robinson he was no particular champion of workingmen or of their claim to possess *social rights* to engage in collective action. Robinson's 1834 July Fourth oration before the Trades' Union of Boston had clearly aligned him with the ten-hours movement and the workingmen's defense of their right to organize unions. "If we have not the social right to fix the price of our own labor, it is perfectly useless to allow us the right at all. For how can an unaided individual without wealth, without education, ignorant of the world, and even of the value of his own labor, who must command immediate employment or starve, enjoy this right as an individual right. If he enjoy it at all, the interests of others engaged in the same or other employments must secure it to him." For Robinson, in short, trades unions which set prices and controlled the hours of labor enabled the powerless individual to regain control of his destiny.[40] Rantoul, in contrast, opposed both the ten-hours movement and combinations to fix the price of labor:

Our time . . . is our own, to devote to the service of others, in such portions as we please, with or without an equivalent, or directly to our own convenience, comfort or improvement. We have a right to make the best bargain for it with those who employ us. We have a right to make the best bargain for it with those whom we employ. If we ask more than the highest market price for it, when we have it to sell, we must not be surprised if no one is willing to buy. If we offer less than the lowest market price for it, when we wish to procure it, we must not be surprised if no one will furnish it to us. No one has any authority to dictate the price to the buyer or the seller, it must be settled by agreement between them; and the competition between the buyers on the one hand and the sellers on the other will induce them to fix it at a point where both parties can profit by the bargain. We have a right to sell our time for ten hours every day, for twelve, for fifteen, for more or for less, to anybody that will buy it. But if we offer to contract to labor ten hours a day and nobody wants less than twelve, we must not wonder that nobody accepts our offer.[41]

---

[40] Robinson, *Oration*, 12, 27–8.
[41] Robert Rantoul, Jr., "An Address to the Workingmen of the United States of America" (1833), in Luther Hamilton, ed., *Memoirs, Speeches and Writings of Robert Rantoul, Jr.* (Boston, 1854), 219–50, at 233.

The discourse of law *reform* was, by the late 1830s, to become the dominant language in which workingmen's relations with the courts were discussed. Yet that discourse, even the Democratic variant which Rantoul represented, does not do full justice to the legal consciousness of the antebellum labor movement.[42] Among the Boston Working Men, at least, one may find fragments of a very different critique, spearheaded by Seth Luther, whose vantage point on "law" was so far outside the parameters of "law reform" as to suggest no commonality at all.

In Luther's rendition, the history of law for working people in America had been, almost unrelieved, the history of oppression. "We are told that it 'is the first duty of an American citizen to respect the laws,'" he commented sarcastically in the course of his July Fourth address to the Working Men of Brooklyn in 1836.

Law hung old women in Salem because it was *proved*, said the courts of *law*, that they were witches. *Law* hung the Quakers in Boston, because they wore strait coats and broad brimmed hats. *Law* whipped the members of the same sect, at the cart tail, from town to town in New Hampshire. Law bared the backs of the Baptists in Boston, and lashed them until the skin was flayed off, because they said 'every man has a right to worship God according to the dictates of his own conscience;' and law in Connecticut compelled every body to cut their hair in a particular manner and prosecuted men for kissing their wives on the first day of the week. Law laid the stamp tax, and the tea tax, and our fathers resisted those unjust laws even unto blood. . . . Must we be told to submit in silence to *law*, merely because it *is* law, without reference to its constituent principles? No law will ever command the respect of any, not even a slave in every sense, unless that law is just.[43]

Luther drew here on rich veins of popular antilegalism in American culture.[44] The influence of that antilegalism on the political conflicts of the 1830s has been noted by many previous historians, so to discover it in Luther's discourse is no more than mildly interesting. What is more important is what he did with it. By the 1830s, it has been argued, the values connected with eighteenth-century outbursts of popular antilegalism – corrosive antagonism to property and hierarchy, the desire for a simple and fundamental statement of principles of justice – had mutated into the familiar "demands for a formal equality of legal rights, most importantly the right to compete on equal terms in the market," which are taken to be the epitome of the Age of Jackson's individualistic mien.[45] Undoubtedly such a mutation did occur, and we may observe its tracks in many places.[46] Take, for example, Rantoul's famous 1836 July Fourth "Oration at Scituate," in which a stentorian assault on the

---

[42] On the varieties of law "reform" see Robert W. Gordon, "Book Review: The American Codification Movement," *Vanderbilt Law Review*, 36, 2 (Mar. 1983), 431–58, at 443, 445–58.

[43] Luther, *An Address delivered before the Mechanics and Working-Men of the City of Brooklyn, on the Celebration of the Sixtieth Anniversary of American Independence* (Brooklyn, 1836), 9–10 (emphasis in original).

[44] For the roots of the antilegalism manifested by the 1830s labor movement, see Gordon, "American Codification Movement," 436–41. See also Chapters 1–5, this volume.

[45] Gordon, "American Codification Movement," 454.

[46] Not least, as I have already pointed out, among the Jacobin lawyers of the early conspiracy cases. See Chapter 5.

"folly, barbarism, and feudality" of the common law was but the prolegomenon to a rhapsodic invocation of the joys of negative liberty.

The leading idea of the American policy is freedom. The sole purpose of government is to prevent the rights of the citizens from being infringed or encroached upon. Every man should be left in the full enjoyment of his natural liberty, so long as he does not thereby interfere with any of the natural rights of his neighbor. When he invades the hallowed boundary of another's rights, then the government should put forth its strong arm to protect them: but so long as he refrains from any such invasion, an American citizen may claim, as his birth-right, perfect and unrestrained liberty of action. Within these limits, wherever his interests, wherever his inclination may lead him, he may take his own course, and government has no right to place in his path the very slightest impediment. He may rove free as the free air which he breathes, calling no man his master, acknowledging no power above him but in heaven, subject to no other restraint but the obligations of virtue and the dictates of conscience and honor, unshackled by arbitrary, vexatious and galling restrictions, untrammelled by human legislation, so long as he obeys the guidance of an enlightened monitor within. For him the whole object of government is negative.[47]

But that mutation is not all of what occurred. In Luther's version of apposite Independence Day discourse (a striking counterpoint to Rantoul's, both delivered the same year on the same day, probably at the same hour) antilegalism fed not a celebration but a profound sense of alienation from the institutions created in the aftermath of the Revolution. "It might be deemed hazardous and to say the least injudicious to assert that the Workingmen of the United States are not so well situated as they were before the Revolution. But I am prepared to make that assertion," Luther told the Working Men of Brooklyn. "Previous to the revolutionary war there was an equality of condition among the people which does not now exist." Now it would take a second revolution to undo the damage done to the condition of the people since the first. "We will try the ballot box first; if that will not effect our righteous purpose, the next and last resort is the cartridge box."[48] In

---

[47] Robert Rantoul, Jr., "Oration at Scituate," in Hamilton, ed., *Memoirs, Speeches and Writings*, 251–96, at 283. For a study of Rantoul's career and ideas, see Robert D. Bulkley, Jr., "Robert Rantoul, Jr., 1805–1852: Politics and Reform in Antebellum Massachusetts" (Ph.D. diss., Princeton University, 1971).

[48] Luther, *Address delivered before the Mechanics and Working-Men of the City of Brooklyn*, 10–11, 17–18. The sense of alienation and loss which Luther conveys was endemic among the leaders of the 1830s labor movement. Note, e.g., the following *Address to the Cordwainers of the United States and More Particularly the Eastern States. Done by Order of the Convention of Cordwainers Held in New York in March, 1836* (Philadelphia, 1836), 2–7: "The time was, when the laborer was considered as 'worthy of his hire.' Not only so, but he was enabled, by industry and economy, to realize sufficient in his early years of manhood, to support himself and family with decency and respect in his declining years. Labor, too, was deemed, in the early organization of our government, respectable; and the man who earned his bread in the sweat of his brow, and sustained otherwise a reputation for virtue and morality, was esteemed not only as a valuable member of society, but one of its principal supporters. He had no superior, save what intelligence made superior, and he stood an equal chance with his fellow-man, for honorable promotion in the general scale of society. Such was the case, fellow-workmen, when republican simplicity guided the actions and governed the course of republicans. Such was the case when those imperishable words, 'ALL MEN ARE CREATED EQUAL,' first sounded on the ear...."

the meantime, however, the workingmen's only protection was trade unionism – a far different route to social justice than that suggested by Rantoul, whose *Address to the Workingmen of the United States of America* published three years earlier had sternly and somewhat patronizingly advised working people that combinations forcibly to raise or lower the rate of wages were "direct and inexcusable infringements" on the voluntary principle of market determination through the interactions of free and unrestrained individuals.[49]

We are told by the mighty fiat of Judge Edwards that "self-constituted societies will not be permitted to rear their crests in this country." If you can find anything more tyrannical than this in all the history of despotic power, I should like to see it. We can, and do, tell the learned judge that "self-constituted societies" *do* exist, *must* exist, and *shall* exist, even if we have to defend ourselves with the bayonet's burnished point. . . .

The very fact that societies formed by Mechanics and Workingmen, are attacked, with such venomous malignity, by the leaders of the aristocracy, ought to convince us that in union alone there is safety. During the past year I visited the Trades Unions of New York, Albany, Newark, Philadelphia, Baltimore and Washington, and in *all cases*, where the principles on which Unions are founded are carried into effectual practice, there the Workingmen are in a state of progressive improvement. . . . In my opinion, that Mechanic or laborer who opposes Trades Unions is either ignorant, foolish or wicked. He is a kind of suicide. He is like a hog in the water, while he is swimming for life he is cutting his own throat with his own hands, as it is well known a hog will do with his fore feet in the act of swimming.[50]

This was hardly the discourse of a law reformer seeking a mere formal equality of rights. Rather, Luther was talking about the realities of power, public and private. The description of the stand-alone worker as "a kind of suicide" is a particularly arresting rebuttal of Rantoul's negative liberalism.

Yet it was the liberal reformer, not the corrosive radical, who was to dictate the parameters of Massachusetts labor's decisive encounter with the courts. By the end of the 1830s, economic depression had undercut the radical wing of the Working Men's movement, leaving liberal law reform the almost uncontested inheritor of, and simultaneously the most effective response to, the antilegal tradition in American political culture. Thus, when it came to that decisive moment when Massachusetts finally made its late entrance on the stage of spasmodic guerrilla warfare between trade unionism and its judicial critics, it was Rantoul not Luther who took the lead and dictated the tactics. As defense attorney in *Commonwealth v. Hunt*, he

"But, alas! how changed! Revolutionary republicanism and patriotism has given way to speculation and stock-jobbing; love of country to love of gold. . . .
. . . "We see, within the last few years, competition, to an unlimited extent, has entered our business. Not that system of honorable competition which gives life and activity to every business, and engenders a spirit of emulation and pride, but a cold, calculating, heartless system, which is founded on the utter prostration of the rights of the Journeymen, and the usurpation of those rights by the employers" (2–4, 5).
[49] Rantoul, "Address to the Workingmen," 234.
[50] Luther, *Address delivered before the Mechanics and Working-Men of Brooklyn*, 18 (emphasis in original).

helped Lemuel Shaw craft a quintessentially *legal* response to the tensions of the previous decade, one that neatly placed the Supreme Judicial Court's imprimatur on the rewritten rules of engagement that had already begun to appear piecemeal in other states, one that thereby made the law of criminal conspiracy *usable* because, ostensibly, it had at last been emptied of political significance. Indeed, the continued ironic juxtaposition of the careers of the reforming lawyer and the radical artisan becomes almost painful: At virtually the moment that Rantoul's liberal discourse was carrying the day for the journeymen bootmakers in Shaw's courtroom, Luther was experiencing the beginnings of an altogether less triumphant and ultimately pathetic denouement, caught up in the trials of Rhode Island's Dorr Rebellion.[51]

Peter Oxenbridge Thacher and Seth Luther represented the opposed extremes of a universe of postrevolutionary discourse on the location and uses of civic power in a republic. Luther's was the discourse of popular democracy: police located in the unmediated will of the people. Thacher's was the discourse of the common law state: police located in the juridical rule of law. These, however, were opposites within the same universe. What they shared even as they disagreed about everything important was agreement, relatively speaking, on the realm of human activity that was determinative. That realm was the civic realm – the realm of politics and public action. And although each demonstrated in his own way his awareness of the social and political salience of the civic realm's major competitor – the realm of the market, of commerce and industry, of money, of the economy – and sought to address that salience through various strategies of acknowledgment or accommodation or rejection, the shared essence of their discourses was that both treated the fate of the material world as determined, and contests in the civic realm as determining. To Luther the sovereign people, to Thacher the law and the state, remained the principal text.

Lemuel Shaw and Robert Rantoul, Jr., inhabited a different conceptual universe, one in which the polarity of the postrevolutionary era was reversed. They represented the world as constituted by the economic behavior of the actors within it; as powered by a different agent of change – competition; and as centered on a different mechanism – the market. In its two trials, *Commonwealth v. Hunt* reveals something of the old world and something of the shape of the new.

COMMONWEALTH v. HUNT

It should not surprise us that Boston's journeymen bootmakers turned to Robert Rantoul in the fall of 1840 for assistance in answering before the austere Judge Thacher to the criminal conspiracy indictment brought against them by Suffolk

[51] On the Dorr Rebellion see George M. Dennison, *The Dorr War: Republicanism on Trial, 1831–1861* (Lexington, 1976).

County Attorney Samuel D. Parker. Like Frederick Robinson, Rantoul was a strong Democrat, a principled political opponent of the conservative Whig elites with whom the prosecution was unambiguously identified. He was also an accomplished attorney with a deserved reputation for taking on unpopular causes.[52] Nor was Rantoul's liberal discourse by any means alien to the workingmen. As we have seen, though Luther was a major voice for most of the 1830s throughout New England and, to a lesser extent, up and down the East Coast, the early labor movement was in no sense ideologically uniform, and there were others just as sincere as Luther whose ideas were closer to the mainstream of Jacksonian negative liberty inhabited by Rantoul. "We ask no protection," Theophilus Fisk told the mechanics of Boston in the course of his fiery 1835 address *Capital Against Labor*. "We simply desire TO BE LET ALONE."[53]

The indictment in *Commonwealth v. Hunt* grew out of a fairly petty squabble within the ranks of the Boston Society of Journeymen Bootmakers over a fine levied by the society against one of its members, Jeremiah Horne, for a minor infraction of its rules. Horne refused to pay, was expelled, and then became liable to pay additional fines and an initiation fee before he could rejoin and avoid being scabbed. Horne continued to refuse. Under pressure from a threatened walkout of the society men in his shop, Horne's employer, Isaac Wait, then dismissed him. Horne took the matter to the county attorney, who in turn took the matter before the grand jury and procured from it a somewhat lurid indictment, charging that the society was a criminal conspiracy which oppressed and impoverished employers and noncomplying workmen. Instituted in the run-up to the 1840 elections and in a charged partisan atmosphere, the prosecution excited considerable local interest.[54]

The substance of the prosecution's case was very weak. Notwithstanding the text of the indictment, employing bootmakers were only peripherally involved. Wait made it clear in testimony that he considered the matter one between the society and Horne, that he had not been injured by the society's activities, and that he would have preferred that Horne remain in good standing with the society so as to avoid trouble in his shop. Other master bootmakers joined Wait in testifying that

[52] Merle E. Curti, "Robert E. Rantoul, Jr., The Reformer in Politics," *New England Quarterly*, 5, 2 (1932), 265–80, at 267–9. On Rantoul's role in the trial and appeal of *Commonwealth v. Hunt*, see Bulkley, "Robert Rantoul, Jr.," 293–300; Walter Nelles, "Commonwealth v. Hunt," *Columbia Law Review*, 32, 7 (Nov. 1932), 1128–69.

[53] Theophilus Fisk, *Capital Against Labor, An Address Delivered at Julien Hall, Before the Mechanics of Boston, on Wednesday Evening, May 20* (Boston, 1835), 7. On Fisk, see David R. Roediger, *The Wages of Whiteness: Race and the Making of the American Working Class* (London, 1991), 74–5. As Bulkley says of the approach taken by Rantoul in *Commonwealth v. Hunt*, "He accepted the wages-fund theory of the classical economists, and therefore believed that a wage increase in one craft would come at the expense of another; combinations of workers to raise wages were, therefore, unjust. However, he strongly opposed the courts' stepping into this area . . . this was, he believed, a private matter which would best be left to the natural workings of the economy" ("Robert Rantoul, Jr.," 296–7).

[54] Nelles, "Commonwealth v. Hunt," 1132–3; Levy, *Law of the Commonwealth*, 185–6; *Boston Evening Transcript*, 14 Oct. 1840. Bulkley describes the atmosphere in which the trial was conducted as one "of intense partisanship" ("Robert Rantoul, Jr.," 293).

they had been neither oppressed nor impoverished but in fact had benefited from the society's existence.[55] As for Horne, he did not get to tell of his oppression at all. On Rantoul's objection, Thacher ruled that as a professed atheist Horne was incompetent to testify, thus depriving the prosecution of its most important witness.[56] All in all, the *Boston Morning Post* reported after the trial had been in progress about a week that "the number of witnesses sworn was very great, but the testimony of all may be summed up in a brief space, as much of what they said had no material bearing on the case."[57]

Legal arguments were reported at greater length. For the prosecution Parker rehearsed Massachusetts case law and the full array of American and British precedents. He insisted, following *Commonwealth v. Judd*, that a confederacy to do an unlawful act, or even to do a lawful act with an unlawful purpose, was an indictable conspiracy, and that the conspiracy was the gist of the offense, no overt act being required to prove it. No part of this common law had been abrogated by the state's recent revision of statutes. By undertaking "to prevent a man from working lawfully, as he pleases, and for whom he pleases, and at what price he pleases," Parker argued, the bootmakers' society had fulfilled all the requirements of the law, demonstrating an intent to coerce that was grossly tyrannical and illegal. Such interference with the freedom of others was despotic and an unlawful invasion of the liberty of the subject. Recalling themes from the whole forty-year saga of journeymen's conspiracies, Parker went on to denounce the society as antirepublican and as an illegitimate incursion upon the prerogatives of the state. "Such a Society and power amount to a government within a government."[58]

Arguments for the defense turned on the adequacy of the prosecution's proof

[55] It is noteworthy that, notwithstanding Thacher's clear signals in 1832 and 1834 that he was more than ready to entertain prosecutions of journeymen, employers in general had apparently either felt no need or had been unwilling to seek grand jury indictments. Thus despite the renewal of organization among Boston workers in 1834 and their continued professions of determination to ensure a ten-hour day, and despite strikes of journeymen carpenters in 1835 and of the journeymen bootmakers themselves in 1835 and 1836, no conspiracy charges were attempted, far less brought to trial, at any time during the 1830s. See Boston Municipal Court Docket (1833–40), Massachusetts State Archives. In announcing the indictment of Hunt et al., the *Boston Evening Transcript* (8 Oct. 1840) noted that theirs was "the first indictment of the kind ever found in this State."

[56] Rantoul must have particularly enjoyed the ruling excluding Horne's evidence, given Thacher's role six years previously in the prosecution and conviction of Abner Kneeland on an indictment for "wilfully blaspheming the holy name of God, by denying God, his creation, &c." and the subsequent use of charges of atheism against law reformers. On the Kneeland case, see *Commonwealth v. Abner Kneeland*, Thacher's Criminal Cases 346 (1834), and 37 Mass. 206 (1838). On its role in codification debates, see Karen Orren, *Belated Feudalism: Labor, the Law, and Liberal Development in the United States* (New York and Cambridge, 1991), 66.

[57] *Boston Morning Post*, 19 Oct. 1842. Earlier, the *Post* (16 Oct.) had commented, "Thus far the testimony in support of the indictment has been of a vague and uncertain character, both as to time and facts. Much of the time of the Court has been taken up in the discussion of rules respecting the rights of witnesses and the admissibility of testimony." According to the *Post* (21 Oct.) this "technical warfare" had gone on for two days and a half.

[58] *Boston Morning Post*, 21 Oct. 1842. See also Christopher L. Tomlins, *The State and the Unions: Labor Relations, Law, and the Organized Labor Movement in America, 1880–1960* (New York and Cambridge, 1985), 41.

of a conspiracy. Embracing without query the by then familiar definition that "a conspiracy is a combination to do a lawful act by unlawful or criminal means; or to do an unlawful or criminal act by lawful means," Rantoul and his co-counsel, John S. Kimball, argued that the prosecution had done nothing more than show that the society did indeed exist and thereafter had simply relied on the imputation to the defendants of an intent to injure and on extravagant rhetoric for the rest of its case.

It is not proved, that any injury has been done or intended in this case. We have the express agreement of the accused among themselves; and it does not express or imply any intent to injure third persons, or do an unlawful or criminal act. They agreed, for purposes beneficial to themselves, without intending to injure others. The acts done under it have been lawful, and have not violated the rights of others; and it was a part of their agreement that nothing should be done under it, violating the laws of the commonwealth. There is no evidence that any master-workmen have been impoverished; but on the contrary, the evidence shows that they have been benefited by the work being better done. There is no evidence that workmen have been impoverished. Sums contributed by the members have been voluntary. Those not members have been employed and as well paid as the members.[59]

Given that mere association was not in itself unlawful, the defense argued, the question was whether the defendants could be shown to have committed any injurious act, criminal *or* unlawful. This they denied, pointing to the existence of similar societies for similar purposes among all professions and trades, to the innocence of action and motive in the journeymen's combination, and to the absence of injurious consequences of their actions. As Rantoul put it in his preliminary notes on the indictment, "We contend they have a perfect right to form a society for their mutual interest and improvement. . . . To substantiate these charges and allegations we shall contend that it is not enough to prove that the accused did form a society and agree together that they would not work for the masters if they employed other workmen than those who belonged to the club – but they must prove actual force, fraud and nuisance – so in regard to compulsion."[60]

[59] John S. Kimball, opening for the defense, in *Commonwealth v. John Hunt, et al.*, Thacher's Criminal Cases 609 (1840), at 618–19. The report of this passage in the *Post* (21 Oct.) has Kimball making the somewhat different claim that the defendants' agreement "does not express or imply any intent to injure third persons, or to do any criminal act." The *Post*'s report also shows Kimball arguing at this point that "when members have refused to work in the same shop with others, as they had a right to do, it does not appear that any other workman has lost a day's work in consequence thereof." On the contrast between the idiom of coercive collectivity in the early nineteenth century's corporative craft combinations and of voluntarism in the voluntary associations that succeeded them, see Tomlins, *The State and the Unions*, 42–5. On this contrast in Britain see John V. Orth, "English Combination Acts of the Eighteenth Century," *Law and History Review*, 5, 1 (Spring 1987), 175–6. See also Wood, "Conspiracy and the Paranoid Style," 438–41. Some years ago David Montgomery noted that the voluntary decisions of individual workers, within self-imposed constraints of honor and solidarity, were the means relied upon in the mid-to-late nineteenth century to maintain a union's presence in American shops. It could be argued, however, that this was as much the consequence of a pragmatic decision to avoid activities which could result in conspiracy indictments for coercive activity as it was the expression of some deep ideological or cultural impulse. See David Montgomery, *Workers' Control in America: Studies in the History of Work, Technology, and Labor Struggles* (New York and Cambridge, 1979), 16.

[60] Papers of Robert Rantoul, Jr., Massachusetts Historical Society, Boston. Rantoul's file on the case included a pamphlet copy of a House of Commons speech of 4 February 1840 on "The State of the Poorer

The defense's stress on the innocence of the defendants' intent and the absence of injury recalled Gibson's opinion twenty years before in *Commonwealth v. Carlisle*. Kimball and Rantoul also gave some attention to the argument, debated at considerable length in intervening cases, that a criminal conspiracy indictment could only be a remedy against a threat to the public and not merely private injuries. Both suggested that even if an injury had been done by the dependents, it was a private injury only and therefore not indictable but answerable only through a civil action.[61] But neither dwelt much on the point, and the question of demarcating public and private played a distinctly second fiddle to the questions of means and ends, and impact on others, whether public or private. The defense, that is, was operating very much within the restated tenets of the conspiracy doctrine that had been emerging over the previous decade. Although they hotly disputed the substance, such as it was, of the prosecution's case, Rantoul and Kimball advanced a doctrinal position not much at variance from that outlined by Recorder Bouvier four years earlier in Philadelphia.[62]

Traces of that consensus can even be found in Judge Thacher's charge to the jury. Thacher was careful to inform the jury, as had the county attorney, that the journeymen were not on trial for associating per se. "There is no doubt that these defendants and their brother craftsmen may assemble in societies, and discuss the value of their work, and the wages to which they are reasonably entitled for their skill and labor. So long as they shall not assume to restrain the liberty and rights of others, no offence will be done."[63] What they were on trial for was their "design and tendency, by a concentrated action, to injure and control" masters and other journeymen, whether by interfering in their subsisting contracts, or by compelling them to join or, in the case of masters, at least to abide by the rules of their

---

Classes in Great Towns," by Robert A. Slaney, Esq., M.P. Rantoul had marked the following passage (at 39–40): "Trade clubs, intended to keep up wages and give an allowance when out of work, existed in several of the best paid and skilful trades, as among the brushmakers, tailors, coachmakers, hatters, &c.; and in these trades we shall find, whatever the fluctuation of wages, there seldom were any riots or disturbances, and the sufferings of their families were much less. It is true they often acted unjustly . . . yet nevertheless on the whole, there was great advantage to the community and themselves in these trade societies. For a long time they were forbidden by the unjust combination laws, which are now repealed, and since then their character has improved, and as long as violence and fraud are prevented, they ought to be extended instead of discouraged."

[61] Thus according to Kimball, "all the injuries alleged here to be done, or intended, are mere private injuries and a conspiracy to commit a private injury is not indictable by the English common law, as at present understood, unless the injury itself would be an indictable offence – *King v. Turner*, 13 East 229–231, also 14 Johnson's R., 271, *People v. Mather*. But the injured individual may have his civil action, *ex delicta*, on the case, for all damages, and ample justice" (*Boston Morning Post*, 21 Oct. 1840). In fact, as we have seen, the accuracy of Kimball's claim of a distinction between private and public injuries was dubious whether as a statement of current English or American doctrine, at least outside New York (and even there highly questionable after 1836; see Chapter 5). Certainly the distinction was explicitly criticized in Massachusetts by the commissioners for revising the criminal law in the commonwealth. See Chapter 5, n. 59. See also *Commonwealth v. Eastman*, 55 Mass. 213 (1848).

[62] As we have seen, this was also the position adopted by the Democratic Party press. See, e.g., *Philadelphia Public Ledger*, 14 June 1836. See also *Boston Morning Post*, 9 Oct. 1840 and 16 Oct. 1840.

[63] *Commonwealth v. John Hunt, et al.*, 652.

association.[64] As we have seen, however, Thacher saw no necessity for proof of an overt act in order to find a conspiracy, and predictably, given his earlier pronouncements, his instructions were unambiguously antagonistic to the defendants.[65] Never one to put much trust in the natural resilience of the social order to whose defense he was so committed, Thacher stressed the catastrophic consequences should journeymen's associations be left free to exist unhindered. The Society of Journeymen Bootmakers, he told the jury, was "a new power in the state, unknown to its constitution and laws, and subversive of their equal spirit." It threatened to become the first of a new species of "secret and unknown tribunals" which, if allowed to exist, would subject citizens "to varying laws by which their property will be taken from them against their consent, and without trial by jury." It was a threat to civic harmony.

If such associations should be organized and carried into operation through the varying grades, professions and pursuits of the people of this commonwealth, all industry and enterprise would be suspended, and all property would become insecure. It would involve in one common, fatal ruin, both laborer and employer, and the rich as well as the poor. It would tend to array them against each other, and to convulse the social system to its center. A frightful despotism would soon be erected on the ruins of this free and happy commonwealth.[66]

Under Thacher's prompting, the jury returned a verdict of guilty. That outcome, like the trial itself, occasioned considerable local protest. Thacher was defended, cautiously, in the Whig press but vigorously denounced in the Democratic press.[67] The Third Grand Rally of the Working Men of Charlestown[68] on 23 October greeted the verdict handed down earlier that day with resolutions condemning attacks upon the right of combination and denouncing "our courts of justice, so called" as "partial and oppressive, striving to punish us for forming associations." The rally called for immediate reforms to establish an elective judiciary "making the Judges . . . the

---

[64] Ibid., 643. "It is undoubtedly true, that each of these defendants might lawfully refuse, individually, to work for any one, as he should think fit." But "[i]f the defendants intended and expected, by means of this confederacy, to benefit themselves, at the expense of the rights of others, and by an unlawful invasion of those rights, it was an offence. It is an unlawful means to effect an unjust and injurious purpose" (ibid.).

[65] "It has ben argued by Mr Rantoul . . . that no indictment for conspiracy will lie, unless it be founded on a combination of two or more persons to commit a *criminal* act, which would of itself be an indictable offence. But this is not, in my opinion, a correct estimate of the law [citing *Commonwealth v. Boynton* (1803), *Commonwealth v. Pierpont* (1803), *Commonwealth v. Warren* (1809), and *Commonwealth v. Judd* (1807) to show that the offense of conspiracy consisted in a confederacy or combination to commit an unlawful act]. . . . The gist of the offence consists in the unlawful confederacy, and it is complete when the confederacy is made; and any unlawful act done in pursuance of it, is no constituent part of the offence, but merely an aggravation of it" (ibid., 640–2, emphasis in original). As this underlines, the conspiracy – the confederacy to commit an unlawful act – is complete and indictable on the basis simply of the expression of agreement by two or more people, as in a constitution. No actual injury is necessary.

[66] Ibid., 653–4.

[67] For Whig comments see *Boston Daily Atlas*, 23 Oct. 1840; *Boston Daily Advertiser*, 23 Oct. 1840.

[68] See Prologue, above.

servants, instead of the masters of the people."[69] More such protests would likely have followed had sentencing proceedings not been stayed by Rantoul's filing of a bill of exceptions to Judge Thacher's instructions (apparently the subject of an argument between them).[70] Attacks upon Thacher nevertheless continued, criticism of his role in *Commonwealth v. Hunt* feeding a deep-seated unpopularity perhaps inevitable after twenty years dispensing criminal justice from the lonely and utterly unloved bench of the Boston Municipal Court, and certainly in any case an unpopularity which Thacher did little to avoid, preferring to remain obstinately aloof in his rectitude, "never suffer[ing] the clamors of the populace or the intercessions of friends to exercise a 'malign influence' over his conduct on the bench."[71] After Thacher's death early in 1843, Boston's criminal courts were reorganized with a haste bordering on the indecent.[72]

Rantoul argued his exceptions to Thacher's instructions before the Supreme Judicial Court in June of 1841. Three were minor disputes about the admissibility of evidence. It was the fourth, "that none of the acts discussed in the five counts in the indictment constitutes an indictable offence," upon which the opinion of the court was desired.

[69] *Third Grand Rally of the Workingmen of Charlestown, Mass., Held October 23d, 1840*, Kress Library, Harvard Business School.

[70] The *Post* (23 Oct.) reported that at the conclusion of Thacher's charge to the jury, "Mr Rantoul presented to the judge several propositions of law, with the request that he would charge the jury accordingly, or definitely decline so to do. – This led to a little altercation the result of which was the handing of the paper back to Mr R, without any positive expression of opinion on the part of the judge." Rantoul's propositions became the basis of the bill of exceptions which he filed several days later. See the defense's bill of exceptions in "Commonwealth v John Hunt and others, Trades Union Conspiracy," Boston Municipal Court File Papers (1840), no. 41, in Records of the Massachusetts Superior Court, Suffolk County, Massachusetts State Archives, Boston.

[71] "Obituary," *Law Reporter*, 5 (Mar. 1843), 528. In the Municipal Court "Proceedings" occasioned by Thacher's death and later published, John M. Williams, chief justice of the Suffolk County Court of Common Pleas, provides a sad picture of a lonely and somewhat misanthropic man who had endured in what was evidently an unpleasant job for twenty years of "almost solitary confinement and hard labor." The nature of a criminal trial court, Williams observed, was such as to rank it and its doings low in the public estimation. Further "an idea has become extensively prevalent, that a judge whose jurisdiction is exclusively over crimes and punishments, necessarily becomes prejudiced against those who stand accused before him, and eager for their conviction." Thacher had "suffered under the imputation and suspicion of this unworthy feeling." He had also had to bear the brunt of popular odium in enforcing laws for the protection of public morals thought "oppressive" by the majority. The knowledge of popular enmity had produced in him "a feeling of difficulty and embarrassment which added new weight to his solitary cares and anxieties" but he "did not shrink from the painful duty." See John M. Williams, *Proceedings in the Municipal Court of the City of Boston, Occasioned by the Sudden Death of Hon. Peter O. Thacher, Late Judge of that Court, with a Sketch of his Judicial Character* (Boston, 1843), 9–12, 14–15.

[72] Thacher died on the morning of 22 February. Within seven days, legislation reorganizing the Municipal Court and providing that its presiding judge would be drawn on a rotating basis from a panel of all the Common Pleas judges for Suffolk County had been drafted and passed through both houses of the legislature. The legislation was approved by the governor on 1 March, four days before Thacher's memorial service in the Brattle Square Church. See *Massachusetts. Statutes* 1843, c. 7, An Act Relating to the Court of Common Pleas, and the Municipal Court of the City of Boston. I have been unable to determine whether the governor at least waited until after Thacher's funeral to complete the abolition of his position, or whether the legislation was signed before it took place. Either way, it must have been a close-run thing.

Rantoul's appearance before the Supreme Judicial Court was a second airing of the lengthy discussion of the common law of conspiracy which had featured in his closing speech to the Boston Municipal Court jury the previous year. The offense charged, he argued, was not punishable by statute in Massachusetts. If it were to be considered an offense at all, therefore, it could only be at common law. As such two issues arose. First, whether it was an offense punishable under English law; and second, if so, whether such English law had been received in Massachusetts under the Constitution.[73]

The law of the mother country was in force in the colonies as far as was appropriate to their condition, but such common law did not include those elements addressing "the artificial refinements of a numerous people." It was in light of these – "the laws of police and revenue" – that the common law of conspiracy was to be construed. Conspiracy had first been provided for in the reign of Edward I and until the time of Hawkins had remained confined to the vindication of abuses of legal procedure in the courts of justice. Hawkins had described a common law broadened to include all confederacies wrongfully to prejudice a third person, as for example "a confederacy by indirect means to impoverish a third person." Here indirect means meant unlawful means, and indeed in all the English cases the doctrine had been that an unlawful act, or a lawful act by unlawful means, had to be shown. Only one case could be found apparently to the contrary, that of the journeymen tailors convicted of a conspiracy to raise their wages, but that case could not be explained except as tried under the old statutes of laborers regulating trade and manufactures. These, however, had not been introduced into the colonies. "Now I contend that all these cases regulating the prices of labor, hours of labor, authorizing justices to fix prices and so forth are all local police regulations confined to the Island of Great Britain."

What of the American cases? Here conspiracy convictions had generally been secured in cases of confederacies to do unlawful acts, not acts against trade. Indeed, no American higher court had heard a case of conspiracy in restraint of trade except in New York, where such an indictment was possible under the Revised Statutes. There had been prosecutions in lower courts, but close examination showed that the true ground on which these cases had been tried was that of unlawful means, as in *Commonwealth v. Moore* (1827), "which also charged unlawful means, by assault and battery." In Massachusetts there had of course been previous indictments for conspiracy, but none for a conspiracy to affect trade. Insofar as restraint of trade was

---

[73] The following account of arguments before the Supreme Judicial Court in *Commonwealth v. Hunt* has been reconstructed from a number of sources: Rantoul's notes on the case located in the Papers of Robert Rantoul, Jr., Massachusetts Historical Society; the account of closing arguments at the trial stage before the Boston Municipal Court in Thacher's *Criminal Cases*, 622–37; the account of the Municipal Court trial published in the Suffolk County Bar journal, *The Law Reporter*, 3, 8 (Dec. 1840), 290–304; the report of the Supreme Judicial Court hearing and decision in 45 Mass. 111; and in particular the minutes of argument before the Supreme Judicial Court at its adjourned law term, June 1841, kept by Chief Justice Shaw. For the last see Lemuel Shaw, Supreme Judicial Court Minute books, 27:593–604, Social Law Library, Boston.

part of the common law of conspiracy in England, then, it had not been received in America. For this indictment to be proven, it had to be shown that the journeymen bootmakers had had resort to ends or means unlawful in local law.

Rantoul then turned to a detailed inspection of the indictment. In Massachusetts, conspiracy had been defined as an agreement to do an unlawful act or to do a lawful act by unlawful means. One might, on the basis of most of the cases, say that in fact a criminal act was required. But even if merely unlawful, it had at least to be an act for which the law would give an action for damages. This indictment did not satisfy such requirements, for it charged neither an unlawful purpose nor unlawful means to accomplish a lawful purpose. The first two counts simply alleged a combination, which was not per se unlawful. The remaining counts alleged various means, but none were unlawful. Thus in the third count "the object is [to] prevent a man from following his trade, but this is not necessarily unlawful. A temperance lecturer induces men to forbear buying rum, to the impoverishing of sellers of rum." In the fourth count there was alleged an intention to impoverish Horne and wrongfully to prejudice him by indirect means. "This must be criminal or actionable or done by means criminal or actionable. If the means are intended to be shown to be unlawful means, those means must be specially set forth, for they constitute the gist of the crime." In the fifth count, alleging an intention to impoverish various employers and to prevent them from employing any person not a member, "prejudice and impoverishment in a trade may be lawfully done, as when a person does the something better and cheaper than another, and thereby takes away his custom and impoverishes him."[74]

Rantoul's argument was answered for the commonwealth by its attorney general, James T. Austin. The charge in the indictment was that the defendants had conspired to establish an unlawful monopoly of one branch of labor, that of making boots, and that they had used unlawful means to effect this purpose. In the first count the defendants were accused of a combination to regulate and govern their own conduct and the conduct of others. The unlawful means averred was a refusal to work for anyone who employed a person not a member of their society. In the second count, the unlawful object stated was that they had conspired not to work with any person who would not pay a penalty into their fund.[75] "It was a conspiracy to compel one to pay a sum of money which he was not bound to pay. It was to extort money unlawfully." The third and fourth counts charged the object of the conspiracy to be to prevent Horne from exercising his lawful trade and profession

---

[74] In support Rantoul cited *Nichol et al. v. Martyn*, 170 E.R. 513 (1799), where Lord Kenyon stated, "A servant, while engaged in the service of his master, has no right to do any act which may injure his trade, or undermine his business; but every one has a right, if he can, to better his situation in the world; and if he does it by means not contrary to law, though the master may eventually be injured, it is *damnum abs. injuria*" (513).

[75] Shaw's minutes show that Austin misstated this count of the indictment as charging "that they conspired not to work *for* any person who should not pay a penalty into their fund" (Shaw, Minute Books, 27:599).

contrary to his liberty and right, and the fifth charged it to be to prevent the master workmen from employing persons who did not belong to their association.[76]

Whether the general crime set forth was indictable in Massachusetts was not a matter for dispute but a fact already decided by the adjudged cases. The definition of conspiracy in Massachusetts had been clearly and explicitly stated by Chief Justice Parsons in *Commonwealth v. Judd* as "to do a lawful act by unlawful means." This, however, did not limit the object indictable by law. And indeed, in the unreported case of *Commonwealth v. Boynton et al.* (1803) an attempt to establish an unlawful monopoly in restraint of trade had been held indictable as a conspiracy. Further, the offense was completed by the act of conspiring, and no overt act, in pursuance, was necessary. As to the defense's "great objection that there can be no unlawful conspiracy unless the act contemplated by the combination, if done, would be a criminal act, or at least an unlawful act which would be the ground of an action of damage," this was countermanded as a principle of law by the evidence of successful indictments of conspiracies to accomplish a purpose contrary to good morals[77] or to raise the price of government funds.[78] Indeed, any confederacy affecting public trade or public health, public morals or public peace, or to effect some unlawful object might be the subject of indictment for conspiracy.[79]

The defense had suggested that the modern law of conspiracy had grown originally out of the harsh, absolute, and barbarous statutes of laborers that were not part of the common law of Massachusetts, but these acts had all now been repealed and in recent cases of conspiracy to raise wages[80] nothing had been said about the statutes of laborers. Rather, these cases had been decided upon principles of the common law. For evidence that these principles of the common law had been adopted in Massachusetts, Austin first pointed to the New York case *People v. Melvin* (1809), tried well prior to the adoption of the Revised Statutes. Exception had been taken there to the indictment, he stated, but overruled. The present indictment followed the same form. Subsequent New York statutes had thus *affirmed* the criminality of such conspiracies, and this had been borne out by the decision in *People v. Fisher*. The same principles had also long since been affirmed in Massachusetts in *Commonwealth v. Boynton* and also, in the same year (1803), in a second unreported case *Commonwealth v. Pierpont*.[81] Subsequently the principle

---

[76] On this point Shaw records Austin's subsequent observation that it was "an illegal act to prevent an individual from exercising his freedom in employing such persons and upon such terms as they may think just and proper" (ibid., 602).

[77] Citing *R. v. Mawbie*, 101 E.R. 796 (1796).

[78] Citing *R. v. De Berenger*, 105 E.R. 536 (1814).

[79] Austin stated: "The manifest object [of the bootmakers' society] is to coerce employers by means of a strike, which would affect his business. The rules all aim at that object. Combination to black one's character by verbal slander is an indictable conspiracy. An agreement of many officers of the [East India Company] if one were removed all would resign [was found to be an indictable conspiracy]. An unlawful combination to hiss a play is the subject of an indictment " (in Shaw, Minute Books, 27:600–1).

[80] Citing *R. v. Hammond and Webb*, 170 E.R. 508 (1799); *R. v. Journeymen-Taylors*, 88 E.R. 9 (1721).

[81] Austin also cited *Commonwealth v. Judd* (1807), *Commonwealth v. Kingsbury* (1809), and *Commonwealth v. Warren* (1809).

had also been recognized as a common law principle in the Revised Statutes of Massachusetts.[82]

Rantoul replied briefly. "The great question important to the defendants and to the public, [is] whether workmen are guilty of a crime punishable by law, in disposing of them[selves], at what price, to whom and on what terms, that they may respectively think fit. Whatever any individual may lawfully do, several may agree together to do. If a labourer may prescribe whatever terms and conditions they [*sic*] think fit, any or all those in the same trade may agree to do the same thing."[83] Cases of conspiracy to defraud were abundant in Massachusetts, but there had been none that could be shown to be for conspiracy to raise wages or to affect trade. This was strong evidence to show that such law had never been adopted in Massachusetts. As to the "irrelevance" of the statutes of laborers to recent English journeymen's conspiracy cases, as contended by Austin, these had in fact remained in force until late in the reign of George III. As to the relevance of *People v. Melvin*, it had been overruled by *Lambert v. The People*. And as to the decision in *People v. Fisher*, it had been founded wholly on that provision of the New York Revised Statutes making it indictable to conspire to restrain trade or commerce. Indeed, *People v. Fisher* had been the first such case in any state. That there had been none until after the New York statute was passed afforded the strongest proof that a common law restraint of trade principle had *not* been adopted before the Revolution. Such regulation regarding commerce, "the colonists did not bring with them."

The Supreme Judicial Court's opinion was not delivered until almost a year later. Then, at its March 1842 term, the court arrested judgment. Written by Chief Justice Shaw, the court's opinion has generally been regarded as a masterpiece, although precisely of what it was a masterpiece has remained a matter of debate. Walter Nelles, for example, thought the decision a landmark, but also a paradox in that an outcome so apparently progressive should have emanated from so conservative a court. He solved the paradox by giving the decision a sly political twist. Shaw, he thought, was attempting to defuse workers' suspicion of local Whig elites in order to improve the chances for the Whig program of protective tariffs.[84] Leonard Levy, by contrast, had little time for either Nelles's paradox or his explanation. *Hunt* was "the Magna Charta of American trade-unionism" in that it "removed the stigma of criminality from labor organizations."[85] Like Nelles, Levy gave some weight to exogenous variables. Shaw, he thought, might have been influenced by a desire to neutralize the "threat" of the codification movement by demonstrating that traditional processes of common law adjudication could result in reasonable and fair

---

[82] Citing *Massachusetts Revised Statutes*, c. 82, s. 28; c. 86, s. 10.

[83] In his minutes of Rantoul's argument (Minute Books, 27:603) Shaw here added one of his rare annotations. "Check to the extent stated. Suppose a court [has] evidence to be heard in a town on a particular day, which necessarily makes it the duty of a great many people to attend there and all the town's keepers of houses combine to refuse to entertain any person but at exorbitant prices, and this without previous notice, would not the conspiracy be unlawful?"

[84] Nelles, "Commonwealth v. Hunt," 1151–62.

[85] Levy, *Law of the Commonwealth*, 183, 192–6.

outcomes.[86] Levy, however, thought the "most plausible" explanation lay in Shaw's own legal consciousness, his "latitudinarian" willingness to entertain the idea that there might be social gains to be had from competition between interests, even competition overshadowed by an element of coercion, as long as it remained peaceable.[87] Others have also regarded the decision as primarily an attempt to restore an aura of fairness and legitimacy to a system of common law adjudication damaged by the egregious biases of judges like Moses Levy, Savage, Edwards, and Thacher. At the same time they have denied that the outcome was in fact anything other than a perpetuation of that same bias skillfully reconstituted the more ably to serve the needs of an evolving capitalism.[88]

Shaw's opinion came in two parts. He began by offering an extended discussion of the offense of conspiracy in the law of Massachusetts, the first such discussion at so authoritative a level since Parsons's opinion in *Commonwealth v. Judd*, and far more comprehensive. Here, citing the numerous cases from early in the century, Shaw affirmed that "the general rules of the common law, making conspiracy an indictable offence" were in force in Massachusetts, by which he meant that it was "a criminal and indictable offence, for two or more to confederate and combine together, by concerted means, to do that which is unlawful or criminal, to the injury of the public, or portions or classes of the community, or even to the rights of an individual."[89] Following Rantoul, however,

---

[86] Ibid., 196–202.   [87] Ibid., 203–6.

[88] See, e.g., Wythe Holt, "Labour Conspiracy Cases in the United States, 1805–1842: Bias and Legitimation in Common Law Adjudication," *Osgoode Hall Law Journal*, 22, 4 (Winter 1984), 591–663, at 595. Holt writes that Shaw's opinion restored "the appearance of justice" to the law of labor conspiracy, but that the opinion hid the same "pro-entrepreneurial" biases expressed in earlier verdicts less favorable to the defendants. Holt later refines his argument as follows: "Shaw intended to write a good common law legal opinion – which meant carefully giving judges the leeway appropriate for further interpretation and adumbration of a *necessarily* loosely-defined common law crime. He would have fought to suppress any of his own biases he might have noticed expressly intruding themselves, but he would have failed to understand the way that his entrepreneurial interests and High Federalist upbringing organically molded his entire thrust of thought and patterns of activity; and he certainly would have failed to notice that those biases were to a large extent inherent both in the substantive law of labour conspiracy and in the common law method of adjudication. . . .

"I do not say that Shaw intended to fool the world, but I do say that the structures of liberal thought and common law judicial decision-making are such that they allow the intelligent ideologue to express an apparent concession in a manner which actually negates that concession and, in the end, keeps the ideologue's deep economic interests intact, all entirely 'unconsciously' " (645, n. 267).

Like Holt, Raymond Hogler in his article "Law, Ideology, and Industrial Discipline: The Conspiracy Doctrine and the Rise of the Factory System," *Dickinson Law Review*, 91, 3 (Spring 1987), 697–745, sees the decision in *Hunt* as advancing "the interests of capitalism" (745). Hogler, however, is critical of Holt and others for the "ideological" thrust of their analyses. Although recognizing the salience of exogenous variables, he says that they have failed to ground their explanations on "economic realities" (737, 739; and see, generally, 734–9). Unfortunately Hogler's own account is marred by his misunderstanding of the essentials of Leonard Levy's argument. Contra Hogler, at 735–6, Levy did not argue that Shaw's decision was to be explained by his antipathy for codification. In Levy's opinion this was at most a secondary issue.

[89] 45 Mass. 111, at 121–2.

Shaw observed that what was unlawful or criminal was clearly dependent upon "the local laws of each country." Thus it did not follow that every common law conspiracy indictment anywhere was a precedent for a similar indictment in Massachusetts. Rather, the cases already decided in the state were the best guide in defining or describing the offense there. "Without attempting to review and reconcile all the cases, we are of opinion, that as a general description, though perhaps not a precise and accurate definition, a conspiracy must be a combination of two or more persons, by some concerted action, to accomplish some criminal or unlawful purpose, or to accomplish some purpose, not in itself criminal or unlawful, by criminal or unlawful means."[90] Shaw then discussed such "rules" as seemed well established in dealing with the issue – that the unlawful agreement was the gist of the offense and that it was not therefore necessary to allege execution; that if execution were alleged, it was by way of aggravation – and drew a conclusion: that acts in execution could not therefore be used to prove the offense of conspiracy absent averment of an unlawful purpose or unlawful means; and therefore that an indictment which failed to set out such purpose or means was – "as a necessary legal conclusion" – insufficient.[91]

Shaw then inserted the particular circumstances of the prosecution of the bootmakers into his general discussion of common law conspiracy. For an association of journeymen to be prosecuted successfully for a criminal conspiracy the prosecution had to be based on an indictment which met the standards outlined. This indictment, however, failed to aver unlawful purpose or means. In the first count, as to purpose, the indictment, once stripped of "introductory recitals . . . alleged injurious consequences and . . . qualifying epithets" averred no more than that "the defendants and others formed themselves into a society, and agreed not to work for any person, who should employ any journeyman or other person, not a member of such society, after notice given him to discharge such workman." Their intent was to induce all engaged in their occupation to join with them in their association. This was not unlawful per se. To sustain a charge of conspiracy a "dangerous and pernicious" purpose in associating needed to be alleged and proved. Nor had unlawful or criminal means been demonstrated in this count. "The case supposes that these persons are not bound by contract, but free to work for whom they please, or not to work, if they so prefer. In this state of

---

[90] Ibid., 123.

[91] Conspiracy was an offense "which especially demands the application of that wise and humane rule of the common law, that an indictment shall state, with as much certainty as the nature of the case will admit, the facts which constitute the crime intended to be charged. . . . [W]hen the criminality of a conspiracy consists in an unlawful agreement of two or more persons to compass or promote some criminal or illegal purpose, that purpose must be fully and clearly stated in the indictment; and if the criminality of the offence, which is intended to be charged, consists in the agreement to compass or promote some purpose, not of itself criminal or unlawful, by the use of fraud, force, falsehood, or other criminal or unlawful means, such intended use of fraud, force, falsehood, or other criminal or unlawful means, must be set out in the indictment" (ibid., 125–6).

things, we cannot perceive, that it is criminal for men to agree together to exercise their own acknowledged rights, in such a manner as best to subserve their own interests."[92]

As with the first count, so with the rest. Shaw's opinion analyzed each and found it wanting in its averment of unlawful purposes or means. As he did so, however, he kept the focus of the rebuttal narrowly confined. Had the defendants refused to work in violation of a contract, or had they sought to compel an employer to discharge a workman in violation of a contract, a very different question would have been presented. "If a large number of men, engaged for a certain time, should combine together to violate their contract . . . it would surely be a conspiracy to do an unlawful act, though of such a character, that if done by an individual, it would lay the foundation of a civil action only."[93] Had the indictment "averred a conspiracy, by the defendants, to compel Wait to turn Horne out of his employment, and to accomplish that object by the use of force and fraud, it would have been a very different case." The conclusion was, as a result, heavily qualified. "Looking solely at the indictment . . . and confining ourselves to facts so averred as to be capable of being traversed and put in issue, we cannot perceive that it charges a criminal conspiracy punishable by law."[94]

The immediate impact of *Commonwealth v. Hunt* is perhaps best evidenced in the reaction of the local bar. "In the opinion of the court," stated *The Law Reporter*, journal of the Suffolk County Bar Association, in a very brief notice, "the general direction of the law of conspiracy, as laid down in the municipal court, was affirmed, but the court were of the opinion that the present indictment could not be maintained."[95] *Hunt*, that is, was not perceived as sanctioning any kind of departure

[92] Ibid., 128–30. Here Shaw adapted Rantoul's example of a temperance lecturer (see Rantoul's argument before the Supreme Court discussed above) to his own purposes, using it to show how self-interested association might actually do harm to another, yet remain innocent of pernicious intent: "Suppose a class of workmen, impressed with the manifold evils of intemperance, should agree with each other not to work in a shop in which ardent spirit was furnished, or not to work in a shop with any one who used it, or not to work for an employer, who should, after notice, employ a journeyman who habitually used it. The consequences might be the same. A workman, who should still persist in the use of ardent spirit, would find it more difficult to get employment; a master employing such an one, might, at times, experience inconvenience in his work, in losing the services of a skilful but intemperate workman. Still it seems to us, that as the object would be lawful, and the means not unlawful, such an agreement could not be pronounced a criminal conspiracy" (130).

[93] In his charge to the trial jury, Thacher had argued that indeed the defendants *had* been guilty of such "unlawful interference" (*Commonwealth v. John Hunt, et al.*, Thacher's Criminal Cases, 644). The point upon which the Supreme Judicial Court and its Municipal Court colleague differed was not whether such behavior merited indictment but whether, in this case, the indictment had successfully alleged such behavior. For a fuller discussion on this point, see also below, the section entitled Fidelity, Obedience, Control, in Chapter 8, esp. n. 73.

[94] 45 Mass. 111, at 132, 136.

[95] *The Law Reporter*, 5 (Aug. 1842), 168. See also the 1844 *Report of the Penal Code of Massachusetts*, c. "Conspiracy," holding inter alia that the "conspiracy may be unlawful, though the act proposed to be done would not be unlawful if done by an individual without any confederation with others . . . [as] to raise or reduce the wages of any particular class of persons."

or shift in general conspiracy doctrine. On the fundamental issue exciting most debate during the first half of the nineteenth century in both English and American courts – whether conspiracy could be used to vindicate merely private injuries – the opinion in Hunt was, on the surface, noncommittal. However, in making the averment of criminal or unlawful means or ends the test of the sufficiency of indictments, Shaw strongly implied that no other limitation existed on the reach of the doctrine, and his definition and description of the offense lend weight to the conclusion that he saw no particular limitation on its use other than such as was derived from the procedural safeguards described in his critique of the indictment. Such a move toward elevating procedural safeguards over substantive delimitation was indeed at one with the whole thrust of Anglo-American conspiracy doctrine in the first half of the nineteenth century.[96]

On the specific matter of journeymen's combinations, *Commonwealth v. Hunt* was plainly at one with the doctrine that had been articulated elsewhere, most clearly in Pennsylvania – that the test of criminality lay in the intentions and behavior of the journeymen in association – and was important primarily for giving that doctrine its most authoritative statement to that point. "Associations may be entered into, the object of which is to adopt measures that may have a tendency to impoverish another, that is, to diminish his gains and profits, and yet so far from being criminal or unlawful, the object may be highly meritorious and public spirited. The legality of such an association will therefore depend upon the means to be used for its accomplishment."[97] That this represented no particular restraint on the application of criminal conspiracy to journeymen's combinations in Massachusetts is evident from Shaw's own qualifying remarks. Although it might now be acknowledged lawful for men to agree to exercise their right to contract with others for their labor collectively, once executed the contract was guarded by criminal sanction from any interference. A collective quitting of employment was a criminal interference; so too was an attempt by some employees to prevail upon others to abandon their engagements. It is hardly surprising that in light of this the 1853 edition of *Davis's Criminal Justice*, a standard guide to Massachusetts criminal law, should quote *Commonwealth v. Hunt* as authority in *support* of the statement that combinations "to prevent another, by indirect and sinister means, from exercising his trade" or "to raise the rate of labor" were indictable at common law.[98] Elsewhere, too,

---

[96] See "Conspiracy," *American Law Journal*, n.s. 4 (1852), 312–15; *Commonwealth v. Eastmann* (1848), 55 Mass. 189. See also Chapter 5.

[97] 45 Mass. 111, at 134.

[98] Franklin Fiske Heard, ed., *Davis's Criminal Justice*, 3d ed. (Boston, 1853), 388–9. Heard indicated that the effect of the procedural guidance given by the Supreme Judicial Court over the years was that it had made the law of conspiracy easier to employ: "These cases fully sustain the doctrine, that when a conspiracy is plainly and technically alleged, overt acts done in pursuance of it need not be set out, or, if set out, need not be proved. The unnecessary and troublesome forms heretofore used in setting out the conspiracy, and all the overt acts and circumstances which followed or accompanied it, are hereby avoided" (390).

criminal conspiracy continued to be invoked as a counter to combinations among employees.[99]

Because the decision in *Commonwealth v. Hunt* was at one with its doctrinal universe, it does not require explanation as a puzzle or a paradox. This is not to say that the court was insensible to the stimuli of local debate, whether over the tariff, over the legitimacy of common law adjudication, or, more parochially, over the lack of restraint of its Municipal Court colleague. It is to say merely that no particular determinative exogenous variable need be invoked to explain the conclusion at which it arrived.[100] This does not, however, make the decision any the less interesting. Indeed, considered as an event in the history of legal ideas it was a major statement and was intended by the court so to be understood.[101] Ideologically, no

---

[99] The known antebellum instances are *Lehigh Boatmen* (Pa. 1843), settled before trial; *Tredegar Iron Workers* (Va. 1847), dismissed; *Baltimore Machinists* (Md. 1853), no prosecution instituted; *Philadelphia Compositors* (Pa. 1854), outcome not recorded; *Glassboro Glass-Blowers* (N.J. 1859), outcome not recorded. For the Lehigh case, see *Philadelphia Public Ledger*, 2 Sept. 1843. For the Tredegar case, see Kathleen Bruce, "Slave Labor in the Virginian Iron Industry," *William and Mary Quarterly*, 2d ser., 6, 4 (Oct. 1926). For the Baltimore, Philadelphia, and Glassboro cases, see Commons et al., *History of Labor*, 1:611–13.

In the Tredegar case, according to Bruce, tradesmen recruited from northern states struck in protest at the employment of slave labor within the works. They were prosecuted for forming "a mutual combination," summonsed, "and shown that whether their intention were such or not, they were effecting a combination which in 1847 the laws of Virginia forbade." In the absence of proof of an agreement to strike and in light of expressions of regret on the part of the strikers at the appearance of law breaking, the case was dismissed. (So, however, were the striking tradesmen.) The Tredegar works' ironmaster, Joseph R. Anderson, justified his actions on the grounds that it was "a rule of public law which has been recognized in states in which there are no slaves, that combinations against any interest, or to accomplish private ends are public offences, and as such are prohibited and punished" (see Bruce, "Slave Labor," 296, 299).

The Baltimore case is also particularly interesting in that there the machinists' employers obtained an opinion on the legality of journeymen's associations from four leading local attorneys that read as follows (in Commons et al., *History of Labor*, 1:611–12): "It is the undoubted right of every individual in society to determine for himself the proper compensation or wages for his own labor, and to refuse to labor for anyone who will not pay the wages he demands. But although the right of each individual to determine for himself the wages proper for his own labor is universally conceded, there is not the same agreement as to the legality of combinations of individuals for the avowed purpose of controlling or regulating wages, generally, in any trade or community – and it is proper for us to state that, by the highest judicial authority of Maryland, its Court of Appeals, it has been expressly declared that combinations or conspiracies to raise wages, although they are combinations for a purpose neither illegal nor immoral, and which each individual in the combination had a perfect right to accomplish for himself, are yet indictable at the common law as mere conspiracies for that purpose, because of the tendency of such combinations to prejudice the public" [citing *State v. Buchanan*, 5 H. & J. 317 (1821), at 360, 361, 368].

In both the Philadelphia and Glassboro cases, strikers were arrested on conspiracy charges. No further details of the Glassboro case are forthcoming. In the Philadelphia case a preliminary hearing resulted in indictment of the strikers on a charge of conspiracy "to injure the business" of the strikers' employer through intimidation and coercion of the employer and nonstriking employees. No record of a prosecution has survived. See Commons et al., *History of Labor*, 1:612–13.

[100] Starting from different premises, Roscoe Pound reached a similar conclusion in *The Formative Era of American Law* (Boston, 1938), at 88. "When one studies the history of the law as to conspiracy and [its] relation . . . to received professional ideals of the social order in America, it is perfectly possible to understand . . . *Commonwealth v. Hunt* without attributing political motives to a man whose whole judicial career is a refutation of such a charge."

[101] Note the opening sentences of Shaw's opinion: "Considerable time has elapsed since the argument of this case. It has been retained long under advisement, partly because we were desirous of examining, with some attention, the great number of cases cited at the argument, and others which have presented

214

less than procedurally, it was an attempt at signifying what would no longer, and what would henceforth be, correct juridical practice; it was a discursive summary of the ongoing changes that had transformed the American political economy since the turn of the century and a description of a new agenda for courts to pursue.

All this may best be seen in Shaw's manifest indifference in his opinion to the priorities suggested by either the communitarian or the civic conservative (Thacherite) concerns expressed in earlier opinions and in his invocation in their stead of a social world constructed wholly by contracts. Instead of a preconceived culturally, politically, or legally-constituted whole, Shaw represented society as the sum of a congeries of diverse material interests that individuals pursued, self-consciously, by entering into voluntary transactions that bound them according to the terms they were able to negotiate with each other. Contract supplied the transactional mechanism, and the competitive marketplace principle – that the maximization of opportunities to pursue self-interest maximized the good of all – provided the justification. Because maximization of opportunity implied no inherent limitations on the form in which opportunity might be pursued, associations might be created for that purpose through the same contractual devices that constituted all forms of social relation whenever interests were held sufficiently in common to warrant collective rather than individual action.

The measure of acceptability of any species of human behavior having become its tendency to contribute to a competitive marketplace society, pursuit of self-interest, either singly or – through a self-constituted association – collectively, was legitimate even should it prove to be injurious to another, as long as, *but only as long as*, it was perceived to be congruent with the maximization of efficiency in the use of resources through application of the principle of competition.[102]

Suppose a baker in a small village had the exclusive custom of his neighborhood, and was making large profits by the sale of his bread. Supposing a number of those neighbors,

themselves in course, and partly because we considered it a question of great importance to the Commonwealth, and one which had been much examined and considered by the learned judge of the Municipal Court" (45 Mass. 111, at 121).

[102] Shaw dealt at some length with the apparent contradiction between Horne's right to work and the defendants' assertion of their right in association not to work with him, the effect of which had been to procure his dismissal. His comments provided a guide to how a prosecution should proceed in dealing with that contradiction: "If, for instance, the indictment had averred a conspiracy, by the defendants, to compel Wait to turn Horne out of his employment, and to accomplish that object by the use of force or fraud, it would have been a very different case; especially if it might fairly be construed, as perhaps in that case it might have been, that Wait was under obligation, by contract, for an unexpired term of time, to employ and pay Horne. As before remarked, it would have been a conspiracy to do an unlawful, though not a criminal act, to induce Wait to violate his engagement, to the actual injury of Horne. . . . [E]very free man, whether skilled laborer, mechanic, farmer, or domestic servant, may work or not work, or work or refuse to work with any company or individual, at his own option, except so far as he is bound by contract. But whatever might be the force of the word 'compel,' unexplained by its connexion, it is disarmed and rendered harmless by the precise statement of the means, by which such compulsion was to be effected. It was the agreement not to work for him, by which they compelled Wait to decline employing Horne longer" (ibid, 132–3).

believing the price of his bread too high, should propose to him to reduce his prices, or if he did not, that they would introduce another baker; and on his refusal, such other baker should, under their encouragement, set up a rival establishment, and sell his bread at lower prices; the effect would be to diminish the profit of the former baker, and to the same extent to impoverish him. And it might be said and proved, that the purpose of the associates was to diminish his profits, and thus impoverish him, though the ultimate and laudable object of the combination was to reduce the cost of bread to themselves and their neighbors. The same thing may be said of all competition in every branch of trade and industry; and yet it is through that competition, that the best interests of trade and industry are promoted.[103]

Because injurious outcomes might result from socially beneficial actions, the mere fact of an injurious outcome was not sufficient to justify condemnation of the behavior leading to it. At the same time, given that society had no existence apart from the myriad of individual transactions, any injury was potentially socially deleterious. Whereas courts in previous conspiracy cases had attempted to distinguish between public and merely private injuries, the competitive principle brooked no such limitation. Hence the legality of an injurious outcome would be judged by the end sought or, where the end was judged laudable or meritorious or public-spirited, by the means used.

By treating the courts as judges of the consequences of behavior rather than as gatekeepers of the community or as constitutors of the commonwealth responsible for preemptive declaration of what would and would not be allowed, *Commonwealth v. Hunt* tended to place them at one remove from the front line of controversy over journeymen's combinations. In effect, this was a "privatization" of the issue of combination, turning it from what had been primarily a confrontation between working people and the courts over the legitimacy of the postrevolutionary polity into a matter of industrial relations – a conflict between working people and their employers over the degree of control each would exercise at the point of production, a conflict that the courts would mediate. But as Shaw's example of the baker indicated, *Hunt*'s "decriminalization" of unions had effect only as long as they fell within the ambit set by the market economy's discourse of efficiency. Nor did *Hunt* do anything to erode the courts' decisive role in the determination of that ambit, and hence of the degree of criminality to be read in the intentions or actions of associated workers. In the industrial struggles which became endemic during the second half of the nineteenth century the courts' use of criminal conspiracy was to prove devastating.[104]

---

[103] Ibid., 134.

[104] On this, see, e.g., Victoria Hattam, "Economic Visions and Political Strategies: American Labor and the State, 1865–1896," *Studies in American Political Development*, 4 (1990), 82–129; idem, *Labor Visions and State Power: The Origins of Business Unionism in the United States* (Princeton, 1992), Chapter 2. See, generally, Karen Orren, *Belated Feudalism: Labor, the Law, and Liberal Development in the United States* (New York and Cambridge, 1991), 118–59; William E. Forbath, *Law and the Shaping of the American Labor Movement* (Cambridge, 1991), 59–166.

CONCLUSION

Sean Wilentz has recently argued that the 1820s and 1830s saw a major and lasting change in conservative thought about popular behavior and politics.[105] In the postrevolutionary era, fears of disorder, the specter of democratic majoritarianism and of accompanying conflict between the wealthy few and the propertyless many, and the turbulence and instability of mass society had all dictated the creation of institutional checks on popular access to and participation in government. By the end of the 1830s, however, conservatives had realized that the reinforcements for the social order and stability that they craved might actually be found in the very behavior peculiar to mass democracy that they feared. Accepting as regrettable fact the ascension of "the self-interested many," they sought to turn it to their advantage. America, they now proclaimed, was "a country of self-made men."[106] But it was one held in place "by mutual dependence and an overarching harmony of interests."[107] This, then, was a *self-constituted* society, made possible by continuous interaction among a multiplicity of individual pursuits of self-interest but also by an imputed shared regard for the framework of contractual freedoms which made "self-constitution" realizable.

In the evolution of labor conspiracy doctrine since the turn of the century one may observe that new ideological consensus taking shape. Declamation against illegitimate "self-created" combinations which threatened the general welfare had given way to attention to the manner in which an interest concededly legitimate – at least in the abstract – was being pursued. *Commonwealth v. Hunt* was the capstone, marking the completion of a transition from a political economy for which republicanism had supplied the discursive frame of reference and within which protagonists had counterposed different conceptions and locations of regulatory authority – police of the community, police by the trade, juridical supremacy, the ascendancy of the legislature – to one in which market liberalism's umpired contest of selfish interests was the embracing discourse, and the issue had become, pragmatically, the relative utility of labor combinations to the achievement of a contractually created society's proclaimed objective of an overarching comity among distinct interests.

Yet for three reasons, the ideology of freedom implied in contractualist discourse was really quite deceptive. First, the years of its efflorescence were years of growing inequalities in American life. The material realization of freedom, as distinct from its ceremonial proclamation, was beyond the capacities of growing numbers of Americans. Second, even in its formal garb the freedom of self-creation that the contractualist vision celebrated was not reflected in the essential constitutive relations

---

[105] Sean Wilentz, "Many Democracies: On Tocqueville and Jacksonian America," in Abraham S. Eisenstadt, *Reconsidering Tocqueville's* "Democracy in America" (New Brunswick N.J., 1988), 207–28, at 217–220.
[106] Calvin Colton, quoted in ibid., 219.   [107] Ibid., 218, 219.

217

of everyday productive and reproductive life – of parent and child, husband and wife, employer and employee. These were susceptible to self-creation neither by democratic process nor through contractual negotiations. These were relationships whose essentials were secured elsewhere, in common law texts and in the official discourse of the courts.

The meanings of these relationships were secured elsewhere, by other than those persons who actually lived them, because, for all their ideologizing, conservatives' fundamental reliance upon the moderation of social action through institutional restraints remained decisive. This was the third reason that contractualist discourse was deceptive. "Subject and citizen are, in a degree, convertible terms," wrote Chancellor Kent in 1836, for, "though the term *citizen* seems to be appropriate to republican freemen, yet we are, equally with the inhabitants of all other countries, *subjects*, for we are equally bound by allegiance and subjection to the government and law of the land."[108] Institutional checks, others said, were "a necessary foil against encroachment by the 'tumultuous mob' upon the rights of the 'moral, prudent, industrious, and well-disposed' minority."[109]

As *Hunt*'s careful qualifications on the exercise of "acknowledged rights" showed, law stood tall among those restraints. Indeed, the more the many threatened to impress their interests upon political institutions, the more power migrated to just such less-accessible locations.[110] This meant, for example, that so far as working people's "social right" to collective action was concerned, even the achievement of its legislative recognition after the Civil War in several states would make no practical difference. Working people's encounter with legality did not end in 1842; it merely shifted ground.

In the highly visible, surface world of labor conspiracy and collective activity, law had come to furnish the medium of restraint in large part by dint of its role in supervising the processes through which popular will was expressed in the polity. But law also furnished a preeminent medium of restraint in daily life, as a back-channel, so to speak, of elite rule amid the goings-on of the democracy. Hence the next part of this book examines law's constitution of employment – one of the key

[108] Chancellor James Kent, *Commentaries on American Law*, 3d. ed. (New York, 1836), 2:258n. On the persistence of this strain of discourse throughout the antebellum period, see Michael P. Rogin, *Subversive Genealogy: The Politics and Art of Herman Melville* (New York, 1983), 265; George M. Fredrickson, *The Inner Civil War: Northern Intellectuals and the Crisis of the Union* (New York, 1965); Daniel T. Rodgers, *Contested Truths: Keywords in American Politics since Independence* (New York, 1987), 102–43. As Rodgers puts it, "the democratic revolution of the early nineteenth century had barely gotten under way before a movement gathered strength – not merely to co-opt or compromise the rhetoric of the people's sovereignty – but to inter it altogether. Spilling out of the great revivals of the nineteenth century, full of counterrevolutionary confidence, men of these convictions burst into mid-nineteenth-century political argument talking not of the people's sovereignty nor of rights but of the claims, the powers, even the divinity of governments"(111).

[109] *Note*: "Political Rights as Political Questions: The Paradox of *Luther v. Borden*," *Harvard Law Review*, 100, 5 (Mar. 1987), 1125–45, at 1133.

[110] See, generally, L. Ray Gunn, *The Decline of Authority: Public Economic Policy and Political Development in New York State, 1800–1860* (Ithaca, 1988).

relations of routine social existence. In the particular instance of the employment relationship, we shall see, the law of the early republic established not self-constituted freedom but an asymmetrical realm of "masters" and "servants," a realm in which the subjection of the employee was the sign of employment, a sign rendered in official discourse not only socially acceptable but in fact utterly commonplace – a fact of working life.

PART 3

Law, authority, and the employment relationship

Jessamy. I say, Sir, I understand that Colonel Manly has the honour of having you for a servant.

Jonathan. Servant! Sir, do you take me for a neger, – I am Colonel Manly's waiter.

Jessamy. A true Yankee distinction, egad, without a difference.

Royall Tyler, *The Contrast: A Comedy in Five Acts*

Introduction: the nomenclature
of power

"There is no such relation as *master and servant* in the United States," observed a British-born attorney, John Bristed, in 1818. "Indeed, the name is not permitted: – '*help*' is the designation of one who condescends to receive wages for service."[1] His was no isolated impression. Commentators on the society of the early nineteenth-century United States commonly used the antipathy of working people toward the language of servitude to impress on their readers the depth of antagonism toward the accoutrements of traditional society which they had found in the new republic.[2] Charles W. Janson, whose *The Stranger in America* dwelt on "the arrogance of domestics in this land of republican liberty and equality," reported the following conversation with a "servant-maid" who had opened the door to his knock on a visit to an acquaintance:

Is your Master at home? – I have no Master.
Don't you live here? – I stay here.
And who are you then? – Why, I am Mr. ——'s help. I'd have you to know, *man*, that I am no *sarvant*. None but *negers* are *sarvants*.[3]

In 1805 the self-styled "working shoemakers" of Philadelphia had roundly condemned their "masters" for their adoption of "the slavish style of Europe." Thirty years later, the journeymen tailors on strike in New York held up not only the actions but also the titular pretensions of their "would-be *masters*" as the acme of tyranny. Whether articulating their objections in a defensive racism, in a radical republican scorn of aristocracy, or, fleetingly, like the Workingmen of Charlestown, in an explicit politics of countervailing power, antebellum white working Americans

---

[1] John Bristed, *America and Her Resources* (London, 1818), 460.
[2] See, e.g., Richard Parkinson, *A Tour in America in 1798, 1799, and 1800* (London, 1805), 1:18–19, 30–2; Francis Grund, *The Americans, in their Moral, Social and Political Relations* (Boston, 1837), 236–8; Frances Trollope, *Domestic Manners of the Americans*, ed. Donald Smalley (New York, 1949), 52–8; Thomas Colley Grattan, *Civilized America* (London, 1859), 1:256–9. See, in general, Albert Matthews, *The Terms Hired Man and Help* (Cambridge, 1900), 28–31.
[3] Charles William Janson, *The Stranger in America* (London, 1807), 88.

did not take kindly to those who used terms of domination and subordination in the employment relationship.[4]

The social and political antipathies of the populace were one thing, however; the professional discourse of law quite another.[5] Late in May of 1832, for example, one Charles R. Codman, a storekeeper of Lindall Street in Boston, contracted with Frederick Lincoln, master mason and drain digger, to lay a drain to connect his store with the common sewer. During the course of the excavation water from the sewer penetrated several adjoining cellars, causing damage to the goods of a number of Codman's neighbors. One of those neighboring proprietors, Robert Stone, filed suit against Codman in the Suffolk County Court of Common Pleas to recover damages for the injury he had sustained from the negligence of those whom Codman had employed to dig his drain. At a trial before a Supreme Judicial Court jury that November Stone's claim was allowed,[6] but Codman's attorneys took the matter on appeal before a full bench of the court, arguing that Lincoln had been an independent contractor in the excavation and thus that the defendant had no case to answer. According to Theophilus Parsons, Jr., appearing for Codman, "The plaintiff was bound to employ a person of suitable skill and knowledge of his business." Having done so, "such workman is liable himself. The relation of master and servant does not exist." Codman's other attorney, Samuel Hubbard, underlined the point just as emphatically. "When a master mechanic is employed to do work in this Commonwealth the relation of master and servant does not subsist. The mechanic acts upon his own skill and judgment and not under the immediate orders of the employer."[7] The court, however, gave no weight to these arguments:

Without reviewing the authorities, and taking the general rule of law to be well settled, that a master or principal is responsible to third persons, for the negligence of a servant, by which damage has been done, we are of opinion, that if Lincoln was employed by the defendant to make and lay a drain for him, on his own land, and extending thence to the public drain, he Lincoln procuring the necessary materials, employing laborers, and charging a compensation for his own services, and his disbursements, he must be deemed in a legal sense, to

---

[4] On the working shoemakers of Philadelphia, see the Introduction to Part 2 and the section entitled The First Wave, 1806–1815, in Chapter 5. On the New York tailors, see the section entitled The New York Cases, in Chapter 5; and Sean Wilentz, *Chants Democratic: New York City and the Rise of the American Working Class, 1788–1850* (New York, 1984), 290. On the Workingmen of Charlestown, see the Prologue. On racist and misogynist antipathies to the use of terms of servitude to describe employment relations, see David R. Roediger, *The Wages of Whiteness: Race and the Making of the American Working Class* (London, 1991), 43–64; Elizabeth Blackmar, *Manhattan for Rent, 1785–1850* (Ithaca, N.Y., 1989), 116–22.

[5] For contemporary judicial recognition of and commentary on this divergence between legal and popular discourse, see *Ex Parte Meason*, 5 Binney 168 (1812), and *Boniface v. Scott*, 3 Sergeant and Rawles 349 (1817). These cases are discussed further in the section entitled The Mid-Atlantic and North Atlantic Regions, in Chapter 8.

[6] *Stone v. Codman*, Supreme Judicial Court (Suffolk County, Mass.) *nisi prius* session, Nov. term 1832 (New Entry 19).

[7] Lemuel Shaw, Supreme Judicial Court Minute Books, 9:125, 126, 128, Social Law Library, Boston.

have been in the service of the defendant, to the effect of rendering his employer responsible for want of skill, or want of due diligence and care.[8]

The argument in the Supreme Judicial Court over the applicability of the language of master and servant to the relationship between Codman and Lincoln in this case was in large part technical. Nonetheless it is of major significance. First, it was not an isolated event. Resort to the same nomenclature in the generality of cases involving employment issues coming before the courts in the industrializing states during the first half of the nineteenth century testifies to the tendency of lawyers and the judiciary to construe the broad spectrum of employment relationships using a comprehensive common law discourse of master and servant. Second, legal discourse has social consequences. It is thus of considerable importance to note that at a time when popular discourse treated linguistic claims to vested status and authority in the employment relationship as highly controversial, legal discourse did not. In *Sproul v. Hemmingway* (1833), for example, Chief Justice Shaw's opinion for the court represented employment as properly a relationship between a superior and a subordinate, a master and a servant. In Shaw's contemplation, the legal test of the existence of a relation of employment was the extent to which the alleged employee was subject to the "order, control and direction" of the employer. Similarly, in *Inhabitants of Lowell v. Boston and Lowell Railroad Corporation* (1839), the court found that men performing work for the defendants' subcontractor on a construction project were working for the defendants' benefit, "under their authority, and by their direction," and hence were their employees and servants. In *Earle v. Hall* (1841), it determined that two parties did not stand "in the relation of superior and subordinate, or employer and person employed," despite the existence of a contract between them providing for one to build a house on the land of the other, because the putative employer could not be shown to be exercising "power and control" over the activities of the putative employee. And in *Elder v. Bemis* (1841), the court confirmed that master/servant's discourse of power and control was determinative of employment for all practical purposes by finding that where a person in the employment of another was acting under the direction of a third party, he was to be considered the servant of the person under whose direction he labored rather than of the person with whom he had contracted.[9]

In having recourse to master/servant's language of power and control as its preferred strategy for dealing with the employment relation in these cases, the Supreme Judicial Court advertised its conclusion that, notwithstanding their ostensible contractual provenance, employment relations were properly to be conceived of as generically hierarchical. Nor were courts alone in adopting this course. A similar path was being blazed by the profession's intellectual elite: people like Tapping Reeve, Zephaniah Swift, Chancellor Kent, Nathan Dane, Timothy Walker – the

---

[8] *Stone v. Codman*, 32 Mass. 297 (1834), at 229. cf. *State v. Higgins*, 1 N. C. 36 (1792) (see n. 18).
[9] *Sproul v. Hemmingway*, 31 Mass. 1; *Inhabitants of Lowell v. Boston and Lowell Railroad Corporation*, 40 Mass. 24; *Earle v. Hall*, 43 Mass. 353; *Elder v. Bemis*, 43 Mass. 599. See also *Yates v. Brown*, 25 Mass. 2 (1828).

writers of the treatises which, in the words of one historian, were "americanizing" the common law.[10] Take Walker's *Introduction to American Law*, published in 1837. "The title of *master and servant*, at the head of a lecture, does not sound very harmoniously to republican ears," Walker acknowledged. Yet, disharmony notwithstanding, he then proceeded to affirm that common law master/servant doctrine was the core of the law of employment in the American republic. Indeed, "the legal relation of master and servant *must* exist," he wrote, "wherever civilization furnishes work to be done."[11]

Walker's treatise represented resort to master/servant doctrine to construe the employment relation as little more than a routine encounter between the autonomous realm of human activity called "work," a realm with its own social arrangements and relations that required nothing more than descriptive juridical cataloging, and the specialized legal concepts appropriate to that function. It was, he wrote, "differences of condition" that made some persons employers and others laborers. Law did no more than provide appropriate names for social relationships.[12] But this was an unduly modest claim.[13] Legal discourse does *not* simply catalogue social relations received from elsewhere. Rather, through its intellectual and professional practices, law is constituted as a system of authoritative knowledge, one that helps determine the conditions of social existence and thus the very nature of social relations. Indeed, what is particularly noteworthy about early nineteenth-century American courts' resort to master/servant discourse to construe the generality of employment relationships is the extent to which it involved them in engineering an extensive doctrinal migration of vested authority beyond the more specific kinds of social relations that the law concerning "masters" and "servants" had described in the colonies.[14]

[10] See William E. Nelson, *Americanization of the Common Law: The Impact of Legal Change on Massachusetts Society, 1760–1830* (Cambridge, Mass., 1976).

[11] Timothy Walker, *Introduction to American Law* (Philadelphia, 1837), 243. Walker here was perhaps unable to hide a certain contempt for the performers of manual labor, an attitude more fully revealed in his other writings. On this see Jonathan A. Glickstein, *Concepts of Free Labor in Antebellum America* (New Haven, 1991), 38.

[12] Walker, *Introduction to American Law*, 243. Such denials of history were a feature of nearly all the early master and servant treatises. In his pioneering study of English law on the subject, *Treatise on the Law of Master and Servant* (1852; 4th ed., Philadelphia, 1886), e.g., Charles Manly Smith wrote that "it seems to be unnecessary to enter into any discussion of the various opinions which have been expressed by different authors as to the first origin of that relationship; for since it is obvious that, in the complicated intercourse of modern society, a great proportion of the business of human life must be carried on through the instrumentality of others," it seemed to follow inevitably "that the relationship of master and servant must exist" (51). See also the first specifically American work on the subject, Horace Gray Wood's *Treatise on the Law of Master and Servant* (Albany, 1877): "It will serve no practical end to attempt to trace the rise, changes or improvements in this relation. . . . It is enough for all practical purposes to know how the relation *now* exists" (2, emphasis in original).

[13] In fact, I chose the epigraph to Part 1 of this book to advertise my suspicion of the implicit modesty of such claims.

[14] "Were the writer untrammelled by authority, his treatment of this topic, as one of the domestic relations, would be confined to what are denominated as common law menial servants, so called from being *intra moenia*, or rather to domestic servants, extending the definition to all such as are employed in and about a family in carrying on the household concerns, whether their occupations be within or

The carryover of the magisterial claim to authority meant that the nineteenth-century employment relationship failed in vital respects to comport with the "liberal illusion" of formal legal equality.[15] Rather than facilitating the development of employment in the early Republic as a transaction between juridical equals, courts and treatise writers' resort to master/servant doctrine instead helped establish employment as a legally asymmetrical relationship in which the parties coexisted under conditions of structured inequality. On some occasions courts can be found denying this inequality; on others as we have just seen, they affirmed it as both natural and necessary – essential, indeed, to the proper functioning of the relation. Sometimes they can be found attempting to do both simultaneously.[16]

The most obvious expression of legal asymmetry in the nineteenth-century employment relationship may be found in the presumption that a contract to deliver labor for money delivers the employee's assent to serve; assent, that is, that for as long as the relationship continues the employer shall control and direct the disposition of the labor to be delivered.[17] The presumption is illustrated in the course of many of the century's judgments, but nowhere more succinctly than in the words in 1851 of Judge William B. Caldwell of the Supreme Court of Ohio, in *The Little Miami Railroad Company v. John Stevens*:

When a man employs another to do work for him, each incur their obligations. The person hired is bound to perform the labor according to the agreement, and the employer is bound to pay; besides that, neither party has parted with any of his rights. The employer has no more control over the person he has employed, *outside of the service to be rendered*, than he has over the person of any other individual.[18]

without of doors, so long as they constitute part of the family. In this restricted sense, the law of master and servant is manifestly of little importance to-day. But . . . legal precision must sometimes be sacrificed to legal usage; and as terms have been carried . . . beyond their original signification, for the sake of analogy, we are bound to follow, even though it be into logical confusion" (James Schouler, *A Treatise on the Law of Domestic Relations* [Boston, 1870], 600). See also Wood, *Treatise on the Law of Master and Servant*, 3–4 (emphasis supplied): "By the common law, servants were divided into three classes, or grades, as menial servants; apprentices; agricultural laborers and agents. Indeed, those only were regarded as coming strictly within the term *servant* who were employed for domestic purposes, and were hirelings for money to serve about the master's house and to attend upon him personally. All others, as clerks, farm hands, etc., were denominated laborers or workmen, and were, in many respects subject to different rules from merely menial servants. . . . But in this country, no such distinction exists, and *all who are in the employ of another, in whatever capacity, are regarded in law as servants*."

[15] On the liberal illusion see William Reddy, *Money and Liberty in Modern Europe: A Critique of Historical Understanding* (New York and Cambridge, 1987), 62–106.

[16] See, e.g., *Ryan v. Cumberland Valley Railroad Company*, 23 Penn. St. R. 384 (1854). This and other examples are discussed in Chapter 8. See also Chapter 10.

[17] Long ago, we should note, John R. Commons argued that the modern labor contract should not be seen as an exchange of payment for work but rather as the sale of a promise to obey commands. See John R. Commons, *Legal Foundations of Capitalism* (New York, 1924), 284. See also Ton Korver, *The Fictitious Commodity: A Study of the U.S. Labor Market, 1880–1940* (Westport, Conn., 1990), 1 (the essence of the labor contract is the employer's authority to direct and command the employee).

[18] 20 Ohio R. 416 (1851), 433 (emphasis supplied). Note, in contrast, the contention of the prosecution in *State v. Higgins*, 1 N.C. 36 (1792), at 39, in the course of an argument otherwise urging a wide definition of the term "servant": "the mechanic to whom we send a job, is not our servant. . . . There is no authority on one side, no subjection on the other. The mechanic is *employed*, not *directed*. His time is

The employer's right of control over "the service to be rendered," however, is precisely the issue. As Caldwell's statement confirms, the operative enjoys autonomy (legally, although not of course materially) prior to entry and after exit from employment. That is, the operative enjoys civic autonomy. But the relationship itself appears as a realm in which the subjection of the employee is a routine incident, a "fact of working life." This fact of life is consequent upon the additional right of control imputed in legal descriptions of employment to inhere in the employer. The operative's decision to enter employment is thus a decision to enter a realm in which the employer enjoys not just the material capacity (the power) to put the employee in action but also the legal authority, vested in the employer as a matter of policy and in certain circumstances backed by criminal sanction.[19]

Sociolegal theorists have recognized that this juridical resort to master/servant concepts was of substantive importance in underpinning workplace discipline and establishing the legitimacy of supervisory prerogative during America's industrial transformation.[20] Nevertheless, they have tended to deal with master/servant reasoning in the nineteenth century's law of employment as an increasingly outmoded "survival" of older forms or as the outcome of an evolutionary process of conceptual "fusion" or "merger" between traditional status-derived ideas of employment and more modern notions of freedom of contract. At least in the American case, however, the contradictory coexistence of freedom and subordination represented in the law of employment cannot be fully accounted for by conceiving the issue in quite this way.[21] Rather, employment law in the nineteenth century must be considered in large part a new-minted discourse, the product of an extension of master/servant

his own, not ours. He may postpone our work to make room for another's. The relationship between him and us supposes no superiority on our side, and therefore it is not the relation which exists between master and servant"(emphasis in original). Many historians have argued that the resort to a language of *employment* in Anglo-American culture in the eighteenth and nineteenth centuries was a sign that traditional inequalities of *service* were being discarded. See, e.g., E. P. Thompson, "Patrician Society, Plebeian Culture," *Journal of Social History*, 7, 4 (Summer 1974), 382–405, esp. 384; Daniel T. Rodgers, *The Work Ethic in Industrial America, 1850–1920* (Chicago, 1979), 30. And indeed, in *State v. Higgins* the language of employment is being used to distinguish independent self-directed labor from the circumstances of direction and hierarchy associated with service. Over the following fifty years, however, the essence of the legal meaning of employment became, quite precisely, direction and hierarchy. This is a trend of which historians have shown insufficient awareness.

[19] This issue is explored further in the section entitled Legal Reinforcement of the Employer's Authority and the section entitled Fidelity, Obedience, Control, both in Chapter 8.

[20] According to Philip Selznick, e.g., once a contract "was defined as an *employment* contract, the master-servant model was brought into play. The natural and inevitable authority of the master could then be invoked, for that authority had already been established as the defining characteristic of the master-servant relation." More recently, James B. Atleson has also pointed to the expectations and obligations carried over from traditional master/servant law which litter the modern employment contract. See Philip Selznick, *Law, Society, and Industrial Justice* (New York, 1969), 136; James B. Atleson, *Values and Assumptions in Labor Law* (Amherst, 1983), 11–16. See also Marc Linder, *The Employment Relation in Anglo-American Law: An Historical Perspective* (Westport, Conn., 1989).

[21] This interpretation has in fact also been criticized in Britain. See Ken Foster, "From Status to Contract: Legal Form and Work Relations, 1750–1850," *Warwick Law Working Papers*, 3, 1 (May 1979), 1–41.

concepts to encompass a circle of work relationships previously outside the master/servant ambit.[22]

During the colonial era, work for another in America comprehended not one but at least two basic types of relationship: that between a householder and dependents (menials, bound servants, apprentices) and that between principal and independent contractor, or customer and supplier. Of these, only the former was governed by master/servant concepts.[23] Importantly, as adult hired labor (work for wages)

---

[22] This point will be argued exhaustively in the next two chapters. For a brief foretaste, compare the conception of employment in *State v. Higgins*, 1 N.C. 36 (1792), quoted in n. 18, with that in *Matthews v. Terry*, 10 Conn. 455 (1855), at 457, where the court's conception of the relation of master and servant plainly extends it to persons "*employed* in husbandry, in manufacturing business, or in any other manner" (emphasis supplied). On the expansive quality of master/servant, see also, generally, Lea VanderVelde, "The Gendered Origins of the *Lumley* Doctrine: Binding Men's Consciences and Women's Fidelity," *Yale Law Journal*, 101, 4 (Jan, 1992), 775–852; Adrian Merritt, "The Historical Role of Law in the Regulation of Employment," *Australian Journal of Law and Society*, 1, 1 (1982), 56–86; G. De N. Clark, "Industrial Law and the Labour-Only Sub-Contract," *Modern Law Review*, 80 (1967), 6–24. The point is supported in the British context, albeit indirectly and unintentionally, by Otto Kahn-Freund, "Blackstone's Neglected Child: The Contract of Employment," *Law Quarterly Review*, 93 (Oct. 1977), 508–28.

[23] For insight into the latter employment relationship see Joseph Story, *Commentaries on the Law of Bailments* (Cambridge, Mass., 1832), 275–88; Theophilus Parsons, *The Law of Contracts* (Boston, 1853), 1:610–17; John Bouvier, *Institutes of American Law* (Philadelphia, 1858), 1:393–405. See also, generally, R. Millward, "The Emergence of Wage Labor in Early Modern England," *Explorations in Economic History*, 18 (1981), 21–39. As commentators on the law of bailments explained, *locatio operis*, or the hiring of labor and services for reward, could be taken to cover any situation in which a person contracts with another to perform a certain undertaking or to do work on materials furnished by that other. Commentators described the obligations owed by each party to the other: on the part of the employer, to pay the agreed price, to do everything necessary to enable the engagement to be completed, and to receive the article when completed; on the part of the employee, to do the work according to agreement, to employ properly materials furnished, and to show the appropriate degree of care and skill in performing the work.

A body of doctrine descriptive of a wide range of reciprocal, artisanal, and outwork transactions, *locatio operis* was no less appropriate to the generality of industrialism's work relationships than the preferred preindustrial discourse of master and servant. Nor was it in any sense less available to common law authorities. Crucially, however, the law of *locatio operis* made no presumption that the relationship of employer and employed was one of authority and subordination, of the exertion of control and subjection to it. It was in large part the juridical decision that employment should be considered such a relation which, during the course of the nineteenth century, confirmed master and servant as its legal paradigm. Indeed, in nineteenth-century employment cases one can observe the master/servant paradigm being invoked to reinterpret bailment relations as relations of authority and subjection, a development of no little significance given the mushrooming resort to outwork networks in the mass production of goods such as garments, shoes, and so forth. In *Harmer v. Cornelius*, 140 E.R. 94 (1858), for example, the plaintiff had entered into a contract with the defendant to undertake a month's work at panorama and scene painting. After two days, however, the defendant refused to proceed with the contract, provoking the plaintiff's suit. The defendant's justification was that the plaintiff had misrepresented his skill and ability and had proven to be incompetent to do the work required. The defendant prevailed. Less important than whether that outcome was justified or not is the question how the judgment treated the issue. It began as a discussion of bailment: "When a skilled labourer, artizan, or artist is employed, there is on his part an implied warranty that he is of skill reasonably competent to the task he undertakes. . . . The public profession of an art is a representation and undertaking to all the world that the professor possesses the requisite ability and skill." No employer was bound to honor an engagement with an employee whose profession of skill proved false. But, crucially, in the court's discourse, the performance of the work could only be framed as service. It quite abruptly ceased to debate whether *incompetence* on the part of one

229

became increasingly significant as a mode of performance during the eighteenth century, and in some places well before then,[24] it appears to have been considered a relation distinct in important respects, both social and legal, from servitude. During the first half of the nineteenth century, however, as employment in America became reconceived socially and legally as primarily a single universal and impersonal relation founded on wage labor, the ambit of master/servant discourse widened, bringing hired labor decisively under the umbrella.

In the course of this expansion the emerging generic employment relationship was progressively freed of most of the colonial era's specific statutory descriptions of particular personal statuses inhabited by significant groups of working people – indentured servant, indentured apprentice, and so forth – and of the specific statutory disciplines that went with those descriptions. The result, as Robert Steinfeld has recently shown, was the burgeoning nineteenth-century celebration of employment as "free labor" – a relation universally available through the medium of contract.[25]

But processes of legal transformation were at work, simultaneously, in the opposite direction, implying nonnegotiable common law incidents of authority and direction hitherto identified with personal service into contractual relationships of employment. These changes underwrote an employer's right and capacity, *simply as an employer contracting for the performance of services*, to exert the magisterial

contracting party justified the other's refusal to honor the bargain and translated the issue before it into the language of *misconduct*. The defendant employer was a master justifiably disciplining his servant by dismissing him for his incompetence. "Misconduct in a servant is, according to every day's experience, a justification of a discharge. *The failure to afford the requisite skill which had been expressly or impliedly promised, is a breach of legal duty, and therefore misconduct.* . . . So, in *Spain v. Arnott*, 2 Stark. N.P.C. 256, Lord Ellenborough, speaking of a servant who had refused to perform his duty, says, – 'The master is not bound to keep him on as a burthensome and useless servant to the end of the year.' And it appears to us that there is no material difference between a servant who will not, and a servant who cannot, perform the duty for which he was hired" (98–99, emphasis supplied).

On outwork in nineteenth-century production, see Christine Stansell, *City of Women: Sex and Class in New York, 1789–1860* (New York, 1986), 106–19; Wilentz, *Chants Democratic*, 119–32; Blackmar, *Manhattan for Rent*, 124–6. To be sure, one should not take from these observations a presumption that a bailment model of employment could necessarily have offered workers greater autonomy absent any significant alteration in their social and material circumstances. As Stansell shows, gender and poverty rendered the growing population of single female outworkers acutely vulnerable to exploitation by contractors, irrespective of their legal relations. All the same, it is worth noting how, in New York, the extreme deterioration of outwork conditions of employment in the middle decades of the nineteenth century does seem to coincide with the continuing generalization of the master/servant model of employment. On a separate but related issue, one should also note how, in the case of outwork performed by women and children in families, the employer's disciplinary claim increasingly cut across the traditional patriarchal claim to control wives' and children's labor. On the impact of legal relations of employment on family relations see also below, Chapter 8, n. 88.

[24] For a summary survey of the incidence of free (hireling) labor in colonial America, see David W. Galenson, "Labor Market Behavior in Colonial America: Servitude, Slavery, and Free Labor," in David W. Galenson, ed., *Markets in History: Economic Studies of the Past* (New York, 1989), 52–96, at 84–95.

[25] Robert J. Steinfeld, *The Invention of Free Labor: The Employment Relation in English and American Law and Culture, 1350–1870* (Chapel Hill, 1991).

power of management, discipline, and control over others.[26] During the first half of the nineteenth century, indeed, the exercise of power became decisive in determining whether relations of employment between two parties existed. To the courts, exerting power over another became a routine feature of what they recognized employment to mean as a legal relationship.[27]

Notwithstanding, then, the growth in the postrevolutionary decades of a vibrant *popular* culture clearly unwilling to accept that concepts of master and servant had relevance to any but a tightly defined circle of explicitly servile relationships, one finds by the middle decades of the nineteenth century American courts and treatise writers routinely describing the official *legal* culture of employment in an Anglocentric common law discourse of master and servant.[28] To be sure, the popular culture of free labor had enough political strength to ensure that no American state could adopt a statutory law of employment after the fashion of eighteenth-century innovations in English law or, for that matter, the innovations being introduced in less-democratic nineteenth-century Anglophone cultures (provincial Canada, the Australian colonies). But its influence on the routines of common law discourse – the daily life of the courts, the developing conceptual apparatus of treatise writers – was much less sustained.[29] Acting piecemeal, largely remote from the glare of public attention attracted by the conspiracy issue, the law courts and law writers of the early republic built their approach to the employment relationship on the back of English master/servant law. In the process, they vested in the generality of nineteenth-century employers a controlling authority over their employees founded upon the preindustrial master's claim to property in his servant's personal services.

[26] On this see Alan Fox, *Beyond Contract: Work, Power and Trust Relations* (London, 1974), 181–4; Foster, "From Status to Contract," 25–41; Richard Kinsey, "Despotism and Legality," in Bob Fine et al., eds., *Capitalism and the Rule of Law: From Deviancy Theory to Marxism* (London, 1979), 46–64.

[27] Wood, *Treatise on the Law of Master and Servant*, 2.

[28] In addition to the references already cited on the popular rejection of the language of servitude, see Lea VanderVelde, "The Labor Vision of the Thirteenth Amendment," *University of Pennsylvania Law Review*, 138, 2 (Dec. 1989), 441–3. As with conspiracy, developments in the law of master and servant in antebellum America were almost wholly at common law. Unlike England, none of the industrializing American states adopted a statutory law of master and servant. For the contrasting political and legal experience of Canada, see Paul Craven, "The Law of Master and Servant in Mid-Nineteenth-Century Ontario," in David Flaherty, ed., *Essays in the History of Canadian Law* (Toronto, 1981), 1:175–211. On Australia see Merritt, "The Historical Role of Law in the Regulation of Employment," 56–86; John B. Hirst, *Convict Society and Its Enemies: A History of Early New South Wales* (Sydney, 1983), 101–3. See also Michael Quinlan, "Labour Control, Organisation and Resistance in Three Australian Colonies, 1830–1850," unpublished paper.

[29] Its strength is demonstrated in Timothy Walker's acknowledgment of the "strangeness" of master/servant discourse to republican ears. The limits to that strength are demonstrated immediately after by Walker's use of that discourse in his analysis of employment in any case. (*Introduction to American Law*, 243).

7

The law of master and servant

The Clothier told his Story first, and his complaint was as follows; that *Edmund Pratt*, the Person brought before him, was a Journeyman Weaver; that he had given him a Piece of Work to do, which he promis'd to finish for him out of hand, and that now he had neglected it . . . that at last, when he entreated him to go to work, he answer'd him *flat* and *plain*, he would not work; that he did not want Money, and would not work, not he; and for this Reason he came to his Worship for a Warrant to bring *Edmund* before him.

The Justice answer'd him very sencibly; *first*, that as he (*Edmund*) was not an Apprentice, or a hir'd Covenant-Servant, bargain'd with for the year, that is, for a certain time *and the like*; the Case did not lie before him; and that if the Fellow was a Knave, and would not perform his Agreement, he must sue him for his Bargain. . . .

This I mention, because I think, if the Laws of *England* are deficient in any thing, it is in this, namely, that they do not empower the Justices to compel labouring People who undertake work, to finish it. . . . [I]f this was the Case, much of the Mischief would be remedied that way.

But this Deficiency of the Law, it seems the Fellow knew, and this made him not only saucy and peremptory to his Employer, but very pert and impudent before the Justice himself, as you will see.

Daniel Defoe, *The Great Law of Subordination consider'd; or, the Insolence and Unsufferable Behavior of* SERVANTS *in England duly enquir'd into*

Even in England, a law of master and servant did not exist as such – a body of doctrine describing a generic, disciplined relation of employment – much before the early eighteenth century. "Masters" and "servants" of course were known well before then. In her classic account of the enforcement of the Statutes of Labourers, for example, Bertha Putnam held that the word *servant*, or *serviens*, was used in the fourteenth century to describe the broad range of persons who worked in some capacity for another or owed them duties of service.[1] In this most general of senses,

---

[1] Bertha Puttnam, *The Enforcement of the Statutes of Labourers* (New York, 1908), 79–80, 181–4. See also Frederick Pollock and Frederic W. Maitland, *The History of English Law before the Time of Edward I* (Cambridge, 1923), 1:282–90; Elaine Clark, "Medieval Labor Law and English Local Courts," *American Journal of Legal History*, 27, 4 (Oct. 1983), 337–9. And see C. B. Macpherson, *The Political Theory of Possessive Individualism: Hobbes to Locke* (Oxford, 1962), 107; idem, "Servants and Labourers in Seventeenth-Century England," in his *Democratic Theory: Essays in Retrieval* (Oxford, 1973), 207–23.

the description "servant" might be applied to persons of considerable status. "To a medieval lawyer the class might include people as far apart in rank and status as a bailiff and a mason, or a steward and a household labourer."[2] Others, however, have argued for a more precise meaning for the term associating service with particular forms of manual labor and especially with the institution of service in husbandry;[3] and indeed, when we turn to the bulk of early modern English law relating to the regulation of labor, notably that growing out of the Statute of Artificers, the evidence for a diversity of legal relations of employment, rather than a single universal master/servant relation, is quite strong.[4] For example, Michael Dalton's *Countrey Justice*, for a century following its first publication in 1619 the standard work of reference for English justices of the peace, treats servants as a subgroup of a more general category, "labourers." Distinct legal procedures, conditions, and disciplines were applicable to servants by virtue of characteristics peculiar to servitude that distinguished it as an employment relation from the situations in which other working people (variously entitled labourers, workmen, artificers, or handicraftsmen) might be found.[5] "Servants," for example, were differentiated from "artificers" and "labourers" by their performance of work according to a definite term of hire, in common practice one year, as opposed to casual labor or the performance of particular functions or tasks;[6] by their identification with employment in husbandry, the regulation of which, historically, had tended to be rather more extensive than that of other occupations; and by their domicile in the household of their employer, or *intra moenia*, giving rise to the description "menial servant."[7] Overall, service was distinguished from other relations of employment in providing the master with unlimited call upon

[2] Gareth H. Jones, "Per Quod Servitium Amisit," *Law Quarterly Review*, 74, 293 (Jan. 1958), 39–58, at 54.

[3] See, e.g., Peter Laslett, "Clayworth and Cogenhoe," in H. E. Bell and R. L. Ollard, eds., *Historical Essays, 1600–1750, Presented to David Ogg* (London, 1963), 169n.; idem, "Market Society and Political Theory," *Historical Journal*, 7, 1 (1964), 150–4; idem, *The World We Have Lost* (London, 1965), 15; idem, *The Earliest Classics* (London, 1973), ix; and idem, *Family Life and Illicit Love in Earlier Generations: Essays in Historical Sociology* (Cambridge, 1977), 61–3. See also Keith Thomas, "The Levellers and the Franchise," in G. E. Aylmer, *The Interregnum: The Quest for Settlement, 1646–1660* (London, 1972), 57–78, at 70–3. See generally Ann Kussmaul, *Servants in Husbandry in Early Modern England* (Cambridge, 1981), 3–10.

[4] For an analysis of the making of the Statute of Artificers richly suggestive of the diversity of relations and regulations represented therein, see S. T. Bindoff, "The Making of the Statute of Artificers," in S. T. Bindoff et al., eds., *Elizabethan Government and Society: Essays Presented to Sir John Neale* (London, 1961), 56–94.

[5] Michael Dalton, *The Countrey Justice: Containing the Practice of the Justices of the Peace Out of Their Sessions* (London, 1619), 68–75. Reference hereafter is to the 1697 edition, 119–30.

[6] Ibid., 123, 127–30. See also Richard Burn, *The Justice of Peace and Parish Officer* (1743; 2d ed., London, 1755), 213:"[I]n general, the law never looks upon any person as a servant, who is hired for less than one whole year; otherwise they come under the denomination of labourers." See also *R. v. Inhabitants of St. George Hanover Square*, Burrow's Settlement Cases 12 (1734). And see Thomas, "The Levellers and the Franchise," 71–2.

[7] Kussmaul, *Servants in Husbandry*, 5–7. See also Sir William Holdsworth, *A History of English Law* (London, 1936), 2:461; Robert W. Malcolmson, *Life and Labor in England, 1700–1780* (New York, 1981), 35–8, 54, 65–7.

the capacity of the servant to perform undifferentiated labor over an extended period.[8]

Such distinctions in terminology and regulation gave legal recognition to differences in age, marital status, skill, and craft training existing within the working population, all of which contributed to differences in the mode and term of employment. The work of English social historians confirms that these distinctions were adhered to in both legal and social usage into the second half of the eighteenth century.[9] As one English historian has recently concluded, working people "may well have been the least homogenous of all the orders in early-modern society."[10] Their legal regulation reflected that heterogeneity.

One of the most important characteristics distinguishing service in early modern England from other conditions of labor was that its incumbents were overwhelmingly young people entering adolescence rather than adult workers. Thus, according to Ann Kussmaul, "Servants were youths hired into the families of their employers."[11] Peter Laslett's evidence drawn from a number of European societies of the early modern era shows that "servants in fact were, to a very large extent, young, unmarried persons . . . [and] four-fifths of male servants and two-thirds of female servants were under the prevalent age of marriage."[12] More recently, Marjorie McIntosh has similarly concluded that almost without exception servants were young people who had left their parental homes to work in other households until financially able to set up their own households and marry. "During this interim between childhood and adulthood," McIntosh writes, "young men and women worked as servants or formal apprentices. Servants were employed in agriculture, in trade and crafts, and as domestic workers. They were a distinct group from the wage laborers – adult men who lived in their own homes and were generally married." Like Laslett, McIntosh also draws our attention to the wider European context, arguing that youthful service "formed a necessary part of the characteristic Northwest European household formation system during the seventeenth and eighteenth centuries, linked to a late age of marriage and the requirement that after marriage a couple be in charge of its own separate household." In general, McIntosh estimates that these youthful servants provided between one-third and one-half of all labor in early modern English

---

[8] "A hired Servant is always under the Government, Discipline and Control of the Master, even on Sundays" (*R. v. The Inhabitants of Winton*, Burrow's Settlement Cases 280 [1748]. See also *R. v. Inhabitants of Macclesfield*, Burrow's Settlement Cases 458 (1758).

[9] See e.g., Kussmaul, *Servants in Husbandry*, 135–42; K. D. M. Snell, *Annals of the Labouring Poor: Social Change and Agrarian England, 1660–1900* (Cambridge, 1985), 73–84.

[10] A. Hassell Smith, "Labourers in Late Sixteenth-Century England: A Case Study from North Norfolk [Part I]," *Continuity and Change*, 4, 1 (1989), 11–52, at 31. See also A. J. Tawney and R. H. Tawney, "An Occupational Census of the Seventeenth Century," *Economic History Review*, 5, 4 (Oct. 1934), 25–64.

[11] Kussmaul, *Servants in Husbandry*, 3; and see 4, 31. See also Snell, *Annals of the Labouring Poor*, 83–4, 322–34.

[12] Laslett, *Family Life and Illicit Love*, 34.

agriculture; they probably comprised approximately 15 per cent of the whole population.[13]

In one crucial respect, however, English law displayed a tendency to treat the different sorts and conditions of working people similarly. When dearth or disease threatened serious social crisis, the response was the adoption of strict restraints on mobility through criminalization of the abandonment of employment before the term or task agreed to be performed had been finished.[14] Responding to the labor shortages in husbandry occasioned by the Black Death, the Statutes of Labourers (1349 and 1351) not only compelled able-bodied persons without means of support to serve "him that doth require him" but also prohibited any "reaper, mower, or other workman, or servant" from departing service "without reasonable cause or licence" before term. The statutes sought to prescribe a yearly term for service in husbandry and to limit the mobility of covenanted farm servants, and attempted to cap wages paid in husbandry and in the artisan crafts.[15] Even in this respect, however, early English law was uneven and ad hoc in its application outside periods of crisis. Criminal restraints were most clearly applicable to unskilled agricultural workers. These people, whether laborers or servants were "virtually the sole targets of enforcement of the statutes."[16] More ambiguous was the position of artisans agreeing to perform particular tasks rather than entering into service. Such persons tended to be treated as liable only to common law actions of assumpsit for nonperformance rather than statutory prosecutions for departure.[17]

The piecemeal ad hocery of early English law was addressed by the Statute of Artificers in 1562. The statute reaffirmed both the principle of compulsory service in husbandry for the able-bodied without means of support and the liability of laborers and servants to prosecution for premature departure. It further confirmed that liability would extend to artisans retained to perform any piece of work "taken in great, in task or in gross." Premature departure would incur a penalty of imprisonment for one month and the forfeiture of five pounds to the party abandoned. The

---

[13] Marjorie K. McIntosh, "Servants and the Household Unit in an Elizabethan English Community," *Journal of Family History*, 9, 1 (Spring 1984), 3–23, at 3–4. See also Malcolmson, *Life and Labor*, 64; R. M. Smith, "The People of Tuscany and Their Families in the Fifteenth Century: Medieval or Mediterranean?" *Journal of Family History*, 6, 1 (Spring 1981), 123; John Hajnal, "Two Kinds of Pre-industrial Household Formation System," in Richard Wall, ed., *Family Forms in Historic Europe* (Cambridge, 1983), 92–9. The ongoing scholarly investigation of the relationship between service and youth in early modern Europe is ably summarized in Michael Mitterauer, "Servants and Youth," *Continuity and Change*, 5, 1 (1990), 11–38.

[14] Robert J. Steinfeld, *The Invention of Free Labor: The Employment Relation in English and American Law and Culture, 1350–1870* (Chapel Hill, 1991), 25–41; Marc Linder, *The Employment Relationship in Anglo-American Law: A Historical Perspective* (Westport, Conn., 1989), 45–55.

[15] The Statutes of Labourers, 23 Edw. III (1349) and 25 Edw. III (1350).

[16] Linder, *Employment Relationship in Anglo-American Law*, 49.

[17] Ibid., 50. However, see also A. W. B. Simpson, *A History of the Common Law of Contract: The Rise of the Action of Assumpsit* (Oxford, 1975), 48–9.

statute emphasized that artificers or labourers "retained in any service" were liable to one month's imprisonment for departing that service.[18]

By thus using criminal sanctions to restrain unauthorized mobility, the statutes underwrote an employer's claim to a property right in his employee's services, a claim already recognized in the common law *actio per quod servitium*.[19] Later commentary, however, allows us grounds to doubt both the scope and effectiveness, and the persistence, of these sanctions.[20] In particular, we cannot assume their applicability, nor the applicability of their common law analogues, to the very substantial population of artisans and independent contractors involved in outwork industries.[21] Moreover, because employment relations were still highly diverse, even the existence of a general restraint on departure cannot be assumed to have otherwise homogenized the legal character of the employment relationship. The severity of the restraint, for example, is not the same for both task and time work. Servants remained the only category of work people liable to perform undifferentiated labor over a lengthy period of time, rather than short-term casual labor or the performance of specific tasks, and restriction of their mobility seems to have been significantly more an object of policy than restriction of the mobility of artificers and laborers.[22]

During the eighteenth century, the diversity of employment relations in English law underwent reorganization and significant homogenization as the variety of statuses recognized in law began to crumble into the single status of wage labor.[23] This change did not occur overnight. "Even when the factory system developed it by no means necessarily followed that the relationship between the factory owner and the work-people was immediately transformed into the modern one of master and servant. The old attitudes died hard: on the one side the factor or merchant, who did not interfere – and did not seek to interfere – in the process of production itself; on the other the domestic worker, choosing his own hours and methods of work, nominally at least his own master."[24] Nevertheless, by midcentury we may

---

[18] The Statute of Artificers, 5 Eliz. I, c. 4 (1562).

[19] On the history of this action, see Jones, "Per Quod Servitium Amisit," 39–58.

[20] See, e.g., Daniel Defoe, *The Great Law of Subordination consider'd; or, the Insolence and Unsufferable Behavior of* SERVANTS *in England duly enquir'd into* (London, 1724). (An example of Defoe's description of English law is quote in the epigraph to this chapter. As this indicates, Defoe was a trenchant critic of the shortcomings of English law on this subject.) See also Burn, *Justice of the Peace and Parish Officer*, 4th ed. (London, 1757), 240.

[21] Defoe, *Great Law of Subordination*, 91–4; Linder, *Employment Relationship in Anglo-American Law*, 55. See also Tawney and Tawney, "An Occupational Census of the Seventeenth Century," 46–9, 54–7; R. Millward, "The Emergence of Wage Labor in Early Modern England," *Explorations in Economic History*, 18 (1981), 21–39.

[22] Lawrence Stone, *The Family, Sex, and Marriage in England, 1500–1800* (London, 1977), 22, 27; Steinfeld, *Invention of Free Labor*, 40.

[23] Brian W. Haines, "English Labour Law and the Separation from Contract," *Journal of Legal History*, 1, 3 (Dec. 1980), 271–4.

[24] G. De N. Clark, "Industrial Law and the Labour-Only Sub-Contract," *Modern Law Review*, 80 (1967), 6–24, at 7. Here "domestic worker" refers to a worker engaged in outwork and not to a domestic servant. See also John Smail, "New Languages for Labor and Capital: The Transformation of Discourse in the Early Years of the Industrial Revolution," *Social History*, 12, 1 (Jan. 1987), 54–61.

detect the emergence of "master and servant" for the first time as a generic description of the employment relation.

One of the earliest examples of the use of the phrase in this way can be found in Sir Matthew Hale's *Analysis of the Law*, first published in 1713, which refers to "Master and Servant" as one of the "Relations Oeconomical," that is, one of the domestic relations (the others being "Husband and Wife" and "Parent and Child"). Hale's *Analysis* was confined to civil law, however, and the very lack of substance – "Touching the Third Oeconomical Relation of Master and Servant," Hale commented, "little is to be said," – suggests little more than an innovative categorization at this point.[25] Hale did indicate that several "kinds of servants" were to be comprehended under this heading (although without further specifying who they were),[26] and he listed the civil remedies that masters might have against a third party for retaining his servant "before his Time is expir'd" or for rendering him incapable of performing by beating him. On the other hand Hale dealt with "tradesmen," such as "a common taylor," separately and in a manner indicating that he regarded their relationship with employers as one of bailment, in which their skills might be hired but without entry into service, and therefore not as one properly comprehended under the master/servant title.[27] Charles Viner's *General Abridgment of Law and Equity*, which began to appear in 1742, also used the category of "master and servant." Viner's was a more comprehensive rendering, covering both civil actions and the provisions of the criminal statutes in some detail. It was, however, a relatively traditional description, for example including both the "higher" servants – bailiff, factor, steward – and those manual workers whose movements were subjected to legal controls by the Statute of Artificers.[28]

The beginnings of a newer approach are more fully revealed in Richard Burn's *Justice of the Peace and Parish Officer*, first published in 1743 as a revision and extension of Dalton's *Countrey Justice*. Burn's *Justice* dealt exclusively with the lesser occupations, thus helping to identify servant as a legal category associated generically with manual employment. This association was strengthened by Burn's reorganization of Dalton, lumping the different statuses ("labourers, journeymen, artificers, and other workmen") together under the title of "servants."[29] Finally, Burn for the

---

[25] Sir Matthew Hale, *The Analysis of the Law* (London, 1713), 45, 50. I am indebted to Robert Steinfeld for bringing Hale's work to my attention.

[26] Ibid., 50. Hale's contemporary Daniel Defoe listed apprentices, menial servants, and clerks, and also made reference to "the Labouring Poor" as "Servants without Doors" (*Great Law of Subordination*, 8–9).

[27] Hale, *Analysis of the Law*, 117–8, 123. On bailment see above, Introduction to Part 3, n. 23.

[28] Charles Viner, *A General Abridgment of Law and Equity* (Aldershot, 1742-), 15:308–34.

[29] Burn, *Justice of the Peace and Parish Officer*, 4th ed., 3:229–65. Although Burn is the best known of the successors to Dalton, his was by no means the only justice of the peace book circulating in eighteenth-century England. See, e.g., William Nelson, *The Office and Authority of a Justice of Peace* (London, 1704); Joseph Shaw, *The Practical Justice of Peace* (London, 1728). Shaw also used "servants" as the appropriate category for all labor regulation, but Nelson's alphabetical mode of organization used "apprentices". Nelson became the organizational model for abridgements published in the American colonies during the first half of the eighteenth century, whereas Burn was increasingly resorted to for abridgements in the second half. See generally John A. Conley, "Doing It by the Book: Justice of the Peace Manuals and English Law in Eighteenth Century America," *Journal of Legal History*, 6, 3 (Dec. 1985), 257–98.

first time grouped under this category all the old statutes regulating disputes over putting-out between employers and domestic workers in the cloth trade (dealing mostly with embezzlement of materials and methods of payment) and also more-recent statutes dealing with the urban handicraft trades passed in the wake of the degeneration of the trading companies' guild controls.[30] In subsequent editions Burn's *Justice* reflected the further expansion of legislation regulating the employment relation both in husbandry and in craft industries, passed to remedy the "insufficient and defective" laws then in being. These general acts, passed in 1747, 1766, and 1777, revived and reinforced the disciplinary incidents of the Statute of Artificers and extended their regulatory ambit to encompass by name practically the whole range of artisanal and laboring occupations making up the bulk of the work force.[31]

Twenty years after Burn's first edition, Blackstone's *Commentaries on the Laws of England* confirmed the emergence of the single category of "Master and Servant" as the operative legal description for all relations of manual employment, whether inside or outside the household. Following Hale's general typology, Blackstone gave details of the "kinds of servants" to which Hale had alluded but which he had not defined. These were menial servants "so called from being *intra moenia*, or domestics"; apprentices; and laborers "who are only hired by the day or week, and do not live *intra moenia*." Blackstone referred to the last as those persons "concerning whom the statute so often cited [the Statute of Artificers] has made many very good regulations," in effect like Burn filling the empty civil category created by Hale by bringing under the single title "servant" the great diversity of occupational statuses to which varying sanctions had been applied in the Statute of Artificers.[32] At the same time Blackstone indicated that the "higher" servants were now more properly regarded separately from manual workers, "being rather in a superior, a ministerial, capacity." Such persons, Blackstone allowed, were at best "servants *pro tempore*" and only "with regard to such of their acts as affect their master's or employer's property."[33] The result was a classification of master and servant that reduced to a single legal relation the heterogeneous manual labor statuses of early modern England and

---

[30] Burn, *Justice of the Peace and Parish Officer*, 4th ed., 3:244–65.

[31] The new wave of legislation began in 1747 with 20 Geo. II, c. 19, An Act for the Better Adjusting and More Easy Recovery of the Wages of Certain Servants; and for the Better Regulation of Such Servants and of Certain Apprentices. This act extended to "servants in husbandry, who shall be hired for one year, or longer . . . and artificers, handicraftsmen, miners, colliers, keelmen, pitmen, glassmen, potters, and other labourers employed for any certain time, or in any other manner." Further legislation followed in 1766 (6 Geo. III, c. 25, An Act for better regulating Apprentices and Persons working under Contract) and 1777 (17 Geo, III, c. 56, An act . . . for the more effectual preventing of Frauds and Abuses by Persons employed in the Manufacture of Hats, and in the Woollen, Linen, Fustian, Cotton, Iron, Leather, Fur, Hemp, Flax, Mohair, and Silk Manufactures), culminating in 4 Geo. IV, c. 34 of 1823, An Act to enlarge the Powers of Justices in determining Complaints between Masters and Servants. See generally Brian W. Napier, "The Contract of Service: The Concept and Its Application" (D.Phil. diss., Cambridge University, 1975), 71–5, 85–6.

[32] Sir William Blackstone, *Commentaries on the Laws of England* (Chicago, 1979), 1:410–20, at 414–15. See also Otto Kahn-Freund, "Blackstone's Neglected Child: The Contract of Employment," *Law Quarterly Review*, 93 (Oct. 1977) esp. 511.

[33] Blackstone, *Commentaries*, 1:415.

that separated out from that relation those statuses not associated with manual labor.[34]

MASTER AND SERVANT IN COLONIAL AMERICA

In colonial America, even more than in early modern England, work and employment were highly diversified social phenomena. Labor practices varied markedly from region to region, running the gamut from the considerable reliance on indentured and race servitude common in many parts of the Chesapeake and, during the eighteenth century, the middle colonies, to the family-centered labor found everywhere but particularly dominant in New England. Relations of clientage (the combination of tenancy and labor obligations) and reciprocation (the transfer of goods and services among interdependent neighbors and in transactions between customers and independent artisan proprietors) were commonly found among both the urban and rural populations of the middle and northern colonies. Vocational duality was also common, particularly in the case of rural artisans. Wage labor, known in all regions from early on, grew in importance during the course of the eighteenth century, both in husbandry and in the artisan trades.[35]

---

[34] Such a classification tended to bring within the master/servant relationship those whose relation with their employers had theretofore been one of bailment rather than service. Thus, as Lord Mansfield put it in the Court of King's Bench in 1774, a journeyman "is a servant by the day; and it makes no difference whether the work is done by the day or by the piece." And that, tellingly added Mr. Justice Aston, would be the case "even supposing . . . that the [journeyman] did live in his own house" and "took in work from employers at large" (*Hart v. Aldridge*, 1 Cowp. 55 [1774]). See also *Blake v. Lanyon*, 6 Term Rep. 221 (1795), at 222: "A person who contracts with another to do certain work for him is the servant of that other till the work is finished." Cf. Defoe, *Great Law of Subordination*, 91–103. Cf. also the contemporaneous American case *State v. Higgins*, 1 N.C. 36 (1792).

The pattern of master/servant's development as a generic legal category suggested here – stressing qualitative alteration and expansion in the middle to late eighteenth century – accords with others' investigations of master/servant's disciplinary enforcement, which point to an increased volume of master/servant proceedings in the later eighteenth and the nineteenth centuries. See in particular Douglas Hay, "Masters, Servants, Justices, and Judges: The Law of Master and Servant in England in the Eighteenth and Nineteenth Centuries" (paper presented to the Postgraduate Seminar on Law and Labour in the Commonwealth, Institute of Commonwealth Studies, University of London, 1988).

[35] See generally Stephen Innes, "Fulfilling John Smith's Vision: Work and Labor in Early America," in idem, ed., *Work and Labor in Early America* (Chapel Hill, 1988), 18–32, 43–4; Richard S. Dunn, "Servants and Slaves: The Recruitment and Employment of Labor," in Jack P. Greene and J. R. Pole, eds., *Colonial British America: Essays in the New History of the Early Modern Era* (Baltimore, 1984), 157–94; David W. Galenson, "Labor Market Behavior in Colonial America: Servitude, Slavery, and Free Labor," in David W. Galenson, ed., *Markets in History: Economic Studies of the Past* (Cambridge, 1989), 52–96; Marcus Rediker, "Good Hands, Stout Heart, and Fast Feet: The History and Culture of Working People in Early America," in Geoff Eley and William Hunt, eds., *Reviving the English Revolution: Reflections and Elaborations on the Work of Christopher Hill* (London, 1988), 221–49, at 228–31. Innes notes that "the major social divisions in the colonies were not between labor and capital, but between the free and unfree" and that "rather than class, the boundaries to these categories largely were set by age in the northern colonies and race in the plantation South" (18–19). See also Sharon V. Salinger, *"To Serve Well and Faithfully": Labor and Indentured Servants in Pennsylvania, 1682–1800* (New York and Cambridge, 1987); Jean B. Russo, *Free Workers in a Plantation Economy: Talbot County, Maryland, 1690–1759* (New York, 1989); Christine Daniels, "Alternative Workers in a Slave Economy: Kent County, Maryland, 1675–1810" (Ph.D. diss., Johns Hopkins University, 1989).

In America, as in England, the law of employment emerged through a process of conflation and differentiation among existing legal categories. In America, however, this development occurred during the first half of the nineteenth century rather than during the eighteenth century. It was propagated, largely, by the professional juridical elite through treatise writing and common law judging activities heavily informed by English legal discourse. That is, in institutional terms this development was almost entirely the result of juridical not legislative initiative. And it was a development, finally, which grew out of a colonial legal landscape different in important respects from that of contemporary England, a landscape in which criminal penalties against departure protecting an employer's claim to property in service, and also the analogue common law actions themselves, had by the end of the seventeenth century, and in some regions well before then, become focused in their application largely on the institutions of indentured servitude and slavery. To the extent that the variety of legal compulsions regulating wage labor in English law were imported into the mainland colonies during the period of first settlement (and as we shall see, the comprehensiveness of that importation is highly debatable),[36] they do not appear to have survived beyond the turn of the eighteenth century except in those specific, and increasingly distinct, instances.

Hence, although it is indisputable that, wherever it applied in colonial America, the criminal disciplining of labor was severe, what remains very much at issue is the

Although definite figures are hard to come by, it is clear that indentured servants were not a significant proportion of the New England working population at any point after first settlement, that they peaked as a majority of the working population in the Chesapeake colonies during the middle decades of the seventeenth century but declined in importance thereafter, and that in the middle colonies they peaked at about 25 percent of the urban working population in the mid-eighteenth century, followed by a rapid decline. (On the last see Salinger, *"To Serve Well and Faithfully"*, 57–61, and see generally 178–80. Because Salinger's data are drawn entirely from Philadelphia, where indentured servants were particularly prominent in the labor force, the 25 percent figure likely overstates their importance in middle colony urban areas in general. Certainly it overstates their importance in the performance of all middle colony work, rural and urban, for as Salinger notes on the basis of an examination of rural Philadelphia County, the incidence of indentured servants in the rural work force was less than half that in the city [71].) The considerable variation over time and region prevents any close comparisons between the incidence of indentured servants in the mainland colonies' working population and that of servants in the English working population, but there seem to be some rough parallels. Further, as we shall see, the demographic characteristics of the colonial servant population are very similar to those of English servants.

[36] Aspects of the general relationship between English law and colonial practice have already been explored in Part 1. In regard to that relationship, Shannon Stimson has recently observed that "the American court system, which virtually collapsed all English common law jurisdictions, often rendered the wholesale incorporation of English law inapplicable and pointless . . . . All the colonies claimed the 'benefits' of general common law rights, but they accepted only limited categories of British statutes." As a result, "what constituted the 'common' law was in many colonies a product of selective and conscious incorporation of English law placed side-by-side with an indigenous colonial product" (*The American Revolution in the Law: Anglo-American Jurisprudence before John Marshall* [Princeton, 1990], 56). The reception or influence of English law regulating wages labor is addressed in some detail in this chapter. It is worth noting at the outset, however, that as eminent an authority as Benjamin Franklin, when preparing characteristically terse comments in response to Josiah Tucker's *A Letter From a Merchant in London to His Nephew in North America* in 1771, asserted flatly that "the Statutes for Labourers" were not then in force in America, "nor ever were." See William B. Willcox, ed., *The Papers of Benjamin Franklin* (New Haven, 1973), 17:352.

ambit of that criminalized discipline as compared with England.[37] Certainly, there were no colonial American equivalents of the English eighteenth-century master and servant statutes upon which nineteenth-century jurists could build a generic indigenous criminalized labor law.[38]

New England

In New England, evidence of either a customary or a legal identification of un-indentured wage labor with a condition of criminally disciplinable service is meagre from the outset. In seventeenth-century Massachusetts, for example, anecdotal evidence suggests that virtually from the time of first settlement hired laborers were not regarded as servants. Wage labor was colloquially referred to as "help."[39] The General Court early adopted labor regulations directed at the mobilization of all persons for harvest work and also attempted the regulation of "excessive" wages paid to laborers and prices charged by artificers in the colony. Wage and price regulation proved ineffective, however, and the General Court subsequently devolved regulatory authority to the towns. Resort to regulation at that level was no more than spasmodic.[40] Outside the lone directive (backed by no specified sanction) "that all workmen shall work the whole day, allowing convenient time for food and rest," there is little evidence of statutory regulation of hireling labor. Indeed, Governor John Winthrop commented in 1641 that "being restrained, they would either remove to other places where they might have more, or else being able to live by planting and other employments of their own, they would not be hired at all."[41]

---

[37] Something of the antipodal disjunction between labor as disciplined servitude and labor as autonomy which seems so important a characteristic of early America is conveyed by Michael Zuckerman's wide-ranging interpretive essay "Identity in British America: Unease in Eden," in Nicholas Canny and Anthony Pagden, eds., *Colonial Identity in the Atlantic World* (Princeton, 1987), 115–57, at 126–8.

[38] On the application of "the general lines" of English labor statutes to indentured servitude in the colonies, see Bradley Chapin, *Criminal Justice in Colonial America, 1606–1660* (Athens, Ga., 1983), 135–7; Steinfeld, *Invention of Free Labor*, 41–54. On the growing distinctiveness of indentured servitude in colonial law in the later seventeenth and the eighteenth century see Steinfeld, *Invention of Free Labor*, 103. On the relationship between indentured servitude and service-in-husbandry, see David W. Galenson, *White Servitude in Colonial America: An Economic Analysis* (Cambridge, 1981), 6–8; and Jack P. Greene, *Pursuits of Happiness: The Social Development of Early Modern British Colonies and the Formation of American Culture* (Chapel Hill, 1988), 10.

[39] Albert Matthews, "The Terms Hired Man and Help," reprinted from *Publications of the Colonial Society of Massachusetts*, 5 (Cambridge, 1900), 21–8; Eric G. Nellis, "Labor and Community in Massachusetts Bay, 1630–1660," *Labor History*, 18, 4 (Fall 1977), 525–44, at 528.

[40] Richard B. Morris, *Government and Labor in Early America* (New York, 1975), 55–77; see also Nellis, "Labor and Community," 535–8. David Galenson has commented that the New England colonies "had active markets for hired labor from a very early date, and these operated with little effective government intervention" ("Labor Market Behavior in Colonial America," 92).

[41] *Records of the Court of Assistants of the Colony of the Massachusetts Bay, 1630–1692* (Boston, 1901–28), 2:37 (hereinafter *RCA*); James K. Hosmer, *Winthrop's Journal, 1630–1649* (New York, 1908), 2:24 (the Winthrop quotation appears in Galenson, "Labor Market Behavior in Colonial America," 92–3). It is worth noting that early colony legislation rendered "servants" departing their masters before term liable to return by force of arms, but not workmen or laborers (*The Book of the General Lawes and Libertyes Concerning the Inhabitants of the Massachusets* [Cambridge, Mass., 1929; first printed by order of the General Court, 1648], 38).

The colony's Court of Assistants promulgated a number of orders and decisions in regard to servants during the early years of settlement, which, piecemeal, reproduced some elements of English law and introduced innovations.[42] These included, for example, a requirement of a minimum term of one year when hiring unsettled servants[43] and the punishment of enticers and runaways.[44] Early on, however, servitude began to appear as a specific condition identified with persons entering the colony bound to multiyear indentures and distinct as such from the remainder of the laboring population.[45] Measures specifically regulating "servants" during the early years speak to such a special – and temporary – status. These required faithful performance during service as a condition of taking up grants of land and forbade masters from allowing servants to buy out their time or otherwise releasing their servants early. The authority of the master was enforced – for example, servants were forbidden to "give, sell, or trucke any commodytie whatsoever, without licence from their maister, dureing the tyme of their service" – but provision was made to protect the servant from ill-treatment.[46] Reinforcing the identification of servitude with a multiyear indenture to be followed by freedom, it was also provided that "servants that have served diligentlie and faithfully to the benefitt of their maisters seven yeares, shall not be sent away emptie."[47]

Court proceedings carry the same message. Runaways, for example, were normally required to serve an additional period "att the end of their tyme," implying the existence in almost all such cases of an indenture specifying a term of service and not merely a parol agreement.[48] Other cases also strongly imply that a written indenture or covenant was required as a basis for claims of property in service and for the invocation of criminal restraints. For example, in 1639 Israell Stoughton was fined forty shillings by the Court of Assistants "for releasing his man before the expiration of his time" but had his fine remitted after demonstrating that "hee could not hold his servant haveing no covenant."[49] During the course of the seventeenth

---

[42] *RCA*, 2:2–35 passim.

[43] In June 1631 the Court of Assistants ordered that "noe man within the limits of this jurisdicon shall hire any person for a servant for less time than a yeare, unless he be a settled housekeep" (*RCA*, 2:15).

[44] *RCA*, 2:27, 43, 51, 57, 59, 86, 97.

[45] Lawrence W. Towner, "A Good Master Well-Served: A Social History of Servitude in Massachusetts, 1620–1750" (Ph.D. diss., Northwestern University, 1954), 36–9, 50–7.

[46] Nathaniel B. Shurtleff, ed., *Records of the Governor and Company of Massachusetts Bay in New England* (Boston, 1853–4), 1:157 (Order of 3 Sept. 1635), 186 (Order of 13 Dec. 1636), 76 (Order of 28 Sept. 1630); and see *The Body of Liberties* (1641), tit. "The Liberties of Servants," in William H. Whitmore, ed., *The Colonial Laws of Massachusetts* (Boston, 1890), 52–3. See also Record Commissioners of the City of Boston, *Second Report: Boston Town Records, 1634–60* (Boston, 1877), 142 (Order of 25 Nov. 1657).

[47] *The Body of Liberties* (1641), tit. "The Liberties of Servants."

[48] In England, in contrast, oral retainers were criminally enforceable. See Jones, "Per Quod Servitium Amisit," 50–1.

[49] *RCA*, 2:84, 88. Note also *William Deane v. Mr Jonathan Wade* ("For prosecuting him after the manner of a runaway, the plaintiff being free"), in *Records and Files of the Quarterly Court of Essex County, Massachusetts, 1636–83* (Salem, Mass., 1911–21), 2:62 (1658) (hereinafter *RFQE*). In 1634 Edward Winsloe of Plymouth carefully and expressly covenanted with William Hamonds and Nicolas Prestland that they were to serve him and were "not to depart the service of him, the sayd Edw:, till haruest be at home; in the mean time to do what buisnes the said Edw: hath to do" on penalty of payment of five pounds each in sawn boards (Nathaniel B. Shurtleff, ed., *Records of the Colony of New Plymouth in New England:*

century, court records strongly suggest that the distinction between work for wages and service by indenture or by other form of written covenant became legally explicit; "servants" subject to restraint were increasingly identified as one or other form of bound labor – "covenant" servants, debt servants, apprentices, African-Americans, or Indians.[50] Persons working for hire, including artisans contracting to perform specific tasks, were not held criminally liable for failure to perform and at common law appear at most to have been held liable to pay damages in lieu.[51]

Compared with other regions, indentured servitude was never a particularly significant institution in colonial New England's social and economic organization.[52] Legislation regulating "servants" nevertheless continued to be passed periodically

Court Orders [Boston, 1855], 1:30). The implication here is that remedies for premature departure in such situations were unavailable by other than express contractual provision.

[50] The court records thus reflect the conclusions reached by Lawrence Towner. See, e.g., "A Good Master Well-Served," 331–2. See also Lawrence W. Towner, " 'A Fondness for Freedom': Servant Protest in Puritan Society," *William and Mary Quarterly*, 3d ser., 19, 2 (Apr. 1962), 201–19, at 205. And see Samuel Willard, *A Compleat Body of Divinity in Two Hundred and Fifty Expository Lectures* (Boston, 1726), sermon 179 (delivered 24 Aug. 1703), 613–17 (2d set), considering "the Relation which is made between the *Master & Servant*" (emphasis in original). Willard argued that the relation of master and servant had a precise meaning, that it was not a general or natural relation but one founded upon and exercised within households, and that it encompassed four different degrees or statuses of servitude: service by binding indenture or covenant (the "most honourable"); debt service; service resulting from captivity in war; and service "by natural generation" – that is, slavery. The term *covenant servant* refers to one bound by the form of written indenture known as a "covenant merely personal." On this see Warren M. Billings, "The Law of Servants and Slaves in Seventeenth Century Virginia," *Virginia Magazine of History and Biography*, 99, 1 (Jan. 1991), 45–62, at 46–7.

[51] See, e.g., *Waldron agt. Henderson*, *Records of the Suffolk County Court, 1671–80*, Colonial Society of Massachusetts, Publications, 29–30 (Boston, 1933), 2:901, 924, 1038 (1678) (hereinafter *RSCC*). See also *Pennell agt. Pendell*, *RSCC*, 2:620 (1675); *Yardley agt. Boden*, *RSCC*, 2:775 (1677). In the case of *Ursellton v. Godfrye*, *RFQE*, 2:175, 185 (1659), the plaintiff obtained judgment against the defendant "for not performing a summer's work," but when she then tried to recover the five pounds forfeiture prescribed by the Statute of Artificers as part of the penalty for early departure in English law, she was nonsuited. In *Joyliffe agt. Nick* and again in *Davie agt. Hall*, both *RSCC*, 2:825 (1675) and 876 (1678), the action was for nondelivery of goods and the verdict was for delivery or damages in lieu of performance. Cases of courts apparently ordering specific performance with no opportunity to avoid performance by paying damages in lieu do show up in the records earlier in the century. See, e.g., *Henry Archer v. John Fullar*, *RFQE*, 1:147 (1648); *Thomas Cooper, complt, v. John Bliss; Hugh Dudley, complt, v. Thomas Mirack; John Lamb, complt, v. Thomas Mirack; Henry Burt, complt, v. John Henryson*; all in Joseph H. Smith, ed., *Colonial Justice in Western Massachusetts (1639–1702): The Pynchon Court Record* (Cambridge, Mass., 1961), 236 (1655), 246 (1660), 247 (1660), 252 (1661). But such cases are very rare, and by the 1670s, if not before, damages in lieu appears to have become standard practice. (Richard B. Morris was in fact roundly criticized when *Government and Labor in Early America* first appeared for claiming as examples of specific performance cases in which courts ordered performance *or* damages. See Joseph H. Smith, "Review of *Government and Labor in Early America*," *Columbia Law Review*, 46 [1946], 688.) Thus see *Morgan agt. Ferry*, in Smith, *Colonial Justice*, 279 (1674). See also *RSCC*, 1:liv.

[52] Galenson, *White Servitude in Colonial America*, 156; Gary B. Nash, *The Urban Crucible: Social Change, Political Consciousness, and the Origins of the American Revolution* (Cambridge, Mass., 1979), 104–6; Bernard Bailyn, *Voyagers to the West: A Passage in the Peopling of America on the Eve of the Revolution* (New York, 1986), 204–70; Jackson Turner Main, *Society and Economy in Colonial Connecticut* (Princeton, 1985), 182. Legislation passed in 1709 "for the encouragement of the importation of white servants, of the kingdom of Great Britain" attests to a desire in the colony to improve the supply of indentured servants through payment of a bounty to importers. See *Province Laws* 1708–9, c. 11. The scheme lapsed after three years, however, and was not renewed. The bounty, it should be noted, was applicable only to males between the ages of eight and twenty-five.

throughout the colonial period. With few exceptions, these measures made clear that what was intended was a regulation of adolescents; the statutes clearly did *not* contemplate regulation of adult labor. In other words it was youthful labor, not labor as such, that was made the object of statutory definition and sanctioning.[53]

As in England, colonial New England's social and economic organization was founded on households, whose members were parents, the children of those parents, and servants. As in England, moreover, the servants in these households were overwhelmingly young people.[54] To be sure, nothing in colonial legislation indicates that "servant" described a status *legally confined* to a particular stage of the population's life cycle. (The narrower category of apprentice was, of course, so confined in English law and became so established in Massachusetts.)[55] The presumption that "servant" as a general description also meant "youth," however, is clear in practically every legislative measure and order dealing with servants in seventeenth and eighteenth-century Massachusetts.[56] In 1651, for example, the General Court

[53] The importance of youthful labor in seventeenth-century Massachusetts has recently been emphasized by Daniel Vickers, who has argued on the basis of a study of Essex County that heads of farm households relied heavily on the labor of their own children, supplemented where necessary by exchanges of labor services among interdependent households ("Working the Fields in a Developing Economy: Essex County, Massachusetts, 1630–1675," in Innes, ed., *Work and Labor in Early America*, 56–60). See also Main, *Colonial Connecticut*, 183, 190–4. For a study of eighteenth-century farm labor that also stresses the centrality of young workers, see Ross W. Beales, Jr., "The Reverend Ebenezer Parkman's Farm Workers, Westborough, Massachusetts, 1726–82," *Proceedings of the American Antiquarian Society*, 99, 1 (1989), 121–49. See also, generally, Francis G. Walett, ed., *The Diary of Ebenezer Parkman, 1703–1782* (Worcester, 1974), pt. 1, *1719–1755*.

[54] John Demos asserts that "much the greatest portion of persons in servitude were children" (*A Little Commonwealth: Family Life in Plymouth Colony* [New York, 1970], 71). See also Towner, "A Good Master Well-Served," 50–5, 75, 84–8, 106. There has long been a scholarly consensus that the inhabitants of colonial North America, like their counterparts in England, often sent their children, and particularly the children of their poor, into service. My aim here is not to challenge the consensus as such (although for a valuable qualification, see Vickers, "Working the Fields in a Developing Economy"), but rather to suggest that the direction of the correlation of "child" and "servant" needs examination and that the appropriate conclusion to draw is not that children were overwhelmingly servants but rather that servants were overwhelmingly children.

[55] Record Commissioners of the City of Boston, *Boston Town Records*, 157 (Order of 20 June 1660); *Province Laws* 1692, c. 28, An Act for Regulating of Townships, Choice of Town Officers and Setting Forth Their Power (in which town officers were empowered to bind out children of the poor as apprentices). See, however, W. J. Rorabaugh, *The Craft Apprentice: From Franklin to the Machine Age in America* (New York, 1986), 4; Towner, "A Good Master Well-Served," 37–9.

[56] Indeed, the Boston town order cited in n. 55, besides establishing the importance of apprenticeship, indicates that *apprentice* and *servant* were used interchangeably, that *both* implied youth, and that on reaching the age of twenty-one the young adult was considered fit to "govern" others (that is, other apprentices and youthful servants): "Whereas it is found by sad experience that many youthes in this Town, being put forth Apprentices to several manufactures and sciences, for but 3 or 4 years time, contrary to the Customs of all well governed places, whence they are uncapable of being Artists in their trade, besides their unmeetness at the expiration of their Apprenticeship to take charge of others for government and manual instruction in their occupations . . . it is therefore ordered that no person shall henceforth open a shop in this Town, nor occupy any manufacture or science, till he hath completed 21 years of age, nor except he hath served seven years Apprentice-ship, by testimony under the hands of sufficient witnesses. And that all Indentures made between any master and servant shall be brought in and enrolled in the Town's Records within one month after the contract made, on penalty of ten shillings to be paid by the master at the time of the Apprentices being made free."

bracketed "servants" with "children . . . apprintizes and schollers belonginge to the colledge or any other Latine schoole" in an order seeking to keep "the younge people of this country" from dissipation and idleness.[57] In 1654 the General Court joined "children and servants" in an order seeking to punish youths for rude behavior.[58] The following year children and servants were again joined in a law governing trespass, as they were in 1679 in the act creating the office of tythingman.[59] The act of March 1695 prohibiting masters of outbound ships from taking onboard persons absconding from service identified "men's sons or servants" as the potential miscreants.[60]

Eighteenth-century legislation addressed to the regulation of servants exhibited a heightened tendency to identify service with youth. A new version of the 1695 act passed in 1718 was "for the Preventing of Persons Under Age, Apprentices or Servants, Being Transported Out of the Province."[61] The act of 1759 empowering the courts of general sessions of the peace to hear complaints relating to the treatment of servants or apprentices by their masters or mistresses and to punish their unlawful absences clearly identified the persons described as juveniles.[62] This

[57] The order provided that any person who did not "hasten all such youthes to theire severall imployments and places of abode or lodgings aforesaid . . . or any servant or other helpe in the family, or supplyinge the place of a servant" would be liable to fine. Shurtleff, *Records*, 3:242 (Order of 14 Oct. 1651); and see also ibid., vol. 4. pt. 1, 325 (Order of 19 May 1658).

[58] Ibid., 3:355 (Order of 22 Aug. 1654).

[59] Ibid., 2:180 (Order of 23 May 1655); Whitmore, *Colonial Laws*, 270.

[60] *Province Laws* 1694–5, c. 23, An Act for Preventing of Men's Sons or Servants Absenting Themselves from Their Parent's or Master's Service Without Leave. See also Shurtleff, *Records*, 1:115 (Order of 1 Apr. 1634, emphasis supplied): "It is ordered that if any *boy* (that hath bene whipt for running fro his master) be taken in any other plantacon, not having a note from his maister to testifie his business there, it shallbe lawfull for the constable of the said plantacon to whip him and send him home." Court records dealing with runaways and abused servants very often identify the servant as a minor. See, e.g., *RFQE*, 8:92 (1681) (the runaway described as "a very naughty boy"); *RFQE*, 8:314 (1682) (the abused servant described as "one of his [master's] boys").

[61] *Province Laws* 1718–19, c. 14.

[62] *Province Laws* 1758–9, c. 17, An Act in Further Addition to an Act Intitled "An Act for Explanation of and Supplement to an Act Referring to the Poor." The act reads, where relevant, as follows (emphasis supplied): "[I]t shall and may be lawful for the courts of general sessions of the peace for the respective counties, upon complaint made by the overseers for the poor selectmen of any town in such county, or by the overseers appointed for the county where *any indented, bought, or any way legally bound, servant or apprentice* shall not be within any town or district, that *any such servant or apprentice* have been abused or evil treated by their masters or mistresses, or that the education of *such children* in reading or writing and cyphering, according to the tenor of their indentures, has been unreasonably neglected, to take cognizance of such representation or complaint, and if upon inquiry there shall appear to have been just cause therefor, such master or mistress shall forfeit a sum not exceeding five pounds. . . . [T]he said court may order *such child or children* to be liberated or discharged from their masters or mistresses, *and any male so discharged being under the age of twenty-one years, and any female under the age of eighteen years, may, by order of such court, be bound to other persons until they arrive to the age of twenty-one or eighteen years respectively.*" As its title indicates, this legislation, dealing with "any indented, bought, or any way legally bound, servant or apprentice," regulated the binding of *poor* apprentices. Lawrence Towner shows that the binding of poor apprentices assumed a growing importance from the late seventeenth century on as the incidence of voluntary bindings declined ("A Good Master Well-Served," 56, 86, 106–8). See also idem, "The Indentures of Boston's Poor Apprentices: 1734–1805," *Publications of the Colonial Society of Massachusetts*, 43 (1966), 417–68.

presumption was reiterated and reinforced in legislation passed in 1795 "to Secure to Masters and Mistresses, as well as to apprentices and minor servants bound by Deed, their Mutual Privileges" in which *servant* was throughout used interchangeably with the term *apprentice*, as it had been throughout the previous 150 years, to describe an indentured minor.[63] Eighteenth-century court records similarly indicate that the terms *servant* and *apprentice* were used interchangeably. A 1733 Worcester County proceeding, for example, was summarized as follows:

George Wicker, *servant* of _____ Baldwin now living in Leicester in this county having absented himself from his said masters service and yᵉ charge and recovering him amounting to eight pounds sixteen shillings and the said George being before the Court and acknowledging yᵉ same the Court therefore order that the said *apprentice* serve his said master his heirs executors or administrators eight months next after the determination of the present indenture.[64]

A second proceeding, over thirty years later and at the other end of the colony, illustrates the same point:

Complaint having been made against Mr Jacob Thayer by his *servant* Thomas Vaux, and the same having been considered. It was Agreed between the Partys that all past behavior on either side should be overlooked, that the *Prentice* will serve five weeks after he is free to make up the time he has been absent and that he is to have everything done and provided according to the indentures.[65]

Both legislative and court records thus appear to confirm that beginning long before the beginning of the eighteenth century, the regulation of "servants" in Massachusetts had become predominantly and consciously a regulation of juveniles.[66] Indeed, there are few references to servants in colonial statutes that do not identify service with youth.[67] Adult debtors were liable to be bound out to service in the

---

[63] *Massachusetts Acts* 1794, c. 64.

[64] "Records of the Court of General Sessions of the Peace, for the County of Worcester, Massachusetts, 1731–37," session of 6 Feb. 1733, in Worcester Society of Antiquity, *Collections*, 5, 18 (1883), 62–3 (emphasis supplied).

[65] See "Selectmen's Minutes, Meeting of 26 May 1772," in Record Commissioners of the City of Boston, *Twenty-Third Report: Selectmen's Minutes, 1769–75* (Boston, 1893) (emphasis supplied).

[66] Contemporary observations of servitude lend support to this conclusion. In his famous sermon *A Good Master Well Served*, e.g., Cotton Mather explicitly addressed himself to servants as young people: "Servants, you are under a yoke in your youth; but that so few of you do, while you are young, affect the easy yoke of the Lord Jesus Christ, this is a lamentation. . . . Come then young servants, make your choice this day." At the end of the sermon Mather widened the scope of his remarks to include black slaves with the white "Prentices" and "Handmaids" (*A Good Master Well Served: A Brief Discourse on the Necessary Properties and Practices of a Good Servant in Every Kind of Servitude* [Boston, 1696], 30, 31, 51–5).

[67] The legislation passed in 1695 and 1718 applied to absconding apprentices and "covenant" servants (1695) and to apprentices and "bought or hired" servants (1718). The legislation of 1759 applied to "indented, bought, or any way legally bound" servants or apprentices. As we have seen, *apprentice* and *servant* were used as synonyms throughout the colonial period, the only detectable difference being that an apprentice was a juvenile bound out specifically to learn a trade and a servant was simply a juvenile bound out to work. The term *covenant servant* could refer to any person, minor or adult, who had entered into or been bound by an explicit contract or indenture providing for an extended period of service,

seventeenth century,[68] but their actual numbers were never large, and involuntary servitude for debt was abolished in 1737.[69] Adult criminals might also be bound out, as might vagrants. These forms of involuntary binding were reaffirmed by the act of 1756 which provided that any person "liable, by virtue of any law or laws of this government, to be sent and committed to the house of correction or workhouse, from any county, town or district in this province" might instead be bound out to service for a term not exceeding one year.[70] Again, however, the numbers were insignificant.[71] More important as a guide to variations in the composition of the servant population is the increasing resort following the turn of the century to the enactment of public order legislation singling out "Indian, negro or molatto servants or slaves" for exemplary punishment and restricted freedom of movement. As this would suggest, the incidence of Indian servitude and African slavery was increasing rapidly as a proportion of all bound labor between 1690 and 1750, stimulating concern to develop additional controls on this permanent servile population of nonwhite adults.[72]

In Massachusetts, then, there is little evidence of any effective reproduction of English labor law's generalized statutory restraints during the colonial period.[73] This conclusion fits well with what we know of colonial society and economy. The

probably several years in duration. *Bought* or *hired* servants could refer to persons whose indentures, or services, had been purchased from, or otherwise assigned by, their original masters (assignment was possible in the case of both indentured servants and apprentices); *hired servants* could also refer to persons covenanting to serve voluntarily for a definite term. There is no indication that *hired servant* was used generically to refer to *any* person entering an employment relationship.

Voluntary bindings by adults for a term not exceeding one year at a time and by written instrument did clearly take place. This was acknowledged indirectly in the 1756 act dealing with the involuntary binding out to service of indigent persons, which provided that such involuntary bindings by overseers of the poor or selectmen "shall be as valid and effectual, in law, to bind and hold the person so put to service, as if any such person, by his or her own act and consent, being of the age of twenty-one years, had bound and put out him- or herself a servant for the like term [i.e., not exceeding one year], by indenture, or by any other legal form or manner of covenant or contract" (*Province Laws* 1755–6, c. 43). I have come across no indication in the case records, however, that such persons were restrained from premature departure, and as we have seen, the act of 1718 that encompassed "hired servants" confined its restraints to "persons under age." See also the Conclusion to this chapter.

[68] Morris, *Government and Labor in Early America*, 356–8. For examples, see *RFQE*, 6:393–5 (1678), 7:153 (1678), 8:441 (1682). On the role of debt servitude in furnishing a labor force see Daniel Vickers, "The First Whalemen of Nantucket," *William and Mary Quarterly*, 3d ser., 40, 4 (Oct. 1983), 560–83.

[69] See Towner, "A Good Master Well-Served," 115–16; Peter J. Coleman, *Debtors and Creditors in America: Insolvency, Imprisonment for Debt, and Bankruptcy, 1607–1900* (Madison, 1974), 41.

[70] *Province Laws* 1755–6, c. 43, An Act in Addition to the Several Acts and Laws of this Province Now in Force Respecting Poor and Idle, Disorderly and Vagrant Persons. This legislation was intended primarily as a means of reducing demands on community poor relief by forcing "idle, dissolute and vagrant persons" into work to support their families.

[71] For the period through 1750, Towner finds approximately 100 cases of criminals bound out but very few instances of adult vagrants forced into service ("A Good Master Well-Served," 115–21).

[72] See, e.g., *Province Laws* 1703–4, c. 11, An Act to Prevent Disorders in the Night; *Province Laws* 1752–3, c. 16, An Act to Prevent the Breaking or Damnifying of Lamps Set Up In or Near Streets, for Enlightning the Same, and c. 18, An Act for Further Preventing All Riotous, Tumultuous and Disorderly Assemblies. On the increasing incidence of bound Native American and African labor see Towner, "A Good Master Well-Served," 438.

[73] For contemporary confirmation, see Greenleaf, quoted below at n. 109.

white adult male population of Massachusetts tended to be self-employed, mostly in family farm agriculture, with additional but smaller groups of rural and urban craftsmen, similarly self-employed.[74] Both sectors were characterized by reciprocal transfers of goods and services among relatively interdependent households; that is, most employment relations were in the form of contractor–contractee, customer–producer, or principal–agent transactions.[75]

The same was largely true of the New England region as a whole. Indeed, of the New England colonies only Rhode Island – significantly, the New England colony with the greatest concentration of bound labor[76] – adopted statutes clearly reproducing the English labor statutes' generalized disciplinary incidents.[77] Under the terms of a 1647 statute, any servant retained "by promise or covenant" for some period who departed that service before the end of the term covenanted for should be "committed to Ward without Baile or Mainprize" until bound by sufficient sureties to perform the engagement. In 1676 these terms were amended slightly so that one hired "for one year's service, or more or less time" was prohibited from departing prematurely on pain of imprisonment. Under the 1647 enactment prohibition against departing work also applied to "any Artificer or Handicraftsman" who "shall depart and leave his said work before finished" without the employer's assent. In this case, however, the English penalty of imprisonment was not carried over, the legislation

---

[74] See Richard L. Bushman, *King and People in Provincial Massachusetts* (Chapel Hill, 1985), 84–5; David Brody, "Time and Work during Early American Industrialism," *Labor History*, 30, 1 (Winter 1989), 13–14; Rorabaugh, *The Craft Apprentice*, 5; Sean Wilentz, "Against Exceptionalism: Class Consciousness and the American Labor Movement, 1790–1920," *International Labor and Working Class History*, 26 (Fall 1984), 1–24, at 7–8; Main, *Colonial Connecticut*, 196, 200, 241, 242–3. Adults primarily dependent on their own farming for sustenance can be found hiring out as wage labor on a casual basis. For examples, see Walett, *Diary of Ebenezer Parkman*. And see Galenson, "Labor Market Behavior in Colonial America," 93, 94. In addition, in his study of Kent, Connecticut, Charles S. Grant estimates a population of "hired hands" (adult men without houses, farms, or other significant property holding) varying from 25 to 40 percent of the town's population during the second half of the eighteenth century. Although these hired hands had formerly experienced considerable upward mobility, Grant finds that by the end of the century they were fast becoming a permanent propertyless class (*Democracy in the Connecticut Frontier Town of Kent* [New York, 1961], 94–8).

[75] See Daniel Vickers, "Competency and Competition: Economic Culture in Early America," *William and Mary Quarterly*, 3d ser., 47, 1 (Jan. 1990), 4–12. See also Wilentz, "Against Exceptionalism," 7–8; James A. Henretta, "Families and Farms: *Mentalité* in Pre-industrial America," *William and Mary Quarterly*, 3d ser, 35, 1 (Jan. 1978), 3–32; Richard Bushman, "Family Security in the Transition from Farm to City, 1750–1850," *Journal of Family History*, 6, 3 (Fall 1981), 238–56, at 239–44; Betty Hobbs Pruitt, "Self-Sufficiency and the Agricultural Economy of Eighteenth-Century Massachusetts," *William and Mary Quarterly*, 3d ser., 41, 3 (July 1984), 334–64; Jonathan Prude, *The Coming of Industrial Order: Town and Factory Life in Rural Massachusetts* (New York and Cambridge, 1983), 4–13. See, in general, William E. Nelson, *Americanization of the Common Law: The Impact of Legal Change on Massachusetts Society, 1760–1830* (Cambridge, 1975), 54–63.

[76] Galenson, "Labor Market Behavior in Colonial America," 86.

[77] Plymouth Colony, New Hampshire, and Connecticut all largely echoed Massachusetts' identification of servants with youth in their enactments. Unlike Rhode Island, none adopted statutes clearly disciplining the generality of hired manual labor. See, e.g., *The Book of the General Laws of the Inhabitants of the Jurisdiction of New Plimouth* (Cambridge, Mass., 1672), 26–7 (tit. "Education of Children"); *The General Laws and Liberties of Connecticut Colonie* (Hartford, 1672), 13–14 (tits. "Children" and "Rebellious Children and Servants"), 47–8 (tit. "Master, Servants and Sojourners").

providing for a fine of five pounds to be recovered "by Action of the Case." Labor in Rhode Island appears to have remained formally subject to these legal restraints throughout the eighteenth century. The Act for Punishing Criminal Offences of 1728 imposed criminal penalties on all departing workmen, servants, and artificers, as in the Statute of Artificers. By 1757, artificers were no longer covered, although departing hired servants remained punishable. Provision for the criminal liability of workers for hire departing before term finally disappears in Rhode Island's Act to Reform the Penal Laws of 1798.[78] Colonial Rhode Island's singularity in the matter of criminal justice has been noted by John Murrin, who finds that the colony "enacted a highly romanticized version of English criminal justice," intended to advertise, in contrast to its neighbors, "the colony's dedication to English law."[79]

The Chesapeake and the Carolinas

In the Chesapeake colonies and the Carolinas there is far more compelling evidence than in the New England jurisdictions that at least during the seventeenth century indentured servitude and unindentured wage labor represented variations on the same criminally disciplinable legal category. As in Massachusetts, indentured servants in Virginia departing before term were, of course, liable to restraint[80] but so were employed former indentured servants who had served out their time and "hired freemen." Like the testimonials required of English servants in husbandry, freed servants and hirelings leaving an engagement were required to obtain a certificate attesting that they were free from obligation to their previous master or employer. Certificates were to be produced when agreeing to a subsequent engagement. Anyone hiring a person without a certificate who should subsequently prove to be already in the employ of another was liable to compensate the previous master or employer, while "the party hired shall receive such censure and punishment as shall be thought fitt by the Governor and Counsell."[81] Subsequent legislation required

[78] See John R. Bartlett, *Records of the Colony of Rhode Island and Providence Plantations in New England* (Providence, 1858), 1:182–4; An Act for Punishing Criminal Offences, 16 Car. II (1676), in John D. Cushing, ed., *The Earliest Acts and Laws of the Colony of Rhode Island and Providence Plantations, 1647–1719* (Wilmington, Del., 1977), 140, 146; An Act for Punishing Criminal Offences (1728), in *Acts and Laws of His Majesty's Colony of Rhode Island* (Newport, 1730), 169–75; An Act for the Punishment of Sundry Crimes and An Act to Prevent Masters and Mistresses Putting Away their Hired Servants, both in *The Charter Granted by His Majesty, King Charles II, To the Governor and Company of the English Colony of Rhode-Island and Providence-Plantations, in New-England in America* (Newport, R.I., 1767), 63, 176; An Act to Reform the Penal Laws, in *The Public Laws of the State of Rhode Island and Providence Plantations, as Revised by a Committee* (Providence, R.I., 1798), 584–605.

[79] John Murrin, "Magistrates, Sinners, and a Precarious Liberty: Trial by Jury in Seventeenth Century New England," in David D. Hall et al., eds., *Saints and Revolutionaries: Essays on Early American History* (New York, 1984), 168.

[80] See, e.g., the 18 Car. I, Act XXII (1642–3), in William Waller Hening, *The Statutes at Large* (New York, 1823), 1:254.

[81] 18 Car. I, Act XXII (1642–3), in ibid., 253–4. These provisions were reenacted with minor modifications (devolving punishment to the discretion of the court) in 9 Commonwealth, Act XV (1657–8), Concerning Hireing of Servants, in ibid., 439–40.

the party hired not merely to carry and produce the certificate but to surrender it to the new employer, thereupon becoming liable to restraint as a runaway on premature departure.[82] As for any person who "comeing free into the country shalby any contract agree with any person, and before the time agreed for be accomplished shall depart to another, hee shall performe the tenor of his contract first made, and pay the apparent damage that shall arise by his breach of covenants, and shall after that satisfyed, be lyable to the payment of what damages any other contractor with him shall recover of him by law."[83] The colony also early adopted, virtually word-for-word, the Statute of Artificers' prohibitions on premature departure of artisans and laborers employed on task work.[84] Court records from the 1630s and 1640s reveal that hired laborers were indeed made subject to court orders to perform agreed terms of service in the face of refusal to enter service subsequent to agreement or early departure, and on the basis of parol as well as written agreements.[85] Artisans contracting to perform specific tasks were also made subject to court orders to perform, though less consistently.[86]

After the middle of the seventeenth century, however, this regime appears to have eased somewhat, and there are indications that, legally as well as socially, indentured servitude and hireling labor in the Chesapeake became more distinct conditions.[87] The 1632 prohibitions on abandonment of work by artificers and laborers

[82] 14 Car. II, Act CI (1661–2), Hired Servants, in ibid., 2:115–16.

[83] Ibid., 116. See also, generally, *An Abridgement of the Laws in Force and Use in her Majesties Plantations* (London, 1704), 59–61.

[84] 8 Car. I, Act XXVIII (1632), in *Statutes at Large*, 1:193. Unlike Rhode Island, the Virginia version included the sanction of imprisonment.

[85] See, e.g., *Matter of Michael Bryant*, in Susie M. Ames, ed., *County Court Records of Accomack-Northampton, Virginia, 1632–1640* (1954: Millwood, N.Y., 1975), 29 (1635); *Matter of William Standley, John Parramoore v. Edward Robins, Matter of Rowland Vaughan*, and *Matter of Christopher Bryan*, all in idem, ed., *County Court Records of Accomack-Northampton, Virginia, 1640–1645* (Charlottesville, 1973), 61–2, 63 (1640); 218–9 (1642); 285, 289 (1643); and 326 (1644).

[86] See, e.g., *Matter of William Johnson and Martin Kennett*, and *Matter of John Knight*, both in Ames, ed., *Court Records of Accomack-Northampton, 1640–1645*, 257(1643), 229–41 (1643); *Ambrose Daniel v. Thomas Paicie*, in John F. Dorman, ed., *Westmoreland County, Virginia, Order Book, 1690–1698* (Washington, D.C., 1962), 18 (1691); *Hunt v. Dawson, Durant v. Weavor*, and *Fisher v. Charleton* (1699), all in Mattie E. Parker, ed., *North Carolina Higher Court Records, 1697–1701* (Raleigh, 1971), 144 (1697), 248 (1698), 341 (1699).

[87] In 1688, e.g., we find the Charles City County Court holding that "it is very dubious whether or not a hired servant shall be equally punishable as an indentured servant if he strikes his master" (*Petition of Thomas Reeve*, in Benjamin B. Weisiger, ed., *Charles City County, Virginia, Court Orders, 1687–1695* [n.p., 1980], 161). Also, in the Maryland case *Glover v. Davis*, 54 Md. Arch. 393 (Talbot County, 1666), the defendant's failure to perform an agreement to work for the plaintiff resulted in a verdict of damages rather than an order to perform or the invocation of criminal sanctions.

It is worth noting that even in the earliest statutes (cited above at n. 81) hirelings and indentured servants were treated as distinct categories of persons. See also the early cases *Parramoore v. Robins*, where a departing hired servant was treated by the court in a manner substantially different from the normal treatment of a runaway indentured servant; and *Elizabeth Savage v. John Pyle*, where the court upheld the contention of the plaintiff that her employment by the defendant (on an oral agreement) was at will. Both cases are in Ames, ed., *Court Records of Accomack-Northampton, 1640–1645*, 219 (1642), 353 (1644). Also, in a couple of early cases there are hints of what may have been a practice of requiring employees to post a surety against early departure, implying the insufficiency of statutory disciplines to control hired labor. See, e.g., *Articles of Agreement between William Roper and John Booth*, in Ames, ed., *Court Records*

were not reenacted by Virginia's "Grand Assembly" of 1661 and therefore lapsed. Nor did the subsequent omnibus Virginia statutes regulating servant and slaves reproduce the earlier provisions requiring specific performance of contracts by persons coming free into the country. The first of those statues, passed in 1705, continued to require that all freed servants obtain freedom certificates and lodge these with successor employers so that "poor people may not be destitute of emploiment, under suspicion of their being servants" and continued to apply, at least in some of its elements, not only to "imported" servants (whether bound by indenture or according to the custom of the country) but also to those "become servants of their own accord here" and "hired" servants; but the majority of its clauses were devoted to the regulation of indentured servants. The 1748 omnibus statute, however, conspicuously omitted all reference to persons "become servants of their own accord" and confined itself to servants "by act of parliament, indenture or custom" alone. The 1748 act also omitted the 1705 act's direct requirement that freed indentured servants lodge their certificates of freedom with successor employers.[88] This pattern of differentiation between imported servants and hirelings continued in the second half of the century. Thus in 1774, "it must be understood that Servants are here distinguished from Slaves, and that they are also different from Hirelings, who engage themselves in the Service of another, without being obliged thereto by Transportation, or indenture."[89]

of Accomack-Northampton, 1640–1645, 279–80 (1643). A distinction between servants and hirelings is also implied by midcentury Maryland cases involving suits brought by prematurely departing hired laborers for unpaid wages. See *Knages v. Bouls*, 53 Md. Arch. 158 (Charles County, 1661); *Price v. Wheeler*, 53 Md. Arch. 385 (Charles County, 1663). On changes in the condition of free and indentured labor in the seventeenth- and eighteenth-century Chesapeake in general see Edmund S. Morgan, *American Slavery, American Freedom: The Ordeal of Colonial Virginia* (New York, 1975), 295–387; Lorena S. Walsh, "Servitude and Opportunity in Charles County, Maryland, 1658–1705," in Aubrey C. Land et al., eds., *Law, Society, and Politics in Early Maryland* (Baltimore, 1977), 118–28; Lois Green Carr and Russell R Menard, "Immigration and Opportunity: The Freedman in Early Colonial Maryland," in Thad W. Tate et al., eds., *The Chesapeake in the Seventeenth Century: Essays on Anglo-American Society* (New York, 1979); Allan Kulikoff, *Tobacco and Slaves: The Development of Southern Cultures in the Chesapeake, 1680–1800* (Chapel Hill, 1986), 30–44; Russo, *Free Workers in a Plantation Economy*, 314; Daniel, "Alternative Workers in a Slave Economy."

[88] See 4 Anne, c. 49, An Act Concerning Servants and Slaves (1705), in *Statutes at Large*, 3:447–62; and cf. 22 Geo. II, c. 14, An Act Concerning Servants and Slaves (1748), in ibid., 5:547–58. In 1726 an act amending the 1705 act was passed inter alia in response to complaints that persons "under pretence of understanding several trades and misteries, have procured large sums of money, to be advanced to them, and have entered into covenants with merchants, and others, in Great-Britain, for the paiment of large wages, yearly, though they were totally ignorant of, and unable to perform, such trades and misteries." See 12 Geo. I, c. 4, An Act for Amending the Act Concerning Servants and Slaves (1726), in ibid., 4:168–75, at 174–5. The amending act added provisions to the 1705 act making any person "imported into this colony, as a tradesman or workman, on wages" who "shall be found not to understand such trade, or emploiment," liable to prosecution by their "master or owner." A verdict confirming the fraud would result in compensation to the master or owner "of such servant," if money had been advanced, by deduction of wages or further time of service. The 1726 amendments also provided that such an "imported" tradesman or workman who refused or neglected to perform was liable to serve two days for every day of nonperformance, "after his time, by indenture or former order of court, is expired." These provisions were reenacted in 1748.

[89] Richard Starke, *The Office and Authority of a Justice of Peace* (Williamsburg, 1774), 318–19. Noting further that masters were held responsible for the maintenance of their "servants," Starke concluded (319,

As in Virginia, so in South Carolina. South Carolina's first (1717) omnibus statute "for the better governing and regulating white servants," although aimed largely at indentured servants, also contained provisions reproducing Virginia's requirement of specific performance by freemen and regulating persons become servants "by contract for wages" and also "hired labourers." By 1744, when a new act was passed, however, the latter references had disappeared. The 1744 act dealt solely with indentured servants.[90] The North Carolina act of 1741 "Concerning Servants and Slaves," in contrast, was broader, its ambit extending to all servants engaging for a term of years by importation, indenture, "or otherwise."[91] But James Davis's 1774 manual for local justices, *The Office and Authority of a Justice of Peace*, made it clear that by then, as in Virginia, "servant" meant an imported indentured servant.[92]

As in New England, throughout the colonial era one finds in both the Chesapeake colonies and the Carolinas a clear correlation between servitude and youth. In their study of Middlesex County, Virginia, for example, Darrett Rutman and Anita Rutman found that preslavery Virginia's indentured servant population was heavily skewed toward adolescent and unmarried young adult males in the age range 15–25.[93]

emphasis added) that "the Labor *and Obedience* of Servants are intended as a Compensation to their Masters for their Care and Protection."

The Act Concerning Servants of 1785 expressly limited its jurisdiction by defining servants as "white persons not being citizens of any of the confederated states of America, who shall come into this commonwealth under contract to serve another in any trade or occupation." See 10 Commonwealth, c. 83, in *Statutes at Large*, 8:190–1. Further confirmation came in the Act Reducing into one, the several Acts concerning Servants of 1792. See 17 Commonwealth, c. 132, in *A Collection of All Such Acts of the General Assembly of Virginia, of a Public and Permanent Nature, as are now in Force* (Richmond, 1803), 247–9.

[90] For South Carolina see An Act for the Better Governing and Regulating White Servants (1717), in Nicholas Trott, *The Laws of the Province of South Carolina* (Charlestown, S.C., 1736), 312–19, esp. at sec. 7; and cf. the act of 1744, in William Simpson, *The Practical Justice of the Peace and Parish Officer, of His Majesty's Province of South Carolina* (Charlestown, S.C., 1761), 227–38, at the same section. Simpson's reproduction of sample legal forms (summonses, warrants, etc.) show that "servant" meant "indented servant" (237–8).

[91] See *A Collection of all the Public Acts of Assembly, of the Province of North Carolina: Now in Force and Use* (New Bern, N.C., 1751), 161–73, at 161. The act also copied Virginia's provisions in regard to tradesmen or workmen imported on indenture. See n. 88 above.

[92] James Davis, *The Office and Authority of a Justice of Peace* (New Bern, N.C., 1774), 310–20.

[93] Darrett B. Rutman and Anita H. Rutman, *A Place in Time: Middlesex County, Virginia, 1650–1750* (New York, 1984), 71. See also Walsh, "Servitude and Opportunity," 113–15; James Horn, "Servant Emigration to the Chesapeake in the Seventeenth Century," in Tate et al., eds., *The Chesapeake in the Seventeenth Century*, 61, 65. It seems clear that both in age and in demographic and social background emigrant indentured servants and English servants in husbandry were substantially the same genus. See Dunn, "Recruitment and Employment of Labor," 161–3; David Souden, " 'Rogues, Whores, and Vagabonds'? Indentured Servant Emigrants to North America and the Case of Mid-Seventeenth-Century Bristol," *Social History*, 3, 1 (Jan. 1978), 23–41. See also Russell R. Menard, "British Migration to the Chesapeake Colonies in the Seventeenth Century," in Lois Green Carr et al., eds., *Colonial Chesapeake Society* (Chapel Hill, 1988), 99–132, at 128–9. Menard finds that throughout the seventeenth century servants were overwhelmingly young, single males "aged between sixteen and twenty-five at arrival," and that once the initial and more heterogeneous flow of migrants had slackened, the age profile of incoming servants tended to become more markedly youthful as the century progressed. For additional evidence on the youth of indentured migrants, together with exploration of reasons for their decisions to emigrate, see Farley Grubb, "Fatherless and Friendless: Factors Influencing the Flow of English Emigrant Servants," *Journal of Economic History*, 52, 1 (Mar. 1992), 85–108.

Available court records tend to confirm this pattern. In Maryland, for example, of 49 servants imported without indenture presented to the Prince George's County Court between 1696 and 1699, 48 were judged to be 20 years of age or younger. Their average age was 15.3 years.[94] In the longest run of published North Carolina county court records I have been able to access, those of the Court of Pleas and Quarter Sessions of Cumberland County, 1755–1791, all indentures of servitude recorded before the court are of minors, and there is no example of a court proceeding involving an indentured servant who is clearly an adult.[95]

The Middle Colonies

The same patterns hold elsewhere. In Delaware, Kent County court records describe a servant population at the end of the seventeenth century consisting overwhelmingly of orphans and imported juveniles, together with a few voluntarily or involuntarily bound adult debtors.[96] All these "servants" were indentured: There is no indication that wage labor, as such, was identified with unfreedom or criminal discipline.[97] Subsequent Delaware statutes regulating servants dealt only with bound labor.[98] In New Jersey, too, local statute law regulating servants was directed exclusively at the institution of indentured servitude, with unindentured wage labor thought of socially and legally as a distinct – and unregulated – status.[99] The same appears to be the case in New York[100] and also in Pennsylvania, one of the major

[94] See Joseph H. Smith and Philip A. Crowl, eds., *Court Records of Prince Georges County, Maryland, 1696–99* (1964; Millwood, N.Y., 1975).

[95] See William C. Fields, ed., *Abstract of the Minutes of the Court of Pleas and Quarter Sessions of Cumberland County, 1755–1791*, 2 vols. (Cumberland County, N.C., 1977–81), 2v. See also Morris, *Government and Labor in Early America*, 391–2.

[96] Leon de Valinger, ed., *Court Records of Kent County, Delaware, 1680–1705* (Washington, 1959).

[97] One may, e.g., note that Captain William Darvall's notice of appointment of his friend William Borne as his attorney to manage a Kent County plantation empowered Borne "to take In att his pleasure any freemen or buy any saruant or saruants" (ibid., 61).

[98] See 13 Geo. II, c. 77 (1739), An Act for the Better Regulation of Servants and Slaves Within This Government, in John D. Cushing, comp., *The First Laws of the State of Delaware* (Wilmington, 1981), I, i:210–16.

[99] See the act of 1713/14, An Act for Regulating of White Servants, in Bernard Bush, *Laws of the Royal Colony of New Jersey, 1703–1745* (Trenton, 1977), 2:140–3. The preamble of this statute indicates that it was conceived as a regulation of *indentured* servants and that it confined that category to persons *imported* into the province. This also seems to have been the case at the time of passage of the earliest general enactments for the Jersey colonies. See the Bill for the General Laws of the Province of East Jersey (March 1682) and the Acts and Laws of the General Free Assembly for the Province of West New Jersey (May 1682), both in *The Grants, Concessions and Original Constitutions of the Province of New Jersey* (Philadelphia, 1758), esp. 236–7, 447. New Jersey's provisions for taxation also reproduced the common eighteenth-century distinction between servant and hireling, categorizing "single Man that works for hire" separately from "bought servant". See, e.g., the act of 1752 "for the Support of Government," in Bush, *Laws*, 3:200–1. On the other hand, the colony's 1758 settlement provisions recognized a category of "hired servant" (although the Act to explain what shall be a legal Settlement of 1740 did not). Bush, *Laws*, 3:599–615, and 2:526–9.

[100] See the act of 1684 "Concerning Masters, Servants, Slaves, Labourers and Apprentices," in *Records of the States of the United States* (microform), ser. B2, New York, reel 1, amending the Duke of York's Laws (1665), tit. "Masters, Servants and Labourers," in John D. Cushing, ed., *The Earliest Printed Laws of New*

recipients of indentured servants in the eighteenth century.[101] In the latter colony, for example, we find the assembled representatives in 1756 distinguishing between their "hired labourers" and their imported "servants" in the course of petitioning the governor for relief from the pressures of enlistment:

The House being informed, by Petition from the Masters, that a great number of bought Servants are lately inlisted by the Recruiting Officers now in this Province . . . we beg Leave to lay this Grievance before the Governor. We presume that no one Colony on the Continent has afforded more free Recruits to the King's Forces than Pennsylvania. . . . By this, and the Necessity we are under of keeping up a large Body of Men to defend our own extensive Frontiers, we are drained of our hired Labourers; and as this province has but few slaves we are now obliged to depend principally upon our Servants to assist us in tilling our lands. If these are taken from us, we are at a Loss to conceive how the Provisions that may be expected out of this Province another year, for the Support of the King's Armies, are to be raised."[102]

So far as the day-to-day regulation of labor in the middle colonies is concerned, published court records are as yet scarce. One can gain considerable insight into the routine activities of local courts and justices, however, by reference to the abridgements of English justice of the peace manuals compiled locally for the guidance of colonial justices. During the eighteenth century six editions of the so-called *Conductor Generalis*

York, 1665–1693 (Wilmington, Del., 1978), 151–2. New York's legislation was sparse. The colony passed no omnibus servants statute during the colonial period. What it did pass, however, indicated that "servants" comprehended minors or other persons bound by written indenture rather than the generality of hired labor. Thus the act of 1766 "For the Regulation of Servants" (*Laws of New York*, 7 Geo. III, c. 1306) covered minors or others bound by written contract "for a Term of Years, or any shorter Time" and provided "that no such Contract shall bind any Infant longer than until Arrival to the full Age of twenty-one Years, excepting such as are or shall be brought into this Colony from beyond Sea, and are and shall be bound in Order to raise Money for the Payment of their Passages." These provisions were reconfirmed in the act of 1788 "Concerning Apprentices and Servants" (*Laws of New York*, 11th Session, c. 13), and in the act of 1802 "Concerning Apprentices and Servants" (*Laws of New York*, 24th Session, c. 11). Robert Steinfeld has argued that legislation limiting indentured servitude to minors and immigrants was a postrevolutionary development (*Invention of Free Labor*, 132–3). As the New Jersey and the New York examples indicate, however, such limitations were a common feature of colonial legislative practice well prior to the Revolution.

[101] See the Duke of York's Laws (1664), tit. "Masters, Servants and Labourers" (N.B. the "American Addendum"); "Laws Agreed Upon in England" (1682), paras. 23 and 29; and "Laws Made att an Assembly Held att Philadelphia" (1683), chaps. 139 and 153; all in Gail McKnight Beckman, ed., *The Statutes at Large of Pennsylvania in the Time of William Penn* (New York, 1976), 1:98, 123, 157, and 165. See also An Act for the better Regulation of the Servants in this Province and Territories (1700), in John D. Cushing, ed., *The Earliest Printed Laws of Pennsylvania, 1681–1713* (Wilmington, Del., 1978) 15–17; and the "Supplement" of 1771, in *Records of the United States*, ser. B2, Pennsylvania, reel 3.

[102] The Pennsylvania legislature is quoted in Benjamin Franklin, *An Historical Review of the Constitution and Government of Pennsylvania* (London, 1759), 322–3. See also Matthews, "The Terms Hired Man and Help," 14. On the regulation of indentured servitude in Pennsylvania, see Salinger, "*To Serve Well and Faithfully,*" 80–1. It is worth noting that, according to Franklin, the distinction between indentured servants and other forms of labor was that their "purchaser, by a positive Law, has a legal Property in them during the Term they are bound for" (Franklin, *Historical Review*, 93). See also Benjamin Franklin to Sir Everard Fawkener (27 July 1756) in Leonard W. Labaree, ed., *The Papers of Benjamin Franklin* (New Haven, 1963), 6:472–6, at 474 (identifying servants in Pennsylvania as indentured emigrants and as largely children, and distinguishing "servants" from "hired Labourers" and "Journeymen"). See also the discussion of the court in *Respublica v. Catharine Keppele*, 1 Yeates 233 (1793), esp. 235–7.

were published in New York, Pennsylvania, and New Jersey for the use of northern and middle colony justices. According to the American manuals' leading historian, "the similarity of content between the English and the American manuals is striking" and attests to the closeness with which the colonies followed local English practice. All the more striking in this instance, then, is that out of all those manuals not a single one reproduced *any* of the English law dealing with wage labor – case or statute – which appears voluminously in the English manuals. In other words, so far as the abridgers were concerned, colonial justices would have no use for anything that appeared in English manuals concerning the legal regulation of wage labor.[103]

CONCLUSION

The legal discipline of service, then, appears to have been largely and increasingly confined during the colonial period to the case of persons imported as indentured servants or bound out by local authorities,[104] as governed by local legislation. What Zephaniah Swift said at the end of the eighteenth century in his discussion of Connecticut law he might well have extended to the prerevolutionary mainland colonies as a whole:"labourers, or persons hired by the days work, or any longer time, are not by our law or in common speech considered as servants."[105] The

[103] See *Conductor Generalis; or a Guide for Justice of the Peace* (New York, 1711); *Conductor Generalis; of the Office, Duty and Authority of Justices of the Peace* (Philadelphia, 1722); James Parker, *Conductor Generalis: or the Office, Duty and Authority of Justices of the Peace* (New York, 1749). Before the Revolution further editions of the last were published in Philadelphia in 1749, 1750, and 1764; and in Woodbridge, New Jersey, in 1764 and 1767. After the Revolution editions were published in New York in 1788 and 1790; in Philadelphia in 1792; and in Albany in 1794. See also Conley, "Doing It by the Book," 265. Conley's is the most complete account of colonial justice of the peace manuals. He shows that the *Conductor* was in all essentials an abridgement of the English manuals compiled by Michael Dalton, Richard Burn, and, particularly, William Nelson, all of which, as we have seen, included extensive sections outlining English statute and common law governing labor. The work of abridgement was largely undertaken by editors who were themselves colonial justices and thus intimately acquainted with the scope and nature of the justice's business. Parker's 1764 Woodbridge, N.J., edition, e.g., was abridged out of Burn and stated in its introductory pages that its purpose was to provide a clear guide unencumbered by "matters which no way concern these parts of America" (iii).
All editions of the *Conductor* carried sections on "apprentices" based closely on their English counterparts. It is clear, however, that this apprenticeship regulation had no carryover effect on wage labor. This conclusion may be confirmed by examination of those editions of the *Conductor* based on William Nelson's English original. Nelson organized his manual alphabetically and included law governing servants and laborers under the title of apprenticeship. The *Conductor*'s editors copied his organization and his section on the law governing apprentices but carefully cut out of that section all references to anything other than juvenile apprenticeship.
[104] As in service for debt or on conviction of crime or, in the case of the children of paupers, bound out as apprentices or servants by local authorities.
[105] Zephaniah Swift, *A System of the Laws of the State of Connecticut* (Windham, Conn., 1795), 1:218. We have already encountered a similar statement from Richard Starke in the case of prerevolutionary Virginia. See n. 89 above. In *Government and Labor in Early America*, at 446, Richard B. Morris provides evidence allowing the same conclusion to be drawn with reference to Pennsylvania. In 1771 the glass manufacturer Henry Stiegel attempted to resolve a dispute with a skilled craftsman who had quit his employment in an argument over wages owed by offering a reward for the man's apprehension as a

description *servant* can be found applied, as in English husbandry, to the young and the single put out or hiring themselves out to others for extended terms during adolescence or early adulthood,[106] although Swift's comment suggests that use of the term varied according to region.[107] It may also have been a description more in the eye of the European beholder than the local population. Writing of his travels in the late 1740s in the northern and middle colonies, for example, the Swedish visitor Peter Kalm reported, "The servants which are employed in the English-American colonies are either free persons or slaves," and those who were entirely free (that is, not indentured) "serve by the year." Crucially, however, Kalm went on to observe that "they are not only allowed to leave their service at the expiration of their year, *but may leave it at any time when they do not agree with their masters.*" In other words, Kalm's contemporary account, like the legal record, evidences no carryover to the colonies of English law disciplining wage labor, even when voluntarily covenanting by the year.[108] Further support for this conclusion may be found in the preface to

---

runaway. The workman offered the following public rejoinder (in the *Pennsylvania Packet*, 11 Nov. 1771): "I am not, by the laws of nature, to drudge and spend my whole life and strength in performing my part of the articles, and Mr. Stiegel not paying me my wages. I have taken the opinion of an eminent gentleman of the law upon the articles, who declares, no person can be justified in apprehending me, as I am no servant, and that any person so doing will subject himself to an action of false imprisonment." See also William Deane's suit against his employer some hundred and forty years earlier in Essex County, Massachusetts, "for prosecuting him after the manner of a runaway, the plaintiff being free" (above, n. 49).

[106] Instances of voluntary covenants to serve may be found in all the published colonial court records used in this study, although they are not common. For one group of examples, see de Valinger, *Court Records of Kent County, Delaware*. Such covenants are also noted by Eric G. Nellis in his study of labor in colonial Massachusetts, "Communities of Workers: Free Labor in Provincial Massachusetts, 1690–1765" (Ph.d. diss., University of British Columbia, 1979), 120–4. See also Cheesman A. Herrick, *White Servitude in Pennsylvania: Indentured and Redemption Labor in Colony and Commonwealth* (Philadelphia, 1929), 100–12. Considering involuntary (e.g., servitude for misdemeanor) as well as voluntary bindings, Herrick concludes that only a small minority of indentured servants came from domestic sources.

[107] Albert Matthews's work also suggest regional variation. See "The Terms Hired Man and Help," 243–54.

[108] Adolph B. Benson, *Peter Kalm's Travels in North America; The English Version of 1770* (New York, 1987), 204 (emphasis supplied). See also Steinfeld, *Invention of Free Labor*, 51; Beales, "Ebenezer Parkman's Farm Workers," 132–3; *Tirrel v. Read*, in David T. Konig, ed., *Plymouth Court Records, 1686–1859* (Wilmington, Del., 1978), 5:388 (1731). An examination of the Plymouth court records – easily the most comprehensive set of eighteenth-century court proceedings available in published form – discloses no instance of resort to the common law actions against enticement, beating, and so forth that protected an employer's property rights in services except in cases involving apprentices or indentured Indian or black servants or slaves. See *Crymble v. Graffton, Bailey v. Cutler, Hayward v. Clark, Morton v. Morton, and Alden v. Delano*, all in Konig, *Plymouth Court Records*, 5:233 (1727), 267 (1727), and 573 (1736); 6:8 (1736); and 7:56 (1746). It is also worth noting Charles Grant's observation that Kent's adult hirelings do not feature in the town's court records (*Democracy in the Connecticut Frontier Town of Kent*, 95). On mobility as a distinguishing characteristic of the colonial labor force see Rediker, "Good Hands, Stout Heart, and Fast Feet,"237–9. On this see also generally Laurel Thatcher Ulrich, "Martha Ballard and Her Girls: Women's Work in Eighteenth Century Maine"; Paul G. E. Clemens and Lucy Simler, "Rural Labor and the Farm Household in Chester County, Pennsylvania, 1750–1820"; Billy G. Smith, "The Vicissitudes of Fortune: The Careers of Laboring Men in Philadelphia, 1750–1800"; and Marcus Rediker, "The Anglo-American Seaman as Collective Worker, 1700–1759"; all in Innes, ed., *Work and Labor in Early America*, 70–105, 106–43, 221–51, and 252–86. In "Good Hands," Rediker argues that throughout the colonies "well-oiled" legal machinery ruthlessly punished labor mobility. It is certainly the case that

Joseph Greenleaf's *An Abridgment of Burn's Justice of the Peace and Parish Officer*, published in Boston in 1773, which repeated explicitly what the several editions of the *Conductor Generalis* had indicated earlier in the century, that English laws regulating labor simply had not been adopted. "The circle of a justice's business in [England] is vastly extensive, and is founded chiefly on acts of the British Parliament, which can never have any relation to this colony, such parts are therefore not taken into this abridgment. What we have rejected relates to acts made for the regulating their . . . servants . . . and a number of articles under other heads of no possible use or importance to us in *America*."[109] On this subject, local statute law, with its fairly specific delimitations of the ambit of servitude, was all the law there was.[110]

indentured servants were liable to strict controls but not, as I have tried to demonstrate, the generality of nonbound labor. The only significant but important exception to this rule involved seamen, who were subject to extensive statutory controls in some colonies. See Tomlins, "The Ties That Bind," 208n. For further confirmation see also Jonathan Prude, "To Look upon the 'Lower Sort': Runaway Ads and the Appearance of Unfree Laborers in America, 1750–1800," *Journal of American History*, 78, 1 (June 1991), 124–59, at 124, 139. Prude finds that "runaways were overwhelmingly unfree workers," that is, bound apprentices, indentured servants, convict laborers, and chattel slaves. The only exceptions were fugitive soldiers, criminals, and absconding family dependents (children and, occasionally, wives).

[109] Joseph Greenleaf, *An Abridgment of Burn's Justice of the Peace and Parish Officer* (Boston, 1773), preface (emphasis in original). See also the preface to the 1722 Philadelphia edition of the *Conductor Generalis*. Like the prerevolutionary justice of the peace books, Eliphalet Ladd's *Burn's Abridgment, or the American Justice* (Dover, N.H., 1792) also omitted those sections of Burn dealing with servants.

[110] As the colonial justice of the peace guides indicate, there was no general colonial reception of English labor statutes. As far as Massachusetts is concerned, Chief Justice Lemuel Shaw stated in *Commonwealth v. Hunt*, 45 Mass. 111 (1842), 122: "All those laws of the parent country, whether rules of the common law, or early English statutes, which were made for the purpose of regulating the wages of laborers, the settlement of paupers, and making it penal for anyone to use a trade or handicraft to which he had not served a full apprenticeship – not being adapted to the circumstances of our colonial condition – were not adopted, used or approved, and therefore do not come within the description of the laws adopted and confirmed by the [reception] provision of the [Massachusetts] constitution." The reception statutes of South Carolina (Act 312 of 1712, in Thomas Cooper, ed., *The Statutes at Large of South Carolina* [Columbia, S.C., 1837], 401) and of North Carolina (Ch. 1 of 1749, in Walter Clark, ed., *The State Records of North Carolina* [Goldsboro, N.C., 1904], 23:317) also both ignored the English labor statutes, as did the 1808 *Report of the Judges of the Supreme Court of Pennsylvania, of the English Statutes, which are in force in the Commonwealth of Pennsylvania*, in 3 Binney 595–626; also *Journal of the Nineteenth House of Representatives of the Commonwealth of Pennsylvania*, for 20 Dec. 1808 (Lancaster, Pa, 1808), 88–117. And see the opinion of Brackenridge J. in *Ex Parte Meason*, 5 Binney 167, 180 (1812). A full list of the English statutes judged to have been received in Pennsylvania during the colonial period may be found appended to the *Report*. None of the labor statutes are mentioned. In Virginia it was early announced that "the statutes for artificers and workmen are thought fitt to be published in this colony," 7 Car. I, Act XXX (1631–2, in *Statutes at Large*, 1:167), but this referred to the 1 Jac., c. 6 of 1604, establishing procedures for wage regulation, not to the statutes of laborers and artificers, which had preceded it. Nor in any case did this "publication" survive the Grand Assembly of March 1661/2 and its wholesale reform of Virginia legislation (although the Northampton County Court appears to consider this statute still in force in a case brought before it in 1663. See Morris, *Government and Labor in Early America*, 89). Some elements of the Statute of Artificers were, as we have seen, adopted piecemeal during the first half of the seventeenth century through local enactment, but little of its regulation of unindentured labor survived the seventeenth century, and in 1803, St. George Tucker noted briefly, "The statute 5 Eliz. c. 4 [The Statute of Artificers] . . . is not in force in Virginia" (*Blackstone's Commentaries* [Philadelphia, 1803], 2:425). Rhode Island appears to be the only colonial jurisdiction where the Statute of Artificers had any eighteenth-century resonance.

Precisely because the ambit of master/servant relations and the construction of authority and subordination were thus explicitly delimited during the colonial era, the discourse of servitude was uncontroversial. The scope of its application was known to both those who fell within that scope and those who did not, and the means of passage from servile to nonservile status were reasonably clear. Nor was there any trace, during the eighteenth century, of any American reproduction of the English move toward punitive statutes generalizing master/servant discipline. Rather, the opposite was the case.

That the discourse of servitude became more controversial in the early nineteenth century is perhaps as good a sign as any of an intrusion of uncertainty, an undermining of older delimitations and categories. To be sure, some of the heightened attention can be attributed to the egalitarian republican sensitivities aroused during the Revolution and its aftermath – some, but not all. For in fact, postrevolutionary appraisals did not expunge the discourse of master and servant from American law in deference to the popular culture of freedom and democracy. Far from dying out, the discourse of master and servant underwent generalization.

Democracy nevertheless shaped the process and results of this generalization in the early republic. Thus, in contrast to England, where the re-creation of master and servant as a generic law of employment had a major legislated component of criminalized restraint, in America legislatures stood by and let the delimited statutory regimes of the colonial era fall into irrelevance. In America, the project of creating a generic law of employment was a juridical enterprise. Hence what resulted was a common law regime. This regime provided the modality of rule for the early republic's employment relationship.

8

Master and servant in republican America

"When I use a word," Humpty Dumpty said, in rather a scornful tone, "it means just what I choose it to mean – neither more nor less."

"The question is," said Alice, "whether you can make words mean so many different things."

"The question is," said Humpty Dumpty, "which is to be master – that's all."

Lewis Carroll, *Through the Looking Glass, And What Alice Found There*

During the first half of the nineteenth century, the number of Americans employed by others, in agricultural and nonagricultural pursuits, increased markedly. Nonagricultural employment grew particularly rapidly. Off the farm, between 1820 and 1850 the number of persons working rose from approximately 800,000 to slightly less than 3 million. Over the same period the number of agricultural workers increased at a lower rate, from slightly over 2 million in 1820 to almost 5 million in 1850. By midcentury, on and off the farm, it seems likely that the proportion of productively engaged Americans employed by others – about one-third in 1820 – had increased to about one-half. In the Eastern industrializing states (Massachusetts, Pennsylvania, New York) the proportion was probably closer to three-fourths.[1]

The most obvious sign of this sociological transformation in the organization and

---

[1] See Bureau of the Census, *Historical Statistics of the United States: Colonial Times to 1970* (Washington, D.C., 1975), vol. I, series A 6–8, A 119–34, C 75–84, and D 167–81. See also Bryan D. Palmer, "Social Formation and Class Formation in North America, 1800–1900," in David Levine, ed., *Proletarianization and Family History* (Orlando, 1984), 229–309, at 249. The first U.S. occupational census was not conducted until 1870. This showed, according to David Montgomery, that at that time 67 percent of "productively engaged Americans" were dependent upon employment by others. Working with the same census, Daniel T. Rodgers concludes that in agricultural states "probably half the labor force was employed" but that in industrializing states the proportion varied from a range of 65–75 percent in Pennsylvania to a high approaching 85 percent in Massachusetts. See David Montgomery, *Beyond Equality: Labor and the Radical Republicans, 1862–1872* (New York, 1967), 26–30; Daniel T. Rodgers, *The Work Ethic in Industrial America, 1850–1920* (Chicago, 1979), 37. See also William E. Forbath, "The Ambiguities of Free Labor: Labor and the Law in the Gilded Age," *Wisconsin Law Review*, 1985, no. 6: 767–817, at 779n.

performance of work was the appearance of an increasingly numerous population of free hireling laborers. By 1850, outside the southern slave economy, work in America had become a far less heterogeneous relationship than it had been throughout the colonial period, acquiring a uniform definition and set of characteristics as a single universal and impersonal relation founded on wage labor.[2]

This transformation in the social relations of employment was attended – indeed it was heralded – by major changes in American law.[3] No area of the country was untouched, as changes almost everywhere in the law of employment attest. Their effect was twofold. On the one hand the declining social importance of indentured servitude brought a steady erosion of the specific locally defined statutory disciplines associated with that status and refined throughout the colonial era. Property rights in the person of another came increasingly to be perceived as anomalous and as politically indefensible in the new world of free exchange of labor. Bound labor was acceptable only when the parties could be represented as involved in something other than an exchange relationship – in the case of apprenticeship, for example, as fiduciaries.[4] As Robert Steinfeld has shown, this atrophy of voluntary servitude lent American conceptions of "free labor" added clarity through the increasingly unambiguous association of compulsion with the "other" of chattel slavery.[5]

Simultaneously, however, American legal texts began to make reference to a new

---

[2] See Christopher Clark, *The Roots of Rural Capitalism: Western Massachusetts, 1780–1860* (Ithaca, N.Y., 1990), 304–8; Alexander Keyssar, *Out of Work: The First Century of Unemployment in Massachusetts* (New York and Cambridge, 1986), 16; Stephen Innes, "Fulfilling John Smith's Vision: Work and Labor in Early America," in idem, ed., *Work and Labor in Early America* (Chapel Hill, 1988), 29–30. See generally Montgomery, *Beyond Equality*, 3–44.

[3] As we shall see, signs of discursive change begin to appear in American legal texts around the turn of the century. This is somewhat earlier than one would expect were one to explain legal change simply as a functional *response* to socioeconomic transformation, although see Sanford Jacoby, "The Duration of Indefinite Employment Contracts in the United States and England: An Historical Analysis," *Comparative Labor Law*, 5, 1 (Winter 1982), 85–128, who argues for significant socioeconomic transformation from the mid–eighteenth century. "The customary occupational structure became increasingly complex after the mid–eighteenth century. The rapid expansion of trade and industry shifted employment into occupations that did not easily fit the traditional categories for master and servant law"(91). The fact of change is undoubted. Revisiting the general argument of the first two parts of this book, we shall see that the American law of employment was a distinctly nineteenth-century creation, based upon a postrevolutionary "reception" of an Anglocentric common law discourse.

[4] On apprenticeship see, e.g., *Hall v. Gardner*, 1 Mass. 172 (1804), and *Davis v. Coburn*, 8 Mass. 299 (1811) (apprentices not assignable), and cf. *R. v. Inhabitants of St. George Hanover Square*, Burrow's Settlement Cases 12 (1734) (apprentices assignable). Nathan Dane, *A General Abridgment and Digest of American Law* (Boston, 1823), 1:254, commented that "the apprentice is with his master on a personal trust." Apprentices had generally been considered assignable in the colonies, and when not formally assigned their services were often hired out by the erstwhile master. On assignability see, e.g., Richard Starke, *The Office and Authority of a Justice of Peace* (Williamsburg, 1774), 12–13; Joseph Greenleaf, *An Abridgment of Burn's Justice of the Peace and Parish Officer* (Boston, 1773), 19. For examples of the hiring out of apprentices see *Shurtleff v. Burbanks* and *Foord v. Hooper*, both in David T. Konig, ed., *Plymouth Court Records, 1686–1859* (Wilmington, Del., 1978) 6:139 (1738) and 361 (1743). On the erosion of apprenticeship as a personal relation see generally William J. Rorabaugh, *The Craft Apprentice: From Franklin to the Machine Age in America* (New York, 1986), 57–75.

[5] See, generally, Robert J. Steinfeld, *The Invention of Free Labor: The Employment Relation in English and American Law and Culture, 1350–1870* (Chapel Hill, 1991), 137–60.

"generic" law of master and servant encompassing all employees rather than the carefully delimited categories of servants to whom colonial statutes had been addressed. As William E. Nelson has put it, courts began early in the nineteenth century to use master/servant concepts in dealing with persons, notably industrial laborers, "whose economic position was quite different from that of . . . traditional sorts of servants."[6] From this process there emerged eventually a single paradigmatic legal form, the contract of employment, in which were expressed simultaneous juridical commitments to the liberty of the individual to sell labor to all comers and to the right of the buyer of that labor to exercise disciplinary power over its disposal; that is, to continue to assert a property in the commodity – the labor power – that had been bought. "Free labor," then, did not mean free of legal incidents; and those incidents implanted in the employment relationship by the resort to the common law of master and servant meant that the emerging world of wage labor in the republic would be a world riddled with important and lasting asymmetries of power.[7]

THE LEGAL CONSTRUCTION OF THE EMPLOYMENT RELATION

The changes in American law and the manner of their propagation may best be described as a systematic juridical exegesis on English texts. In this process, as local statute law relevant only to the situation of bound labor fell into desuetude it was replaced by a new and pronounced juridical tendency to resort to English common law principles and precedents. Such developments are observable in all the regions of the country discussed in the previous chapter.

The South Atlantic Region

In Virginia, the changes can best be tracked by comparing successive editions of William Waller Hening's *New Virginia Justice*, a revised and updated sequel to Richard Starke's earlier *Office and Authority of a Justice of the Peace* (published in 1774). Unlike the abridged English justice of the peace manuals in use in the northern and middle colonies, Virginia manuals, beginning with George Webb's *Office and Authority of a Justice of the Peace*, had always attempted to integrate the provisions of local labor

---

[6] William E. Nelson, *Americanization of the Common Law: The Impact of Legal Change on Massachusetts Society, 1760–1830* (Cambridge, Mass., 1975), 125–6.

[7] This did not go unnoticed in contemporary opinion. Stephen Simpson commented in the "Preliminary Dissertation" to his *The Working Man's Manual: A New Theory of Political Economy, on the Principle of Production the Source of Wealth* (Philadelphia, 1831) that "we are bound by the highest and most sacred ties of moral, religious, and political obligation, to bring the condition of the people, in respect to the wages of labour, and the enjoyment of competence, to a level with their abstract political rights, which rights imply necessarily the possession of the property they may produce. . . . To substitute LAW for the distribution of labour, is to introduce the chief feature of the feudal systems of Europe, into the free, self-formed, and equitable republic of this country" (19).

statutes into their borrowings from English manuals. That is, rather than simply excising the irrelevant English sections and leaving it at that, the Virginia manuals spliced in details of local practices. In Hening's first (1795) edition, as in Starke and Webb before him, the section on servants was confined to a description of local practice and its local statutory basis. Just as Starke had reported twenty years before, Hening indicated that in local law "servant" and "hireling" were distinct statuses, the former referring only to servants imported under indenture, the latter describing citizens who worked for wages. About hirelings, local law was silent.[8] In his second (1810) edition, however, Hening noted that "the relation of master and servant" had become "of general concern" and in consequence added a completely new section entitled "Master and Servant" dependent for its substance entirely on Blackstone's *Commentaries* and other late eighteenth-century English sources, and reflective of their inclusion of wage labor within the ambit of the relation. Hening continued to carry a section on the local law of servants as he had in the 1795 edition, wherein it was stated that in Virginia law servants were "such as were formerly denominated indented servants." Concerning such persons, Hening went on, however, "many laws have been enacted, which have now become obsolete."[9]

The Mid-Atlantic and North Atlantic Regions

The same process of revision and extension may be observed in Connecticut, Pennsylvania, and New York. In his *System of the Laws of the State of Connecticut*, published in 1795, Zephaniah Swift did not attempt to hide the lack of consistency between the specific content of local law and social practices and the new generic legal category of "master and servant" derived from the accelerating postrevolutionary reception of English common law categories. Following Blackstone in entitling the relevant chapter "Of Master and Servant," Swift wrote that "a servant is a person subjected to the power and authority of a master for a limited time, upon a particular contract." He then proceeded to consider "who may be servants"; that is, the "several descriptions" of persons who actually were considered servants in local law. In Connecticut, servants might be "children ... bound out in service" until age twenty-one either by their parents or by civil authority. They might be apprentices similarly bound. Finally, they might be debtors "assigned in service for the payment of their debts." In addition, the word *servant* in Connecticut might also signify "menial servants or domestics." Such persons, however, were not "particularly recognized" in local law "and are so denominated from the nature of their employment." Most important, however, was Swift's categorical statement, which we have

---

[8] William Waller Hening, *The New Virginia Justice, Comprising the Office and Authority of a Justice of the Peace in the Commonwealth of Virginia* (Richmond, 1795), 405–7. (The 1795 edition was reprinted in 1799 without alteration.) Cf. George Webb, *The Office and Authority of a Justice of Peace* (Williamsburg, 1736); and Starke, *Office and Authority of a Justice of Peace*.

[9] William Waller Hening, *The New Virginia Justice. . . . The Second Edition, Revised, Corrected, Greatly Enlarged, and brought down to the Present Time* (Richmond, 1810), 393–5, 527–8; see also the third edition (Richmond, 1820), 466–8, 625–6.

already noted, that in Connecticut neither "labourers" nor indeed any person "hired by the day's work, or any longer time" were "by our law, or in common speech, considered as servants."[10]

The limited social and legal ambit of servitude in Connecticut revealed by Swift's description of local practice is striking. No less striking, however, is how rapidly this limited ambit disappeared from the books. Thus only twenty years after Zephaniah Swift had reported that hired laborers were not considered servants either in speech or in law, Tapping Reeve's *Law of Baron and Femme* (1816) followed Blackstone's lead without mention of local difference in stating just as categorically that day laborers *were* servants, along with apprentices, menials, and slaves.[11] Indeed, Reeve prefaced his entire discussion of master and servant with the general assertion that *anyone* who, by virtue of "some compact," had by law gained a right to exercise a personal authority over another was to be counted a master, and that *anyone* over whom such authority might rightfully be exercised was a servant. According to Reeve the master's authority originated in the agreement made between the parties and was thus independent of the provisions of local statute dealing with the several relations of servitude known in Connecticut.[12] *Any* agreement to labor for another, that is, was presumed to be agreement to the exercise of authority by that other over one for as long as the agreement continued.[13] This was a conception of master and servant much broader than that founded on particular life conditions or statuses – minor, debtor, indentured servant, vagrant – as reflected in the colonial statutes.[14] It was also one whose decisive influence Swift acknowledged when he published a revised edition of his *System* in 1822. First restating his original observation that hired laborers were clearly not servants according to local (that is, statute) law or practice, he then found it necessary to add for the first time that "yet while employed, the relative duties and liabilities of master and servant, subsist between them and their employers."[15] In other words, even as he continued to advance his

---

[10] Zephaniah Swift, *A System of the Laws of the State of Connecticut* (Windham, Conn., 1795), 1:218–20. The same conflict appears in other parts of Swift's treatise. The chapter entitled "Of Master and Servant" in volume 1 reflected almost entirely local authority. In his chapter "Of Actions for Injuries that Affect the Relative Rights of Individuals" in volume 2, however, Swift – this time drawing almost entirely on English sources for authority – held that the common law actions protective of a master's rights to property in his servant's services were applicable in the case of persons "whether hired or under any other obligation to serve" (see 1:218–24 and cf. 2:59–67, esp. 66). As in Hening, though less completely, the organization of Swift's treatise reproduces the separation between local and English law.

[11] Tapping Reeve, *The Law of Baron and Femme* (New Haven, 1816), 339. Reeve's treatise thus eclipsed the separation between local and English law reflected in Swift's treatment in favor of the latter.

[12] Ibid., 339. Reeve left unstated whether he considered the master's right to exercise authority to be common law right activated by the parties' agreement to enter into a contract for services or purely a creation of the parties, but the former was implied.

[13] Ibid., 482.

[14] We have already seen Blackstone do this. Tapping Reeve took the same tack in including the higher-status occupations – factors, brokers, auctioneers, and attorneys – in his classification of kinds of servants, while simultaneously, like Blackstone, denying that relationships involving these occupations were personal-service relationships.

[15] Zephaniah Swift, *Digest of the Laws of the State of Connecticut* (New Haven, 1822), 1:60–1 (here citing Blackstone's *Commentaries*).

earlier contention regarding the effect of local law, Swift felt required to confirm the reception of a whole new body of other-sourced common law doctrine to which hired labor in Connecticut was now to be considered subject.

Connecticut's "restatement" was followed in New York when Chancellor James Kent published his *Commentaries on American Law* in 1826. "The several kinds of persons who come within the description of servants," Kent wrote in his lecture "Of Master and Servant," were "subdivided into (1) slaves, (2) hired servants, and (3) apprentices." Indeed, in subsequent editions Kent emphasized that "servants" comprehended the generality of employed persons, with "no legal distinction" separating "hired" from "menial" or "domestic" servants.[16] During the second quarter of the century, New York courts relied heavily on Kent's authority, and also that of English precedents, in allowing hirers of wage labor access to the common law actions that previously had been used to protect a master's property in his *menial* servant's services; that is, his governmental authority as a head of household. In *Woodward v. Washburn* (1846), for example, the New York Supreme Court quoted extensively from Kent's description of the relation of master and servant in sustaining a suit brought by an employer against a neighboring bank to recover damages for the loss of the services of his adult clerk. The clerk, it seems, had been sent to the bank to make the plaintiff's deposit and had been involuntarily detained there when the defendant insisted on locking the doors at the close of business. The circumstances were risible but the implications of the court's decision to allow the plaintiff to recover were not. The court held that for the action to be good it was "enough that the relation of master and servant exists between the plaintiff and the person who is disabled or prevented from performing the service he has contracted to perform by the tortious act of the defendant." There was in particular no need for the plaintiff to demonstrate "that the person whose service has been lost was either his apprentice or child." All that was necessary to found the action was that the person disabled from performing was an employee. As the court put it, the plaintiff had a right to recover on the grounds that "every man has a property in the service of those whom he has employed, acquired by the contract of hiring, and purchased by giving them wages." Interestingly, the last passage was taken more or less verbatim from Blackstone, except that where Blackstone had written "domestics," the New York court had substituted "those whom he has employed," thus using Blackstone's eighteenth-century affirmation of the master's property in the personal service of his *domestics* as authority to recognize that nineteenth-century businesses had a similar property in the labor of adult wage workers. And this would apply, said the court, whether the employee was hired by the year, as here, or by the month or even by the day.[17]

[16] James Kent, *Commentaries on American Law* (New York, 1826), 2:201; reprint ed. (New York, 1827), 214n.; 2d ed. (New York, 1832), 2:261.
[17] *Woodward v. Washburn*, 3 Denio 369 (1846), 371–5. For evidence of the extent of the expansion illustrated here, cf. *Taylor v. Neri*, 1 Esp. 384, 170 E.R. 393 (1795), and also, in turn, *Lumley v. Gye*, 2 El, & Bl. 216, 118 E.R. 749 (1853).

In Pennsylvania, William Graydon adopted the Blackstonian definition of master and servant's ambit, which of course included laborers, in his *The Justice's and Constable's Assistant*, published in 1803.[18] Cases before the Pennsylvania courts during the 1790s and 1800s suggest that the prior local understanding had been far more limited, conforming to the "prereception" practices already recorded for other states. In *Respublica v. Catherine Keppele* (1793), for example, the Pennsylvania Supreme Court discussed who might be considered a servant in terms of bound labor alone, confirming, in *Zieber v. Boos* (1798), that this was "the common acceptation of the term."[19] Fourteen years later, in *Ex Parte Meason* (1812), "common parlance" and "the common understanding of the country" were still recognized to have that same limited ambit. Reflecting the same division between local and more recently received meanings exhibited elsewhere, however, the court now also acknowledged the "very comprehensive import" that "servant" was given "in its legal acceptation," applying not only to indentured servants but to all persons "employed by any one to do service for him."[20]

The issue before the court in *Meason* was whether hired workmen were "servants" within the terms of the state's 1794 intestacy statute and hence entitled to preference for payment of their wages out of the estate of a deceased. It was ruled that "the common understanding" should guide the court's construction of the statute. Five years later, however, in *Boniface v. Scott*, the issue was revisited and the court's definition broadened to include persons working for wages in a family's employ, to whom the court variously referred as "domestics," "hirelings," and "all who are employed for hire in the domestic concerns of the family, in whatever station they may be." To restrict the operation of the act to servants in the popular sense, the court said, would leave few indeed within its scope. "None but indented servants or coloured hirelings; for they, in common parlance, alone are called servants."[21]

Massachusetts

The Pennsylvania court's struggles to recategorize the relations of employment to fit both tenacious local meanings and received doctrine underscore the extent of the doctrinal changes under way in all the states. The same story may be told in some detail in Massachusetts, where the social transformation of employment was perhaps more pronounced than elsewhere. "Between 1815 and 1860," Robert Dalzell has argued, "the economy of Massachusetts underwent a transformation fully as dramatic as the one that swept across England in the half century prior to 1815."

[18] William Graydon, *The Justice's and Constable's Assistant* (Harrisburg, Pa., 1803), 281. Graydon's text included a specimen of a warrant for harboring that, as in other texts here considered, existed alongside the received English category as a colonial era survival indicating the more limited ambit of the relation then: ". . . that _____, his *indented* servant, is concealed and entertained by _____" (283, emphasis supplied).
[19] *Respublica v. Catherine Keppele*, 1 Yeates 233 (1793); *Zieber v. Boos*, 2 Yeates 321, 323 (1798).
[20] 5 Binney 167 (1812), at 168–9, 174. See also, generally, argument of counsel at 171–2 and, particularly, the opinion of Brackenridge J. at 179–83.
[21] 3 Sergeant and Rawles 351 (1817), 352–5.

During that period the state became "the most thoroughly industrialized portion of the globe outside Great Britain."[22] The displacement of the eighteenth century's predominantly family-centered agricultural economy by capitalist manufacturing turned labor into a commodity and the majority of working people into wage earners permanently dependent on others for employment. "Self-employment became the exception rather than the rule," writes Alexander Keyssar. The "era of the independent artisan came to a close, and even in agriculture the ratio of laborers to owners increased. The industrial development of Massachusetts meant that most working people came to labor in shops that they did not own or control, at a pace that was often determined by others."[23]

Significantly, local commentary on the legal relation of master and servant during the late eighteenth and early nineteenth centuries was virtually nonexistent. What there was equated it with apprenticeship. As we have seen, the several abridgements of Burn's *Justice of the Peace* published in New England both before and after the Revolution had not even bothered to reproduce the sections on servants appearing in the English editions. Similarly, the only references to servants in the first justice of the peace manual based specifically on local law to be published in Massachusetts, Samuel Freeman's *Massachusetts Justice* (1802), appeared under the title "Apprentice." This section was wholly confined to minors, drawing its description of the law prevailing locally from the act of 1795 dealing with apprentices and minor servants.[24] William Charles White's *Compendium and Digest of the Laws of Massachusetts*, published in 1809, likewise used the title "Apprentice and Servant." Of the ten clauses under that title, the only one not clearly assuming that the subject was a minor was the final clause, which described the powers given overseers of the poor to bind out vagrants and criminals.[25]

Like Freeman, White's definition of servants was based on local statute. As was beginning to be the case in other states (for example, in Hening's later editions for Virginia and in Swift's *System of the Laws* for Connecticut), White elsewhere in the *Compendium* made implicit reference to a wider legal relation of master and servant, here citing authorities entirely English in origin. Thus, in the course of a section on "Assumpsit," White considered the extent to which contracts made by servants could bind masters. In the section on "Trespass on the Case," he included details of actionable injuries that could be done "to a person standing in the relation of a

[22] Robert F. Dalzell, Jr., *Enterprising Elite: The Boston Associates and the World They Made* (Cambridge, Mass., 1987), 3. See also Oscar Handlin, *Boston's Immigrants, 1790–1880* (Cambridge, Mass., 1979), 1–9; Francis X. Blouin, *The Boston Region, 1810–1850: A Study in Urbanization* (Ann Arbor, 1980), 53–132).

[23] Alexander Keyssar, *Out of Work*, 16, and generally 10–18. And see Sean Wilentz, "Against Exceptionalism: Class Consciousness and the American Labor Movement, 1790–1920," *International Labor and Working Class History*, 26 (Fall 1984), 6–13; Jonathan Prude, *The Coming of Industrial Order: Town and Factory Life in Rural Massachusetts* (New York and Cambridge, 1983), 65–237.

[24] Samuel Freeman, *The Massachusetts Justice: Being a Collection of the Laws of the Commonwealth of Massachusetts Relative to the Power and Duty of Justices of the Peace* (Boston, 1802), 124–7.

[25] William Charles White, *Compendium and Digest of the Laws of Massachusetts* (Boston, 1809), vol. 1, tit. XII.

master," namely enticement and beating his servant; he also gave passing consideration to the action of *respondeat superior*.[26] But as we have seen, these actions had certainly been known during the seventeenth and eighteenth centuries, when they had been applied within the ambit of the local definition of servant. And nothing in White's *Compendium* revised that limited local definition. Thus, the only references to hired labor or "workmen" that one finds in White place them in the context not of master and servant but of bailment.[27]

The first Massachusetts treatise to use a definition of the master/servant relationship more encompassing than the apprenticeship/minor servant focus of the colonial and revolutionary era writers was Nathan Dane's encyclopedic *General Abridgment and Digest of American Law*. Initially, Dane approached the issue in the manner of his contemporaries in other states, by constructing, with reference to both local and English law, a list of the situations in which the relationship had theretofore been held to apply. This gave rise to a significantly wider sense of *servant* than that conveyed by either Freeman or White. A servant, said Dane, was "any one the public employs to do its business ... any one it employs to bargain and contract for it ... and to bind it as far as the power is extended." Also "any one I employ and expressly or impliedly empower to bargain and contract for me so as to bind me, is my servant." In addition a servant was "any one to whose labour and earnings I am entitled." In all these cases "the one employed is serving the employer or is in his service; therefore, in these cases, one hired in my family or other business as my apprentice, factor, bailiff, master of my vessel, my steward, child, or even my wife, is my servant; so a journeyman by the job, is a servant until the job is done."[28] Dane then introduced an essential distinguishing characteristic to bring order to this somewhat haphazard agglomeration of instances; a servant was any person "over whom an authority may be rightfully exercised by another." As Reeve's *Law of Baron and Femme*, published seven years earlier, had done, Dane's *Abridgment* thus made the legitimate exercise of authority to direct labor the paradigmatic test of who fell into the categories of master and servant. Dane held that only certain kinds of employed persons could be considered appropriately subject to the controlling authority of another. These – slaves, apprentices, menial servants, hired laborers, criminals and debtors sold into service – Dane denominated as "proper servants." The other sorts of persons previously listed – factors, auctioneers, brokers, attorneys, masters of ships, and so forth – were "best considered under their proper names."[29]

For Dane, then, the migration of master/servant's authoritarian concepts outward into employment at large suggested, as it had to Blackstone sixty years earlier, the necessity of separating out those statuses or occupations in which the incumbents were employed by others but not considered subject to their control. The result was simultaneous processes of homogenization (of master/servant with employment) and differentiation (of employment situations where the employer did not "control" the

---

[26] See ibid., tit. XVI, at 166; tit. CLXVI, at 1260–2.
[27] Ibid., tit. XXIII, at 228–9; tit. CXLVI, at 1253.
[28] Dane, *Abridgment*, 2:312.   [29] Ibid., 312–13.

incumbents). This illustrates both the way master/servant concepts were beginning to be used paradigmatically in the realm of employment and a simultaneous move to set off those employment relations in which the status of the employee was such as to recommend different treatment.[30] Chancellor Kent's *Commentaries on American Law*, published four years later, displayed the same tendency. According to Kent, as we have seen, the term *servant* covered slaves, apprentices, and the broad catchall category of "hired servants." Kent, however, separated out factors, attorneys, and others and dealt with them under the distinct heading of "Principal and Agent."[31]

THE NEW EMPLOYMENT RELATION

Although writers such as Kent and Dane were moving to define the master/servant relationship far more widely than had been the case thirty years before, their descriptions of its doctrinal ambit still tended to be constructed in part through reference to the categories of *persons* considered properly subject to its rules. When Timothy Walker came to address the matter in 1837, however, he succeeded in engineering a major refinement. Whereas in previous treatise writers' hands master/ servant had described the sorts of employment relationships in which one of the parties was considered routinely subject to the controlling authority of the other, Walker reinterpreted *all* employment relations in that light. He did this by dispensing altogether with the strategy of constructing master/servant doctrine out of the rules applicable to those employed persons to whom the appellation *servant* could properly be applied and instead established it as a description of a universal relationship coextensive with employment itself. "Servitude, strictly so called, does not exist in this country," Walker wrote. But he went on, as we have seen, to state that "the legal relation of master and servant must exist, to a greater or less extent, wherever civilization furnishes work to be done." In fact, Walker concluded, "we understand by the relations of master and servant, nothing more or less, than that of the *employer* and the *employed*."[32]

Walker's treatise was the culmination of the transformation in legal discourse about employment begun some forty years earlier. The transformation occurred in two overlapping stages. In the first stage writers had generally followed Blackstone

---

[30] We have noted similar processes of homogenization and differentiation under way during the colonial period. In that period, however, what underwent homogenization as "servants" were the various categories of "unfree" labor; what was differentiated was free wage labor. In the first half of the nineteenth century, the etiolation of most other forms of bound labor left chattel slavery as its increasingly isolated and extreme example; free wage labor, however, was increasingly clearly brought within the common law of master and servant while the higher nonmanual occupations were differentiated.

[31] Kent, *Commentaries* (reprint ed., 1827), 2:477–508.

[32] Timothy Walker, *An Introduction to American Law* (Philadelphia, 1837), 243 (emphasis in original). Walker underlined the revolution in legal discourse that had occurred by proceeding to treat apprenticeship and agency as special cases that, because they were not standard examples of the employment relation, were best thought of as sui generis exceptions to the paradigm he had identified rather than prime illustrations of it.

in creating a descriptive taxonomy of social relationships and their particular legal incidents; within this taxonomy they had broadened the categories of persons considered appropriate for designation as servants. In the second stage writers had moved beyond categorization, seeking instead to reconceptualize master and servant as a universally available relation. By Timothy Walker's time the only trace of the older taxonomic approach remaining was Walker's broad reference to the foundation of master and servant law in "differences of condition."[33] Employment and the relation of master and servant were effectively synonymous.

Ostensibly, the form of this new universal relation of employment was wholly contractual, the design of any particular employment situation the product of the parties' joined wills and interpreted as such. Certainly according to Walker all matters between the employer and the employed were settled as matters of contract, implying, as it were, that authority was negotiable.[34] Theophilus Parsons spoke to the same point sixteen years after Walker. Whereas in England "the relation of master and servant is in many respects regulated by statutory provisions, and upon some points is materially affected by the existing distinction of ranks, and by rules which have come down from periods when this distinction was more marked and more operative than at present," in America "we have nothing of this kind. With us, a contract for service is construed and governed only by the general principles of the law of contracts."[35] Certainly, as we shall see, midcentury courts did have resort to just such formal contractualist discourse in employment cases. All the same, Parsons's claim was disingenuous, for as we have seen, the essential characteristic of the relationship created by the employment contract was that it was assumed to reproduce the magisterial authority of the master in the person of the employer. And indeed, Parsons's subsequent discussion tended to confirm that the relation of master and servant was less a discrete instance of the more general phenomenon of contract than itself a particular species of legal relation with its own particular incidents, in this case incidents geared to the representation of the authority of the master as a matter of law.[36]

In short, Walker and Parsons notwithstanding, the shape of the employment relation did not originate with the law of contracts. It originated in received common law understandings of what was entailed in being a master and a servant, an employer and an employee.[37] Representing employment relations in the voluntarist language

---

[33] Ibid.   [34] Ibid., 243, 250.

[35] Theophilus Parsons, *The Law of Contracts* (Boston, 1853) 1:86.

[36] This point has been made very effectively by Elizabeth Mensch. See her essay "The History of Mainstream Legal Thought," in David Kairys, ed., *The Politics of Law: A Progressive Critique* (New York: Pantheon Books, 1982), 22.

[37] Thus Chancellor Kent could state that the relation of master and servant (in the case of hired servants) "rests altogether upon contract" and almost in the same breath that "there are many important legal consequences which flow from this relation" (*Commentaries* [reprint ed., 1827] 2:209. See also *Ryan v. The Cumberland Valley Railroad*, 23 Penn. St. R. 384 (1854) (the relation of master and servant was one of the "special relations of life" and therefore was governed by its own particular rules rather than by principles of general application defining "the general relation of man in society." In America this relation was always instituted by a contract to which courts could refer to discover most of its terms.

of contract thus mystified the existence and exercise of power in the employment relationship.[38] Certainly the mechanism of entry into the relation was contractual; but the act of creation visited inherited patterns of duties and expectations upon the parties entering the relationship that were unique to this particular relation. By midcentury those origins were buried beneath several decades' accumulated strata of doctrinal creativity.

The perhaps somewhat abstract quality of the discursive revolution in which the treatise writers were involved might yet tempt the conclusion that processes of doctrinal change, although clearly of importance, were still at best somewhat remote from the ongoing social processes that were turning the late eighteenth-century republic's citizenry into the mid–nineteenth century's industrial work force. The distinguishing characteristic of this work force, however, was that it was mobilized and organized through contracts. The process of its creation was one, therefore, in which the interpreters of contracts – the courts – were always going to have a key role to play. Having attempted to demonstrate, through an analysis of the treatise writers, that although inevitable differences of condition might result in some citizens becoming employers and others laborers, it was law rather than nature or capital that would make the employers the masters and their employees the servants, I now turn to the courts, where the issue was joined more concretely.

LEGAL REINFORCEMENT OF THE EMPLOYER'S AUTHORITY

The emerging master/servant relation described by the treatise writers was, as we have seen, very different from the colonial relations of indentured servitude and apprenticeship/minor servitude. The key characteristic of the latter was, after all, that the servant was restrained from premature abandonment of his or her service by statutory provisions reinforcing – and delimiting – the personal authority of the master.[39] Where the colonial relation persisted – as in the case of apprenticeship and

But the contract never defined the relation of master and servant completely. As with other special relations, "the special duties of each party are so well understood in society that they are left entirely undefined in the contract, and each is presumed to have undertaken them without their being formally specified" [386–7]).

[38] The language of the document itself was another matter. A contract between Henry Roberts and Christopher Lippitt of the Slater Company's Jewett City Mill, 6 January 1815, provided that Roberts was "to do anything that he may be set about by the agent or the principal overseer in said mill & to render all the service to the Company at all times whatever Branch of Business he may be set about – Subject to be discharged by said agent whenever he refuses to do anything that he may be set about that is reasonable for a man to do." See David A. Zonderman, "Aspirations and Anxieties: New England Workers and the Mechanized Factory System, 1815–1850" (Ph.D. diss., Yale University, 1986), 190, now published as *Aspirations and Anxieties: New England Workers and the Mechanized Factory System, 1815–1850* (New York, 1992).

[39] Darrett Rutman and Anita Rutman note that although the law "coerced [servants] back to their proper labor," it also became a site of compromise between servants who "used flight as a bargaining chip" and their masters in need of their labor (*A Place in Time: Middlesex County, Virginia, 1650–1750* [New York, 1984] 132–3). See also Joseph H. Smith and Philip A. Crowl, eds., *Court Records of Prince Georges County, Maryland, 1696–1699* (1964; Millwood, N.Y., 1975), 490.

minor servitude – court records show that criminal sanctions continued to be invoked throughout the first half of the nineteenth century. Thus the bench books of one Boston magistrate, Stephen Gorham, covering the period 1806–20, include 7 cases in which charges of absconding and neglect of duty were brought against apprentices or minor servants.[40] The records of the Boston Police Court covering the period 1822–59 show 80 cases of charges against apprentices or minor servants, 61 for absconding and 19 for being "stubborn and disobedient."[41] Occasional cases suggest that criminal sanctions might also be invoked indirectly to coerce departing laborers to return to employment. In *Commonwealth v. Catherine Cutler* (1826), for example, the Boston Police Court heard that a defendant charged with behaving in a "wanton, lewd and lascivious" manner – one of a number of variations on a theme of vagrancy – had left her employment in a Watertown cotton factory two days earlier. The court discharged her "on condition of returning immediately to the Factory."[42] Both the courts and the legislature also displayed some interest in other indirect uses of the criminal law to regulate aspects of the employment relation, notably by redefining the scope of bailment and the crimes of embezzlement and larceny to guard employers against appropriations of goods and breaches of trust which were otherwise legally ambiguous.[43] There is, however, no indication that the

[40] Bench Books of Justice Stephen Gorham, 1806–20, in Adlow Collection, Rare Book Room, Boston Public Library. Gorham's records also include four cases in which masters sought the return of runaway slaves and fifty-seven cases of absconding/neglect of duty brought against seamen deserting ships in Boston harbor.

[41] Boston Police Court, Docket Books 1822–60 in care of the Clerk of Court, Boston Municipal Court, Criminal Division, Suffolk County Court House, Boston. As a municipal court the Police Court did not exercise jurisdiction over deserting seamen. When cases of absconding seamen were brought before the Police Court, they were referred elsewhere, usually to federal courts. In 1857, however, the Massachusetts legislature passed An Act to Protect Mariners and Ship-Owners From Imposition, providing at section 4 that "No person shall entice or persuade, nor attempt to entice or persuade any member of the crew of any vessel [in any port in this Commonwealth] before the expiration of his term of service in such vessel, under a penalty of not more than fifty dollars for each offence," and at section 5 that "If any person shall knowingly and wilfully persuade or aid any person who shall have shipped on a voyage from any port in this Commonwealth, and received advanced wages therefor, to wilfully neglect to proceed on such voyage, he shall forfeit a sum not exceeding one hundred dollars." See *Massachusetts Acts* 1857, c. 139. For illustrative Boston Police Court actions enforcing this legislation, see *Commonwealth v. Karlson*, BPC docket 7975 (1857); *Commonwealth v. Bryant*, BPC docket 599 (1859); *Commonwealth v. Smith*, BPC docket 1478 (1859).

[42] *Commonwealth v. Catherine Cutler*, BPC docket 578 (1826). See also *Commonwealth v. Isabella*, BPC dockets 689 and 1052 (1824); and *Commonwealth v. Elizabeth Daily*, BPC docket 1195 (1824). On the policing of vagrancy and its relationship to employment see Amy Dru Stanley, "Contract Rights in the Age of Emancipation: Wage Labor and Marriage after the Civil War" (Ph.D. diss., Yale University, 1990). See also Chapter 3, n. 126.

[43] See "Of Offences Against Private Property," *Massachusetts Revised Statutes* 1836, c. 126, sec. 16, 27–30; Willard Phillips et al., *Report of the Penal Code of Massachusetts* (Boston, 1844), "Larceny" and "Embezzlement." And see *Commonwealth v. James*, 18 Mass. 375 (1823); *Commonwealth v. Woodward*, Thacher's Criminal Cases 63 (1824); *Commonwealth v. Thomas Stearns*, 43 Mass. 343 (1841); *Commonwealth v. Doane*, 55 Mass. 5 (1848). In his charge to the Suffolk County grand jury at the opening of the Boston Municipal Court, 13 Mar. 1837, Peter Oxenbridge Thacher described these changes as follows: "The offence of Larceny is consummated by the felonious taking and carrying away of the property of another from his possession. . . . It is no longer a ground of defence for a party, accused of this crime, to allege that a special confidence was reposed in him, and that, in taking the property, he only committed a

individual adult wage laborer could in any way be held criminally answerable for breaches of contract as such.[44]

Civil actions were a different matter. Suits by employers seeking damages for an employee's departure prior to the expiry of an agreed term or for other forms of breach of contract constituted one form of legally sanctioned economic discipline of some importance in shaping the employment relations of the nineteenth century.[45] Such suits had of course been known previously. As wage labor for an agreed period became the paradigm for employment, they became more common. Importantly, however, lower court records indicate that at least in the early years of the century juries tended to allow plaintiffs compensation only for actual loss rather than the full value of the defendant's promise.[46]

---

breach of trust. If an apprentice or clerk, who is of the age of sixteen years, should embezzle the money or property, which his employer has entrusted to him; or if a carrier should convert to his own use property delivered to him to be carried for hire; or if the clerk, or other officer of a bank, or other incorporated company, should embezzle the money or other property of the corporation; – these all incur the guilt of Larceny, and must suffer its penalty" (*Two Charges to the Grand Jury of the County of Suffolk* [Boston, 1837], 21).

[44] But then, it is important to remind ourselves, neither had the wage laborer of the eighteenth. We have already traced the disappearance of the seventeenth century's statutory restraints in those few colonies where they were adopted, and we have noted Peter Kalm's midcentury observation that in the colonies hired agricultural workers were free to depart their employment at any time they chose (Chapter 7). Similar evidence is available from later in the century in Pennsylvania. When Caleb Brinton hired James Greenway and John Cuff to work on his Chester County farm in 1781, for example, their agreement provided that should Greenway and Cuff neglect or refuse to work, Brinton would have the right to hire other workers in their place, with Greenway and Cuff liable for the cost. The inference is plain that Brinton was not in any position to have his hirelings forced to perform their agreement and could only seek damages for the breach (Paul G. E. Clemens and Lucy Simler, "Rural Labor and the Farm Household in Chester County, Pennsylvania, 1750–1820," in Innes, ed., *Work and Labor*, 106–43, at 106–7). William Nelson's work on colonial Massachusetts similarly indicates that employers confronted by quitting or nonperforming employees had no recourse to penal sanctions but only to the recovery of damages through a civil suit for nonperformance (*Americanization of the Common Law*, 57–8). For further evidence of eighteenth-century Massachusetts practice see below, n. 52. These findings are consistent with the evidence of seventeenth- and eighteenth-century court records discussed in Chapter 7. As we have seen, when a defendant had breached an obligation to do work for a plaintiff, seventeenth-century courts would sometimes order performance – that is, order involuntary labor – as an alternative to assessing damages. Neither I nor, to my knowledge, anyone else has found examples of colonial courts ordering performance in such cases after the end of the seventeenth century, however, and the cases where the orders appear generally arise in circumstances where a specific task has been undertaken but not carried out. Such orders need to be perceived in the context of the rural economy of interdependent obligation described in the scholarly literature; as cases, that is, involving reciprocal transfers of goods and services. In the records I have surveyed there are very few examples of courts using specific performance to enforce commitments to perform labor in exchange for wages, and these appear to be confined almost exclusively to the first half of the seventeenth century. See also Karen Orren, "Organized Labor and the Invention of Modern Liberalism in the United States," *Studies in American Political Development*, 2 (1987), 324.

[45] See, e.g., Zonderman, *Aspirations and Anxieties*, 171–2.

[46] See, e.g., *Smith v. Knoepsel*, Suffolk County Court of Common Pleas (hereafter Suffolk CCP), July term 1797, 147; and Supreme Judicial Court, *nisi prius* session, Feb. term 1798, 4; *Frothingham v. Barbeau*, *Frothingham v. Torline, President and Directors of the Ransellaer Glass Factory v. Warn, Frothingham v. Jackson* and *Frothingham v. Weatherwax*, all in Suffolk CCP, Oct. term 1811, 145, 149, 152, 288, 291; *Boston Glass Manufactory v. Welser* and *Boston Glass Manufactory v. Roesch*, Suffolk CCP, Oct. term 1816, 50, 53; *Dorchester Cotton and Iron Factory v. Howard*, Suffolk CCP, Jan. term 1823, 209; *Kimball v. Robinson*, Suffolk

Potentially much more intimidating than damages was the denial to employees departing their engagements prior to term any right to recover such wages as they might be owed at the moment of departure. At first, lower court trials of this issue tended to result in the employee's recovery of wages owed on a plea of *quantum meruit* (what the plaintiff reasonably deserved to have), compensating employers for actual costs where appropriate by deducting expenses accruing from the premature departure in setoff.[47] As in employer suits for damages, then, lower courts allowed compensation for actual loss but did not grant the employer the full value of the employee's promise.[48] Almost unanimously during the first half of the century,

CCP, July term 1831, 122; *Tenney v. Weeks*, Suffolk CCP, Apr. term 1837, 44; *Hubbell v. Robinson*, Suffolk CCP, Apr. term 1855, 147.

[47] See, e.g., the references to lower court decisions in *M'Millan and M'Millan v. Vanderlip*, 12 Johnson 165 (N.Y. 1815), at 165; *Jennings v. Camp*, 13 Johnson 94 (N.Y. 1816), at 95; *Hoar v. Clute*, 15 Johnson 224 (N.Y. 1818); *Reab v. Moor*, 19 Johnson 337 (N.Y. 1822), at 337; *Stark v. Parker*, 19 Mass. 267 (1824), at 267.

[48] In England it had long been stated as well-established doctrine, in the case of service, that "if the Servant depart himself before the End of his Time, he loses all his Wages" (William Nelson, *The Office and Authority of a Justice of Peace* [London, 1704], 44). See also Michael Dalton, *The Countrey Justice: Containing the Practice of the Justices of the Peace out of Their Sessions* (London, 1619); also the 1697 ed. at 129. See also Peter Karsten, "'Bottomed on Justice': A Reappraisal of Critical Legal Studies Scholarship Concerning Breaches of Labor Contracts by Quitting or Firing in Britain and the U.S., 1630–1880," *American Journal of Legal History*, 34, 3 (July 1990) 213–61, esp. 220–1; Brian W. Haines, "English Labor Law and the Separation from Contract," *Journal of Legal History*, 1, 3 (Dec. 1980), 277–80.

Yet in *Cutter v. Powell*, 6 T.R. 319, 101 E.R. 575 (1795), a case often cited as conclusive proof of the rule, the bench in fact adverted to a crucial distinction between the circumstances of parties agreeing (as in *Cutter*) to an express written contract, which "speaks for itself," and the more usual circumstance of hirings "in the general way," that is oral retainers for the customary annual term. Speaking directly to this distinction, Lawrence J. held that "with regard to the common case of an hired servant . . . such a servant, though hired in a general way, is considered to be hired with reference to the general understanding upon the subject, that the servant shall be entitled to his wages for the time he serves though he do not continue in the service during the whole year" (577). That is, what decided the court in *Cutter v. Powell* (unanimously) against the recovery of wages on a *quantum meruit* was the existence of a written contract between the parties, the terms of which expressly departed "the general understanding." See *Cutter v. Powell*, 573, 576–7. See also *Countess of Plymouth v. Throgmorton*, 3 Mod. 153, 87 E.R. 99 (1687); *Worth v. Viner*, 3 Vin. Abr. 8–9; *Ex Parte Smyth*, 1 Swans 337, 36 E.R. 412 (1818), at 421n; J. L. Barton, "Contract and *Quantum Meruit*: The Antecedents of *Cutter v. Powell*," *Journal of Legal History*, 8, 1 (May 1987), 49, 60–1.

The rule as stated by Lawrence J. was reproduced by William Selwyn, citing *Cutter v. Powell* as authority, in his *Abridgment of the Law of Nisi Prius* 1807; 7th ed. (London, 1827), 2:285–6: "If a servant be hired in the general way, he is considered to be hired with reference to the general understanding upon the subject, viz. that he shall be entitled to his wages for the time he shall serve, though he do not continue in the service during the whole year." See also Samuel Comyn, *A Treatise of the Law Relative to Contracts and Agreements Not Under Seal* (London, 1807), 1:229 (distinguishing express written contracts, which were entire, from "the common case of an hired servant," where "the servant shall be entitled to his wages for the time he serves"). However, in *Spain v. Arnott*, 2 Stark 255, 171 E.R. 638 (1817), when confronted by the necessity of justifying the denial of wages owed to a servant who had been dismissed without pay before the end of the year for disobeying his employer, the court held that the servant could not recover on an apportionment because all yearly hirings of farm servants were entire.

In the first edition of his *A Practical Treatise on the Law of Contracts, Not Under Seal* (London, 1826), Joseph Chitty cited *Spain v. Arnott* as establishing *only* that a servant *discharged for misconduct* "is not entitled to any wages from the day he is so discharged, if they had not then accrued due" and made no mention of any general doctrine of entirety in yearly hirings. Indeed, like Selwyn before him, Chitty continued to cite Lawrence J.'s statement from *Cutter v. Powell* in support of the proposition "that a master and

however, courts of record hearing cases on appeal disallowed lower court recoveries, holding that an employment contract was an entire contract, and therefore that no obligation to pay wages existed until the employee had completed the agreed term.[49]

The first reported instance of this is the New York case *M'Millan and M'Millan v. Vanderlip* (1815), where Vanderlip, having abandoned his engagement with the defendants as a spinner (an oral agreement to spin for ten and a half months at three cents per run) sued for the wages owed him for the 845 runs he had actually spun. A lower court jury granted him $22.35, being the balance less $3 already advanced by the employer. The New York Supreme Court, however, ruled that Vanderlip had no right of recovery. Citing "the good sense of modern times" the court interpreted the parties' agreement as an entire contract upon which Vanderlip could not sue until he had completed his term of service. The court's statement clearly implied innovation. It also expressed a more general concern that its ruling should be understood to apply to all wage labor engagements, including those made "in the general way":

servant contracting for the hire of the latter, may be presumed to agree, subject to terms which are almost universally adopted on these occasions" (see 172–3). Subsequently, however, in *Huttman v. Boulnois*, 2 Car. & P. 509, 172 E.R. 231 (1826) the reversal of the relationship between "express contracts" and "the general understanding" hinted at in *Spain v. Arnott* was fully carried through, Abbott C. J. now affirming that in the *absence* of an "express" agreement providing otherwise, the law's presumption that general hirings were hirings for a year was sufficient to defeat claims for unpaid wages litigated by hirelings departing prior to the expiry of a year's service, *because it was also to be presumed that yearly hirings were entire.* Abbott also now affirmed that the doctrine "that a general hiring is a hiring for a year" extended beyond farm and domestic servants to encompass the generality of hirings (including, in this case, a clerk). See also *Beeston v. Collyer*, 130 E.R. 768 (1827). In the wake of *Huttman*, and citing that case as authority, the second edition of Chitty's *Practical Treatise* (London, 1834) included *for the first time* reference to a rule that "where the payment is to be quarterly, or yearly, or at fixed periods, and the servant improperly leave his master . . . it seems that he is not entitled to wages for any part of such quarter, &c. even to the day he quits; as there can no apportionment of an entire payment under such circumstances" (458). As this last statement of Chitty's indicates, yearly hirings could be considered apportionable in cases where the servant was not dismissed for misconduct or had not left improperly, underlining that the "entire contracts" doctrine was disciplinary in intent. See also *Archard v. Hornor*, 3 Car. & P. 349, 172 E.R. 451 (1828). On disciplinary discharges see *Pagani v. Gandolfi*, 2 Car & P. 369, 172 E.R. 167 (1826); *Atkin v. Acton*, 4 Car. & P. 208, 172 E.R. 673 (1830); *Callo v. Brouncker*, 4 Car & P. 518, 172 E.R. 807 (1831); *Turner v. Robinsons and Sanford*, 6 Car. & P. 15, 172 E.R. 1126 (1833).

[49] It is worth noting in this connection that Selwyn's, Comyn's, and Chitty's statements of the applicable rules (detailed in n. 48) were faithfully reproduced in the American editions of their works. See, e.g., Selwyn's *Abridgment* (Philadelphia, 1807), 3:948, and (Albany, 1811) 2:1067; Comyn's *Contracts and Agreements* (New York, 1809), 1:228–9 (see also the later annotated American edition of Comyn's treatise published under the title *The Law of Contracts and Promises Upon Various Subjects and with Particular Persons* [New York, 1826], 753); Chitty's *Practical Treatise* (Boston, 1827), 171–2. Not until the 1834 American edition of Chitty (Philadelphia), at 172, was an American "rule" of entirety invoked.

So far as native treatises are concerned, Reeve's *Law of Baron and Femme*, published in 1816, made no mention of any entirety rule. Indeed, Reeve stated of *menial* servants in Connecticut merely that "if they leave their master, they are liable for *damages*" (at 347, emphasis supplied). In fact, the entirety rule did not make its appearance in Reeve's treatise until the annotated third edition was published in 1862. Nor did either the first (1826) or revised (1827) editions of Kent's *Commentaries* make any reference to an entirety rule in the case of "hired servants" (at 209). The rule was not introduced until the second (1832) edition, citing *Huttman v. Boulnois* (at 258).

It appears to me, that the construction I have put on this contract, is not only warranted by the agreement itself, but that it is a very useful and salutary one. The general practice, in hiring laborers or artisans, is, for 6 or 12 months, at so much per month: the farmer hires a man for 6 or 12 months, at monthly wages; and he takes his chance of the good, with the bad months. It is well known, that the labor of a man, during the summer months, is worth double the labor of the same man in winter; but upon the principles contended for by the defendant's counsel, if the farmer hires in the autumn, for twelve months, at monthly wages, the laborer may quit his employ on the first of May, and sue for his wages, and recover them, leaving the farmer the poor resort of a suit to damages. The rule contended for holds out temptations to men to violate their contracts.[50]

A more complete statement of the issue, one more directly underscoring both its innovatory character and its disciplinary incidents, came from the Massachusetts Supreme Judicial Court in 1824. Here John Stark, a farm laborer engaged for a year but departing early, had sued Thomas Parker to recover unpaid wages owed for labor on the latter's farm.[51] As in New York the lower court had allowed recovery, instructing the jury to deduct such sum as it might think proper compensation for the defendant's loss of service.[52] Again as in New York, the higher court denied it.

[50] 12 Johnson 165, 166–7.

[51] As in *M'Millan* there was no written contract. Plaintiff's counsel cited Lawrence's rule from *Cutter v. Powell* in support.

[52] "If such sum should exceed the sum claimed by the plaintiff," the trial judge ruled, "they might find a verdict for the defendant" (*Stark v. Parker*, 19 Mass. [1824], at 267). That it was customary well before the end of the eighteenth century in New England agriculture to reckon wages on departure with compensatory damages where applicable in setoff is suggested by the circumstances of James Hopkins's departure from his employment with Ebenezer Parkman in April 1780. Hopkins had been hired by Parkman for the season but had been at work only three days when a dispute arose between them. Hopkins indicated that he would leave, to which Parkman agreed, though "somewhat reluctantly" as there was no prospect of his finding a replacement. Hopkins had received board and lodging for the three days and asked no wages for the work he had done. Significantly, he also offered to pay Parkman "the Damage of Disappointment" (see Ross W. Beales, "The Reverend Ebenezer Parkman's Farm Workers, Westborough, Massachusetts, 1726–82," *Proceedings of the American Antiquarian Society*, 99, 1 [1989], 121–49, at 133, 149). Parkman's diaries offer some grounds for believing such a practice of apportionment may have been in existence some fifty years earlier. In March 1726 Parkman had hired Robert Henry for the coming year but dismissed him after only three months for what Parkman clearly believed was ample cause. Parkman nevertheless paid Henry for the work he had done to that point without any hint of an "entirety" claim based on dismissal for cause (ibid., 121, 142). A practice of apportionment is also implied in George Washington's contract with his carpenter, Benjamin Buckler, where the parties agreed that should Buckler prove "in any respect dishonest or unfaithful or if upon trial he should prove idle, or negligent" he might be dismissed without notice "upon paying him for the time he has worked in proportion to the number of days and season he has been in the said Washington's service" (reproduced in Richard B. Morris, *Government and Labor in Early America* [Boston, 1981], 220–1; Morris describes this as a "typical" agreement).

This evidence is, of course, no more than suggestive, and is to some extent balanced by evidence tending in the opposite direction. Thus we should note the Swedish visitor Peter Kalm's cautionary comment from the mid–eighteenth century that colonial farm laborers departing before term risked losing their wages. See Adolph B. Benson, *Peter Kalm's Travels In North America; The English Version of 1770* (New York, 1987), 204. Likewise, Richard B. Morris indicates on the basis of seventeenth-century research that masters would allege departure of the employee before term in defense of suits for payment of wages owed (*Government and Labor*, 216). Although Morris provided no specific examples, support can be found in the Maryland cases *Knages v. Bouls*, 53 Md. Arch. 158 (Charles County, 1661), and *Price v. Wheeler*, 53 Md. Arch. 385 (Charles County, 1663). See also *Pennell agt. Pendell, Records of the Suffolk*

"The plaintiff was to labor for one year at an agreed price." It would be "repugnant to the general understanding of the nature of such engagements" and "a flagrant violation of the first principles of justice" to permit him to avoid his agreement and simply recover wages owed for time actually spent laboring. Brushing aside the plaintiff's counsel's observation that "no laborer would make such a contract unless he were imposed upon," the court held that "the performance of the year's service was "a condition precedent to the obligation of payment" and must be performed in its entirety "before he is entitled to anything."

Although the court made reference to "ancient and well established principles" and "the usages of the country and common opinion" in support of its ruling in *Stark*, both its own comments and local reaction to the decision indicate that the ruling in fact represented a major innovation in local law. "It has been urged that . . . a different rule of construction has been adopted in this commonwealth," the court noted. "And we are bound to believe that such has sometimes been the fact, from the opinion of the learned and respectable judge who tried this cause, and from instances of similar decisions cited at the bar, but not reported." Such had indeed been the fact, as the *Boston Courier*'s report of the case (reprinted from the *Massachusetts Yeoman*) makes clear:

It is an evil of which almost every farmer has had cause to complain, that labourers, after being hired for a term of time, for six months or a year, frequently leave the service of those with whom they have so contracted before the expiration of the term, and at a time when their labor is the most valuable; and afterwards claim payment for the time they have worked, precisely as if there had been no hiring for the specific time. This claim, unfair and unreasonable as it seems to be, has been sustained by Courts, which have allowed the labourer to recover "as much as he reasonably deserved to have," taking into consideration the time he has worked, and the damages, if any, which his employer has suffered by his failing to serve out the stipulated time. *This has been generally understood to be the common law of the State.*[53]

Hailing *Stark* as a decision of great importance to the community in general, and "agriculturists" in particular, the *Courier* informed its readers that the quitting worker

County Court, 1671–80, Colonial Society of Massachusetts Publications 29 (Boston, 1933), 2:620 (1675). Karsten, however, cites a number of eighteenth-century cases "which allowed appropriate recovery to laborers and artisans who had sued for wages" ("Bottomed on Justice," 224n). Examination of Suffolk County Massachusetts Common Pleas records shows that numbers of actions were heard there in the late eighteenth and the early nineteenth century for both breach of covenant and *quantum meruit* for work, labor, and services.

[53] 19 Mass. 267, at 271–5; *Boston Courier*, 23 July 1824 (emphasis supplied). As we have seen, New York's lower courts had also tended to allow recovery in such cases. That they were reflecting common practice in cases of premature departure is suggested by testimony in the Pennsylvania case *Libhart v. Wood*, 1 Watts and Serg. 265 (1841), at 265–6, where canal boat captains testified that crewmen were customarily hired by the season but were nevertheless paid in full for the time spent in employment if they left prematurely, or at most docked two or three dollars. For an example of an explicit agreement for deduction of a fraction of weekly wages owed to be held over for payment at the end of the year as security for faithful performance, see *Meyer v. Lombard* and *Wentz v. Lombard*, Suffolk CCP Apr. term 1834, 29, 38. On the holding back of wages as security against premature quitting see also Anthony F. C. Wallace, *Rockdale: The Growth of an American Village in the Early Industrial Revolution* (New York, 1978), 179.

would no longer be able to recover for part performance. "It is decided that where this is a contract to labour for a certain term, at a stipulated price for the term, and the labourer voluntarily leaves the service of his employer before the expiration of the term, without sufficient cause and without the consent of the employer, he cannot recover any part of his wages."[54]

The decision in *Stark* came in the wake of increasing resort to term hire of wage labor in New England agriculture and appears to evince a desire to give Massachusetts law a disciplinary capacity in regard to such labor that it had theretofore lacked.[55] Certainly it was very much to the fore in the court's consideration, as indeed it appeared to have been in New York, that "in this commonwealth . . . the important business of husbandry leads to multiplied engagements of precisely this description."[56] There was, of course, no hint here of resort to the criminal restraints on departure that had characterized English service-in-husbandry.[57] But this is hardly surprising: As we have seen, there is little evidence that such restraints had ever been applied in America to other than bound servants. Particularly in light of what appears previously to have been customary in Massachusetts and elsewhere – that the departing worker could sue for wages owed at the moment of departure and be held liable to the employer in setoff only for the cost of finding a replacement – the

[54] *Boston Courier*, 23 July 1824.

[55] See also *Olmstead v. Beale*, 36 Mass. 528 (1837); *Davis v. Maxwell*, 53 Mass. 286 (1847). In those cases, as in *Stark*, plaintiffs continued to press for compensation up to the moment of departure, with damages for the employer in setoff. "I only contend that the party shall have his whole wages," stated plaintiff's counsel in *Olmstead*. "He shall pay out of his compensation all damage which the employer has suffered, by reason of the nonperformance of the whole contract" (Lemuel Shaw, Supreme Judicial Court Minute Books, 18:285, Social Law Library, Boston). The court was unimpressed. See discussion of Olmstead below, this chapter, at nn. 91–3. That *Stark* may indeed have had an impact on agricultural practice is suggested by Thomas Ward's reaction in 1830 to the premature departure of two of his hired laborers, David Jennings and John Holyoke. Jennings left on 6 September, two months early, "on account of health." He "had his pay, and went home." Holyoke left on 11 December, three months early, saying that the work had become too hard. He did not get his pay but was required to wait out the full year for which he had agreed to work for Ward. See Jack Larkin, " 'Labor Is the Great Thing in Farming': The Farm Laborers of the Ward Family of Shrewsbury, Massachusetts, 1787–1860," *Proceedings of the American Antiquarian Society*, 99, 1 (1989), 189–226, at 197.

[56] 19 Mass. 267, at 275. According to Christopher Clark, before 1820 the hiring of labor had been "a normal, frequent part of farmers' strategies" but most wage work had been done "in small amounts, intermittently, and by people who had other things to do as well." Households "preferred to rely on their own labor whenever possible, hiring help or swapping work in the neighborhood when they had to." This pattern of reciprocation among interdependent households, as we have seen, the eighteenth-century norm. After 1820, however, Clark notes "a progressive increase in contract hiring of farm labor for five, six, or seven months each summer and, in fewer cases, for a year at a time." See his *The Roots of Rural Capitalism*, 304–5. See also Larkin, " 'Labor is the Great Thing in Farming' "; Richard B. Lyman, Jr., " 'What Is Done in My Absence?' Levi Lincoln's Oakham, Massachusetts, Farm Workers, 1807–20," *Proceedings of the American Antiquarian Society*, 99, 1 (1989), 151–87; Daniel Vickers, "Competency and Competition: Economic Culture in Early America," *William and Mary Quarterly*, 3d ser., 47, 1 (Jan. 1990), 3–29, esp. 7–9; Winifred B. Rothenberg, "The Emergence of Farm Labor Markets and the Transformation of the Rural Economy: Massachusetts, 1750–1855," *Journal of Economic History*, 48, 3 (Sept. 1988), 537–66, esp. 544–5. See generally Allan Kulikoff, "The Transition to Capitalism in Rural America," *William and Mary Quarterly*, 3d ser., 46, 1 (Jan. 1989), 94–119.

[57] Robert Steinfeld has argued that it is the absence of any discussion of criminal restraint that lends *Stark* its real significance (*Invention of Free Labor*, 150).

loss of wages owed on an agreement to labor for a specific term (a parol agreement at that) seems a significant move toward enhanced contractual discipline.[58]

FIDELITY, OBEDIENCE, CONTROL

The cases denying departing employees *quantum meruit* recovery of wages owed not only exhibited the courts' increasingly explicit tendency to have resort to an Anglocentric master/servant paradigm in comprehending employment relationships as a whole but also underscored the judiciary's tendency to articulate their approval of the paradigm's hierarchical incidents in terms of their social utility: It was a necessary and desirable feature of the social organization of work across the full range of agricultural and industrial occupations that the employer's authority should

---

[58] The practice of *quantum meruit* recovery with damages to the employer in setoff was endorsed in the New Hampshire decision *Britton v. Turner*, 6 N.H. 431 (1834), but the "entirety" construction prevailed everywhere else until the 1850s. See Wythe Holt, "Recovery by the Worker Who Quits: A Comparison of the Mainstream, Legal Realist, and Critical Legal Studies Approaches to a Problem of Nineteenth Century Contract Law," *Wisconsin Law Review*, 1986, no. 4:677–732, at 678–700. Holt's analysis has been criticized by Peter Karsten, who argues that the application of entire contracts' nonapportionment rules to the hiring of labor was not an early nineteenth-century innovation but followed established English and colonial practice with regard to retainers for hire. Karsten, however, does not give adequate attention to the doctrinal issues raised in n. 48 above, nor does he take proper account of the contrary evidence supplied in the *Courier*'s reporting of *Stark v. Parker*. Nor is Karsten's claim that American courts were in fact moving away from the entirety standard prior to the 1850s particularly convincing, given that *Britton v. Turner* is the only instance he can cite. See Karsten, "'Bottomed on Justice,'" 213–47.

Karsten makes a stronger case in contending that courts held employers to as strict standards of behavior in construing their liability in breaches of contracts as their employees, punishing employer breaches of "entire" contracts by awarding the *full value* of the contract to the plaintiff employee ("'Bottomed on Justice,'" 248–55). Standards, of course, dwell in the eye of the beholder. In *Marsh v. Rulesson*, 1 Wend. 514 (N.Y. 1828), at 515, for example, Chief Justice Savage found that a farmhand who had been sworn at by his employer for his refusal to work on Sundays had not been justified in quitting, though he admitted that the language used "was extremely improper." See also *Singer v. McCormick*, 4 Watts and Serg. 265 (Pa. 1842), where it was held justifiable for a clerk ordered by one partner in a firm to alter certain ledger entries on a partnership account to be discharged for so doing by the other partner. Some courts also appeared to think distinguishing among employees of different status not inappropriate in considering claims for damages as a result of their employers' breaches of contract. In *Costigan v. The Mohawk and Hudson Rail-Road Co.*, 2 Denio 609 (N.Y. 1846), for example, the New York Supreme Court granted a railroad superintendent discharged without cause the full value of his contract and rejected the defendant company's contention that the plaintiff was obliged to mitigate his damages by seeking employment. Seven years earlier, in *Shannon v. Comstock*, 21 Wend. 457 (N.Y. 1839), at 462, the same court had indicated in dicta that a manual laborer faced with an employer's breach of a contract of hire could recover only actual loss, which he would also be required to mitigate. "A mason is engaged to work for a month, and tenders himself and offers to perform, but his hirer declines the service. The next day the mason is employed at equal wages elsewhere for a month. Clearly his loss is but one day; and it is his duty to seek other employment. *Idleness is in itself a breach of moral obligation. But if he continues idle for the purpose of charging another, he superadds a fraud, which the law had rather punish than countenance*" (emphasis supplied). For an English court's discussion of the salience of status, see *Beeston v. Collyer*, 172 E.R. 276 (1827). See also Jay Feinman, "The Development of the Employment at Will Rule," *American Journal of Legal History*, 20 (1976), 118–35, at 131–5.

be reinforced in this way.[59] In *Stark*, for example, the court had indicated that it conceived of the parties as necessarily unequal by dint of the kind of relationship in which it found them. The service of the plaintiff for a year was a condition precedent to his recovery of the stipulated compensation, and this, the court announced, was how "employer and employed alike universally so understand it." Not only, moreover, was the laborer worthy of his hire "only upon the performance of his contract," he was worthy of it only if he had performed *faithfully*. Wages were not just the price of labor – payment for work done – they were "the reward of fidelity."[60] The same sentiments were aired in other states. "Faithful service," said the Supreme Court of Pennsylvania, was a condition precedent to the right to recover wages. It was a matter of the soundest policy that conduct "inconsistent with the relation of master and servant" be penalized by their loss.[61] Thus, "when a servant . . . is turned away by his master before the period for which he has engaged to serve has expired, and his dismissal be in consequence of his own misconduct, he will be entitled to no wages."[62] In New York, Supreme Court Chief Justice Savage similarly held that failure to perform according to an employer's "lawful and reasonable commands" rendered a servant "burthensome and useless" and warranted immediate dismissal without wages and without compensation.[63] Employment relationships, that is, had a necessary authoritarian component distinguishing them from other kinds of contracts: The employer was entitled not only

[59] This was expressed in a progressive broadening of the paradigm's ambit to encompass more and more employment situations. See, e.g., *Thayer v. Mann*, 56 Mass. 371 (1841); *Denny v. Cabot*, 42 Mass. 82 (1843). Often the outcome in the individual case was to the benefit of the employee/servant. In *Thayer v. Mann*, e.g., Mann was an insolvent putter-out of materials for bootmaking, whom Thayer was suing for payment for boots made, using the provisions of the statute of 1838, c. 163, An Act for the Relief of Insolvent Debtors, which gave preference to a creditor who was "an operative in the service of" an insolvent. Mann's attorney argued that Thayer was not an operative within the meaning of the statute, given that he performed the work on his own premises and used his own tools and was not under the defendant's supervision. The court disagreed, and Thayer recovered. The case is significant in its illustration of the process by which the law creates structures into which litigants have to fit themselves in order to benefit, and that those structures have consequences. Here, Thayer – an independent artisan – becomes an "operative" and is described throughout the court's opinion as a "laborer." See also a different line of cases illustrating the distinct but related point that employees/servants are purveyors of services alone and can claim no property in the goods they produce, even where they add material in the process of production: *Eaton v. Lynde*, 15 Mass. 242 (1818); *Stevens v. Briggs*, 22 Mass. 177 (1827); *Judson v. Adams*, 62 Mass. 562 (1851). See generally *King v. Indian Orchard Canal Company*, 65 Mass. 231 (1853).

[60] 19 Mass. 267, at 275 (emphasis supplied). Nineteenth-century courts, as we see here and as we shall see further in the following chapter, demonstrated considerable resourcefulness in constantly adding to the list of what an employer supposedly bought with the offer of wages. Thus in judicial imagination a wage rate reflected the price of labor in current conditions of supply and demand but also a premium that the employer agreed to pay the employee in return for the latter's assumption of the perils of the occupation. It bought the value-added by the employee in performing the labor agreed but also the employee's fidelity in performance. As far as the courts were concerned, there was seemingly no end to the number of purchases an employer could be held to have made at any given wage rate.

[61] *Libhart v. Wood*, 267; *Singer v. McCormick*, 4 Watts and Serg. 265 (1842), at 266–7.

[62] *Libhart v. Wood*, 267.

[63] See *Lantry v. Parks*, 8 Cowen 63 (1827), at 64; *Marsh v. Rulesson*, 1 Wend. 514 (1828), at 515.

to receipt of the services contracted for in their entirety prior to payment but also to the obedience of the employee in the process of rendering them.

Courts demonstrated their readiness to extend the master/servant paradigm and its authoritarian incidents in the case of wage labor not only in the language they employed to describe wage workers and their implied contractual obligations of respect and obedience but also by allowing hirers of wage labor access to common law rules and actions which had hitherto governed the narrower arena of "traditional" master/servant relationships; rules and actions, that is, which previously had been used to protect a master's property in his *menial* servant's services. We have already noted the New York Supreme Court's willingness in *Woodward v. Washburn* to allow an action *per quod servitium amisit* in the case of an employer not in loco parentis and an adult hired worker. The court also confirmed that employers might police the property they had acquired in the labor of their wage worker employees through actions of enticement or harboring against others interfering with the master/servant relation. "Every master has, by his contract, purchased for a valuable consideration the services of his domestics," held the court, quoting Blackstone. "The inveigling or hiring his servant, which induces a breach of this contract, is therefore an injury to the master."[64] The point was underlined six years later in *Haight v. Badgeley*. "No absolute property can in this state be acquired in the person or personal services of an adult, by an executory contract. Nor have we, and probably we never shall have here, criminal proceedings to enforce such a contract of hiring, as in England. But unless there is something in the genius of our institutions that renders the law of the mother country inapplicable, it is here, as there, actionable, to entice from the service of another, one who is in the employment of the latter, under a contract not fully executed."[65]

The same point was made by courts in Pennsylvania.[66] In *Dunlop's Lessee v. Speer*

---

[64] 3 Denio 369, 372. See also *Dubois v. Allen*, 1 Anthon NP 94 (1809); *James v. Le Roy*, 1 Anthon NP 117 (1809), 6 Johnson 274 (1810); *Scidmore v. Smith*, 13 Johnson 322 (1816); *Stuart v. Simpson*, 1 Wend. 376 (1828). See also the New York Common Pleas case *Wallack v. Gilfert* (1827), reported in the *Boston Courier*, 7 Mar. 1827, where the plaintiff theater manager successfully sued the defendant, also a theater manager, for persuading a husband and wife team of performers then under contract with the plaintiff to abandon their contracts with the plaintiff in favor of performing instead for the defendant. (One should note that in this case only nominal damages were awarded. At this time such "professional" employees were not generally considered subject to master/servant law. Consistent with the argument of this chapter, they were later to become so. On this, see Lea S. VanderVelde, "Hidden Dimensions in Labor Law History: Gender Variations on the Theme of Free Labor," in Christopher L. Tomlins and Andrew J. King, eds., *Labor Law in America: Historical and Critical Essays* (Baltimore, 1992), 99–127; idem, "The Gendered Origins of the *Lumley* Doctrine: Binding Men's Consciences and Women's Fidelity," *Yale Law Journal*, 101, 4 (Jan. 1992), 775–852.

[65] 15 Barbour's SC 499 (1853), at 501.

[66] In his *Institutes of American Law* (Philadelphia, 1858), 1:532–3, John Bouvier stated, "As the master is entitled to the services of his servant . . . [e]nticing a workman who is employed by another for a definite time, before such time has expired, is an injury committed to his employer, and this though he be but a journeyman. And if a servant leave his master's employment, without just cause, and a third person retain him, and knowingly harbor him, so as to deprive the master of his services, an action lies." In support he cited the English case *Hart v. Aldridge*, 1 Cowp. 55 (1774), two New York cases involving menials (*Scidmore v. Smith* and *Dubois v. Allen*), and the Massachusetts case *Boston Glass Manufactory v. Binney*, for details of which see below.

(1810), for example, the Supreme Court of Pennsylvania noted that inciting workmen in the employ of another to quit was a tort that, on proof, would give rise to a claim of damages against the inciter.[67] The issue was adverted to more directly two years later by Brackenridge J., in *Ex Parte Meason*: "Will it be said that an action in Pennsylvania will not lie for enticing away a laborer at husbandry hired by the day, week, month or year?" Brackenridge asked, again quoting Blackstone for authority. "Much less that it will not for enticing away hands employed at a manufactory?"[68]

As in New York and Pennsylvania, so in Massachusetts: After the turn of the century, actions for enticing and/or harboring, previously confined to bound servants, begin to crop up in the case of workers who had simply left one employer and gone to work for another.[69] In 1808, for example, the firm of John Brooks and Company, merchant tailors of Boston, recovered damages from one Daniel Dunwell for harboring and employing two tailors, George Hamilton and Robert Gray, who had both previously contracted to work for the plaintiff for three years.[70] The issue arose again some years later in *Boston Glass Manufactory v. Binney* (1827), where the plaintiffs alleged that representatives of a rival firm had enticed a number of skilled workmen in several departments of their establishment to leave and go to work for the rival. In this action the court found that there was no case to answer: The workmen allegedly enticed were not bound by any current contract or engagement, their contracts having expired, their continuing employment was based simply on a "mutual understanding" shared with the plaintiff company that neither party would withdraw from their relationship without giving a fortnight's notice. Yet there was clearly no doubt in the court's mind that the plaintiff's action would have been quite appropriate had it been able to produce acceptable evidence that the defendant's intervention had disrupted a continuing relationship with the workers in question.[71]

---

[67] 3 Binney 169 (1810), at 170, 173. See also *Heck v. Shener*, 4 Sergeant and Rawles 249 (1818), at 259.

[68] *Ex Parte Meason*, 181. For an account of Delaware manufacturing employers' contemporaneous attempts to invoke enticement to protect their interests in hired labor, see George H. Gibson, "Labor Piracy on the Brandywine," *Labor History*, 8, 2 (Spring 1967), 175–82.

[69] Nelson, *Americanization of the Common Law*, 125–6. See also Orren, "Organized Labor and Modern Liberalism," 329; Morris, *Government and Labor*, 433; Reeve, *Law of Baron and Femme*, 377. Like my own, Morris's research suggests that enticement actions were confined during the colonial period to formally bound (that is, apprenticed or indentured) servants (414–34).

[70] *Brooks v. Dunwell*, Supreme Judicial Court (Suffolk County, Mass.) *nisi prius* session, Nov. term 1808 (Continuing Action 224). See also *Dorr v. Winship*, Supreme Judicial Court (Suffolk County, Mass.) *nisi prius* session, Mar. term 1810 (Continuing Action 75). In Massachusetts as elsewhere, most early nineteenth-century enticement actions continued to involve minor servants and apprentices. See, e.g., *Carlton v. Joy*, Supreme Judicial Court (Suffolk County, Mass.) *nisi prius* session, Feb. term 1803 (Continuing Actions 98 and 99); *Gammell v. Major*, Suffolk CCP, Oct. term 1805, 161; *Rayner v. Waite*, Suffolk CCP, Oct. term 1825, 79. And see *Massachusetts Acts* 1793, c. 59, An Act Providing for the Relief and Support, Employment and Removal of the Poor, where it was stated that "every person enticing any . . . apprentice or servant [bound out to service by the Overseers of the Poor] to elope from his master, or harbouring him, knowing him to have eloped, shall be liable to the master's action for all damages sustained thereby."

[71] 21 Mass. 425. In fact, at the *nisi prius* hearing of the Suffolk Supreme Judicial Court, Chief Justice Parsons had advised the jury that notwithstanding the absence of a current agreement, *any* approach by another party constituted enticement as long as actual employment continued, even if notice to quit had

Subsequently the enticement action was placed fully on the contract of employment and reconceptualized as a "tort of interference with contractual relations," effectively confirming the employment contract as an enforceable grant to the employer of property rights in the employee's labor, in the enjoyment of which the employer was entitled to both common law and also equitable protections.[72] As we have already seen in the conspiracy cases, under certain circumstances that property right was also considered protectable by criminal indictment. In *Commonwealth v. Hunt*, for example, Chief Justice Shaw clearly indicated that interferences with contractual relations were criminal where persons engaged in a dispute with an employer sought to restrain other employees from fulfilling existing agreements, or engaged in a concerted breach of their own. Men might lawfully agree together "as to the manner in which they would exercise an acknowledged right to contract with others for their labor." Once bound by contract "for a certain time," however, interference, as in a collective quitting of employment, was criminally sanctionable.[73]

been given. At the full bench hearing, however, the court inclined to the view that there had been no attempt to entice from actual employment but only the offer of a new agreement to commence after the requisite notice was given to the original employer. The court offered no criticism of Parsons's statement of the law, simply questioning whether there was sufficient evidence of a subsisting engagement to justify a finding in favor of the plaintiff in this case (426, 427–8). For later examples of resort to enticement actions in Massachusetts see *Pelby v. Barry*, Supreme Judicial Court (Suffolk County, Mass.) *nisi prius* session, Nov. term 1835 (New Entry 269) and Nov. term 1836 (Continuing Action 145); *Ayer v. Chase*, 36 Mass. 556 (1837); *Brown v. Burnett*, U.S. Circuit Court (First Circuit, District of Massachusetts), Oct. term 1847, in Charles Greeley Loring Papers, unprocessed manuscript collection, Social Law Library, Boston; *Butterfield v. Ashley*, 60 Mass. 249 (1850); *Butterfield v. Ashley*, 68 Mass. 254 (1854); *Walker v. Cronin*, 107 Mass. 555 (1871).

[72] See *Lumley v. Wagner*, 42 E.R. 687 (1852); *Lumley v. Gye*, 118 E.R. 749 (1853); John Nockelby, Note, "Tortious Interference with Contractual Relations in the Nineteenth Century: The Transformation of Property, Contract, and Tort," *Harvard Law Review*, 93 (1980), 1510–39; VanderVelde, "The Gendered Origins of the *Lumley* Doctrine." As VanderVelde shows, equitable restraints on employees breaching employment contracts became a notable feature of employment in the second half of the century. In one of the first such cases, *Hayes v. Willio*, 11 Abb. Pr. N.S. 167 (1871), at 176, the New York Court of Common Pleas upheld a request for injunctive relief from a theater manager seeking to prevent an actor from performing for a rival contrary to a term in his contract requiring the plaintiff's consent. "It is indisputable, that when theatrical managers with large capital invested in their business, making contracts with performers of attractive talents, and relying upon such contracts to carry on the business of their theaters, are suddenly deserted by the performers in the middle of their season, the resort to actions at law for damages must fail to afford adequate compensation. It is not always that the manager is deprived of his means of carrying on his business, but that his performers, by carrying their services to other establishments, deprive him of the fruits of his diligence and enterprise, increase the rivalry against him, and cause him an injury. It is as much his right, if he have a contract to that effect, that no other establishment shall have the services of his performers as that he shall have them himself." The judgment was subsequently reversed, but on an unrelated point. See *Hayes v. Willio*, 4 Daly 259 (1872). On the later development of equitable remedies against third-party labor unions held to be interfering in an existing employment relationship, see Felix Frankfurter and Nathan Greene, *The Labor Injunction* (New York, 1930); William E. Forbath, "The Shaping of the American Labor Movement," *Harvard Law Review*, 102, 6 (Apr. 1989).

[73] 45 Mass, 111 (1842), at 130–1. As I have pointed out in Chapter 6, in his charge to the jury at the original trial in the Boston Municipal Court, Peter Oxenbridge Thacher had argued that indeed the defendants *had* been guilty of exactly the kind of collective "unlawful interference . . . with a subsisting contract between other persons" that Shaw regarded as criminally indictable. See *Commonwealth v. Hunt*, Thacher's Criminal Cases 609 (1840), at 644. In the Supreme Judicial Court, however, Shaw held that

The widening scope accorded the enticement action by American courts during the first half of the nineteenth century exemplifies the carryover into the generic nineteenth-century law of employment of key disciplinary characteristics from the narrower sphere of master/servant household relations. Early in the century American courts had already indicated the continuing availability of enticement as an action to protect a master's property in the personal services of his apprentice or his indentured servant, and a parent's property in the services of a child. As its catchment area expanded, however, master/servant migrated from its home among the personal relations where Tapping Reeve et al., following Blackstone, had left it, toward what Timothy Walker called "the business relations." This relocation made eminent sense to Walker: Master and servant "has in fact very little to do with domestics, or domestic life," he wrote in 1837.[74] It also made sense to American courts, and by midcentury the tendency to remove master and servant from among the personal relations was becoming manifest in judicial opinion.[75] Simultaneously, however, American courts used Blackstone's affirmation of the master's property in the service of his *domestics* as authority to recognize a similar property in business employers and allowed them resort to actions founded on the personal relations (*per quod*, enticement, harboring) to protect their "property" in the labor of adult wage workers (farm laborers, factory operatives, skilled artisans).[76] In this way, the presumption that employment as a social relation was necessarily defined by the exercise of authority by a superior over a subordinate in whatever processes of production in which the latter was engaged was joined by the recognition of a capacity in the

the *Hunt* indictment had not successfully alleged an indictable interference. The point upon which Thacher and Shaw differed, then, was not whether a collective interference with an existing engagement was sanctionable as a common law conspiracy but whether, in this case, the behavior of the defendants amounted to such an interference. It is important to note that in this regard the position adopted by both Shaw and Thacher contrasted markedly with that of the court in the *Philadelphia Tailors'* case fifteen years earlier, where it was held that a violation of a contract "might be the subject of a civil action, but not of a criminal charge." See Marcus T. C. Gould, *Trial of Twenty-four Journeymen Tailors, Charged With Conspiracy* (Philadelphia, 1827), 158. On the continuation of conspiracy indictments after the Civil War see Victoria C. Hattam, "Economic Visions and Political Strategies: American Labor and the State, 1865–1896," *Studies in American Political Development*, 4 (1990), 108–9; idem, *Labor Visions and State Power: The Origins of Business Unionism in the United States* (Princeton, 1992), Chapter, 2.

The point debated in their different judgments by Shaw and Thacher – whether the collective action of the journeymen constituted an indictable or actionable third-party interference in subsisting contractual relations – would become a key element in American labor law's treatment of labor unions in the late nineteenth and twentieth centuries (Christopher L. Tomlins, "Labor Law," in Stanley L. Engerman and Robert E. Gallman, eds., *The Cambridge Economic History of the United States*, vol. 3, forthcoming). And see also Dianne Avery, "Images of Violence in Labor Jurisprudence: The Regulation of Picketing and Boycotts, 1894–1921," *Buffalo Law Review*, 37 (1988/9), 1–117. Karen Orren has argued that in fact from the beginning a subtext of enticement pervades all nineteenth-century American labor conspiracy cases. See her *Belated Feudalism: Labor, the Law, and Liberal Development in the United States* (New York, 1991), 106–7, 122–8.

[74] Walker, *Introduction to American Law*, 250.

[75] See, e.g., *Ryan v. The Cumberland Valley Railroad Company*, 23 Penn. St. R. 384 (1854), at 387.

[76] In his opinion for the court in *Boston Glass v. Binney*, e.g., Wilde J. clearly identified the skilled workers involved as "laborers" and then proceeded to identify "laborers" as "servants" (21 Mass. 425, at 428). For an example of the insinuation of hierarchical master/servant incidents into the nonhierarchical bailment relationship see the Introduction to Part 3.

employer to protect that authority from outsiders on the basis of a property right enjoyed by the employer in the labor performed. During the first half of the century, these were established as the key elements in the legal definition of the kind of "business" relationship that a contract of employment actually constituted.[77]

EMPLOYER RULES

In choosing to construe relations between the new generation of *business* employers and their employees through resort to common law rules and procedures previously protective of the master's property rights in, and dispositive authority over, the labor of household servants, American courts ensured that master/servant law's indubitably hierarchical conception of the social relations appropriate to productive labor would be indelibly imprinted on the early republic's emerging industrial society. One might think of this as a kind of functional response to the "demands of capitalism," but as we have seen, the response largely predated the demands. Hence, although such an approach retains considerable appeal in a general structural sense, it seems inadequate as an explanation of human decision making.[78] Rather, I think the early republic's jurists were behaving in this corner of their juridical lives more or less as they did across the whole spectrum of their activities. At a time of considerable social fluidity, democratic pressure, and political stress – a time shown by Martin Wiener's recent dissection of nineteenth-century discourses of criminality and penality to be one of widespread concern at the apparent social chaos inherent in uncontrollable individual willfulness[79] – they staked their faith in law, particularly the common law, as *the* great rock of cultural stability and ideological certainty. In the law of employment relationships, as elsewhere, their efforts were emblematic of a process of putting in place what were deemed to be the essential elements of an orderly society.

As manufacturing and transportation enterprises increased in scale during the 1830s and 1840s, however, one begins to encounter instances of a further restatement of master and servant, extending the magisterial authority vested in the person of the employer to the disembodied figure of the corporation. Significantly, in addition, whereas the personally authoritative employer had been subject to rules of law which retained for the courts the role of ultimate exponents of authority's ambit, as exemplified in the case of apprenticeship, this further restatement saw courts concede to the employer the capacity to exercise powers of detailed regulation in workplace relations for itself.[80] What emerged was a legal discourse of employment

[77] See Otto Kahn-Freund, "Blackstone's Neglected Child: The Contract of Employment," *Law Quarterly Review*, 93 (1977), 510–12, 521–3; Philip Selznick, *Law, Society, and Industrial Justice* (New York, 1969), 122–37.

[78] I return to this point below, in An Interlude: On Law and Economy.

[79] Martin J. Wiener, *Reconstructing the Criminal: Culture, Law, and Policy in England 1830–1914* (New York and Cambridge, 1990).

[80] Similar developments had occurred earlier in England. See Hay, "Masters, Servants, Justices, and Judges," 16–18.

increasingly leaving it to employers to exercise detailed control over the employed, a translation of master/servant's concepts of the authoritative employer and the subordinate employee into the secular language of "management" – *internal* and *internalized* regulation. This was a devolution justified in the name of free contractual assent.

The law-described and law-enforced authority of the master was invoked by the new corporate employers as the foundation for their *additional* claim to exercise powers of detailed regulation in workplace relations. Take, for example, the concluding paragraph of the "General Regulations" of the Lawrence Manufacturing Company of Lowell, Massachusetts, in the early 1830s, describing the basis upon which all other regulations promulgated by the corporation rested. "Persons in the employ of the Company will reflect, *that it is their voluntary agreement to serve*, and *the consequent mutual relations of the parties*, which renders it proper on their part to conform to regulations, and warrants the Agent in promulgating rules for their observance. They will perceive that where objects are to be obtained by the united efforts and labor of many individuals, some must direct and many be directed." Assent to enter employment, then, bound the employee to certain consequences built automatically into their contractual relationship.[81]

Such claims by corporate employers had implications for the place of the courts in the regime of employment law, which thus far the courts had been instrumental in constructing. In most of the cases we have examined, the courts' work of adaptation involved their adjudication of the application of available legal rules to new American circumstances but not any particular change in the historical position of the court itself as the arbiter of the master/servant relationship. In a series of cases in the 1830s and 1840s in Massachusetts, however, courts began to consider how far the rule-making activities of corporate employers could themselves determine the legal consequences, for employees, of entering an employment relationship; how far, that is, regulations promulgated unilaterally by the employer in the course of business would be treated as incidents of the contract of employment supposedly produced by negotiation between the parties.

In the earliest of these cases, *Stevens v. Reeves* (1829), the Supreme Judicial Court was faced with a complete clash of work cultures. Reeves, a weaver and a recent emigrant from England, engaged to occupy a loom in the weaving shed of an

---

[81] "General Regulations, to be Observed by Persons Employed by the Lawrence Manufacturing Company, in Lowell," 21 May 1833, broadside, Kress Library, Harvard Business School, Cambridge, 2 (emphasis supplied). The company's 1833 regulations were lengthy, wordy, and written in a tone of appeal to the reasonableness and good sense of the work force, inviting compliance. The revised regulations issued some ten years later were, in contrast, curt and commanding. They concluded without elaboration: "these regulations are considered a part of the contract with all persons entering into the employment of the Lawrence Manufacturing Company" ("Regulations to be Observed by all Persons Employed by the Lawrence Manufacturing Company," 1842 [?], broadside, Kress Library, Harvard Business School). For a survey of early factory rules, see Zonderman, *Aspirations and Anxieties*, 144–55. David Roediger has concluded that, by the 1840s, "[t]he factory system tended to confine and discipline workers to an unprecedented extent" (*The Wages of Whiteness: Race and the Making of the American Working Class* [London, 1991], 69).

Andover wool factory and to be paid by the piece. He wove for a few days, left for a few days, returned and wove a few days more, then sought payment for what he had produced and left permanently. The factory then brought an action to recover damages for Reeves's "breach of contract" on the grounds that he had failed to comply with a rule requiring two weeks' notice of intention to quit. The court found that Reeves had not been made aware of the rule nor been given an opportunity to make himself aware of it, and thus that the rule could not be held to be an implied term of his engagement.

Reeves had behaved, as any skilled artisan working in his own shop might, as an independent mechanic producing goods at his own convenience for a customer from materials supplied by that customer. The alteration in the physical circumstances achieved by the customer's centralization of production in his own shed equipped with his own tools had not altered Reeves's perception of what their relationship entailed, as expressed in his behavior. Reeves had acted as an independent contractor and treated the factory as a customer. The question for the court was whether the factory's rule – promulgated, as the Lawrence Manufacturing Company example demonstrates, as a means of expressing the factory's authority in its relations with its employees – was sufficient to vacate Reeves's own perception of himself. The court's answer affirmed the power of the rule while denying its applicability in the instant case. Had Reeves's situation been such that it might reasonably support the inference either that he knew the rule or that he could have known the rule, the rule would have been determinative of his relationship with his employer.

Buried in the court's decision, then, was an endorsement of the employer's determinative rule-making authority. Nor was the protection against its invocation – the requirement of knowledge in the employee – particularly comprehensive; there was considerable elasticity in the court's conception of the appropriate test for reasonable opportunity to know. "As the usage supposed is a particular one [that is, particular to this employer] . . . it should have appeared, that the defendant knew of the usage when he entered upon the work or before he left it." Had the plaintiff company been able to show the court that its particular usage was an expression of a general requirement common to like establishments, the court would have presumed the defendant's knowledge without more ado. Contemporary managerial practice was thus to be conclusive of the issue. In effect, the court left the possibility for Reeves's self-perception to endure to turn, rather delicately, on whether the generality of his potential employers would decide to allow it to endure.[82]

The next such case, *Hunt v. The Otis Company* (1842), rendered the court's accommodation of the employer's rules in interpreting the employment relationship

---

[82] 26 Mass. 198, at 200–1. Employer rules did, of course, demonstrate precisely this tendency to become standardized over time. See the Lawrence Company rules in n. 81, and cf. the 1842 version with the "Regulations to be Observed by all Persons Employed in the Factories of the Middlesex Company," 1846, broadside, Kress Library, Harvard Business School; and the "Regulations to be Observed by all Persons employed by the Dwight Manufacturing Company," n.d., reproduced in *Mary Rice v. The Dwight Manufacturing Company*, 56 Mass. 80 (1848), at 81.

more explicit. In this case, Elvira Hunt sued the Otis Company for sixty dollars in unpaid wages. The company contended that the accrued wages were wholly forfeit as a result of Hunt's failure to give four weeks' notice of her intention to quit. The company offered proof that the plaintiff knew of the regulation when she entered its employ, contending that the regulation had therefore become part of her contract of employment. The court found that the plaintiff was bound by the regulation and had therefore broken her contract and was liable in damages to her employer but that her liability extended only to such a sum as would compensate the defendants for losses actually sustained as a result of the breach. The breach of the defendants' regulation did not justify a forfeiture of the whole sum owed by them to her, for "the defendants' regulation . . . did not contain in its terms the stipulation, that in case of quitting without giving the four weeks' notice, the wages accrued should be forfeited." As in *Stevens v. Reeves*, however, it endorsed the power of the employer to achieve the desired result for itself simply by altering its own rules. Indeed, having noted that "this regulation of the defendants is important to them in the due management of their business, not merely in regard to this case, but as to others," it invited the defendant so to act:

[I]f the construction now given to this regulation, in respect to the damages for the breach thereof, is calculated in its tendency to produce injurious effects to the defendants, they have only to enlarge their rule by adding to it a clause of forfeiture of wages accrued, and a requisition that operatives entering their service sign it.[83]

The determinative status of such a regulation was confirmed in the third of these "employer rules" cases, *Rice v. The Dwight Manufacturing Company* (1848).[84] Here Mary Rice sought to recover $13.64 for three weeks' employment in the defendant's mill. The company alleged that the wages were forfeit on the grounds that its rules provided only for annual engagements with four weeks' notice of an intention to quit. To prove the nature of the contract the company offered in evidence a copy of its rules, which were posted in the mill and which were handed to every person hired, inscribed with the employee's name. These provided, inter alia, that "all persons entering the employ of the company . . . are considered as engaged to work one year, if the company require their services so long" and that "all persons intending to leave the employment of the company are to give four weeks notice of their intention to their overseer; and their engagement with the company is not considered as fulfilled, unless they comply with this regulation."[85]

At the initial lower court trial of the suit, the presiding judge ruled that it was for the jury to decide whether the defendant's regulations determined Rice's

[83] 45 Mass. 464, at 467–8. As we shall shortly see, an employee's signature did not turn out to be necessary for courts to infer their acknowledgment of employer rules. Simply giving an employee a copy of the establishment's regulations was sufficient. See *Rice v. The Dwight Manufacturing Company; Mitchell v. Pennsylvania R.R. Company*, 1 American Law Register 717 (1853).

[84] The case was described by the defendants, on appeal, as one involving but a small amount of money but "of a class important" (Shaw, Minute Books, 42:39).

[85] 56 Mass. 80, at 81. These were standard requirements, varying from company to company only in the length of the period of notice required.

contract of employment.[86] He also left open the question whether, in any case, there was sufficient mutuality in the terms of the alleged agreement to constitute it as a binding contract.[87] The company took exception, arguing that the only question to be decided was the factual question whether or not the plaintiff had been furnished with the company's regulations. If so, then as a matter of law the plaintiff was bound by all their provisions whether she had understood them or not. The jury found for the plaintiff, but on appeal the company's exceptions were granted and the lower court judge held to have erred in allowing the jury to determine the import of the defendant's regulations. "It was, no doubt, the province of the jury to decide all questions of fact; but it was the duty of the court to instruct the jury, hypothetically, that if a particular fact or combination of facts was proved, certain legal consequences would follow." Whether or not the plaintiff had received the regulations was a question for the jury, but not whether those regulations, once proved to have been received, were terms of her contract. That followed automatically. The lower court judge was also criticized for allowing the jury to consider the possibility of a want of mutuality or understanding. "When a contract is reduced to writing, it may, and probably does, sometimes happen, that one or both of the contracting parties misapprehend the legal effect of the writing. Yet if it be not altogether unintelligible, the court will read the contract for the parties, and they will be bound by its legal effect. . . . If the plaintiff had read the regulations, or if she had received from the operatives in the mill, or from other sources, general information as to their contents, and was content to waive further inquiry, and, with the imperfect information which she possessed, entered into the contract, it appears to us that she would have been bound, and that the jury should have been so instructed."[88]

---

[86] The trial court judge instructed the jury, "that as the regulation paper was not signed by the defendants, nor delivered by [the plaintiff], as a contract, to the defendants, she was not, by the acceptance of the paper and promise, as before stated, necessarily bound by its provisions, according to their legal interpretation, as a contract; that the fact, that she took the paper under the circumstances stated, was strong evidence, tending to prove that she regarded it as a contract binding upon her, and that she had read and understood its contents, but it was only evidence of the fact; that as the regulations professed to make but a part of the contract, and the evidence of the rest of the contract must be sought from other sources, and as these regulations contained various stipulations, which could not enter into the contract of the plaintiff and defendants, and it was claimed that they were so obscure that they could not be understood by common minds, it was not a question of law to the court, as to the legal construction to be given to the several stipulations contained in the regulation paper; but the whole evidence presented a question of fact for the jury to decide, which question was, whether a contract had been made, and, if made, whether it had been broken by the plaintiff" (ibid., 82–3).

[87] "The jury, when determining the question, whether there was any misunderstanding of the parties in the present instance, might take into account the alleged obscurity of the regulation paper. . . . It was incumbent upon the defendants, in order to maintain their defence, to satisfy the jury, that there was an agreement between the parties, embracing all the particulars essential to a valid contract, and understood alike by both, in all its essential particulars" (ibid., 83–4).

[88] Ibid., 82–4, 85–7. See also a distinct line of cases dealing with the employment of children that have the same effect of underlining the employer's undiluted authority over the employee (in these cases at the expense of parental control): *Adams v. The Woonsocket Company*, 52 Mass. 327 (1846); *Dodge v. Favor*, 81 Mass. 82 (1860); *McIntyre v. Fuller*, 84 Mass. 345 (1861). On the erosion of the family system of labor in the Slater mills of southwestern Massachusetts and its replacement by managerial control, see Barbara

The Supreme Judicial Court's increasingly formalistic disquisition on the law of contracts in the employer rules cases, in particular its resort to formal rules of contractual construction in Rice's case, obscured the impact on the employment relationship of the disparities in the parties' relative capacities to act that the parallel juridical resort to master/servant reasoning had helped so effectively to entrench. Once having voluntarily entered employment, the employee was left subject to the employer's *managerial* exercise of authority, an authority rendered remote from its legal base, private, and largely unaccountable. Those who sought to dilute the employer's directive power by invoking public authority as intervenor found themselves simply referred back to their employers. "Labor is intelligent enough to make its own bargains and look out for its own interests."[89]

Increasingly, courts justified this outcome through resort to a discourse of labor freedom and liberty of contract. As free persons owning their own capacity to labor, employees who entered into employment signified by that action their assent to be bound by the terms and conditions upon which employment had been offered – terms and conditions that, presumptively, they had been given opportunity to negotiate.

Free labor, however, had multiple meanings. To the antebellum labor movement, free labor ideally meant economic independence through the ownership of productive property, or proprietorship. Failing this, free labor at the very least meant a far more substantive conception of contractual freedom for the wage laborer than the abstract formalism of mere self-ownership would allow.[90] We find that substantive conception expressed in *Olmstead v. Beale* (1837), a suit on appeal before the Massachusetts Supreme Judicial Court to recover wages owed to an agricultural laborer departing before term. Counsel argued on behalf of the plaintiff that courts were particularly obliged to construe contracts for personal labor with attention to the relativities of power pertaining between the parties.[91] Failure to do so would deny the less-powerful party the elementary comity that republican ideals "of liberty and independence" required American courts to preserve. It would reduce labor to "a species of slavery," inviting eventual "collision and controversy."[92]

M. Tucker, *Samuel Slater and the Origins of the American Textile Industry, 1790–1860* (Ithaca N.Y., 1984), 214–49.

[89] *Report of the Special Committee of the Legislature of the Commonwealth of Massachusetts on the Petitions Relating to the Hours of Labor*, Massachusetts House Document no. 50 (March 1845), in John R. Commons et al., eds., *A Documentary History of American Industrial Society* (Cleveland, 1910–), 8:133–51, at 150.

[90] On the meanings of free labor in the antebellum north see William E. Forbath, "The Ambiguities of Free Labor: Labor and the Law in the Gilded Age," *Wisconsin Law Review*, July 1985, no. 4:767–817. See also Lea S. VanderVelde, "The Labor Vision of the Thirteenth Amendment," *University of Pennsylvania Law Review*, 138, 2 (Dec. 1989), 437–504.

[91] "If any species of contract ought to be construed favorably to give the party a compensation, when he has not performed his contract, it must be that for personal labor" (Shaw, Minute Books, 18:284).

[92] The plaintiff, said counsel, should have his whole wages, paying out of his compensation "all damages which the employer has suffered by reason of the nonperformance of the whole contract." This was consistent with law, good policy, and sound principle. In cases involving bonds, mortgages, and so forth, "the obligation is only to pay an actual indemnity and be exonerated from the legal obligation of the contract." In all such matters courts had recognized "a tacit condition that either party may quit when he becomes dissatisfied" (ibid.).

Unsurprisingly, Olmstead's counsel was not successful. The court's was a rather more dessicated liberty than that which counsel had invoked. Assuredly the condition of laborers might merit sympathy, but sympathy had no place in a court of justice. Laborers lived under a government of equal laws and must hence "be subject to the same rules and principles as the rest of the community." Such were "elementary principles," which "admit of no exceptions in favor of any class or description of persons."[93]

Having created the authoritative employer as the central and essential fact of working life through their original resort to master/servant doctrine, antebellum courts refused, in the name of free labor and freedom of contract, to mediate the asymmetrical employment relationship they had created. Even when the asymmetries of the relationship were too visible to be ignored, as in Rice's case, where we find the Supreme Judicial Court expressing its incomprehension "that any person of sound mind, without circumvention, would enter into an agreement in the manner supposed," the result was not reconsideration of the incomprehensible but instead resort to deeper levels of formalistic discourse in which the issue became the protection of law's own prevailing ideational coherence. "When a party enters into a written contract, in the absence of fraud or imposition, he [*sic*] is conclusively presumed to understand the terms and legal effect of it, and to assent to them." Whether she realized it or not, by going to work for the company Rice had assented to the regulations. Even were it to be proved beyond doubt that she had no practical understanding of the regulations' import, "it would be dangerous to permit the contract to be avoided on the ground of ignorance."[94] Dangerous? To whom, one might ask? Not, surely, to Mary Rice, nor to that "class or description of persons" – laborers, operatives, employees; servants all, in legal contemplation – of whom she was one.[95] As Olmstead's counsel had argued, for them a greater freedom lay in intervention. If there were danger to be perceived in such an outcome, it had to be danger to the legal discourse by which Rice's case had been produced. Quite simply, if courts acknowledged that daily interactions between free working people and their employers were structured by relations of domination and subordination, they would also have to acknowledge how those relations were actually sustained by the very modes of reasoning they used to attribute meanings to those interactions. This, quite understandably, they were not disposed to do.

[93] 36 Mass. 528, at 528–9.

[94] 56 Mass. 80, at 87. It is worth keeping in mind that what the court was here describing as a written contract, as we have seen, was in fact a copy of the company's rules upon which its agent had written Rice's name.

[95] 36 Mass. 528, at 528. In *The Fall of the House of Labor: The Workplace, the State, and American Labor Activism, 1865–1925* (New York and Cambridge, 1987), at 65–6, David Montgomery draws attention to the social processes of naming workers and work. I hope to have demonstrated, in the course of this chapter, the signal role of the courts and of legal writers in these processes throughout the first half of the nineteenth century.

CONCLUSION

Two compelling images of the meaning of employment, one dominant, the other subterranean, became current in the American republic during the first half of the nineteenth century. The dominant image was of employment as a mutually beneficial relationship constructed by free and equal parties and secured by the courts. As Henry Williams of Taunton put it in 1853 during debates in the Massachusetts constitutional convention on the adoption of a secret ballot amendment to the state constitution, "In a free government like ours, employment is simply a contract between parties having equal rights. The operative agrees to perform a certain amount of work in consideration of receiving a certain amount of money. The work to be performed is, by the contract, an equivalent for the money to be paid. The relation, when properly entered into, is one of mutual benefit. The employed is under no greater obligation to the employer than the employer is to the employed. . . . In the eye of the law they are both freemen – citizens having equal rights, and brethren having one common destiny."[96] The subterranean image, in contrast, was one of legally sanctioned exploitation and inequality; "a cruel system," Seth Luther called it, "of exaction on the bodies and minds of the producing classes."[97]

Such contrasting images seem to have little in common. Yet they were related. Williams partly and Luther fully recognized the contradiction between the equality enjoyed by citizens as legal subjects and as electors of democratic governments and their manifest inequality in the employment relationship. Luther, for example, decried the viciously ironic contrast between the equality of the polls and the tyranny of the mills. "We have appealed to [the mill owners'] sense of justice, their sense of humanity, their love of country, to consider the evils they are bringing on the poor." What had been the reply? "'I will shut down my gates, and you will starve in a week, and rather than do *that* you will work on our terms.'" But at election time, "when these same men want the votes of the Working Men, they will say, in strains as sweet as angels use, 'Fellow Citizens, we want your assistance, give us your voices, your voices, your *sweet* voices.'"[98] Williams, observing the same contrast, feared for the republican equality of the franchise in the face of the coercion endemic in the workplace, where, inevitably, distinctions – of propertied and propertyless, rich and poor, employer and employed – dominated. "The practice of intimidation, has become with us an evil of great magnitude. It has increased, is increasing, and ought to be diminished. It has boldly entered the political field – controlled elections, and will, unless arrested, control our legislation, and determine the character of our institutions."[99]

[96] *Official Report of the Debates and Proceedings in the State Convention Assembled May 4th, 1853, to Revise and Amend the Constitution of the Commonwealth of Massachusetts* (Boston, 1853), 1:550. I am indebted to Robert J. Steinfeld, whose own work on this subject drew Williams's remarks to my attention.

[97] Seth Luther, *An Address to the Working Men of New England* (New York, 1833), 29. See also Orestes Brownson, *The Laboring Classes, an Article from the Boston Quarterly Review* (Boston, 1840).

[98] Luther, *Address to the Working Men of New England*, 25–6 (emphasis in original).

[99] *Debates and Proceedings*, 555.

291

Williams's solution was to seek the passage of a secret ballot law. His priority, that is, lay with the public appearance of formal civic equality at the polls. Manifestly this ignored the root cause of the problem, a cause he had himself identified, the growing disparity of power in the workplace. To address that cause would be to admit to the unreality of the dominant image of the employment relationship, something Williams, like the courts, seemed reluctant to do. Yet even acknowledging the threat and identifying its source was admission enough. Certainly "in a free government like ours" employment *ought* to be "simply a contract between parties having equal rights." Unfortunately, as Williams appeared to recognize despite himself, it wasn't.

The courts' choice of a discourse of master and servant to construct the meaning of employment was a major reason why employment was not all that Williams wished it to be. It was not by any means the only reason, nor even – at a time of accelerating disjunction in the *material* resources available to parties on either side of the bargain – the most obvious. But the asymmetries of the employment relationship in the nineteenth century were more than simply the outgrowth of economic power rendering nugatory formal juridical equality. For, as the treatise writer James Schouler was to put it in 1870: "The relation of master and servant *presupposes* two parties who stand on an unequal footing in their mutual dealings. . . . This relation is, in theory, hostile to the genius of free institutions. It bears the marks of social caste."[100]

Assuredly, the inequality Schouler described was not quite of the same order as the traditional master/servant relationship: an encompassing "relation of domination, established in the form of the individual will of the master."[101] In legal contemplation employees had the right to enter the employment relationship on the best terms they could negotiate. Their right of exit, too, was protected, though encumbered by significant legally imposed costs. And outside employment they enjoyed civic freedom. But although the power asymmetries on display in the contract of employment represented a more measured inequality than that characterizing the old master/servant relation, the inequality was more permanent and more universal. Service had been but one form of work relation, and in most cases a temporary one. By the middle of the nineteenth century, in contrast, the contract of employment, and the official discourse of master and servant that construed it, had become the paradigm of the employment relationship.

[100] James Schouler, *A Treatise on the Law of Domestic Relations* (Boston, 1870), 599 (emphasis supplied).
[101] Michel Foucault, "Two Lectures," in *Power/Knowledge: Selected Interviews and Writings, 1972–77*, ed. Colin Gordon (New York, 1980), 104.

An interlude: on law and economy

A very short chapter, containing infinitely more time and less matter than any other in the whole story.

Epigraph to Chapter 7 of Henry Fielding's The Life of
Mr. Jonathan Wild, The Great

One of my chief concerns while writing this book has been to avoid the imputation that there existed a functional relationship between "the needs of capitalism" and the legal discourses construing labor and employment to which courts and treatise writers had resort in the early republic. This is not because I believe that law had no significance for the processes of industrialization and capital accumulation under way during the first half of the nineteenth century. Indeed I think it was of vast significance. What I would wish to deny is simply the implication, as I put it at the outset, that this significance lies in a relationship that is unilinear and founded in the economy. What is "law" at any given moment is determined by legal discourse's own rules of formation rather than by its proponents' obedience to an overweening exterior influence. Law's relationship to economy, as to any social process, is hence mediated by the particularities and anomalies of its own process of creation.[1]

If it is to enjoy social authority as a modality of rule, however, legal discourse must remain consistent with "the principles structuring the dominant or hegemonic discourses" abroad in society at large.[2] Concern for consistency demonstrates law's sensitivity to its social context, but as a discursive practice in itself consistency is also the foundation upon which is built law's potent "ideology-effect" of legitimation. The *pursuit* of consistency thus demonstrates law's responsiveness to its context; the *achievement* of consistency simultaneously reinforces law's claim to authority over that context – its claim to tell the truth.

During the course of this study we have seen law encounter and take on board the discourses of property, political economy, the market and self-ownership, and

---

[1] I first developed some of the points of argument in this paragraph and the next in the course of preparing a review of Anthony Woodiwiss, *Rights v. Conspiracy: A Sociological Essay on the History of Labour Law in the United States* (New York, 1990), to whose stimulating discussion of relative autonomy (at 4–11) I am indebted.

[2] Ibid., 11.

civic equality; and we have seen law establish ascendancy over "oppositional" discourses – corporate collectivity, locality, police, democracy, substantive equality. In the next and final part of this book I seek to explore law's encounter with hegemonic discourses of specific and immediate importance to the course of American industrialism – "management" and "free labor." I have touched briefly on these already. This discussion, I hope, will serve to elucidate what I see as the nature of law's relationship with the economy.

Central to the processes of industrialization and capital accumulation under way during the first half of the nineteenth century, I will argue, was the unending struggle of employers of labor to secure profit through the physical organization and reorganization of the process and technology of production and, in particular, through the exercise of disciplinary power over their employees.[3] In attempting the former – the organization and reorganization of physical assets – employers exerted a power grounded in the asserted right to exclusive control of their property (that is, the means of production). The role sought of law in this was the vital but relatively straightforward and essentially negative one of protection.[4] As we have seen, this was the role envisaged and endorsed by pivotal late eighteenth-century figures like Adam Smith, Patrick Colquhoun, and James Madison.

In attempting the latter, however – the assertion of disciplinary power – employers made a rather more extensive bid for legal aid, for although one may recognize in security of possession a necessary condition for the creation of social relations of domination between individuals, possession by itself is not sufficient to guarantee the successful reproduction of such relations within the work process. Success here requires in addition recognition of the employer's claim to act as a private legislator. It is here, in its relation to the attempts by employers of labor to exercise a power to discipline as well as a power to exclude, that the key to law's role in the process of creating an industrial economy in America lies.[5]

---

[3] By *disciplinary power* I do not mean simply the power to command obedience. Rather, I mean the "mechanism of power which permits time and labor . . . to be extracted from bodies," which Michel Foucault identified some years ago as the singular invention of the seventeenth and eighteenth centuries. According to Foucault, disciplinary power is power in detail. It "implies an uninterrupted, constant coercion, supervising the processes of the activity rather than the result." It is administered "according to a codification that partitions as closely as possible time, space, movement." Disciplinary power became possible "when an art of the human body was born, which was directed not only at the growth of its skills, nor at the intensification of its subjection, but at the formation of a relation that in the mechanism itself makes it more obedient as it becomes more useful." See Michel Foucault, "Two Lectures," in *Power/Knowledge: Selected Interviews and Writings, 1972–77*, ed. Colin Gordon (New York, 1980), 104; and idem, *Discipline and Punish: The Birth of the Prison* (New York, 1979), 137–8.

[4] See generally Karl Renner, *The Institutions of Private Law and Their Social Functions*, ed. Otto Kahn-Freund (London, 1949).

[5] Alan Fox, *Beyond Contract: Work, Power, and Trust Relations* (London, 1974), 188–9; Richard Kinsey, "Despotism and Legality," in Bob Fine et al., eds., *Capitalism and the Rule of Law: From Deviancy Theory to Marxism* (London, 1979), 46–64. What we see here, if I may place my own twist on the allusive title of Alfred Chandler's justly admired work on American business in the nineteenth century, is the culmination of a process whereby the eighteenth century's "visible hand" – police – became reinvented as the very different and private hand of management. See Alfred DuPont Chandler, *The Visible Hand: The Managerial Revolution in American Business* (Cambridge, Mass., 1977).

295

Already in this book we have had some occasion to explore the interaction and intersection of law with the disciplinary power of employers. The subject of the final part – the question whether employers should be made liable for the consequences of industrial accidents – allows us to grapple directly with the issue. Industrial accidents began to occur in increasing numbers in the late 1830s and 1840s, largely because of employers' attempts to increase the intensity of the accumulation process. Suits seeking to attribute responsibility for work injuries to employers and to compel them to pay substantial sums in compensation threatened a significant level of legal regulation of employers' capacity to exercise power over their employees. In the circumstances of the particular "moment" at which this interference was mooted, circumstances of crisis in and challenge to the intensification of the accumulation process, the refusal of courts to admit the possibility of intervention established that the contested territory of production was a private sphere, occupied by the employer's disciplinary power and not by the state.

Law's part in determining the course that the new industrial economy was to follow in the United States was not, however, one that could be effective only by being instrumental. Turning aside challenges from employees to employers' disciplinary power, that is, was only one aspect of the intersection of law and economy. Of no less importance was the courts' careful doctrinal exegesis on the law of torts and the no less painstaking elaboration of the immanent rationality of the way things were that accompanied it. Through these ideational processes, the courts reassured those appalled at the "mysterious" power of employers to crush "humble industry" without redress of the perfect lawfulness, the sense, the necessity, indeed the justice, of such outcomes. "We are all in danger hourly," said the Huntingdon County Pennsylvania Court of Common Pleas in 1853, "either from our own carelessness or want of foresight of others around us. Almost every step through life is one of peril. The prosecution of every employment or business has its incident risks, with which one engaging in it is fairly supposed to be as well acquainted as his employer, and which it is but reasonable to say he undertakes to encounter."[6] Or again, as the Illinois Supreme Court put it five years later, the case before it – a speeding train, a shifting load, a laborer riding on the car thrown off and killed – was "*but an ordinary accident*, a casualty to which the employment he was engaged in, exposed him," something to be dealt with routinely, simply one more example of a class of incidents whose risk employees routinely bore.[7]

---

[6] *Mitchell v. Pennsylvania R.R. Company*, 1 American Law Register, 717 (1853).

[7] *Illinois Central Railroad Company v. Cox*, 21 Ill. 20 (1858), 26 (emphasis supplied). See also *Michigan Central Railroad Company v. Leahey*, 10 Mich. 193 (1862), at 200, where the risk of accidental injury was held to be integral to the nature of work *as such*. The risk, moreover, was in the nature of things one borne by the person at work, not because of any contractual agreement so to do but simply as a fact of working life. "[T]he reason of the rule depends more upon the fact of doing the work than upon the . . . nature of the hiring. It is a risk incident to the *work*; and that risk in no way depends of necessity upon the form of the contract." For an account of bureaucratic processes resulting in a similar routinization of the perception of work accidents in England see W. G. Carson, "The Conventionalization of Early Factory Crime," *International Journal of the Sociology of Law*, 7, 1 (1979), 37–60.

In this aspect of what they did, courts reveal themselves as central actors in the reproduction of the social order, creators of representations – facts – of daily working life that make the present "usable" by imparting to what is merely contingent a powerful aura of certainty.[8] In the case of industrial accidents, the present that the courts assisted to prevail was one in which the maiming or death of employees at work simply blended into the topography of industrialism, ordinary, if regrettable, occurrences that were part of the price society paid for the wealth that industry brought and for the rights and liberties, such as freedom of contract, that were the attributes of free and equal citizens. In this way the courts helped to render the structure of power that lay behind and effected such outcomes not merely mysterious but in fact virtually invisible.

[8] Robert W. Gordon, "New Developments in Legal Theory," in David Kairys, ed., *The Politics of Law: A Progressive Critique* (New York, 1982), 286–92. And see Paul Q. Hirst, *On Law and Ideology* (London, 1979), 113, 146–50; Jacqueline Tombs, "Law and Slavery in North America: The Development of a Legal Category" (Ph.D. diss. University of Edinburgh, 1982), 54–63.

PART 4

The new industrial order

to the Hon. Nathan Hale Esq.
President of the Corporation of the Boston & Worcester Rail Road

Sir,

Mr Gilham Barnes has requested to me to explain to you the nature of the injury sustained by him on the road last June and his situation.

The left arm was so injured that amputation was necessary. The back was seriously injured. The nervous system underwent a concussion, which disturbed his consciousness many days.

Mr Barnes has a wife [and] three or four boys. The eldest is just recovering from typhus fever. He is an industrious poor man, who and whose wife are cheerful laborers and maintain and train their children to become good citizens If your Corporation ever indulge in a generous sympathy toward humble industry crushed by the mysterious power of your road, Mr Barnes presents a strong example.

With great respect I have the honor to be, Dear Sir, yours & c.

Geo. C. Shattuck
Boston, Sept. 6, 1837

Introduction: a sign of the times

On 16 June 1837, at a little after six o'clock in the morning, a train of cars carrying lumber and gravel and crowded with twenty or more Irish track laborers and other workmen left the Boston depot of the Boston & Worcester Railroad Corporation bound for Worcester, Massachusetts. About four miles out, just after the train had passed the City Mills and was nearing the Brookline Road, a wheel on one of the cars broke. The train was thrown from the tracks. Two men were killed and several others severely injured.

Among the injured was a man named Gilham Barnes, engaged by the corporation about two weeks before to carry out maintenance work on several bridges between Boston and Worcester. The previous day Barnes, his brother Luther, and one of the men that worked with them had ridden the same train (an unscheduled track maintenance train known to the corporation as the "gravel" train) as far as the Arsenal Bridge, which carried the railroad over the Watertown Road in Brighton to deliver materials and tools. On the morning of the sixteenth, Barnes sent the others by wagon via the Mill Dam toll road to begin work on the Arsenal Bridge while he made arrangements with the conductor of the gravel train for additional materials to be carried to the Worcester Bridge. Barnes intended, it would seem, to ride the gravel train as far as the Arsenal Bridge, where he would jump off and join his workmen. "We saw the train going out just after we paid [the] toll," Luther Barnes later recounted. "Then near City Mills we saw shingles all about. I saw my brother running towards us. He waved his hat twice. And he held up his arm and I saw blood and flesh."[1]

Luther put his brother in the back of the wagon and carried him back to the house in Charles Street which Gilham shared with his sister's family. By the time they got there, Gilham was "all distressed." His sister found him "seriously wounded . . . disfigured and bruised and his face full of gravel." Shortly after, his left arm was amputated. He was to remain confined to the house for several months.

Early in September Gilham Barnes approached the corporation to seek

[1] These and all subsequent details of the case are drawn from files of case notes and testimony referring to *Barnes v. The Boston & Worcester Railroad Corporation* in the Charles Greely Loring Papers, unprocessed manuscript collection, Social Law Library, Boston.

301

compensation, using his doctor, George Shattuck, as an intermediary.[2] The corporation had already furnished relief to others injured in the accident and to the families of those killed (Oliver Everett, for example, had been allowed "full wages during all the time he was unable to work" because of his injury), and the president of the corporation, Nathan Hale, indicated that the board of directors would entertain a request for assistance if Barnes made a personal plea. Rather than approach the board in the deferential manner specified by Hale, however, Barnes chose to retain an attorney, Abraham Moore, to act on his behalf. Moore wrote to Hale on 16 September requesting that he respond formally to the letter from Dr. Shattuck.[3] Barnes "would gladly avoid any unpleasant altercation," Moore indicated, but "finds himself in a situation which calls on him, in duty to himself and his family, to seek some remuneration for the injuries he has sustained as he thinks by the unwarrantable carelessness of your agents." Moore indicated that unless the matter received the "early attention" of the board of directors, Barnes would sue the railroad. Hale ignored the letter, and three days later Moore filed a suit in the Suffolk County Court of Common Pleas seeking damages of $10,000 in compensation for injuries that had rendered the plaintiff "wholly unable to earn a support for himself and family during his natural life."[4]

The Common Pleas hearing resulted in a decision for Barnes, forcing the railroad to appeal to the Supreme Judicial Court. At this point, by mutual agreement, the matter was referred to a panel of referees. After extensive hearings the corporation was found to have owed Barnes a duty of care rendering it responsible for injuries caused by the negligence of its agents, and Barnes was awarded $3,000 and his costs.[5]

Gilham Barnes's case is one of the earliest examples to come before an American court of a suit alleging that employers were legally obliged to compensate their employees in damages for injuries occurring in the course of their employment.[6] The next quarter century would see many more, both in Massachusetts and elsewhere.[7] This new phenomenon of employer liability suits marked a decisive moment in

---

[2] Shattuck to Hale (6 Sept. 1837), in *Barnes v. The Boston & Worcester Railroad Corporation*, Loring Papers. Shattuck's letter is reproduced as the epigraph to Part 4 of this book.

[3] Moore to Hale, in Loring Papers.

[4] *Barnes v. The Boston & Worcester Railroad Corporation*, Suffolk County Court of Common Pleas, Oct. term 1837 (New Entry 216).

[5] Supreme Judicial Court Dockets, Mar. term 1838 (Continuing Action 313) and Mar. term 1839 (Continuing Action 172). The referees' award was filed with the clerk of court on 10 Apr. 1839, and an execution was issued from the clerk's office on 18 Apr. In Office of the Clerk of Court, Supreme Judicial Court (Single Justice Session), Suffolk County Court House, Boston.

[6] The first example anywhere seems to be the English case *Priestley v. Fowler*, 3 M. & W. 1, 150 E.R. 1030 (1837), originally heard at the summer 1836 term of the Lincolnshire Assizes. The first in America was *James Murray v. S.C. Rail Road Company*, 1 McMullen 385 (1841), originally heard in Charleston in July 1838. Earlier American cases, however, had dealt with suits brought by masters of slaves against hirers to recover the value of slaves injured or killed while in the hirer's employ, some of which became the occasion for significant expressions of opinion on general matters of liability. See Chapter 10.

[7] For a full listing see Jerrilyn Marston, Comment, "The Creation of a Common Law Rule: The Fellow-Servant Rule, 1837–1860," *University of Pennsylvania Law Review*, 132 (1984), 579–620.

American labor and legal history, for it confronted courts with a demand that they impose on employers a clear legal obligation to safeguard their employees' present and future earning capacity commensurate with the employer's claim to the employees' obedience on the job. Gilham Barnes's success suggests that at the outset the possibility of legal intervention in the employment relationship to impose such an obligation was by no means foreclosed. As far as the legal responsibilities of employers in their relations with employees were concerned, that is, it was a moment of openness and uncertainty in American jurisprudence.

Yet the moment was short-lived. Just over a month after Barnes's attorney filed suit, an engineer, Nicholas Farwell, lost an arm in a derailment. Parallels between his suit and that of Gilham Barnes abound. Both sought restitution from the same employer. Both retained the same attorney, Abraham Moore. Moore delayed filing Farwell's suit until the result of the Barnes case was known and then modeled his declaration on Barnes's experience.[8] But whereas the Common Pleas had found for Barnes, in Farwell's case the court found for the railroad. Thus it was the plaintiff who was forced to appeal. Once before the Supreme Judicial Court, the case went to a jury trial (*nisi prius*) rather than to referees. When that jury could not agree whether the defendant was liable or not, the parties agreed to submit the case to the full court for a decision on the defendant's liability as a matter of law. The outcome was a trenchant denial of the plaintiff's right of recovery. Led by its chief justice, Lemuel Shaw, the Supreme Judicial Court of Massachusetts delivered itself of an interpretation of employer liability that effectively left the railroad immune from suits brought by its employees. The product of the early republic's leading state court, over the following decade *Farwell v. The Boston & Worcester Railroad* became *the* case in the common law of employer liability, treated not only in Massachusetts but throughout the Anglo-American jurisprudential world as the requisite authoritative statement of the limits to an employer's responsibilities, the point of departure in all subsequent litigation in any industrial situation.

Historical analysis of early employer liability jurisprudence has tended to focus on its revenue effects, for Shaw's judgment was clearly a substantial saving for the railroad. Having sought $10,000, Nicholas Farwell eventually received about $700 in benevolent assistance.[9] Writ large, it would appear that, as Leonard Levy put it thirty years ago, "American capitalism, at a critical stage in its development, was relieved of an enormous financial burden for industrial accidents which it would otherwise have incurred."[10] Others have built on this focus to suggest that Shaw's embrace of a highly restricted doctrine of employer liability was one element in a more general move toward the purposeful reformulation of private law to subsidize

---

[8] *Farwell v. The Boston & Worcester Railroad Corporation*, Suffolk County Court of Common Pleas, Oct. term 1839 (New Entry 150).

[9] For a breakdown of this payment, see the section entitled Contract and Power, in Chapter 10.

[10] Leonard W. Levy, *The Law of the Commonwealth and Chief Justice Shaw* (Cambridge, Mass., 1957), 166. See also Lawrence M. Friedman and Jack Ladinsky, "Social Change and the Law of Industrial Accidents," *Columbia Law Review*, 67 (1967), 50–82.

new enterprise and promote the social and economic interests of entrepreneurs, an instrumental response to capitalism's "need" during the early phases of industrialization for a legal environment facilitative of capital accumulation.[11]

Yet although of explanatory value, such a focus on material consequences may not be the best way, and is certainly not the only way, to approach the issue. First, it may misrepresent the origins of the impulse for legal change. Recent research on the history of tort law suggests that the conflicts over liability that accompanied industrialism were sparked by pressures to *widen* the arena of tortious liability rather than to restrict it. According to Robert Rabin, for example, injurious behavior in the preindustrial era was governed not by strict liability principles but by a (rebuttable) assumption of no liability outside carefully demarcated areas.[12] Considered from this perspective, the rejection of employer liability seems to have been more an attempt to preserve the status quo in the face of a move by wage workers to present new and literally unprecedented claims for adjudication than an aggressive assault on previously uncontroversial assumptions of employers' responsibility for the welfare of those working for them.[13]

Second, the "needs of capitalism" analysis suggests too reductionist, and perhaps too universal, a level of causal determinacy between social and legal phenomena.[14]

---

[11] See, e.g., Morton J. Horwitz, *The Transformation of American Law, 1780–1860* (Cambridge, Mass., 1977), 208–10. See also Marston, "Creation of a Common Law Rule," 580–1.

[12] Robert L. Rabin, "The Historical Development of the Fault principle: A Reinterpretation," *Georgia Law Review*, 15 (1981), 925–61. See also Gary T. Schwartz, "Tort Law and the Economy in Nineteenth Century America: A Reinterpretation," *Yale Law Journal*, 90 (1981), 1717–75; idem, "The Character of Early American Tort Law," *UCLA Law Review*, 36, 4 (1989), 641–718; M. J. Pritchard, *Scott v. Shepherd (1773) and the Emergence of the Tort of Negligence* (London, 1976); Alfred S. Konefsky and Andrew J. King, eds., *The Papers of Daniel Webster* (Hanover, N.H., 1982), *Legal Papers*, vol. 1: *The New Hampshire Practice*, 421–2; Horwitz, *Transformation of American Law*, 85–99. And see Mark Tushnet, "The American Law of Slavery, 1810–1860: A Study in the Persistence of Legal Autonomy," *Law and Society Review*, 10, 1 (Fall 1975), 119–84, at 161.

[13] It is noteworthy that, as Schwartz shows in "The Character of Early American Tort Law," courts appeared far more concerned to contain the extension of tort liability in the realm of employer liability than in any other realm of tort law. Schwartz's explanation for what he finds, however, is no more convincing than the explanations offered by instrumentalist scholars for what they found. Schwartz argues that courts were not sympathetic to suits arising from workplace dangers because "throughout the nineteenth century the problem of workplace dangers was disproportionately a problem of railroad dangers," that most employer liability suits were hence filed by railroad workers, that railroad workers enjoyed high social status, and that their high status eroded the sympathy that courts might otherwise have been expected to feel for them (710–15). There are two problems here. First, as we shall see, workplace danger in the nineteenth century was not *disproportionately* associated with railroads. Were one to single out any one industry, both construction and mining would have at least as strong a claim; but in any case, it is an error to explain workplace risk through an imagined causal association with any particular technology. Second, the status argument does not work. Although it is true that during the period under consideration more liability suits were filed by railroad workers than by workers in any other industry, many of these involved unskilled brakemen and common track laborers – according to accident reports the most dangerous categories of railroad work (see below, Chapter 9, n. 60). Courts drew no distinction between suits filed by these "low-status" employees and "high-status" engineers and conductors. Nor do courts appear to have distinguished between suits filed by railroad workers and those filed by factory operatives.

[14] See Robert W. Gordon, "Tort Law in America" (review article), *Harvard Law Review*, 94, 4 (Feb. 1981), 903–17, at 907.

More is involved here than courts lowering the costs of investment. Court decisions limiting employer liability in industrial accident cases need to be understood in relation to the particular form that industrial capitalism was taking in the United States by the middle decades of the nineteenth century. Like other issues in the early republic's labor and employment law, that is, the issue of employer liability was as much one of how power in the republic was understood, where it was located, and how it was organized and expressed, as of the instrumental necessity that a narrowly drawn doctrine of tortious liability be adopted in order to guarantee the success of American capitalism.

9

Mechanism

Were we required to characterise this age of ours by any single epithet, we should be tempted to call it, not an Heroical, Devotional, Philosophical, or Moral Age, but, above all others, the Mechanical Age. It is the Age of Machinery, in every outward and inward sense of that word; the age which, with its whole undivided might, forwards, teaches and practises the great art of adapting means to ends. Nothing is now done directly or by hand; all is by rule and calculated contrivance.

Thomas Carlyle, "Signs of the Times"

In Thomas Carlyle's remarkable "Signs of the Times," Leo Marx argued nearly thirty years ago, one sees encapsulated the philosophical consequences of the vast industrial sea change sweeping through the society and culture of the first half of the nineteenth century.[1] Carlyle's essay acknowledged and traversed the new and apparently beneficial technological artifacts that were revolutionizing everyday life. "Our old modes of exertion are all discredited, and thrown aside. . . . For all earthly and for some unearthly purposes, we have machines and mechanic furtherances; for mincing our cabbages; for casting us into magnetic sleep. We remove mountains and make seas our smooth highway; nothing can resist us. We war with rude Nature; and, by our resistless engines, come off always victorious, and loaded with spoils." Yet for Carlyle machines were but an aspect of something for more important, something he denominated "mechanism" and which he saw at the heart of the new era. "Men are grown mechanical in head and in heart, as well as in hand. . . . Not for internal perfection, but for external combinations and arrangements, for institutions, constitutions, – for Mechanism of one sort or other, do they hope and struggle. Their whole efforts, attachments, opinions, turn on mechanism, and are of a mechanical character."[2] Far transcending mere machinery, mechanism stood for the triumph of universal rationality and the new sciences of human behavior over metaphysics. It was the essence of the era's dominant social philosophies – utilitarianism, laissez-faire economics, political economy[3] – encompassing all their manifold attempts

[1] Leo Marx, *The Machine in the Garden: Technology and the Pastoral Ideal in America* (New York, 1964), 170–80.

[2] "Signs of the Times," in *Carlyle: Selected Works, Reminiscences, and Letters,* ed. Julian Symons (Cambridge, Mass., 1963), 22–3, 25.

[3] See Alan Shelston, ed., *Thomas Carlyle: Selected Writings* (Harmondsworth, England, 1971), 16–17.

to achieve a purposeful rearrangement of human energy through the creation of functionally specific institutions and organizations dedicated to the reconstruction of intellectual and material life as a taxonomy of rules, procedures, and behavioral laws.

Carlyle's essay traced the impact of mechanism "in all the great manifestations of our time" – intellectual, practical, political, artistic, religious, moral. Everywhere, he argued, it threatened a distortion in the human condition: "excessive emphasis upon means as against ends, a preoccupation with the external arrangement of human affairs as against their inner meaning and consequences." Mechanism signified the displacement of spirituality by selfishness, of the "primary, unmodified forces and energies of man" by "immediate 'motives', as hope of reward, or as fear of punishment." Mechanism enshrined self-interest as the guiding principle of human affairs. "Self-denial, the parent of all virtue, in any true sense of that word, has perhaps seldom been rarer," and virtue itself had become "but a calculation of the Profitable."

Such a turn of events might well be productive of many palpable benefits, Carlyle acknowledged. "By our skill in Mechanism, it has come to pass, that in the management of external things we excel all other ages." Ultimately, however, "this faith in Mechanism, in the all-importance of physical things" was "a threat to the necessary balance in the human situation," one that risked the destruction of "Moral Force."[4]

Thousands of miles to the west of Carlyle's Edinburgh, the misgivings that haunted the Scottish essayist seemed remote. In August 1830, for example, at a meeting in Faneuil Hall in Boston called to promote the construction of a railroad to the Hudson River, Benjamin Hallet gave voice to an understanding of the human situation which located moral force, not in abstention from the untrammeled pursuit of self-interest, but rather precisely in the release of self-seeking industrial and entrepreneurial energies from inhibiting restraints. To Hallet, the capacity to extend "facilities of intercourse" such as railroads to ever-wider segments of the populace exemplified the "vast moral power" of capital investment. Drawing an explicit parallel between the railroad and "the development of resources once deemed quite as visionary, through another medium of industry and enterprise – domestic manufactures," Hallet argued that it was in "great enterprises" such as these that Americans could find "a practical demonstration of the doctrine of the greatest good of the greatest number." Who would have dared, forty years before, to "conjure up the visions of such manufacturing cities as Lowell and Fall River, your Ware, Waltham?" Yet now they held in their hands the keys to the commonwealth's future prosperity. The wealth generated by these great factory communities, Hallet concluded, confirmed the truth of the principle that he saw at the center of the American political economy: "Develop the resources of the country – place the means of wealth within the reach of industry, and you produce the happy medium in society."[5]

---

[4] "Signs of the Times," 41, 35.
[5] Quoted in George S. White, *A Memoir of Samuel Slater* (Philadelphia, 1836), 53–7.

Men like Hallett were celebrants of industrialism as a new moral, political, and economic order. As Anthony Wallace has put it, they "articulated a mystique of industrial progress, seeing it as the means by which poverty, ignorance, violence, and vice could be eradicated, and prosperity, education, cooperation, and virtue could take their place." Theirs was an ideology that created "an ambience of respect for the economic hero" and for heroic entrepreneurial activities, and that placed the industrialist at the center of the new social order. In their unquestioning embrace of the panacea of "development," their invocation, as in Hallett's case, of the example of "great enterprises" such as the textile mills of Lowell to ram home the material benefits self-evident in America's political economy, they displayed none of Carlyle's disquiet.[6]

Others were less sure. The brash confidence of men like Hallet contrasted visibly with sentiments abroad among America's working population. Northern workingmen did not reject industrialism as such. Indeed, they prided themselves as its foot soldiers. "*We* have erected these cities and villages which smile where lately was the Indian's wigwam, or the lair of the wild beast. *We* have called into existence American manufactures, and been the instruments by which Commerce has amassed her treasures; *our* labor has digged the canals, and constructed the railways, which are intersecting the country in all directions, and opening its resources. *We* have built and manned the ships which navigate every ocean, and furnished the houses of the rich with all their comforts and luxuries."[7] Their argument, rather, was with the political economy – the means – that had emerged with industrialism. In that argument we can detect something of the tension between mechanism and moral force which inhabited Carlyle's critique of the old world and which gave his words, for all their sententiousness, considerable resonance in the new.

Writ large, the argument was about wealth and its distribution. More precisely, however, it was about the asymmetries of power, public *and* private, which structured the generation of wealth and affected its distribution. To working people, as indeed to many of its advocates, industrialism's promise had been the steady alleviation of general want and social inequality. Yet neither seemed decisively on the wane. If anything, disparities were growing. "Our labor has done it all," claimed the Workingmen of Charlestown. But what was their condition? "We toil on from morning to night, from one year's end to another, increasing our exertions with each year, and with each day, and still we are the poor and dependent. Here as

[6] Anthony F. C. Wallace, *St. Clair: A Nineteenth Century Coal Town's Experience with a Disaster-Prone Industry* (New York, 1987), 230, 237, and generally 228–47. On the moral primacy of business and the pursuit of a capitalist ethics by Hallet and his peers, see Frederic Cople Jaher, *The Urban Establishment: Upper Strata in Boston, New York, Charleston, Chicago, and Los Angeles* (Urbana, 1982), 37–44, 50–4. For an interpretation of the manifestation of such sentiments in law, see James Willard Hurst, *Law and the Conditions of Freedom in the Nineteenth Century United States* (Madison, 1956), 3–32. For an account of their provenance more generally, see Steven Watts, *The Republic Reborn: War and the Making of Liberal America, 1790–1820* (Baltimore, 1987). On the American response to Carlyle, see Marx, *Machine in the Garden*, 180–90.

[7] *Third Grand Rally of the Workingmen of Charlestown, Mass., Held October 23d, 1840*, Kress Library, Harvard Business School, 5–6 (emphasis supplied).

everywhere else, they who pocket the proceeds of our labor, look upon us as the lower class, and term us the mob. We are but laborers, operatives, *vulgar* workingmen. We are poor; our wages barely suffice to supply us the necessaries of life. . . . Our rights and interests attract no general attention."[8] To society's defenders, in contrast, the poverty and inequality of which working people complained seemed, if personally unfortunate, socially inconsequential, even useful. To Jonathan Wainwright, D.D., the rector of Trinity Church in Boston, for example, poverty was not at all a curse but a salutary social condition, development's engine rather than its target. Growth, Wainwright pronounced, "required" inequality of wealth and condition to propel over forward the "admirable principle" of the division of labor. "Many employments essential to the existence of civilized society are yet so unpleasant in themselves, that no one would undertake them but from the excitement of such a motive." Equality of condition would undermine industry. "Those, therefore, who would throw down the distinctions created by wealth, may justly be denounced as the deadly enemies of all human enterprise."[9]

Where then look for freedom and happiness? Charlestown's Workingmen looked hopefully to collective political and economic action to redress their grievances and revive their lost independence.[10] In Wainwright's industrial order, in contrast, one looked to individual self-improvement; behavior, that is, obedient to the "sound principles of political economy" – what Carlyle had called "the laws of mechanism." Individual pursuit of self-interest was the only route to freedom and happiness, a route signposted by laws giving "to each, as far as was practicable, equal opportunities of success" but equally solicitous for the "sacred" rights of property, particularly capital's right to the whole fruit of its increase. This was a route that was to be free from the "legalized violence" of legislative impediment:

Can we accomplish the object, and keep the happy medium through legislative interference, by checking the increase of capital, by forcing the wealthy under a process of unequal taxation

---

[8] Ibid., 6 (emphasis in original). On growing material inequality, see James Henretta, "Wealth and Social Structure," in Jack P. Greene and J. R. Pole, eds., *Colonial British America: Essays in the New History of the Early Modern Era* (Baltimore, 1984), 262–89; Jeffrey G. Williamson and Peter H. Lindert, *American Inequality: A Macroeconomic History* (New York, 1980), esp., 36–46; and, generally, the sources cited in Chapter 2, n. 62.

[9] Jonathan M. Wainwright, D.D., *Inequality of Individual Wealth the Ordinance of Providence, and Essential to Civilization: A Sermon Preached . . . on the Annual Election, January 7, 1835* (Boston, 1835), 26–7, 29. Seth Luther replied to Wainwright the following year in the course of his Fourth of July *Address Delivered Before the Mechanics and Workingmen of the City of Brooklyn* (Brooklyn, 1836). "The history of the Workingmen in all ages of the world has been a history of oppression on the side of wealth, and a base submission to that oppression on our part. The man who denies this is either a fool or a knave; and he who attempts to persuade us that we ought to submit to the present state of things under the consideration that it is the order of Divine Providence, must be both fool and knave. A man who tells you that the great Author of our existence designed that the *many* should be poor and miserable, in order that the *few* may roll and riot in splendid luxury, would pick your pocket if he had a good opportunity, let him profess what he may. He may even profess to be a minister of him who had not where to lay his head, and hypocritically pretend to great regard for his fellow creatures, but he is not worthy of his profession and does not fulfill the duties of his 'high calling'" (12).

[10] See the Prologue.

to give up a portion of their superabundance, or by an agrarian system of the division of property? None but a madman, an ignorant enthusiast, or an unprincipled demagogue could propose [such] remed[ies].

Once take away stimulus to individual exertion and accumulation, the capital of the country would be diminished. "With the reduction or loss of capital, manufactories must cease, all works of public improvement must be put an end to, the whole community must step by step go backward."[11]

ORDER AND CHAOS

The seeds of this argument about labor freedom had been sown years before. At its beginning, as we have seen, the new republic's peculiar claim to uniqueness had inhered principally in the prospect that it offered its citizens – the promise of both material sufficiency and personal liberty through the successful reconciliation in one republican ideology of values supportive of economic growth with those embracing a social order of free and independent men.[12] Precisely their concern for the realization of that promise had led many of the revolutionary generation – predominantly Jeffersonian Republicans – to oppose the pursuit of any economic trajectory that would take the new nation in the direction of the old world and the "loathsome dependence, subservience, venality and corruption" in which its form of industrialization was steeped, and to identify instead the enjoyment of an interdependent self-sufficiency as the new world ideal, the sine qua non of republican virtue.[13]

Theirs was not a critique of industrial development per se. As both John Kasson and Leo Marx indicate, one finds among late eighteenth-century American republicans such a keen sense of alliance between liberty and "invention" or "technology" that it is impossible to put their suspicions down to some atavistic urge to escape back to simpler times.[14] What aroused their apprehension, rather, was the prospect of the appearance in America of "great manufactures . . . which cannot be carried on, but by rigid system and immense capitals," for these would undermine rather than reinforce the unique social relations of production which might be achieved in a republican political economy.[15] As Marx puts it, "From Jefferson's perspective, the machine is a token of that liberation of the human spirit to be realized by the young American Republic; the factory system, on the other hand, is but feudal oppression in a slightly modified form." Applied to the needs of small-scale producers in households or workshops, machine power would be "a welcome ally in the republican

[11] Wainwright, *Inequality*, 36–7, 47–8.

[12] Joyce Appleby, *Capitalism and a New Social Order: The Republican Vision of the 1790s* (New York, 1984), usefully evokes the confluence of these ideas.

[13] Drew McCoy, *The Elusive Republic: Political Economy in Jeffersonian America* (Chapel Hill, 1980), 15, 62–7.

[14] John Kasson, *Civilizing the Machine: Technology and Republican Values in America, 1776–1900* (New York, 1976), 3–51, esp. 13; Marx, *Machine in the Garden*, 145–50.

[15] McCoy, *Elusive Republic*, 111, 104–19.

enterprise," for such manufacturing "would not threaten, but rather enhance, the independence and virtue of American society." A specifically *republican* industrialism, in other works, could help steer America permanently away from the corrupt social systems of Europe. It was the social relations of the factory that Jeffersonians feared, not manufacturing.[16]

The concerns of those sharing this perspective may be detected by examining the reaction to Alexander Hamilton's 1791 blueprint for industrial growth, the *Report on Manufactures*. Hamilton's *Report* underscored how an industrialism animated by the political economy of federalism would be a far different phenomenon from that implied in the Jeffersonian vision, seeming to many staunch republicans "to describe a society ominously reminiscent of the English system." Rather than a republican industrialism predicated on the diffusion of wealth and energy, the *Report* recommended policies to encourage the concentration of capital and its investment in large-scale manufacturing through the creation of subsidized corporate monopolies. To Hamilton's opponents, these "artificial" monopolies "would ruin private, 'natural' producers and foster dangerous, unrepublican disparities in wealth." Indeed, many of them "came to fear nothing less than a conspiracy to corrupt American society and smash the republican experiment by imitating British forms, manners and institutions." This same contest of world views was renewed ten years later when the revival of commercial tensions between America and Europe brought Congress "a deluge of petitions seeking public support of domestic manufactures." Shrugging off bitter Federalist criticism, the Jeffersonians rejected the petitions, pointing to the "excellent and extensive" achievements of the artisan trades and treating the virtual absence of larger-scale factory production of textiles and metal goods as a positive good. "We may felicitate ourselves that, by reason of the ease of gaining a subsistence and the high price of wages, our fellow-citizens born to happier destinies are not doomed to the wretchedness of a strict discipline in such manufactories."[17]

The approach to industrialism implicit in what Joyce Appleby has called "the Republican vision of the 1790s" complemented other components of that ideology: its politics of participation, its antagonism to great disparities in property and wealth, its denial of natural inequalities and of the inevitability of hierarchy in human affairs, its promise of a universal prosperity through moderate toil.[18] In the organization of the economy no less than society as a whole the goal was the preservation of the "free and independent man" from control, whether by authoritarian institutions or privileged elites.[19]

Yet what to the Jeffersonians was an exhilarating attempt to democratize and demystify the exercise of economic and political power in American society was to

---

[16] Marx, *Machine in the Garden*, 150; Kasson, *Civilizing the Machine*, 24–5. See also McCoy, *Elusive Republic*, 230.

[17] See McCoy, *Elusive Republic*, 148–65, 223–4.

[18] See, generally, Appleby, *Capitalism and a New Social Order*, 79–105.

[19] Ibid., 45, 3–23.

their political opponents no more than the encouragement of anarchy, of assaults on property, of disorder. "After finding power to originate in the free and independent man," wrote one Federalist sardonically, "we have yet to inquire whether this free and independent man will voluntarily submit to the restraints which the good of the community requires of him." As we have seen, defending the good of the community from unthinking majorities by prescribing involuntary restraints was central to Federalist law and politics during the early years of the republic. Federalists looked upon "the independence of individuals and the voluntary cooperation of private persons" as an unwelcome democratic cacophony threatening society's fabric.[20]

As the battles of "the worthy" against "the licentious" grew in intensity, condemnation of contemporary life as impossibly chaotic and disorderly widened in influence, becoming a pervasive and enduring theme of American life.[21] Particularly in a postrevolutionary world of rapidly increasing spatial and, it seemed, social mobility, elite values of discipline, hierarchy, and control acquired increasing resonance in the definition of what constituted a properly republican social order when compared to the "democratic" alternatives – spontaneous association, freedom, independence, and equality. "Some writers complained about the whirl of commercial activity and the concomitant lack of fixed social positions: others worried that political democracy bred a social libertarianism which often degenerated into license. Still others took alarm at the complex and artificial character of civilization. All of them agreed that antebellum America acutely suffered from a lack of order and stability. All feared for the cohesion of the community."[22]

One result, as David Rothman and others have demonstrated, was the multiplication of specialized institutions designed for the inculcation of orderly practices in subordinate populations. "The almshouse, orphanage, penitentiary, reformatory, and insane asylum were all erected and meticulously systematized to deal with the deviant and the dependent."[23] Represented as re-creations of the mythical organic, hierarchical, *stable* communities of prerevolutionary times, these were all, in fact, disciplinary institutions, dedicated, to use Carlyle's words, to the production of order "by rule and calculated contrivance." They were procedural machines, the means by which "social victims" might be reprocessed and transformed ("ground" as Bentham once put it) into honest and respectable citizens.[24]

[20] Ibid., 94; Kasson, *Civilizing the Machine*, 31–2.

[21] See, in general, Rowland Berthoff, *An Unsettled People: Social Order and Disorder in American History* (New York, 1971).

[22] David J. Rothman, *The Discovery of the Asylum: Social Order and Disorder in the New Republic* (Boston, 1971), 217; see also 69–78, 114–19.

[23] Kasson, *Civilizing the Machine*, 64. See, generally, Rothman, *Discovery of the Asylum*; Michael B. Katz, *The Irony of Early School Reform: Educational Innovation in Mid–Nineteenth Century Massachusetts* (Cambridge Mass., 1968); David Tyack and Elisabeth Hansot, *Managers of Virtue: Public School Leadership in America, 1820–1890* (New York, 1982).

[24] Thus Michael Ignatieff notes how Bentham conceived of the penitentiary "as a machine for the social production of guilt" (*A Just Measure of Pain: The Penitentiary in the Industrial Revolution, 1750–1850* [London, 1978], 213). More earthily, Bentham referred to his Panopticon as a "Machine for grinding rogues honest" (quoted in ibid., 68). See also, generally, Martin J. Wiener, *Reconstructing the Criminal: Culture, Law, and Policy in England, 1830–1914* (New York and Cambridge, 1990), 14–156.

Each of these institutions has its own history and its own explanatory discourse of professionalization and reform wherein, in large part, its origins and inspiration are to be found. Those discourses, however, shared certain characteristics. Of these none was more important than their common point of departure, that human beings could be "managed"; that is, their behavior and motivations altered through the employment of appropriate disciplinary techniques. "By management," the English Whig James Burgh had rhapsodized in 1775, "the human species may be moulded into any conceivable shape."[25] Rothman's description of the penitentiary as "a conscious effort to instill discipline" by means of an institutional routine characterized by a number of established elements – "a set work pattern, a rationalization of movement, a precise organization of time, a general uniformity" – is equally appropriate as a description of any of the great multitude of social settings in which this new discourse of management may be detected, for in each of those settings the goal was the same. "A regimen applied to the body by the external force of authority would first become a habit and then gradually be transformed into a moral preference. Through routinization and repetition, the regimens of discipline would be internalized as moral duties."[26]

Of all the settings into which the techniques and practices of management were introduced, none was to prove more enthusiastic or enduring in its reception than the industrial enterprise. The overwhelming tendency of historians to locate the genesis of "management" in the Industrial Revolution and to identify it as preeminently an industrial practice amply attests to this.[27] In England it was the first generation of factory masters – men such as Watt, Boulton, Strutt, Wedgewood, and Arkwright – who brought the discourse of management to bear on the world of work in the service of establishing the rational and methodical deployment of labor which their new large-scale enterprises demanded. "Besides introducing mechanization, extended division of labor, and systematic routing of the work process, they also devised the new disciplines of industrial labor: punch clocks, bells, rules, and fines. In order to reduce turnover and to stabilize the labor force in their early factories, they provided schools, chapels, and homes for their workers in model villages."[28] The establishment of a factory system in the early nineteenth century in the United States brought comparable developments, notably in the attempt by the Boston Manufacturing Company to create the factory as a "total institution" which would allow the company exclusive supervisory control over the environment in which work was performed.[29]

Because to many in the revolutionary generation the distinguishing quality of a truly *republican* industrialism had to be precisely its *avoidance* of any such system of

---

[25] Quoted in Ignatieff, *A Just Measure of Pain*, 67.

[26] Rothman, *Discovery of the Asylum*, 108; Ignatieff, *A Just Measure of Pain*, 67.

[27] See e.g., Sidney Pollard, *The Genesis of Modern Management: A Study of the Industrial Revolution in Great Britain* (London, 1965). The same assumption animates Alfred DuPont Chandler's *The Visible Hand: The Managerial Revolution in American Business* (Cambridge Mass., 1977).

[28] Ignatieff, *A Just Measure of Pain*, 62. [29] Kasson, *Civilizing the Machine*, 64.

labor discipline and supervisory authority, the impulse of America's early industrial proprietors to achieve a disciplined labor force through "management" of their employees was highly controversial. Many Jeffersonians, according to Anthony Wallace, found the very idea of management immoral, objecting vociferously to the principle of subordination that it entailed. Believing that men were accountable not to their superiors but to their peers, Jeffersonians "did not think very seriously about the problems of designing efficient bureaucratic management," trusting instead that human reasonableness would flower once "artificial restraints of property, class, government, and religion were removed, and spontaneous associations could arise."[30] Yet the mounting uncertainty as to the value of that unsettling spontaneity, that absence of traditional "restraints," which we have observed in the post-revolutionary social order offered American factory masters considerable opportunity to convince their peers of the propriety of their vision of the industrial order. Just as in England, where Jeremy Bentham described the work of moral reformation as a "species of manufacture," American factory masters proclaimed that the ordered discipline of their establishments served social and not merely self-interested economic purposes.[31]

Thus, throughout the Massachusetts textile industry, whether in the small rural mills of southwestern Worcester County or the larger Waltham-style establishments of Lowell, proprietors "adopted the rhetoric of uplift" to explain and justify the authority they sought over the lives and work of their employees. In the Lowell mills, where the labor force was composed predominantly of single females recruited from "virtuous rural homes" throughout New England, the transition from family member owing service to a family master to employee owing service to a factory master was negotiated via patriarchy. Corporate authority was presented as the surest means of reassuring farm families of the safety of their daughters from the corruption and seduction endemic in a turbulent society. In more isolated rural areas the message was rather different. Here proprietors like Samuel Slater identified their mills almost as missionary outposts, agents of education and civilization in a backward and brutish countryside. In either case, however, mills "under right management" would help combat "the natural tendency of accumulating vice, ignorance and poverty," introducing in their place "habits of order, regularity and industry" and establishing thereby a "broad and deep foundation" for "public and private future usefulness." As in the orphanage, the penitentiary, and the asylum,

---

[30] Anthony F. C. Wallace, *Rockdale: The Growth of an American Village in the Early Industrial Revolution* (New York, 1978), 263. See also David A. Zonderman, *Aspirations and Anxieties: New England Workers and the Mechanized Factory System, 1815–1850* (New York, 1992), 113–14.

[31] Ibid., 57–86. Indeed, according to Andrew Fraser, what one sees represented in the early business corporation is not at all the budding capitalist's exclusive focus on profits and production but a traditional elite's political concern for an institutional form to underpin the hierarchical order of propertied authority in the face of the ravages of Jeffersonian democracy. As much a political as an economic institution, the early corporation was "a little republic," whose relationship with its employees (that of "benevolent but firm patriarch[y]") reflected a conservative republican communitarian ideology, ("The Corporation as a Body Politic," *Telos*, 57 [Fall 1983], 5–41).

314

so in the mill, "management" was the means by which improvement in the moral character of the population might be achieved, bringing into existence the "exemplary republican work force" which would be the salvation of a society in the throes of disorder.[32]

Historians have not failed to appreciate the potential for oppression in the disciplined control sought by factory proprietors. By and large, however, we have generally accepted the creation of an ordered and regularized work environment as one of the facts of life of the transition to industrial capitalism.[33] But on close examination the proposition seems more open to question. Certainly the expanded scale of the organization of labor in New England's new textile enterprises and, later, on the railroads altered the prevailing character of work. In both instances, employers sought to substitute routinized regimes of employment for the "discretionary and spasmodic" mien of the craft–agrarian past through the creation of disciplinary and supervisory hierarchies.[34] Yet just as contemporary research in industrial sociology has indicated that formal descriptions of the structure of workplace relations usually conceal a far more contingent, even chaotic, reality, so we may be justified in suspecting that precisely the same was true of early nineteenth-century workplaces.

Consider first the working conditions prevailing in most antebellum industrial establishments. In many cases factory work was physically a miserable experience. "The ceilings were too low, the rooms were too small, and as a result the operatives were crowded together in narrow quarters."[35] Coping with machinery, too, proved a daunting experience. Encountering "the buzzing and hissing and whizzing of pulleys and rollers and spindles and flyers" for the first time was "bewildering and oppressive."[36] A fictionalized contemporary account of an operative's first encounter with a Lowell loom conveys the idea:

[S]he went into the Mill; and at first, the sight of so many bands, and wheels, and springs, in constant motion, was very frightful. She felt afraid to touch the loom, and she was almost sure that she could never learn to weave; the harness puzzled and the reed perplexed her; the shuttle flew out, and made a new bump upon her head; and the first time she tried to spring the lathe, she broke out a quarter of the treads. . . . There was a dull pain in her head, and a sharp pain in her ankles; every bone was aching and there was in her ears a strange noise,

---

[32] Kasson, *Civilizing the Machine*, 69–86; Jonathan Prude, *The Coming of Industrial Order: Town and Factory Life in Rural Massachusetts* (New York, 1983), 111–16; White, *A Memoir of Samuel Slater*, 113–20.

[33] As Keith Tribe puts it in his own critique of this representation, when we think of the Industrial Revolution we think "of factories and steam power, of fat capitalists and impoverished wage workers," and above all "of machinery, discipline and regulation" (*Genealogies of Capitalism* [London, 1981], 111).

[34] Walter Licht, *Working for the Railroad: The Organization of Work in the Nineteenth Century* (Princeton, 1983), 79. Thomas Dublin, *Women at Work: The Transformation of Work and Community in Lowell, Massachusetts, 1826–1860* (New York, 1979), 58–74. See, generally, E. P. Thompson, "Time, Work-Discipline, and Industrial Capitalism." *Past and Present*, 38 (1967) 56–97; Sidney Pollard, "Factory Discipline in the Industrial Revolution," *Economic History Review*, 2d ser., 16 (1963–4), 254–71.

[35] Wallace, *Rockdale*, 181.   [36] Kasson, *Civilizing the Machine*, 78.

as of crickets, frogs, and jews-harps, all mingling together; and she felt gloomy and sick at heart.[37]

Visitors referred to "the din and clatter" of the looms in operation "as something frightful and infernal" and "an atrocious violation" of the senses.[38]

Work under such conditions was enervating enough, but mills also suffered acute problems of dampness and ventilation,[39] compounded in the case of textiles by the high ambient temperatures required for successful cotton spinning and the choking dust that was one of the textile production process's most unpleasant by-products. Anthony Wallace quotes the testimony of a Pittsburgh physician before a Pennsylvania Senate committee at some length:

The factories are ill ventilated; their atmosphere is constantly impregnated, and highly surcharged with the most offensive effluvia – arising from the persons of the inmates, and the rancid oils applied to the machinery.

The temperature of their atmosphere is generally high, approaching a medium of from sixty to seventy degrees in winter, and rising to eighty and even ninety degrees in summer. Their atmosphere is constantly filled with floating particles of cotton; the finer the yarns to be spun, the higher the temperature must be. Cotton yarns cannot be spun in any atmosphere other than this. The cotton wool, when impregnated with the oil used to diminish friction in the machinery, and in the usual temperature of the rooms, emits a most offensive fetor. This fetor, acted on by the azote and hydrogen abounding in the rooms, gives an atmosphere which none but those accustomed to it can respire without nausea.

In the rooms where the cotton wool undergoes the first process of carding and breaking, the atmosphere is one floating mass of cotton particles, which none but those accustomed to it, can breathe, for an hour together, without being nearly suffocated.

Unsurprisingly, contemporaries considered factory work "not congenial to activity or health." Sickness, or "mill fever," was an almost invariable consequence of commencing work in a textile mill.[40]

Contradictions between the image of managed machine-paced order and a more disorderly reality were not confined to the physical environment of work. They were

---

[37] *Lowell Offering* (Aug. 1841), 1: 169–70, quoted in Zonderman, *Aspirations and Anxieties*, 23. See also, generally, 33–42.

[38] In John R. Commons et al. eds., *A Documentary History of American Industrial Society* (Cleveland, 1910), 7: 134.

[39] Ibid., 134. See also, e.g., Judith A. McGaw, *Most Wonderful Machine: Mechanization and Social Change in Berkshire Paper Making, 1801–1885* (Princeton, 1987), 309–10. McGaw quotes one Berkshire, Mass., paper mill worker's expressed desire to alter his employment "on account of the Room in which I work, it is very wet and is ingering my health." His wages, he reported were good, "But money will not purches health."

[40] Wallace, *Rockdale*, 181–2; Carl Siracusa, *A Mechanical People: Perceptions of the Industrial Order in Massachusetts, 1815–60* (Middletown, Conn., 1979), 115. See also Dublin, *Women at Work*, 70; Zonderman, *Aspirations and Anxieties*, 75–6, 81–4; McGaw, *Most Wonderful Machine*; 309–10. *The Minority Report of the Massachusetts House Special Committee of Inquiry into the Limitation of the Hours of Work*, Massachusetts House Document no. 153 (1850), in Commons et al., eds., *Documentary History*, 8: 151–86, at 164, cited "conclusive" evidence that operatives "were exposed to extraordinary causes of disease, while engaged at their daily toil."

also implicit in the work rhythms and habits of the largely rural work force. Drinking and gambling at work, visiting and talking with other operatives, and in particular absenteeism and transiency, all rendered the formal regularity of the mill somewhat superficial.[41] Managers could invoke disciplinary sanctions in individual cases (at least one Hamilton Manufacturing Company employee was discharged because she was caught "dancing in the work room"[42]), but their capacity to enforce those sanctions systematically was in fact quite limited. At Lowell millowners organized authority hierarchically through delegation to workroom supervisors of immediate supervision and control of employees, but the exercise of discipline could easily clash with the interests of those same overseers in keeping up production in their respective sections. When it suited him, an overseer faced with a breach of the mill's "order" would simply turn a blind eye.[43] In the Slater mills of Dudley and Oxford, considerable disciplinary authority was effectively delegated by managers to heads of family; that retained in supervisors' hands was all the time subject to negotiation, rendering its systematic application uncertain. As Jonathan Prude remarks in his study of the Slater mills, "not all directives were always enforced. It was, in fact, precisely amid these 'rules and regulations' that managers and employees would develop many significant compromises in the regimens of local factories."[44]

Outside the mills, even these basic attempts at creating systems of authority were lacking. Most early American entrepreneurs, Richard C. Edwards has noted, tended to rely on their own personal power and authority for control of their establishments. This was hardly conducive to the achievement of an orderly industrial environment for, as Edwards finds, the exercise of that power "was typically erratic and arbitrary."[45] In assessing the performance of English entrepreneurs, Keith Tribe has similarly argued that the development of techniques for systematic supervision of large bodies of labor did not really begin until after midcentury, and that until then "size meant chaos."[46]

There is, therefore, a not-inconsiderable irony in the imagery of regularity and

[41] Zonderman, *Aspirations and Anxieties*, 255–6.

[42] Hamilton Manufacturing Company, Registers of Employees 1830–60, Baker Library, Harvard Business School.

[43] Dublin, *Women at Work*, 60, 73.

[44] Barbara M. Tucker, *Samuel Slater and the Origins of the American Textile Industry, 1790–1860* (Ithaca, N.Y., 1984), 147–62; Prude, *The Coming of Industrial Order*, 130. See also Zonderman, *Aspirations and Anxieties*, 97–118.

[45] Richard C. Edwards, *Contested Terrain: The Transformation of the Workplace in the Twentieth Century* (New York, 1979), 23–7.

[46] Tribe, *Genealogies of Capitalism*, 115. Note the experience of the early eighteenth-century English ironmaster Ambrose Crowley. Crowley had attempted to run his works according to rules "defining duties, compensations and penalties in the minutest detail." When it came to the actual operation of his works, however, Sidney Pollard tells us that he was soon reduced to "a constant sense of despair about the efficiency of control" (*Genesis of Modern Management*, 55–9). Pollard concludes that the modern industrial proletariat which emerged in England in the first half of the nineteenth century experienced not so much disciplined regularity as "compulsion, force and fear" (207). For a vivid sense of the chaos of industrialism in England, see Raphael Samuel, "The Workshop of the World: Steam Power and Hand Technology in Mid-Victorian Britain," *History Workshop*, 3 (1977), 6–72.

orderliness to which early nineteenth-century industrialists resorted in attempting to describe the reality of their enterprises. Industrial "order" was to an important extent a mask for confusion and arbitrariness, a facade behind which employees daily confronted an unpredictable terrain.[47]

ACCIDENTS

Of all the "manifold uncertainties" with which workers had to contend each day at work, none was more serious in its consequences than their constant vulnerability to violent accidents.[48] Fleeting glimpses of work injuries available through surviving records underscore how closely violent death attended working people. Take, for example, the case of Charles Goddard, thrown twelve feet head first into a brick wall by machinery in operation at the Marine Railway in Boston; or Jeremiah Menzies, whose life ended abruptly on the Fourth of July in 1829 when his ribs were crushed and his back broken by a blow from a hawser at Barnes' Wharf. Then there was David Sullivan, found "hanging by the legs, in fragments," following the bursting of a locomotive steam engine boiler on the Eastern Railroad; and Charles Miller, who died at the Massachusetts General Hospital of injuries received at Merrill & Brother's paper manufactory, "by being accidentally caught by a shaft in said mill while revolving with great rapidity, he being carried round several hundred times, coming in contact with the ceiling above thereby bruising his flesh and breaking many of his bones."[49]

Examined individually, incidents such as these lend a certain descriptive weight to the proposition that the course of industrialization in antebellum America was chaotic and disorderly. They give added meaning to Seth Luther's charge that "the whole system of labor . . . is a cruel system of exaction on the bodies and minds of the producing classes."[50] Examined in aggregate, however, one may detect patterns in their incidence that suggest they signify a lot more besides.

[47] This point owes much to Michel Foucault's pointed observation that a disciplinary society does not imply a disciplined society; or in other words that disciplinary "simply refers to the deployment of certain techniques rather than to the achievement of desired effects as well" (see Mark Cousins and Athar Hussain, *Michel Foucault* [London, 1984], 188). Rothman implies a similar conclusion in testifying to the inability of prisons and asylums, behind their respective institutional facades, actually to achieve "order" in their populations (*Discovery of the Asylum*, 237–64). See also Ignatieff, *A Just Measure of Pain*, 207–15.

[48] Alf Lüdtke, "The Historiography of Everyday Life: The Personal and the Political," in Raphael Samuel and Gareth Stedman Jones, eds., *Culture, Ideology, and Politics: Essays for Eric Hobsbawm* (London, 1982), 48. Walter Licht comments on railroad work: "Employment was erratic and uncertain, and the hours were long. But an even greater specter haunted nineteenth-century American railwaymen. Railroad work was dangerous. Accidents were not just common; they were an integral component of the work. If many men ultimately escaped accidental injuries and death, the fear and threat of such happenings were inescapable and hung over everyone working on the line" (*Working for the Railroad*, 181).

[49] Report no. 100 (3 May 1827), no. 210 (4 July 1829), no. 1026 (2 Apr. 1849), and no. 1247 (19 June 1851), all in Suffolk County Coroners, Reports of Inquests, Adlow Collection, Rare Book Room, Boston Public Library.

[50] Seth Luther, *An Address to the Working Men of England on the State of Education and on the Condition of the Producing Classes in Europe and America* (New York, 1833), 29, and see also 19–20.

The absence of any requirement for the recording of industrial accidents in Massachusetts or any other state prior to the late nineteenth century makes reliable estimates of their incidence during the antebellum period next to impossible.[51] Business records of this era are generally silent about injuries on the job, and few of the recent histories of antebellum manufacturing have had anything substantial to offer on the subject.[52] What evidence there is, however, suggests that industrial accidents were actually relatively rare during most of the first two or three decades of the century. An inspection of the records of various medium-to-large construction projects of the prerailroad era, for example, discloses few mentions of injury to any participant. During the ten years from 1794 to 1804 that Loammi Baldwin was superintendent of the construction of the Middlesex Canal he recorded only three instances of injury to anyone involved in the project.[53] Similarly, at the conclusion of construction of the new Suffolk County Court House in Boston in 1813, the architect in charge, Charles Bulfinch, reported that only one injury had occurred during the project.[54] A similar story is told by the records of Loammi Baldwin, Jr., engineer in charge of the construction of a naval dry dock at Charlestown. Throughout the period of construction only two accidents are mentioned, the first in 1831 when one man was killed and several injured by the collapse of a wooden retaining wall in a major excavation, and the second some fifteen months later when Baldwin's deputy, George M. Dexter, reported that a carpenter named Johnson had dropped a large chisel he had been sharpening, "cut[ting] off his big toe and half the next, as clean as possible."[55]

---

[51] By *industrial accident* I mean an injury or illness occurring within the scope of employment and causally linked to employment.

[52] Thomas Dublin makes passing reference to "the risk of personal injury" attending particular mill occupations but provides no details (*Women at Work*, 65). In *Rockdale*, 149–50, Anthony Wallace argues that industrial accidents were a common occurrence, but that assertion is based on nothing more than a few incidents recorded by the artist John Rogers while a journeyman machinist in the early 1850s. Wallace has pursued the issue much more systematically in *St. Clair*, esp. 249–75. In this book, however, his evidence is drawn mostly from the 1860s and 1870s. Walter Licht's excellent study *Working for the Railroad* pays considerable attention to accidents but unfortunately he also has little concrete to offer on the early period.

[53] Simeon Farmer, who "had his leg broke in two places by the return of an iron crow bar in turning over a stone" in June 1797; Richard Briggs, "who had his leg broke blowing stones" in September 1800; and Mr. Malseed, who was fatally injured when he fell into a lock pit in August 1804. In Baldwin Papers, box 2 "Reports"; and box 1, James F. Baldwin to Loammi Baldwin (13 Aug. 1804), Baker Library, Harvard Business School.

[54] A laborer, Martin Nolan, had been injured while engaged in digging the drains from the new courthouse to the adjacent street. "The earth caved in upon him, and so injured him in the limbs as to confine him to his house fourteen weeks" (Charles Bulfinch to William Donnison, Esq. (10 Aug. 1813), in Adlow Collection.

[55] Loammi Baldwin, Jr., to Commodore John Rogers, president of the Navy Board (2 Nov. 1831), in Baldwin Papers, box 21; Dexter to Baldwin (11 Feb. 1833), in Baldwin Papers, box 19. Although there is no reason to doubt the comprehensiveness of Baldwin's and Bulfinch's records, one must still be careful about drawing conclusions in regard to the frequency of industrial accidents based on employer records alone. Employers on large construction projects often took steps to limit their involvement in large-scale direct employment of labor. Rather than create its own semipermanent work force, for example, the Middlesex Canal Corporation attempted to subcontract most of the unskilled construction work to local farmers or to gangs of laborers, who associated themselves more or less spontaneously to bid for digging

Work accidents, therefore, appear to have been relatively unusual in the 1820s and early 1930s.[56] They became considerably less so in the 1840s and 1850s. Analysis of the reports of coronial inquests conducted within Suffolk County between 1830 and 1860 indicates that the proportion of deaths resulting from work-related accidents to all deaths by violence rose from roughly 1 in 26 in the 1830s to 1 in 15 in the 1840s and 1 in 7 in the 1850s.[57] This increase is not on the face of it all that surprising, given that the period from the late 1830s on witnessed the diffusion of technological innovations – the railroad, the steamboat, the stationary steam engine – that historians have commonly associated with an increase in workplace risk.[58] When considered carefully, however, few of the fatal industrial accidents reported by Boston's coroners could be attributed to the risks of operation at the frontier of the era's technological capacity. Rather, the circumstances of accidents were typically mundane. Austin Fenlee, a seaman on the brig *Emir*, was killed on 4 December 1828 because a flimsy staging made of oars collapsed as he worked at putting a hoop on the brig's foremast. Samuel Welch, at work in the rigging of the schooner *Eliza Ann* on the morning of 1 September 1829, fell from the main top because the masthead, "being very rotten," broke off.[59] Numbers of common laborers died in

by the rod. Skilled work, particularly masonry, was also usually subcontracted to master artisans, who supplied their own journeymen and assistants. Delays in completing sections of the work were often attributed to the absence of a pool of labor on call, but the practice of subcontracting had the valuable benefit of spreading the economic risks associated with the enterprise beyond the investors in the corporation. These forms of work organization make accidents difficult to trace because there is no particular reason why injuries to employees of subcontractors or to members of gangs of laborers would show up in the primary contractor's records. Indirect confirmation of this can be gleaned from a letter from George Whistler, chief engineer of the Western Railroad Corporation, to the corporation's board in answer to a claim made by Elias Whipple of Springfield for compensation for the death of his son in a construction accident. The son, Whistler indicated, "was unfortunately killed while on the road as a hired laborer of the contractor . . . it has never been the custom elsewhere to my knowledge, for Railroad corporations to make provision, in cases of accident among these laborers." See Whistler to the President and Directors, Western Railroad Corporation (8 June 1841), WRR Case 1, Clerk's Files, in Edward J. O'Day, "Construction the Western Railroad: The Irish Dimension," *Historical Journal of Massachusetts*, 11, 1 (Jan. 1983), 20–1.

[56] During the mid-1820s, the *Boston Courier* carried on average one report every two months of a work accident in Massachusetts and four reports every two months of accidents occurring outside the state. (These estimates are based on a reading of every issue of the *Courier* for the years 1824–7 inclusive.) Of these, the majority in each year examined involved construction. Interestingly, contemporaries noted both the dangers of construction projects in comparison with other pursuits but also, in the 1820s at least, the comparative infrequency of accidents. In May of 1825, for example, the *Courier* complained of a lack of local news, stating that although there was considerable demolition and construction of buildings in the city, "the people who superintend this business are so confoundedly careful that there is seldom any 'crash' of limbs to be recorded" (*Boston Courier*, 27 May 1825). Andrew Prouty, *More Deadly than War! Pacific Coast Logging 1827–1981* (New York, 1985), at 4, also seems to suggest work accidents were comparatively rare before the middle decades of the nineteenth century. We should note, however, that Daniel Vickers finds a high accidental death rate among seventeenth-century Essex County cod fishers ("Maritime Labor in Colonial Massachusetts: A Case Study of the Essex County Cod Fishery and the Whaling Industry of Nantucket" [Ph.D. diss., Princeton University, 1981], 98–9).

[57] Suffolk County Coroners, Reports of Inquests nos. 230–1595, in Adlow Collection.

[58] See, e.g., Paul Finkelman, "Slaves as Fellow Servants: Ideology, Law, and Industrialization," *American Journal of Legal History*, 36, 4 (Oct. 1987), 269–305, at 269–70.

[59] Suffolk County Coroners, Reports of Inquests nos. 180 and 212, in Adlow Collection.

falls through the unguarded scuttles of warehouses, slipped from icy scaffoldings, or perished when banks of earth collapsed in construction projects. Among railroad workers, brakemen were the most liable to injury simply because railroad bridges were generally constructed with insufficient clearance to allow safe passage of the car *and* the brakeman on top.[60]

Scholars in the field of industrial sociology and other present-day commentators have argued that although it is common to see industrial accidents attributed to the "inevitable" risks of operating at the cutting edge of technological capacity, they are in fact far more often caused by the pressures brought to bear on employees by their employers' desires to minimize costs and maximize productivity. An employer determined to keep work moving and costs low will quite routinely place his employees in physical danger in their day-to-day employment. "The more rationalized the work, the faster the machines run, the less time wasted between operations . . . the greater the chance that in the short or medium term the work force will be palpably injured by its labor."[61] Evidence detailed enough to permit rigorous testing of this hypothesis as an explanation of the occurrence of work injuries in the first part of the nineteenth century is hard to come by. Such illustrations of workplace pressures as are available, however, tend to support the proposition that the causes of accidents are to be found in the sociology of production rather than in the pressure of economic growth against the outer limits of technical achievement and human knowledge.

Take, for example, a series of letters describing the use of a diving bell in the construction of the Charlestown navy yard dry dock during the winter of 1833 written by George Dexter, clerk to the superintendent of the yard, to Loammi Baldwin, Jr., the chief engineer. On the first morning of work involving use of the bell, Dexter told Baldwin, the men "all held back and seemed unwilling to go." Some demanded double wages before they would go in the bell; others simply declined "from fear." Dexter described to Baldwin how he had "sent out of the yard for an Irishman who had been working the last summer on the bank at the bottom of the yard, and put him 'nolens volens' into the bell and descended with him." The experience was "not very unpleasant, excepting the pressure of air on the ears," and the demonstration apparently sufficed in allaying the men's anxieties and persuading them to work in the bell at their regular wages. Dexter indicated, however, that operation of the bell was going to

---

[60] Of twenty-five railroad workers whose deaths in accidents were recorded by the Suffolk County coroners between June 1845 and January 1859, eleven were brakemen. The next largest category was yardmen, with five (see Reports of Inquests in Adlow Collection). Over the same period on the Boston & Worcester alone, eight brakemen were killed and four injured. After one particularly nasty incident in January 1848 the directors appointed a committee to report on the cost of raising all bridges on the line. There is no indication, however, that any further action was taken (Boston & Worcester Railroad, Directors' Minutes, vol. 6 [meeting of 4 Jan. 1848], in Boston & Albany Railroad Collection, Baker Library, Harvard Business School).

[61] Charles F. Sabel, *Work and Politics: The Division of Labor in Industry* (New York and Cambridge, 1982), 199. See also W. G. Carson, *The Other Price of Britain's Oil: Safety and Control in the North Sea* (Oxford, 1982).

be problematic. The air hose was faulty and "the scow on which it is placed is an old affair and leaks badly."

Dexter's next letter shows that by the time operations began in earnest the following week the yard men, although now willing to go in the bell, were not adapting to the task. "The men were awkward and did not work to much advantage." Dexter arranged for a subcontractor to take over the underwater excavation and proudly told Baldwin of the 40 percent saving in costs which this had effected. His letter, however, shows that the price to which the subcontractor had agreed had placed his workers under enormous pressure to avoid delays. "Our men would not work in the bell when the thermometer was below 32. Mitchell and his men are at work today and the thermo. at 10." Dexter reassured Baldwin that "we are daily gaining information and experience about the use of the bell," yet his letter was a catalogue of near-disasters. "The air pump is good for its size, but is not large enough, and the divers often have to ring for more air. When the bell is full of air, by constant pumping, it will keep a supply, but when the men are at work and cant the bell a little the air escapes and the pump cannot replace it quick enough." Even raising and lowering the bell was a major problem. "The rope by which the bell is suspended is 5 in. white rope, roved through 2 three fold blocks 14 in. sheave. This rope, however, by being in the water has become an 8 in. and sticks badly in the mortices of the blocks." Moreover "the barrel on which the rope is wound up does not answer well. The slope is too gradual which causes the rope to surge badly." Dexter indicated that he had contemplated substituting a chain for the rope, but had not done so because it would prevent the use of the bell in cold weather.[62]

Notwithstanding the difficulties described in Dexter's letters, there is no evidence that the operation of the navy yard bell was not accident-free. Certainly no report of any mishap appears in the chief engineer's papers. The example, nevertheless, is instructive, in that it reveals how considerations of cost and speed could impinge upon considerations of safety to the detriment of the latter. An old leaky scow, an inadequate air pump, a rope which swelled in water and stuck in its blocks, a badly designed windlass – none of these were exactly problems beyond the leading edge of early nineteenth-century technology. Yet Dexter never so much as hinted that he was considering suspension of the bell's use until the faults were corrected. Neither the weather nor shoddy equipment nor the anxiety of the workmen involved was to interfere with the schedule of construction operations.

Similar hints of the negative impact of considerations of cost and speed of operation upon the safety of the working environment appear in the reports of the Suffolk County coroners. When Isaac Tirrell's steam engine boiler blew up on Christmas Eve 1845, killing his son William and fellow worker William Ford, Tirrell told the inquest that the accident had been caused by Ford's incompetence in regulating the quantity of water in the boiler. According to the testimony of master machinist Stillman Chubbuck, however, just the previous week Tirrell had

---

[62] Dexter to Baldwin (14–28 Jan. 1833), all in Baldwin Papers, box 19.

called him in to examine and repair the boiler only to be told that the boiler "was very old, hardly worth repairing, and if he was not careful it would burst and kill somebody." Tirrell, said Chubbuck, had reluctantly agreed to have the boiler patched but had told Chubbuck's workmen to "be as quick as you can about it, for we are in a great hurry." Other workmen in Tirrell's shop claimed that the boiler had been leaking badly and that Tirrell had acknowledged the need to do something about it "when over with his hurry." They described how Tirrell's careless management had "often led us to fear and to remark that we should either be blown up or burnt up."[63]

Evidence culled from the work of other writers confirms that a rising curve of injury was a general accompaniment of higher speeds and greater intensification of production pressures. In textiles and in other industries, according to David Zonderman, "letters from workers, and the labor press, were filled with reports of men and women being maimed or killed by machinery."[64] Judith McGaw writes similarly. Papermaking, she tells us, underwent transformation from "a relatively safe craft" to a mechanized industry characterized by "increasingly demanding work, longer hours, and dangerous, unhealthful working conditions."[65] Anthony Wallace's recent study of anthracite mining in Pennsylvania finds poor colliery design and maintenance responsible for most colliery accidents, the legacy not of technical ignorance but of rapid speculative development and deliberate decisions to keep operating costs as low as possible. "Maximum profit could only be achieved by spending no more than the minimum on casualty prevention; maximum safety could only be secured by accepting less than maximum profit. With few exceptions . . . the operators chose to solve the dilemma by minimizing expenditures on safety."[66]

In Massachusetts, the pivotal importance of the cost–safety nexus took on its peculiar clarity in the 1830s and 1840s. Employers found themselves participating

---

[63] Suffolk County Coroners, Reports of Inquests no. 753 (24 Dec. 1845), in Adlow Collection. Another example of the cost–safety nexus at play comes from Connecticut in 1846 in this description of difficulties arising from the mechanization of metalworking and the accompanying replacement of skilled craftsmen with unskilled operatives. The author is Samuel Collins, Superintendent of the Collins Axe Company in Collinsville. His comments are reproduced in David A. Zonderman, "Aspirations and Anxieties: New England Workers and the Mechanized Factory System, 1815–1850," (Ph.D. diss., Yale University, 1986): "The effect of running our grinding with green Irishmen now became visible by the increase[d] 'wear and tear' of machinery. The three breast wheels failed one after the other though they had been running but ten years. The pine shaft of one of them broke, the life of the wood being destroyed by allowing the gudgeons to heat. Grindstone dust fills the holes for oiling unless watched with care. *We could not possibly suspend our business to build wood wheels which would delay several months so we put in cast iron breast wheels.* The aproning, gearing and large wheels or drums for belting being all ready for that kind of wheel but they did not live much longer than the wood wheels and *we finally put in iron turbine wheels which cost much less though they don't run as steady and we have more accidents by the bursting of stones*" (65–6, emphasis supplied).

[64] Zonderman, *Aspirations and Anxieties*, 43, and see generally 42–4.

[65] McGaw, *Most Wonderful Machine*, 311.

[66] Wallace, *St. Clair*, 260–1. On the technology of colliery design and the social and economic context of its application, see also Anthony F. C. Wallace, *The Social Context of Innovation: Bureaucrats, Families, and Heroes in the Early Industrial Revolution* (Princeton, 1982), 103–50.

in an increasingly competitive local economy and reacted by intensifying the pace of work. By the late 1830s, indeed, the performance of work in Massachusetts had become entangled in what W. G. Carson has trenchantly described as a "political economy of speed."[67] With entrepreneurs scrabbling for advantage in an increasingly rapacious competition for new markets and scarce investment capital, rapidity of development and operational intensity became the essence of industrialism in the state.

What was particularly noteworthy about the political economy of speed was the dramatic intensification of workplace pressures that it brought, with predictable results for the safety of the environments in which people worked. In the New England textile industry, for example, the rapid expansion of mill capacity that occurred during the 1830s greatly increased competition in the industry, precipitating a fall in revenues and profits. Slackening consumer demand after 1837 rendered the situation acute. Mill agents under pressure to increase productivity and reduce unit costs turned to the intensification of work through the techniques of speed-up and stretch-out and the introduction of premium payments to the most productive overseers. At Lowell the "leisurely atmosphere of the early mills" was transformed over the succeeding decade as work loads effectively doubled while working conditions deteriorated. As one overseer put it: "The necessity which [the supervisor] is under of producing work, of the quality, and in the quantity his employers desire of him, *compels* him (even when he has a disposition to do otherwise) frequently to be apparently harsh and unmindful of those employed under him."[68] A similar story was unfolding in the smaller, southwestern Massachusetts mills, where the traditional "family" system of labor organization slowly disintegrated under the pressure of speed-up and stretch-out.[69]

The same stresses can be discerned compromising the safety of operations on the region's early railroads. Here, however, the story is more complex. First, the railroads had to compete with preexisting modes and routes of carriage. Owing their origin in large part to the desire of Boston's merchant capitalists to win themselves a share of the booming trade with the West, New England's railroads were intended to counteract New York merchants' water-borne dominance over what was seen as Boston's commercial hinterland. Maintaining their edge in competition with road and water transport was clearly always going to be an important constraint upon the railroads' freedom of operation. Operational success, however, itself presupposed success in attracting sufficient investment capital to make the railroad a going concern, and success in competing for capital was in turn dependent upon holding out a realistic prospect of a decent return on investment. In 1828, for example, the proponents of the projected railroad linking Boston to Albany estimated that a

---

[67] Carson, *The Other Price of Britain's Oil*, 84–138.
[68] Dublin, *Women at Work*, 108–12, 132–8 (emphasis supplied).
[69] Tucker, *Samuel Slater*, 214–49. And see, generally, Siracusa, *A Mechanical People*, 160–1.

minimum return of 6 percent per annum was necessary to attract the capital required. Significantly, they were able to demonstrate their project's capacity to achieve this return only by deliberately underestimating its recurrent costs. Annual maintenance costs, for example, were set at a quite unrealistic 0.25 percent of invested capital.[70] The Boston & Worcester Railroad, chartered in 1831 to undertake the development of the first stage of the route to Albany, followed a similar strategy, deliberately minimizing costs and predicting healthy returns in order to compete for investment.[71] Indeed, so intense was the desire of the directors "to prove, once and for all, that railroads were a profitable investment" that it led them consistently to underestimate operating (particularly maintenance) costs in order to justify devoting operating revenues to the payment of dividends.[72]

As in Wallace's Pennsylvania anthracite example, a clear threat to operational safety arose from these circumstances. Having staked the survival of its enterprise upon the promise of substantial dividends, the Boston & Worcester's board of directors was committed to maximizing speed and minimizing costs in both construction and operation of the road.[73] Given the intensity of competition for capital and the ceiling on freight and passage charges imposed by the existence of alternatives, fulfillment of its pledges was not possible any other way.

The railroad that resulted was, unsurprisingly, "a superintendent's nightmare" – a single-track line operating without signals on which "collision lurked around every corner."[74] Collisions at unmarked crossings between road and rail traffic began to occur almost immediately. These were soon joined by a quickening flood of derailments and collisions between trains bringing injury and death to passengers and employees alike.[75]

A rigid scheduling system was adopted as the main, indeed only possible (given the physical plant available), guarantee of operational safety. Yet this was inevitably compromised by constant pressures from the board to increase the intensity of

[70] Stephen Salsbury, *The State, the Investor, and the Railroad: The Boston & Albany, 1825–67* (Cambridge, Mass., 1967), 64–5.

[71] Ibid., 109.

[72] Ibid., 112. So desperate was the board to demonstrate profitability that it committed itself to a first dividend which exceeded earnings by $5,000. As Salsbury comments, "In effect, the [board] proposed to pay out as a dividend the money the stockholders paid in as capital" (130). Not to be outdone, the board two years later declared a half-year dividend of 3 percent, which it proposed to finance by raising a loan (Boston & Worcester Railroad, Directors' Minutes, vol. 2 [meeting of 20 June 1837]).

[73] On this as a general characteristic of American industrialization, the product of distinctive conditions encouraging both labor and capital saving, see H. J. Habakkuk, *American and British Technology in the Nineteenth Century: The Search for Labor-Saving Inventions* (Cambridge, 1962), esp. 53–131.

[74] Salsbury, *The State, the Investor, and the Railroad*, 114–15.

[75] Examination of the directors' minutes indicates that in operations through 1850 the railroad's superintendents reported 32 incidents in which trains were derailed or involved in collisions with each other, and a further 19 collisions with road traffic at crossings or with straying cattle. Over the same period some 40 employees were reported killed or injured, along with 49 passengers and 22 pedestrians who had strayed onto the tracks (Boston & Worcester Railroad, Directors' Minutes, vols. 1–7; see also Suffolk County Coroners, Reports of Inquests). It is likely that these figures understate the full total of death and injury, as the superintendents did not always offer full details of the incidents they reported.

operations. Early in 1839, for example, the board can be found expressing its "great concern" at the "various accidents, disasters and occurrences which have recently happened on the Rail Road," especially "the several instances of the merchandize trains running with a much greater speed than are allowed by the regulations heretofore adopted." Less than three months later, however, we find the same board instructing the superintendent "to rescind the regulation by which the enginemen are required to run the passenger trains over the road in three hours, and to direct them to run carefully over every part of the road, especially over all uneven places, and to perform the whole distance in not less than two hours and three quarters." Apart from the board's implicit acknowledgment that the roadbed was not in the best of conditions, its instruction rather contradicted its earlier profession of concern at the speed of the merchandise trains, for it is clear that on a single-track railroad an instruction to increase the speed of one class of traffic was de facto an instruction to increase the speed of all.[76]

The board's need to increase the intensity of operations and the resulting increase in the incidence of accidents originated in the board's initial strategy of minimizing the capital costs of the road. This was underscored in the report of an independent committee set up by the railroad's stockholders at their annual meeting in June 1840 to investigate "why the dividends of this company have not yet exceeded six per cent," a rate, according to the committee, "altogether too low, when compared with the reasonable expectations of the stockholders and the eligible position of the road." The committee – whose very existence evidences the constant pressures on the board to improve returns – focused on the deficiencies of the corporation's locomotive department. The road's engines, it reported, were "of antiquated patterns, deficient in power and decrepit for want of repairs and requiring a constant outlay to keep them in motion." Too small and weak for the roles they had to play, the mechanical strain under which they had been placed had resulted in constant break-downs and accidents, considerable expenditure in repairs, and the loss of revenue through delays and lost business. Given, moreover, that even when operating smoothly their small size meant they were incapable of hauling large loads, persistent use of small locomotives had necessitated that the volume of traffic on the road be increased to an extremely high level. Not only had this meant additional operating expenses in the form of track maintenance and fuel and labor costs, it had also materially increased the risk of catastrophic accidents. The committee called for the introduction of heavier locomotives, which "will perform the work of three [existing locomotives], will save the expense of two firemen and enginemen, will obviate the necessity of frequent trains of freight which on Roads with a single track materially retard the transportation of passengers and occasion a waste of fuel and labor and frequent accidents," and "will cause less damage to the Road." It also called for the immediate commencement of work on a second track. "The perils of the way are increasing and must continue to increase with the accession of business. . . . [T]he security of the

---

[76] Directors' Minutes, vol. 3 (meetings of 16 Jan. 1839 and 10 Apr. 1839).

travelling public imperatively demands a second track, [for] without such a safe-guard it will be impossible for this road to perform its own business and the business derived from the other great roads that unite with it and avoid the recurrence of similar disasters."[77]

The deterioration of working conditions in the state's mechanizing industries in the second half of the 1830s and the traveling exhibition of injury and dismemberment on the railroads point up the decisive impact of the political economy of speed on the safety of work in early industrial Massachusetts. Equally important, however, these developments helped bring to the surface the completeness of the contradiction between employers' idealized image of industry as ordered regularity and the actuality of their employees' daily lives. The result was a growing consciousness of industrial crisis.[78]

Reactions were forthcoming from both employers and workers. For their part, employers placed redoubled emphasis upon the transformative powers of "management." Unsavory or dangerous working conditions were to be addressed through the further bureaucratization of supervisory authority and the establishment and enforcement of more elaborate codes of rules and workplace procedures.[79] Once promulgated, these rules and procedures took on a life of their own as a necessary and sufficient condition of the existence of a safe and orderly workplace. Accidents were to be explained not by the pressures visited on the work force and the fabric of the workplace as a consequence of their employer's desire to produce competitively, but by an employee's violation of the rules.[80] But in fact, as we have already

---

[77] Report of the Committee of Stockholders appointed "to examine and consider the report of the directors," in Boston & Albany Railroad Collection, case 6.

[78] For a description of this growing consciousness of crisis in Massachusetts, see Siracusa, *A Mechanical People*, 155–62. See also, generally, David M. Gordon et al., *Segmented Work, Divided Workers: The Historical Transformation of Labor in the United States* (New York and Cambridge, 1982), 54–78.

[79] See, e.g., Wallace, *Rockdale*, 326–37; Tucker, *Samuel Slater*, 223–9. As Licht shows, this was a particular strategy of railroad managers faced with the accumulation of intractable operating problems (*Working for the Railroad*, 80–9).

[80] Thus when, early in 1842, the Committee on Rail-roads and Canals of the Massachusetts General Court mounted an investigation into "the causes of the frequent accidents upon the Western rail-road," it determined that the most notorious accident – a head-on collision on 5 October 1841 at Westfield – had been caused by the failure of one conductor to keep to his timetable. However, in investigating a second major accident which had occurred in early February 1842 at Richmond, the committee professed itself unable to explain why an engineer (unfortunately deceased in the accident) had run his locomotive through a damaged section of track at normal speed (causing it to derail) without pausing to consider the impact on train crews of injunctions from the corporation to stick rigidly to the timetable on pain of dismissal. See Commonwealth of Massachusetts, Senate Document 55 (Feb. 1842), 5–8.
Wallace makes the same point in the Pennsylvania anthracite setting: "It is obvious . . . with respect to firedamp explosions, that the "careless miner" with his naked light could not ignite the gas if the ventilation system, for which the operator was responsible, had done its job. Of course, there were careless miners and careful miners guilty of moments of carelessness, who entered old workings against the rules in order to urinate or defecate, or who climbed up into gassy breasts against the fire boss' orders, or who failed to use safety lamps when they were told to do so because they could work faster with naked lights. But in every explosion there was the contributing factor of an inadequate ventilation system for which the operator, the superintendent, the engineer, and the inside boss were responsible, and which the individual miner could control only to the most limited degree. Thus for the operators and their associates routinely to blame the miners alone for explosions which could have been prevented by better

327

seen, when rules got in the way of production and profit, employers and supervisors could often be found surreptitiously conniving in their breach.[81] In other words, whether rules accurately described the realities of production, and thus provided a means for its regulation, was in fact highly debatable.[82] Just how debatable has been demonstrated in the work of historians such as Walter Licht, whose research well attests to the "diffuseness" and "indeterminacy" of early industrial work. "An effort at labor control," Licht writes, "rules often are presented as descriptions of the normal working day. The true picture – of what actually occurred on the job on a daily basis – was more complicated." Whatever those rules tell us about managers' desires to proclaim at least the appearance of rationality, the reality, on the railroads, was that "work for all grades of [employees] was characterized by contingency and an absence of specification."[83]

During the 1830s and early 1840s Massachusetts workers also addressed the contradiction between the appearance and the reality of industrial work. In part, they and those who spoke for them did so simply by offering a counterimage of industrial order to that embraced by their employers. Strikes, speeches, and demonstrations became occasions to air grievances about the depraved and tyrannical factory system and to invoke a contrasting egalitarian ideal that recalled the republican industrialism of the Jeffersonians.[84] Increasingly, however, this by now somewhat utopian critique of wage slavery and class division metamorphosed into something more deliberate. "Unable to halt what they perceived as the degradation of work," writes Thomas Dublin, "operatives sought at least to mitigate its ill effects," mounting a series of campaigns for the legal regulation of conditions and hours of work in textile mills. Beginning in 1843 and climaxing in 1845, operatives petitioned repeatedly for legislative protection of the employed through the limitation of the

---

ventilation was obviously a self- serving position. By placing responsibility for prevention on the miners' shoulders, and demanding of them the moral qualities of prudence and foresight, the operator community avoided the 'extra' expense of the extensive 'dead work' involved in extending gangways and headings, installing large fans, and enlarging air holes" (*St. Clair*, 269–70).

[81] See above, n. 43 and accompanying text. Connivance ranged from employers tampering with clocks to lengthen the measured working day to overseers tampering with machinery to speed production and win bonuses. On the former see Luther, *Address to the Working Men of New England*, 20. On the latter see Caroline Ware, *The Early New England Cotton Manufacture: A Study in Industrial Beginnings* (Boston, 1931), 265.

[82] As Charles Sabel has pointed out, "rules are supposed to be constructed so carefully that following them blindly produces a perfect product every time. But . . . in factories as elsewhere, reality is so complex and rapidly changing that no plan can be comprehensive enough to be a completely reliable guide to action" (*Work and Politics*, 104). Similarly, Craig Littler states that "simple models of an organizational structure which assume unilateral rule-determination and unilateral rule-enforcement are extremely simplistic." Littler stresses how rule evasion can quite easily become acceptable behavior to management and how this "collaborative violation" becomes "stabilized as a permanent aspect of the work organization" (*The Development of the Labor Process in Capitalist Societies* [Exeter, N.H., 1982], 40–1). See also Michael Burawoy, *Manufacturing Consent: Changes in the Labor Process under Monopoly Capitalism* (Chicago, 1979), 46–94.

[83] Licht, *Working for the Railroad*, 89–93.

[84] Kasson, *Civilizing the Machine*, 86–97. Zonderman, *Aspirations and Anxieties*, 195, 247–8.

working day in factories to ten hours. The power of their employers and the disorder and danger of their lives in the mills – the pace of work, the abominable conditions, the lack of safety, the high incidence of disease and death in the work force – bulked large in the operatives' submissions.[85]

The operatives' efforts bore fruit in 1845 with the appointment of an investigative committee by the Massachusetts legislature, before which textile workers presented their evidence of the "pain, disease and privation" attending millwork and of the necessity of reducing hours.[86] The committee, however, declined to recommend legislation. The committee did not wish "to be understood as conveying the impression, that there are no abuses in the present system of labor." But it held that a reduction of hours in Massachusetts mills would so raise the costs of production as to place "capital, enterprise and industry" in the state at a severe competitive disadvantage. The committee would therefore heed pressures to "keep clear and mind [its] own business." Matters between the operatives and their employers were best settled by the parties themselves. The committee therefore referred the petitioners back to their employers, who, it hoped, would demonstrate their "ardent love for social happiness," and who were in any case in the best position to judge what remedies to institute.[87]

One might argue that by accepting "time and work discipline" as appropriate categories within which to pursue their contest with their employers, the operatives' petitioning strategy had allowed the whole argument to move decisively onto the employers' terrain, with predictable results when it came to the expression of official opinion. As we have seen, however, although the image of that terrain was one of regularity, its reality was one of oppressive arbitrariness and unpredictability. By campaigning to achieve the regulation of working conditions through public intervention, even though unsuccessful, workers were not simply attempting to press on their employers variations to the content of those mutually agreeable categories of time and work discipline. Rather, they were seeking to remold the terrain itself, to legislate in their own terms a modicum of the "order" that was absent from the reality of "management."[88]

[85] Dublin, *Women at Work*, 112, and see also 113–5; Zonderman, *Aspirations and Anxieties*, 234–60; Siracusa, *A Mechanical People*, 203; Frances H. Early, "A Reappraisal of the New England Labor-Reform Movement of the 1840s," *Histoire Sociale – Social History*, 13 (May 1980), 33–54. For an example see the "Circular of the Fall River Mechanics," reprinted from the *Fall River Mechanic* in the *Workingman's Advocate* of 29 June 1844; in Commons et al., eds., *Documentary History*, 8:86–91.

[86] Ware, *Early New England Cotton Manufacture*, 251.

[87] See the *Report of the Special Committee of the Legislature of the Commonwealth of Massachusetts on the Petitions Relating to the Hours of Labor*, Massachusetts House Document no. 50 (Mar. 1845), in Commons et al., eds., *Documentary History*, 8:133–51; John Q. A. Thayer, *Review of the Report of the Special Committee of the Legislature of the Commonwealth of Massachusetts on the petition Relating to Hours of Labor* (Boston, 1845), esp. 29–32. See also Dublin, *Women at Work*, 113–15.

[88] Zonderman, *Aspirations and Anxieties*, 239, 268–301. As Zonderman puts it elsewhere: "Most operatives probably realized that factories could not be argued away, and that the nation might be worse off without any mechanized manufacturing. The answer was not to destroy the factories but somehow to master them" (295).

CONCLUSION

This, then, was the material and ideological context in which the question of employer liability arose in the late 1830s and 1840s. During these years, deteriorating conditions in industrial establishments provoked an attempt by employees to expose the hidden abode of production to the gaze and the intervention of public authority and, in particular, to employ legal institutions as a means both of protecting themselves from the disorder of a competitive economy and of challenging the ideology of "management." The result was a confrontation with employers determined to avoid regulation potentially restrictive of their capacity to pursue production and profits.

No less than the ten-hours campaign, the common law of employer liability should be seen as one of the sites where this confrontation took place. Suits brought by workers against their employers were "little struggles" conducted at the level of everyday life, attempts to involve the courts in making employers responsible for injuries suffered by employees in the course of their work. By attempting to clarify the nature of the "managerial" power claimed by employers of labor and to hold them accountable for the chaotic consequences of its exercise, the plaintiffs were also implicitly demanding that the courts define the limits of their employers' authority over the organization of production. Thus, like the struggles in the larger arena of the ten-hours movement, the issue became a test of the social acceptability, legitimacy, and ambit of managerial discourse.

10

The law of industrial accidents

[F]ree in hand and foot, we are shackled in heart and soul with far straiter than feudal chains. Truly may we say with the Philosopher, "the deep meaning of the Laws of Mechanism lies heavy on us."

Thomas Carlyle, "Signs of the Times"

Gilham Barnes's suit against the Boston & Worcester Railroad was not resolved until almost two years after his accident. After the preliminary hearing in September 1837 before the Court of Common Pleas resulted in a decision in Barnes's favor, the parties retained additional counsel for an appearance before the Supreme Judicial Court in November.[1] The well-respected Charles Greely Loring took over the principal role in representing the railroad from George Morey, and Abraham Moore sought the assistance of one of the Massachusetts bar's rising luminaries, Rufus

---

[1] The plaintiff's action was on the case. The declaration for the Supreme Judicial Court trial asserted that "in consideration that the plaintiff would perform a certain piece of work, for and at the special instance and request of" the Boston & Worcester Railroad Corporation, the corporation had agreed to pay the plaintiff $1.75 per day and to convey him and his tools and materials to and from the place of work "in and upon certain carriages, called Railroad cars, owned and used by them, the said Corporation in the transportation of certain lumber, gravel and other materials" and that they would do so "in a careful and safe manner, using due care and diligence in and about the condition of said cars and the wheels, attached to the same." Relying "upon the skill, care and diligence of the said Corporation," the plaintiff had entered the defendant's train, which was "then and there under the care and government, inspection and direction of the servants and agents of the said Defendants." But the corporation, "by their said agents and servants" had "negligently and carelessly used in and upon the cars . . . two broken, cracked and insufficient wheels" and further had "so overloaded said cars" and had "so carelessly, unskilfully and improperly governed, managed and directed" them that "the car upon which the said Plaintiff was then and there sitting and riding . . . [was] broken and destroyed," and the plaintiff "thrown in and upon the ground with so great force and violence, and was so wounded, bruised and injured, that the left arm of him the Plaintiff has been amputated above the elbow, and his head, side and leg so greatly bruised, wounded and injured, that his life has been greatly despaired of." As a result, the plaintiff had "suffered great pain of body and anxiety of mind, has been put to great expense for Doctors, surgery and nurses bills, to wit the sum of three hundred dollars, and has been rendered by the injuries aforesaid wholly unable of earning a support for himself and family, during his natural life." These and all subsequent details of the case are drawn from files of case notes and testimony referring to *Barnes v. The Boston & Worcester Railroad* in the Charles Greely Loring Papers, unprocessed manuscript collection, Social Law Library, Boston.

Choate, on Barnes's behalf.[2] At a subsequent appearance before the court in March 1838 the parties reported their agreement to resolve the matter before a panel of referees. Hearings finally began on 27 February 1839 before Emory Washburn, Edward Brooks, and Prince Hawes.[3]

As was his custom, Loring kept extensive records of the arguments and testimony offered by both sides. From these it is possible to reconstruct the hearings more or less word for word.[4] What is revealed is a contest between conflicting doctrinal approaches to the occurrence of an occupational injury. The plaintiff asserted that the railroad owed a duty of care to all whom it conveyed. The corporation contended that the extent of its liability to compensate the plaintiff was determined exclusively by the terms of its contract with its employee.

Abraham Moore opened for the plaintiff. Barnes had come to Boston a poor and penniless man. Through hard work – "we shall prove that he had the reputation of doing more work in a day than any other man in his way in Boston" – he had acquired a small property, which he had nearly freed from mortgage when the accident happened. He was "a moral man of sterling worth," the father of four boys and the principal means of support for aged and infirm parents. Denying any intention to cast aspersions on the character of the corporation or the "numerous excellent gentlemen who comprise it," Moore nevertheless suggested that the burden of any damages ultimately awarded would be "but slightly felt."

Having thus painted the case as one between a poor but virtuous man and a powerful corporation, Moore introduced the plaintiff's case. Barnes had been retained by the assistant superintendent of the road, William Jackson, to tar and gravel several bridges belonging to the corporation. He had been promised transportation to and from the various locations. On 16 June he had resorted to the corporation's track maintenance train, which had subsequently been derailed when a wheel broke on one of the cars. The plaintiff's case rested on the corporation's violation of its obligation to provide Barnes with a safe means of transportation. Moore called witnesses to testify that the defendant had promised to provide Barnes with transport; that Barnes had been directed to take this particular train on the day in question; that many of the wheels on the cars making up this train were cracked – and indeed that it was the corporation's policy to recycle wheels deemed unsafe

---

[2] Of Loring it was said "that he was a cool, deliberate speaker, with great concentrative power and logical force." Rufus Choate, in contrast, was "all excitement, wit, and imagination." See James Spear Loring, *The Hundred Boston Orators* (Boston, 1854), 395.

[3] A letter from Choate to Emory Washburn of 10 Dec. 1838 seems to indicate the plaintiff's impatience at the long delay. "Do let us know the *earliest moment* you can try the case against the Rail Road" (in the collections of the Houghton Library, Harvard University, emphasis in original).

[4] It was said of Loring that he "was in the habit of taking very full notes at the trial of his cases, and of writing out his arguments – generally by dictation – almost at length" (Theophilus Parsons, *Memoir of Charles Greely Loring, Prepared Agreeably to a Resolution of the Massachusetts Historical Society* [Cambridge, Mass., 1870], 9). Because the record is reconstructed from notes rather than from transcripts or reported speech, one cannot be totally confident that the words quoted were actually spoken. One can be confident, however, that they accurately convey the lines of argument employed.

for use on its passenger cars by putting them on the gravel cars, and that as a result the train had been derailed.

In his opening remarks for the corporation, Loring attempted to alter Moore's characterization of the dispute so as to recast the roles of victim and oppressor. The corporation, he indicated, commiserated with Barnes. "The defendants and counsel do deeply sympathize with [him]." But instead of availing himself of the defendant's compassion and appealing to its benevolence and generosity as he might have done, Barnes had chosen to stand upon "his merely legal rights." Having taken that route his case had to be judged according to strictly legal considerations. "Feelings of sympathy and commiseration are among the most operative and powerful of any of humanity, wisely so ordained that our hands may be ever ready to succour and relieve." Fairness to the defendants demanded, however, that the referees banish such feelings from their minds. "If suffered to mingle in and influence [your] enquiry, their agency becomes a direct injustice and oppression upon the defendants and a greater injury is done to them than the plaintiff has suffered for injustice is a greater evil than bodily injury. . . . {I}t *must not for a moment be forgotten* that the appeal which plaintiff has elected to make to you is *not one* to your sense of what is due from the sympathy or generosity of defendants but what is due from them as [a] matter of strict right according to the rules of law and evidence."[5] According to those rules, Loring would argue, Barnes had no right of recovery.

IN SICKNESS AND IN HEALTH?

Loring's denial of the corporation's liability was consistent with the status quo then prevailing so far as concerned an employer's responsibilities in the event of illness or accident involving an employee. Prior to the appearance of employee suits for damages in the late 1830s, the question had been litigated on a few occasions in both England and America, though sparingly and in many cases indirectly. Scattered eighteenth-century English cases had made reference to a master's moral and legal obligation to support domestic servants and yearly servants in husbandry in the event of sickness,[6] but during the second half of the century, precisely at the time that the occupational ambit of the relation was widening to encompass an ever-greater segment of the laboring population, courts became increasingly reluctant to acknowledge that "masters" owed "servants" anything in the way of

---

[5] Emphasis in original.

[6] *R. v. Inhabitants of Christchurch*, Burrow's Settlement Cases 494 (1760) (domestic servant); *R. v. Inhabitants of Wintersett*, Cald. 298 (1783) (farm servant). See also *Dominus Rex v. Inhabitantes de Hales Owen*, 1 Strange 100 (1717) (apprentice). Michael Dalton's *The Countrey Justice* (London, 1619), at 74, stated, "If a seruant reteyned for a year, happen (within the time of their seruice) to fall sicke, or to be hurt or lamed, or otherwise to become *non potens in corpore*, yet it seemeth the Master must not put such seruant away, nor abate any part of his wages, for such time." The rule was reiterated by Richard Burn, *The Justice of the Peace and Parish Officer*, 4th ed. (London, 1757), 3:234.

reciprocal duties of care. Rather, the cost of curing a sick or injured servant, and also the responsibility to provide support when the servant was left dependent or destitute, was judged to be borne by the parish in which the servant had a settlement or, in the case of casual injuries, the parish in which the accident had occurred.[7] "I think, in general, a master ought to maintain his servants, and take care of them in sickness," Lord Mansfield stated in *Newby v. Wiltshire* (1784). "But the question now is, what is the law? There is, in point of law, no action against the master to compel him to repay the parish for the cure of his servant: no authority whatsoever has been cited; and it seems to me that it cannot be. The parish is bound to take care of accidents."[8] In *Scarman v. Castell* (1795) ten years later, Lord Kenyon held in a case heard *nisi prius* that a master was under a legal obligation to care for and maintain a sick or injured servant "while he was under his master's roof" as long as the illness or injury was not "the consequence of his own misconduct or debauchery,"[9] but in *Wennell v. Adney* (1802), Kenyon's opinion was dismissed in most devastating fashion by a full court of King's Bench. Aside from *Scarman v. Castell*, stated Lord Alvanley Ch.J., there was no authority in English law for the assertion that a master was obliged in law to care for his servant. "I have no doubt whatever that parish officers are bound to assist where such accidents as these take place; and that the law will so far raise an implied contract against them as to enable any person who affords that immediate assistance which the necessity of the case usually requires, to recover against them the amount of money expended." But there was no question that the law would raise as an implied term of the master's contract with the servant an undertaking to pay the costs of an injury even if incurred in the master's

[7] Servants or employees crippled or injured in accidents occurring in the course of their employment were "casual poor," the responsibility of the parish in which the accident occurred, on the principle that responsibility under the poor laws lay with the parish where the pauper "really became poor and impotent by being disabled there" (*Lamb v. Bunce*, 4 M. & S. 276 [1815]). See also *Simmons v. Wilmott*, 3 Esp. 91 (1800); *R. v. Kynaston*, 1 East 117 (1800). Although disputes over the relief of injured servants were not an uncommon occurrence in English courts, they were almost invariably disputes among parishes over attempts to "export" injured paupers or actions brought by surgeons and apothecaries against parishes to recover attendance fees. See, e.g., *R. v. Inhabitants of St. James in Bury St. Edmunds*, 10 East 26 (1808); *Wing v. Mill*, 1 B. & Ald. 104 (1817); *R. v. Inhabitants of St. Lawrence, Ludlow*, 4 B. & Ald. 660 (1821); *Tomlinson v. Bentall and Another*, 5 B. & C. 738 (1826). No action appears to have been brought by a servant against a master for medical expenses and relief prior to *Priestley v. Fowler*, 3 M. & W. 1 (1837). See, however, *Sellen v. Norman*, 4 Car. & P. 80 (1829); *Cooper v. Phillips*, 4 Car. & P. 580 (1831); *R. v. William Smith*, 8 Car. & P. 151 (1837). For an excellent summary of the law in England prior to *Priestley v. Fowler* see Brian W. Napier, "The Contract of Service: The Concept and Its Application" (D.Phil., University of Cambridge, 1975), 129–35.

[8] 2 Esp. 739, 4 Dougl. 284. Counsel in this case referred to a "general practice" among gentlemen of sending sick or injured servants to hospitals as proof of "the understanding that masters are not liable; for if they were it would be a breach of trust in the guardians of the hospitals to receive, and an act of meanness in the master to send, the servant." (Hospitals were, of course, charitable institutions.) Counsel conceded that masters of servants might be obliged to maintain sick servants, but only if they were menials, and then only as long as they remained in the master's house (4 Dougl., at 285–6). In *Simmons v. Wilmott* (1800), Lord Eldon observed that servants in husbandry were "not . . . of that description of servants for whom the master is bound to provide" (3 Esp., at 93).

[9] 1 Esp. 270.

service. Such an obligation would only be recognized if expressly entered into by the master.[10]

Scattered evidence from Massachusetts indicates a similar legal and social situation.[11] In 1823, for example, Nathan Dane's *Abridgment* acknowledged *Wennall v. Adney* as decisive in determining the extent of a master's responsibility for sick servants, noting that "the court thought the parish in which the accident happened was liable."[12] That this was already the case in Massachusetts is confirmed, albeit somewhat indirectly, by *Kittredge v. The Inhabitants of Newbury*, heard by the Supreme Judicial Court in 1817.[13] Following an accident at a Newbury woolen manufactory, Kittredge, a surgeon, had been called in to amputate the leg of Thomas Dennett, the injured employee. Kittredge subsequently applied to the Overseers of the Poor of Newbury for payment of his fee. Their refusal prompted a suit. Kittredge lost, but the reason was not that Dennett's employer was liable. Rather, the overseers were excused because the operation had been performed without their approval and the bill presented too late for them to recover the cost of casual relief from the overseers of Newburyport, Dennett's town of settlement. Their obligation, absent these extenuating circumstances, was not challenged.

Cases arising out of controversies over the eligibility of indigent former slaves and their descendants for relief from their town of residence reinforce the point, for decisions in these cases invariably turned upon an explicit comparison between the legal obligation of masters to attend to the welfare of their slaves and the absence

[10] 3 Bos. & Pul. 247, at 252–3. It is worth noting the comments of Alvanley's brother judges. Heath J. observed that Lord Kenyon had been misled by considerations of humanity in deciding *Scarman v. Castell*. He was "perfectly sure" that it was to the advantage of servants that the legal claim for assistance should be against the parish rather than against their masters, "for the situation of many masters who are obliged to keep servants, is not such as to enable them to afford sufficient assistance in cases of serious illness" (253). Rooke J. concluded that if the general principle maintained by the plaintiff were to be adopted as a rule of law, "many persons who are obliged for the purpose of their trade, to keep a number of servants, would be unable to fulfill the duty imposed upon them by the law" (253–4). Chambre J. held that the master's obligation, if any, could arise solely from his contract and that it "cannot be contended that a master impliedly contracts to furnish his servant" with the support contended for. "What has passed at Nisi Prius upon this subject has been somewhat hasty; and I think the rule there laid down would be very disadvantageous to the servants themselves if it were adopted" (254). All the judges dismissed as legally groundless the obligation to support sick or injured servants referred to in Dalton's *Countrey Justice*.

[11] The earliest involvement of local courts in the determination of liability for injuries arising from a work-related accident that I have been able to discover is *Stuart and Ludden's Case, Records of the Suffolk County Court, 1671–80*, Colonial Society of Massachusetts Publications 29–30 (Boston, 1933), 1:404–8. In this case the defendants were accused of "carelessness in fitting the tackling of theire Sloope," occasioning the death of one man and injury to another. Although nowhere explicitly stated, it is implied in one part of the court record that the dead and injured men were crewmen on the sloop. See "Joseph Luden [*sic*] and James Stuart theire reasons of Appeall," at 406, second paragraph. In the County Court Stuart and Ludden were found liable and sentenced to pay compensation to the injured sailor and to the widow of the deceased. On appeal to the Court of Assistants, however, the County Court judgment was reversed.

[12] Nathan Dane, *A General Abridgment and Digest of American Law* (Boston, 1823), 2:319.

[13] 14 Mass. 448.

of any such obligation toward free laborers. Thus in *Littleton v. Tuttle* (1796), the Overseers of the Poor of the town of Littleton sued Tuttle for money laid out in relief of his former slave Cato. Tuttle had bought Cato, then six years old, from Joseph Harwood in 1779 and had retained him in his service until 1794, when Cato had been injured in some unspecified manner. "He being then a cripple, and unable to labor, the defendant delivered him to the overseers of the poor of Littleton and left him with them, refusing to make any provision for him." The overseers claimed Tuttle was liable to make recompense, but the court found that Cato, "being born in this country, was born free" and thus had a lawful settlement in Littleton, relieving his master of the obligation to support him and obliging the overseers to treat him as they would any other free pauper with a settlement in the town. Slaves, the case underlined, were the responsibility of their masters. Free persons, in contrast, were to be supported, if left destitute, by the community.[14]

As in the case of slaves, the relief of sick or injured apprentices was considered to be the personal responsibility of their masters.[15] Thus in *Powers v. Ware* (1824)[16] the Supreme Judicial Court denied, *arguendo*, that a master might discharge his apprentice on the grounds that, by reason of incurable illness, the apprentice had become unable to perform the services required of him in his indenture. According

---

[14] *Littleton v. Tuttle* is reported at 4 Mass. 128. See also *Inhabitants of Winchendon v. Inhabitants of Hatfield*, 4 Mass. 122 (1808); *Inhabitants of Andover v. Inhabitants of Canton*, 13 Mass. 546 (1816); and *Inhabitants of Stockbridge v. Inhabitants of West Stockbridge*, 12 Mass. 399 (1815) and 15 Mass. 256 (1817) in review. In the last of these cases the Overseers of the Poor of Stockbridge sought recovery of expenses incurred in maintaining one Frank Duncan from the overseers of West Stockbridge on the grounds that Duncan had been the slave of Elijah Williams, resident of West Stockbridge, until Williams's death in 1815 and had thus gained a derivative settlement in West Stockbridge through his former master. The West Stockbridge overseers countered that Duncan had been Williams's servant, not his slave, and had thus gained no derivative settlement, but the court found otherwise. "While Frank continued in Williams's service he was to every intent his slave. He had a legal right to keep him in service for life; and in case of his sickness or inability to labor, his master must have supported him at his own expense" (261). As in *Inhabitants of Andover v. Inhabitants of Canton* it was acknowledged that if the master died or himself became a pauper, the slave became the responsibility of the local overseers; hence the finding here that the West Stockbridge overseers were liable. The larger point, however, is that relief of the indigent slave was the master's responsibility, whereas relief of indigent free persons was the responsibility of their town of settlement.

[15] According to Dane, "The master of an apprentice is bound to pay for medical attendance on the apprentice, from the very nature of the relation between master and apprentice, and the father of the apprentice is only bound, when the services have been rendered at his request." Dane emphasized the contrast with nonindentured labor: "As to hired servants, the employer is not bound to pay for medical attendance" (*Abridgment*, 9:35–6). See also James Kent, *Commentaries on American Law*, 2d ed. (New York, 1832), 2:261: "the master is not bound to provide even a menial servant with medical attendance and medicines during sickness," citing *Sellen v. Norman*, 4 Car. & P. 80 (1829).

Although it is not directly on the point, the following observation drawn from Dane's *Abridgment* sheds light on the basis of the distinction between a master's responsibilities to a slave or juvenile servant and his responsibilities toward a hired laborer. "If a slave or a servant, in the place of a child, be beaten or injured by a third person, and sickness, &c. follows, the master recovers for the whole loss, as he must pay the expense, and lose the servant's time; but not where his hired servant has been beaten, for then he bears the loss, and is not entitled to wages during the time he is disabled by the battery, and he finally pays the expense, and such expense will be part of the damages he will recover" (1:315).

[16] 19 Mass. 451.

to the court, the law in the commonwealth was as stated in the English case of *Rex v. Inhabitantes de Hales Owen*, that "the master took him for better or worse, and was to provide for him in sickness." If a master should neglect his duty to care for his apprentice, his neglect would normally provide sufficient grounds for a suit to be brought against him, either by the apprentice's parents or, in the case of poor children bound out to apprenticeships by the town, by the town's selectmen. The grounds for the action, however, were provided by the specific statutory provision that "it shall be the right and duty of parents and guardians, and of selectmen, for the time being . . . binding minors as aforesaid, to inquiry into their usage, and defend them from the crueltieo, neglects or breach of covenant of their masters or mistresses," rather than any general statutory or common law provision facilitating recourse by servant against neglectful masters.[17]

As in the case of slaves, then, a duty of maintenance was required of the masters of apprentices as one element in a highly regulated personal relationship. Both apprentices and slaves were explicitly specified as exceptions to the rule that in the event of sickness or accident the sufferer was left to depend upon his own resources or, more likely, on those of the community through the medium of poor relief.[18] In

---

[17] The provisions of the laws of settlement applying to the maintenance of indigent apprentices reinforce the conclusion that the legal responsibilities of the master to sick or injured apprentices were derived from a specific responsibility levied on masters to act in loco parentis, rather than from any general residual rights of servants. Unlike slaves, whose legal status denied them the right to a settlement of their own, apprentices did not acquire a derivative settlement through their masters but instead had their own settlement through their parents. This meant that where the maintenance of an apprentice was thrown into doubts by the pauperization of his master, the indenture was annulled and responsibility for care reverted to the apprentice's parents and thus ultimately to the community where they had their settlement. Prior to 1794 an apprentice deprived of maintenance by the death of his master could become the responsibility of the master's estate, to be maintained by the estate's executor until such time as the indenture was reassigned or the parties to the indenture agreed that it should be annulled. After 1794, however, the indenture was held to be annulled automatically by the master's death, and the apprentice was returned to his parents or to the Overseers of the Poor to be bound out afresh. See Eliphalet Ladd, *Burn's Abridgment, or the American Justice* (Dover, N.H., 1792), 34–6; *Massachusetts Statutes* 1793, c. 59, 1794, c. 64.

[18] In some states this exceptional status was affirmed only in limited circumstances. Outside those circumstances both slaves and apprentices were held no more privileged than hirelings in the matter of a master's responsibility for their care. Thus in *Dunbar v. Williams*, 10 Johnson 249 (1813), the Supreme Court of New York held that a master was not liable to pay for a physician's care bestowed upon his slave without his knowledge unless the injury was one that required instant and indispensable assistance. In *Percival and Johnson v. Nevill*, 10 SCL 452 (1819), the South Carolina Court of Appeals held similarly that a master was not responsible for treatment of his sick apprentice, absent a special contract, where the master did not request the physician's attendance and the services were not rendered under his roof. In both cases the courts cited the English sick-servant decisions approvingly, the South Carolina court denying that, except for what was expressly specified in the indenture of apprenticeship, an apprentice stood in any different relation to his master than a hireling. This is further confirmation that, at least in the case of apprentices, their exceptional status was a creature of policy.

In *Government and Labor in Early America* (Boston, 1981), at 18, Richard B. Morris notes that in the case of indentured servants, as with slaves and apprentices, it was colonial *policy* to hold masters responsible for their welfare. Employers had no liability for unbound labor, however, the burden falling by default upon the locality (the town in the case of Massachusetts) in which the accident or sickness occurred. When the injured party was a stranger, the town would then attempt to determine where the injured person's settlement was and seek reimbursement. This was often a hopeless task, as is evidenced

neither case was the relation of the parties one that could realistically be generalized to other employment relationships, because in neither case was the relation one grounded on the provision of services for wages.[19]

in the following petition of the Selectmen of the Town of Palmer (24 Jan. 1767), *Massachusetts Archives Collection*, vol. 303, p. 128, Massachusetts State Archives, Boston: "To His Excellency Francis Bernard Esq., Captain General and Governor in Chief over His Majesties Province of the Massachusetts Bay in New England &C, and to the Honorable His Majesties Counsell. The petition of William Scott, Seth Shaw and Robert Roggers, Selectmen and overseers of the poor of the District of Palmer Humbly sheweth, viz

"That whereas one John Ryan, a Transient person not being an inhabitant of our District, nor having any regular place of abode in America that we know of: as he was passing threw our District was Hired to work one Day to assist in pulling down a bridge and to erect another: the bridge fell with him and others on it; and a large quantity of Heavy Timber fell on him: by which he was exceedingly bruised: and also Broke his arm: shoulder: collar bone and Ribs: by which means it Required our Emediate assistance to take Care of Him in his Destressed Condition which your Petitioners have done: and by Extraordinary Care and Expence he is Considerably Recovered and Likely to have the use of his Limbs to a Considerable degree; but is No way able to pay the Cost or ever likely to be able. Nor is there any other Town in America as we know of by Law liable to Reimburse the Cost of his Cure to us: and have no other Remedy but by applying to your Excelency and Honor that the same may be made a province charge."

[19] There was, however, one relation which did have this character and which, nevertheless, did not conform to the rule of self-reliance. Seamen who were injured in the service of their ship or who fell sick during its voyage were held entitled in maritime law to be cured at the ship's expense and to suffer no diminution of wages while incapacitated. See, e.g., *Natterstrom v. The Hazard*, 17 Fed. Cas. 1243–50 (1809), at 1246: "The law marine in relation to mariners converts into an obligation what, in other instances of hire, is the result of benevolence" (citing Pothier, *Louage des matelots*). It did so, according to the court, "for the encouragement of seamen, and as a compensation for the risk which they run of an entire loss of wages, from inevitable accidents occurring to the ship, or from a destruction of the voyage." See also *Harden v. Gordon*, 11 Fed. Cas. 480 (CC, Me.) (1823). In *Reed v. Canfield*, 20 Fed. Cas. 426 (CC, Mass.) (1832), Joseph Story expressly distinguished as a matter of law compensable mariners' injuries from non-compensable injuries incurred by landed workers. "It has been suggested, that a seaman . . . cannot be entitled to any claim against the owners of the ship for injuries received in the ship's service, any more than a mechanic or manufacturer . . . for like injuries in the service of his employer. If the maritime law were the same in all respects with the common law, and if the rights and duties of seamen were measured in the same manner, as those of mechanics and manufacturers at home, doubtless the cases would furnish a strong analogy. But the truth is, that the maritime law furnishes entirely different doctrines upon this, as well as many other subjects, from the common law" (428).

There were, however, relatively stringent limits to the duty to compensate in maritime law. First, the party obliged to meet the expense of maintaining sick or disabled crew members was not the master or owner of the ship but the ship itself (see Dane, *Abridgment*, 9:202). To the extent that the ship and its cargo represented the total available assets from which wages could be paid (see *The Saratoga. – Keating, claimant*, CC Mass., Oct. 1814, reported in *American Law Journal*, 6 [1815], 12–20), the expense of maintaining sick crew members was an operating expense shared by all rather than one borne exclusively by the owner. The analogy to the parish or town's obligation to maintain sick or injured servants is imperfect, but it would be incorrect to claim that in the case of seamen the obligation to maintain was exclusively a charge on their masters. Second, the obligation extended only to sickness or disabilities that were "not produced by [the seaman's] own criminality or fault." (In Nathan Dane's version of this exclusion, the ship was not responsible for injuries caused by the "vicious or unjustifiable conduct" of a seaman [*Abridgment*, 2:480].) In such circumstances the seaman "is not entitled to his wages during the time he does no duty; and subsistence, during the same time, may be charged to him." Finally, in the event of the death of a seaman in the service of the ship, no obligation was incurred to pay any form of compensation beyond what was owed to him in wages at the time of his death. See also below n. 94. Among all categories of hired labor, therefore, seamen alone appear as an exception to the common law rule of self-reliance alleviated by an entitlement to relief by the community when rendered incapable; and even seamen were at best a qualified exception, one grounded in considerations of "policy."

That employers might not be legally obliged to relieve their sick or injured employees is not, however, necessarily conclusive of what their practice actually was. Benevolence, the French jurist Pothier advised employers, was an important virtue, "becoming indeed to persons well-off and following distinguished professions."[20] As Loring told the referees in *Barnes*, it was not to be understood "that the defendants feel such indignation or resentment at the bringing of this suit that their sympathies are chilled or their generosity extinguished. Should your award be against the plaintiff (as they believe it must be) the door of friendly application for relief will still be open."[21]

Evidence of practice in Massachusetts as regards the relief of injured employees in almost nonexistent prior to the 1830s. What little there is suggests a wide variety of attitudes. In 1803, for example, William Niles, "blacksmith, of Charlestown," sued William Ratchford, "blacksmith, of Boston," for payment of wages owed for "certain work and labor" Niles had performed between April 1798 and May 1802 while employed by Ratchford in his shop in Boston.[22] Throughout that period he had also lived in Ratchford's house. Ratchford contested the amount claimed and produced witnesses to testify that Niles had been lame and unable to work for a significant period of his term of employment. He sought to have the cost to him of boarding Niles while he was unable to work and the costs of medical treatment for which he had paid set off against his debt to Niles. He also sought the reduction of wages owed Niles by an amount equivalent to the period Niles was off work. The jury agreed, placing the entire cost of his lameness on Niles.[23]

Others fared even less well. Ratchford had at least maintained Niles during his illness, even if Niles eventually had to pay for it. That this was by no means the

---

[20] Robert Joseph Pothier, *Treatise on the Contract of Letting and Hiring (Contract de Louage)*, trans. G. A. Mulligan (Durban, 1953), 66.

[21] Morton Horwitz has suggested that prior to the era of employer liability litigation, most sick or injured workers were probably helped by their employers from motives of benevolence or charity (*The Transformation of American Law, 1780–1860* [Cambridge, 1977], 208). Against this, one finds among the goals of those calling for the formation of a General Trades' Union of Boston and Vicinity the creation of a "general fund . . . to be devoted to the relief and assistance of those out of employ by accidents, or by any other cause" (see "Circular to the Mechanics of the City of Boston and Vicinity," *The Man* [20 Feb. 1834], in John R. Commons et al., eds., *A Documentary History of American Industrial Society* [Cleveland, 1910], 6:87–90, at 89). The proposal to create a worker-subscribed relief fund suggests both an awareness of accidents as a problem and the absence or insufficiency of alternative forms of relief. On the lack of any generalized practice of benevolent relief of accident victims among contemporary English employers, see P. W. J. Bartrip and S. B. Burman, *The Wounded Soldiers of Industry: Industrial Compensation Policy, 1833–1897* (Oxford, 1983), 28–31.

[22] Suffolk County Court of Common Pleas, July term 1803; Supreme Judicial Court, Nov. term 1806 (on appeal) (Continuing Action 280); Nov. term 1807 (on review) (New Entry 307). See also *Ratchford v. Niles*, Supreme Judicial Court, Nov. term 1807 (Continuing Action 58).

[23] Gary Nash has argued that, in the case of eighteenth-century Philadelphia, workers hired on a casual basis would not be supported in the event of sickness but that those lodging with masters for extended periods would be paid despite missing time as a result of sickness or injury (*The Urban Crucible: Social Change, Political Consciousness, and the Origins of the American Revolution* [Cambridge, Mass., 1979], 258–9).

rule is suggested by an article in the *Boston Medical and Surgical Journal* in July 1829 complaining of the "extremely cruel and dishonorable" manner in which sick or injured domestic servants were often treated by their employers. Physicians, stated the author, were "not infrequently" embarrassed by masters who forced their servants to pay their own physician's bills. "The payment of wages should cease during medical attendance, but all further loss belongs to the family whose misfortune it is to have any of their domestics taken sick." The article went on to condemn those who would send a sick servant away to "poor, confined and dirty lodgings" or would "have him confined to a hospital." Masters should be more willing to suffer the expense and inconvenience involved for the sake of a closer relationship with their domestics. "A little feeling shown by a master or mistress to a sick servant would generally be well bestowed, and might be equally well repaid by his future faithful services."[24] Few, it seemed, took any notice. Analysis of the returns of free (charitable) patients prepared during the late 1830s by the superintendent of the Massachusetts General Hospital shows that between one-quarter and one-third were female domestic servants.[25]

An ideology of benevolence may have played a rather more prominent role in the practices of Massachusetts corporate employers.[26] This should not surprise us unduly for historians have generally agreed that a paternalistic sense of social responsibility or "stewardship" was a key component of early corporate ideology. Thus, some years ago Caroline Ware argued that Francis Lowell established the Boston Manufacturing Company not only to facilitate the concentration of capital and the organization of textile production but also "to provide a scheme for protecting his working population." Anthony Wallace similarly finds the millowners and "managerial people" of Rockdale imbued with a strong sense of responsibility for the welfare of their employees.[27]

By the end of the 1830s, however, corporate social responsibility was well on its way to becoming another casualty of the political economy of speed as the decade's growing emphasis upon profit and productivity began to strip the business coporation

[24] "Sickness of Domestics," *Boston Medical and Surgical Journal*, 2, 23 (21 July 1829), 353–4.

[25] Massachusetts General Hospital, *Annual Report to the Board of Trustees* (Boston, 1836–9) (inclusive).

[26] Some evidence of corporate benevolence earlier than this can be found in Loammi Baldwin's Middlesex Canal Corporation records, which show that two of the workers reported injured during construction of the canal had payments voted to them by the corporation's board of directors. In the case of Simeon Farmer, the board voted that Baldwin pay for his board "one month or more in consideration of his suffering occasioned in the work of the canal." Later correspondence reveals that Farmer was off work for fourteen weeks and confronted by bills for medical attendance and board totaling over fifty dollars. Again in September 1800 the Committee on Operations voted thirty-five dollars toward the expenses of Richard Briggs, "who had his leg broke blowing stones." That this was by no means the rule, however, is indicated by the case of Martin Nolan, the laborer injured during construction of the Suffolk County Court House. Despite strong support from the architect in charge, Nolan went uncompensated. See Chapter 9, nn. 53–4.

[27] Caroline Ware, *The Early New England Cotton Manufacture: A Study in Industrial Beginnings* (Boston, 1931), 61; Anthony F. C. Wallace, *Rockdale: The Growth of an American Village in the Early Industrial Revolution* (New York, 1978), 296–397. See also Frederic Cople Jaher, *The Urban Establishment: Upper Strata in Boston, New York, Charleston, Chicago, and Los Angeles* (Urbana, 1982), 57–64.

of all but an economic identity.[28] For all their protestations of responsibility in their actions toward their employees, the priority that Massachusetts industrialists increasingly accorded economic factors in determining their policies left them possessed of but a cramped notion of what stewardship meant.[29] In proclaiming that "the door of friendly application" was open to the increasing flood of accident victims generated during the late 1830s and 1840s, for example, those owners and managers restated the responsibilities of "stewardship" in the banal terms of the cash nexus, simultaneously teaching their employees that they counted only as the embodiment of their labor. In such circumstances it is hardly surprising that employees so taught should eventually seek counsels' aid to realize a truer approximation of their lost property's worth than corporate handouts, which, by the end of the 1840s, had in any case dwindled to the merest pittance.[30]

THE RIGHT TO MANAGE

In this context, each party to *Barnes v. Boston & Worcester Railroad* was addressing the question whether common law institutions should now be made available to facilitate the imposition of social duties on employers in the name of the common good. Moore and Choate stressed the devastation visited on the plaintiff by his injury and insisted that a corporation's legal liabilities should be made coextensive with its legal advantages and properly reflect the moral responsibilities which its privileges had brought. Loring, in contrast, attempted to strip the case of ethical content and pare it down to bare contractual essentials – a purely private tussle.

In their canvassing, in microcosm, of the nature of the relationship which should pertain between law and economy, the two sides employed different legal strategies. For the plaintiff, Choate stressed that liability derived from an extensive legal duty of care owed by the corporation to all who rode its cars, employees and passengers

---

[28] See Chapter 9; Andrew Fraser, "The Corporation as a Body Politic," *Telos*, 57 (Fall 1983), 5–40, esp. 25–40. See also Sean Wilentz, "The Rise of the American Working Class, 1776–1877: A Survey," in J. Carroll Moody and Alice Kessler-Harris, eds., *Perspectives on American Labor History: The Problem of Synthesis* (DeKalb, Ill., 1989), 92–3.

[29] Philip Scranton, *Proprietary Capitalism: The Textile Manufacture at Philadelphia, 1800–1885* (New York and Cambridge, 1983), 30–1.

[30] Reports of employee injuries and deaths in the minutes of the board of directors of the Boston & Worcester Railroad reveal that a tendency in the late 1830s to offer employees or their families fairly substantial cash payments in the event of injury or death while in the railroad's service had virtually disappeared by the mid-1840s. See, e.g., Boston & Worcester Railroad, Directors' Minutes, vol. 3 (meeting of 9 Oct. 1838), detailing payment of $500 to the widow of Hiram Bridges, engineer, killed in a collision, and cf. Directors' Minutes, vol. 5 (meeting of 11 Feb. 1845), instructing the superintendent to provide relief to John Smith, machinist, severely injured in a machine shop accident "not exceeding thirty dollars"; and Directors' Minutes, vol. 6 (meeting of 20 Apr. 1847), instructing that a subcommittee created to inquire into the circumstances of an accident to John Mitchell, brakeman, in which Mitchell lost his leg, be empowered to pay Mitchell's hospital expenses and also the cost of a wooden leg "if they judge [the latter] expedient." All in Boston & Albany Railroad Collection, Baker Library, Harvard Business School.

alike. As the owner and operator of the gravel cars the corporation was to be held to the responsibilities of a common carrier of passengers. It was therefore bound to exercise such a level of diligence in the management of its business as would ensure protection to all those riding legitimately, save only from extraordinary accidents. The law would infer from the circumstance of breaking down without apparent cause a prima facie proof of negligence for which the defendant was liable. The burden was on the defendant to show that there was no negligence. But this it could not do, for defective – cracked – wheels were in use on the cars and it was their use which had occasioned the accident. The defendant had admitted by its own actions in ordering cracked wheels to be removed from the passenger train that it did not consider them safe – "except," Choate noted sarcastically, "for Irish labourers" – and it had failed to show any sort of usage of cracked wheels on other roads which might justify it in seeking to place the risk of riding on the gravel train on the shoulders of the plaintiff. Once the corporation had agreed to employ Barnes and to furnish him with transportation to and from his work it had brought him within the sphere of those to whom it was obliged to offer indemnity in the event of loss resulting from its neglect of that duty.[31]

For his part Loring retorted that no basis existed in law for the imputation of any duty of care which could encompass Barnes, and further that the presence of cracked wheels on the gravel train's cars was not prima facie proof of anything, given that such wheels were put to like use on other roads. The question whether anything was owed in this particular case, he continued, could only be resolved through an examination of the precise terms of the plaintiff's contract. This showed that the defendant had not explicitly promised transportation but had merely undertaken to supply conveyance for men and materials at its discretion.

The distinction was important, for Loring sought to imply into Barnes's contract a "general rule" promulgated by the corporation that no one in its employ was allowed to use the gravel train other than the gang of laborers specifically assigned to it. It was, said Loring, the defendant's custom to allow its employees the privilege of riding free, but they were directed to use the first car of the passenger train, which, as a result, had become widely known as "the labourers' car" or "the Irish car." Barnes was to be presumed to have been aware of this rule, having worked for the defendant on previous occasions. Thus, if Barnes had chosen to ride

---

[31] Choate's argument is reconstructed here from the sketchy notes scribbled by Loring during the hearing. See *Barnes v. Boston & Worcester Railroad*, in Loring Papers. The argument appears to have had two components. One was an attempt to bring Barnes within the ambit of *respondeat superior* by alleging negligence on the part of those acting for the corporation in the management of the road, for which the use of the cracked wheels was evidence. The other stressed the corporation's breach of a duty of care it owed its employee by failing to provide a mode of transportation free of defect. Given the state of Loring's notes, it is not possible to reconstruct the precise relationship between these two lines of argument or to indicate with any assurance whether one was more important than the other. On contemporary arguments in regard to the ambit of *respondeat superior*, see below, n. 94. On attitudes toward Irish laborers, see David R. Roediger, *The Wages of Whiteness: Race and the Making of the American Working Class* (London, 1991), 133–4.

on the gravel train in breach of the defendant's rule, he had done so at his own risk.[32]

Loring presented the corporation's rule as an objective fact of life, a managerial pronouncement determinative of the reality of railroad work. As he put it in his closing argument, the testimony of the defendant's witnesses had clearly shown "that no men at work on the road except the gang attached to the gravel train were ever directed or authorized to ride upon it" and that on the contrary "such act was contrary to the [corporation's] express rules and orders, well known and understood." Yet testimony given by witnesses for Barnes during the hearing had shown that Loring's "rule" was less than prescriptive in practice. Other employees testified that they too had ridden on the gravel train, usually when accompanying materials being dispatched to points along the right-of-way for use in track maintenance operations. Loring attempted to diminish the significance of their evidence: "No one witness proves it to be customary for any to ride but the gang. A few instances only can be found in which others have been permitted to go [on the gravel train]," and these "*were in no case instructed* to go there and knew that this was not the regular place, but that another was provided." His protestations were rather beside the point, however, given that the plaintiff did not seek to prove that he had contracted specifically to use the gravel train but rather hoped to convince the referees that the corporation had a duty to compensate him for its negligence because he had been on the gravel cars with its consent or, as Choate put it, "under such circumstances that a man of sense would suppose himself to have such consent."[33]

Loring's argument that the corporation's rule was decisive of its obligations toward its employee foreshadowed what would in later years become familiar employer defenses against accusations of liability for industrial injuries: the defense of contributory negligence on the part of the injured employee and the defense that the employee had assumed the risk of injury. It was, quite obviously, an argument severely restrictive in its implications insofar as legal imputation of social responsibilities to employers was concerned. Loring sounded the same theme – that the management of the railroad was a matter to be left to the corporation and its rules – in the final segment of his presentation where he turned from his narrow focus on the contract between Barnes and the corporation to an examination of the plaintiff's claim that the defendant owed him a duty of care equivalent to that it owed to its passengers.

Loring's particular target was the plaintiff's contention that the defendants "by their agents and servants *negligently* and carelessly used in and upon the cars, in and

---

[32] "Suppose the *contract general* to carry plaintiff and his materials – which is the only reasonable supposition – it is manifest that plaintiff must in such case adopt the usual mode, or some [other] one pointed out by defendants" (emphasis in original). If, knowing the rule, he chose to exercise the privilege of free transportation extended to him by the corporation by taking another mode of conveyance, either to avoid loss of time or for preference, it was at his own risk.

[33] Emphasis in original.

upon which plaintiff was riding *two broken cracked* and *insufficient* wheels."[34] That the defendants had indeed equipped the train with wheels they knew to be cracked – "say 3 or 4" – was conceded. Loring insisted, however, that the mere use of such wheels proved nothing. Rather, two separate issues were involved: first, "whether the use of cracked wheels is ipso facto negligence and carelessness"; and, second, if not, "whether there was any neglect or carelessness in this [particular] instance," for example, by using wheels that were particularly badly cracked or by failing to exercise sufficient precaution or examination.

Here arose the legal question of whether *any* degree of care and prudence was actually required of the defendants in their use of the train sufficient to sustain the plaintiff's contention that they owed him a duty of care. Loring's answer was – virtually none. "The defendants in *the use of this train* are not *common carriers*. This is not a train used for the transportation of goods for hire – but [is] for the sole use of defendants [in] carrying occasionally materials to be used on their road." As such it was "perfectly manifest . . . that the general principles of law making common carriers liable for all losses except by acts of God do not apply." Nor were the defendants liable as carriers of passengers "as [for example] stage coaches, hackney coaches & c," for the plain truth of the matter was that this particular train "is not suited nor intended for the conveyance of passengers *for hire*." Indeed, the train was "*not a public* train which every one has a right to use on tendering payment for fare or freight" at all. Rather, it was "the private vehicle of the defendants to be used for their own purposes."[35] Loring's conclusion? "The public has therefore no right or interest in the gravel train; no right to use it on any terms [and] no interest in having it kept safe or strong, any more than it has in having the *private* waggon or carriage of any individual kept safe or strong."[36] Barnes's case, that is, fell outside that narrow circumstance in which the law would recognize an overriding public interest in regulating the management of a concern and impose a penalty in cases of default in the shape of a presumption of liability. Consequently "no greater degree of care or prudence or skill can be required of defendants than is required of persons of common prudence in the management of their own concerns."[37]

[34] Emphasis in original.

[35] Emphasis in original. As already stated, we may conceptualize early nineteenth-century tort law as defining islands of liability in a sea of no-liability. See above, Introduction to Part 4. Here we find Loring attempting to exclude Barnes's case from those categories of circumstances in which a tort liability has been recognized. A responsibility to the public has been allowed in certain circumstances – hence the existence of what the defense in *Farwell v. Boston & Worcester* would call the "severe" rule of *respondeat superior*. See below, nn. 62–3. But the ambit of liability is restricted and certainly does not extend to incidents where the public is not involved.

[36] Emphasis supplied.

[37] To illustrate his point, Loring offered the following analogy: "Suppose a private individual not acting as owner of a line of coaches or baggage waggons undertakes to remove a family and its furniture from one place to another. He is held to no greater care, prudence and skill in his vehicle horses and driver than men ordinarily receive. And if this carriage break or be overturned and loss of property or life ensue – he is not accountable unless owing to want of ordinary care and diligence. Whereas if he were acting as Common Carrier or stage coach proprietor he would be liable in one case *at all events*, and in the other for any want of utmost care and prudence." Moreover, "this case would be the same, if a

Having thus defined the parameters of the defendant's obligations, the question became whether the defendant's actions had breached those parameters or not. "The first question then is, is the use of cracked wheels on gravel trains consistent with *ordinary care and prudence?*"[38] Whether the defendant had breached this standard, Loring argued, could only be determined by reference, first to the conduct of other railroad corporations and second to the actual experience of this corporation. As to the latter, Loring claimed that no previous accident on the Boston & Worcester Railroad had been attributed to cracked wheels and that the corporation had always been careful to inspect their condition. As to the former, "the evidence proves that all other corporations did use these wheels on some or all of their trains. If these gravel trains were generally used with cracked wheels, how can the defendants be said to have been deficient in ordinary care and prudence?" It was "monstrous to say that a system used from one end of the continent to the other [and] on every road – is not consistent with ordinary care and discretion."

In short, Barnes's contract promised him nothing more than transporation and furthermore contained an implied term barring him from using the train upon which he had been riding at the time of the accident. In choosing to ride on the gravel train despite that implied term, Barnes had violated his contract, freeing the corporation from liability. As to any general duty of care owed by the corporation, the train itself was a private train and not subject to the public interest in maintaining safe modes of transportation. Hence the corporation owed Barnes only ordinary care and prudence in the running of the train. The only possible standard for the ordinary care and prudence required of the railroad in this instance was that of the actual practices followed by the generality of railroad corporations in the management of their affairs. As in the matter of the rule supposedly implied in the plaintiff's contract, the managerial position was actually conclusive of the issue. Outside the exceptional situations of common carriers and carriers of passengers, circumstances already demonstrated to be inapplicable to this case, public prescription of a formal standard of care was not appropriate because there was no "public interest."

Loring's forensic efforts notwithstanding, Barnes prevailed and was awarded $3,000 in damages. The costs of the hearing – $436 (including $300 in referees' fees) – were also paid by the railroad. No record of the referees' reasons for their finding of liability was kept, so it is impossible to ascertain the precise basis of the decision. Loring himself, however, noted cryptically during Choate's closing argument that the referees seemed to be attaching particular importance to that part of the plaintiff's case which alleged that the corporation's use of cracked wheels was a demonstration of negligence sufficient to render it liable. Certainly Loring himself devoted the preponderance of his argument to persuading the referees that liability was a creature of the parties' contract and that the question of negligence should not therefore be admitted. And when Loring finally did address the negligence argument directly,

person were thus carrying materials and men to do work upon his home or farm." In either case "reasonable diligence is all that could be required." (Emphasis in original.)

[38] Emphasis in original.

345

it was in order to demonstrate that it could not apply in the circumstances of this case.

Barnes v. Boston & Worcester Railroad reveals the potential within the realm of common law discourse in the late 1830s and early 1840s for the development of an approach to industrial injuries predicated upon the existence of a public interest in the conditions prevailing in industrial workplaces. As we have seen, by the early 1840s the existence of such an interest was being canvassed quite actively in the legislative arena by working people, notably in the form of the ten-hours movement. As my examination of the course of argument in Barnes has indicated, recognition of such an interest would have had important implications for the counterclaims of the owners and managers of industrial enterprises that their establishments and work practices were their own private affair, not subject to public oversight.[39] *Barnes* is almost the only available example of precisely how those claims might have been affected at common law, but it is not entirely isolated. In *Randolph v. Hill*, heard in 1836, for example, the Virginia Court of Appeals upheld a jury verdict awarding damages to Hill for the death of his slave by asphyxiation in a mining accident.[40] The verdict was based inter alia on the jury's inference from facts presented to it that the defendant's overseer had not exhibited the necessary degree of care and that the defendant's establishment was dangerously deficient in providing only one bucket to draw up laborers from a seventy-foot-deep shaft. On appeal, the defense argued, as in *Barnes*, that such matters were irrelevant unless measured against a standard of practice, that the appropriate standard was that prevailing in mines in the district, that the jury had clearly ignored evidence tending to show that the defendant's overseer was no more neglectful of his duties than other overseers in his position, and that the mine was no more dangerous than other coal mines in that locality. By upholding the verdict, however, the Court of Appeals appeared to leave it open to plaintiffs to invite courts and juries (or referees) to apply their own standards in determining the substantive question of what constituted a safe working environment[41]

---

[39] In her outstanding biography of Rufus Choate, Jean V. Matthews has noted that although industrialists had never been averse to public *aid* to industry, most obviously in the shape of the tariff and eminent domain provisions, they were highly resistant to attempts by government to *regulate* it. "Their property might be social, both in the benefits it dispensed and the fostering it deserved, but its management they regarded as a purely private matter" (*Rufus Choate, The Law and Civic Virtue* [Philadelphia, 1980], 74).

[40] 34 Va. (7 Leigh) 383. One must, of course, be extremely cautious in relying upon cases involving slave workers in the area of employer liability. Here I wish only to use *Randolph v. Hill* to illustrate how, in the 1830s, courts were confronted with debates over public intervention in the management of a workplace. For excellent, though quite distinct, accounts of how and why the law of employer liability for the death or injury of hired slaves differed from that concerning wage workers, see Mark Tushnet, *The American Law of Slavery, 1810–1860: Considerations of Humanity and Interest* (Princeton, 1981), 46–54, 183–8; and Paul Finkelman, "Slaves as Fellow Servants: Ideology, Law, and Industrialization," *American Journal of Legal History*, 31, 4 (Oct. 1987), 269–305.

[41] The possibility that plaintiffs would be able to introduce jury deliberations into the determination of the cause of occupational death is of particular importance in the American context, given the rapid withering away after the Revolution of any recognition of a capacity in coroners' juries to levy fines or "deodands" on the objects (and thus on the owners of the objects) that had "moved to the death" of a victim. On deodands see Harry Smith, "From Deodand to Dependency," *American Journal of Legal History*,

rather than leave the standard to be set by the practices of a majority of the industrialists in a given area.[42]

Barnes v. Boston & Worcester Railroad was not, however, a case of record and as such was accorded no role in doctrinal debates over the extent of an employer's liability for industrial injuries. Indeed, the principal cases of record in which and from which employer liability doctrine was wrought during the following decade all rejected the claim for a widened sphere for tort liability, which had been at the heart of the plaintiff's case in *Barnes*. Either indirectly, by counterposing various doctrines of mitigating circumstance or employee culpability, or directly, by straightforwardly asserting that the extent and limits of an employer's liability were purely contractual issues, Massachusetts courts rendered employers substantially immune from injury claims. Their example was widely followed.

THE FELLOW-SERVANT RULE: PRECURSORS

Central to this new trajectory was the suit brought by Nicholas Farwell against the Boston & Worcester Railroad in 1839. As we already know, Farwell sued the railroad for $10,000 in damages to compensate him for the loss of his arm in a derailment caused by another employee's error. Farwell had been the engineer in charge of a passenger train that had run off the tracks at an improperly set switch. Farwell's attorney – Abraham Moore again – filed the suit almost as soon as his success in *Barnes* was confirmed,[43] but at the October 1839 term of the Suffolk County Court of Common Pleas he got a taste of what was to come when the court

---

2 (1967), 389–403. On the role of coroners' juries in the determination of cause of occupational death in England see Elizabeth Cawthon, "Thomas Wakley and the Medical Coronership – Occupational Death and the Judicial Process," *Medical History*, 30 (1986), 191–202. According to the *Corpus Juris Secundum* "the doctrine (of deodand) was so repugnant to the American concept of justice that it was not included as a part of the common law of this country" (C. J. S. 26A, 185). See also *Parker-Harris Company v. Tate*, 135 Tenn. 510 (1916).

[42] See, however, *Williams and Hitchcock v. Taylor*, 4 Porter 234 (Ala. 1836). This case is discussed at n. 51.

[43] Suffolk County Court of Common Pleas, Oct. term 1839 (New Entry 150). The plaintiff's Common Pleas declaration, in a plea on the case, read that "in consideration that the Defendants would pay him, the said Plaintiff the sum of two dollars per day, he said Plaintiff agreed with said Defendants undertook and promised to serve them faithfully and diligently in the capacity and employment of an Engineer" and did so "till the thirtieth day of October eighteen hundred and thirty seven, when at a place called Newton . . . the said Defendants by their servant so carelessly, negligently and unskilfully managed fixed placed and put the iron match rail called the short switch across the rail or track of the Defendants said Rail Road that the Engine and Cars upon which the Plaintiff was engaged and employed in the discharge of his said duties of Engineer were thrown from track of said Rail Road, and the Plaintiff by means thereof was thrown with great violence in and upon the ground by means of which one of the wheels of one of said Cars passed over the right hand of the Plaintiff crushing and wholly destroying the same in so much that his right hand has been amputated and the Plaintiff by means aforesaid greatly bruised maimed and wounded, and has been for ever incapacitated for earning his living in his said business as Engineer or by manual labour of any kind, and has been put to great expense for Doctors, Surgeons and Nurses Bills to wit the sum of five hundred dollars, and hath suffered great pain of body and anxiety of mind."

decided in favor of the railroad. The plaintiff appealed the Common Pleas judgment to the supreme Judicial Court, sitting *nisi prius*. At that hearing, however, the jury could not agree whether the defendant was liable.[44]

At this point the parties agreed to refer the case to a full bench of the court for it to determine whether, in the wake of the recent decisions in the English case *Priestley v. Fowler*[45] and the American case *Murray v. South Carolina Rail Road Company*,[46] the defendants could as a matter of law be held liable to one employee for an injury alleged to have resulted from the negligence of another. Ironically enough, the attorney retained by Abraham Moore for Farwell's Supreme Judicial Court appearance was none other than the same Charles Greely Loring who had represented the railroad in Barnes's case.[47] Loring's performance is worth examining closely because at least one analysis of the outcome in *Farwell* has attributed the result in large part to Loring's poor performance on the plaintiff's behalf. "Rarely in the history of American law," according to Morton Horwitz, "has so significant a case of 'new impression' . . . been so thoroughly determined by the intellectual impoverishment of counsel."[48]

Priestley v. Fowler and *Murray v. South Carolina Rail Road Company* were both suits brought by injured employees against their employers. Priestley was a butcher's boy whose leg was broken when an overloaded cart driven by another of the butcher's employees overturned while he was riding on it; Murray was a fireman injured in a derailment. As in *Barnes* the actions were both "on the case," the plaintiffs seeking to found their claims on an assertion of a duty of care owed them by the employer and extending to protect them from the negligence of other employees, rather than in contract. Also as in *Barnes* the defendants' response was in each case, first, that no such action was available because no duty was owed beyond those provided for, expressly or implicitly, in the parties' contracts; and, second, that even had the plaintiff sued in contract he would have failed because close examination disclosed no evidence that the parties' contract in fact extended to a promise on the part of the employer to indemnify his employee against the consequences of injury while in his service.

The referees, as we have seen, had found for Barnes. In each of these cases of record, however, the court found for the defendants. The English court, for example,

[44] *Farwell v. Boston & Worcester Railroad*, Supreme Judicial Court (Suffolk County) Nov. term 1840 (Continuing Action 215).
[45] 3 M. & W. 1 (1837). This case was originally heard at the Lincolnshire Assizes in July 1836, where it was decided in favor of the plaintiff.
[46] 1 McMullen 385 (1841). This case was originally heard before a jury at Charleston in 1838, where it was decided in favor of the plaintiff.
[47] Commentary on the arguments of counsel in *Farwell v. Boston & Worcester Railroad* is based on a reconstruction derived from a combination of three sources: Charles Greely Loring's case notes, in Loring Papers; the entries concerning *Farwell* in the minute book of the Chief Justice of the Supreme Judicial Court, Lemuel Shaw (vol. 29, 244–49), Social Law Library, Boston; and the entries concerning the case in the minute book of Justice William Hubbard (vol. 1, 184–95), Social Law Library, Boston. Unless otherwise indicated, Loring's case notes are the prime source.
[48] Horwitz. *Transformation of American Law*, 210.

rejected out of hand the possibility that a general obligation to indemnify servants against unanticipated injury occurring in the course of employment could be inferred to exist.[49] If such a liability were found, Lord Abinger stated, "the principle of that liability will carry us to an alarming extent." The narrowly drawn and carefully demarcated boundaries of tort liability would collapse in a welter of suits. "If the owner of the carriage is therefore responsible for the sufficiency of his carriage to his servant, he is responsible for the negligence of his coach-maker, or his harness-maker, or his coachman. The footman, therefore, who rides behind the carriage, may have an action against his master for a defect in the carriage owing to the negligence of the coach-maker, or for a defect in the harness arising from the negligence of the harness-maker, or for drunkenness, neglect, or want of skill in the coachman." Matters would not end there. "The master, for example, would be liable to the servant for the negligence of the chambermaid, for putting him into a damp bed; for that of the upholsterer, for sending in a crazy bedstead whereby he was made to fall down while asleep and injure himself; for the negligence of the cook, in not properly cleaning the copper vessels used in the kitchen; of the butcher, in supplying the family with meat of a quality injurious to the health; of the builder, for a defect in the foundation of the house, whereby it fell, and injured both the master and the servant by the ruins." Merely to contemplate "the inconvenience, not to say the absurdity of these consequences," was sufficient answer to the plaintiff's plea on the case. As to a plea in contract, although none had been made, a master was "no doubt" obliged to take steps to secure the servant's safety while in his employment to the best of his "judgment, information, and belief"; but "the mere relation of the master and the servant never can imply an obligation on the part of the master to take more care of the servant than he may reasonably be expected to do of himself."[50]

Similar fears were expressed by the South Carolina Court of Appeals in *Murray*. The lower court had instructed the jury "that the plaintiff's service subjected him to all the ordinary risks and perils of the employment," but that if the jury were satisfied that the plaintiff fireman had been endangered by careless conduct on the part of a superior officer of the company (the engineer) and that the plaintiff had had no means of avoiding the danger, then the company would be liable if injury resulted. A majority of the higher court disagreed. If the plaintiff were entitled to recover in this suit, said Evans J. on behalf of the majority, "a new class of liabilities would arise, which I do not think has ever heretofore been supposed to exist," rendering employers vulnerable to an avalanche of suits. Evans canvassed the circumstances in which a court would have found the railroad rendered liable by the act of an agent; the law, he acknowledged, would annex a responsibility in the case

---

[49] Defendant's counsel in the original hearing in *Priestley* propounded the same standard that Loring had put forward, unsuccessfully, in *Barnes*. "A master is only to use such ordinary care and diligence as he would use over himself; so long as their waggons, ladders, &c., are in such repair as any prudent man's would be, they are not liable for any of the accidents that may befall their servants, or others by them." See Bartrip and Burman, *Wounded Soldiers of Industry*, 24–5; and n. 37, above.

[50] 3 M. & W. 5–6.

of an injury to a passenger or other stranger or for the loss or damage of goods. But this was for a specific reason: "unless [the principal] be liable, the great operations of life can not be carried on – no man would have adequate security for his person or his property."[51]

Because the plaintiff's case did not fit within these established boundaries of tort liability he was unable to recover unless he could show that the railroad had assumed the responsibility by contract. This he could not do. "With the plaintiff, the

[51] 1 McMullan 398–9. Here also, as in the submissions of defense counsel in *Barnes* and *Priestley*, a limited standard of "ordinary care" on the part of the employer was acknowledged. See 389–90. Just how limited a standard this was is suggested in a little-noticed American case, *Williams and Hitchcock v. Taylor*, decided in Alabama in 1836. In this case the court had been asked to rule on the liability of the plaintiffs-on-appeal to make good the value of a slave killed while under hire to them to work on their steamboat. The slave had fallen into the unfenced engine pit of the boat and had been killed by the flywheel. The lower court instructed the jury that if they believed that running the boat with an unfenced engine demonstrated negligence, then they should allow recovery. Reversing the trial court, the state Supreme Court held that the owner of the slave could not recover. Its opinion is worth quoting at length, for although the decision itself was confined to slave workers, the court's opinion ranged more widely (4 Porter 234, at 238–9, emphasis supplied): "From the instructions which the Court [below] gave to the jury, we understand it was the opinion of the Court, that any degree of negligence makes owners of boats liable for the injuries suffered by their agents and servants, while they are engaged in the business they had undertaken to do on a boat.

"It was anciently held, that a carrier of goods, for hire, was responsible only for ordinary neglect. This rule, so far as it related to the conveyance of mere goods, was changed long since; but the strict rule upon the subject, which is now recognized, does not apply to the conveyance of slaves as passengers, by a carrier for hire, as the Supreme Court of the United States decided, in the case of *Boyce* against *Anderson* [27 U.S. 150 (1829), see below]. For such passengers, a carrier is liable only for ordinary neglect. In that case, it was determined also, that if slaves paid no hire for their passage, the carrier would be responsible only in a case of gross neglect. A less degree of negligence makes a carrier liable to a passenger, who has, or is bound to pay his hire, than is required to make him responsible to one, from whom he is to receive no reward. *It must require as great a degree of negligence to make an owner of a boat liable to an agent, or a servant, engaged in business in his boat, as it would to give a right of action against him, to a passenger, who was bound to pay no reward for his passage.* Neither such a passenger, nor a servant, who is hired to do business on a boat, pays any reward for his passage. By the engagement of such a servant, were he a free man, he would incur an obligation to go on the boat, and acquire a right to be there, and for his services while there, would be entitled to compensation; but for his passage he would pay nothing.

"In this view of the case, if the servant be a slave, his owner would be entitled to the compensation for his services, and the owner of the boat would be liable to the master only, for the degree of negligence, which would make him responsible to the servant, if he had been a free man, and had suffered an injury, which did not cause his death. *In such a case, a carrier is liable only for gross negligence, which is defined to be the want of slight diligence, or a failure in the lowest degree of prudence, or an omission to exercise the diligence, which men habitually careless, or of little prudence, generally take in their own concerns.*"

In the 1829 case *Boyce v. Anderson* cited in the court's opinion in *Williams and Hitchcock*, the U.S. Supreme Court had been asked to address the liability of a carrier for the value of four slaves stranded as the result of a steamboat accident and drowned while being rescued. (The defendant was the rescuer, accused of negligence in mismanaging the rescue.) For the court, Chief Justice Marshall had recognized (at 154–5) that the "doctrine is, that the carrier is responsible for every loss which is not produced by inevitable accident" but had held that a distinction should properly be drawn "between a human being in whose person another has an interest, and inanimate property." Slaves had volition and could not be subject to the same control as packages of goods. Marshall had then continued: "There are no slaves in England, but there are persons in whose service another has a temporary interest. We believe that the responsibility of a carrier, for injury which such person may sustain, has never been placed on the same principle with his responsibility for a bale of goods. He is undoubtedly answerable for any injury sustained in consequence of his negligence or want of skill; but we have never understood that he is responsible farther."

defendants contracted to pay hire for his services. Is it incident to this contract that the company should guarantee him against the negligence of his co-servants? It is admitted he takes upon himself the ordinary risks of his vocation; why not the extraordinary ones? Neither are within his contract – and I can see no reason for adding this to the already known and acknowledged liability of a carrier, without a single case or precedent to sustain it."[52]

Although the authority of these cases to determine the outcome of Farwell's suit remained to be established, Loring chose a strategy not of challenge but of avoidance. Assuming that the court would affirm the general applicability of the fellow-servant principle – the issue that the parties had agreed to place before the court for examination[53] – Loring took no steps to dispute the decisions enunciating the principle and concentrated instead on arguing that the circumstances of Farwell's suit made it an exception. Loring also appears to have decided prior to the hearing that the Supreme Judicial Court would be unwilling to entertain a suit based upon an expansive reading of the employer's tort liabilities. Thus he sought to avoid the problem of a negligence-based argument by putting his case almost entirely on the contract between the railroad and Farwell.[54]

[52] 1 McMullan 400. The issue of contract had also been addressed by the Alabama court in *Williams and Hitchcock v. Taylor*: "The instruction of the Court to the jury, that if they believed there had been negligence, without specifying the degree of it, the defendants to the action were liable, was erroneous. But we do not think the rule, which regulates the liability of a carrier, to passengers, who pay no reward for their passage, is applicable to the case of an agent, or servant, who is a free man, and knows when he enters into an engagement with a carrier, that the seat of the coach, which he agrees to drive, is without a railing, or that the coach itself is unfit to be used; or, that there is a defect in a boat, which must be a source of danger to him, while he shall pursue the business, that he undertakes to do. The agent, or servant, takes upon himself the risk of accidents and injuries from causes, of which he has knowledge. He acquires a right by his contract, to go on the boat, and to compensation for the business he may do there, and knows when he enters into his engagement, that he will be exposed to danger while he shall be employed in earning his wages. The carrier exposes himself to the peril for the purpose of earning freight, and the prospect of gain induces the agents and servants to incur the same hazard. But the only object of a passenger of any description is to be carried safely. If the servant be a slave, and the master, or his agent, who made the engagement for the servant, knew, when he entered into it, of the defects in the boat, the same rule is applicable, which would apply, were the servant a free man, and had made the contract himself" (239–40).

In tort, then, the court considered the employer liable to his worker (free or slave) only for gross neglect. As for contract, by entering into an agreement to work for the employer the free worker was to be understood as assenting to the condition of the workplace as it stood at the moment of entry. In juridical presumption the worker knew, or had the opportunity to know, the dangers of the job to be performed. By contracting, the worker assumed the risk in return for "the prospect of gain."

[53] As put to the Supreme Judicial Court, the joint declaration of the parties of the question at issue read as follows: "If the Court shall be of opinion that as matter of law the defendants are not liable to the plaintiff, he being a servant of the Corporation, and in their employment, for the injury he may have received from the negligence of . . . another servant of the Corporation, and in their employment, then the plaintiff shall become nonsuit; – but if the Court should be of opinion as matter of law, that the Defendants may be liable in this case, then the case shall be submitted to a jury upon the facts, which may be proved in the case, – the Defendants alleging negligence on the part of the plaintiff." Supreme Judicial Court (Suffolk County), Nov. term 1841 (Continuing Action 101).

[54] Shaw was not impressed with Loring's attempt to avoid the action on the case. "It is questionable whether this action is founded in tort or contract," he recorded in his minutes. "It falters between both." As we have already seen Loring's argument in *Barnes* was contract-based.

FARWELL v. BOSTON & WORCESTER RAILROAD

In attempting the removal of *Farwell* from beneath Lord Abinger's umbrella, Loring relied heavily on the circumstances of Farwell's working environment. The duties of the plaintiff, Loring told the court, were confined exclusively to running the locomotive and had nothing to do with the road itself or its condition. He was thus utterly dependent upon others for its proper construction and good condition. The plaintiff had sustained his injury by reason of the negligence of another person employed by the defendants to have charge of the switches, whose duties were likewise peculiar and confined. Thus whereas Priestley's case "was clearly one of equal knowledge on the part of the servant and of voluntary exposure on his part to a known hazard not required by his duty," *Farwell* just as clearly turned on the engineer's inability to know of the hazard of the open switch. Were the court to ignore the distinction and allow the principle contended for by the defendants to be applied in these circumstances, all persons employed by them in all their various departments – clerks, messengers, machinists, carriage builders, porters, ticket sellers – being employed for one ultimate purpose, could be classed as servants together, "and no one therefore could have any remedy against the defendants for the default of another, however distinct and independent might be their departments." Such an outcome, Loring told the court, was too absurd to contemplate.

Loring had, however, not merely to address the different circumstances of *Priestley* but also Lord Abinger's all-encompassing rejection of the plaintiff's attempt in that case to infer a rule of employer liability upon which to sue. In this "interesting and peculiar" case, Loring continued, the court had undertaken to affirm a general rule of no liability applying to all cases of injury befalling a servant in the employment of his master without discrimination as to the particular nature of the employment relationship or the cause of the injury. In justification it had cited the master's causal remoteness from the injuries for which he might be made liable. Now, as numerous applications of the rule *respondeat superior* showed, remoteness per se was no argument against attributing liability, because carriers for hire and tavern or boardinghouse keepers were held responsible to parties suffering injury however remote the cause and however careful they personally might have been. Nevertheless, Loring accepted that there was no rule of law imposing obligations on employers in their relations with their employees analogous to those imposing obligations upon carriers and tavern keepers.[55] Rather, the question as to the duty of the master to care for his servant was one to be settled by reference to the nature of their contract. "In each case that arises, reference must be had to the *contract* existing between them as stipulated in terms or implied from the nature

[55] "We do not go upon the principle that the defendants are liable in this case upon the rule regulating their liability to passengers carried for hire. In that case they are liable for the want of the utmost care and prudence of which human foresight is capable. But the servants in their employment do not come within the reason for that rule . . . Nor do we rest our claim upon the same principle which lies at foundation of the liability of principals for the acts of their servants."

of the service, and the question of the master's liability must depend upon that contract as applied to that particular case." And if examination of the contract should affirm that the master was responsible for ordinary carelessness or negligence in regard to the means that he stipulated to provide to enable the servant to discharge the duty he had undertaken, "it matters not how remote the cause may be nor whether the carelessness was his own or that of another agent employed by him in that behalf."[56]

In construing contracts to determine the extent of the liability that the master had incurred, Loring argued that the proper rule was that "the master contracts to be responsible to the servant for the carelessness or negligence of those employed by the master in distinct services or departments, over which the servant has no supervision or control." Thus in the example of the footman used by Lord Abinger, whose employment it was to tend at table and ride behind the coachman as the personal attendant of his master and who had no care, control, or knowledge of the carriage or its equipment, "it seems fair if not necessary to infer as the *mutual understanding*, that when the master contracts with the servant to ride upon his coach, giving him no right or authority to control it or to see to its sufficiency or equipment and no opportunity of doing so in the regular discharge of his duty, he contracts that he will have a coach which is *safe* to ride upon, so far at least as ordinary care on his part and those employed by him in that behalf is involved; for no one can suppose that a footman would enter upon such service with any other understanding. And as the *knowledge* and *power* in reference to the *true condition* of the carriage are *entirely confined to the master* or those *employed by* him and the footman has *none*, nor *any* means of *obtaining* them, it seems reasonable and just that the obligation in this behalf should be entirely upon the master."[57]

This did not mean that the indemnity for the servant implied in the employment contract was absolute. Indeed, Loring continued, the same reasons that required the master to be held liable to the servant for injuries suffered by acts of those employed in different services over whom he had no control and against whose conduct he could not guard himself were just as persuasive in exonerating the master from liability in those cases where the servant could exercise control or supervision or had an opportunity to protect himself by caution and prudence. "By the contract between the master and servant it may reasonably by inferred that the servant agrees to take the hazard of the carelessness or negligence of his fellow servants or those employed with him in the same business because they are necessary and natural incidents to his ordinary occupation – in the same manner as all the ordinary chances of like injuries are to all men in all cases – and because they have to a great extent the

---

[56] Chief Justice Shaw's minute book reveals the judge noting to himself at this point, "It may be that the remedy in tort is mistaken, causing him to amend the form of action." Similarly, Justice Hubbard's minute book notes that no contract was alleged in the plaintiff's declaration, where trespass on the case had been the plea.

[57] Emphases in the original.

means of guarding against such injuries by the exercise of mutual caution and forbearance or prudence, while the master has none whatever, and because between persons employed in any joint agency or service there is a *privity* of *control* that renders them liable to each other for their carelessness or neglect in the discharge of it." But in Farwell's case, no such control by the servant had been possible. "Neither could interfere with the other nor even have any means of knowledge of the conduct or deportment of the other prior to the accident." The corporation, on the other hand, had complete power to control and supervise the switchman in the discharge of his duty[58] and was actually under the most imperative obligation to exercise that power, for it owed a great and paramount duty to the world at large to keep the road in perfect order at all times.

Inevitably, Loring's notes of the case presented by the opposing counsel are briefer than those on his own. Nevertheless, together with the minutes of Chief Justice Shaw and Justice Hubbard they are sufficient to enable a detailed reconstruction of the defendants' arguments.

The plaintiff's claim, defendants' counsel stressed, was new and unprecedented.[59] If allowed, it would bear adversely upon every person and company having others in their employ. The plaintiff claimed that he should be indemnified from danger resulting from the actions of all other servants employed by the defendants, save only those whose actions he could directly influence. The plaintiff, however, had not been employed to act alone but in conjunction with others. This was the nature of his employment. "To say that these persons were acting different parts and were therefore not acting jointly is a non sequitur: each was performing a different part, but for one object, and so they were fellow servants and copartners."[60] "Infinite mischief" – an avalanche of actions crippling employers in all walks of life – could be expected if the rule contended for by the plaintiff were adopted.[61]

In order even to maintain an action, counsel stated, plaintiff had to establish his claim upon some rule of law. Being unable to find one, his attorney had first sought to invent a principle whereby the defendants could be charged with the negligence of another according to the maxim *respondeat superior*. The defendants' first answer to this was simply that no precedent could be found to support the application of the maxim in such circumstances. There was "not a single case where this principle has been applied to a case like the present" even though cases like this "must have

---

[58] The switchman "contracts alone with the defendants and is directly accountable to them." It was the corporation "from whom he receives his compensation [and] who alone can control or dismiss him."

[59] "I have looked through all [the] digests and books. [I] have examined [the] civil codes," stated George Morey. Nowhere was there a hint of a rule remotely similar to that for which the plaintiff was contending.

[60] According to Justice Hubbard's minutes, Morey likened the relationship between the engineer and the switchman to that pertaining between different parts of the body. "Could the eye complain of the hand and the hand of the foot?" Defense counsel also used the examples of a blacksmith's shop, actors in a play, and farmers making hay as illustrations of their point.

[61] Ibid.

happened in great numbers in the various trades." This absence of precedent "presses strongly against the plaintiff."[62]

Second, and more important, suits such as this one fell outside the ambit of the rule. *Respondeat superior* was a severe maxim, for it rendered the principal liable even though guilty of no personal misconduct. As such, the rule was an exception to the law governing relations between parties, one that had been created solely as a matter of policy to answer to the "convenience" and "general interest" of the public. Being thus an "artificial" rule "founded in wisdom" for "the benefit of society," it was pertinent to ask whether it was in the public interest for the court to entertain the extension of the rule in the manner called for by the plaintiff to the point where it assigned liability to the master for the acts of servants in reference to each other.[63] Once examined from this perspective it was plain that the public interest required that the servant should not have an opportunity to recover from the master, but rather that the several servants of the same employer should be treated as sureties for each other. Such would be the obvious intent of public policy in these circumstances, for the intent would be to supply "a strong motive to constant vigilance."[64] By turning each servant into "a form of superintendent," accidents might be avoided, for "if they cannot look to the company [they] will better look out for each other."

Nor, finally, was there any support to be had for a suit such as this in public opinion, for although the legislature had recently taken action to specify the duties owed by railroads to their passengers, its brief had not extended to employees.[65] Therefore, although the plaintiff had argued that the general good would be served by the adoption of the principle for which he contended, it seemed clear that public opinion, judging at least by legislative action, was against him.

This discussion showed, defendants' counsel argued, that an action on the case founded on the principle of *respondeat superior* could not be maintained. Counsel for the plaintiff was apparently in agreement because, notwithstanding the original declaration, he had declined in argument to maintain his action on the general

---

[62] Ibid. Shaw records counsel's remarks slightly differently: "[*Respondeat superior*] prevails in the civil or cases at the common law yet there has been no case in either code when the legal principle has been so applied. The cases must have happened, time without number, and no such [action] was brought, till lately, and never sustained. It would be a new era in legal history if maintained."

[63] Originally, Morey told the court, *respondeat superior* had been expressly limited to the protection of travelers on the highway and their property from injury. Succeeding cases had, for sound reasons of public policy, subsequently extended the master's obligation to encompass all third persons. It had, however, never been held to extend to indemnify other servants. See Shaw's minute book.

[64] Ibid.

[65] *Massachusetts Statutes* 1840, c. 80: "If the life of any person, being a passenger, shall be lost by reason of the negligence or carelessness of the proprietor or proprietors of any rail-road, steam-boat, stage coach, or of common carrier of passengers, or by the unfitness or gross negligence or carelessness of their servants or agents, in this Commonwealth, such proprietor or proprietors, and common carriers, shall be liable to a fine not exceeding five thousand dollars, nor less than five hundred dollars, to be recovered by indictment, to the use of the executor or administrator of the deceased person, for the benefit of his widow and heirs." Here, as elsewhere, one may note how the "public" granted protection was defined by its gender no less than by its absence from production.

principle of the master's liability for the torts of servants, effectively "conced[ing] that the plaintiff is not entitled in the principle *respondeat superior*."[66] The case instead had been put wholly on the contract.

There was, however, no more justification for plaintiff's contention considered as an action of contract than as one of tort. What was the parties' contract? "To set in motion an engine – a movable machine – on a fixed machine . . . a single track rail road."[67] Clearly the contract had been made in contemplation of the nature of the road and thus in the knowledge that there were turnouts with switches tended by switchmen, whose character the plaintiff had ample opportunity to know by reason of his daily passage along the road. The plaintiff thus "makes a continuing contract applicable to the state of things which must arise on such employment." His contract "was made in reference to the labor and risk incident to the nature of the service" and with "a full knowledge thereof . . . for a fixed and agreed compensation." In construing the contract to see what was implied, therefore, the true rule was that "*the plaintiff takes upon himself the risks and perils incident to his situation*" in exchange for "a satisfactory compensation."[68] The plaintiff, moreover, had conceded that there were certainly circumstances in which the master would not be liable – for example, where the negligence of those acting with the servant in the same department was at issue. What basis, however, could there be for holding the master free of liability in these circumstances other than the conclusion that the servants had assumed the risks? "He says the master is not responsible to the servant for an injury received from the negligence of one acting in the same department. But why not, unless the servant takes the risk of negligence in his department?" And if the servant was held to have assumed the risks in those circumstances, why not in all circumstances? To hold that the master contracted to be responsible to each in his own department for the carelessness of those in another and that the engineer had the control of those employed with him and was answerable for their negligence but not for that of other parties was, defense counsel emphasized, not a serious position. Rather, it was to adopt "*arbitrary positions argued to fit this case*," to assume that there could be no general rule to be laid down but rather to adapt the contract implied in each case to fit the circumstances of that case.

Defendants' counsel admitted that there were circumstances where the defendants would be bound to indemnify injured parties even where no express contract had been agreed – as, for example, in the case of passengers, who had paid for their

---

[66] When it came to his rebuttal Loring hedged his bets, but, at least as recorded in Shaw's minutes, he did so rather unconvincingly. "[We] do not place the case on the ground of [the] liability of [the] master for the negligence of servants, but do not decline it, and if the court think it applicable, it [could] be applied."

[67] In Hubbard's minute book.

[68] Emphasis in original. Hubbard's minutes show counsel emphasizing here that Farwell's wages as an engineer were higher than those he had received as a machinist, and that there was also a differential between the wages he had been paid as the engineer of the merchandise train and those he received for driving the passenger train. These details had also been included in the agreed statement of facts jointly submitted to the court by the parties at the outset.

carriage and therefore had a right to safe carriage. But the plaintiff had not sought indemnification on that ground but only on the ground that the employer was rendered liable by the contract of employment. "He says that the master contracts to use ordinary care and diligence to enable the servant to perform his engagements." Even admitting this to be so, it could not affect the defendants, because they had not been wanting in proper care and diligence. If a master were to be held accountable to his servant in the exercise of care to any degree at all, it could be for nothing more than his responsibility to select and employ careful servants to act with the complainant. "And if such an one is employed, [the] superior is no further responsible."[69] There could be no question that the defendants had not performed this duty "faithfully and fully." The servants they had employed were fit and suitable – the switchman's general reputation was one of competence and care – and the road itself was in proper condition.

In short, the plaintiff's argument posed a new and untried theory that threatened established rules of tort law and that distorted the effect of the parties' contract as to the care owed by the employer. By conceding that a master was not answerable to employees for injuries arising from the actions of others engaged in the same department, the plaintiff had effectively conceded the entire case because by this he recognized that the employee "takes the risks incident to his employment." *Priestley* and *Murray* – the only available precedents – settled the matter.

In rebuttal, the onus fell upon Loring to reestablish his case in the face of the defendants' denunciation of its novelty. From what the defendants' counsel had said, Loring commented, one would think that the plaintiff "was going for a revolution of the law," that a decision in his favor "would be such an astonishing novelty as to shock the whole professional world from the Chancellors and Chief Justices down to the turnkeys." Far from it. The plaintiff's sole object was to demonstrate that his claim was an exception to the rule that a master was not liable to his servant for damages caused by the negligence of a fellow servant by showing that the engineer and the switchman were not fellow servants or joint agents within the sense of that rule. The only vestige of novelty in the case was that the exception for which the plaintiff contended could not have arisen under the circumstances of "the ordinary occupations of life in former times" but had its origins in the unprecedented scale and novelty of organization of contemporary enterprise and in the vastly complicated relations of master and servant resulting therefrom.

Defendants' counsel, Loring stated, had insisted that plaintiff and switchman were joint agents and fellow servants because they were employed together for the same general purpose or object, namely conducting cars over the road. They had illustrated their argument with analogies to farmers making hay, to blacksmiths at work in their shop, to actors on stage. "Now in all these cases the parties are joint agents and fellow servants because they are not only employed for the same general object but all [are] employed to *act together* for one purpose, requiring their joint

[69] Shaw's minute book.

357

action *with each* other at the same place and time, and for the same end." The "vast enterprises of the present day," however, were characterized above all by "the great extent and variety of [their] departments . . . combining almost indefinite space and numerous operations independent of each other in their administration although cooperating in their results." In the case of the railroads "the machine shop may belong to one [department], the Rail Road to another, the cars and locomotive to another." Employees no longer had the same master but "different masters [in] different departments" and were employed for distinct and separate duties involving no immediate personal connection of the agents with each other – duties to be performed at different times in different places and of essentially different natures. "Each in his department is a coservant with those employed *there with him*, but he is *not a fellow servant* with the others employed in their distinct and independent departments [even though his performance] may be essential to the common or general object to be attained." The machinist in his shop, the switchman out on the tracks, the ticket seller in his office, and the carriage builders in their shed were all indisputably employees of the same employer, but in each case "the relation of joint agents or coservants ceases beyond the regular sphere of each individual's occupation."

It was crucial to Loring's case that the court accept his analysis of the relationship between the plaintiff and the switchman, for this was his only answer to the brooding presence of *Priestley*. Having established, at least to his own satisfaction, that the plaintiff and the switchman were not fellow servants, however, he still faced the task of undermining the defense's "assumption of risk" argument. The plaintiff, he argued, had been hired exclusively to perform the duty of running the engine. In thus limiting his powers and rights of control and supervision – his exercise of discretion or autonomy – to that function, the defendants had by implication agreed that the road upon which the engine would be run would be suitable and safe. Admittedly, it might be said that plaintiff had entered into his contract in the knowledge that the operation of the railroad depended in part upon switches and that those who manned the switches might well be careless, and therefore that he had assented to run the risk of that carelessness. "But no one would listen to that argument." Rather, in light of the inability of the plaintiff to control the switchman or guard against his negligence, the master should be held to have contracted with the engineer that the switches would be faithfully tended "as much as if he agreed to tend them himself."

Finally, Loring addressed the question of public policy, invoked by the defendant as an explanation of and justification for the assignment of risk to the employee. "They argue that servants should have no remedy . . . because the want of one will make them more careful of each other. . . . This was the argument used in the South Carolina case.[70] But that can only be when they have the means and opportunity of

[70] Here Loring referred to the argument of counsel for the railroad in *Murray v. S.C. Rail Road* that co-servants "must look to each other for protection and safety, and be thence induced to stimulate each other to care and diligence, and prevent, by the efforts of one, the consequences of the negligence of another. On this the public security depends, and it would be greatly endangered were a different principle adopted" (1 McMullan 385, at 397).

such watchfulness and care." When they had none, the rule, to achieve the intended public policy effect, should necessarily be applied directly the other way, "giving a remedy against the master to compel him and his servants in that department to greater fidelity and care." In this case the argument would apply if the engineer had had an opportunity to overlook or guard against the carelessness of the switchman, or if their relationship was one in which there reposed mutual care and oversight. "But as the engineer can have no such oversight or knowledge, there is the more reason for making the master liable, as an additional inducement to be careful for the sake of passengers."

Loring's argument was notable primarily for its caution and its conservatism. At only one point, when trying to explain the complete absence of precedents for claims by servants against masters under any circumstances, did he even hint that the plaintiff's suit afforded the court an opportunity for innovation. "The [defendants'] counsel says he has researched the library and that he nowhere found the *protection* of *the servant alluded to*."[71] But the books in the library were "from a country where the distinction between master and servant in all its relations is very different from that here, [which] doubtless must affect judicial opinions as it does all society." In America "a very different relation, and very different public sentiment prevails . . . and requires a careful and equal distribution of the rights of protection and indemnity for the employed and the employer."[72] But this implied criticism of American doctrine's Anglocentricity was out of character, for Loring was certainly no radical. On the contrary, here, as elsewhere, the entire structure of his argument turned on a reverence for English precedent (he seemed almost mesmerized by *Priestley v. Fowler*), dictating a narrow focus on seeking individual exceptions to what he assumed to be well-established rules.

Given Loring's conservatism, in particular his effective abandonment of the action on the case in the face of *Priestley* and *Murray*, the result was a foregone conclusion. The plaintiff had accepted the premises of the defendants' argument and contested only the detail of the conclusions to be drawn from those premises. The court was not challenged to depart from those premises, and so it did not.[73]

The general rule in such circumstances, Chief Justice Shaw indicated for the court, was one of no liability. As the defendants had maintained, and as plaintiff's counsel had himself conceded, there was no basis within the existing bounds of tort principles upon which such a suit might be maintained. The only possible candidate, *respondeat superior*, "presupposes that the parties stand to each other in the relation

---

[71] Emphasis in original.

[72] Justice Hubbard noted in his minutes at this point that Loring "thinks servants very degraded in England – and so poor [that they] cannot try their cases."

[73] As Roscoe Pound put it many years ago, although spoken of "as if it set up an arbitrary exception to a rule of law which expressed a fundamental and universal idea of justice," in fact the judgment in *Farwell* did no more than refuse "to extend further an exception to a then generally received doctrine that liability must flow from fault." It would, Pound continued, "have been quite impossible for American judges trained in the common-law tradition, acting in the light of the received ideals of the times, to come to any other conclusion" (*The Formative Era of American Law* (Boston, [1938], 87).

of strangers, between whom there is no privity. . . . But this does not apply to the case of a servant bringing his action against his own employer to recover damages for an injury arising in the course of that employment," because the parties not being strangers, "all such risks and perils as the employer and the servant respectively intend to assume and bear may be regulated by the express or implied contract between them, and . . . in contemplation of law, must be presumed to be thus regulated."[74] As to the construction of that contract, "the general rule . . . is, that he who engages in the employment of another for the performance of specified duties and services, for compensation, takes upon himself the natural and ordinary risks and perils incident to the performance of such services, and in legal presumption, the compensation is adjusted accordingly." The court was "not aware of any principle which should except the perils arising from the carelessness and negligence of those who are in the same employment."[75] Had such an exception been established by law "it would be a rule of frequent and familiar occurrence, and its existence and application . . . would be settled by judicial precedents." But it was the court's opinion that no such exception had been established, "and the authorities, as far as they go, are opposed to the principle."[76]

Left at that, Shaw's decision would have amounted to little more than an affirmation of the sufficiency of the defendants' legal reasoning. As has been pointed out elsewhere, however, *Farwell v. Boston & Worcester* was self-consciously a broad defense of the immunity of employers from liability for industrial injuries.[77] The explanation for this lies in the "considerations of policy and general convenience" that, no less than legal principle, were cited by the court as determinants of its decision.[78]

As we have already seen, both parties to *Farwell* addressed the implications that decision of the suit one way or the other would have for the prevention of accidents. This was not an abstract debate but an issue of considerable moment. Take, for example, the accident record of the Boston & Worcester Railroad in the four and one-half years that the case had been pending. All told, there had been twenty incidents: ten collisions (five at crossings); a derailment; one instance each of people and cattle killed while walking on the track; injury to four employees and two more killed; and some twenty-five passengers injured, twenty of these in a collision in June 1840 at Grafton.[79] Even this sorry record was eclipsed, however, by the Boston & Worcester's sister railroad, the Western. Beginning in the winter of 1840 that road experienced a series of disasters that left seven employees dead and two injured, along with one passenger dead and at least another fifteen injured.[80]

---

[74] 45 Mass. 49, at 56.

[75] Ibid., 57.   [76] Ibid.

[77] Jerrilyn Marston, Comment, "The Creation of a Common Law Rule: The Fellow-Servant Rule, 1837–1860," *University of Pennsylvania Law Review*, 132, 3 (1984), 579–620, at 590–4.

[78] 45 Mass. 49, at 57.

[79] See, generally, Boston & Worcester Railroad, Directors' Minutes, vols. 2–4 (1837–42).

[80] Western Railroad, Director's Records, vol. 2 (1836–41), and Clerk's Files, case 1, in Boston & Albany Collection, Baker Library, Harvard Business School. See also Stephen Salsbury, *The State, the Investor, and the Railroad: The Boston and Albany, 1825–67* (Cambridge, Mass., 1967), 182–5.

Early in 1842 (18 January) the state legislature created a special committee of inquiry into the accidents on the Western Railroad. The committee was directed to investigate the causes of the accidents and to report on "the expediency of enacting such laws as will have a tendency to prevent a recurrence of similar accidents." The committee's interpretation of this task was that it should determine whether the railroad's agents were "chargeable with any negligence in the discharge of their duties, which should expose them to the censure of the public," and whether "the expression of such censure by the Legislature" would "prevent the dangers which attend travel upon this and other similar roads." Its report of 18 February chose specifically to absolve the board of directors from any culpability. "We are not satisfied, from the investigations that we have been able to make, that the directors have been justly chargeable with any neglect of duty, which has caused these accidents." Rather, their management of the railroad was such as to inspire confidence. "They adopt the regulations which their judgment, aided by experience, pronounces best. They employ men whom they suppose to be the best qualified to discharge the duties required of them." Having found no evidence of any neglect on the directors' part "to use every reasonable precaution to prevent accidents," the committee declined to recommend any action "which may censure the directors in this matter." Nor, as a result of their confidence in the director's management of the railroad, was the committee prepared to counsel legislative intervention. In what Stephen Salsbury has described as "a classic argument for an unfettered management," the committee earnestly expressed the hope "that increased vigilance and care will hereafter prevent the recurrence of the accidents which have so alarmed the community," but found itself unable to "suggest any legal enactment which can aid in producing this desirable result."[81]

The public interest in railroad safety, the legislature had indicated through its committee, would not be served by the imposition of new responsibilities on management to care for the well-being of passengers and employees.[82] Rather, the best means for the prevention of accidents was an unencumbered management, free to promulgate suitable rules and regulations to govern its business, to pursue contravention of those rules and regulations, and to "discharge [any employee] from service, upon the slightest evidence of negligence, or wantonness, or incompetency."[83] The public interest could thus be best served by the reinforcement of public confidence in managerial expertise and in the promotion of management's disciplinary capacity.

Shaw's common law judgment reached the same conclusion. Considered in relation to the unspoken alternatives canvassed by the committee – the imposition of duties of care on employers through judicial or legislative intervention – his decision, like theirs, strongly endorsed the unfettered corporation. An employer was liable in tort to third persons for the negligence of his servant in the conduct of his business, but that was a strictly limited liability founded in policy rather than law

---

[81] *Report of the Committee on Rail-roads and Canals*, Senate Document 55 (1842), 6–9; Salsbury, *The State, the Investor, and the Railroad*, 189.

[82] Salsbury, *The State, the Investor, and the Railroad*, 189.   [83] Senate Document 55 (1842), 8.

and encompassing only those with whom the employer had no contractual relations. "Considerations of policy and general expediency forbid the extension of the principle, so far as to warrant a servant in maintaining an action against his employer for an indemnity which we think was not contemplated in the nature and terms of the employment, and which, if established, would not conduce to the general good."[84] Given that the relations between the parties were contractual, it was the contract that properly defined the extent and limits of the employer's responsibility. Where the contract contained no express warrant of indemnity for injury arising from the acts of other employees, the court would not imply one, for in establishing the existence of implied terms in contracts between parties what a court did was to infer the existence of a duty on the basis of its consideration of what would best promote the benefit – "the safety and security" – of all persons concerned. No duty of care that would justify plaintiff's suit was to be found following this route either.[85]

In endorsing the unfettered corporation, Shaw's decision in *Farwell*, like the report of the committee of inquiry just a few weeks earlier, also recognized and endorsed the structure of disciplinary power that permeated the employment relationship and yoked the public interest in industrial safety to its perpetuation. Indeed, Shaw went the committee one better, for his decision also invoked a responsibility on the part of employees to police themselves. Where, as here, "several persons are employed in the conduct of one common enterprise or undertaking . . . the safety of each depends much on the care and skill with which each other shall perform his appropriate duty." Shaw proposed to take advantage of this interdependence by making each worker responsible for potentially injurious negligence or misfeasance on the part of the others. "Each is an observer of the conduct of the others, can give notice of any misconduct, incapacity or neglect of duty, and leave the service if the common employer will not take such precautions, and employ such agents as the safety of the whole party may require." The incentive of each to take care and to ensure that others did likewise would, however, be destroyed if the employee could have resort to the common employer for indemnity in case of loss through injury. Hence the prospect of indemnity should be foreclosed. "By these means, the safety of each will be much more effectually secured, than could be done by resort to the common employer."[86]

In conjunction with the doctrine that an employee contracted to "assume the risk" of his employment, this rather chilling conclusion placed all employees under the constant gaze of self-imposed or peer-imposed discipline. As defendants' counsel had advocated, Shaw's decision turned each employee into "a form of superintendent," not only of others but also of self.[87] These, of course, were responsibilities without

---

[84] 45 Mass. 49, at 59.

[85] Ibid., 58   [86] Ibid., 59.

[87] That such self- and other-discipline were two sides of the same coin in Shaw's decision is confirmed by his reaction to Loring's attempt to distinguish Farwell's claim on the grounds that he and the switchman were employed in different departments. If employees were to be responsible for policing each other, Loring argued, that responsibility could extend only so far as their enjoyment of the means – notably, the requisite knowledge – to do so. Shaw, however, refused to entertain the point. First, he

concomitant power to realize them, for they were imposed within the context of a structure of managerial power that gave no role in the direction of the enterprise to the employees save that of policing each other's obedience to company rules and regulations. In contrast, the authority of the employer over the direction of the enterprise – identified by Shaw implicitly and by the committee of investigation into the Western Railroad disasters explicitly as the sine qua non of an orderly and rational industrial environment – was power without responsibility, carrying with it no duty upon which the employee subjected to it could sue.

CONTRACT AND POWER

Shaw's denial of a legal right of recovery threw Nicholas Farwell back onto the mercy of his employers. On 19 September 1842 the railroad's board of directors recorded that he had been paid seven hundred and twenty dollars in full of all claims against the corporation. This sum included wages for the period from the date of the accident until the end of 1837 (approximately $120), an additional sum of $500 that had been voted to him by the board in January 1838 in response to his initial application for assistance, and a contribution (approximately $100) toward his medical expenses. The directors could congratulate themselves for maintaining their record of benevolent treatment of injured employees and for successfully avoiding the vastly larger expenses that a victory for Farwell's suit would have meant.[88]

Succeeding cases in Massachusetts confirm the reluctance of the courts to intrude any liabilities upon the state's employers. Thus in *Hayes v. The Western Railroad Corporation* (1849) and *Albro v. The Agawam Canal Company* (1850),[89] the Supreme Judicial Court indicated that an employer was no more liable to an employee injured through the negligence of another employee who was either temporarily (*Hayes*) or permanently (*Albro*) in a position of authority over the injured employee than would have been the case had the two been fellow servants of identical status. In *King v. Boston & Worcester Railroad* (1851) it held that the employer could not be

---

challenged Loring on whether the different departments could in fact be distinguished from each other. "When the object to be accomplished is one and the same, when the employers are the same, and the several persons employed derive their authority and their compensation from the same source, it would be extremely difficult to distinguish, what constitutes one department and what a distinct department of duty. It would vary with the circumstances of every case." But in any case, Shaw continued, Loring's distinction assumed a principle of employer responsibility that the court did not accept. "The exemption of the master . . . from liability for the negligence of a fellow servant, does not depend exclusively upon the consideration, that the servant has better means to provide for his own safety, but upon other grounds." Those other grounds were the employee's contractual assumption of the risks of his employment. The master was exempt from liability "because the implied contract of the master does not extend to indemnify the servant against the negligence of any one but himself" (45 Mass. 49, at 60–1).

[88] Farwell's suit had cited medical expenses of $500, which offers a different perspective on the corporation's generosity in this matter.

[89] 57 Mass. 270, and 60 Mass. 75. These were the first cases to come before the Supreme Judicial Court on the question of an employer's liability for occupational injuries after Farwell's suit.

held liable for an injury caused by defective equipment, on the grounds that "keeping the road in proper repair . . . would seem to be the work of servants or laborers," the risk of whose negligence was assumed by the plaintiff.[90] In *Gillshannon v. Stony Brook Railroad* (1852) it held that a laborer injured while being transported to his place of work on a gravel train could not recover against the employer because the transportation was a "permissive privilege" granted the plaintiff under his contract "to facilitate his labors and service." The risk was hence assumed in his contract of employment.[91] Finally, in *Albro v. Jaquith* (1855) it held that a servant injured by the negligence of another servant in the employ of the same master not only could not sue the master but could not even sue the negligent servant.[92]

In light of the legal and social history of employee sickness and injury in the late eighteenth and early nineteenth centuries, it is not particularly surprising that the Massachusetts courts should so consistently have rejected claims of employer liability for injuries to their employees at work. This history must tend to qualify those accounts of the issue that place particular stress on *Farwell* as a decisive doctrinal innovation that "carved out an exception to the well-established rule of *respondeat superior*."[93] If anything, it shows that the true revolutionaries and innovators were not the judges who defined the fellow-servant rule but the plaintiffs who sought to press the new claim.[94]

[90] 63 Mass. 112, at 115. The plaintiff in this case was an apprentice in the defendant corporation's machine shop but was injured while acting temporarily as a fireman at no advance in his wages. Although the risk premium had been an important element in Shaw's justification of the assumption of risk doctrine, the court in King's case studiously ignored the inconsistency.

[91] 64 Mass. 228, at 231. The circumstances of Gillshannon's case were, of course, identical to those in the suit brought by Gilham Barnes. See also *Seaver v. Boston and Maine Railroad*, 80 Mass. 466 (1860).

[92] 70 Mass. 99.

[93] Marston, "Creation of a Common Law Rule," 579. On this point see also Pound, *Formative Era of American Law*, 87.

[94] As far as the potential of *respondeat superior* is concerned, there is no evidence that the principle had ever been applied or even much thought about as a rule of sufficient generality as to encompass the imputation of negligence to the employer in cases of injury occurring within an employment relationship. (*Respondeat superior*, as we have seen, was not invoked in Barnes's case, nor was it in *Priestley v. Fowler*.) Indeed, early nineteenth-century Massachusetts lawyers with an interest in the origins of this "ancient customary principle" might reasonably have been led to the conclusion that *respondeat superior* specifically excused the master from liability for injuries done by one servant to another. In 1808 the *American Law Journal*, published in Boston and Philadelphia, carried a translation of those elements of Justinian's *Pandects* dealing with the responsibilities of masters of ships and of inn- and stablekeepers. "The master must answer for the acts of all his mariners, whether slaves or freemen," indicated the *Journal*, translating from the eighteenth book of Ulpian; "and it is very proper he should answer, as he himself appoints them." But "he does not answer further than for damage done on board of his vessel; and he is not to answer for any thing done out of the vessel although by mariners." And crucially, "if the mariners occasion damage to each other, no action lies against the master" (*American Law Journal*, 1, 4 [1808], 496). See also discussion at nn.55, 62–65 above.

The argument that in industrial accident cases judges had to confront *respondeat superior* as relevant doctrine to be distinguished (or that in *Farwell*, as Horwitz would have it, the court was spared the necessity of so doing only because of Loring's ineptitude) grows out of the assumption that these cases were part of a larger trend in legal development in which a judiciary sympathetic toward entrepreneurial capitalism reacted to the increasing incidence of tort claims accompanying the industrialization of the northeastern economy by radically diluting preindustrial principles of strict liability through the introduction of liability-limiting criteria such as the fault principle. As I indicated in the introduction to this

Simply to assert that Shaw and his fellow judges reacted to the attempt to press claims of an employer's liability by refusing to depart from the status quo does not, however, do justice to their achievement. In the context of a rapidly changing social structure, a refusal to innovate can be just as revolutionary in its effects as a dramatic policy shift (particularly where, as here, the refusal is articulated not in a piecemeal fashion but in the form of a broad rule). Here, in the context of severe social and economic stresses emerging from an industrialism predicated on the concentration rather than the diffusion of economic power and, more immediately, on a political economy of speed, the courts' refusal to innovate was a rejection of the possibility – and indeed of the desirability of reconstructing the social relations of employment through the imposition of public duties on employers. This left the social and organizational structure of the new industrial "order" to be defined very much as the outgrowth of employers' discretionary authority.

The centrality of this approach to the trajectory being followed by Massachusetts courts in the liability cases was rendered progressively clearer with each of the successive judgments reinforcing *Farwell v. Boston & Worcester*. Always treating *Farwell* as their point of departure, these cases fleshed out the assumptions about the nature of industrial order – the social relations of production, the appropriate distribution and location of power and authority, the foundations of discipline – that had been embedded in the common law doctrine of employer liability as a result of Shaw's ruling.

These were as follows: First, industry was the private domain of the employer, not amenable to public oversight. This argument, advanced by the defendant in *Barnes* but denied by the referees, had been affirmed by Shaw in *Farwell*. It was confirmed by the court in *Hayes v. Western Railroad*. There the defendant railroad corporation argued that the derailment in which the plaintiff had been injured had occurred

---

section of the book, however, recent research has suggested that injurious behavior in the preindustrial era was governed not by principles of strict liability but by an assumption of no liability outside carefully demarcated areas. Seen from this perspective, *respondeat superior* appears less as the doctrinal expression in master/servant relations of wide-ranging strict-liability assumptions than as one of a limited number of carefully defined enclaves existing in a predominantly no-liability world. Into this enclave the courts admitted injuries suffered by strangers at the hands of servants if they were the consequence of acts expressly or impliedly commanded by the master and occurring within the usual course of his business, but not injuries judged to be the consequence of a servant's "willful" acts. (Given that the courts' definition of willful action could extend to any act whose performance was not involuntary or uncoerced, the realm of potentially uncompensated injuries was left wide indeed. See *M'Manus v. Crickett*, 1 East 105 [1800], for a discussion of the meaning of willful action.) A master was also held liable where an injury appeared to be the result of negligence or want of skill on the part of a servant, "because it was a neglect and fault in the master to appoint a careless and negligent person to do his business." As Nathan Dane indicated, however, there was no guarantee that the principle would extend liability to masters if they could show that the servant they had appointed had otherwise exhibited a "good and faithful character," for it had never been settled "how far one negligent act, as the one complained of, is conclusive evidence of a negligent character in the servant" (see Dane, *Abridgment*, 2:495, and generally 315–16, 494–5). Even in third-party relations, therefore, *respondeat superior* did not render the master automatically liable for any injury resulting from his servant's negligence. Rather, the liability of the master was due to his own fault in appointing an insufficient servant and might be avoided by demonstrating appropriate care in the choice of the servant.

because of the negligence of a fellow employee, a brakeman, who had been away from his post when the accident occurred. The plaintiff sought to have the trial court jury given leave to consider facts tending to show that the derailment had been caused by the negligence of the corporation in assigning too few brakemen to control the train. On appeal, the Supreme Judicial Court disallowed the plaintiff's contention. "When it is established, that the injury complained of was occasioned by the neglect of the man on the train, and not by reason of the absence of the man, then surely the absence of the man becomes immaterial. . . . The proximate cause is the object of inquiry, and when discovered, is to be regarded and relied on." The trial court had thus been quite correct to instruct the jury to disregard the question of whether there were enough brakemen, for this was not a matter appropriate for the jury to consider. "It was within the province and the duty of the court to instruct the jury, that a fault, if any, of the defendants, from which the plaintiff had not suffered, and of which he had no right to complain, was immaterial."[95]

Second, employers might create hierarchies of supervision and control in order to project their authority within that private domain without rendering themselves liable for any adverse consequences suffered by their employees. Thus employers might freely delegate power temporarily or permanently to officers to whom subordinates were required to show obedience on pain of dismissal, but they would not be held accountable for the consequences of negligent actions on the part of those to whom they had delegated that supervisory authority. As the court put it in *Albro v. The Agawam Canal Company*: "The injury of which the plaintiff complains appears to have happened while she was acting in the discharge of her duty to the defendants, as her employers, in their factory, and to have been occasioned by the negligence of another person [that is, the factory superintendent], who was also engaged in the defendants' service, in the same factory. The duties of the superintendent may be different, and perhaps may be considered as of a somewhat higher character than those of the plaintiff; [but] inasmuch as they are both the servants of the same master, have the same employer, are engaged in the accomplishment of the same general object, are acting in one common service, and derive their compensation from the same source . . . [they] must be considered as fellow-servants."[96]

Third, the officers to whom power was delegated in a hierarchically organized enterprise were not to be held accountable in its exercise to their subordinates, but only to their superiors. Thus, courts in their decisions accommodated the distribution of power and the lines of accountability created privately by the employer. This was made abundantly clear in *Albro v. Jaquith*, where, having failed in her attempt to hold the Agawam Canal Company liable for the actions of its superintendent, the plaintiff, Mary Albro, tried to sue the superintendent himself. She was told she could not. "His obligation to be faithful and diligent in this particular resulted either from an express contract with his principal, or is to be implied from the nature and character of the service in which he was engaged. And because this is

---

[95] 57 Mass. 270, at 274. [96] 60 Mass. 75, at 77.

the sole origin and foundation of his duty, he is responsible only to the party to whom it was due for the injurious consequences of neglecting it. It is not pretended that he had entered into any stipulation, or made any positive engagement with the plaintiff, in relation to the service which he had agreed to render to their common employer. She therefore had no legal right to complain of his carelessness or unfaithfulness; for he had made himself, by no act or contract, accountable to her."[97]

Fourth, following directly on Shaw's lead in *Farwell*, courts acknowledged that the exercise of supervisory power by the employer through the hierarchical structures created for that purpose was appropriately to be supplemented by the exercise of self- and peer-superintendence on the part of the work force. Shaw having attempted to encourage work force self-superintendence by denying a right of recovery against the common employer, a lead followed by the courts in the subsequent cases, the court in *Albro v. Jaquith* sought to add to the incentive by denying a right of recovery against the negligent peer – the immediate perpetrator – as well. "Many of the considerations of justice and policy, which led to the adoption of the general rule, now perfectly well established, that a party who employs several persons, in the conduct of some common enterprise or undertaking, is not responsible to any one of them for the injurious consequences of the mere negligence or carelessness of the others in the performance of their respective duties, have an equal significancy and force, when applied to actions brought for like causes by one servant against another." According to Justice Merrick, for the court, "the knowledge, that no legal redress is afforded for damages occasioned by the inattention or unfaithfulness of other laborers engaged in the same common work, will naturally induce each one to be not only a strict observer of the conduct of others, but to be more prudent and careful himself." By thus encouraging increased vigilance, "the welfare and safety of all" would be promoted.[98]

The influence in these judgments of prior assumptions about the appropriate sources and conditions of industrial order seems incontestable. Yet their presence was obscured because, as we have seen, the courts' rejection of the applicability of tort concepts meant that the issue of employer liability was dealt with within a contractarian doctrinal discourse representing the relationship between injured employee and defendant employer as the product of freely exercised choice. Once the issue had been brought within this doctrinal category, the question of the actual allocation of power in the employment relationship was rendered irrelevant to the courts' determination of where responsibility for the occurrence of occupational injury should lie. Rather, questions about the allocation of authority and the imputation of responsibility in the employment relationship were transformed into questions about the character of the agreement which the individual parties, employer

---

[97] 70 Mass. 99, at 101. She, of course, remained accountable to the superintendent or any other agent to whom the employer had delegated supervisory authority, on the basis of her contract with the employer.
[98] Ibid.

and employee, were held at some prior stage to have entered into, questions which courts would answer in the event of a dispute by having reference to that agreement – and with due regard to the civil liberties enjoyed by both parties as equivalent legal subjects – but with no concern for the actual structures of domination and subordination within which, as employer and employee, the parties moved.[99] Thus construed, the employment relationship was rendered impervious to any attempt to invoke the existence of a structure of authority within the enterprise as justification for asserting the utility of building a commensurate structure of protective or compensatory duties. Instead, the courts' presumption "that employees understand and appreciate the ordinary risk and peril incident to the service in which they are to be employed" and that they "predicate the compensation they are to receive, in some measure, upon the extent of the hazard they assume" made the exercise of power in the employment relationship a thoroughly mysterious affair.[100]

RULE OR EXCEPTION? THE EVIDENCE OF NEW YORK AND PENNSYLVANIA

The implications of the Massachusetts decisions did not pass uncriticized by contemporary commentators. According to Thomas Shearman and Amasa Redfield's *Treatise on the Law of Negligence*, for example, the Massachusetts courts had been far more severe on employee litigants than courts in other jurisdictions. "We think the [Massachusetts] courts have had a tendency to narrow the remedies for negligence by technical and unsound decisions, and especially to favor corporations and employers at the expense of servants."[101] Measured against developments elsewhere, however, the Massachusetts cases were not at all atypical. Both doctrinally, as precedents, and ideologically, as a mode of reasoning, they were central to employer liability jurisprudence throughout the country.[102]

Decisions in other major Eastern industrializing states – New York and Pennsylvania – followed the Massachusetts example closely, always citing the cases decided there as leading precedents. In New York, *Farwell* was endorsed *arguendo* in 1844[103]

[99] As Horwitz puts it, in this contractarian world "the only measure of justice was the parties' own agreement" (*Transformation of American Law*, 209).

[100] *Albro v. Jacquith*, 70 Mass. 99, at 101. On the invisibility of power within the contract of employment see Alan Fox, *Beyond Contract: Work, Power, and Trust Relations* (London, 1974), 182–4.

[101] Thomas G. Shearman and Amasa A. Redfield, *A Treatise on the Law of Negligence*, 2d ed. (New York, 1870), 128.

[102] It is thus inaccurate to claim, as does Gary T. Schwartz, that the Massachusetts cases were "sharply out of line" with the law of other American jurisdictions ("The Character of Early American Tort Law," *UCLA Law Review*, 36, 4 [Apr. 1989]), 641–718, at 694).

[103] *Brown v. Maxwell*, 6 Hill 592 (1844), at 593–5. Here the injury was to a minor whose leg was broken in the course of work with several co-workers all acting under orders from a foreman. A lower court jury had found for the plaintiff, on advice from the court that the common employer was responsible for an injury arising in the course of employment supervised by the common employer's foreman. The New York Supreme Court found the lower court's directions erroneous and reversed judgment on the ground that the plaintiff was as much a party to the negligence that had caused the injury as the

and confirmed in 1851 as "part of the common law of the country."[104] As in Massachusetts, New York courts repeatedly resisted plaintiffs' requests to narrow the effect of the rule. In *Sherman v. The Rochester and Syracuse Railroad Company*,[105] for example, the plaintiff was the estate of a brakeman who had been killed in a derailment resulting from his train running into a cow while traveling at a speed of eighty miles per hour. The brakeman was required to obey the orders of the engineer or conductor. Neither had called for brakes to be applied. The court ruled that the brakeman had by his contract assumed the risk of injury from "the usual perils of the business," including the risk of negligence of co-servants, and that it was "just and reasonable to both [employer and employee], and strongly calculated to secure fidelity and prudence on the part of the servant that he should rely solely on the skill and prudence of himself and his fellow servants in the business for protection from injury." Such rules of liability "must necessarily apply as well where the employments of the servants are distinct, as to cases where they are one; and to the several grades of employments, where those in the inferior are subject to the direction and control of those in the higher grades, as to cases where all occupy a common footing and possess equal authority." If proximity or remoteness of position were to be taken into account, "where is the line? And what substantial difference is there between a case of injury from the negligence of a servant with superior authority, and one from like negligence of a servant with equal authority? ... It is manifest that no distinction or exception as to liability of the principal, resting on the inability of the injured party to protect himself in the particular case, could be made without practically abrogating the entire rule."[106] Succeeding cases confirmed that employers' immunity from liability would hold in circumstances where the injury to the employee was attributable to negligence on the part of persons in supervisory or even managerial positions,[107] where the persons held to be

---

foreman who gave the orders. The court observed that in *Farwell* a plaintiff who had been "in no sense a party to the negligent act which produced the injury" had still been held unable to recover. The court "entertain[ed] no doubt of [the] correctness" of that decision.

[104] *Coon v. The Syracuse and Utica Railroad Co.*, 5 N.Y. 492 (1851), affirming 6 Barb. 231 (1849). Here a track laborer sent onto the track in a handcar to make repairs had been run down by a track-repair train that had been dispatched without notice, without lights although running at night, and at an unusual hour. He was held unable to recover against the common employer for injury arising from negligence in the management of the train on the ground that the laborer and the managers of the train were "engaged in the same general business" (496).

[105] 17 N.Y. 153 (1858).   [106] Ibid., 156–7.

[107] In addition to *Brown v. Maxwell*, *Coon v. Syracuse and Utica*, and *Sherman v. Rochester and Syracuse*, see *Wright v. New York Central Railroad Company*, 25 N.Y. 562 (1862); *Faulkner v. The Erie Railway Company*, 49 Barb. S.C. 324 (1867); and *Warner v. The Erie Railway Company*, 39 N.Y. 468 (1868). In *Wright* the plaintiff was a brakeman injured in a collision as a result of the negligence of the train's engineer. The court held that the engineer and brakeman were fellow servants and therefore that the company was not liable for the engineer's "gross, even culpable negligence" (567). It also denied the plaintiff's other contention, that the managing agent of engineers had rendered the company liable by his negligence in employing an incompetent engineer on the run in question. Evidence given showed that the engineer had been told by the managing agent to relieve the regular engineer on a night run unfamiliar to him and that the replacement engineer had indicated that he did not feel competent to take the assignment. Nevertheless, the court rejected the plaintiff's claim that the accident was the result

369

co-servants were employed in different departments of the business with no opportunity for mutual oversight,[108] or where the injury occurred outside the immediate
scope of employment.[109] Employers would be held liable for injuries caused by
defective plant or equipment or by incompetent co-servants only where the employer's
actual negligence or misfeasance could be demonstrated in creating the defect or
failing to remedy it once known, or in selecting and retaining the incompetent
person.[110] Not until after the Civil War did New York courts begin to move toward
the adoption of a so-called vice-principal exception, which broadened employer
liability somewhat to include liability for injuries caused by the negligence of those
"standing in the place of" the employer.[111]

of the assignment of an incompetent engineer to the train, holding instead that the accident was caused
by the engineer's failure to abide by the company's running regulations and that "it required no skill
as an engineer or conductor, or experience in running a railway train" to follow instructions (569). It also
discounted the claim that the managing agent's role in assigning the engineer rendered the company
liable: "In running this particular train, to meet an emergency occasioned by sickness in the family of
the regular engineer of the train, [the managing agent] was acting as the foreman or servant of the
company, and in concert with every other person having any duty to perform in respect to it. . . . Had
he caused the trains to be run short-handed, it would have been an act of negligence on the part of one
of the servants of the company, for the consequences of which the defendants would not have been liable
to their other employees. All that [the managing agent] did upon that occasion, he did as the agent or
servant of the defendant, and there is nothing to distinguish the case from any other in which an inferior
or subordinate servant is injured by the negligence of a superior agent of the same principal or employer"
(571). In dicta (at 571) the court found "debatable" the proposition that the company owed its servants
any general responsibility to ensure the proper performance of delegated powers in the selection and
hiring of co-servants.

[108] *Coon v. Syracuse and Utica; Sherman v. Rochester and Syracuse; Russell v. The Hudson River Railroad
Company*, 17 N.Y. 134 (1858); *Boldt v. New York Central Railroad Company*, 18 N.Y. 432 (1858). In
Boldt, a laborer employed to assist in the construction of a new track parallel to the existing track was
hit as he walked to work along the new track by a train that had been switched onto the unopened new
track to avoid an obstruction on the old track. The court held that "the plaintiff who suffered and the
persons who caused the injury were in the service of one employer – the railroad company – the plaintiff
in preparing a track and the others in running trains." Had the plaintiff been injured while engaged in
repairing the old track he could have had no case, and his employment in construction of the new track
did not distinguish his situation. "He must be taken to have contracted with reference to the possibility
of cars being run on the new track, whenever it became so nearly finished as to render such running
practicable" (433–4).

[109] *Russell v. Hudson River; Boldt v. New York Central.*

[110] *Faulkner v. Erie; Warner v. Erie; Keegan v. The Western Railroad Corporation*, 8 N.Y. 175 (1853); *Ryan
v. Fowler*, 24 N.Y. 410 (1862); *Connolly v. Poillon*, 41 Barb. S.C. 366 (1864); *Loonam v. Brockway*, 3 Rob.
S.C. 74 (1864); *Kunz v. Stuart*, 1 Daly 431 (1865); *Anderson v. New Jersey Steamboat Company*, 7 Rob. S.C.
611 (1867); *Brickner v. New York Central Railroad Company*, 2 Lans. 506 (1870). In *Anderson v. New Jersey
Steamboat* it was noted that "to constitute such actual negligence or misfeasance of the principal, actual
notice to the principal of the defect in the materials or machinery through which, or the unskillfulness
or unfitness of the servant through whose negligence or unskillfulness the injury in question occurred,
must be shown" (611).

[111] Thus, in *Laning v. The New York Central Railroad Company*, 49 N.Y. 521 (1872), the court retreated
from the position it had identified with in *Wright v. New York Central*, holding that injury resulting from
the negligence of "some general agent, clothed with the power, and charged with the duty to make
performance for the master," would render the common employer liable (532). See also *Spelman v. The
Fisher Iron Company*, 56 Barb. S.C. 151 (1870). The extent and limits of this vice-principal exception were
spelled out in *Hofnagle v. The New York Central and Hudson River Railroad Company*, 55 N.Y. 608 (1874),
where the court made it clear that the imputed vice-principal would have to exercise much more than
mere supervisory or directive authority before a plaintiff could escape the fellow-servant rule: "The duty

The story was much the same in Pennsylvania, where early cases established extensive employer immunity. In *Strange v. McCormick*,[112] for example, it was held that an employer was under no legal obligation to see that machinery in use in his factory was safely constructed, nor was the employer answerable to one servant for the injurious negligence of another even where that negligence was "actual careless-ness" and the person guilty of the negligence was the manager of the factory. As far as the risk of working with defective machinery was concerned, "the law very properly presumes that every man who undertakes a business understands the char-acter of the business and of the tools and machinery with which it is to be done. . . . If the machinery is dangerous in its character, or by reason of its want of repair, a proper workman is presumed to know it at least as well as his employer, and has a right to decline the work, and if he does not, he takes the risk."[113] As to the manager's carelessness, "the manager himself is (as far as concerns the plaintiff) but one of the instruments by which the defendant carries on his business; an instrument just as likely to be defective as any of the unintelligent instruments by which the business is effected, and the persons employed are all subject to the risk of his occasional negligence and unskilfullness, and cannot transfer the risk to the em-ployer."[114] Pennsylvania courts, in short, saw no more reason than Massachusetts courts to treat employers' liability as if it could be affected by the actions of those

which [a corporate body] owed to [its employee] was to place beside him and over him competent fellow-servants, and to supply him and them, with adequate materials and appliances for the performance of any labor, which was laid upon him or them. It was liable for the negligence of a fellow-servant, who was charged by it with the performance of that duty, *and who thereby, for the occasion, stood in its place as master*. It was not liable for the negligence of a competent fellow-servant who was not thus charged, though he might have had some authority and power of direction over [the employee] and [other] servants of his grade" (610–11, emphasis supplied). On the later course of this exception see "Master and Servant," *Albany Law Journal* (11 Mar. 1876), 174–6.

[112] 3 *American Law Journal* 156 (1851).

[113] Ibid., 400. See also *Hayden v. Smithville Manufacturing Company*, 29 Conn. 548 (1861), where the plaintiff (a boy of ten years) had been injured after being caught in unfenced machinery. The court stated that "every manufacturer has the right to choose the machinery to be used in his business, and to conduct that business in the manner most agreeable to himself, provided he does not thereby violate the law of the land. He may select his appliances, and run his mill with old or new machinery . . . as he pleases. The employee having knowledge of the circumstances, and entering his service for the stipulated reward, can not complain of the peculiar taste and habits of his employer, nor sue him for damages sustained in and resulting from that peculiar service" (558).

[114] Ibid., 401. See also *Frazier v. The Pennsylvania Railroad Company*, 38 Pa. 104 (1860). Contemporary cases in New England spelled out similar views. Thus, in *Beaulieu v. The Portland Company*, 48 Me. 291 (1860), where the plaintiff had protested the danger of an assignment to his foreman but had been ordered to work and had been injured, the company was held not responsible. "They do not guaranty to their employees the faithfulness and diligence of their co-laborers in carrying on the business, or in keeping the machinery in such repair, or the works in such condition, that they shall be always safe. This is a part of the hazard which the employees impliedly assume themselves. . . . And this rule applies to all who are engaged in the common business, *whatever relation of subordination they sustain to each other* (295–6, emphasis added). See also *Hard v. The Vermont and Canada Railroad Company*, 32 Vt. 471 (1860), where the plaintiff was the estate of an engineer killed by a boiler explosion attributable to the failure of the company's master mechanic (superintendent of all locomotives) to keep the locomotive in good repair. Here the court held that the superintendent and the engineer were co-servants, and thus the company was not liable.

in whom the employer vested workplace authority.[115] As in New York, no modification of this position took place until the development after the Civil War of a limited vice-principal exception covering situations where employers delegated their "direct, personal and absolute obligation" of ordinary care – the provision of "a reasonably safe place in which to work, and reasonably safe instruments" – to an agent. Where that agent by delegation had entire charge of a business or a distinct branch of it, with complete oversight and discretion, the fellow-servant rule no longer applied in regard to the actions of the agent insofar as they impacted injuriously on employees.[116]

RULE OR EXCEPTION? THE EVIDENCE OF THE MIDWEST

Midwestern state courts also underwrote employer immunities during the 1850s and 1860s. Initially they did so with less enthusiasm than in the eastern states and with much more attention to countervailing argument.[117] The result during the 1850s was that in some midwestern jurisdictions, notably Ohio and Indiana, employers enjoyed a rather less comprehensive immunity than in the eastern states. Indeed in one state, Wisconsin, the very principle of employer immunity was fundamentally challenged. During the 1860s, however, these midwestern jurisdictions uniformly fell into line with the eastern states, expanding the realm of employer immunity and distinguishing or overruling their earlier stands as they went.

In Ohio, the first case in which an appellate court ruled on a tort claim by an injured employee against an employer was *Little Miami Railroad v. John Stevens*.[118] Stevens was an engineer injured in a train collision caused by a schedule variation.

[115] And see *Ryan v. The Cumberland Valley Railroad Company*, 23 Penn. St. R. 384 (1854) (common laborers and engineers/conductors are co-servants); *Weger v. Pennsylvania Railroad Company*, 55 Pa. 460 (1867) (track laborers and foremen are co-servants); *Delaware and Hudson Canal Co. v. Carroll*, 86 Pa. 374 (1879), and *Waddell and Walter v. Simoson*, 112 Pa. 567 (1886) (miners and mine bosses are co-servants); *Lewis v. Seifert*, 116 Pa. 628 (1887) (train dispatcher and locomotive engineer are co-servants). This was also the case in Maryland. See *O'Connell v. Baltimore and Ohio R.R. Co.*, 83 American Decisions 549 (1863) (common laborer and engineer are co-servants). In *Lewis v. Seifert*, at 646, the court summarized the rule in Pennsylvania as follows, showing its extent and limits to be much the same as summarized for New York in *Hofnagle*: "To constitute fellow-servants the employees need not be at the same time engaged in the same particular work. It is sufficient if they are in the employment of the same master, engaged in the same common work and performing duties and services for the same general purpose. The rule is the same, although the one injured may be inferior in grade, and is subject to the direction and control of the superior whose act caused the injury, provided they are both co-operating to effect the same common object."

[116] *Lewis v. Seifert*, 647. And see *Mullen v. Philadelphia and Southern Steamship Company*, 78 Pa. 25 (1875) stating: "Where a master places the entire charge of his business, or a distinct part of it, in the hands of an agent, exercising no discretion and no oversight of his own, it is manifest that the neglect by the agent of ordinary care in supplying and maintaining suitable instrumentalities for the work required, is a breach of duty for which the master should be held answerable" (32).

[117] In *Pittsburg, Fort Wayne and Chicago Railway Company v. Devinney*, 17 Ohio St. R. 198 (1867), at 212, this early tendency to follow a distinct trajectory on the matter was attributed to local antagonism to "railways and other rich and powerful corporations."

[118] 20 Ohio 416 (1851).

The railroad superintendent had passed word of the variation to the conductor, who was in overall charge of the train's operation, but neither had informed the engineer. In the lower court trial Stevens recovered a verdict of $3,700 damages against the railroad, which appealed on the ground that it was not liable for any injury to Stevens occurring as a result of the conductor's negligence. The Ohio Supreme Court, however, upheld the verdict. According to Caldwell J., the railroad was obligated to show "care and prudence in the management of [its] business." Such risks as were assumed by employees did not extend to risks arising from negligence, particularly the negligence of those placed in authority by the company. Nor was Caldwell impressed by the policy argument of enhanced safety through the encouragement of mutual policing on the part of employees. "It is a matter of universal observation, that in any extensive business, where many persons are employed, the care and prudence of the employer is the surest guaranty against mismanagement of any kind. The employer would, we think, be much more likely to be careless of the persons of those in his employ, since his own safety is not endangered by any accident, when he would understand that he was not pecuniarily liable for the careless conduct of his agents. Indeed, we think that those who have others in their employ are under peculiar obligations to them to provide for their safety and comfort, and we think they should at least be held legally responsible to them as much as to a stranger."[119]

Neither of Caldwell's colleagues on the court was prepared to go to the same extent in denying the employer's immunity.[120] One, Spalding J., dissented strongly, citing *Murray, Priestley, Farwell*, and numerous New York decisions, endorsing both their legal and their policy rationales, and urging that "the solemn adjudications of courts of recognized authority should be followed, unless not applicable to our condition."[121] The other, Hitchcock C. J., concurred only to the extent of excepting *Little Miami* from the rule created by those decisions, which he otherwise endorsed, on the grounds that the railroad superintendent had shown negligence in failing to ensure that the engineer was told of the schedule change. That concurrence, however, committed Ohio well in advance of other states to a broad vice-principal exception to the fellow-servant rule.

The extent of the exception was revealed in Ohio's next appellate case, *Cleveland, Columbus and Cincinnati Railroad Company v. Keary*.[122] Here a brakeman had sued for an injury received in a collision caused by the negligence of the conductor of the train upon which he was employed. The court confirmed his suit, holding that

---

[119] Ibid., 432, 434. One could, Caldwell admitted, suppose a case "where two persons employed by the same individual, and standing on a perfect equality – where the business was managed as much by one as the other – where they would stand on the same footing as men in the community generally do – in which the employer would not be liable for an injury done to one by the negligence of the other" (435–6). But this was not such a case.

[120] Caldwell acknowledged that the reasoning in *Murray* and *Farwell* covered the circumstances in *Little Miami* but argued that those cases were "contrary to the general principles of law and justice" and should not be followed (ibid., 436).

[121] Ibid., 438–53, esp. 440, 450.   [122] 3 Ohio St. R. 202 (1854).

having made the brakeman answerable to the authority of the conductor, the company was itself answerable to him for the conductor's negligence in exercising that authority.

[The plaintiff] engaged to serve the company in the capacity of brakeman, and to submit in all things to the orders and control of the conductor who might be placed over him by the company, and put in charge of the train. While performing his duties faithfully, in accordance with his contract, he is injured by the carelessness of the conductor, to whose control he has been subjected by the company. He had no power to determine who this conductor should be, and no right to control or participate in the duties which the company had devolved upon the conductor. He had, by his contract, promised obedience; and this the company had a right to require, and they received it.

The quid pro quo of the employee's obedience was the employer's liability for the acts of those placed in positions of command – in this case, the conductor. "His will alone controls everything, and it is the will of the owner that his intelligence alone should be trusted for this purpose." Employees bound to obey the orders of the superior placed over them, and performing as directed, could not be made to bear losses arising from the superior's carelessness "until we are prepared to say that justice and public policy require the consequences of duty omitted by one party to be visited upon the other, although stripped of all power to prevent such consequences."[123]

Ohio's vice-principal exception thus made the employer liable for the negligence of all those placed in positions of authority. This was a striking expansion of liability when compared with contemporary eastern state doctrine, and a much broader statement of employer responsibility than that to which those states would move in the 1870s with their vice-principal rule.[124] Yet at the same time *Keary* also stilled any doubts that Ohio had adopted the fellow-servant principle. Unlike Caldwell in *Little Miami*, the court did not disparage but rather endorsed precedents from elsewhere. It professed "to administer the common law of England, in so far as its principles are not inconsistent with the genius and spirit of our own institutions." *Priestley, Farwell*, et al. were all cases well decided, and by courts for which the Ohio Supreme Court entertained "the highest respect."[125] Indeed, so clearly did the *Keary* court place itself behind the fellow-servant principle that Warden J., the trial court judge in *Little Miami* and now a member of the Supreme Court bench, was moved to offer a qualified dissent. English master and servant law had denied an employer's liability, he argued, because it was a law developed out of the relationship of master and menial, of superior and inferior, a relationship governed by principles of paternal intimacy and benevolence, not of legal right. To follow that rule was hence to endorse the application of a law for menial servants to all employment relationships, greatly damaging the rights of employees. The "policy" arguments articulated in *Farwell* for

[123] Ibid., 208, 211, 219.
[124] See above, nn. 107, 111, 114–6 and accompanying text, and compare.
[125] 3 Ohio St. R. 202 (1854), 205–6, 212.

so doing were specious. As far as the notion that wages included a "risk-premium" was concerned, "the rate of compensation in dangerous employments, and the well-known motives of inclination or necessity which cause men to undertake them, are against such a supposition." As to mutual policing, "in the instance of an equal such watchfulness would be fruitless unless it were accompanied by tale bearing; and what an equal would disdain to do, an inferior would not dare to attempt – while no officer in command would submit to such conduct in an inferior." Even the Ohio court's vice-principal exception was nonsense, for all employees from highest to lowest acted as the employer's agents, not simply those given some authority over others. Because all acted in pursuit of the common employer's interests, the common employer should be held liable for the negligence of *anyone* into whose hands, in the course of doing business, the circumstances of employment had placed "the power of doing hurt."[126]

Succeeding cases confirmed that Ohio was still marching to the same drummer as the eastern states. In *Mad River and Lake Erie Railroad Company v. Barber*,[127] a conductor injured by freight cars that ran out of control as a consequence of insufficient brakemen and faulty brakes was held to have assumed the risk of running the cars with insufficient brakemen and, through his negligence when inspecting the cars for defects, to have contributed to his own injury. The company was liable for a failure to show ordinary care, but if the agent continued in the business of the company knowing of its failure to show ordinary care, he waived his own rights and took the risk on himself.[128] In *Whaalan v. Mad River and Lake Erie Railroad Company*,[129] the court found that a track laborer injured by a log thrown from a passing locomotive by a tender-hand was the fellow servant of the tender-hand and thus could not recover damages against the common employer, notwithstanding their employment in distinct departments of the railroad. In *Manville v. The Cleveland and Toledo Railroad Company*,[130] a conductor injured by the negligence of other employees while traveling to take charge of a train was held to be within the scope of his employment and therefore unable to recover against the common employer. As in *Whaalan*, the conductor in *Manville* was held to be in the "common service" with other employees in the performance of "active operations" upon the railroad. The court acknowledged that the concept of "common service" could and did encompass "servants somewhat disconnected in their respective duties" yet refused to allow such disconnection to interfere with its application of the fellow-servant rule.[131] A similar result transpired in *Columbus and Xenia Railroad Company v. Webb*,[132] where the estate of a brakeman killed in a fall from his train caused by a defective brake

---

[126] Ibid., 219–29, at 225, 226.   [127] 5 Ohio St. R. 541 (1856).
[128] Ibid., 564.   [129] 8 Ohio St. R. 250 (1858).
[130] 11 Ohio St. R. 417 (1860).
[131] Ibid., 425. "In this sense, those employed in facilitating the running of the trains, by ballasting the track, removing obstructions, or keeping guard to prevent obstructions, and those employed at stations, attending to switches, and other duties of a like nature upon the road, as well as those upon the trains, operating, may all be well regarded as fellow servants in the common service" (426).
[132] 12 Ohio St. R. 475 (1861).

was found to have no right of recovery against the company, the detection and repair of defects being the responsibility of co-servants, for whose negligence the company could not be held responsible. The court's statement of the degree of care owed by the company confirmed its headlong retreat from the broad principle of publicly accountable responsibility articulated by Caldwell in *Little Miami* to the vague standard of industry practice long since endorsed in the East:

> It is hardly necessary, or practicable, to state the degree of care due from the company in this case to the brakeman. It can only be correctly expressed by saying, that it was incumbent upon the company to use all that care and precaution for the safety of the brakeman, that might reasonably be expected of a railroad company on the part of an intelligent brakeman acquainted with the care and precaution used by other well-conducted railroad companies in like cases.[133]

Finally, in *Pittsburgh, Fort Wayne and Chicago Railway Company v. Devinney*,[134] the Ohio court disowned its own extensive vice-principal exception. A brakeman injured in a collision between two trains occasioned by the negligence of the conductor of the other train was held to have no recourse against the common employer. Without formally overruling the earlier Ohio decisions that had established employers' responsibility for the acts of those they had put in authority, the court defined the law to be settled according to precedents from England, Massachusetts, New York, and Pennsylvania, and set out to rejoin what it quite clearly regarded as a jurisprudential mainstream from which earlier decisions in the state had foolishly and inexplicably deviated:

> The true general rule is, and so it must be, that when men are employed for the prosecution of a lawful but hazardous business, they assume the hazards of such employment arising from the negligence of co-employees, and stipulate for compensation according to their estimate of such hazards; subject, however, to this exception, that the master is liable for such injuries as accrued to the servant from the negligence of a fellow-servant in the selection of whom the master has been culpably negligent; and to this we in Ohio have added the further exception of a case where the servant injured is subordinate to, and acting under the orders of the culpable fellow-servant.
>
> For the reasoning on which the decisions establishing this exception are based, the members of this court, as now constituted, are not responsible; nor are we at all bound to carry out their logic to its ultimate consequences . . . we have already diverged from the general current of judicial decision elsewhere. A majority of the court are unwilling to increase the divergence.[135]

---

[133] Ibid., 497. The employer was "in no sense, from the relation they so sustain to each other, a warrantor of the safety of the employee" (495). According to precedents quoted by the court, the extent of the employer's duty went no further than providing equipment it believed to be reasonably safe and selecting competent fellow servants to attend to its upkeep (490–5).

[134] 17 Ohio St. R. 198 (1867).

[135] Ibid., 212–13. As Welch J. put it in dissent, the majority's decision in *Devinney* "does not overrule the former Ohio decisions on the subject . . . yet it narrows the ground upon which they stand, so as to make them utterly indefensible" (213).

A similar story may be told in Indiana. Here the court's immunization of employers was conditioned by its adoption of a "different-departments" exception similar to that contended for, unsuccessfully, by plaintiffs in many eastern states. The issue arose in Indiana's first appellate-level employer liability case, *Gillenwater v. Madison and Indianapolis Railroad*, in 1854.[136] In *Gillenwater*, the plaintiff was a house carpenter employed by the railroad to build a bridge. He was injured by the derailment of a train carrying timbers for the bridge, upon which he had been traveling with the company's consent. The Indiana Supreme Court held that "the business of a house-carpenter, even as applied to the specific case of building a railroad bridge, is an employment under the company, too remote to be embraced within the rule laid down in [*Farwell*]." So clear was the distinction that the court felt under no obligation "either to approve or dissent from the doctrine there held." Its opinion, however, was overall cool toward adoption of the fellow-servant rule and was clearly influenced by the Ohio court's decision in *Little Miami*, which it cited as a rejection of the rule.[137]

Indiana's coolness lasted only a few months, and in *Madison and Indianapolis Railroad Company v. Bacon*,[138] the Supreme Court adopted the fellow-servant rule. There had been no repudiation of the rule in Ohio, it now noted, but only "the *dictum* of a single judge."[139] All other courts that had considered the rule had endorsed it. As a matter of policy the rule was justified as an encouragement of mutual policing; its tendency was to make employees "anxious and watchful, and interested for the faithful conduct of each other, and careful to induce it." It worked no hardship on the employee "because his entering upon the service is voluntary, is with a knowledge of its hazards, and with a power and right to demand such wages as he shall deem compensatory."

For the time being, affirmation of the rule did not mean abandonment of the Indiana court's *Gillenwater* doctrine. Thus in *Fitzpatrick v. Albany and Salem Railroad Company*,[140] the court found the company liable to a plaintiff laborer injured in a collision while traveling to work on the company's gravel cars. The collision was found to be the result of negligence on the part of the gravel train's engineer. The court held that the circumstances of the case brought the laborer within the *Gillenwater* exception. "His employment – that of loading and unloading the cars – at once shows that he had no connection with or control in the movement of the train. The plaintiff could not, therefore, have contributed to produce the injury."[141] Three years later, however, the court significantly narrowed the effect of its exception

---

[136] 5 Ind. 339 (1854).   [137] Ibid., 346–7.

[138] 6 Ind. 205 (1855).

[139] Ibid., 208. The court blamed its erroneous interpretation of *Little Miami* in its *Gillenwater* decision on the editors of *American Railway Cases*, who had incorrectly cited *Little Miami* as a repudiation of the fellow-servant rule (207).

[140] 7 Ind. 436 (1856).

[141] Ibid., 438–9. The court also denied that the plaintiff could be held to have contracted to assume the risk of injuries where these were the result of the "gross negligence and unskilful conduct" of an agent acting outside the scope of the plaintiff's oversight (439).

when it found that a plaintiff in virtually identical circumstances to those pertaining in *Fitzpatrick* could not recover. This case, *Ohio and Mississippi Railroad Company v. Tindall*,[142] involved a laborer killed in a derailment while riding on the company's gravel cars. The derailment was found to have been caused by the engineer's carelessness. In *Gillenwater* and *Fitzpatrick* the court had premissed the plaintiffs' recovery on their separation from control of the movement of the trains whose accidents had injured them, but in *Tindall* the court held that the laborer and the engineer were "engaged in the same general undertaking." Its opinion clearly demonstrated a desire to conform its findings to the Massachusetts case *Gillshannon v. Stony Brook*. Of its own *Fitzpatrick* decision it stated without elaboration that the decision was distinguishable. Indiana's effective abandonment of its *Gillenwater* doctrine came three years later in *Wilson v. Madison &c. R.R. Co.*,[143] where a yardman injured while uncoupling a freight car was held to be "in the same general undertaking as the engineer and conductor having charge of the cars" whose negligence had caused his injury. Citing *Gillshannon v. Stony Brook* as the leading case, the court declared the question of the company's liability "conclusively settled." The court also cited *Whaalan* and three New York cases, but failed to mention any of its own previous decisions on the subject.[144]

The Indiana different-departments exception thus followed the same course as the Ohio vice-principal (or "superior-servant") exception.[145] In each case a strong initial statement qualifying the immunity of employers in liability suits by attending to the realities of industrial structure and circumstance was progressively diluted until it ceased to have any effect. Confronted with the accumulating weight of English and American precedent interpreting employer immunities broadly, both courts exhibited a striking desire to conform themselves to juridical authority elsewhere rather than persist in putatively idiosyncratic deviations of their own.[146]

This tendency to retreat from the dictates of circumstance in the face of doctrine was even more strikingly illustrated by the behavior of the Wisconsin Supreme Court in its consideration of the fellow-servant rule. The issue initially came before the court somewhat indirectly in 1858 in the case *Chamberlain v. Milwaukee & Mississippi Railroad Co.*[147] The case involved an express messenger whose business

---

[142] 13 Ind. 366 (1859).

[143] 18 Ind. 226 (1862). [144] Ibid., 230.

[145] The two "exceptions" were closely related in that circumstantially authority and functional separation usually went hand in hand. This is demonstrated, for example, in *Wilson v. Madison*. The Indiana court was not confronted with a request for a ruling explicitly on the vice-principal issue until 1864, when a brakeman sued for an injury incurred while acting under the direct supervision of his conductor. In that case, *Thayer v. St. Louis Alton and Terre Haute R.R. Co.*, 22 Ind. 26, the court denied the plaintiff's claim, again on the grounds that brakeman and conductor were "engaged in the same undertaking" (29). By that time the court's doubt that an employee by contract assumed the risk of the negligence of co-employees had long since abated.

[146] On the force of precedent in the fellow-servant cases, see Marston, "Creation of a Common Law Rule," 579–620. Marston, unfortunately, significantly exaggerates the deviationist tendencies of the Ohio and Indiana courts by discussing only the cases which established their deviations and not those in which the courts subsequently abandoned them (605–13).

[147] 7 Wisc. 367 (1858).

made him a regular passenger on the company's trains. Just prior to setting off on a trip from Milwaukee to Madison aboard a freight train he was asked if he would stand in as an emergency brakeman in return for payment. During the trip the messenger was injured and brought suit against the company. The lower court instructed the jury that if it considered he had been injured by the negligence of those operating the train, he was entitled to recover, but also that if the jury considered him a fellow servant of those in charge of the train, he could not recover. The jury found for the plaintiff, and the company appealed the sufficiency of the lower court's instructions. The Supreme Court found error in some of the lower court's instructions but left the fellow-servant instruction undisturbed and uncriticized. The case was then sent down for a new trial.

The new trial resulted in *Chamberlain*'s prompt reappearance before the Supreme Court,[148] this time on appeal by the plaintiff against instructions to the jury that had resulted in a decision for the defendant. Again the Supreme Court reversed the lower court, and ordered a second new trial. If the plaintiff were considered a passenger, the court stated, he could not be held negligent simply because (this was the company's contention) he had agreed to expose himself to risk by acting as an emergency brakeman. More important, the court now held, even if he were considered a servant of the company, the plaintiff could still recover, unless he had himself been personally negligent in discharging the duties he had agreed to perform. Denying that it had endorsed the fellow-servant rule in its earlier *Chamberlain* decision, the court held the proper rule was that "having set a force in motion for their own benefit [the company] are bound to see that it is conducted with proper care and skill, so as not to injure others." It thus held the fellow-servant rule incorrect as contrary to reason and justice. As long as not *actually at fault* themselves, employees could maintain actions against their employers for injuries arising from the negligence of other employees.

The Wisconsin Supreme Court considered the efforts of the Ohio and Indiana courts to craft exceptions rather than reject the rule outright and found them incoherent. The different-departments exception provided no basis on which to draw the lines where difference was established. After all, distinct duties fell to different employees within the same "department" of service. "Can it be maintained that [the company] may, through their engineer, so negligently manage the engine, as to mangle the brakemen and all their other servants on the train, and yet be entirely irresponsible" simply because all were judged within the same "department"?[149] As to the vice-principal or superior servant, exception, the Wisconsin court simply repeated Judge Warden's critique of the majority opinion in Ohio's *Keary* decision six years earlier. *All* employees were the agents of the company, not simply those in authority. If a company chose to manage the force it had set in motion by giving directions through a figure placed in authority over others, and he was negligent, that was the company's negligence: It had failed in its duty and

---

[148] *Chamberlain v. Mil. & Miss. R.R. Co.*, 11 Wisc. 238 (1860).   [149] Ibid., 252–3.

should be responsible. "But . . . is it not equally clear that, in order to manage the force which they have set in motion properly, that proper directions must be properly *executed* as well as *given*? This is too obvious for question. Can the same court which has said to one brakeman that the company is bound so to manage the force it sets in motion, as not to injure him by negligence, and has given him a judgment for the negligence of the conductor, with any consistency say to another who has been injured by the negligence of the engineer, that he cannot recover, because he was not subordinate?"[150]

If these courts' attempts to craft exceptions were incoherent, in the Wisconsin court's opinion, so were the justifications that other courts had offered for the existence of the fellow-servant rule. The servant was said to assume all risks contractually, but as the Indiana court had well said, the negligence of others should not be counted among the ordinary risks incident to any employment. Nor was the public policy argument for the necessity of encouraging mutual supervision any more worthy of respect:

The only possible ground upon which it could rest, would be the supposition that employees upon railroads and other improvements which the public use, would be more vigilant to prevent injuries from the negligence of each other, if they knew they could not recover damages against the company, than they would with the opposite belief. But this notion is based upon a false estimate of the motives which govern human action. The lives and limbs of these employees are at hazard along with those of the public, and all human experience and consciousness, abundantly testify that to the motives which these furnish, the right to an action for damages could add nothing.

Considerations of public policy led, rather, to completely opposite conclusions. First, "*employees are a portion of the public*, and the safety of the rest not requiring it, there can be no just reason for excluding them from that protection, which it is the policy of the law to furnish to every one, against injury by the negligence of others." Second, "by just so much as the liability of the employer for the negligence of his servants is reduced, by just so much are the motives diminished which induce him to employ servants of the greatest skill and vigilance. And if from this relaxation, negligent servants are employed, the public at large, as well as the other employees, run the hazard of the calamities arising from it."[151]

The result of the second new trial in Chamberlain's suit against the Milwaukee & Mississippi Railroad is not recorded, but one may presume Chamberlain was successful. The general issue was revisited for a third time within a few months, however, in the unrelated case *Mosely v. Chamberlain.*[152] Here the plaintiff was the administratrix of the estate of her son, Willis Mosely, a baggageman on the La Crosse

---

[150] Ibid., 256 (emphasis supplied).   [151] Ibid., 253, 253–4 (emphasis supplied).

[152] 18 Wisc. 731 (1861). The report of this case did not appear until 1865, when it was issued as an appendix to the state reports. The case is erroneously identified in Marston's "Creation of a Common Law Rule," 215, as a further step in the saga of *Chamberlain v. Milwaukee & Mississippi.* In fact, the railroad involved in *Moseley v. Chamberlain* was the La Crosse and Milwaukee; the defendant, Chamberlain, was operating the road at the time as mortgagee in possession.

and Milwaukee Railroad who had been crushed to death in an accident. The lower court jury had found for the plaintiff, and the defendant appealed citing a technical jurisdictional issue and the fellow-servant rule. When it came to the latter the Wisconsin Supreme Court once again reversed itself, overruling *Chamberlain* and falling into line with other jurisdictions. The court was not unanimous – nor had it been in *Chamberlain v. Mil. & Miss* – and the majority in favor of the rule was created by Chief Justice Dixon's decision to switch sides. Dixon gave little time to a further discussion of the issue. His own views on the matter, he said, had not changed. His reasons for changing his vote lay in "that deference and respect which is always due to the enlightened and well considered opinions of others ... the almost unanimous judgments of all the courts both of England and this country." Against this "unbroken current of judicial opinion," the Wisconsin Supreme Court could not stand alone. *Chamberlain v. Mil. & Miss.*, said the chief justice, "must be overruled." Like Indiana and Ohio, Wisconsin had rejoined the pack.

CONCLUSION

And so it went. Elsewhere in the Midwest, courts adopted doctrinal positions protective of employer immunities with little dissent.[153] Southern courts also had little trouble with the fellow-servant rule in abstract, though almost uniformly they found it impossible, because of the peculiarities of their situation, to apply the rule "to any other than free white agents."[154] North Carolina was the only partial exception, allowing in *Ponton v. Wilmington and Weldon R.R. Co.*[155] that a slaveowner who had hired out his slave to another could not seek compensation for the slave's injury or death resulting from the negligence of another servant of the hirer. Unlike other southern judges, it has been said in explanation, North Carolina's chief justice, Thomas Ruffin, was a great judge who saw himself aligned with a national legal culture rather than a sectional culture. "He may very well have been unable to break

---

[153] See, e.g., *Honner v. Illinois Central Railroad Company*, 15 Ill. 550 (1854); *Illinois Central Railroad Company v. Cox*, 21 Ill. 20 (1858); *Michigan Central Railroad Company v. Leahey*, 10 Mich. 193 (1862); *Davis v. Detroit and Milwaukee Rail Road Company*, 20 Mich. 105 (1870); *Sullivan v. Mississippi and Missouri Railroad Company*, 11 Iowa 421 (1860); *Hoben v. Burlington and Missouri River Railroad Company*, 20 Iowa 562 (1866).

[154] *Scudder v. Woodbridge*, 1 Ga. 195 (1846), at 198. See also *Shields v. Yonge*, 15 Ga. 349 (1854). Legislatures in both regions were less prepared to concede employer immunity. Georgia (1855), Iowa (1862), Wyoming Territory (1869), and Kansas (1874), all adopted legislation attributing liability to employers, although only in regard to railroads and then only where the injured employee was innocent of any taint of contributory negligence. Courts responded by zealously protecting employees' rights to absolve their employers from liability by contracting out, a position they also pursued with respect to the limited common law intrusions on immunity represented by the eastern states' development of their narrow vice-principal exception in the 1870s. On post–Civil War developments in employer liability, see Charles W. McCurdy, "The Roots of 'Liberty of Contract' Reconsidered: Major Premises in the Law of Employment, 1867–1937," *Supreme Court Historical Society Yearbook*, 1984, 20–33, at 30–3.

[155] 51 N.C. 245 (1858). See also *Heathcock v. Pennington*, 33 N.C. 640 (1850).

from the *Farwell* precedent, simply because all other major courts . . . seemed to follow it."[156]

Across the country, as courts endorsed employer immunity, they also endorsed the reasoning that explained and justified it. Employers were not omniscient, said the Supreme Court of Ohio; it was unreasonable to hold them responsible where the negligence of one employee resulted in injury to another. "And if it be a crime, or *quasi* crime, as some who argue the question of the master's responsibility seem unconsciously to intimate, to put in operation the tremendous and dangerous enginery and natural forces which modern civilization has discovered, invented and applied, it is surely a sufficient answer to a claim of responsibility on that ground against the employer, on the part of the employee, that the latter is a voluntary *particeps criminis*."[157] Had the law made it a duty of the master to indemnify his servants against injury, asked the Supreme Court of Pennsylvania? Such a duty would be "substantially one of protection,which cannot exist without implying the correlative one of dependence or subjection." Such was not the relation of master and servant in America. "Both are equal before the law, and considered equally competent to take care of themselves." Employees were free actors, equals in a mutually designed relationship. They might therefore reasonably be held responsible for the consequences of their decision to enter. To immunize the servant against the ordinary dangers of his occupation "would violate a law of nature."[158]

In its invocation of the virtues of abstention, its perception that protection meant "a sacrifice of liberty on the part of those intended to be protected,"[159] the Pennsylvania Supreme Court was powerfully expressing the centrality of one kind of labor freedom – freedom as contractual liberty, as self-ownership – to its conception of the employment relationship and the equality of the parties therein. Nor should one doubt even for a moment the court's genuine belief that abstention was socially more appropriate than protection. Yet its claim that liberty of contract of itself guaranteed equality sat oddly with its equally strong commitment to the presumption that employment was a relationship of inequality and subjection, requiring fidelity, obedience, and sacrifice of control on the part of the employee[160] – a presumption, as we have seen, that echoes throughout the case law of the first half of the nineteenth century. The superior-servant exception was one, somewhat half-hearted response to this contradiction, but one that, in fact, robbed employees of civic personality by making their rights hostage to their willing participation in a private world of unilateral employer-promulgated rules. "The servant will be allowed his action," wrote Ohio's Welch J., dissenting in *Devinney* in forlorn attempt to maintain the superior-servant exception in the face of the majority's abandonment

---

[156] Finkelman, "Slaves as Fellow Servants," 304. On Ruffin see also Tushnet, *American Law of Slavery*.
[157] *Pittsburgh, Fort Wayne and Chicago Railway Company v. Devinney*, 212.
[158] *Ryan v. Cumberland Valley Railroad Company*, 386, 387.   [159] Ibid., 388.
[160] Indeed, as we have seen, while proclaiming that the equality of master and servant was ensured by their exercise of freedom of contract, the Pennsylvania Supreme Court was quite willing to imply asymmetrical duties into the contract, notably the duty of the employee to obey commands.

of it, "in such cases, when it appears he could not have participated, or interfered to prevent the injury, without a *breach of duty*; in other words, where he could not have done so without going out of his proper *sphere of action*, and thus violating the *rules and regulations* of the business – which are nothing more or less than the *laws of his employer*." To go out of his proper sphere of action would be an act of "*insubordination*," laying the servant open to his employer's correction. "His business lies within the circle prescribed for him by the laws of his employer. . . . As long as he remains within it and does his duty *there*, his employer is bound to protect and indemnify him."[161] But why should employees' rights be thus contingent? Were employees not, as had been asserted in Wisconsin, "a portion of the public"? If injured while pursuing their employer's interests, should they not be entitled to full recompense without more ado?

As critics on both sides of the fellow-servant rule argued, modifications like superior-servant and different-departments were incoherent. The courts that developed them discarded them. The courts that resisted the full logic of the rule bowed to the majority that enforced it. In justifying their conformity, courts found refuge in the rule's portrayal of a voluntaristic workplace, in its blend of contract reasoning, with its injury premium and freely bargained allocation of risk, and social policy reasoning, with its population of self-willed workers exercising a manly mutual police. Yet the constant companion of these, as we have seen, was a consciousness of the necessities of power. It was "right and proper," said the Illinois court, that one servant should not recover against the common master for the negligence of others. Each had contracted according to a calculation of the hazards of the particular service to be performed. Each had to be encouraged to check that all co-servants did their duty "with proper care and fidelity" and to report to the principal those who did not. "This will make them all prompt and vigilant, and their master's interest be closely interwoven with their own." Were this not so, "no great enterprises could be safely undertaken and carried on, nor would there exist that vigilance and care on the part of the employed, which is so vital to their success."[162] Indeed, authority untrammeled by the restraint of legal responsibility for the consequences of its exercise was the bottom line. "If this were [not] the rule, it would embarrass the conduct of all business, where any risk is to be run," said the Supreme Court of Pennsylvania in *Ryan v. The Cumberland Valley Railroad Company*. "How could a sailor be ordered aloft in a storm, without the employers being liable to the charge that the captain had shown want of proper skill and care in giving such an order in the circumstances?"[163] How indeed?

As we have seen throughout this book, from the early years of the republic the equalitarian discourse of civic society existed side-by-side with significant and growing disparities of power in the social relations of production and employment. In part, those disparities emanated from the asymmetry of monetary exchange that

---

[161] *Pittsburg, Fort Wayne and Chicago Railway Company v. Devinney*, 214 (emphasis in original).
[162] *Illinois Central Railroad Company v. Cox*, 26–7.
[163] *Ryan v. The Cumberland Valley Railroad Company*, 388.

undermined the possibility of substantive equality in the wage bargain. But they also emanated from the asymmetries inscribed on the subjects employer/master and employee/servant in American law, asymmetries that the courts, in the name of contractual freedom or social necessity, refused to mediate.

Working people were thereby doubly disadvantaged. For them, the symmetry promised in the republic's revolutionary claim of civic equality outside the employment relationship always became asymmetry within. Contrary to the brave but lonely and ultimately futile stance of the Wisconsin Supreme Court, employees, considered as such, were not "a portion of the public" at all. People at work were not citizens but servants. By midcentury, they were already fast disappearing into the legal black hole whose all-encompassing existence was to become the central fact of modern working life.[164]

[164] The "black hole" metaphor is suggested by James Gray Pope, "Labor and the Constitution: From Abolition to Deindustrialization," *Texas Law Review*, 65, 6 (May 1987), 1071–136, describing the absence of constitutional protections for labor protest. Pope attributes the black hole to "the commodity theory of labor dominant during the *Lochner* era." My argument in this book suggests some strong common law foundations dating from rather earlier in the republic's history.

Epilogue: "free Ameriky"

"You, my worthy friend, to my concern, have reflected upon the government under which you live and suffer. Where is your patriotism? Where your gratitude? True, the charitable may find something in your case, as you put it, partly to account for such reflections as coming from you. Still, be the facts how they may, your reflections are none the less unwarrantable. . . . [W]hile in general efficacious to happiness, the world's law may yet, in some cases, have, to the eye of reason, an unequal operation, just as, in the same imperfect view, some inequalities may appear in the operations of heaven's law; nevertheless, to one who has a right confidence, final benignity is, in every instance, as sure with the one law as the other. I expound the point at some length, because these are the considerations, my poor fellow, which, weighed as they merit, will enable you to sustain with unimpaired trust the apparent calamities which are yours."

"What do you talk your hog-latin to me for?" cried the cripple. . . .

"To mere reason your case looks something piteous, I grant. But never despond; many things – the choicest – yet remain. You breathe this bounteous air, are warmed by this gracious sun, and, though poor and friendless, indeed, nor so agile as in your youth, yet, how sweet to roam, day by day, through the groves, plucking the bright mosses and flowers, till forlornness itself becomes a hilarity, and, in your innocent independence, you skip for joy."

"Fine skipping with these, 'ere horse-posts – ha ha!"

Herman Melville, *The Confidence Man*

Some months prior to the election of 1840, there appeared in the *Boston Quarterly Review* what has been described as "one of the most remarkable of the documents of Jacksonian democracy."[1] The document was Orestes Brownson's essay "The Laboring Classes,"[2] a lengthy rumination on the debased condition of wage labor in America inspired by the publication in Boston earlier that year of Thomas Carlyle's *Chartism*, a similar disquisition on wage labor in England. Brownson and Carlyle had much in common[3] – just how much would become clearer in succeeding years

[1] Arthur M. Schlesinger, Jr., *The Age of Jackson* (Boston, 1953), 299.

[2] *Boston Quarterly Review*, 3 (July 1840), 348–95. The article was republished as a pamphlet, *The Laboring Classes, An Article from the Boston Quarterly Review* (Boston, 1840). All references are to the pamphlet version.

[3] Like Carlyle, Brownson consistently lamented the retreat of metaphysics in the face of materialism.

as the mature Brownson turned from the passionate radicalism of his youth to the profession of an austerely conservative social organicism.[4] But in 1840 Brownson's democratic convictions still burned with an intensity that made Carlyle's sophistic disquiet at the course of modern life seem in comparison somewhat effete. In "The Laboring Classes," Brownson far outstripped his Scottish counterpart both in the urgency with which he denounced the deteriorating prospects confronting working people and in the conviction with which he advocated regenerative remedies of the most fundamental kind.

Throughout the world, Brownson wrote, desperation and deprivation were the lot of wageworkers. Everywhere they were poor and depressed, rewarded in inverse proportion to the amount of service they performed, worn out in health, spirit, and morals through incessant exploitation by their employers.[5] Americans might fancy their society the exception – and indeed in America history and material abundance had combined to allow wage labor to be experienced "under its most favorable aspects," had made it "as good as it can be," had allowed it to reach "all the excellence of which it is susceptible." Yet even in America the story was one of physical and moral decline. "The actual condition of the working-man today, viewed in all its bearings, is not so good as it was fifty years ago." Once, given reasonable health and industrious habits, "almost any man might aspire to competence and independence." But no longer. "The wilderness has receded, and already the new lands are beyond the reach of the mere laborer, and the employer has him at his mercy." In America as elsewhere, "if the present relation subsist, we see nothing better for him in reserve than what he now possesses, but something altogether worse."[6]

Polemicizing against the wages system, which exploited labor by denying it both opportunity and capacity to attain competence, Brownson also attacked particular social institutions – principally, organized religion and the laws of inheritance – which in his analysis were preventing working people from realizing independence by starving them of the spiritual and material resources necessary to its accomplishment. His answer was not the cautious amelioration proposed by Carlyle (universal education to improve them and general emigration to get rid of them) but an altogether more dramatic set of remedies: a decisive shot of spiritual energy through mass recommitment to the unmediated and radically egalitarian "Christianity of Christ," to be followed by massive majoritarian democratic reform. That is, having aroused all minds to the need for reform, having "quickened in all souls the moral power to live for it or die for it," resort was to be had to government – "the agent of society . . . the organ through which society effects its will" – and to its legislative capacities to make the desired alterations in the structure of society.[7]

---

[4] George M. Fredrickson, *The Inner Civil War: Northern Intellectuals and the Crisis of the Union* (New York, 1968), 144. On Brownson's essential conservatism see, generally, Leonard Gilhooley, *Contradiction and Dilemma: Orestes Brownson and the American Idea* (New York, 1972).

[5] *Laboring Classes*, 10.   [6] Ibid., 14.

[7] Ibid., 13–20, 21, 22–3. On the early Brownson's doctrine of Christianity as a weapon of class struggle, see Anne C. Rose, *Transcendentalism as a Social Movement, 1830–1850* (New Haven, 1981), 33–4.

Resort to government was as fundamental to success as spiritual regeneration, because it was in the constitution of society, no less than in its metaphysic (in the institutional as well as the imaginative), that the problems besetting labor lay:

The evils of which we have complained are of a social nature. That is, they have their root in the constitution of society as it is, and they have attained to their present growth by means of social influences, the action of government, of laws, of systems and institutions upheld by society, and of which individuals are the slaves. This being the case, it is evident that they are to be removed only by the action of society, that is, by government, for the action of society is government.[8]

Control of government was to be used first to effect a great *un*doing, the repeal of "all laws which bear against the laboring classes." There had theretofore been too much government, said Brownson, in orthodox Jacksonian fashion. But the objective was not the rhetorical regulatory tabula rasa of laissez-faire and competitive individualism. It was, rather, to get rid of government "of the wrong kind." The problem with government was not so much that it had been too active but that its activity had been devoted to the upbuilding of "PRIVILEGE": banks, employers, the business community, hereditary wealth. The goal, once the legal foundations of privilege were destroyed, was hence not inactivity but activity differently directed, the enactment of such new laws as would be necessary to enable working people to achieve and maintain social equality. "We have no faith in those systems of elevating the working classes, which propose to elevate them without calling in the aid of government. We must have government, and legislation expressly directed to this end."[9]

Because Brownson saw in the October 1840 "Address" of the Workingmen of Charlestown an identical commitment to democracy as substantive "equality before society" rather than mere political equality, he dubbed the Workingmen social democrats, true successors of Jefferson, seekers after the revolutionary heritage of liberty and independence embarking on the next logical step beyond Jeffersonian radicalism that salvation of the laboring classes required. A social democrat, he said, was "a Jeffersonian Democrat, who having realized political equality, passed through one phase of the revolution, now passes on to another, and attempts the realization of social equality, so that the actual condition of men in society shall be in harmony with their acknowledged rights as citizens."[10]

Yet even as he wrote, Brownson's democratic impulse was living on borrowed time. Shattered by the outcome of the 1840 election, a "profoundly disillusioned" Brownson swapped faith in majoritarian democracy for Catholic statism, enthusiastically embraced government as the master of society rather than its servant, and spent the rest of his life excoriating social democracy as socialistic centralism.[11]

---

[8] *Laboring Classes*, 23   [9] Ibid., 23, 24.

[10] *Boston Quarterly Review*, 4 (Jan. 1841), 112–19, at 117. On the relationship between social democracy and Jeffersonian radicalism, see also Richard J. Twomey, *Jacobins and Jeffersonians: Anglo-American Radicalism in the United States, 1790–1820* (New York, 1989), 214–40.

[11] Fredrickson, *Inner Civil War*, 28, 186–8; Gilhooley, *Contradiction and Dilemma*, 134–6.

Brownson's abandonment of "social democracy" and the ideal of equality before society was more than a curtain falling on the enthusiasms of one idiosyncratic radical. It was another sign of the times. Even as the surge of political participation dating from the era of the Revolution was reaching its apogee, a half-century after the creation of the republic, the effective capacity of that participation to register a social impact was being set ever more comprehensively at nought by the structural and ideological limitations inscribed on governmental activities. American democracy, it appeared by the 1840s, had acquired mass but not substance. Democracy in America was "exclusively political and procedural", with most of social and economic life comfortably ensconced outside its boundaries.[12]

This is not to say that working people did not continue to attempt the turn to social equality via governmental reconstitution that the youthful Brownson had recommended. We have seen the signs of their interest arising in the 1830s. Take, for example, the resolutions of the National Trades' Union convention of 1834 on the condition of the laboring classes of the country, notably their goal of a strategic marriage between "the complete organization of the working classes throughout the United States" – still the only sure foundation for their "social happiness" – and the active pursuit of "correct legislation" to regain and protect positions lost by laborers' "inattention to their own best interests."[13] The programs and platforms of the Working Men's movement of the 1840s were, likewise, full of calls for regulation of hours and working conditions, sought the functional representation of labor in all departments of government (both state and federal), and proposed the creation of wholly new governmental forms: industrial congresses, industrial legislatures, even an "industrial revolutionary government."[14] But they were singularly unsuccessful against a configuration of politics and governance geared to the satisfaction of entrepreneurial elites and the expansion of their market economy. "The separation of the political and economic spheres, the decline of legislative power, the growth of administration, and institutional decentralization provided the political stability and predictability necessary for the establishment of a self-regulating market system." Private not public authorities dominated the resolution of economic issues; "the economy was effectively insulated from democratic control."[15] Government was for disciplining subjects, not empowering citizens, a "mere instrument of preventing wrong and dispensing justice," as one of Brownson's many critics put it, and nothing more.[16] Government in America supposed "in the case of each individual,

---

[12] L. Ray Gunn, *The Decline of Authority: Public Economic Policy and Political Development in New York State, 1800–1860* (Ithaca, N.Y., 1988), 16.

[13] In John R. Commons et al., eds., *A Documentary History of American Industrial Society* (Cleveland, 1910–), 6:205–9. I discuss these resolutions and the policy program they embraced in more detail in Chapter 5, n. 89.

[14] Ibid., 8:81–209, 315–34; Carl Siracusa, *A Mechanical People: Perceptions of the Industrial Order in Massachusetts, 1815–1860* (Middletown, Conn., 1979) 158–62.

[15] Gunn, *Decline of Authority*, 9.

[16] Charles Grandison Thomas, *Hereditary Property Justified: Reply to Brownson's Article on the Laboring Classes* (Cambridge, Mass., 1841), 7.

a perfectly separate and independent dominion over his own affairs, with which it does not and cannot interfere." To go beyond this was to threaten "a rapacious distribution of the rightfully acquired fruits of industry," which would "lay a great restraint on the production of wealth" and do "gross injustice" through "wanton violation of the sacred right of property."[17]

The autonomous individual subject and the restrained democracy it exercised were creations of the early republic's legal discourses. These discourses had established a society of safeguarded property, separated public and private spheres of action, and disciplined actors. These were the republic's facts of life. Legal discourse, further, had been the prime carrier seeding and reproducing these facts throughout the myriad social locations in which action took place. Law, "that science which is to direct the actions of mankind," taught the republic what it looked like.[18]

No more important a location can be found, I have argued here, than labor. Labor is the essential creative activity underpinning every social formation. But labor is also a category of social action and, as such, a subject of the discourses through which humans create, imagine, or invent their societies. Indeed, precisely because it underpins the social formation, it is its quintessential liability, the ultimate condition of what is invented.

The labor invented in the years of the early republic was, scholars have urged,

---

[17] Ibid., 8. Hence we may see the juridical and political dynamics of the post–Civil War period's substantive due process jurisprudence somewhat prefigured in the debates and conflicts described in this book. Both in its title and its content, Christopher Gustavus Tiedeman's *The Unwritten Constitution of the United States: A Philosophical Inquiry into the Fundamentals of American Constitutional Law* (New York, 1890) serves to display the parallels. Just as the early nineteenth century's legal writers had claimed for the common law both a constitutional role and an independent and autonomous role in checking, balancing, and restraining popular politics, so Tiedeman claimed that an "unwritten constitution" expressing society's "prevalent sense of right" empowered courts to act against legislative majorities threatening to intrude upon individual freedom. "Under the stress of economical relations, the clashing of private interests, the conflicts of labor and capital," Tiedeman wrote in 1890, the "old superstition that government has the power to banish evil from the earth" had been revived. "The State is called on to protect the weak against the shrewdness of the stronger, to determine what wages a workman shall receive for his labor, and how many hours he shall labor." Confronted with such "extraordinary demands" leveled by "the great army of discontents," confronted too by "their apparent power, with the growth and development of universal suffrage, to enforce their views of civil polity upon the civilized world," conservatives were well justified in fearing "the advent of an absolutism more tyrannical and more unreasoning than any before experienced by man – the absolutism of a democratic majority." Only the courts, empowered by the unwritten constitution, could allay those fears, could "lay their interdict upon all legislative acts which interfere with the individual's natural rights" of life, liberty, and property. The courts's disposition so to act, Tiedeman concluded, was "in these days of great social unrest" especially to be applauded (79–81). Tiedeman's *Unwritten Constitution* is briefly discussed in Herbert Hovenkamp, *Enterprise and American Law, 1836–1937* (Cambridge, Mass., 1991), 174. On the intellectual history of substantive due process, see idem, "The Political Economy of Substantive Due Process," *Stanford Law Review*, 40, 2 (Jan. 1988), 379–447. For elaboration of Tiedeman's views, see his *Treatise on the Limitations of Police Power in the United States Considered from both a Civil and Criminal Standpoint* (St. Louis, 1886).

[18] *American Quarterly Review*, 12 (1832), 267. And see, generally, Robert A. Ferguson, *Law and Letters in American Culture* (Cambridge, Mass., 1984), 23–6, 69–70; Ralph Lerner, "The Supreme Court as Republican Schoolmaster," *Supreme Court Review*, 1967, 127–80. As Ferguson puts it, "Others might comment, but the business of defining the republic remained the particular prerogative of those who joined the legal profession" (24).

fundamentally different from the modes of activity underpinning colonial America.[19] I have no argument with this contention, as far as it goes. Let us, though, understand the detail of the legal regime which constructed labor as a category of social action in the early republic before we label the result. Perhaps then we will see that the direction of the innovation involved was not quite as unambiguous as scholars have tended to believe. Examined in detail, the law of the seventeenth and eighteenth centuries yields a backdrop somewhat different from the more conventional blur of a "traditional" or "premodern" society of presumptively uniform unfreedoms. On close inspection, the vista of freedom celebrated as the early republics's mark of modernity dissolves to reveal a less-elevated landscape.

There is little doubt who is in charge of today's workplace, who has "exclusive control over the conception of work." Courts defend employers' "right to demand obedience to commands" and their right to the "loyalty" of employees, particularly in the face of the threat of "outside forces," as facts of working life.[20] But such facts, I have tried to show, are not immutable. Rather, they are the products of legal discourse, their origins to be found in the great burst of juristic activity that did so much to define the nature of American existence in the first half-century of the Republic. Consequently, even as we recognize that the legal asymmetries inscribed then continue to mold the social relations of today – that, in Kent's words, the "law knowledge" we have dug up is still churning away busily "in constant action"[21] – we should also recognize their contingency. Law may have taught the republic what it looked like, but law's kind of republic was never the only kind possible; after considering all of what has been argued here one might even judge the outcome ultimately too pinched in the freedoms of which it could conceive or the happiness that it could admit. Other republics also deserve inquiry. Some may offer fuller kinds of freedom.

[19] See Robert J. Steinfeld, *The Invention of Free Labor: The Employment Relation in English and American Law and Culture, 1350–1870* (Chapel Hill, 1991); Gordon S. Wood, *The Radicalism of the American Revolution* (New York, 1992).

[20] For recent commentary on the employment relationship in these terms, see Regina Austin, "Employer Abuse, Worker Resistance, and the Tort of Intentional Infliction of Emotional Distress," *Stanford Law Review*, 41 (1988), 1–59; Richard M. Fischl, "Labor, Management, and the First Amendment: Whose Rights Are These Anyway?" *Cardozo Law Review*, 10 (1989), 729–46; idem, "Self, Others, and Section 7: Mutualism and Protected Protest Activities under the National Labor Relations Act," *Columbia Law Review*, 89 (1989), 789–865. On the persistence of asymmetry in labor law, see also Christopher L. Tomlins, "Labor Law," in Stanley L. Engerman and Robert E. Gallman, eds., *The Cambridge Economic History of the United States*, vol., 3, forthcoming.

[21] James Kent, *A Lecture Introductory to a Course of Law Lectures in Columbia College, Delivered February 2, 1824* (New York, 1824). See also the epigraph to Part 1 of this book (p. 17).

Index

391

Index

311–12; Hamiltonian, 62–64, 86; on judiciary, 67–72; and law, 59, 70–71, 105–6; and local sovereignty, 61–62; Madisonian, 62–64, 86; and majoritarianism, 59, 64, 312; and manufactures, 311; model of government of, 72–73, 88–89, 91, 92; and "self-created societies," 125; on social order, 312

fellow-servant rule: exceptions to, discussed, 352–63, 370, 372, 372–78; precursors of, 347–51; principle of, admitted by plaintiff in *Farwell*, 351; temporarily rejected in Wisconsin, 379–81, 383, 384

Fenlee, Austin, killed at work, 320

Ferguson, Robert, on law and American Revolution, 27

"Few," the, 1, 4–5, 10

Fielding, Henry: his *The Life of Mr. Jonathan Wild, The Great* quoted, 294; as police theorist, 79

Fielding, John, 79

Fisk, Theophilus, 200

Fitzpatrick v. Albany and Salem Railroad Company (1856), 377, 378

force laws, 60, 64

Ford, William, killed at work, 322

Fortescue, Sir John, on monarchy and police, 44–45

free labor: conceptions of, 308–12; and contractualism, 382, 383–84; discourse of, 289–90; and distributive justice, 308–12; and law, 260–61, 268–70, 291–92, 295; maintenance of, when indigent, 336; and management, 313–15, 329, 330; Herman Melville on, 385; multiple meanings of, 289; and republicanism, 289, 383–84

freedom: Thomas Jefferson on, 84–85; Peter Oxenbridge Thacher on, 103–4

Freeman, Samuel, on master and servant law in Massachusetts, 266

Frieze, Jacob, on wage bargain, 9

General Abridgment and Digest of American Law, A (Nathan Dane), 267, 335

General Abridgment of Law and Equity, A (Charles Viner), 237

General Trades' Union (New York), 156, 158, 160, 161, 170; condemned in *People v. Cooper*, 166

Georgia: and employer liability law, 381n154; and police, 57

Gibson, John, 203; cited, 147, 177; his judgment in *Commonwealth v. Carlisle*, 145, 146–47; on judicial review of legislative acts, 92n115

Gillenwater v. Madison and Indianapolis Railroad (1854), 377, 378

Gillshannon v. Stony Brook Railroad (1852), 364; cited, 378

Goddard, Charles, killed at work, 318

Goebel, Julius, on federal Constitution, 71

Gordon, Robert, on needs of capitalism, 29

Gorham, Stephen, 271

government: Anti-Federalists on, 64–66, 68–73; Orestes Brownson on, 386–88; character of, in colonies, 51–52; culture of, and Revolution, 52, 91–92; debates over, in Confederation period, 60–73; Federalists on, 72–73, 88–89, 91, 92; Thomas Jefferson on, 84–88; labor movement on, 12, 388; and law, 45–47, 92–94; and liberalism, 75; and majoritarianism, 57–58, 59, 64; William Manning on, 1–2, 7, 8; model of, in federal Constitution, 65, 88–89, 92; model of, in Massachusetts Constitution, 3n4; Thomas Paine on, 83; and police, 39–47, 55–59, 61, 64, 78, 94; and popular sovereignty, 67, 72–73; and property, 68, 70, 78, 88, 309–10, 389; and rights, 57–58, 67; and security, 88, 388–89; supremacy of judiciary in, debated, 67–73

Gray, Robert, 281

Graydon, William, on master and servant law in Pennsylvania, 265

Greene, Jack P.: on ideology of improvement, 53–54; on social crisis in late colonial period, 53

Greenleaf, Joseph, on labor and law in colonial America, 257

Grenville, George, 50

guilds: and craft government, 117; and criminal conspiracy, 114–18; evolution of, 116–18; final collapse of, 123; statutory consequences of their disappearance, 238

Haight v. Badgeley (1853), 280

Hale, Sir Matthew, on master and servant law, 237, 238

Hale, Nathan, as president of Boston & Worcester Railroad, 302

Hallet, Benjamin, on enterprise and industrial development, 307, 308

Hamilton, Alexander, 61; on "energetic government", 62, 74; his federalism, contrasted with Jefferson's, 86, 87; his model of government, 88–89; on judiciary and its powers, 67–68, 68n30; on manufactures, 311; nationalism of, 62–64; on state governments, 62

Hamilton, George, 281

Hamilton Manufacturing Company, 317

Hanway, Joseph, 79

happiness, 3–4, 15, 37, 41, 47, 58, 309; in Federalist and Anti-Federalist discourse, 62,

Index

Index

Index

Farwell v. Boston & Worcester Railroad, 303, 347, 348

Moore, Ely, 158–59; on criminal conspiracy, 159

Morey, George, 331; as defendant's attorney in Farwell v. Boston & Worcester Railroad, 354–57

Morgan, Edmund, on popular sovereignty, 52

Morison, Samuel Eliot, on William Manning, 1, 2n1

Morris, Gouverneur: on police, 61; on state sovereignty, 61

Morris, Robert, 61

Mosely, Willis, killed at work, 380–81

Mosely v. Chamberlain (1861), 380–81

Murray v. South Carolina Railroad (1841), 348, 349–51, 359; cited, 373

Murrin, John, on law in colonial Rhode Island, 249

mutual and self-supervision, 362, 383; criticized, 375

Napoleonic Code, 30

Nash, Gary, on social crisis in late colonial period, 52–53

National Convention of Cordwainers (1836), 159; comments on People v. Fisher, 110n5, 161n102

National Trades' Union, 157, 159; on cooperative production, 174–75; on criminal conspiracy, 159; on government, 388; on politics and policy, 157n89

Nelles, Walter, on Commonwealth v. Hunt, 209

Nelson, William E., on master and servant law in early republic, 261

New England: railroads in, 324–25; textile industry in, 313–15, 324

New England Association of Farmers, Mechanics and Other Workingmen, 183; on law, 194; and ten-hour day, 186

New Hampshire, and "agrarian" agitation, 61

New Jersey: conspiracy doctrine in, 148, 150; labor and law in, 253, 254–55; labor conspiracy cases in, 214n99; and police 57

New Virginia Justice, The (William Waller Hening), 261–62

New York (city), 52, 89; journeymen in (early national period), 112; labor conspiracy cases in, 128, 129, 138–42, 151, 160–71; labor movement in (1830s), 156, 157, 158–59, 160–61, 163, 169, 173, 174, 175

New York (state), 106; criminal conspiracy doctrine in, 126, 148–51, 160, 166–69, 178, 181, 187; growth of wage labor in, 259; its revised conspiracy statute of 1828, 149–50, 150–51, 162, 170, 206, 208, 209; labor and law in: (colonial) 253, 254–55, (early

republic) 264, 274–75, 277, 279, 280, 368–70; Utica convention (1836), 169–71, 174; Working Men's Party, in, 153, 154–56

New York General Trades' Union, see General Trades' Union (New York)

New York Herald, on criminal conspiracy, 167, 168

New York Journal of Commerce, on criminal conspiracy, 169

New York Transcript, on People v. Faulkner, 162

New York Union, on People v. Faulkner, 163

Newark, labor movement in (1830), 157, 164

Newark Trades' Union, 161; protests People v. Faulkner, 164–65

Newby v. Wiltshire (1784), 334

Newton, Isaac, 24

Niles, William, plaintiff in Ratchford v. Niles (1803), 339

North Carolina: labor and law in: (colonial) 252, 253, (early republic) 381–82; and police, 57

Novak, William, on police power, 94

Office and Authority of a Justice of Peace, The (James Davis), 252

Office and Authority of a Justice of Peace, The (George Webb), 261

Ohio, and employer liability law, 372–76, 382–83

Ohio and Mississippi Railroad Company v. Tindall (1859), 378

Olmstead v. Beale (1837), 289–90

Ordinance of Conspirators (1293, 1305), 115, 116

outworkers: Daniel Defoe on, 232; employment of, in English law, 236, 238

Owen, Robert Dale, and New York Working Men, 154; and state guardianship, 154, 155

Paine, Thomas, 82–83; on British polity, 83; and commercial society, 82; on democracy, 82–83; on government, 82; on law, 35; on property, 83; on welfare and distributive justice, 83

Palmer, Robert, on police and communalism, 58

pandecticism, 30

paper currency, 60, 64

Parker, Samuel D., 200; as prosecutor in Commonwealth v. Hunt, 201

Parsons, Theophilus, 210; cited, on criminal conspiracy, 187–88, 208

Parsons, Theophilus, Jr.: as defendant's attorney in Stone v. Codman, 224; on law of master and servant, 269

patriarchy, and industrial discipline, 314

Pennsylvania, 58, 82, 106; anthracite mining accidents in, 323, 327n80; campaigns against